The Other Side of Western Civilization: Readings in Everyday Life

Volume I: The Ancient World to the Reformation

Fifth Edition

The Other Side of Western Civilization: Readings in Everyday Life

Volume I: The Ancient World to the Reformation

FIFTH EDITION

EDITED BY
STANLEY CHODOROW
California Virtual University, La Jolla

MARCI SORTOR
Grinnell College

HARCOURT COLLEGE PUBLISHERS

Fort Worth   Philadelphia   San Diego   New York   Orlando   Austin   San Antonio
Toronto   Montreal   London   Sydney   Tokyo

Publisher	Earl McPeek
Executive Editor	David Tatom
Market Strategist	Steve Drummond
Developmental Editor	Tracy Napper
Project Editor	Laura J. Hanna
Art Director	Chris Morrow
Production Manager	Linda McMillan

Cover image: Brueghel, Pieter the Elder, *The Dark Day*, from the series "The Seasons," 1565. Kunsthistorisches Museum, Vienna, Austria, Erich Lessing/Art Resource, NY.

ISBN: 0-15-507851-8
Library of Congress Catalog Card Number: 99-60750

Address for Domestic Orders
Harcourt Brace College Publishers, 6277 Sea Harbor Drive, Orlando, FL 32887-6777
800-782-4479

Address for International Orders
International Customer Service
Harcourt Brace & Company, 6277 Sea Harbor Drive, Orlando, FL 32887-6777
407-345-3800
(fax) 407-345-4060
(e-mail) hbintl@harcourtbrace.com

Address for Editorial Correspondence
Harcourt Brace College Publishers, 301 Commerce Street, Suite 3700,
Fort Worth, TX 76102

Web Site Address
http://www.harcourtcollege.com

Printed in the United States of America

9 0 1 2 3 4 5 6 7 8   039   9 8 7 6 5 4 3 2 1

Harcourt College Publishers

For Peggy
For Dan

PREFACE

Social history continues to broaden and deepen our understanding of people of the past. And as never before, its relevance to the history of institutions and ideas—the stuff of Western Civilization and other survey courses—has become dramatically clear. The fifth edition of *The Other Side of Western Civilization* has been designed to give insights into the daily lives of people from all walks of life. It contains readings that center on people and subjects that receive inadequate attention in texts for survey courses, such as women, commoners, religious minorities, children, the elderly, marriage and households, popular culture, and leisure activities. It reintroduces people into the events, institutions, and ideas of Western Civilization by exploring how these phenomena influenced and were influenced by ordinary folk. Most importantly, it allows us to understand what these historical developments meant to real people: how a teenager understood his Protestant faith when living among Catholics, what it meant to live a cloistered life, how changes in inheritance practices among the nobility in turn changed whom a girl might marry, and how changes in marriage law might make an otherwise respectable young woman an unmarried mother.

One-half of the readings in this edition are new. They represent some of the most recent scholarship on subjects that have just begun to attract serious scholarly consideration as well as on subjects that have been at the heart of long-standing and lively debate. The new selections address topics such as magic, reputation, marriage, and how people might relax and spend a few hours with friends. Others touch on important new insights that research has provided into women's private and public roles in antiquity and the Middle Ages. Youth and childhood are the subjects of three of the new readings. Interior lives and emotions and individual self-expression are treated as well. Some new selections focus on crime and marginality, and on city life and neighborhoods. War from the point of view of a Greek hoplite, and the experience of Roman slavery are the topics of other selections. Many of the readings provide excellent examples of the different types of sources that historians use to reconstruct the outlooks, families, social networks, and daily experiences of people who rarely wrote about such things.

The readings of this book shed light on people's experiences and activities at all levels of society. There are selections pertaining to the nobility as well as to peasants and townspeople. Likewise, this edition includes readings on criminals and village witches. Some of the readings investigate a number of major developments in European history—such as the spread of Christianity, feudalism, the Crusades, the Renaissance, and the Reformation from the individual's point of view. The conduct of warfare among ancient Greeks and during the Hundred Years' War are considered in readings that concentrate on how the participants experienced them. Readings on life as a Roman slave and on life in a monastery and in a medieval city explore the ways in which people participated in the institutions of their time. Other readings explore households in antiquity and the early Middle Ages and the care of the elderly.

The readings in this book are organized chronologically into five parts. Part 1 pertains to antiquity from 500 B.C. to A.D. 500. Cities played an important part in the culture, society, and political organization of both Greece and Rome, and this is reflected in the readings. Part 2 covers the early medieval period, from the sixth through the eleventh centuries, after the collapse of the Roman Empire in the West and the establishment of the Germanic kingdoms in its former territories. During this period some of medieval Europe's most distinctive institutions—such as feudalism and manorialism—emerged. Part 3 concerns the developments of the twelfth and thirteenth centuries, when the achievements of medieval Europeans reached their highest state. The twelfth and thirteenth centuries were a period of relative peace, resulting in economic and geographic expansion and the broadening of Europe's intellectual horizons. Part 4 addresses the late Middle Ages, when Europe was plunged into a series of crises: protracted war, frequent harvest failures, economic contraction, and the demographic and psychic devastation caused by the bubonic plague. Part 5 addresses aspects of European society during the Renaissance and Reformation, from the sixteenth through the seventeenth centuries.

I would like to thank Paul Kern of Indiana University Northwest for his advice on ancient warfare. Jennifer Whartenby and Josh Blue expedited things by photocopying reams of material and provided a veritable courier service between my office and the library. Thanks go to the reviewers: Ron Brown, Charles County Community College; Ginger Frost, Samford University; and Randy Howarth, Cleveland State University. Thanks also go to Tracy Napper, Senior Developmental Editor and Laura J. Hanna, Senior Project Editor, at Harcourt Brace Publishers. I thank my husband Dan Ferro and my daughter Emily for being such good sports about weekends and evenings devoted to this book. Last, I offer deep gratitude to my students at Grinnell College. Their enthusiasm and interest informed the choices made for this edition.

Marci Sortor

Contents

TOPICAL TABLE OF CONTENTS

Work

INTRODUCTION

The importance of a book such as this is as great now as it was when the first edition of *The Other Side of Western Civilization, vol. 1* appeared in 1973. To-day most texts, even large Western Civilization texts, include some treatment of women, humble folk, and popular culture. Such coverage, however, is necessarily brief and cannot keep up with the dynamic changes taking place in social history. Historians of premodern Europe continue to explore ever more deeply people's experiences, circumstances, and outlooks. In addition to doing much important new research into areas such as gender, emotions, deviance, persecution and tolerance, social networks, and families, social historians have demonstrated how these shaped and were shaped by developments in institutions and culture. The centrality of social history to what, twenty-five years ago, was considered "mainstream" history has never been so obvious as it is now, and it calls for a fifth edition.

The readings in this book focus on the life experiences of people from all ranks of society: from slaves to nobles and from peasants to city folk. It considers the distinctive experiences of the very young, the old, and adolescents. A number of the readings explore work, leisure, households, popular religion, public celebrations, marriage, magic and crime. Other readings explore the connection between people and the institutions, ideas, and events of their day.

Social history presents special problems for the historian of preindustrial Europe. Until the modern period, the vast majority of the European population could not read or write. The few who could tended to be found among the cultural elite—such as medieval monks and Renaissance scholars—who in turn were in the service of those who wielded power and dominated society. In most cases, those who generated documents did so for the purposes of running governments, managing estates, or discussing theological or philosophical matters. Documents directly addressing private concerns, such as family life and personal relationships are scarce before the Renaissance. How most people felt about the world around them or the hardships they faced went almost completely unrecorded. Similarly, few documents speak directly to people's inner lives and private beliefs. More particularly, the purposes for which the majority of medieval records were generated have resulted in the documentary underrepresentation of particular groups of people, such as slaves, commoners, women and children, regardless of status, and ethnic and religious minorities. Documents that do refer to these groups almost invariably were written from the point of view of the masculine, adult elite and are frequently distorted by its particular interests and biases.

The problems posed by the documentary evidence have led social historians to develop new ways of looking at these documents and to explore new sources of information. The readings in this book provide excellent examples of the ways in which social historians have been able to discover records—unwritten as well as written—left behind by the underrepresented members of premodern society and to use documents created by and for the elite to learn about what life was like for the rest of the population. For example, Athenian law, written exclusively by men, and long used by historians to study the political history of the ancient Greeks, can speak to how men lived with and understood women. It also sheds light on the social and legal environment within which women lived. Accounts of saints' lives, previously studied as literature and for the information they supplied about the church, are used in one selection to reconstruct barbarian households. Another selection uses records of lawsuits among Jews to catch a rare glimpse of the medieval Jewish community, a glimpse made all the more rare for being generated by the community itself and therefore free of the prejudice and stereotyping that pervades medieval Christian references to Jews. Changes in marriage law and inheritance patterns provide rich material for understanding the experiences of young men and women. Architecture speaks to the social environment in Renaissance Italy. In two other selections, the sociability of ancient Romans and the beliefs of early medieval Franks emerge from the evidence supplied by archeology.

In this edition, some beloved classics remain from the previous editions. Eileen Power's "Peasant Life in the Middle Ages" recreates a day in the life of a Frankish peasant Bodo and his wife. Power's ability to breathe life into the dry economic documents of a Frankish manor continue to make this selection a favorite. Similarly, the account of the childhood and youth of William Marshal in "The Training of a Knight" by Sidney Painter is a masterful biographical sketch. The prospects of this younger son of a minor nobleman were not promising, yet this initially rather unimpressive youth eventually became one of the most powerful men in England. Painter's account follows William through his training as a knight and his early years of service and tournaments. Although William Marshal eventually won considerable fame and fortune, he represents the large proportion of knights who, for the most part, served rather than became powerful men in the feudal system. The distinctive melding of two cultures—Muslim and Latin Christian—in the Crusader kingdoms of the Levant in Joshua Prawer's "The World of the Crusaders" continues to speak to students' interest in pluralistic societies. And Jonathan Sumption's "Pilgrimage and Medieval Travel" remains a fresh and lively account of what people seeking penance, and sometimes entertainment, were likely to encounter on their way to holy places. "Feudal War in Practice" by John Keegan still fascinates with its powerful recreation of a medieval battle scene. The thundering hooves of charging horses and the confusion as something—which those in the rear cannot see—goes wrong up front are brought to life in this moving account of warfare in the Middle Ages.

Making war is the occupation of a few. All people, in contrast, are subject to physical growth, development and, should they live long enough, aging. Age and youth have recently been areas of considerable interest among social historians. The place an individual holds in society as he or she moves through life—as well as the changing expectations concerning behavior, duties, privileges, powers—is central to a host of questions about societies. "Child-rearing in the Middle Ages" by Shulamith Shahar investigates the care and education of children in their earliest years. The advice given to parents regarding the upbringing of their children indicates that medieval parents were just as aware as their modern counterparts of the developmental stages of the very young. Yet certain practices, such as relying on wet nurses and swaddling, indicate that parents and children lived in a world profoundly different than our own. They reveal, too, some distinctive attributes of medieval families and their functions. The care of the elderly is addressed by Barbara Hanawalt in "Growing Old in an English Village." The arrangements that peasants made for their maintenance in their declining years raise important questions about the nature of the rural family in the later Middle Ages. They also suggest a degree of individuality that is often assumed to be the product of a later period. Youth and the transition to adulthood are explored in two readings in the selection "On the Threshold of Independence: Adolescence." In "Apprentices and Masters" Ilana Krausman Ben-Amos describes the experiences and feelings of a teenager who has left home to live with a master. As an apprentice he became, in effect, a member of his master's family. The relationship between the master and mistress and the youthful apprentice could be a profoundly satisfying and profitable one. It could also be full of conflict and anger. In the second reading, Steven Ozment recreates the ups and downs of a university student in "The Private Life of an Early Modern Teenager."

A number of selections treat women, the family and the household. The selection "Women and the Household in Ancient Greece" by Sue Blundell explores the evidence for the seclusion of women in Athens. The rigid segregation of men and women into public and private spheres suggests that, while at a considerable legal and economic disadvantage, Athenian women enjoyed a certain authority within the household. Families are treated in two selections. David Herlihy attempts to reconstruct the family and household of the barbarian tribes migrating into the Roman Empire in "The Early Medieval Household." He discovers a perplexing combination: polygyny and female slavery combined with the influential role of daughters and sisters in family strategies. The influence of the church had produced a profoundly different kind of family by the twelfth century. In the selection "Noble Marriage" Constance Brittain Bouchard assesses the implications that changing family strategies among the nobility had upon the marriage prospects of young men and women. Gender, age, and marital status determined women's participation in the public life of the village in Judith Bennett's "Power, Property, and Gender in Village Life." Natalie Zemon Davis explores women's work in and out of the household in "Women and Work." Davis shows that most women were economically active, but that their income-earning potential was significantly lower than that of men. A woman who had only her labor to support her faced a life of poverty. The division between men's and women's work sharpened in the sixteenth century to a degree not seen in the Middle Ages. Bound up with an increasingly restrictive guild system and a developing, sometimes unstable market economy, the division of labor was an expression of changes in gender roles for both men and women, particularly in the cities.

In both ancient and medieval times, the vast majority of the population was rural, yet cities exercised a powerful influence. Cities were the foundation of Greek and Roman civilization. A central ingredient in the civilized life of the cities of the Roman Empire was the public bath. Baths and their exercise grounds catered to the needs of the body while they invited bathers of all ranks to relax with their friends and neighbors. Fikret Yegül describes this most urbane of institutions in "Roman Baths and Bathers." After a hiatus of several centuries, cities became vibrant centers of commercial and intellectual life once again. Barbara Hanawalt describes medieval London from the point of view of its residents in "London and Its Neighborhoods." Cities like London and Paris exerted a powerful pull. Some came to the city looking for work; some were drawn almost irresistibly, as a moth to a flame. Those without friends and family, and so without a network to help them through hard times, were in danger of falling into a life a crime. The life stories of those who found themselves arrested and brought before the court of the Paris Parlement are the subject of the selection "Down and Out in Paris: Criminals and Their Milieu" by Geremek Bronisław.

Cities were also the home of most of the members of northern Europe's only tolerated religious minority. In "Jews in a Christian Society" Robert Chazan describes Jewish communities in Europe before the religious and military fervor stirred up by leaders of the first Crusade led to widespread attacks against them. The Jewish community was distinctive both for the degree to which it remained separate from the Christian society that surrounded it and for the contribution that it made to the economy and learning of Europe as a whole. The presence of Judaism—which the church revered as the faith from which Christianity emerged but despised for its denial of the divinity of Christ—was a source of tension in medieval Europe. The Crusades, although directed against the Muslim occupation of the Holy Land, ignited these tensions with heartbreaking results.

A number of the readings consider premodern institutions from the perspective of the people who participated in or were affected by them. The effectiveness of ancient Greek armies depended on the ability of the individual hoplites to hold the line at all costs. John Lazenby gives us a clear understanding of what those costs were by describing what the soldier must have seen and felt as he prepared for battle and then finally met the enemy face to face. Keith Bradley, in "Slaves and Society in Rome," describes the importance of slaves in Roman society. The range of occupations held by slaves created great variety in their experiences and in the relationships between slaves and masters. "Life in a Monastery," by C. H. Lawrence, describes a way of life that was highly esteemed in the Middle Ages and explains how monasteries were run. This selection allows us to look inside the walls of these institutions that were so important to scholarship, church reform, and politics, in the Middle Ages. In two selections mentioned earlier, "Peasant Life in the Middle Ages" and "The Training of a Knight," the manorial system is viewed from the perspective of those who worked the land and knighthood is viewed from the perspective of a young military retainer hoping to make good.

Other readings show how premodern people participated in the major developments and events of their day. The expansion of the Roman Empire and its military successes were brought home to the city of Rome itself with parades, the display of the spoils of war, and celebrations. In "Games, Plays, and Races: Celebrating Rome" Joseph Stambaugh demonstrates how the average Roman shared in the glory that was Rome. Over a millennium later, Renaissance scholars studied ancient Rome in the hopes of attaining the accomplishments of antiquity anew in their own day. This cultural and political rebirth had as its ideal the educated man accomplished in a range of disciplines and activities. In the selection "The Scholar in His Study" Dora Thornton asks the question of how any scholar—professional or amateur—pursued the intellectual ideals of Renaissance society. Her answer brings together the intellectual trends of the day with changes in the architecture of homes. It also speaks to Renaissance households and the opportunity that the private study created for the expression of individualism. Tessa Watt shows how common folk drew on Protestant ideas and the new technology of the printing press to express their own beliefs. In "Pictures, Print, and Piety," Watt takes us into humble inns and farmhouses to gaze upon the printed pictures and texts that decorated their walls.

Some of the readings in this book are devoted to how common folk influenced the belief systems of premodern culture. Others speak to the relationship between elite high culture and low, or popular, culture. High and popular culture never existed completely separately from each other, and the ways in which ideas were transmitted between them has proved a fruitful area of research. J. M. Wallace-Hadrill, in the selection, "The Conversion of the Franks," reveals a two-way process of cultural communication. He traces the conversion to Christianity of both the Frankish aristocracy and the peasantry and finds that the processes for the two groups were very different. Moreover, Wallace-Hadrill shows how missionaries had to modify their message if they were to gain a hearing among the peasantry. In turn, the peasants' preexisting beliefs and practices left an imprint on Christianity. The relationships between magic and Christianity are explored in "Love and Magic in the Renaissance." Guido Ruggiero begins this selection with an account of the discovery of a little wax figure stuck with pins and the investigation of those responsible for it—the village matchmaker and a pregnant girl. He describes a magic that was bound up with mainstream Christian belief. Stephen Ozment follows the religious flip-flopping of a Protestant boy attending a Catholic university. Emotional impulse, a certain degree of superstition, and a good deal of prejudice rather than theological principle seem to guide the youth's actions in "The Private Life of an Early Modern Teenager."

The private life of the heart and mind, where emotions and perceptions rule, is perhaps the next great field of exploration for social historians. The promises spoken by lovers in a darkened bedroom, a Protestant teenager caught up by the grandeur of a Catholic ceremony, objects of interest secreted away in a Renaissance study, may seem distant from the grand events of history. They are the other side of Western civilization—the side of the popular, the private, the underrepresented. As the lived experience of events great and small, they are also at the very center of the story of Western civilization and the history of premodern Europe.

Bibliography

The great social historian Marc Bloch wrote an appraisal of his craft which was found among his papers and published as *The Historian's Craft* (New York, 1953). Interest in social history and in the development of theory and methodology that furthered investigation into the lives and thoughts of common folk intensified in the 1960s. In part, that interest was fueled by the groundbreaking work of Natalie Zemon Davis, *Society and Culture in Early Modern France* (Stanford, CA, 1965), who applied anthropological theory to accounts of popular behavior such as festivals and riots. Peter Burke used folktales, literature, and festivals to construct a symbolic language for understanding people's experiences and values in *Popular Culture in Early Modern Europe* (London, 1978). Burke's *History and Social Theory* (Ithaca, NY, 1993, 1992) discusses the use of models and theories from the various social sciences in historical research. See also Eric Wolf, *Europe and the People Without a History* (Berkeley, 1982); Carlo Ginzburg, *Clues, Myths and the Historical Method,* trans. by John and Anne C. Tedeschi (Baltimore, 1989); Edward Muir and Guido Ruggiero, *Microhistory and the Lost Peoples of Europe,* trans. by Eren Branch (Baltimore, 1991); Aron Iakovlevich Gurevich, *Medieval Popular Culture: Problems of Beliefs and Perceptions,* trans. by Jana Bak and Paul Hollingsworth (Cambridge, Eng., 1988), and *Historical Anthropology of the Middle Ages,* trans. by Jana Howlett (Chicago, 1992). A discussion of how medieval women's history fits into the larger scope of medieval history and the special problems involved in investigating the history of medieval women is provided by Susan Mosher Stuard, ed., *Women in Medieval Historiography* (Philadelphia, 1987).

Sixth century B.C. *Greek kylix (drinking vessel) attributed to Exekias, showing the god Dionysus in a sailing boat. (Black-figure style)*

(SOURCE: Hartwig Koppermann, Staatliche Antikensammiungen, Munich)

I

THE ANCIENT WORLD
5th Century B.C.–5th Century A.D.

The five selections of Part 1 treat the social life of ancient Greece and Rome. At the beginning of the fifth century B.C., Greece was the center of Western civilization, extending its influence over the entire Mediterranean world. Athens used its navy and commercial power to establish a far-flung empire of city-states. Aligned against this maritime empire was the Peloponnesian League, a confederation of Greek cities led by Sparta. In the early fifth century, the eastern Greek colonies were attacked and conquered by the Persian Empire. Athens' unsuccessful attempt to assist the colonies militarily brought the wrath of the Persian emperor down upon it. In 490 B.C., Athens' army of citizen-soldiers went up against the invading forces of the Persian war machine in the Battle of Marathon. Athens was fantastically successful; 192 Greeks gave up their lives, a handful compared to 6,400 Persian warriors dead. The key to Athens' military prowess was a kind of warfare well-suited to the Greek city-state, in which men fought side-by-side in ranks in a more or less orderly fashion. John Lazenby recreates the battlefield experience of the hoplite (a foot soldier fighting in close ranks) in the first selection.

The society of ancient Greece was controlled by its male citizens, whether the community government was democratic or oligarchic. But the society of the towns included many other elements beside citizens. The *metics*, or foreigners, formed a large class of merchants, artisans, and laborers, who played important roles in the economic and social life of the cities, but who were excluded from a direct role in politics. Then many persons of substance, although of low status, were former slaves or descendants of them. All women were excluded from the political life of the cities. In Athens, respectable women were expected to withdraw as much as possible from public life. In the second selection, Sue Blundell examines the seclusion of women in ancient Athens.

Cities again played a central role in the Roman Empire. As the Romans expanded their empire, they constructed a network of cities from which they governed the provinces and collected taxes. The city of Rome was huge by ancient standards, with at least 1 million inhabitants by the beginning of the Christian era. The third selection addresses how the largest city in the Western world defined itself politically and religiously through its holidays. Richard Stambaugh shows how the celebration of the Roman civic religion performed a number of functions: It was a way for the powerful to advertise themselves and to curry the favor of the masses; it communicated information about the empire's military successes and the exotic lands it had conquered; and it provided residents with opportunities for rest and relaxation.

Empire brought with it the spoils of war, including human beings captured in battle. Slavery was widespread in the ancient world, but it reached unprecedented proportions and importance in both ancient Athens and imperial Rome. A more benign institution central to the life and culture of Roman cities throughout the empire was the public bath. Any city worthy of the name possessed at least one. As the empire itself waxed, these monuments to health, leisure, and sociability became ever more grand. In the fourth and fifth selections, Keith Bradley describes the variety of experiences of slaves and Fikret Yegül takes us into the baths of the Roman empire.

BIBLIOGRAPHY

See Robert Flaceliere *Daily Life in Greece at the Time of Pericles,* trans. Peter Green
(New York, 1965) for a general overview of Greek society; and P. J. Rhodes, *The
Athenian Empire* (Oxford, 1985). Victor Davis Hanson, *The Western Way of War:
Infantry Battle in Classical Greece* (New York, 1989) rethins the nature of Greek
warfare in light of Greek society and agriculture. See also W. K. Pritchett *The
Greek State at War,* vols. 1-4 (Berkeley, 1971-85); John F. Lazenby, *The Spartan
Army* (Warminster, England, 1985); and John Rich and Graham Shipley, *War and
Society in the Greek World* (London, 1995). For general studies of warfare in an-
tiquity see John Warry, *Warfare in the Classical World: War and the Ancient Civ-
ilizations of Greece and Rome* (London, 1998); and R. Humble, *Warfare in the
Ancient World* (London, 1980). Warfare, of course, leads to casualties. G. Manjo
discusses the treatment of injuries in *The Healing Hand: Man and Wound in the
Ancient World* (Cambridge, MA, 1975).

For women in antiquity, see Sarah Pomeroy's important book, *Goddesses, Whores,
Wives and Slaves: Women in Classical Antiquity* (New York, 1975); Gillian Clark,
Women in the Ancient World (Oxford, 1989); and Michael Massey, *Women in An-
cient Greece and Rome* (Cambridge, England, 1988). Women's condition in
Greece is treated by Roger Just, *Women in Athenian Law and Life* (London,
1989); and David M. Schaps, *Economic Rights of Women in Ancient Greece*
(Edinburgh, 1979). The little-recorded lives of rural women are investigated by
Walter Scheidel, "The Most Silent Women of Greece and Rome: Rural Labour and
Women's Life in the Ancient World (I&II)," *Greece and Rome* 62:2 (1995):202-
17, and 63:1 (1996):1-10. For family life in ancient Greece see Nancy Demand,
Birth, Death, and Motherhood in Classical Greece (Baltimore, 1994); Mark
Golden, *Children and Childhood in Classical Athens* (Baltimore, 1990); and Sarah
Pomeroy, *Families in Classical and Hellenistic Greece* (Oxford, 1997). Mary R.
Lefkowitz and Maureen B. Fant, eds., *Women's Life in Greece and Rome* (Balti-
more, 1982) is a collection of primary sources on women in antiquity.

Slavery in the ancient world is treated by William L. Westermann, *The Slave Systems
of Greek and Roman Antiquity* (Philadelphia, 1955) and Moses I. Finley, *Classical Slavery* (London, 1987). For Greece, see Yvon Garlan, *Slavery in Ancient
Greece,* trans. Janet Lloyd (Ithaca, NY, 1988). For Roman slavery, see Keith
Hopkins, *Conquerors and Slaves: Sociological Studies in Roman History, vol. 1*
(Cambridge, England, 1978); Alan Watson, *Roman Slave Law* (Baltimore and
London, 1987). Keith Bradley investigates slave rebellion in *Slavery and Rebellion
in the Roman World* (Bloomington, IN, 1989). Thomas Wiedeman provides collections of sources in *Slavery* (Oxford, 1987) and *Greek and Roman Slavery* (Bal-
timore and London, 1981).

For the social context of Rome, see Andrea Giardina, *The Romans,* trans. by Lydia G.
Cochrane (Chicago, 1993); Florence Dupont, *Daily Life in Ancient Rome,* trans.
Christopher Woodall, (Oxford, 1992); Peter Garnsey and Richard Saller, *The Ro-
man Empire: Economy, Society and Culture* (Berkeley, 1987); Claude Nicolet, *The
World of the Citizen in Republican Rome,* trans. P. S. Falla (Berkeley, 1980); Ramsay
MacMullen, *Roman Social Relations, 50 B.C. to A.D. 284* (New Haven, 1974); and
P.A. Brunt *Social Conflicts in the Roman Republic* (New York and London, 1971).

ON THE BATTLEFIELD: HOPLITE WARFARE

JOHN LAZENBY

*Around the time of the rise of the Greek city-state (ca. 650–338
B.C.), Greek soldiers abandoned fighting one on one and began fighting on foot in close formation, in a phalanx. In doing so, they abandoned the style of warfare of the Greek heroes, in which individual
confrontations and acts of bravery were emphasized, for a strategy
that deemphasized the individual and made each man dependent on
his fellow soldiers' ability to hold the line. Standing shoulder-
to-shoulder and about eight ranks deep, the hoplite warriors were
invincible. They took their name from the large wooden shield, the
hoplon, used to protect its bearer's left side as well as the right side
of the man standing on his left.*

*Hoplite warfare sacrificed mobility for unity. As long as they did
not break rank, they created an impermeable line. Hoplites were heavily armed, with bronze helmet, breastplate and greaves (armor for the
shin), as well as tunic, spear, and shield. Combined, weapons and armor weighed between fifty and seventy pounds. The shield alone—
three feet in diameter and made of wood—weighed about sixteen
pounds. Not only was the equipment heavy, it was hot; the Greek battle season was summer, when temperatures could reach ninety degrees. Weight and heat placed very real physical constraints on the
hoplites; battles were short. They were also brutal and frightening.
Earlier, Greek soldiers relied on the javelin, striking at their opponents
from a distance. Lightly armed and fighting independently, they could
advance and retreat at will. The success of the phalanx negated all possibility of individual soldiers backing away from danger or seeking a
better position. The front lines of opposing phalanxes came up against
each other, each man thrusting at the opposing line with his spear.
Last, hoplite battles were decisive; these face-to-face engagements did
not allow for protracted wars or withdrawals for rest periods.*

*A man needed to be strong to bear the arms of the hoplite and
to have the stamina to use them in battle, but he did not need much*

From: John Lazenby, "The Killing Zone," in Victor Davis Hanson, ed., *Hoplites: The Classical
Greek Battle Experience* (London: Routledge, 1991, 1993), pp. 87, 88–108.

training. Most hoplites were farmers and craftsmen. They fought alongside their friends and neighbors. Undoubtedly, part of the phalanx's success was due to each man's realization that breaking ranks would endanger members of his own community and shame him before them. These considerations cannot take away the fact that ordinary men had to muster the bravery to go into battle, hold the line regardless of the dangers facing them, and fight opponents standing only a few feet away. How did the phalanx function? Were hoplite warfare and the emergence of democratic city-states related? In this selection, John Lazenby draws on Greek historians, literature, and art to recreate the battle experience, taking us onto the battlefield and into phalanx itself, to stand alongside the Greek hoplite.

No one alive today has ever experienced anything really like a hoplite battle. Contemporary accounts survive, at least one by an eye-witness, but they chiefly take a wide-angle view. There is no 'blow-by-blow' commentary. To try to understand what went on at the 'sharp end', we have to draw on many sources, including poets and dramatists, and the best we can hope to achieve is a composite picture, since no two battles were exactly alike. . . .

We begin with the setting, which was usually a flat terrain. Hills, streams, marshes, the sea, and other features, often play some part, but are rarely, if ever, crucial. There is much truth in the remark Herodotos attributes to Mardonios, that 'when the Greeks declare war on each other, they choose the best and smoothest place and go down and have their battle on that', though it is less true, as we shall see, that they suffered heavily as a result. The area would be enough to accommodate several thousand men, but probably not more than 50,000 at most, if Greek was fighting Greek. Thucydides, for example, evidently thought that First Mantineia was a big battle, yet it is doubtful whether more than about 20,000 hoplites took part, and at the Nemea, possibly the greatest hoplite battle ever fought, there were probably fewer than 50,000.

Since battles were usually fought in the summer, it would be hot and sunny. Bad weather, even thunderstorms, rarely, if ever, interrupted proceedings, though Plutarch alleges that one such aided Timoleon's victory at the Krimisos. Battles could be fought at other times of the year, for example the one between the Mantineians and Tegeates at Laodokeion in the winter of 423/2 BC (i.e. between October and March), but perhaps the only time conditions affected the issue was when snow drove the forces of the 'Thirty' away from Phyle in the winter of 404/3 BC.

Before battle, the hoplites would form up in their files, eight deep or more. The greatest depth recorded is the 'fifty shields' of the Thebans at Leuktra, though the forces of the 'Thirty' also formed up fifty deep at Mounychia in 403 BC, when confined to a single road. Probably in most armies men from the same localities served together—Lysias, for example, implies that in the

Athenian army men from the same deme fought alongside each other. But in the Spartan army, by Xenophon's time, recruitment was no longer on a local basis. Sons, fathers and brothers did not necessarily even serve together in the same *morai*. Nevertheless, the members of the smallest units, the *enomotiai*, presumably knew each other, since they only consisted of forty men, even at full strength, and on campaign probably only contained thirty-five men or fewer. Presumably, too, since the composition of an *enomotia* was based on age-groups, with the younger men in the front ranks, each man also knew his place.

One wonders, however, whether this was true of most armies. There is no evidence that there were units smaller than a *lochos* in national armies other than the Spartan, and although the size of a *lochos* varied from state to state, and from time to time, they always seem to have contained several hundred men. Unless units of this size were broken down into smaller ones, it is difficult to believe that every man would have had a fixed position, and one suspects that before a battle there was a certain amount of jostling as men found themselves a place. This may be part of the point of Brasidas' scornful remark that movement of spears and heads was characteristic of troops who would not stand their ground.

If the battle was at all unexpected, men could still be putting on their armour as they took their positions, as happened before Second Mantineia. In Euripides' *Heraclidae,* it is even suggested that the aged Iolaos should have someone carry his equipment to the battle-line, and in real battles, officers in particular may only have taken their shields from their soldier-servants at the last moment. If there was time to kill before the advance, men would stand with spears at the slope and shields leaning against their legs. Sometimes the pose was kept up to show contempt for an advancing enemy. Spartans possibly sat while waiting, as seems to have been true of Plataia, though there they were being subjected to fire from Persian archers rather than waiting to advance against other hoplites.

Many generals would take this opportunity to harangue their men, perhaps addressing them unit by unit, as Pagondas did before Delion, 'so that they did not all leave the line at once', or walking along the ranks as Archidamos did before the 'Tearless Battle', presumably so that all could hear him. But the Spartans preferred to encourage each other, according to Thucydides, 'knowing that long practice in action is of more help than brief, well-rounded, verbal advice'. Generals and their staff would also be busy with the sacrifice, and perhaps having a drink of wine to steady their nerves, as Kleombrotos and his officers were before Leuktra, though it seems unlikely that wine was normally served out to all.

The signal for the advance was often given by trumpet, and the hoplites would move forward, initially, perhaps, with spears still at the slope. Men would sing the 'Paian', or, in the Spartan army, if Plutarch is right, a hymn to Castor. Most armies did not march in step, judging by Thucydides' emphasis that the Spartan army did, to the sound of pipes. At a further signal, down would come the spears, or at least those of the first two or three ranks, and a good general hoped all would be lowered simultaneously for effect. 'Since there were many soldiers,' Iphikrates is supposed to have said on one occasion, 'they were neither able to level spears nor to sing the paian together; when I ordered "level spears", there was more noise of teeth to be heard [presumably chattering!] than of weapons.' But if it worked, the result could be terrific. It is vividly captured by Plutarch in his description of the moment at Plataia, when 'in an instant the phalanx took on the look of a wild animal, bristling as it turns at bay'.

Armies sometimes advanced at the double, and Thucydides' description of the slow advance of the Spartans at First Mantineia implies that this was unusual. But one suspects that all hoplites started at a walk, and then, unless they were Spartans, broke into a double when they got near the enemy. Xenophon ordered his men to double when the first sling-stones rattled against their shields, and it was probably usually when they came within missile-range that hoplites started to run. The slow approach of the Spartans was designed to preserve their formation. At the Nemea they are even said to have halted within 200 yds (180 m) of the enemy, to perform a final sacrifice to 'Artemis the Huntress', which would also have given them a chance to dress their line. This was clearly a matter of concern. At Kounaxa, when the line started to billow out, Xenophon and his comrades shouted to each other not to 'run races'.

Often, too, Greeks raised a war-cry, evidently sounding something like 'eleleu', and sometimes drummed spear on shield. In Aischylos' *Seven Against Thebes* (385–6) there is even a reference to the fearful clangour of bronze bells, apparently fixed on the insides of shields! Aischylos also remarks on the dust raised by advancing troops, the 'voiceless herald of an army', and Euripides likens the flashing of the bronze accoutrements to lightning.

Many battles, it appears, were virtually decided almost before they began, by the flight of one side or the other. As one of the characters in Euripides' *Bacchae* remarks, 'it is common for fear to strike with panic an army under arms and in its ranks, before the spears touch'. At First Mantineia the centre of the allied line, particularly those opposed to the 300 Spartan *hippeis,* broke and ran, 'the majority not waiting to come to grips', and notoriously at the so-called 'Tearless Battle', 'only a few of the enemy waited for the Spartans to come within spear-range'. As Euripides again says, the test of a man's courage was not the bow, but 'to stand and look and outface the spear's swift stroke, keeping the line firm' or, as Xenophon more succinctly puts it, castigating a coward, 'because he could not look the spears in the face, he did not want to serve'.

Sometimes, too, at least one wing of a phalanx contrived, by luck or judgement, to avoid a head-on collision. Thucydides says that all armies tended to edge to the right, as each man sought the protection of his neighbour's shield for the unguarded right half of his own body, and there was thus a tendency for each side to create an overlap on the right. Euripides refers to the stalemate situation which could result, and this was, presumably, why the battle of Laodokeion was 'ambiguous'. At the Nemea, however, the Spartans appear to have deliberately exploited the tendency, and although the result was that the left was sacrificed, this may have seemed acceptable. The left consisted of allied troops, who would not lose too heavily if they beat a hasty retreat, and the right could then take the victorious enemy right in its shieldless flank, as it broke off pursuit and attempted to retire.

If, however, phalanxes met head on and were prepared to fight it out, the gap between them would have closed rapidly until sometimes the opposing front ranks literally crashed together. More often, one suspects, the advance of both phalanxes slowed as they got 'within spear-range', and the men in the front ranks probed with their spears, trying to stab their opposite numbers.

How were these initial thrusts normally delivered? The language Xenophon uses in the *Anabasis* certainly seems to suggest that spears were lowered from the shoulder to the underarm position, below the waist, as the advance began. This would have had the advantages that there would, perhaps, have been less likelihood of accidentally wounding one's own comrades, and that the thrust could then have been directed below the rims of enemy shields, at relatively unprotected parts of the body. But both Tyrtaios and Kallinos describe soldiers as carrying their spears aloft, and when Tyrtaios exhorts the Spartans to 'brandish the mighty spear in the right hand', he can hardly be thinking of an underarm thrust.

It is true that the latter is sometimes depicted on vases, but where it is, the scenes are invariably duels between individuals. There does not seem to be any example of lines of hoplites advancing with spears levelled below the waist. Admittedly, there are very few such scenes, in any case, but those that have survived, from the Chigi vase onwards, invariably show hoplites carrying spears overarm. Similarly, although wounds to the lower part of the body, and to the legs, are mentioned, it is not usually clear when they were inflicted. In one case where it is, when the Spartan prince, Archidamos, receives a wound through his thigh, right at the beginning of a fight, he is specifically said to be leading his men in column, two by two. Assuming that he was on the right, the position normally occupied by a commander, the right side of his body would have been completely unprotected, and even an overarm thrust could have got him in the thigh.

It may be the case that advancing hoplites carried their spears in the underarm position, but it is unlikely that they delivered their first thrusts underarm, and then changed grip in the melée. More likely they brought their spears to the overarm position, before they came 'within spear-range', though it is difficult to see how this was done. The change, it must be remembered, involves not just raising the spear, but also turning the hand round on the spearshaft, since when a thrust is underarm, the thumb is towards the point, but when overarm, towards the butt.

The change-over could have been effected by sticking the spear in the ground, then picking it up again with the hand reversed. But this would have required a momentary halt—difficult when charging at the double, but perhaps possible for the Spartans, or any other troops who halted during the advance. Alternatively, a momentary shift of the spear to the left hand, gripping the strap or cord near the rim at the right of the shield, might have done the trick. More risky, but perhaps easier, would have been to lift the spear above the head, still with the underarm grip, then let it go for a moment, and catch it as it fell, with the grip reversed. Even lifting the spear from below the waist to above the shoulder would have been much easier if hoplites had not been standing shoulder to shoulder, let alone marching or running, and the difficulties would certainly have been compounded if the change was only made after battle had been joined. But somehow or other it seems to have been done.

With spears probably held high, then, hoplites in at least the front rank, possibly the front two, thrust downwards, aiming for the face, and presumably the throat or shoulders, over the rim of the shield, or for the chest through shield and cuirass. There was, however, no loosening of the close-packed formation, at this point, as some have suggested. Plato's *Laches* makes it clear that this only happened when one side or the other fled the field, and what would have been the point of each man seeking the protection of his right-hand neighbour's shield during the advance if they then parted company when battle was actually joined?

The only evidence that the hoplite phalanx was at all fluid are the occasional references by the poets, from Tyrtaios to Pindar, to 'fore-fighters' *(promachoi),* usually with the implication that this is where a brave man would seek to take his place. Thus Tyrtaios cries, 'let each man direct his shield straight to the fore-fighters', and Pindar talks about the 'throng of fore-fighters' where the best men fought. However, there would, presumably, have been ample opportunities for hoplites to display either their courage by pressing forward, as men fell in front of them, or their faint-heartedness by holding back. . . .

Euripides' description of the fight between Eteokles and Polyneikes, though a description of an imaginary duel, possibly allows us to glimpse something of the preliminary exchanges in a hoplite battle. The two antagonists keep their shields up, apparently eyeing each other through holes pierced in the rims of their shields—was this true, one wonders, of real battles? Then Eteokles turns his foot on a stone and exposes his thigh outside his shield. Immediately, Polyneikes thrusts and drives his spear through his brother's leg, but in so doing exposes his own shoulder to a counter-thrust.

It was, presumably, in such an encounter that the Spartan king, Kleombrotos, got his mortal wound in the opening moments of Leuktra. Eteokles and Polyneikes, however, survive this wounding, and go on to kill each other with swords, and although they were heroes, it is alleged of the perfectly mortal Spartan, Kleonymos, that at Leuktra he fell three times, before finally being killed, indicating that he was not yet shield to shield with the enemy. However, the Thessalian 'trick' which Eteokles finally uses to kill Polyneikes, would not have been appropriate to a hoplite. It involved taking a pace back, which would have been almost impossible for a man in the front rank of a phalanx.

It was, perhaps, this preliminary stabbing and counter-stabbing that Tyrtaios had in mind when he talks about 'slogging it out' (*aloièseumen*—literally, 'we will be threshing'). Men probably still had breath to shout—Euripides, for example, imagines Athenians shouting 'Athens' and their opponents shouting for Argos. But the grimmest description of the sound of battle is Xenophon's of Second Koroneia: 'There was no shouting, nor yet silence, but the kind of noise passion and battle are likely to produce.' Groans and screams no doubt mingled with the clash of spear on shield and of spear-shaft on spear-shaft. In Aischylos the 'spear-shaken air seethes', and in real battles indescribable confusion probably reigned. Thus in his account of the night attack on Epipolai, Thucydides says that even in daylight 'each man hardly knows anything except what is happening to himself', and in Euripides' *Supplices* Theseus says one question he will not ask, in case he is laughed at, is who met whom in the battle. It is significant that there was obviously no clear tradition about how even Epameinondas met his end.

Far from his fighting bringing about any loosening of the phalanx, it was now that its cohesion mattered more than ever. At the beginning of the hoplite era, Tyrtaios adjures the Spartans to fight 'standing by one another', maintaining that 'fewer die' as a result, and that this was so is confirmed by Xenophon's description of a minor skirmish on Aigina in 388 BC, and by many an occasion when hoplites in a difficult situation preserved themselves by maintaining their compact order. As one of Plutarch's *Sayings of the Spartans* puts it, a man carried a shield, unlike helmet and cuirass, 'for the sake of the whole line', and this was not just because of the protection one man's shield afforded to the man on his left, but because an unbroken shield-wall was virtually impregnable.

If we imagine what it would have been like to stand in the front line of a phalanx, swapping thrusts with enemy spearmen only a few feet away, we can understand why Euripides' Amphitryon argues that if a hoplite finds himself ranged alongside cowards, he may be killed by his neighbours' faintheartedness. Demosthenes puts the other side of the case when he says that no one who flees from a battle, ever blames himself, but the general, his neighbours and everyone else. But, as he goes on, 'they are none the less, of course, defeated by all who flee, for it was open to the man who blames the others, to stand, and if each man did this, they would win'. As Brasidas says, 'those who have no line, may not be ashamed to give ground under pressure. Advance or retreat having the same good repute among them, their courage is never tested'. For hoplites, leaving the line, even to challenge the enemy individually, as Aristodemos did at Plataia, was regarded as irresponsible folly, for, as Brasidas again puts it, 'independent action is always likely to give a man a good excuse for saving his own skin'.

Sometimes, it appears, this fighting went on until both sides had virtually wiped each other out. At the Nemea, for example, 'the men of Pellene being opposite the Thespiaians, they each fought and fell in their places'. There may also sometimes have been a certain ebb and flow in the struggle. In the imaginary battle in the *Heracleidae,* for example, Euripides has his messenger describe how 'at first the thrust of the Argive spear broke us, then they gave back', and Xenophon argues that at Leuktra the Spartans must have been winning initially, since otherwise they would not have been able to carry their king, still living, from the field. This also shows that it was possible to get a wounded man to the rear, even in the thronging turmoil of a hoplite battle, though one suspects that an ordinary hoplite who fell stood less chance than a king of Sparta. Even the Spartan second-in-command on Sphakteria, Hippagretas, was left lying among the dead.

If neither side gave way in these preliminary exchanges, the pressure from the rear would sooner or later force the opposing front ranks to close right up to each other, shield to shield, and many sources mention the crash when this happened. Then the fighting would be as Euripides describes it in the second phase of his fictional battle, 'toe-to-toe, man to man', or as Tyrtaios puts it, 'with foot set beside foot, pressing shield to shield, crest against crest, helmet against helmet, chest against chest'. Xenophon's description of the Spartans and Thebans at Second Koroneia, when 'crashing their shields together, they shoved, fought, slew and died', shows that the poets did not exaggerate.

At such close quarters, it is difficult to see how spears 6 ft (1.8 m) and more in length could have been of much use, though one could, perhaps, have aimed for the men in the second and third ranks. It has been suggested that most spears were broken at the first impact, and that swords were then used. But the evidence is not very good, and other passages suggest that swords were only used after prolonged fighting. The spear was certainly the hoplite weapon *par excellence.* Archilochos' spear was his bread and wine and he drank leaning on it, and for Aischylos the typical Greek weapon, as opposed to the bow of the Persians, was the 'close-quarter spear'. Euripides' Amphitryon, in his argument with Lykos over the respective merits of the hoplite and the archer, even declares that the former has only one means of defence—'having broken his spear, he has no means of warding death from his body'. This was, strictly speaking, untrue, but when Xenophon says that after Second Koroneia you could see swords 'bared of their sheaths, some on the ground, some in a body, some still in the hand', does he not imply that you would normally have expected to see them still *in* their sheaths? This battle, it must be remembered, 'like no other of those in our time,' as Xenophon says, consisted of two separate encounters, and, as a result, it is likely that more spears were broken than in normal battles.

There is another answer to how hoplites fought, once they were too close to the enemy to make effective use of their spears. Xenophon's description of the second encounter at Koroneia suggests that the opposing lines, having crashed into each other, shield to shield, literally started to shove, and shoving *(othismos)* evidently was a feature of many a battle. Herodotos, for example, says there was 'much shoving' over the body of Leonidas at Thermopylai and that at Plataia the fighting was prolonged 'until they came to the shoving'; at Solygeia the Athenian and Karystian right wing 'with difficulty shoved the

Corinthians back'; at Delion the engagement took the form of 'tough fighting and shoving of shields'; at Syracuse the Athenians and their Argive allies defeated both wings of the Syracusan army, by shoving, and at Leuktra, the Spartan right was 'shoved' back.

But what form did this 'shoving' actually take? We do not really know, but it is possible that hoplites in the rear ranks literally put their shields against the backs of those in front and pushed. Xenophon advocates that the best men should be placed in front and rear of a phalanx so that the worst men in the middle could be 'led by the former and *shoved* by the latter'. More directly, later writers talk about the men in the rear ranks of a Macedonian-style phalanx using the weight of their bodies to push those in front forwards, and it is arguable that this would be *a fortiori* true of a hoplite phalanx.

None of the earlier sources gives any clear indication how the 'shoving' was accomplished, but Thucydides, in saying of the Thebans at Delion that 'they followed up little by little as they shoved', makes it sound very like the inexorable 'heave' of a well-drilled pack on a rugby football field. The famous story of Epameinondas' cry for 'one pace more' at Leuktra also sounds like the kind of thing the leader of a rugby 'pack' might shout. The story is late and one wonders whether many of Epameinondas' men could have heard him, but Thucydides' account of Sphakteria implies that Spartans normally expected to hear orders, when he says that they were unable to hear them there because of the shouting of the enemy. One suspects that commanders often did call for a supreme effort, and even if they could only be heard by those immediately around them, word could rapidly have been passed to the rest.

Of one thing we can be certain. Epameinondas would have been among his men. He was killed at Second Mantineia, and many another hoplite general also fell in battle. There was sometimes criticism that generals took all the credit, but even an old cynic like Archilochos felt he could trust a commander who was 'short, bowlegged to look at, set squarely on his feet and full of heart', and there was probably a natural camaraderie between hoplites and their commanders. After all, they belonged to the same class. Even in the Spartan army, men about to engage in or in the midst of a battle were not averse to shouting advice to their officers, king included.

It is evident, too, that the depth of a phalanx was significant from at least the time of Marathon onwards. Thus Xenophon says that before the Nemea there was some discussion amongst Sparta's opponents about what depth to adopt. Later he implies that it was decided to form up sixteen deep, though in the event the Boiotians ignored the agreement, and made their phalanx 'really deep'—perhaps twenty-five, as at Delion. Xenophon's remarks here may suggest that 'really deep' formations were defensive, but the significance of the depth of a phalanx was surely not just the defensive strength it imparted. When Epameinondas made his phalanx 'fifty shields deep' at Leuktra, he was not thinking in terms of defence, but of 'crushing the head of the snake'.

It has also been suggested that the point of these 'really deep' phalanxes was to provide a reserve, which could be moved out to attack the flanks of an enemy phalanx, once its front was 'pinned'. But there is no evidence that the rear ranks of a hoplite phalanx were ever used in this way, and there must be some other explanation for the importance attached to depth. The most probable is that it was thought that the deeper the phalanx, the more likely it was to be able to win the 'shoving' and literally smash through the enemy line. Thus, at Second Mantineia, Xenophon says, Epameinondas used his phalanx, deepened just before the advance, 'like a trireme bows on'.

It may, finally, be of some significance that ancient authors occasionally imply that physical strength was a factor in winning hoplite battles. Herodotos, for example, remarks that the Persians at Plataia were 'not inferior in spirit and strength'—it was only their lack of armour and expertise which let them down. Diodoros, too, several times alleges that the bodily strength of the Thebans gave them victory, and Plutarch even claims that their skill in wrestling helped to win Leuktra. This is treated seriously by some scholars, but it seems doubtful whether close-packed hoplites, with shields on their left arms and spears or swords in their right hands, could have wrestled with their opponents. When the Spartans were reduced to fighting with hands and teeth at Thermopylai, it was because all their weapons had gone, and similarly when the Persians tried to grab the Greeks' spears at Plataia, it was presumably because their own spears were too short.

Physical strength would clearly have been important for the 'shoving', but in rugby football it is not necessarily the heaviest and strongest pack that wins—how the pressure is applied is also important. Hoplites needed to be strong, in any case, to stand up to prolonged fighting in the heat, burdened with heavy equipment. The way that men from Archilochos onwards threw away their shields if they turned to run, shows that the shield was particularly burdensome, but the weight of hoplite equipment in general is often contrasted with that of other troops. The physical exertion involved in hoplite fighting is perhaps most vividly brought out in a passage of Euripides, where Hekuba draws attention to the stain on the rim of Hektor's shield, caused by the sweat from his face, 'as he endured the toils of battle'.

Even if the rear ranks did not literally push against those in front, they could have added 'weight' in the general sense that the greater the number of men pressing forward, the greater the force of the attack, and they would also have made it impossible for those in front to turn and run. This is a point made by the later writers Polybios, Arrian and Aelian, and Xenophon's Cyrus orders the commander of his rear-guard bid his men watch for any shirking amongst those in front. Again there may have been a certain amount of ebb and flow at the shoving stage. Herodotos, for example, alleges that the Greeks flung the Persians back four times in the shoving over Leonidas' body, though this was not against hoplites. But, eventually, one side or the other would have had to give way, either because gaps opened in the line as men fell, or because of the sheer weight of their opponents' 'shove'. Often the collapse came in one section of the line and led to the flight of the rest. At Leuktra, for example, the Spartan left gave way when it saw the right 'shoved back'. Epameinondas elevated into a principle the idea that if you could defeat one part of an army, the rest would give way, believing, Xenophon says, that 'it is very hard to find men willing to stand, when they see some of their own side in flight'.

We might, perhaps, have expected to hear of the losers being knocked down and trampled underfoot as the victors surged forward, but possibly the disintegration was gradual. The rear ranks in the losing phalanx would have peeled off to run, and even the front ranks may have stayed on their feet, though the moment of disengagement would have been terribly dangerous. Perhaps they were helped by a momentary pause as the winners realized that the enemy line had given way and that shoving could give place to stabbing. We do hear of fugitives trampling each other in their desperation to get away, for example at First Mantineia, and the situation could be much worse if escape was difficult, as for the Athenians at the ford over the Assinaros. Xenophon has an appalling description of Argive fugitives trying to get away from Spartans between the 'long walls' of Corinth, in the Corinthian War. They were penned up against one of the walls, and were trying to scramble up the steps leading on to it; some were even asphyxiated in the crush. A recent tragedy at a football match in England, in which ninety-five people were killed, is a terrible reminder of what such an incident would have been like.

Undoubtedly the side that lost a hoplite battle tended to lose more heavily than the winners, and this was presumably because men who turned to flee, immediately exposed their backs. As Tyrtaios says, 'it's easy to pierce the back of a fleeing man'. Often, too, as we have seen, they threw away their shields, so that even if they did turn at bay, they would have been at a serious disadvantage. It was in these situations that—according to Plato's *Laches*—weapons-drill finally came into its own. But not every retreating hoplite was a Sokrates, whose belligerent mien in the retreat from Delion, acted as an effective deterrent to anyone who thought of attacking him. Often one imagines, once panic had set in, the mass of fugitives would have been more like the mob of Argives Xenophon describes, 'frightened, panic-stricken, presenting their unprotected sides, no one turning to fight, but all doing everything to assist their own slaughter'. Even on a battlefield, parts of a defeated army could find themselves surrounded, as happened to the Thespiaians at Delion, and once the winners' bloodlust was aroused, they might even slaughter some of their own men, in ignorance, as happened here. Xenophon says that the Spartans who had routed the Argives just described, thought their defenceless state was a gift from heaven.

But for all the horrors of such incidents, where figures are given, the losses suffered in hoplite battles actually seem to represent only a small percentage of those who had taken part. Thus the losses at Delion amounted to just over 7 percent for the Boiotians and just over 14 per cent for the Athenians, if Thucydides' figures are reliable. Figures for other battles are less reliable, but in few, if any, do even the beaten side appear to have suffered more than the Athenians at Delion, and casualties amongst the winners seem sometimes to have been perhaps as low as 2 percent. Such figures pale in comparison with the appalling losses inflicted on the Romans, for example, at Trasimene and Cannae, where about 60 percent of them may have been killed.

These were special cases, but part of the reason for the comparatively low losses in hoplite battles was that hoplites were not really suited to pursuit, and that although cavalry was frequently used instead, not all Greek states had cavalry, and those that did often had very few. Apart from the sheer weight of their equipment, hoplites who broke ranks to pursue, laid themselves open to counter-attack, and cavalry and light troops could also very easily find themselves in difficulties if beaten hoplites rallied. Thus it was no kind-heartedness which led the Spartans only to press the pursuit for a short distance, as Thucydides tells us was their custom, though they may also have felt it was not the 'done thing'.

However, even if losses in a hoplite battle were comparatively low, the nature of the fighting probably meant that the small area in which the decisive clash had taken place would have been a grim sight. We can probably discount some of the more lurid descriptions, for example Aischylos' talk of the 'clotted gore' lying on the soil at Plataia, and of the 'heaps of corpses bearing silent witness to the eyes of mortals to the third generation', though Herodotos claims to have seen the skeletons of men killed at Pelousion during Kambyses' invasion of Egypt. Obviously, too, if fugitives were caught in a situation like the wretched Argives at Corinth, the slaughter would have been more than usually horrific. The heaps of corpses, Xenophon implies, looked like piles of corn, logs or stones. But Xenophon's description of the battlefield at Koroneia, which he saw himself, is bad enough:

> When the battle was over, one could see, where they had crashed into each other, the earth stained red with blood, bodies of friends and foes lying with each other, shattered shields, broken spears, swords bare of sheaths, some on the ground, some in the body, some still in the hand.

The 254 skeletons, laid out in seven rows, around the site of the Lion of Chaironeia, assuming that they are the remains of men killed in the battle, are a reminder that Xenophon's description of Koroneia is probably only too accurate.

At least when the fury died, Greeks usually behaved in a fairly decent manner. There was little exulting over fallen foes, indeed Agesilaos is said to have been saddened at the news that so many had fallen at the Nemea, and Philip to have burst into tears at the sight of the dead members of the Sacred Band after Chaironeia. Then, as now, survivors shook hands with their comrades, and there was the usual boasting: 'Of the seven dead, whom we overtook on our feet,' sings Archilochos, 'we are the thousand slayers.' Sometimes men gathered round their generals to congratulate them.

There are very few references to the care of wounded. Xenophon's statement that the first Spartans wounded in the encounter with Iphikrates' peltasts near Corinth, were got away safely to Lechaion by the *hypaspistai*, is a rare exception. More attention was obviously given to those of high rank.

Agesilaos, for example, is said to have been severely wounded at Second Koroneia, but clearly survived, and Plutarch claims that Pelopidas received seven wounds at First Mantineia, though the story can hardly be true. Philip of Macedonia certainly recovered from a series of horrific wounds. Herodotos' story of how the heroic Aiginetan marine, Pytheas, was patched up by the Persians suggests that this seemed most unusual to a Greek, and one suspects that enemy wounded left on the battlefield were either killed, or left to die. The enemy dead were stripped of their armour, which was then partly used to set up a trophy, or for subsequent dedication to the gods. But the corpses were almost invariably handed over for burial, once the defeated sent a herald requesting a truce for the purpose. The delay after Delion was for special reasons, and Herodotos' evident disgust at the way Xerxes treated Leonidas' body, suggests that such behaviour was most un-Greek.

Prisoners are rarely mentioned, presumably because men who were not killed or too badly wounded, were usually able to escape. Some were certainly taken on occasion, for example, if escape was impossible, as at First Koroneia and on Sphakteria. But the 2,000 Athenian prisoners Philip took at Chaironeia, twice as many as were killed, were quite unprecedented. Willingness to surrender, or at least to consider it, was indicated by holding out hands, or lowering shields and waving. Prisoners were usually returned at the end of the war, although they were sometimes enslaved, or, if they were generals, executed, as happened to the unfortunate Athenians in Sicily.

How, then, were such battles won and lost? It is obvious from Plato's *Laches* that individual skills were not important, and Herodotos' Demaratos says that even Spartans fighting singly were merely 'second to none, though together they were the best of all men'. Thus at Plataia the personal courage of Persians, 'rushing out in ones and tens and in larger and smaller groups', was of no avail: 'they crashed into the Spartans and were destroyed'. Even the desperate courage of Aristodemos earned him no recognition from his fellow Spartans, since they considered he had been 'acting like a lunatic and *leaving the line*'. There was no place for such *virtuosi* in a hoplite line-of-battle.

Unit skills were, however, important, and here the Spartans clearly had an edge. As we have seen, their army was the only one to be articulated into manageable units, and the author of the *Constitution of the Lakedaimonians* attributed to Xenophon says that Spartan infantry tactics were thought to be too complicated for other troops, though he himself believed the reverse to be true. Significantly, the one thing he did think was not easy to learn, except for those 'trained under the laws of Lykourgos', was 'to fight equally well with anyone one found, even if there was confusion'. It was clearly this training in fighting together as units that enabled the Spartans to carry out complicated manoeuvres like the 'forward-bend' *(epikampe)*, 'counter-march' *(exeligmos)*, and 'back-wheel' *(anastrophe)*.

There was, however, a limit to the tactical skills that hoplites could display. The necessity to maintain cohesion made the phalanx an essentially unwieldy formation, and generals were not only untrained, but, as we have seen, in the thick of the fight. The most that even the best could usually hope to do was to set his army in motion according to a preconceived plan. The best of them all, Epameinondas, apparently made no changes to his plan once the massed Theban phalanx started to roll at Leuktra: the Sacred Band's charge at the double was Pelopidas' idea, if Plutarch is right. Similarly, at Second Mantineia, although Epameinondas increased the depth of his phalanx at the last moment, it was before the advance. The Spartans sometimes tried altering their formation during the advance, or after battle had been joined, but each time it went disastrously wrong.

Ultimately the single most important factor in a hoplite battle was undoubtedly what Napoleon thought, many centuries later, counted for three-quarters in war: morale. We have already seen that on many occasions hoplites fled almost before a blow had been struck, and panic was easily communicated. Pindar says that even the sons of gods were not immune, and, as previously mentioned, it was Epameinondas' opinion that it was very hard to find men who would stand when they saw part of their own army in flight. This was one of the reasons why the Spartans were so successful for so long. In effect their battles were 'three-quarters' won before they started, since their enemies feared to face them. As Plutarch says, they were 'irresistible in spirit, and, because of their reputation, when they came to grips, terrifying to opponents, who themselves did not think that with equal forces they stood an equal chance with Spartiates'.

Morale, as Plutarch implies, works both ways: if you think you are going to win, you will gain in confidence; if your enemy thinks you are going to win, he will lose confidence. Spartans were supremely confident. On Sphakteria, for example, the 390 or so hoplites who remained, after their first guard-post had been overwhelmed, 'seeing an army approaching, formed up and advanced against the Athenian hoplites, *wanting to come to grips with them*'. One tends to forget that they were outnumbered by more than two to one by these hoplites alone, to say nothing of some Messenian hoplites, 7,500 armed Athenian sailors, 800 archers and 800 peltasts! Thucydides' description of the advance of the Spartan army at First Mantineia gives a marvellous impression of soldiers who knew exactly what they had to do, and that they could do it.

This kind of confidence goes a long way towards explaining why many Greeks feared to face the Spartans. The mere sight of the *lambdas* displayed on their shields was enough to send a shiver down Kleon's spine, according to the comic poet, Eupolis, and Xenophon's story of the confident advance of a force of Argives against dismounted Spartan cavalry troopers who had borrowed shields bearing *sigmas* (for 'Sikyonians'), implies that the Argives would not have been nearly so confident, had they known that they were facing Spartans. Even the overwhelming numbers the Athenians had at Sphakteria did not prevent them going ashore 'obsessed by the idea that they were going against Spartans'.

What, then, motivated men in these encounters? Obviously their feelings were just as complex as those of men in more recent conflicts, and since we cannot question ancient Greeks, we must, in the end, confess that we shall never know what their motives were. Simple patriotism certainly played a part, and men were clearly concerned to defend their homes and loved ones. Then as now, too, even the aggressors often thought of themselves as engaged in what we would call a 'pre-emptive strike'. Thus, before Delion, the Athenian general, Hippokrates, declared that 'the battle will take place in their country but will be for our own'!

Unlike the soldiers of modern armies, hoplites were not 'the nation in arms', in the sense that in most states, if not all, the poor were excluded because they could not afford to buy the relatively expensive equipment required. In Athens, for example, hoplite service was almost certainly impossible for the *thetes*,* who formed, perhaps, 40 to 60 percent of the population, at various times. It is true that the emergence of hoplites marks a break with the aristocratic past, and that the hoplite *ethos* differed from the aristocratic, as one can see by comparing Homer with Tyrtaios. But hoplites remained an elite, and the non-aristocrats among them probably adopted many aristocratic attitudes. It was not for nothing, after all, that Homer has been called the 'Bible' of the Greeks. Thucydides perhaps expresses the attitude of the hoplite class when he implies that the activities of 'stone-throwers, slingers and archers' before a battle, were of little or no importance, and his comment on the 120 Athenian hoplites who perished at the hands of Aitolian javelineers—'these, so many and of the same age, were the best men from the city of Athens who perished in this war'—seems to contain an added note of bitterness. Moreover, hoplites were 'the nation in arms', in another sense, in states where those who could not afford such service, were excluded from full civic rights.

Thus, although men of the hoplite class were realists enough to know that war was a grim business—neither Homer nor Tyrtaios glosses over the horrors—they also retained sufficient of the aristocratic way of thinking to regard prowess in battle as glorious. 'This is the noblest virtue,' sings Tyrtaios, 'this the noblest prize among men', and he goes on to declare that if a brave man falls, his grave and his children and grandchildren are honoured, and if he survives, he is looked up to by young and old alike. This may just seem like a Spartan speaking, but Alkaios, too, said that 'to die in war is a noble thing', and even Thucydides' Perikles, who so poignantly expresses how death in battle is the end of all a man's hopes and fears, nevertheless maintains that such a death is the final confirmation of his worth.

Obviously there were pressures on a man not to play the coward, as there are now. They may have been strongest in Sparta, where cowardice not only caused a man to be shunned by his fellows, but almost certainly led to his losing his civic rights. Such men were called *tresantes* (tremblers) from Tyrtaios'

Thetes were the lowest class of free men. They were too poor to afford the armor of the hoplites. (ed).

day to Plutarch's. But cowardice could also be an offence in Athens, and failure
to perform one's military duties could lead to execution. The demagogue,
Kleophon, for example, was condemned to death ostensibly on a charge of being 'absent without leave'.

In the end, however, what modern research has shown about today's soldiers, was probably also true of those of ancient Greece—that it was mainly
not wanting to 'let one's mates down' which kept them from shirking, though
the evidence largely concerns the Spartans. Thus one suspects that the reason
for the suicide of the sole Spartan survivor from the so-called 'Battle of the
Champions', was not just the fear that his mere survival might cast doubt on
his courage, but also the thought of being left alive when all his comrades had
perished. Not letting others down was no doubt also partly what Tyrtaios had
in mind when he exhorted the Spartans to fight 'standing by one another', and
said that a soldier who encouraged his neighbour was 'a good man in war'.
Xenophon's Cyrus, possibly thinking of the Spartans, considered that those
who messed together would be less likely to desert each other, and that there
could be no stronger phalanx than one composed of friends.

Athenaios even says that before battle the Spartans sacrificed to Eros,
'since safety lies in the love of those ranged alongside each other', and there
can be no doubt that sometimes the feelings of hoplites for their comrades
were homosexual, particularly in the Spartan and Theban armies. The Sacred
Band was supposed to have been composed of pairs of lovers, which makes
the skeletons at Chaironeia, if they are those of this elite force, all the more
poignant.

Ancient Greek armies, like more modern ones, no doubt contained their
share of thugs and psychotics, and the Spartan way of life may have conditioned them to think of fighting as something normal, or even desirable. But
the epitaph of those who fell at Thermopylai, is as poignant as anything ever
said about war dead, and there is nothing of the berserker about the Spartan
Anaxibios' remark to his soldiers, when he realized that he was trapped: 'Men,
my duty is to die here, but you hurry to safety before the enemy closes'. It is
the impression one so often gets of ordinary men just doing their duty, which
is so moving. Pindar, for example, says of a young man probably killed fighting for Thebes at Oinophyta: 'You breathed out the flower of your youth in
the throng of fore-fighters, where the best kept up the struggle of battle with
hopes forlorn', and an Athenian who fought at the Nemea, confessed in court
that he did so 'not as one who did not think fighting the Lakedaimonians was
a fearful thing'.

But perhaps Simonides should have the final word. A friend of his, the
Akarnanian seer, Megistias, was killed at Thermopylai. Before the last day,
Herodotos tells us, 'on looking into the sacrifices, he declared the death com-
ing would be with them at dawn', but although Leonidas urged him to go, he
sent his only son away instead, and stayed to die with the Spartans he served.
Simonides composed this epitaph for his friend:

This is the memorial of famed Megistias, whom on a day the
  Medes slew, having crossed the Spercheios river.
He was a seer, who all the time knowing well the fate
  approaching, had not the heart to desert the captains of
  Sparta.

WOMEN AND THE HOUSEHOLD IN ANCIENT GREECE

SUE BLUNDELL

Nearly everything we know about Athenian women comes from the men of classical Athens. Literature and law codes mention women frequently, but they were products of male authors. These sources cannot provide us with women's own accounts of their experiences, but they do provide us with a good picture of the circumstances in which women lived, and what men thought and expected of women. Athens' women, even those of citizen families, possessed no active political rights. They were excluded from the proceedings of the citizen assembly; they could hold no public office. They could not own property, make contracts, begin or conduct court proceedings, make major transactions, or enter into a marriage on their own. They always belonged to a man's household; there was no option of independence. These legal disabilities were the product of a society in which, with the exception of some religious ceremonies, public life was almost exclusively male. Women belonged to the household and in the household.

The subordination of women was characteristic of ancient societies, but there were degrees of more or less subordination. Like their Athenian counterparts, women in Sparta had no political rights, but they could own land and conduct business. Roman law gave fathers extreme power over their households. A father's power over his daughters was transferred to their husbands when they married, but only if the father consented to give it up. Nevertheless, Roman law also made it possible for women to participate in public life—going outside the household to social gatherings and public events—and to own land. Women's legal dependence on male heads of household lessened dramatically by the end of the Republic. Emperor Augustus (31 B.C.–A.D. 14) attempted to replenish Rome's dwindling population by granting independence to

From: Sue Blundell, *Women in Ancient Greece* (Cambridge, MA: Harvard University Press, 1995), pp. 135–44.

*freeborn women who gave birth to three children, and to freed
women who bore four.*

*In this selection, Sue Blundell explores the most powerful ex-
pression of women's place in ancient Athenian society: female seclusion. What did the segregation of men's and women's worlds mean
for women? How absolute was women's seclusion? What ramifications might the ideal of seclusion hold for those women—poor
women, servants, and slaves—who could not practice it?*

SEXUAL SEGREGATION

In the first half of this century much of the scholarly discussion about the position of women in Classical Athens centred on the issue of their seclusion.
Nowadays, there seems little doubt that sexual segregation did at least exist as
an upper-class ideal. Xenophon produces a classic statement of it when he puts
into the mouth of Ischomachus the words, 'So it is seemly for a woman to remain at home and not be out of doors; but for a man to stay inside, instead of
devoting himself to outdoor pursuits, is disgraceful'. According to Plato,
women are a race 'accustomed to an underground and shadowy existence';
while the spectacle of Athenian women crouched in doorways, asking passers-
by for news of their husbands, fathers or brothers after a disastrous defeat in
battle, is described in one speech as 'degrading both to them and to the city'.
The market-place was apparently included in the public locations deemed un-
suitable for respectable females, for it seems to have been common for husbands or slave-girls to do the shopping.

The segregation of male and female citizens was also applied to those occasions when the social life of the *polis* penetrated the private house. The *sym-
posium*, the party where men drank and talked with their friends, was not an
event for citizen women, although mistresses and female entertainers might attend. If a woman went out to parties with a man, this was regarded as proof
that she was a courtesan and not his lawful wife. In her own home a wife
would not be expected to have any contact with male visitors. She was not present when guests were entertained, even if the invitation had been an impromptu one. To say that a woman talked to men, or even that she opened the
front door herself, was tantamount to calling her a trollop.

The home was the arena devoted to the private life shared by males and
females, and any violation of the home might be interpreted as an affront to
the modesty of its womenfolk, even if the incursion had manifestly been made
for other purposes. This aspect of the code of honour is highlighted in a number of law-court speeches. In one, the speaker relates how his opponent Simon,
in the course of a drunken raid on his house, had entered the women's rooms
and encountered the speaker's sister and niece, 'who had lived so modestly that
they were ashamed to be seen even by relatives'. Even Simon's companions
felt that this was a monstrous act. In another oration, the speaker is careful to

contrast his own behaviour with that of his opponent's associates. Before entering the house of his opponent Theophemus in order to seize some surety for equipment which should have been handed over to him, he had first ascertained that Theophemus was unmarried. He was not, in other words, likely to run across any women. But later, when Theophemus's brother and brother-in-law broke into the speaker's house, they confronted his wife and children in the courtyard. The resulting commotion brought one of the neighbours running up, but even in these circumstances he did not like to enter the house in the absence of its master.

The issue of sexual segregation is a complex one, however. Those scholars who in the past were anxious to defend Athenian men against accusations of locking up their womenfolk often made much of the fact that in tragedy and comedy females seem to have little difficulty in leaving the house. This, one might argue, is a necessity arising from one of the conventions of Athenian drama, which often deals with relations between family members but is almost always set outside the home. It is also thematically significant, since the interaction between private (feminine) concerns and public (masculine) ones is something which interests many Athenian dramatists, and symbolically the threshold of the house is the location where this occurs. Moreover, male characters in drama sometimes express their discomfort at seeing women engaged in exchanges in a public place. Euripides' Achilles is desperately embarrassed when he is forced into conversation with a free-born woman, Clytemnestra, in the Greek camp; and Electra is warned by her husband that 'It is shameful for a woman to be standing with young men'. In comedy, too, a woman who leaves the house may be suspected of having an assignation with a lover.

Nevertheless, it is important to note that in many references it is the fact that women are seen conversing with unrelated males, rather than their appearance out of doors, which is found to be offensive. Segregation is not the same thing as seclusion, and some people may have thought it acceptable for women to emerge from the house occasionally provided that they kept apart from male company. The belief that 'a woman's place is in the home' is not linked solely to the aim of protecting her chastity. Many women would have had plenty of work to keep them there as well. When a character in the *Lysistrata* says 'It's difficult for a woman to get out of the house', she adds 'What with dancing attendance on her husband, keeping the servant-girl on her toes, putting the baby to bed, bathing it, feeding it . . .' . The domestic and time-consuming nature of women's work must have contributed greatly to the notion that a woman who was seen too much out of doors must be up to no good, so that neglect of one's housewifely duties would have become synonymous with a lack of modesty.

For many women of the lower classes, complete confinement to the home would not have been feasible. In a democratic society, Aristotle asks, 'who could prevent the wives of the poor from going out when they want to?' In those homes where there was no well in the courtyard, and no slave to fetch water, women would have to go to the public fountain. The female chorus in

Aristophanes' *Lysistrata* speaks of the crowd that gathers round the fountain in the morning, and scenes like this are also depicted in vase paintings; there is no reason to assume that all the women represented in these are to be seen as slaves, aliens or courtesans. Lower-class women also went out to work, and even where they were employed indoors (for example, as midwives), they would of course have had to leave the house in order to get to their jobs. Although many of the working women in Athens were probably the wives of resident aliens, there is evidence that citizen women worked as grape-pickers, and that some of them sold goods—such as ribbons, garlands, vegetables and bread—in the market. When Lysistrata summons the 'seed-and-pancake-and-green-grocery-market-saleswomen' and the 'garlic-selling-barmaid-bread-women' among her female followers, she is probably referring to Athenian rather than to alien women.

Clearly, lower-class women—the majority of the female citizen population—had a number of legitimate reasons for appearing out of doors. Segregation does not necessarily break down in these circumstances. Most of the activities which took women out of the home would not have necessitated a great deal of converse with men, and as Gould has suggested, citing comparisons with modern rural Greece, there may still have been a 'residual sense of boundary . . . marking them off from the strange males with whom they must have come face to face'. Women who lived in the country, who may have been responsible for tasks such as tending gardens and feeding chickens, probably had more cause to leave their houses than town-dwellers. The strictest segregation was likely to have occurred in the city, where there were far more un-known men on the streets, and where public space may always have been re-garded primarily as male space, occasionally penetrated by females. Until 431 BC, the majority of the Athenian population lived outside the urban centre, but this picture changed when the outbreak of the Peloponnesian War necessitated the evacuation of the Athenian countryside. The women who at that stage came to live in the overcrowded city may have experienced an intensification of the constraints upon them. It is interesting to speculate that the frustration of these countrywomen, coupled with a growing need for women to go out to work, may have produced an increasing disjuncture between male expectations and female behaviour.

Sexual segregation was often a feature of social gatherings in Athens, but there were some events—such as funerals or weddings—where women would have been in mixed company. These would have been mainly family affairs, but women did attend the large state funeral which was conducted for men who had died in the Peloponnesian War, and they were also present at state festivals. However, occasions such as these probably provided little or no op-portunity for converse with unrelated males.

There is no reason to believe that women were isolated from companions of their own sex. Many women, particularly in the lower classes, would have had their own circle of friends and neighbours, part of an autonomous sphere of female relationships which existed in parallel with the masculine social network. Women went to help each other when they were in labour, and might pop into a neighbour's house to borrow some salt, a handful of barley, or a bunch of herbs. When Euphiletus's wife slipped out one night, she told her husband that she had gone next door to relight a lamp. One speaker in a law-suit informs his hearers that his own and his opponents' mothers had been close friends, 'and used to visit each other, as was natural when both lived in the country and were neighbours, and when, moreover, their husbands had been friends when they were alive'. Female friendships, unlike their male equivalents, were formed and conducted within the home, and some men may well have been suspicious of these 'hidden' relationships. It is, after all, a male playwright who puts these words into the mouth of a female character, Hermione: 'our homes are a sink of evil. Against this/ double-lock your doors and bolt them too./ For not one wholesome thing has ever come/ from gad-about female callers—only grief'.

The seclusion of women, while it may have existed as a masculine ideal, could probably only have been put into practice by the affluent classes. As an effective demonstration of a man's ability to protect the purity of his women-folk, it would have been a mark of masculinity, of status and of wealth, and it is little wonder that it was mentioned by speakers in the law-courts who were anxious to stress their respectability. But by the end of the fifth century a tension may have been developing between ideal and reality. Euripides' Andro-mache reveals a contradiction between expectations about women and their actual behaviour when she delivers this personal apologia:

First, since a woman, however high her reputation,
Draws slander on herself by being seen abroad,
I renounced restlessness and stayed in my own house;
Refused to open my door to the fashionable chat
Of other wives.

In comedy, a woman might well be one of the 'other wives' who ignored her husband's wishes: 'If we visit a friend for a celebration, wear ourselves out and fall asleep, you men turn up and search the place from top to bottom, looking for "the bane of your life"'.

The same tension can be perceived in attitudes to women of the poorer classes. In the fourth century, a man named Euxitheus could be deprived of his citizen rights because his mother, having worked as a nurse and a ribbon-seller, was suspected of not being Athenian; and yet, he argues, many Athenian women have become nurses, wool-workers, and grape-pickers, on account of our city's misfortunes (probably the aftermath of the Peloponnesian War). 'We do not live', he points out, 'in the way we would like'. The theory that it was the mark of an Athenian woman to stay quietly at home had certainly not been demolished, but it was obviously being put under great pressure at a time of considerable economic hardship.

Scholars who earlier this century argued against the Athenian practice of seclusion were troubled by the notion of contempt for women which they believed it implied. In this, they were imposing their own standards of judgement on the men of ancient Athens. It is perfectly possible for women to be 'valued' but also to be denied the same rights as men, and the ideal of seclusion would undoubtedly have been viewed by Athenian males as indicative of their great regard for women and of their own diligence in protecting them. It is perhaps only by women today that it is construed as a mark of a lack of freedom and equality for women which has nothing to do with either contempt or its opposite. Of the extent to which Athenian women themselves felt compelled to challenge the ideal we know very little; but there are at least some clear signs that they were on occasions able to evade male vigilance, and to build up an alternative system of female friendships which ran counter to prevailing notions of feminine decorum.

HOUSES

Our knowledge of Athenian houses is limited, since very few have been excavated, and the literary sources contain no detailed descriptions of them. The evidence that exists suggests that in the city they were situated on narrow winding streets, and that even those belonging to upper-class families were very simple in design and construction. The walls were of mud-brick on stone bases, and the rooms were grouped on two or more sides of a small courtyard, which sometimes had a well. In some cases there were upper storeys. There seems to have been very little in the way of elaborate decoration, and furniture and ornaments were sparse. The port of Piraeus, which attracted a growing population in the fifth century, had similar houses, but they were arranged in regular blocks. Country dwellings also had much the same plan, but some of them had larger courtyards, with porticoes along one side.

The boundary between the public world of males and the private world of females was encountered even within the home, at least among the upper classes. Male guests were entertained in the *andron,* the men's dining room, which was a place for talk and also for flirtations with female entertainers and handsome youths; while women spent much of their time in the *gynaikeion,* the women's quarters. The latter consisted of either a single room or a suite of rooms, and might be located on either the ground floor or, where one existed, on the upper storey. It was here that women did wool-working, looked after their children and entertained themselves. The unmarried women of the household and the female slaves would also have slept there, as might the wife on those occasions when she did not join her husband. Even a humble home which had no slaves may have had a room restricted to the women's use, although there is no direct evidence for this.

The most detailed literary account of household space is to be found in the speech in which Euphiletus defends himself against a charge of murdering his wife's alleged lover. Euphiletus explains that his small dwelling had two storeys, and that at first the women's quarters were upstairs, and were equal in extent to the men's quarters below. However, when their child was born, this arrangement was reversed, and the women's quarters were moved to the ground floor so that his wife would not have to keep going downstairs to wash the baby. This presumably means that there was a well in the courtyard. His wife often slept downstairs so that she could feed the infant in the night. On one occasion when Euphiletus came back unexpectedly from the country, the baby began crying, and he insisted that she go down to feed it. She taunted him with wanting to get his hands on the young slave-girl in her absence, and playfully turned the key in the lock when she left, only returning at dawn. Later, he says, he realised that the lover had been in the house, and that the slave had been making the baby cry on purpose.

Excavated Athenian houses tend to support this picture of partial segregation within the home. Where men's and women's quarters can be identified, they are often, when both are on the ground floor, on different sides of the courtyard, and the men's rooms are generally near the street door or opposite to it. Sometimes, rooms in which loom-weights have been found have the remains of staircases in them, which suggests that women might have been able to move from their workroom on the ground floor to the sleeping area above without having to emerge from the women's quarters. The houses generally had only one entrance, so that there was no back door where women might have a casual chat with neighbours. A husband who was suspicious of female friendships would therefore have found it relatively easy, when at home, to police his wife's activities.

WOMEN IN THE HOME

Although rigorous seclusion may seldom have been put into practice, it is clear that on the level both of ideology and of real life the home was a woman's predominant sphere of activity. The most comprehensive account of the ideal is given by Xenophon in the treatise *Oeconomicus*, where the 'model' husband Ischomachus describes in detail the education which he gave his young wife when they were first married. To modern readers Ischomachus may well come over as an insufferably pompous and patronising character, but credit must be given to the respect which he shows for his wife's managerial role within the home. It must be borne in mind, however, that his attitude probably does not represent the norm among Athenian males, who were more likely to have placed a low value on women's domestic work.

In instructing his young bride, Ischomachus warmly recommends a sexual division of labour which determines that husband and wife will play complementary parts in establishing and maintaining an orderly household. Human beings, he says, need shelter for the storage of goods, for the rearing of children and for the production of food and clothing. While men are constitutionally suited to productive labour in the open air, women are by their natures—being more soft, tender and anxious than men—suited to indoor tasks. According to Ischomachus, a woman is like a queen bee: she despatches others to their jobs outside the home, supervises those who work inside and stores, administers and distributes the goods that are brought into the house. In addition to these duties, Ischomachus' wife will be responsible for training and managing their slaves, and for looking after anyone in the household who falls sick. She has to organise the household equipment and personal belongings according to a rational scheme. When this tractable wife asks for her husband's advice on how she can best maintain her looks, Ischomachus' prescription is to avoid too much sitting about: she should stand over and supervise her slaves when they are weaving, baking or handing out stores, and should go on tours of inspection of the house; when in need of a more vigorous workout she can knead and roll out dough, shake coverlets and make the beds.

Ischomachus' bride, we are led to believe, welcomes her new duties with enthusiasm, and demonstrates her considerable intelligence by her dutiful response to her husband's training. When she modestly points out that none of her work would be of any use if Ischomachus were not such a diligent provider, he replies that his labours too would be to no avail if he had no-one to guard what he had produced: 'Do you not see what a pitiful situation those unfortunate people are in who are forced to pour water into sieves for ever . . . ?' Theirs is a partnership in which their separate natures and roles perfectly complement each other.

A similar if rather less fulsome testimony to the importance of the woman's role is contained in a fragment from the play *Melanippe,* by Euripides: 'Women manage homes and preserve the goods which are brought from abroad. Houses where there is no wife are neither orderly nor prosperous. And in religion—I take this to be important—we women play a large part . . . How then can it be just that the female sex should be so abused? . . .'. Euphiletus shows little respect for the value of his wife's work, which is hardly surprising in the circumstances; but he does make it clear that although he had watched her carefully when they were first married, he had begun to trust her with the control of his possessions once their son had been born. Although women were not allowed to engage in monetary transactions of any significance, it would seem that they were often responsible for managing the domestic finances. Lysistrata supports her contention that women are quite capable of controlling the treasury of Athens by pointing out that they have been in charge of the housekeeping for years; and Plato claims that men in Greece hand over control of the money to their wives.

In addition to the duties already outlined, women in poorer families with no domestic slaves would of course have been responsible for all the cooking, baking, cleaning and washing. They and their more affluent sisters would also have been involved in caring for and educating their children, in the case of the girls probably up until the time they left home. Some reasonably well-to-do women, such as Euphiletus's wife, breastfed their own children, but it seems to have been a fairly common practice to engage a wet-nurse: free-born Athenian women were preferred, but slaves and resident aliens were also employed, especially by the poor.

Women of all social classes would have engaged in the important task of wool-working. Although better-off women had slaves who did the bulk of the work, literature and vase paintings indicate that their mistresses assisted and guided them in their labours. Textile production was a vital part of the domestic economy, and some households would have been completely self-sufficient in this respect, even producing their own wool, although raw wool could also be bought on the market. Women in the home were responsible for preparing fleeces, for spinning thread and for weaving lengths of cloth on the loom. Wool was by far the most common fibre, but flax was also used by the better-off, since linen was prized as a material from which finer garments could be made.

Weaving in particular was viewed as the quintessential female accomplishment, and it was common for women to honour a deity with a gift of a fine piece of work. As well as producing the material, they were also responsible for making it up into finished articles. However, most of the clothes worn by the Greeks required a minimum of sewing, since they consisted in the main of simple rectangles of cloth which were belted or pinned into place. Much of the interior decoration of a home was also supplied by its womenfolk, in the form of wall-hangings, bedcovers and cushions. The best items would probably have been displayed in the men's dining room, the most public part of the house, where they would have served to demonstrate the skill and devotion to duty of the female members of the family. Weaving must have been back-breaking and laborious work, but there can be no doubt that for Athenian women their handicrafts would have been a source of pride.

According to Ischomachus, women naturally have more affection for new-born children than men. This affection must often have been a source of grief to Athenian women. Golden estimates that the infant mortality rate may have been as high as 30–40 percent in the first year of life, and that the majority of Greek mothers could have expected to bury at least one child in their lifetime. In addition, some of them would have had to cope with the exposure of an infant. Some modern scholars have suggested that, in circumstances such as these, mothers become conditioned not to feel too great a sense of loss at the death of a child, and that the experience of maternal love is consequently not such a potent element in women's lives as it is at other times or in other places. Golden, however, believes that children in ancient Greece received loving attention from their mothers, but that their grief at a child's loss was diffused through ritual mourning practices and through sharing their sorrow with other adults involved in their care. The existence of the practice of exposure, he suggests, tells us nothing about the response of parents to the death of any child whom they had decided to raise: it is even possible that children are less likely to be neglected in societies where infanticide is permitted, since the children that are reared are positively wanted.

There is certainly no shortage of references in Classical Greek literature to the agony experienced by mothers at the loss of a child. Aeschylus, Sophocles and Euripides all allow Clytemnestra to speak of the grief which she feels at the sacrifice of her daughter Iphigenia. Hector's widow Andromache, in Euripides' *Women of Troy*, utters a heart-rending speech of farewell to her young son when he is taken away to be executed:

> . . . Dear child, so young in my arms,
> So precious! O the sweet smell of your skin! When you
> Were newly born I wrapped you up, gave you my breast,
> Tended you day and night, worn out by weariness—
> For nothing, all for nothing! Say goodbye to me
> Once more, for the last time of all . . .

The concern of real-life mothers for their children is revealed by Aristotle when he describes how some women (presumably those who are poor or unmarried) give their children up to others to rear, and are content to see them getting on well, and to go on loving them, even though the children are ignorant of their true parentage and cannot love them in return. Numerous dedications were made to healing deities such as Asclepius by mothers on behalf of their sick children; and in one Athenian epitaph of the fourth century a woman named Xenocleia is said to have died of grief for her young son.

Greek tragedy, and Greek myth in general, are nevertheless remarkable for the amount of violence that takes place between parents and children. The tendency to focus attention on murderous mothers can perhaps be attributed to an underlying anxiety about sexually active females which found its most forthright expression in imaginative literature. Although such acts of violence were doubtless not unknown, there is no evidence to suggest that in real life they were any more common than they are in our own society.

A more realistic picture of relations between women and their adolescent sons is probably to be found in a section of Xenophon's *Memorabilia* in which Socrates chastises his son Lamprocles for being bad-tempered with his mother, and treats him to a long recital of the selfless toil undertaken by mothers. Even so, Lamprocles replies, no-one could possibly put up with my mother's vile temper. Admittedly, she hasn't done me any physical injury, but she says things which one wouldn't want to listen to for anything in the world. In Aristophanes' *Clouds* there is a portrait of a more indulgent parent. Young Pheidippides, according to his father, has been hopelessly spoiled by a mother who resented her marriage to a social inferior and helped to foster her son's expensive passion for chariot-racing. These sketches, which hardly present a positive view of mothers, probably reflect more accurately than tragedy the conscious responses of the average Athenian male to the institution of motherhood. A pervasive downgrading of the mother's role was perhaps responsible for the relative dearth of images of mothers and children in Greek art.

These rather bleak representations of motherly love must be considered alongside the adverse publicity which wives often receive in Athenian literature. In tragedy, wives may be murderous, like Clytemnestra, bitterly jealous, like Hermione and Deianeira, lustful, like Phaedra, or horrifically vindictive, like Medea, who murders her own children in order to rob her faithless husband Jason of his triumph over her. Tragedy's only significant depiction of a loving relationship between husband and wife is to be found in Euripides' *Alcestis,* in which the heroine agrees to die in place of her husband Admetus. In Aristophanes' comedies, wives are less violent, but are often seen as wily, devious, prone to adultery and overfond of alcohol. In the fourth century the comic playwright Eubulus provided this ironic comment on wifely virtue: 'Oh honoured Zeus, am I the man ever to speak ill of wives? Zeus, may I perish if I do, for they are the best of all possessions. If Medea was an evil woman, Penelope was a good thing. Some will say that Clytemnestra was wicked. But Alcestis can be set against her as good. Perhaps someone will speak badly of Phaedra. But . . . by God, there must be another good wife. Who? Alas, poor me, I've already got through all the good wives, and I've still got so many of the terrible ones to talk about'.

However, although most Athenian men probably had a utilitarian attitude to matrimony, this would not necessarily have prevented a loving relationship from developing in the course of a marriage. Ischomachus is anxious to point out to his new wife that he has not married her for reasons of passion, but because he believes that she will make a suitable partner in the home and in the rearing of children; but, by his own account at least, a bond of mutual affection does appear to develop between the couple. To the somewhat unreliable testimony of male writers on the subject of marital relations there can be added the fact that from about 420 BC onwards there was a considerable increase in the popularity of family burial plots, and that in grave-reliefs of this period joint commemoration of a husband and wife was relatively common. These changes can perhaps be attributed to a gradual privatisation of male concerns, allowing a growing acknowledgement of the part played by one's domestic life in the securing of personal fulfilment. Nevertheless, the expression of love for a wife remains a comparatively rare feature of Classical Greek literature. Aristotle may express the most common male view of relations between husband and wife when he says that their affection for each other is 'in accordance with merit: the husband, as the superior, receives the greater share'.

Few Athenian authors are prepared to acknowledge that the position of Athenian women in the home may have amounted to one of power. Yet references to female control of a household's possessions invite speculation on the possibility of a domestic inversion of public authority patterns, bolstered by the institution of the dowry. More circumstantial evidence is provided by some law-court speeches. In one, we hear about a family meeting where a mother, in a very competent and forceful manner, tackles her sons' guardian (her own father) about his mismanagement of their estate, at the same time demonstrating her sound knowledge of the family finances. Women might also be present at discussions about the terms of a family member's will, and might even represent their husbands on these occasions. Aeschines in one of his speeches refers to rich young men whose fathers were dead and whose mothers were administering their property.

In many instances women would have wielded power through the more indirect methods of nagging or doing things behind their husbands' backs. Euphiletus bears unwitting testimony to the operation of this power: he clearly sees himself as master in his own home, yet his account reveals that his wife was able to speak to him very freely, that her 'joke' of locking him in the bedroom came off, and that she was moreover able for some time to get away with conducting a love affair under his nose. Aristophanes' comedies are a rich source of information on similar female strategies. In *Thesmophoriazusae* we hear about infertile women who sneak babies into the house, and wives who have duplicate keys made so that they can smuggle extra provisions out of the larder. Praxagora in *Women in the Assembly* is always ready with a smart and often abusive retort in her verbal exchanges with her husband. On the basis of the *Lysistrata* we can surmise that withholding sex may have been another female ploy for gaining control over a spouse. Methods such as these were viewed with disfavour by men, but Aristophanes is quite prepared to acknowledge that they could prove very effective. The contrast between the vigorous and outspoken women characters of comedy and the silent and submissive female of the Athenian ideal can probably be explained in part by the fact that inside some homes at least the public face of family life disappeared, and the obedient wife of male discourse was transformed into a genuinely powerful one.

Comedies and law-court speeches offer in this way a valuable insight into a side of Athenian life rarely referred to in the bulk of Athenian literature, which generally focuses attention on public power structures and views the home, if it is mentioned at all, as an extension of the masculine sphere of authority. In legal terms this authority certainly existed, as we have seen; and the ideal of masculine government of the household is forcibly expressed in works such as Xenophon's *Oeconomicus*. Yet between the cracks of the legal and normative framework there appear these glimpses of an alternative and informal pattern of female power. This may to a small extent have filtered out into the public arena as a result of wifely influence over husbands on political and legal questions. The close relationship established between *oikos* and *polis* in Athenian ideology meant that the importance of male domination of the home was recognised; but it also permitted at least a hypothetical reversal of the flow of power. If women and not men were dominant in the private sphere, were the effects of this not bound to be felt in the public domain?

Few Athenian men would have been willing to voice this question openly. But Athenian awareness of the possibility is demonstrated by the frequency with which tragic and comic playwrights envisage a situation in which women intrude into the world of public affairs. In the *Lysistrata* the heroine produces a brilliant analogy between the processes involved in the preparation of raw wool for weaving and the tactics required to create political cohesion in the city. Aristophanes, for one, seems to have been conscious of the fact that the overlap between private and public concerns meant that women, by drawing on their domestic skills, might be capable of making an intellectual as well as a physical contribution to the well-being of the state. Too much should not be made of the issue of female power, for the allusions to it are rare and, in the case of comedy, may be highly imaginative. But it is by no means impossible that a whole area of alternative power structures has been ignored or suppressed by the patriarchal literature of Classical Athens. Once again one must regret the absence of an authentic female voice from the sources for this period.

Games, Plays, and Races: Celebrating Rome

JOHN E. STAMBAUGH

By the beginning of the Christian era, Rome had approximately one million inhabitants, making it by far the largest city in western Europe and one of the largest cities in the world. The sheer size of the city played a part in the politics of the empire, as various factions used their influence over the urban population in an effort to gain power. Influence over the populace was made easier by the fact that much of the city's population was poor. Soldiers returning from their tours of duty and farmers pushed off their land provided a steady stream of immigrants with few economic prospects. The poor counted on subsidies to help buy their main foodstuff—grain—and looked to handouts from rich patrons to help make ends meet. The poor, then, were a force that could be mobilized by the patrons who purchased their loyalty.

The relationship between patron and client belonged to a system in which private individuals provided many of the functions that today are the responsibility of the city government. Basic services such as law, justice, water supply, and firefighting were performed, at least in part, by the initiative of private individuals. In the case of justice, for example, it was the responsibility of the victims of crimes (or their families) to bring criminals to court. Masters could hire private companies to judge, punish, and even execute law-breaking slaves. Important public works, such as the building of temples, roads, and aqueducts, and the provision of public welfare, often were performed by the Roman nobility, who considered the well-being of the city their private responsibility. The blurring of public and private functions in this way strengthened the power of the patrons. The average resident of Rome had a far better chance of seeing justice done if he ever became a victim of a crime, and had a better chance of receiving a gift of grain or money in hard times if he

From: John E. Stambaugh, *The Ancient Roman City* (Baltimore: Johns Hopkins Press, 1988), pp. 225–39.

had a powerful patron. In exchange for protection and support, the client gave the patron his loyalty. In a similar fashion, gifts that a noble made to the entire community, such as a new temple or the repair of an aqueduct, could rally popular support for the agendas he pursued in the Senate.

Clientage created deep divisions within Rome. At times, conflicting noble factions used their influence as patrons to mass small armies to fight out their disputes in the streets. But political divisions were not the only forces that tore at the unity of Rome. There were also extreme differences between rich and poor. In contrast to the spacious houses of the wealthy, with their private gardens and fountains, the multi-storied tenements that sprang up to house Rome's poorer residents typically crowded a family into a one- or two-room apartment without cooking facilities. Such tenements usually provided a single latrine for the entire complex, if they provided one at all. How could a city with such profound divisions continue to function, let alone rule an empire? One answer is the civic religion, which encouraged a sense of unity among Rome's disparate population. Residents were united in the sacrifices and prayers that they offered to the gods to protect Rome—both the city and its empire—and keep it strong. Festivals that combined religious and public functions brought the inhabitants of the city together in a celebration of Rome, its exploits and its gods. Through these celebrations, all residents could participate in the glory of Rome. In this selection, John Stambaugh describes the entertainments of the Roman holidays.

Looking out at the street from their shops or apartments, or passing grand buildings and monuments as they pushed through the crowds, the residents of Rome were assaulted by the spectacular richness we have surveyed—in buildings, open spaces, monuments, statues, and even the people themselves. With so much visual, aural, and tactile stimulation, it was easy to become numb to the grandeur of it all. In compensation, frequently but with an irregular pacing that prevented complacency, the city offered various types of colorful, glamorous, organized pageantry to bring the populace together, affirm the power and stability of the city, and impose a unity of purpose on all the diverse elements of the population.

ANNUAL GAMES: LUDI

Each year significant chunks of time were dedicated to the gods as official ludi, games, which broke into the city's routine as a series of ludi scaenici, theatrical shows, followed at the end with one or more days of ludi circenses, chariot races. Additional events included solemn public banquets, military parades, animal hunts, athletic contests, and all sorts of wandering entertainments. At the end of the republic 74 days were set aside for ludi. On 17 of them chariot races were held in the Circus Maximus, which could accommodate about 250,000 spectators, men and women alike. That probably amounted to half the free adult population of imperial Rome. Fewer people could be accommodated at the theatrical shows, but there were many other things to do, and the long stretches of ludi in April (17 days, plus 3 in May), July (19 days), September (15 days), October (9 days), and November (14 days) must have disrupted the normal pattern of life to a considerable extent. The games preempted all other official business activities. The senators left the Forum, and the equestrians left their businesses to claim their places of honor at the theater and circus.

The oldest games, the Ludi Romani, originated in the time of the kings, and were celebrated annually in September starting in 366 B.C. In the late third century, just after Hannibal's invasion of Italy, the Ludi Plebeii were added in November. Around the end of the third century B.C. other games were added to propitiate other gods: the Ludi Apollinares in 208, the Ludi Cereales in 202, the Ludi Megalenses in honor of the Magna Mater in 194, and the Ludi Florales in 173 at the latest. Later games were added in honor of the military victories of Sulla (82 B.C.), Caesar (46 B.C.), and Augustus (11 B.C.) Under the principate more ludi were added until, by the fourth century A.D., 177 days of each year were celebrated with games of some sort.

The games filled many important religious and political functions in the city's life. They honored the gods and celebrated Rome's good relations with them. They commemorated political successes like that of the plebeian leader Flaminius, who built the Circus Flaminius (in which to hold the Ludi Plebeii), and military victories like those of Sulla, Caesar, Augustus, and, in time, many other emperors. The administration of the games was entrusted to the aediles, and during the republic politicians who wanted to impress the populace spent vast sums of their own money to make their games memorable. The correspondence of Cicero with Marcus Caelius Rufus lets us glimpse one aedile's zeal in 50 B.C. to give the people something to remember. While Cicero was off in Cilicia as governor and relying on Caelius for information about the political situation in Rome, Caelius kept up a barrage of requests for Cicero to hunt down some panthers in the Cilician mountains and ship them to Rome to be hunted during his games.

The ludi also served economic and social functions. Some workers took the days off and enjoyed the spectacles, while others—actors, charioteers, peddlers of food and souvenirs, prostitutes—found work and opportunity at them. The ludi also provided a well-defined situation in which all the various strata of the population could meet one another. Status distinctions were affirmed—the senators and equestrians had seats down in front, the women were seated in the back rows, and the poor folks had standing room in the gallery at the very top. But status distinctions were also transcended, in that the common citizens had a chance to react to the comings and goings of the nobility, to cheer a favorite or boo an unpopular politician. During the principate, the similar interaction between the crowds and the emperor was the closest approximation to a referendum that existed. The powerful knew what it meant, and the historians recorded it. Furthermore, during the games the routines and standards of life were held in abeyance. The Senate and law courts were in recess. The moneylenders closed their shops, which allowed even the debtor to forget his troubles while he was at the theater.

Theatrical shows came to Rome, according to tradition, in 360 B.C., when a serious plague afflicted the city, and the chariot races, which constituted the main spectacle at the Ludi Romani, did not seem to be enough to make the gods put a stop to the epidemic. So, as they often did during the early republic, the Romans sent off to the Etruscans for help. Help came in the form of *histriones,* dancers who performed to the music of woodwinds and who became a regular feature at the games. In time a plot line was added to these performances, and under the influence of the Greeks, dramatic recitations were included as part of the festivities. The landmark figure is a freedman from Tarentum, Livius Andronicus. Starting in the Ludi Romani in 240 B.C., he translated Greek plays into Latin and performed them at the games for the audience. The word for a stage, *scaena,* was borrowed from the Greeks, and the theatrical events were called *ludi scaenici.* Before long, entrepreneurs assembled troops of actors—slaves, freedmen, Greeks—and hired writers like Naevius and Plautus to translate and adapt Greek classics, both tragedies and comedies. Greek plays were popular for all the reasons Greek art, architecture, and myths were popular, not least because many members of the audience, starting in the third century B.C., had visited Greek cities (at least in southern Italy and Sicily) and could appreciate the Greek words and situations. In addition, the playwrights composed new dramas, based on noble moments in Roman history *(fabulae praetextae)* or the everyday world of the taberna *(fabulae tabernariae).*

References in republican and imperial literature help us chart the tides of changing taste. In the late third and early second centuries B.C., when Plautus was writing and producing his plays, the audience preferred comedy to tragedy, and Terence complained that the first production of one play (at the Megalenses of 165 B.C.) was disrupted by the performance of a rope dancer, a boxing match, the catcalls of claques, and the outcry of women, and at the second production (at the funeral games for Aemilius Paulus in 160 B.C.), by a gladiatorial show. A century later audiences were just as hard to please, and when they became restive they were apt to hoot at overacting or yell "Bring on the bears! Bring on the boxers!" By the time of the late republic, little new material was being written. Sponsors concentrated on extravagant and luxurious production values, which reflected the greater luxury in all phases of urban life at the time. Cicero, for instance, sneered at Pompey for bringing onstage 600 mules in a revival of Accius's *Clytemnestra* and a whole triumphal procession in the *Trojan Horse* (by Livius Andronicus or Naevius) at the opening of his theater in 55 B.C. Horace joins the lament complaining that in his time even the more cultured elements in the audience would rather see an exotic visual spectacle than hear a well-composed piece of literature. In the Augustan Age the official predilection for traditional forms was reflected in the theater. The classics were tastefully performed, and the old Italic tradition of the Atellan farce, a cabaret performance of topical humor acted by Roman citizens, was revived. At the same time, the Greek ballet form known as the pantomime was beginning to become popular, and by the second century of the principate it had become, along with a more burlesque variation known as the mime, the main form of theatrical entertainment. If a performance described by Apuleius is any indication, ambitious producers managed to broaden the appeal of their pantomimes by introducing kinky sex or sensational violence, which trended to blur any lingering distinction between the theatrical stage and the gladiatorial arena.

During the republic the plays were held in the open. The players acted on a portable wooden stage; the spectators sat on the grass or on wooden bleachers. Attempts were made to build more comfortable facilities, but they always aroused conservative opposition. An attempt to build a permanent theater in 154 B.C., for instance, moved Publius Scipio Nasica to forbid the erection of seats for plays, in order to extend the "famous Roman, virile art of standing" from political assemblies to occasions of relaxation as well. In spite of this, some temples that were built in and around Rome in the second and first centuries B.C. had semicircular steps in front to accommodate spectators at dramatic performances. By the middle of the first century B.C., it was usual to spread awnings over the temporary seating to provide shade; Lucretius calls attention to the patterns made by the sun shining through the yellow, red, and purple canvas. The temporary theaters were often astonishingly elaborate, full of technological virtuosity and moving parts, and they in turn aroused the righteous indignation of traditionalists. . . .

The day of the ludi scaenici began, not unexpectedly, with a parade. After a sacrifice at the appropriate temple, *exuviae*, tokens of the gods (a thunderbolt or eagle for Jupiter, a shield or helmet for Mars, a dove for Venus, a turreted crown for the Magna Mater) were placed on chairs and carried in solemn procession, heralded by flutes and trumpets, to the theater, so that the gods could enjoy the show held in their honor. The plays themselves reinforced the sense of holiday, especially the comedies with their plots set in far-off Greek cities in which the serious pursuits of the Forum and the shop were mocked openly, young love always triumphed, and slaves could make utter fools of their masters. We do not know the exact performance schedule, except that Atellan farces tended to follow tragedies, and performances could last all day long. The prologue to Terence's *Mother-in-law* makes it clear that other events were going on at the same time as the plays, creating the atmosphere of a carnival midway. At the end of the day, the exuviae of the gods were returned, in still another procession, to their temples.

At all the games, more days were devoted to ludi scaenici than to other activities. At the two ludi in honor of Jupiter, the Ludi Romani and the Ludi

Plebeii, the theatrical days were followed by the Ides (of September and November respectively), on which the Senate went to the Temple of Iuppiter on the Capitoline to partake of a great banquet, the *epulum Iovis,* in the presence of the god. On the next day, the cavalry of the equestrian order paraded in review through the city at the *Probatio Equitum.*

The final days were devoted to ludi circenses, chariot races in the Circus Maximus. These were the most popular and exciting events of the year. The Circus could accommodate a quarter of a million spectators, and everyone, from the emperor to a lowly cook, had favorite teams, horses, and charioteers. During the republic there were two main *factiones* ("teams"), the whites and the reds. Two more, the blues and the greens, were added during the early principate, when the factiones became major social entities. They were virtual corporations under imperial patronage, managed by *domini,* a board of directors, and investors. Each factio bought and trained horses, bought and maintained chariots, bought or hired drivers. The emperors built stabula for them in the Campus Martius with a full staff of coaches, trainers, blacksmiths, farriers, veterinarians, grooms; the teams also had clerks and secretaries, attendants and waiters, and clubhouses with an imperial suite. At least once the factiones formed a cartel and demanded exorbitant prices before bringing their horses to the starting line. To meet the emergency, the praetor in charge threatened to race dogs instead, but Nero came to the rescue with a subsidy.

On the day of the race, a procession was held into the Circus. The crowd cheered their favorites, consulted their programs, placed bets, jostled for places, and watched in rapture as a trumpet was blown and the presiding consul or praetor signaled the start of the race by dropping a napkin. There were races for chariots with two horses or, more commonly, for those with four. Novelty races with other numbers of horses (as many as ten to a team!), or exhibitions of trick-riding, foot races, or relays also provided variety. Seven laps around the course constituted a race, and a full day's program included 24 races. At the conclusion, the victors received prizes: the victor's palm, crowns, and neck chains of gold. Many of the charioteers started out as slaves, and the successful ones could earn enough in prize money of their own to buy their freedom and become "free agents." One such charioteer was Gaius Appuleius Diocles, who has left us a long inscription listing his many victories and tremendous earnings in the middle of the second century A.D. Martial tells us of another famous charioteer, Scorpus, who won over two thousand races before he was killed in an accident at the age of twenty-seven.

In addition to the regularly scheduled ludi (18 days in the republic, 66 by the fourth century A.D.), other games were held on special occasions. It was sometimes necessary to repeat games spoiled by bad omens, or hold new ones to celebrate a military victory, fulfill a vow, or dedicate a new temple. Sometimes, especially during the fourth and third centuries B.C., when the city was under some such stress as a plague or a military defeat, a lectisternium was declared. For one or more days of the observance, the temples were opened and couches were arranged with images of gods reclining and goddesses sitting on them. Food was set in front of them, and as if to join them in their banquet, citizens opened their houses and entertained anyone who dropped in. Most rarely of all—less frequently than once in a lifetime—the Romans celebrated the *ludi saeculares,* "Centennial Games," to mark the stability and progress of the city.

GLADIATORIAL SHOWS: MUNERA

In addition to the ludi, and sometimes in connection with them, upper-class Romans on occasion paid for *munera* in the form of gladiatorial shows. These munera were originally part of the rites owed to the dead. Borrowed from either the Etruscans or the Campanians, they became a part of noble funerals, and thus were one of the ways members of the upper classes extended their family life out into the life of the city. The first recorded gladiatorial *munus* in Rome was held by the sons of Marcus Iunius Brutus Pera in 264 B.C., in the Forum Boarium. In 216 B.C., 22 pairs of gladiators fought in the Forum Romanum at the funeral of Marcus Aemilius Lepidus, and in 183 B.C., 60 pairs fought when Publius Licinius Crassus was buried, an occasion upon which a great banquet also was given for the citizens at tent-shaded tables in the Forum.

The popularity and political potential of these games was evident as early as 133 B.C., when Gaius Gracchus used an original grandstand play to win the favor of the plebeians. Enterprising contractors had erected bleachers around the Forum Romanum, intending to sell seats to those who could afford to have a good view of the munera; this meant that the poor would not be able to see anything. The night before the show, however, Gracchus (who as tribune had public workmen at his command) dismantled the seats, thus giving his constituency an unimpeded field of vision.

Meanwhile, Roman armies were campaigning in new and exotic foreign lands. It did not take long for them to encounter new and exotic animals, which they captured, shipped back to Rome, and used to impart new excitement to victory celebrations. Leopards, ostriches, lions, hippopotami, and crocodiles were brought to Rome for display, and starting in 186 B.C. were stalked and killed in staged hunts called *venationes.* Such games soon became the occasion for a potlatch of conspicuous consumption, as when Cicero's friend Titus Annius Milo planned to spend what amounted to three fortunes for funeral games in 54 B.C. When Pompey celebrated the dedication of his theater in 55 B.C., he set aside the appropriate number of days for tragedies and Atellan farces in the theater itself, followed by a series of athletic contests in the Greek manner, which turned out to be boring for the Roman audience. The big events took place during the final five days, which were given over to venationes. In the Circus Maximus 600 lions and 400 leopards were killed, working up to a grand climax on the last day. On it, 18 elephants were brought out to be hunted by Gaetulians from Africa armed with javelins. It was all very spectacular, but the huge beasts turned out to be too pathetic—even the tough Roman crowd pitied them—and too dangerous—they nearly stampeded into the spectators' seats.

This, however, was a game Julius Caesar knew how to play. When he celebrated his triumphs in 46 B.C., all the resources of the conquered provinces and of his keen sense of showmanship were marshaled to give the city a spectacle it would remember for a long time. In addition to the normal triumphal procession, and the usual sort of gladiatorial duels in the Forum Romanum, Caesar staged events all over town. Plays, including modern mimes composed for the occasion, were performed in each of the four regions of the city. A special wooden amphitheater was built—presumably in the Campus Martius—for the venationes at which Romans got their first-ever glimpse of a giraffe. Another special facility was built at the marshy Codeta Minor in the Campus Martius; there grandstands were erected, some hydraulic arrangements caused the site to be flooded, and Caesar was able to stage a full-scale naval battle, with 4,000 oarsmen and 2,000 armed marines, the first such show ever held in Rome. Mock battles were also held in the Circus Maximus: 400 cavalry, 1,000 infantry, and special troops mounted in turrets on the backs of 40 elephants. (Caesar had learned from Pompey's mistake in staging the elephant battles. At *his* games, the elephants provided transportation, not targets; and to prevent other trouble, a moat 10 feet wide and 10 feet deep was dug all around the Circus between the battle areas and the spectators. In these battles prisoners and condemned criminals fought, as did professionals from the gladiatorial schools and even some distinguished Romans of the equestrian order. Greek athletic contests had become traditional, and must have had some fans among the population, so Caesar included some of them, even though they were not very popular. Other events had a low-key but exotic attraction, such as the Lusus Troiae, a horseback drill executed by young Romans and later described by Vergil, and the Pyrrhic war dances, performed in armor by noble youths.

The popular appeal of such spectacles was too great for the emperors to ignore. Augustus boasted that on 26 occasions he sponsored venationes in the Circus, the Forum, and a new amphitheater, which Statilius Taurus built in the Campus Martius in 29 B.C. Augustus also constructed a permanent *naumachia* on the right bank of the Tiber, which could be flooded for the performance of naval battles. During the principate these animal hunts and gladiatorial shows were detached from funerals and from the religious ludi. Then the Flavian dynasty built the Amphitheatrum Flavium (the Colosseum), and this marked a significant turning point. In A.D. 80, when Titus dedicated the amphitheater with splendid games that lasted for a hundred days and were described with grisly enthusiasm by Martial, Rome gained a permanent facility that accommodated 50,000 people at a time and proclaimed that the gladiatorial shows were unabashedly performances, entertainments. . . .

An industry grew up to cater to the need for gladiators. The emperors built four training schools for them, and a whole catalogue of specialties arose: heavily armed *hoplomachi*; lightly armed "Thracians"; *retiarii*, who fought with a net and dagger and relied on quick footwork; *essedarii*, who fought from chariots; *equites,* who fought from horseback; *bestiarii,* who specialized in killing animals. Vast sums were spent on training gladiators; on feeding them and outfitting them with weapons, costumes, and medical attention; on capturing animals and shipping, feeding, and storing them; and on supporting the attendants who checked tickets and cleaned up, the vendors who sold food and drink, and the sailors who maneuvered the canvas awnings to shade the spectators. On the day of a spectacle, normally the morning was given over to wild beast hunts, which were often elaborated with scenery suggesting the exotic places where the animals might be at home. At noon, during the lunch break, mock battles or amateur tryouts were held; if criminals were to be executed, this was the time when they were thrust into the arena, unarmed, to face either a gladiator with a sword or a hungry bear or lion. The main event was scheduled for the afternoon, when the skilled gladiators fought in pairs until one in each pair was too seriously wounded to continue. The winner asked the *munerarius,* the sponsor, whether to spare or to kill. The spectators were on their feet by this time, gesturing with their hands to indicate whether the loser should be spared or killed.

The insidious appeal of the gladiatorial shows is conveyed most eloquently by Saint Augustine. He tells how his innocent friend Alypius was induced, reluctantly, to go to a show at the Colosseum. To avoid being contaminated by the sight of the bloodshed, he closed his eyes. But a roar of the crowd made him open them, and, says Augustine, once Alypius drank in the carnage, he became drunk with a blood lust that could be satisfied only by going back again and again for more. The program was a ritualized, systematic violence, but because of the skill of the trained gladiators it could be passed off as sport. The average spectator was far enough away from the swords and knives to feel safe, but close enough to see that real blood was being spilled and to realize that in the safety of the seats he had a very real power of life and death over the performance.

TRIUMPHAL PROCESSIONS

The highest honor the Roman state could bestow was the right to march through the city of Rome as a *triumphator.* This was a proud tradition, which Roman historians traced back through a long line of victorious generals to Romulus himself; indeed, the route of the triumphal procession encircled the old city of Romulus on the Palatine. By the third century B.C. the basic ritual of the triumph had been established, and as Roman armies continued their conquests farther and farther away, the triumphal processions became ever-more-spectacular devices for assuring the citizens back home that the military and political affairs of the city-state were being conducted well.

The victorious general returned to the city to ask for the triumph, but he could not enter it. To cross the pomerium was to lose his *imperium,* his power of command, so the senate went out to meet him, usually in the Temple of Bellona. If a triumph was granted, the general and his army camped out on the old military parade ground of the Campus Martius. For the day of the procession, the triumphant general assumed some of the attributes of Jupiter himself: his face was smeared with the same red paint that was applied to Jupiter's statue on the Capitoline; he wore a tunic embroidered with palm leaves, a symbol of victory; over this he wore an embroidered toga; a golden crown was held over his head as he rode in a gilded chariot. The procession was marshaled in the lower Campus Martius, perhaps in the open space of the Circus Flaminius, and the general made a speech to the troops and presented awards and decorations. Then he mounted his chariot, surrounded by his children and accompanied by a slave who held the crown above his head and was supposed to keep reminding him that he was, after all, mortal. The procession set off: first the spoils captured from the enemy, along with floats and pictures illustrating important battles; then the prisoners of war, with captured princes, kings, or queens as featured attractions; and finally the triumphant general surrounded by his soldiers. It all moved solemnly, impressively, gaudily through the Porta Triumphalis, then past cheering crowds through the Circus Maximus and around the Palatine to the Sacra Via, the Forum Romanum, where important prisoners were taken off to the prison and executed, and up the slope to the Capitoline, where the rite climaxed with a sacrifice to Jupiter and a banquet in his temple. The long day ended when the general was escorted home to the music of flutes.

The focus of all this was the general, whom the rites surrounded with a holy ambiguity. Wearing the garments of Jupiter, the general was reminded of his mortality by a slave; riding as a commander in a golden chariot, he was surrounded by his soldiers, who sang songs that made fun of him; claiming all the honors of a king, he ended the day by losing his military authority. This ambivalence reminds us how suspicious the Romans were of the trappings of kingship during the republic. Such scruples were irrelevant under the principate, when the triumph naturally became the emperor's exclusive prerogative, celebrated rarely but with breathtaking spectacle. The best example is the triumph of Vespasian and Titus after the conquest of Judaea in A.D. 70, described by Josephus and depicted on the Arcus Titi. Of all the special events, triumphal processions must have made the deepest impression. They condensed the attractions of a parade, conquest, bloodshed, and hero-worship into a single day that occurred no more than once a year in the times of republican conquests and once a generation in the principate. They were the most intense, most spectacular pageant the city had to offer.

The pageantry of color, texture, and masses, the blare of trumpets and the squeal of flutes, the smell of people, sacrificial animals, and blood, the solemn processions and raucous games—all were a kinetic expression of the same grandiose taste that produced fora, temples, and baths. In its festivals, gladiatorial shows, and triumphs the city celebrated itself, its history, its gods, its power. In all these events, Rome was the focal point, the center of activity, the model of order imposed on a compliant world. . . .

SLAVES AND SOCIETY IN ROME

KEITH BRADLEY

Sadly, slavery has been a long-lived and pervasive institution. When the Romans encountered the Germanic tribes settling along the imperial frontier, they found that they had at least one thing in common with these otherwise alien peoples: the ownership of slaves. Slave owning was widespread in the ancient world. Only a handful of societies, however, have ever qualified as slave societies: societies where a substantial proportion of the population is unfree and where slavery contributes significantly to economic production. Athens and Roman Italy were slave societies during classical antiquity. They were joined, in the modern era, by Brazil, the Caribbean, and the United States.

Roman slave society emerged with the empire. Slaves made up approximately 35 percent of the population of Italy under Emperor Augustus (31 B.C.–A.D. 14). Their considerable numbers made them an important source of productivity. Prisoners of war, abandoned infants, and desperate folk who sold themselves into slavery to pay their debts supplied Romans' appetite for unfree labor. At one end of the slave-holding scale were the poor who owned a single slave to labor alongside them in the fields or help with the housework. On the other end of the scale were people like C. Caecilius Isidorus, who in the eighth century B.C. owned 4,116 slaves, and the younger Melania who freed 8,000 slaves in the fifth century A.D. Even slaves might own slaves.

Slaves worked the large rural estates of the aristocracy, they labored in the killing environment of the mines, they worked as craftsmen and businessmen for their leisured masters and mistresses. Their presence in Roman households—from the very rich to the humble—was ubiquitous. Was slave-holding a profitable enterprise? The large rural estates of the aristocracy, with their fields and workshops, appear to have been successful economic enterprises, but it is not clear that the landowners' priority was profit. Economic

From: Keith Bradley, *Slavery and Society at Rome* (Cambridge, England: Cambridge University Press, 1994) pp. 24–30, 65–66, 67–71, 71–76, 76–77, 80.

activities on most villae *were primarily devoted to providing for the landowners' own households and local needs. In the case of domestic slaves, the answer to the question is straightforward. Household slaves consumed, rather than contributed to, the owner's resources. Did slave-holding provide other, less tangible benefits? In this selection, Keith Bradley describes the slave society of Rome between 200 B.C. and A.D. 200.*

The cultural and institutional visibility of slavery at Rome, across time and space, implies that for slaveowners slaveowning was a never failing source of personal advantage. The social and economic benefits that accrued to owners derived from their almost limitless abilities to control and coerce human property. From a legal point of view the Latin words for power (*potestas*) and slaveownership (*dominium*) could be regarded as synonymous, which means that, above all, slaveowning was an expression of power. Two ceremonial events that in the nature of things were common occurrences illustrate what was involved.

The Roman triumph, first, was a spectacular ceremony that honoured a general victorious in war against a foreign enemy. Essentially it consisted of an elaborate parade that made its way through the streets of Rome, starting from the Campus Martius and culminating at the Capitol where sacrifices of thanksgiving were made to Jupiter. Apart from the senate and magistrates, the procession was made up of the victorious general and his army, who displayed to the crowds of onlookers the spoils of war they had taken and representations of the cities they had captured and territories they had conquered. Customarily too the procession included prisoners-of-war, some of whom might be withdrawn and executed before or as the ceremony concluded, no matter what their rank. So the Numidian prince Jugurtha was put to death following the triumph of C. Marius on the first day of January, 104 BC, whereas it was quite unusual when Pompey gave orders that none of his captives was to be killed in his triumph of 61 BC. The prisoners were slaves, symbols of Roman power and invincibility whose very lives now lay in the hands of their conquerors, a sorry contrast to the Roman soldiers also in the procession who had been liberated—brought back to life, as it were—from enemy enslavement.

It was also customary, secondly, for newly manumitted slaves to appear in the funeral processions that preceded interment or cremation of the dead. They were in fact slaves who had just been set free in accordance with the wishes of their former owners. The idea was that by appearing in the ceremony as free men and citizens—and again, especially in the case of the elite, the processions could be very elaborate affairs—they would be seen to be living proof of the dead slaveowner's generosity and would ensure that he was well-remembered in the community. Dionysius of Halicarnassus, writing in the late first century BC, complained vigorously that the practice had become excessive in his day. The most telling point of the practice, however, was that for

a few moments in time the almost miraculous capacity of the individual slaveowner to convert the powerless to a state of independence was clear to all who
witnessed the passing of his cortege.

In effect, therefore, the power that lay at the disposal of the Roman slaveowner was the power of life and death, and slavery itself was viewed in many
ways as a state of living death. The idea is apparent in a number of sources,
especially legal texts for instance: 'slavery is equated with death', Ulpian declared categorically, as if the connection needed no explanation, and again: 'In
every branch of the law, a person who fails to return from enemy hands is regarded as having died at the moment when he was captured'. Ulpian was writing at the close of the central period but the sentiment was by no means unique
to his generation. The statement, 'We compare slavery closely with death', appears in a section of the *Digest* headed *Various Rules of Ancient Law*, and a
ruling of Justinian's, that the marriage of a freed person came to an end if
reenslavement occurred, just as if death had intervened, continued the association into the Byzantine age. The association was based on the view that slavery originated in warfare:

> Slaves (*servi*) are so-called, because generals have a custom of selling their
> prisoners and thereby *preserving* rather than killing them: and indeed they
> are said to be *mancipia*, because they are *captives* in the hand (*manus*) of their
> enemies.

The victor in battle had the right to kill the vanquished. If, however, the victor spared the vanquished and enslaved him instead, the latter continued to
live, but only in a condition of suspended death at the discretion of the former.
The slave's very identity, in fact, now depended on his owner. This was the
source of the slaveowner's power.

Slaveowners learned the habit of commanding authority at an early age.
In schools for example the children of prosperous families were given language
exercises as part of their curriculum depicting scenes from everyday life (they
were called *colloquia*), which as they were studied and practised transmitted
from generation to generation the cultural norm of wielding power over dependants and inferiors. The process was indirect and unconscious but effective. In one recently published example a *colloquium* shows a boy rising in the
morning and going off to school, studying for several hours with his teachers
and then returning home for lunch. It assumes that the boy will have a string
of personal attendants to cater to his needs—someone to dress him, someone
to help him wash, someone to feed him, someone to take care of his school
supplies—and it assumes that he is already perfectly used to instructing his servants in their duties, even to the extent of using the humiliating form of address Roman slaveowners commonly used of their slaves: 'Get up, boy, see if
it's light yet: open the door and window'; 'Give me that; hold out my shoes,
unfold my best clothes and put my playclothes away. Hand me my cloak and
mantle'; 'Take some clean water to your master my brother, so that he can go
with me to school'. Reinforcing, presumably, what had already been observed,

absorbed and inculcated at home, the school exercises helped establish in children a structure of authority and an expectation of the capacity, even the right, to give orders that would remain with them for the rest of their lives.

For slaves, in contrast, the consequence of living in a state of suspended death was that they could claim no human rights or privileges of any kind. By definition slaves were kinless and were permitted no legally sanctioned familial bonds. Nor could they own property of any kind. In reality of course some slaves reproduced, at times perhaps with the open encouragement of their owners (the benefits were often obvious), but the slaveowner was under no obligation to respect any quasi-familial ties that may have come into being among them. It was common too for many slaves to have a *peculium,* property in kind or cash at their effective disposal; but its contents, strictly speaking, always belonged to the master and were revocable at any time. To live in slavery, accordingly, was to be utterly disempowered.

Enslaved prisoners-of-war, moreover, were also degraded—demoted that is in a quite literal sense from a state of freedom to a state of servitude. The prevalent Roman attitude was that the downward move was shaming, so that socially low and morally low became one and the same. The degraded slave was the symbol therefore of all that was abject and without honour. In the formula of M. Brutus, the assassin of Julius Caesar, it was possible to live honourably at Rome without exercising authority over others but to be a slave to anyone was not to be alive at all. Merely to label someone or something servile or slavish was to project the disgrace of slavery, and the demeanour of the slave was to be avoided at all costs. Thus Quintilian, towards the end of the first century AD, warned the aspiring orator not to give himself a slavish aspect. 'It is, as a rule, unbecoming to raise or contract the shoulders. For it shortens the neck and produces a mean and servile gesture, which is even suggestive of dishonesty when men assume an attitude of flattery, admiration or fear'. True, not all Roman slaves began their lives in freedom. But as the descendants of those who had once been captured and enslaved they inherited, as a matter of course, their forebears' degradation.

The rightlessness and degradation of the slave were made manifest in countless ways, but particularly through sexual exploitation and physical abuse. Quintilian took the following statements as examples of opposing rhetorical arguments:

> If sexual intercourse with a male slave is shameful for a female slaveowner, so is sexual intercourse with a female slave for a male slaveowner.
>
>   It is not the same for a male slaveowner to have sexual intercourse with a female slave as it is for a female slaveowner to have sexual intercourse with a male slave.

Underlying the arguments is a preoccupation with the moral evaluation of male and female behaviour in a patriarchal society that from its upper-class male perspective betrays the slaveowner's fear of finding his wife or daughter seduced by his slave (a possibility that could never be discounted in a society where body-slaves were ubiquitous). But it is taken without question that slaves can and do become objects of sexual gratification for both the men and women who own them. It is one of the prerogatives of ownership and the servile response is scarcely worth considering. To the emperor Marcus Aurelius it was a source of spiritual satisfaction that he had not taken sexual advantage of two slaves he identifies as Benedicta and Theodotus when it had clearly been in his power to do so; his attitude was remarkable but not the situation which prompted it.

Likewise with physical maltreatment: in a treatise called 'On the Passions and Errors of the Soul', written in the late second century AD, the philosopher and doctor Galen gave advice against reacting in haste to the loss of temper. He told how as a young man he had taken a vow not to strike his slaves with his hand, and of how his father, similarly minded, had reproved people for bruising tendons when striking their slaves in the mouth in the heat of anger: 'They could have waited a little while, he said, and used a rod or whip to inflict as many blows as they wished and to accomplish the act with reflection.' There was nothing untoward in abusing a slave, only in doing so in an uncalculated and undisciplined fashion. Galen continued with remarks on how common it was for slaves to be punched with the fists, to be kicked, to have their eyes put out, on how he himself had once seen a man stab a slave in the eye with a reed pen in a fit of anger, and on how his own mother had been so quick to lose her temper that it had been her habit to bite her maidservants. His remarks are disturbing but their accuracy is not in doubt, as all manner of evidence indicates. To Galen's contemporary Artemidorus, a specialist in explaining the meaning of dreams, it was natural for example to take a slave's dream of dancing as a sign that the slave would soon be flogged, because beating was so common a servile experience that no other interpretation of the image of a writhing body was possible. Again, Plutarch could support his point that physical blows were more suitable for slaves than the free by appealing to the common fact that a beating reduced the slave to an abject state. Artemidorus, it can be noted, was prepared to allow slaves their own dreams, though this was a luxury that some slaveowners denied. Pliny once claimed that he had narrowly evaded persecution from the tyrannous emperor Domitian, but a sign that he would remain unharmed had been given in dreams that a slave and former slave of his had experienced: their hair had been cut during the night by mysterious intruders, the connection being that it was common for those accused of crime to let their hair grow. Pliny appropriated the slaves' dream to himself. It did not occur to him to ask if it could have meant anything for those who had actually dreamed it.

Powerlessness and isolation, rightlessness and degradation were the hallmarks of servitude, permitting slaveowners to use their slave possessions for whatever purposes they chose. In everyday reality the management and manipulation of human property demanded recognition of the property's human character. But the right to enslave and to keep enslaved was taken as axiomatic in Roman society, and in a milieu in which civic freedom was not looked upon as naturally available to all, slaveowning served constantly to validate and enhance the status of those who were free. From a cultural point of view, therefore, slavery was at no time an incidental feature of Roman social organisation and at no time an inconsequential element of Roman mentality.

At the end of the first century BC the servile population of the Roman heartland lay, according to modern estimates, in the order of two to three millions, representing 33–40 per cent of the total population. Most slaves were probably involved in agriculture. Thus if the phrase 'slave society' or 'slave economy' is best reserved for those historical contexts in which slaves have played an extraordinarily prominent role in primary production, Roman Italy of the first century BC and first century AD was a genuine slave society—but to the exclusion of other time-periods and regions embraced by Roman history and culture since a comparable slave population never appeared elsewhere. It is difficult, however, to find any period or region affected by Rome in which slaveowning did not function as a means of demonstrating power and domination. The attitudes and habits of mind evident when the slave economy of Roman Italy was at its height long antedated and long outlasted that economy's chronological and territorial limits. The distinction, moreover, between a genuine slave society and a society in which some slaves have simply been present is a modern, not a Roman, distinction, and it is a construct that can result in a certain narrowness of vision. To the extent that owning slaves always served to express *potestas* in a society highly sensitive to gradations of status, esteem and authority, Rome was always a slave society. . . .

From the simple procedure of surveying slave jobs, it appears that no occupation in Roman society was closed to slaves. The only exception, as it happens, was military service, from which slaves were legally, and uniquely, barred. Yet this did not mean that there were any occupations that were formally reserved for members of the servile population alone. In practice domestic servants tended overwhelmingly to be slaves or ex-slaves as far as can be told, but job titles, especially those from the world of agricultural work, were used of slave and free alike. The free poor of Roman society had to provide themselves with income, which for many meant working as casual wage-labourers in jobs sometimes, and sometimes simultaneously, shared by slaves: at Rome itself under the Principate, for example, the construction of public works sponsored by emperors drew on casual wage-labour to a significant degree but without completely excluding slave labour. Many former slaves also continued after manumission to do the same jobs they had done previously as slaves. Nothing indicates therefore that there was a strict separation of slave labour from free labour, or indeed that there was necessarily any competition between the two. In a society where slaves were primarily a social, not an economic category, any such notion would have been alien to the prevailing mentality. In the famous discussion of occupations in Cicero's treatise *de Officiis,* Cicero makes clear the view that anyone who worked for wages, which of course slaves did not normally do, was living in a state of servitude. But while the Romans passed down from generation to generation a stereotyped portrait of the slave as an unscrupulous, lazy and criminous being, and while they thought of certain races, Asiatic Greeks, Syrians and Jews, as being born for slavery, and while they thought certain punishments like crucifixion and burning alive were suitably servile, they never thought of any one form of work as being specifically appropriate just for slaves.

The wide range of slave employments, whether functional (*officia*) or skilled (*artificia*), appears to have been well established in Roman society by the beginning of the central period. In the late Republic the elite tended to stock their residences with greater and greater numbers of domestic servants as a form of competitive ostentation, while in agriculture, particularly in regions of central and northern Italy, slaves tended to grow in numbers at the expense of the Italian peasantry (though not to the extent of ever eradicating the peasantry). A marked increase in slaves' work-roles could thus be expected in the first century BC, but such a development would only have intensified patterns already well in existence in the second century BC. When C. Sempronius Gracchus returned to Rome from Sardinia to stand for the tribunate in 124 BC, he deemed it prudent to inform the people that he had not surrounded himself while in his province with a retinue of handsome slaves, the implication being that it was already conventional for the Roman aristocrat to regale himself in this way. Earlier Cato took the use of slave labour by his peers as normative when writing his agricultural handbook, while in Plautus a multiplicity of slave occupational titles [are in evidence].

The great diversity of slaves' work roles, however, was not unique to Roman slave society. Because the slave systems of the New World were principally concerned with the production of marketable crops, it is an easy assumption that, save for a few domestics, slaves were field hands and nothing more. But the assumption is false, for in the cities of the Americas slaves worked in all manner of service industries and in trades of every level of skill imaginable, from portering and quarrying, street-cleaning and milling to skilled manufacturing, commerce, slave management and personal service. The city of Rio de Janeiro in the early nineteenth century is an especially apposite example, for there, as at Rome, prosperous slaveowners kept sizeable entourages of specialised retainers in their urban residences both for the personal services provided and as symbols of wealth and status, arranged in carefully nuanced hierarchies. There too slave artisans working in manufactories made cigars and candles, hats and paper, soap, cotton and tiles. And there, in the city at large, slaves were ubiquitous, to quote a partial list, as 'printers, lithographers, painters, sculptors, orchestral musicians, nurses, midwives, barber-surgeons, seamstresses and tailors, goldworkers, gemcutters, butchers, bakers, sailors, ships' pilots, coachmen, stevedores, fishermen, hunters, naturalists and gardeners'. The correspondence with Rome is striking, despite the gulfs of time and distance.

Slaves, of both sexes, were expected to work throughout their lives. On farms children were put to work at early ages tending animals, helping to prune vineyards, harvesting fodder for livestock; and in the artisanal sphere it was common for the young to be trained in handicrafts such as weaving, shoe-making, jewellery-making and so on. In domestic service instruction of some sort might also be required—it could take two months for example to become an *ornatrix*—and at court even the cupbearer had to be taught his art. Slave boys sometimes worked as grooms in the imperial cavalry unit known as the *equites singulares Augusti*: thus a boy named Primitivus, a Cappadocian by birth, is known from an inscription set up by his master when he died, aged only thirteen. In later life slaves could again be assigned the simple tasks of childhood, henkeeping, gathering fodder, watering animals, or else be given jobs like that of a doorkeeper that cannot have been onerous. Others could continue to work as nurses or innkeepers, obstetricians or shepherds, but the concept of retirement did not exist.

Because slaves worked from childhood into adulthood (or simply through the force of circumstance), it was possible to progress from one job to another of greater responsibility. Columella recommended that although he should be prepared for the post from boyhood a slave should not be appointed as farm bailiff (*vilicus*) before the age of thirty-five, so great were the prior knowledge and experience needed for such an important position. The historian Timagenes of Alexandria, who once caused offence to Augustus, is said to have come to Rome as a captive in 55 BC and then to have advanced from the job of cook to that of litter-bearer before gaining the chance to pursue an intellectual interest (the jurists, however, saw the promotion of litter-bearer to cook as more realistic—or else the two were jobs to be held in combination). The dream-interpreter Artemidorus knew of a domestic slave who was promoted to oversee the whole household to which he belonged, a move that of course had been presaged by a dream. Conversely, slaves thought to be in need of punishment could be demoted, the cook suddenly becoming just a messenger-boy, and the privileged urban domestic being sent off to manage a distant rural estate.

Promotion is better understood, however, though still no more than imperfectly, in the case of the slaves of the imperial household who as clerks, record-keepers and financial agents served as low-level operatives in the administration of the Roman empire in the second half of Rome's central period. Their names and occupational titles are often known from sepulchral inscriptions—as with Felix, a *verna* who was *adiutor rationalium* (assistant keeper of accounts), or Hermas, a *dispensator a tributis* (tax-steward), or Rhodon, an *exactor hereditatium legatorum peculiorum* (collector of inheritances and bequeathed *peculia*), or Abascantus, also a *verna*, a *dispensator annonae* (steward of the grain supply), or Quintianus, another *verna*, and *vilicus et arcarius XX hereditatium* (supervisor and treasurer of the 5 per cent inheritance tax), or Alexander Pylaemenianus, *abbybliothece Graeca templi Apollinis* (in charge of the Greek library in the Temple of Apollo), and so on. It was possible for such men, whether born into the imperial *familia* or recruited from outside, to advance through what loosely resembled a career structure, beginning with subordinate positions while still young and proceeding to positions of greater authority after manumission, which typically came when they were about thirty. For some, especially in the first century AD, the way was open to participate directly in the highest levels of Roman government.

Few careers are known in detail. But one that is relatively full, and quite astonishing, is that of a man who can be identified not in his own right but only as the father of a son named Claudius Etruscus. Originally from Smyrna in Asia—he was born about AD 2/3—this man served as a young administrator in the household of the emperor Tiberius, by whom he was set free. He accompanied Caligula when the emperor travelled north in AD 39 and was probably promoted to a provincial financial posting under Claudius and Nero before eventually becoming *a rationibus,* secretary in charge of the emperor's accounts, under Vespasian. Vespasian indeed conferred upon him the rank of *eques,* second only to that of senator, and his marriage, under Claudius, to a woman of free birth produced two sons who also gained equestrian standing. Under Domitian he fell into disfavour and was exiled, but he had been reinstated by the time of his death, close to the age of ninety. His overall advancement was spectacular.

The slave career depended on the fact that within the individual *familia* there was an occupational hierarchy in which, say, the *vilicus* was acknowledged to be the superior of the *pastor,* the *cubicularius* of the *ianitor,* and this in turn depended on the wide range of jobs to which slaves were generally admitted. For slaves to quarrel over who had the highest standing in the household was not unknown. But in society as a whole there was also a *de facto* hierarchy of servile statuses, positioning in which was determined by not only the type of work done but also its context: so *rustici* were automatically inferior to *urbani* (at least in a slaveowner's judgement), the size of the *familia* to which the slave belonged was relevant and the social standing of the owner as well. The situation was again very much like that of Rio de Janeiro in later history, when slaves at the bottom of the scale in wealthy households ranked higher than the top slaves of less prosperous slaveowners, and mulattoes could even have more social prestige than many free whites. At Rome the slaves who enjoyed the most elevated rank in the hierarchy were those like the father of Claudius Etruscus who belonged to the greatest and most powerful slaveowner in the world and who played a role in governing the Roman empire. Their standing was such that they were commonly able to take as wives women of superior juridical status, women that is who were freed or even freeborn. Many of them lived in relatively secure material surroundings, enjoying wealth and power which others could come to resent. And often they were slaveowners themselves.

At the opposite extreme, however, there is the slave world evoked by Apuleius when describing the farm to which his hero Lucius was sent— transformed as he was into an ass—to sire mules. The property, owned by a woman of good standing but a provincial, supported a community of grooms, herdsmen and shepherds who with their wives and children lived in comparative isolation far from their owner's urban residence, working under the supervision of a *vilicus* and a *vilica*. They had little opportunity to acquire wealth or power or status. The *vilica* was resourceful enough to use the new ass to mill grain, some of which she sold to neighbours, and a slave child sold wood that he gathered on the mountainside to cottagers who needed fuel. But these were not sources of great income. The *vilicus* and his wife, the highest ranking slaves on the farm, lived in no more than a cottage (*casula*) and the hands' wives were their juridical peers, not their superiors . . .

Most *rustici*—and most slaves were *rustici*—will have lived in circumstances like these, in relative seclusion, at subsistence or near-subsistence level, with a minimum of social and economic security and few prospects of betterment. As with other groups—the slaves who worked in the appalling conditions of the mines (the silver mines of Spain for example where at New Carthage alone in the second century BC there were 40,000 workers) or those who were kept most of the time in chains—their circumstances were variations on a theme of desperation. They can have had little community of interest with the slaves of the emperor.

The employments to which Roman slaves were admitted, then, required so many different levels of skill, expertise and education and were so great in number and so disparate in nature, context and social meaning that slaves in the Roman world could never come to comprise a single, homogeneous class. A prominent Marxist historian of antiquity has described a social class as 'a group of persons in a community identified by their position in the whole system of social production, defined above all according to their relationship . . . to the conditions of production . . . and to other classes'. Its concomitant, class struggle, he calls 'the fundamental relationship between classes . . . involving essentially exploitation, or resistance to it'. It is indisputable of course that all Roman slaves shared a common juridical status and it is true that the fundamental distinction between slavery and freedom affected everyone; as Quintilian remarked, it made a great difference whether one were free or a slave. Moreover Roman slaveowners exploited all their slaves, their elite slaves included, and exploitation was resisted in a variety of ways. Yet as far as can be told there never developed among the slave population a sense of common identity—or class consciousness—that led to an ideological impulse to produce radical change in society. The slave population was too fragmented for that to happen, one of the reasons being that the multiplicity of slave occupations, compounded by differences of origin and geographical location, utterly prevented the emergence of any idea of making common cause. The antagonism between farm hand and bailiff that popular literature assumed conventional illustrates the point. As the slaveowner's representative on the spot, the bailiff gave the slave orders for work, managed his daily routine, and disciplined him. In so doing he became the object of intense anger and defiance: he was after all only a slave himself. Accordingly a competition between the two for the favour and support of the master, fought out in an atmosphere of mutual antipathy, suspicion and fear, was not an obvious inducement to unity of cause and purpose. The diversity of slave jobs and slave statuses in Roman society served to disperse, not to unite, the slave population, which should never be conceived of as a solid, undifferentiated monolith.

Why was so much stress put on particularism where slaves' jobs were concerned? The most revealing piece of evidence on this question is a passage from Columella discussing slaves' work-roles ('opera familiae'). It refers obviously to agricultural slavery, but there is no reason to doubt that the principles it lays down applied in the domestic sphere too. According to Columella, jobs should not be shared because the individual slave would not work industriously if they were, and no one could be held accountable if it turned out that work had been done poorly. It was thus of great importance on this view to maintain a strong distinction between the *arator* (ploughman) and the *vinitor* (vine-dresser) and to keep both apart from the *mediastini,* the ordinary farm labourers. Columella was concerned with extracting high performance from a work force that had no inherent interest in either the quality or the rate of work being done, his object being to secure as substantial a revenue from the land as possible. He thus clearly recognised the need to create an incentive by which to induce efficiency from slave workers and appealed to their pride in urging that they be held responsible for specific tasks. It was a pragmatic response, one that both acknowledged the human character of the slave property and assumed a similarity of values between slave and master.

The need to adopt a realistic strategy of this kind was present throughout the central period. In the last two centuries of the Republic the numbers of slaves involved in Italian agriculture increased dramatically as free peasants left the land under the impact of Rome's military requirements or in response to pressure from magnates seeking to extend and develop their landholdings with slave labour. Under the Principate, moreover, the profile of slave labour in agriculture remained high. An argument has been made that over time an increase in contiguous slave-staffed holdings necessitated more slave supervisors than was economically rational and that a labour crisis consequently developed by the second century AD; this, however, is a position that cannot be sustained by hard evidence. The maintenance of the agricultural slavery system over a period of four centuries or so—much longer than in any of the slave societies of the New World—implies on the contrary that slaveowners derived satisfactory and uninterrupted levels of profit from it, a view supported by the recent demonstration that slaves working in cereal production and viticulture (in particular) were kept fully occupied throughout the year by the demands of the production process and were not a wasteful form of labour as has sometimes been believed. But slaveowners were aware that lack of motivation (*inertia*) on the slave's part was a basic obstacle to labour efficiency, for while the free peasant had to work in order to feed himself and his family, the slave would always be fed by a master mindful of the need to protect his investment, whether he worked or not.

Not surprisingly, Italian landowners never relied exclusively on slave labour but preferred to use different methods of working the individual farms that made up their holdings. The younger Pliny, for instance, who owned a number of farms in two main units, one at Comum and one at Tifernum Tiberinum in Umbria, worked some of his lands with slaves and leased others to tenants, *coloni*, who might in fact have slaves of their own; likewise Columella advocated free management of estates that the owner could not visit regularly. But when the decision to employ slaves had been taken the obstacle of *inertia* had to be overcome and specialisation was one solution. Another was to use a system of gang labour which, as cliometric studies of New World slavery have shown and as Columella again understood, increased efficiency not by making slaves work longer hours but by making them work faster. The two methods complemented each other. Columella described the gang system in this way:

> You should . . . form groups of not more than ten men each—our ancestors called them *decuriae* and were very much in favour of them, since it is particularly easy to keep watch over this number of men, while a larger crowd can escape the control of the overseer as he leads the way. So if you have a large estate, you must assign these groups to different sections of it, and the work must be distributed in such a way that the men will not be on their own or in pairs, since they cannot be supervised properly if they are scattered all over the place; and conversely they must not be in groups of more than ten, since individuals will not consider that the work has anything to do with them personally if they are part of a large crowd. This system will induce them to compete with each other, and also identify those who are lazy.

To emphasize the variety of slaves' work-roles is to emphasise how visible slaves were in every aspect of Roman economic life, both in primary production (agriculture, mining, manufacturing) and in the provision of services. In the cities, towns and countryside of the Roman world working slaves were a fixed element of reality that could not be missed, no matter what the local overall density of the slave population. In everyday commercial life—that is in activities such as shopkeeping, trading and banking—slaves were particularly noticeable, operating as their owners' managers and agents with a great degree of latitude and independence, a pattern clearly shown by a section of the *Digest* that deals with the contractual liability of those who appointed agents to undertake business for them. The agent, who could be free or slave, a man or a woman, was called an *institor* and was appointed 'to buy or sell in a shop or in some other place or even without any place being specified'. Any number of enterprises could thus be in the hands of slaves—managing a farm, buying houses, cattle or slaves, shopkeeping and innkeeping, banking and moneylending, trading and contracting of every kind. Slaves were to be found too as captains of the vessels that were sometimes needed for commercial activities—the ferries that crossed the Adriatic from Brundisium to Cassiopa or Dyrrachium, for example, and the freighters that carried cargoes of vegetables, hemp and marble. Keeping a shop or an inn was presumably a permanent occupation. But some commissions were short-term, going to slaves who already had more regular jobs, an *insularius* or a *stabularius* or a *mulio*. And the owners who appointed them were not just the very rich: the slaves of tailors and cloth merchants, of launderers and bakers were also appointed to hawk, deliver and sell their masters' products; even the slaves of undertakers conducted business for their masters. . . .

It is frequently said, however, that slaves were outsiders or marginal beings and that their marginality, continually reinforced by their rightlessness, contrasted very sharply with the centrality of those who were able to participate fully in human and civic affairs. 'The essence of slavery', on one formulation, 'is that the slave, in his social death, lives on the margin between community and chaos, life and death, the sacred and the secular.' This conceptualisation is very valuable, as seen earlier, for pointing up the extent of the slave's powerlessness and for emphasising that without the master the slave could not exist; and to recognise the slave's alien aspect makes it easier to understand why the slave, although a dominated being, was also an object of anxiety: for at Rome as in other major slave societies fear of revolt by those cut off from the mainstream was widespread and far more prevalent than the actual incidence of insurrection would suggest.

Yet the social and economic intercourse between free and slave represented by the evidence on commercial life makes it impossible to describe Rome as a society simply comprising those on the inside and those on the outside. Full participation in the life of the civic community was in fact confined to wealthy, adult male citizens, a situation that by definition denied many social groups the full benefits of belonging. Under the Principate for example it was impossible until the time of Septimius Severus for Roman legionaries to marry and to produce legitimate offspring, but their incapacity did not generate a belief that Roman troops were in some way excluded from or did not belong to society. Slaves were a different category of course. But it is still probably better to think not so much in terms of all slaves being complete outsiders as in terms of degrees of relative incorporation into the mainstream of community life dependent on slaveowning interests; or, if the metaphor of marginality is kept at all, at least to acknowledge that the margins of society at Rome had to be very broad indeed. At the individual level, certainly, slaves were at times positively embraced by their masters and treated with personal regard. . . .

What slaves themselves thought of the particularistic work regime that slaveowners imposed upon them it is very difficult to tell. Many, it seems, estimated that their best prospects of survival and success lay in accepting their condition and in living within the confines of the social system around them. But in so doing they may have found in their work-roles the means by which to establish a sense of individuality and a sense of belonging to a community— the community of the *familia*. Many of the job-titles of Roman slaves, especially domestics, are known from commemorative inscriptions that were set up by or for men, women and children who had known the lived reality of slavery. Thus the fact that so many slaves and former slaves chose to leave records of the positions they had held and, if they belonged to the great *familiae* of the elite, where they had stood in the slave hierarchy may well reflect something of the values that they had created for themselves in slavery. The elite disdained physical labour and willingly demanded it of their slave dependants. But by taking the one commodity of which no one wished to deprive them, it may well have been possible for slaves to find some compensation for the human toll that slavery had taken of them. . . .

ROMAN BATHS AND BATHERS

FIKRET YEGÜL

The origins of Roman baths lie in the Greek gymnasium, where young citizens trained their minds through study and musical training and their bodies through exercise. While the Romans shared with the Greeks the ideal of a sound body and mind, they put baths to their own, distinctly Roman uses. Baths were part of public life: in addition to small, privately owned commercial baths usually open to the general public, there were the large public baths. Grand baths— thermae—were built by the emperors as an expression of their concern for the public and as an advertisement of their material and political successes. The imperial thermae were immense complexes that could occupy up to thirty acres or more. They possessed educational facilities, religious shrines, and places to walk and socialize as well as to exercise and bathe. In one case, the complex included parks, gardens, and watercourses for swimming and boating. Some were equipped with stadiums. Lavishly decorated with marble, mosaics, and statues, these "people's palaces" were the architectural expression of the political and social world of imperial Rome.

Considerable resources went into running the baths. Rome in 100 A.D. received some 1 million cubic meters of water per day from its aqueduct system, and a substantial amount of that went to supply the baths. The Thermae of Caracalla possessed a reservoir that could hold 80,000 cubic meters of water. Some baths had their own special branch aqueducts. Baths used copious amounts of wood for heating and oil for lighting. While baths were often subsidized by the public or by a private patron, they were money-making enterprises. People worked in the baths selling food, drink, oil to moisturize the skin, and cosmetics. Others rented towels and linens. Still others provided services such as massage and depilation. All paid the baths' administrators a percentage of their earnings.

While rural estate owners possessed private baths, city folk preferred to use the public baths. These baths were open to all; most

From: Fikret Yegül, *Baths and Bathing in Classical Antiquity,* (Cambridge, MA: The MIT Press, 1992), pp. 30–33, 34, 35, 37, 38, 39–40, 41–43.

entrance fees were very low (though women might be charged twice as much as male patrons). Why was bathing so popular among the Romans? Why did they prefer public bathing to private? Clearly, public bathing and the baths themselves performed a social function. In this selection, Fikret Yegül describes baths and bathing in the Roman world.

"I must go and have a bath. Yes, it's time. I leave; I get myself some towels and follow my servant. I run and catch up with the others who are going to the baths and I say to them one and all, 'How are you? Have a good bath! Have a good supper!'" These beguiling words taken from the pages of a schoolboy's exercise book, used roughly 1,800 years ago, vividly express the importance of bathing in Roman civilization. The universal acceptance of bathing as a central event in daily life belongs to the Roman world and it is hardly an exaggeration to say that at the height of the empire, the baths embodied the ideal Roman way of urban life. Apart from their normal hygienic functions, they provided facilities for sports and recreation. Their public nature created the proper environment—much like a city club or community center—for social intercourse varying from neighborhood gossip to business discussions. There was even a cultural and intellectual side to the baths since the truly grand establishments, the thermae, incorporated libraries, lecture halls, colonnades, and promenades and assumed a character like the Greek gymnasium.

Agrippa's census of 33 B.C. counted 170 small baths in Rome; by the early fifth century their number had grown to 856. Even the smallest villages of remote provinces were proud of their public baths. Among the most effective punishments that could be imposed by the government on a community was the closing down of its baths for a period of time.

For the Romans, bathing was a luxury and a necessity. A man, freshly bathed, appeared and felt radiant. Harking back to Homeric accounts of bathing, it was a pleasure deserved at the end of a hot and dusty day of hard work or travel, a civilized treat expected from a considerate host, or a comfort to be relished on a cold day. The bathing scene described by Apuleius, in the second century, reads like a passage from the *Odyssey:* "And he called his maid . . . and said: 'Carry this gentleman's packet into the chamber and lay it up safely, and bring quickly from the cupboard oil to anoint him and towel to rub him, and other things necessary; and then bring my guest to the nearest baths, for I know he is very weary of so long and difficult travel.'"

Even without such an obliging host, it was customary for the wealthy to instruct their servants to maintain and prepare the private hot baths in their suburban villas in anticipation of their arrival in the country. Cicero's concern is typical: "I think I shall arrive at my Tusculan villa either on the seventh or the day after. See that everything is ready there; for perhaps I shall have several others with me, and I expect we shall stay there for some considerable time. If there is no basin [*labrum*] in the bath see that there is one, and so with everything necessary for everyday life and health." The younger Pliny's description of his Laurentian villa and its very commodious bathing facilities—hot and cold swimming pools, exercise and ball courts, and up-to-date heating system—brims with just pride. Still, he expressed satisfaction in recalling that in the small village of Vicus Augustanus, near Ostia, there were three public baths that could be used conveniently as an alternative to bathing at home during an unannounced arrival or too short a stay.

THE LUXURY OF BATHING

Notwithstanding the luxurious bathing facilities available in the homes and country estates of the wealthy, bathing was a public affair in Roman society; bathing facilities in middle- and lower-class tenements and town houses were virtually nonexistent. Even in the more comfortable dwellings of the atrium type, one or two chambers tucked away with the kitchen (and often sharing its stove) sufficed to serve this function. Elaborately designed and elegantly decorated bathing quarters such as in the House of Menander in Pompeii were exceptional. It is possible that these cramped facilities were used predominantly by slaves and servants when they were unable to go to the public baths.

The quality of design and construction of the public baths, on the other hand, was far above average, and in some cases, luxurious, as in the proverbial "freedman's baths." Unfortunately, it is difficult to visualize the wealth of these interiors because the actual remains of luxury are scantily preserved: the decorations of the lofty vaults are gone; the walls and the floors have been stripped of their polychrome marble veneer; the silver basins and spigots, the bronze lion-head fountains, are missing; the sculpture and ornament exist only in fragmentary form, if at all. However, archaeological excavations on three continents attest the basic reliability of ancient written accounts of the opulence of certain bathing palaces—although some authors cared much less for this ostentatious display of wealth than others.

The most vivid and glowing account of the "perfect bath," by two contemporaries of the first century, Martial and Statius, is the description of the Baths of Claudius Etruscus, a small, luxury establishment belonging to a freedman (possibly located on the Quirinal Hill in Rome). "If you do not bathe in the warm waters of Etruscus, you will die unbathed, Oppianus!" exclaimed Martial. He admired the mildness of its waters and the serenity of its light, but most of all the richness of its multicolored marbles originating from distant quarries: the green Laconian marble, the purple, streaked marble from Phrygia, and the golden yellow (*giallo antico*) from Numidia, and added poetically: "The rich alabaster pants with dry heat, and snakestone [serpentine] is warm with a subtle fire." Statius's eulogy to the same baths is more elaborate. Laden with literary and mythological metaphors, the description is florid to the point of conceit: "Toil and care, depart! I sing of the baths that sparkle with bright marbles! . . . Come, then, ye nymphs of the waters, turn hither your clean countenances and bind up your glass-green tresses with tender wine-shoots, your bodies all unclothed as you emerge from the deep springs and torture your satyr-lovers with the sight." The nymphs of whom Statius was singing were not from the streams of faraway, classical lands, but were those who dwelled on the Seven Hills of Rome and mingled in the waters of its aqueducts, especially the two that served the Baths of Etruscus—the pure Aqua Virgo ("the Maiden"), excellent for swimming, and the chilly Aqua Marcia, born among snowy hills. According to Statius, every room was flooded with daylight, everything was etched in brightness and clarity; nothing was commonplace in Etruscus's baths: the doorways were of solid marble, the ceilings were radiant, walls carried pictorial representations in mosaic, and even the fixtures were not of ordinary bronze but of silver.

There is no denying the pleasurable sensory experiences offered by most public baths: vast spaces filled with light; marble tubs sparkling with clear, warm water; gentle soothing massage; perfumed oils and soft, fresh towels. Martial summed up the public sentiment when he admired the extraordinary luxuries offered by the baths built by an emperor about whom he had nothing good to say: "What was worse than Nero? What is better than Nero's hot baths?" But it was also Martial who was willing to forgo these luxuries and plead with charming modesty for a few basic needs and comforts that dignified human life, among which bathing counted as one: "Rufus, my simple tastes demand but modest things to smooth my path: good wine and food, a barber and a bath; a chessboard and pieces; a friend whose tastes and mine agree. . . . Warrant these things to me Rufus, even at [remote] Butunti, and keep yourself Nero's warm baths."

THE SOCIAL NATURE OF BATHING

The Baths of Etruscus in Rome, and others like it, catered to a wealthy class. Some of the bathing establishments might have appealed to certain interests and professional groups, and even became club-like centers, much like certain cafés or lounges become the preferred meeting places of similar interest groups in modern cities. The great number and diffusion of the smaller baths make such a hypothesis logical. The unique decoration of the Hunting Baths in Lepcis Magna, adorned with paintings of the hunt and the capture of African wild beasts, has prompted the theory that this could have been a special bathing establishment for hunters or for the merchants who supplied live animals for circuses and amphitheaters. In the Baths of Julia Memmia in Bulla Regia, the keystones of some of the smaller arches are decorated with various symbols—crowns and crescents—that belong to associations linked with the theater. In the North (Cluny) Baths of Paris, the consoles that support the main vaulting of the frigidarium are carved in the shape of boats that navigated the Seine. An association of Seine shippers is known to have existed from the time of Tiberius, in the first half of the first century. Could this Seine transportation association be responsible for the construction of the Cluny Baths? Libanius informs us that the eighteen tribes of late antique Antioch owned a bath and each tribe competed with the others to make its baths the finest.

But, as a general rule, a majority of the more than eight hundred small baths and eleven thermae of fourth-century Rome were open to anyone who could pay the trifling entrance fee; some, with special endowments, were even free. People naturally had their favorites where they mixed freely and enjoyed seeing familiar faces—sometimes, that of the emperor himself. The precedent goes back to earlier days: King Antiochus Epiphanes (c. 175 B.C.), one of the Seleucid rulers of Syria, was known for his habit of frequenting the public baths and mixing indiscriminately with the commoners. In a story illustrating the king's odd and misplaced generosity, he had a large jar of the costliest perfumed oil poured over the head of a man who had expressed happiness for the privilege of bathing with a king; the poor man slipped and fell on the oily floor of the baths which greatly amused the monarch and his retinue. Tradition dies hard, especially if it is backed by sound political motives: many a Roman emperor visited the public baths and enjoyed bathing in the company of his subjects. This undoubtedly provided the emperor, or the high powered political aspirant, with a chance to appeal for public support and to increase popularity. The baths were, indeed, the ideal institution with which to create the illusion of a classless society—one where wise man and fool, rich and poor, privileged and underdog, could rub shoulders and enjoy the benefits afforded by the Roman imperial system. The social and recreational component of bathing achieved, for better or worse, the status of fine art under the empire.

According to the stern, republican sensibilities of Seneca, it was certainly for the worse. One of the best descriptions of daily activities in a small city bath is found in his critical, satirical account of the deafening noises coming from the bath over which he once had lodgings: panting and grunting hearties as they swing weights; the smacking noise of body massage; someone yelling out the scores of a ball game; and the commotion caused by a thief caught stealing. To these noises were added the singing of the man who likes his own voice under the vaulted halls; the enthusiast who splashes indelicately in the public pool; the shrill voice of the hair-plucker advertising his trade, or worse, the yelling of his victims; and the incessant cries of the cake-seller, the sausage-seller, the candyman, each with his peculiar tone and style.

Ordinarily, men and women bathed separately, although some of the emperors tolerated mixed bathing. According to Varro, the first public baths in Rome were established as two connected buildings, one for men, the other for women. Many inscriptions indicate a certain physical separation of the sexes in the same building or in different buildings by designating them as "baths of men" (*balneum virile*), or "baths of women" (*balneum muliebre*), but it is not always clear what is meant. The former arrangement is recommended by Vitruvius and it is the solution evident in the Stabian Baths and Forum Baths in Pompeii. In both of these republican establishments, men's and women's sections have separate entrances but share the same exercise courts and the same heating and service facilities. Such independent units for different sexes, even in the largest baths, were extremely rare in the empire. The common practice was to assign the sexes different hours for bathing: women bathed in the morning, men in the afternoon.

Martial's and Juvenal's frequent references to women who exercised in the palaestra or bathed with men suggest an increase of mixed bathing in the second half of the first century. However, these are satirical accounts that question the respectability of heterosexual bathing and suggest that women who visited such baths were of dubious reputation. It may have been the rising scandals that moved Hadrian to place a prohibition against mixed bathing ("lavacra pro sexibus separavit"). Consider this inscription found in 1870 on the premises of a private bath in Trastevere, in Rome: "By the order of the mighty god Sylvanus, women are prohibited from stepping into the swimming pool reserved for men." Could this prohibition be taken as evidence that women, too, could be aggressors? While it is difficult to evaluate this enigmatic notice, Lanciani comments: "This inscription shows that police regulations were not enough to keep fast women in order . . . the owners of the baths were obliged to resort to the intervention of the gods."

THE RITUAL OF BATHING

The Roman workday started with the sun and was confined to the morning hours; by noon, or soon after, all business for the day was finished. After a light lunch, and perhaps a short siesta, men went to the baths and stayed there for several hours. Two o'clock in the afternoon (the eighth hour in the Roman system) is specified as the best time to bathe in a number of Martial's epigrams. In one, he parcels out the day's hours into appropriate activities and assigns the eighth hour to palaestral sports and bathing. "This hour [the eighth] tempers the warm baths [of Nero]"—an hour or two earlier the vapors would be excessive and the heat immoderate. This is convincing enough but part of the reason must also have been the desire to establish regular hours for the public baths, and allow sufficient time for their cleaning and maintenance.

Martial, who had been accused of laziness by one Potitus for not publishing a book for a whole year, tried to defend himself by showing how busy he was with daily responsibilities: completely exhausted by the end of the day, he even visited the baths rather late, at the tenth hour. The rulers themselves were no exception when they were very busy: in a letter to Tiberius, Augustus invoked his friend's sympathy for having to sacrifice his meal and postpone his bath until the first hour of the night (c. 6:00 P.M.) because of pressing duties.

Night bathing was not unheard of, but it was not usual and not encouraged. One of the prime targets of Juvenal's satirical arrows are déclassé society women who failed to visit the baths before evening, leaving their unfortunate guests at home nearly dead of hunger. The drunken ardor of an uncouth drinking party such as Trimalchio's could drive revelers to the baths regardless of the lateness of the hour (but that was a private party and a private bath). There are occasional references to artificial lighting of public baths, and oil lamps have been found in large quantities in the excavation of certain baths. Ordinarily, though, baths depended on large and well-placed windows for their illumination and closed per imperial (or municipal) order before daylight completely faded. If the difficulty and extra cost of artificial lighting were two major impediments to night bathing, security was another. We do not know how strict these municipal or state restrictions were or how long they stayed in effect, but in 424, the Baths of Zeuxippus in Constantinople were artificially lighted and the expenses met from public revenue.

The younger Pliny summarized the essentials in the sequence of bathing: "I am oiled, I take my exercise, I have my bath." This was the rudimentary order of the Roman afternoon—a mild form of exercise followed by hot baths, after which the much enjoyed main meal of the day, dinner (*cena*), was eaten. Two centuries later, the system had scarcely changed: after public business, Alexander Severus read, then exercised, had himself massaged with oil, and bathed.

A well-to-do Roman was accompanied to the public baths by his slaves carrying his bathing paraphernalia: exercise and bathing garments, sandals, linen towels, and his toilet kit—the *cista* (a cylindrical metal box) which contained anointing oils and perfume in flasks (ampulla and alabaster), several strigils (a metal blade with a slightly curved end used to scrape down the excess oil from the body), and probably a sponge. A poor person carried his own bundle, or had it carried by an old, home-grown servant. It was a symbol of status to go to the baths attended by an army of well-groomed slaves and to be carried back on a sedan chair. Most Romans, however, could only afford the services of a single professional attendant who anointed, strigiled, and rubbed them down. Professional masseurs and specialists in depilation could be found in almost every bath.

The first thing to do upon arrival at the baths was to undress; even the humblest bathing establishments had a special room, the *apodyterium,* assigned for this purpose; larger baths might have a number of apodyteria, including heated ones for winter use. The furniture of these rooms must have consisted of wooden cabinets or chests—all since perished—for the safekeeping of clothes and personal effects. More permanent are the niches, shelves, and cubbyholes quite frequently found in baths; in the poorer establishments wooden pegs and wall hangers might have sufficed. Masonry benches are preserved in some of the apodyteria; others might have had wooden ones for servants to sit on and keep watch over their masters' clothes (petty theft in public baths was a common though much despised occurrence). In the baths described by Lucian there was a special room in which slaves could wait while their masters bathed.

Unlike the Greeks, the Romans did not think it proper to exercise or bathe in the nude but neither did they consider it proper to enter the exercise ground or the hot rooms of the baths in street clothes and shoes. Information on bath garments is scanty; they probably varied much according to season, climate, and regional customs. Trimalchio wore a light tunic ("red shirt") while playing ball; masculine Phialenis took her exercises vigorously in a skimpy garment like a bikini, her body covered with the yellow sand of the palaestra. More explicit is the description of the *endromis,* a wrap of rough texture worn over the lighter clothing after gymnastic exercises, probably native to the colder regions of the Alps; Martial sent one to a friend with this appealing message: "This shaggy nursling of a weaver on the Seine [Paris], a barbarian garb that has a Spartan name, a thing uncouth, but not to be despised in cold December—we send you as a gift, a foreign *endromis* . . . [that] the searching cold may not pass into your moist limbs, or Iris overwhelm you with a sudden shower. You will laugh at winds and rains, clad in this gift."

Alexander Severus returned from the public baths to the palace in his bathing costume wearing only a purple cloak over it. Among the traditional gear and clothing supplied by the same emperor for his newly appointed judicial officers were two garments for use in the forum, two for home, and one for the baths. There is no description of these garments but they might have been simple linen wraps covering the lower half of the body, somewhat like a Scottish kilt. Wooden clogs or sandals constituted the proper footwear at the baths since they would protect the feet from dirty water as well as from excessive floor heat in some of the hotter rooms.

It would be a mistake to presume that the average Roman engaged in strenuous exercise before taking his bath, like the stripling athletes of the Greek gymnasium. Roman gymnastics was merely a prelude to bathing, a form of recreation, and not intended as training for competition. It was a social habit that had its roots in preventive medicine. The "athletes" were often elderly and not necessarily in good shape, but they hoped to improve their health and ward off disease through exercise.

Despite variations in detail of theory and application, the ancient medical profession was united in the belief that bathing, exercise, massage, and diet were principal elements in establishing and maintaining a regimen for good health. Celsus, a medical writer who lived in the first half of the first century, recognized the benefits of bathing and exercise for a healthy body, but considered vigorous routines, such as the athletes followed, to be potentially detrimental for ordinary people since ". . . any break in the routine of the exercise, owing to the necessities of civil life, affects the body injuriously." Among the useful exercises, he listed reading aloud, walking, running, drilling, and playing handball. But the workout was to come to an end as soon as a light sweat built up, before the body was completely tired out.

Galen, the famed physician of the court of Marcus Aurelius in mid-second century, also emphasized the medical benefits of exercise in conjunction with bathing. In his essay on "Exercise with the Small Ball" (*De parvae pilae exercitu*), he recommended light ball games over other, more strenuous sports as a form of exercise well suited to those who led an intellectual life; they also provided a good basis for military training. Ball games developed all parts of the body in a balanced way, were not expensive or time consuming, and could be practiced safely by all age groups. For maximum benefits, Galen suggested that they, as all other forms of exercise, should be followed by massage with oil and sometimes by hot bathing.

A special room for ball games, comparable to the *sphairisterion* of the Greek palaestra, must have been fairly usual in Roman public baths; one certainly existed in the Baths of Claudius Etruscus. It seems to have gained considerable popularity among the Romans, existing either as an independent facility or as a part of a fashionable villa.

Among the other palaestral sports, running, wrestling, boxing, and fencing were mentioned, although their practice was not limited to the palaestra; many of the larger baths had spacious halls that could be used for indoor athletics. Juvenal mocked brazen society women, who worked out with weights and dumbbells, for infringing upon a branch of sports (*halter*) that was obviously considered a reserve of the serious male athlete. Swimming or rolling a metal hoop with a hooked stick (*trochus*) might have been thought more suitable exercise for women.

Swimming was a popular sport among the Romans, but it is hard to know if it was done in the baths. Literary evidence suggests that although the ability to swim and to swim well was acclaimed as a worthy skill and included in the education of wealthy young men, the proper place for serious swimming was in the sea or in rivers. Baths often had pools (*piscinae*) large enough to swim in, but even the largest of these pools, the *natatio* of the imperial thermae, barely reached a depth of 1 to 1.20 meters. Few are known that included a deep end for diving or other technical features for competition swimming. Swimming in these pools must, therefore, have been limited to a few easy strokes, with most of the bathers enjoying leisurely wading and splashing. The Great Palaestra in Pompeii and the palaestra in Herculaneum had pools that were well over 2 meters in depth, but these were regular "gymnasia" serving exclusively for athletic training and competitions and were not connected with baths.

The time spent in the palaestra of the baths was pleasant, but the delights awaiting inside were pleasanter still. There were precious few who were so engrossed in their exercise as to not stop everything and hurry inside with the first sounding of the *tintinnabulum,* the bell that announced the opening of the hot baths.

One greeted a friend about to start his bath with the wish for a good bath. *"Bene lava!"* or *"Salvus laves!"* and, afterward, hoped that he had washed well, *"Salve lotus!"* Some might have preferred the eastern (Alexandrian) mode of saluting an acquaintance with a slight bow. *"Peripsuma su"* ("Your humble servant").

Formulaic bathing salutations are particularly common in Latin inscriptions. Often framed in *tabulae* or *tabellae ansatae,* and placed at the entrances and exits of baths, they are accompanied by mosaic representations of typical palaestral implements (*strigiles, aryballi,* and *ampullae*) and, more significantly, by the outlines of bathing sandals (*soleae*) indicating the direction of movement (even a pair of sandals side by side, turned in opposite directions). Although representations of *soleae* do occur in buildings other than baths, and might have a variety of meanings (usually to ward off the evil eye), their significant position in baths hints at the existence of a rudimentary order of circulation. Taken in conjunction with other evidence, these inscribed bathing salutations and representations of *soleae* can help interpret the nature and uses of Roman bath architecture.

The order of bathing required a movement from warm to hot through a number of intercommunicating rooms of varying temperatures; the primary stations in this sequence can be identified as the tepidarium and the caldarium. Bathing terminated with a cold plunge in the frigidarium. Most bathers perceived benefits from spending some time in one of the special sweating chambers, the laconicum or the *sudatorium,* the former often specified as having a hot but dry atmosphere. Anointing was essential to exercise, either before or after (or both), and in many baths special warm rooms with various designations seem to have been provided for massage with oil (*aleipterion, destrictarium, unctorium*). It was also customary to terminate hot bathing by rubbing the body with specially prepared cosmetics, oils, and perfumed unguents. Anywhere along this course, deviations, omissions, or repetitions were possible; one bathed as one wished. The order, if one could call it an order, was not a fixed routine. It was more like a general framework that allowed variations, and it received its inspiration, if not its outward shape, from the current recommendations of doctors and the medical traditions of antiquity.

Bathers must have spent most of their time in the caldarium and the frigidarium, the main halls for hot and cold bathing, as well as for a wide variety of social, sportive, and recreational activities and even performances. A mosaic panel at the entrance of a bath in Antioch shows three jugglers and, perched upon the left arm of one, a monkey-like animal. Mountebank performances given in theaters and amphitheaters were very popular in antiquity. Public baths, with their commodious halls, palaestrae, and gardens—and an everready and enthusiastic audience—seem to have served as ideal stages for traveling jugglers, gymnasts, conjurers, jesters, and musicians. A certain Ursus, who lived during Hadrian's reign, was famed for playing a game with a glass ball; his performances attracted large crowds in four of the thermae of Rome (Thermae of Trajan, Agrippa, Titus, and Nero). Ursus composed his own epitaph and hoped to preserve the memory of his fame and unusual skill for posterity; his wish seems to have been granted in a modest way.

Eating and drinking would have infused merriment into any group in the hot baths since vendors of victuals and wine were readily available. For some, this might have meant a light refreshment, an aperitif before dinner; others took it more seriously and made a meal of it. Aemilius ate lettuce, eggs, and eels and tried to excuse his appetite by commenting that he did not take dinner at home. But Philostratus fell down a long flight of steps to his death on his way back at night from a spirited party at the thermal baths in Sinuessa, famed for its curative waters: "He would not have incurred such great danger, ye Nymphs, if he had drunk your waters instead," Martial sagely comments.

The high-vaulted ceilings and large semicircular or arched windows of the caldaria and frigidaria were much admired by the bathers; references in ancient literature to the pleasing daylight and brightness of these lofty spaces are frequent. The enjoyment of the view through these large windows as one bathed immersed in a pool, or even the possibility of getting a tan (some baths had a solarium or a *heliocaminus,* special rooms with unglazed windows for sunbathing) were among the pleasures that made bathing a sensual experience.

The public, by and large, seems to have enjoyed not only the illumination but also the excessive heat of the caldarium, equating abundance with luxury. Martial poked fun at the baths of one Tucca, whose caldarium, though resplendent in rare marbles and gems, was so chilly that Tucca was advised to use the frigidarium to heat the caldarium! There are anecdotal references and criticism of baths so prodigiously and senselessly heated that direct contact with the floor or walls of the caldarium caused the bather serious burns.

A good bath called for a good dinner to make a perfect day. "It is little consolation to bathe in luxury and perish in starvation," observed Martial, and he proceeded to sharpen his lively wit on the subject of dinner as a culmination of bathing in no less than eight epigrams. To dine alone was something of a social disgrace for some and an outright disaster for spongers who hoped to feast sumptuously at the expense of a rich acquaintance. Philo swore that he never dined at home but he might not have dined at all if no one invited him. Cotta was more discriminating and required serious courting at the baths; even Martial had drawn a blank on him:

If you would feast at Cotta's board,
The baths your only chance afford
To get an invitation.
I never yet with him have dined
My naked charms do not, I find
Excite his admiration.

BATHING AND MORALITY

"What is bathing when you think of it—oil, sweat, filth, greasy water, everything revolting . . ." Such was the assessment of bathing by the emperor and philosopher Marcus Aurelius, or, rather, his assessment of material life in general. "Baths, wine and women corrupt our bodies, but these things make life itself," was the Cynics' acknowledgment of the same question, found frequently on inscriptions, epitaphs, or scratched informally on toilet seats in public latrines. The two views are not, actually, all that divergent, except that popular philosophy was able to come to terms with material life and its transient pleasures, and Stoic philosophy could not.

While resting at the country house that once belonged to the hero of the Second Punic War, Scipio Africanus (c. 200 B.C.), Seneca saw the small, dark baths the famous general had used. Drawing a contrast between old and new, he deplored the accustomed luxury of the baths of his own day: "[Today], we think ourselves poor and mean if our walls are not resplendent with large and costly mirrors; if our marbles from Alexandria are not set off by mosaics of Numidian stone [*giallo antico*]; . . . if our vaulted ceilings are not buried in glass [mosaic]; if our swimming pools are not lined with Thasian marble, once a rare and wonderful sight in any temple; . . . and, finally, if water is not poured from silver spigots. . . . What a vast number of statues, of columns that support nothing but are built for decoration, merely in order to spend money! And what masses of water fall crashing from level to level! We have become so luxurious that we have nothing but precious stones to walk upon." He proceeded to contrast the overly lighted contemporary baths with the welcome darkness of the old ones such as the Stabian Baths or the Forum Baths in Pompeii," . . . for our ancestors did not think that one could have a hot bath except in darkness . . . nowadays, however, people regard baths as fit only for moths if they have not been so arranged that they receive the sun all day long through the widest of windows, if men can not bathe and get a coat of tan at the same time, and if they can not look out from their bath-tubs over stretches of land and sea." Regretting the overheating of the new baths and the habit of bathing every day, instead of once a week as the old Romans used to do, he concluded: "Now that spick-and-span bathing establishments have been devised, men are really fouler than of yore."

Writing during the first half of the first century, Seneca was giving voice to a moralizing attitude that disapproved of the increasingly luxurious lifestyle of his day compared with the frugal manners that accompanied military and manly virtues of the past. Seneca was not alone: the disapproval of the excessive material luxury represented by baths; the objection to the worldly and wasteful lifestyle encouraged by them; and the condemnation of the sexual licentiousness and moral delinquency associated with the baths were among the major issues raised by conservative critics and constituted the basis of Christian opposition to bathing several centuries later.

The elder Pliny deplored displays of luxury in women's baths, with their floors of silver, although he was quite proud of the Roman technical achievement that brought water to the baths. A contemporary of both Pliny and Seneca, Demetrius the Cynic entered the Thermae of Nero during the ceremonies of dedication and delivered to the aristocracy congregated there a speech denouncing luxurious baths and bathing. It was the wrong place and the wrong time for outspokenness; he narrowly escaped with his life. It is noteworthy that the generations hypercritical toward the increasing material comforts of life, and of the baths in particular, belonged to the early decades of the empire. Cicero, of the late republic, had no quarrels with the modest bathing establishments of his day. In the second half of the first century,

Martial, Statius, and the younger Pliny accepted the public baths as legitimate and quite in line with the luxuries offered by the imperial system.

The elder Pliny was also worried about excessive anointing and bathing as grim indications of a spreading social disease; he criticized in a satirical vein the "broiling baths by which they have persuaded us that food is cooked in our bodies so that everybody leaves them the weaker for treatment, and the most submissive are carried out to be buried . . ." Pliny's parabolic humor finds its counterpart in Seneca, who spoke about the "fashionable heat" of his day as a proper conflagration and quipped "that a slave condemned for some criminal offense now ought to be *bathed* alive!"

From their inception in Classical Greece the public baths were censured for their appeal to sensual pleasures, and they were accorded a place at the other end of the moral scale from the gymnasium. Baths were associated with an effete and wasteful lifestyle, which was said to have ensnared the well-born youth of Aristophanes's Athens. Centuries later, the Roman historian Tacitus described this way of life, "the lounge, the bath, the banquet," as a form of vice brought by the conquering Romans to Britain, which seduced the native inhabitants of the island.

These refinements affected every class of society in Rome or abroad. Some of the emperors lived amid baths and banquets in their imperial residences. The parvenu found excellent opportunities to display his wealth and stage his petty affectations in the permissive world of the public bath. The tramp, the vagabond, or the ordinary lout also found in public baths an atmosphere ready for uncouth and boorish behavior. There were those who treated the crowd to unsolicited concerts or vulgar recitals of their own poetry. Young Algernon displayed six rings on his fingers, and young Maro displayed his physique and gathered applause.

Drinking in excess was another offensive habit often connected with public baths: "This is one of youth's popular vices," complained Seneca, "to build up strength [by exercise in the palaestra] in order to drink on the threshold of the baths amid the unclad bathers; nay, even soak in wine and then immediately rub off the sweat which they have promoted by many a glass of liquor!" The elder Pliny went so far as to claim that there were many who used the sweat chambers merely in order to raise their thirst.

Gluttony and overindulgence were generally frowned upon and the wise realized the dangers of bathing on a full stomach. Seneca's fare in his old age was frugal: after the bath he would eat only some bread without even bothering to sit down, a moralizing point made in contrast to the indiscretions of the nouveaux riches, who stumbled into the baths after a gross feast. Such foolishness elicited a mock warning from Juvenal against a mistake few would live to repeat: "But you'll pay the price all too soon, my friend, when you undress and waddle into the bath, your belly swollen with undigested peacock meat—a lightning heart-attack with no time to make your final will."

The subject that attracted the greatest public censure was the alleged immoral and sexual indiscretions associated with baths. Throughout Roman history, many viewed the world of the public baths with varying degrees of distaste and reprobation. Despite the lingering existence of a republican tradition of modesty and restraint, and the frequent prohibitions against mixed bathing by most of the emperors, the baths still provided one of the major opportunities for exposing the naked and seminaked body in public. Athenaeus tells that Phryne, the famed courtesan and model who posed as Aphrodite for the painter Apelles and the sculptor Praxiteles, was very beautiful; one could, however, not easily catch a glimpse of her in the nude because she was too modest to go to the public baths. Most of the Roman courtesans did not share Phryne's bashfulness about visiting the public baths with men although they seem to have been well versed in their own brand of coyness. Martial mentions being teased and taunted by Galla: "When I compliment your face, when I admire your legs and hands, you are accustomed to say, Galla, 'Naked I shall please you more,' yet, you continually avoid taking a bath with me. Surely, you are not afraid, Galla, that I shall not please you?" It is reported that Emperor Elagabalus (218–222) gathered in a public building all the prostitutes from public places, including the baths, and lectured them on sexual matters. A century later, despite growing Christian influence, things had not changed much concerning the attentions some prostitutes received in the baths from those in high places. Ammianus Marcellinus, a historian of the fourth century, looked back with nostalgia upon the moral greatness of Rome's republican past and deplored how the nobles of his day brazenly competed with one another to win the favors of a new prostitute who appeared in public baths.

Obviously, prostitutes of both sexes could be found in or around the public baths, and bathing with courtesans was the proper prelude to intimate relationships. More exclusive "bathing parties" for the rich could be arranged, as indicated in a passage from Plautus, an early-second-century-B.C. playwright, where the pimp Lycus tries to lure Collybius into the baths to enjoy "a nicely cushioned couch with a nice lady to love" and a love-bath with plenty of wine and perfumed unguents from an obliging bath attendant. The baths were certainly not only places to seek illicit pleasures but also to find the cure for the same. In that, they had a clear advantage over other localities because they offered the potion of the purge along with the phial of corruption. One even visited the baths to "sweat out" and "sober up" after a night of indiscretion and indulgence.

The objection to bathing on ethical grounds reflects the beliefs and convictions of its exponents and the overall moral atmosphere of the period as much as it expresses a judgment on the baths themselves. Often, the subject is used only as a vehicle to express views on larger issues and requires consideration of the full context for a fair assessment. Given the order of the typical Roman day, and the characteristics of ancient economy, one cannot seriously fault the baths for taking up too much of the afternoon and promoting laziness. That they provided a wholesome and altogether realistic form of recreation for the great majority of the public is sufficient defense against the perhaps justifiable claim that the baths induced indulgent and crude behavior. Such behavior and sexual promiscuity, too, would have existed in the Roman society with or without the help of the baths.

Even Seneca, a man "who held that the good life was a matter of waging continuous war on bodily pleasure," bathed frequently. Moreover, as a Stoic he could not resist viewing life as a metaphor for a public bath: "The program of life is the same as that of a bathing establishment: sometimes things will be thrown at you, and sometimes they will strike you by accident," has one translation. Had Seneca been carving his philosophy on a toilet seat, he might have preferred a shorter and more popular version: "Life is a bath. All paddle about in its great pool, some sink, some swim." . . .

Panel on the Frank's Casket, eighth century (A.D.), *showing the legend of Weland the Smith (at his forge). Casket is made of walrus ivory.*

(SOURCE: Courtesy of the Trustees of the British Museum)

II

THE EARLY MIDDLE AGES
6th–11th Centuries

In the sixth century, the western Roman Empire fell to the Germans, who replaced the Roman political system with independent kingdoms. These kingdoms expressed the political unity of tribal groups that had been brought into federations just before and during the migrations of the fifth century. In Gaul, it was the Franks, in Spain, the Visigoths; in Italy, the Ostrogoths; in North Africa, the Vandals. These major groups slowly absorbed smaller ones like the Burgundians, the Thuringians, and the Alemans.

After the kingdoms were established, the kings of the principal confederations consolidated their positions by assuming the mantle of Roman authority. Everywhere in Europe, the German kings sought and received confirmation of their new power from the Roman emperors in Constantinople. For their part, the emperors had nothing to lose by granting the kings Roman titles. It preserved the image of imperial power, even though its reality had been gone for decades, and it helped to maintain good relations between the eastern Roman Empire and the occupants of the old imperial territories in Europe.

The new society of barbarian Europe was a compound of the old provincial society of the Roman Empire, and the tribal society of the German invaders. Aware of this compound society, the kings issued dual codes of law for their subjects. The Romans continued, therefore, to live under a simplified version of Roman law, while the Germans lived under their ancient laws. The amalgamation of the two communities took generations.

The first selection in Part 2 explores the make-up of the barbarian household before it was substantially changed by contact with Roman culture and Christianity. David Herlihy, in "The Early Medieval Household," uses descriptions of the early medieval Irish household, which did not change as rapidly as its barbarian counterpart on the continent. In the second selection,

J. M. Wallace-Hadrill describes how Christianity gradually spread among the pagan barbarians and the Celtic peasantry whom they ruled. Using the case of the conversion of the Franks, Wallace-Hadrill shows that the process and speed of conversion was not the same for kings, aristocrats, and peasants. Each group had its distinctive pattern of conversion. Moreover, in the conversion process, pagan beliefs mixed with Christian ones and left their mark on medieval Christianity.

The Germanic lords of Europe changed the countryside as well as the cities. Many old villages remained as they had been for generations, but the invaders carved new ones out of the European forest; in these, they introduced new agricultural techniques. During the early middle ages, a technical revolution occurred in European agriculture; as it spread, it changed the way of life of the great majority of the population, the peasants. In the third selection, Eileen Power recreates the world of a medieval peasant by telling the story of Bodo.

In the fourth selection, we turn from consideration of the majority to consideration of a small but important, minority—the Jews. The Jews came to the towns of northern Europe in the ninth century and formed tightly knit, prosperous communities. The authorities recognized the value of these communities and both encouraged immigration of Jews and protected them. But the population found them alien and mysterious, and persecution was a common experience of the Jews. Robert Chazan's "The Jews in a Christian Society" reveals the experience of this unassimilated minority at the time when the towns had begun to grow into major centers of population and commerce.

The final selection, Joshua Prawer's "The World of the Crusaders," takes us to the Holy Land, where the European conquerors established a colonial society after the First Crusade (1096–1099). In fact, this colony was the most famous of those built by Europeans during the eleventh century. Beginning in the middle of the century, northerners had pushed steadily to reconquer the Iberian peninsula from the Moors, the Islamic North Africans who had occupied it since 711. In Spain, the new conquerors organized their new territories as colonial extensions of the ancient Christian communities that had clung to the southern flank of the Pyrenees since the time of Charlemagne. The colonial state in the Near East had much the same character as those in Spain: it was a plantation of western society in an alien world, which influenced virtually every aspect of the colony's social life.

BIBLIOGRAPHY

On the Germans and Germanic Society, see Patrick Geary, *Before France and Germany: The Creation and Transformation of the Merovingian World* (New York, 1988); Malcolm Todd, *The Northern Barbarians, 100 B.C.-A.D. 300* (London, 1976); and Lucien Musset, *The Germanic Invasions* (State College, PA, 1975). E. A. Thompson brought his studies of Germanic society together in *The Early Germans* (Oxford, 1965). For a survey of medieval households, see Jack Goody, *The Development of the Family and Marriage in Europe* (New York, 1983). Susanne Wemple discusses early marriage patterns and how they changed under the influence of the Christian Church in *Women in Frankish Society: Marriage and the Cloister 500–900* (Philadelphia, 1985). George Duby discusses the effect that Christianity had on marriage in *The Knight, the Lady, and the Priest: The Making of Modern Marriage in Medieval France*, trans. by Barbara Bray (New York, 1983, 1981).

For peasants and village life, see the seminal work of Mac Bloch, *French Rural History*, trans. by Janet Sondheimer (Berkeley, 1966). For more up-to-date surveys see Robert Fossier, *Peasant Life in the Medieval West* (New York, 1988); and Werner Rösener, *Peasants in the Middle Ages* (Urbana, 1992) with emphasis on, respectively, French and German examples. Georges Duby, *Rural Society and Country Life in the Medieval West*, trans. by Cynthia Postan (London, 1968) combines abundant primary source readings with analysis. Excellent local studies are: J. A. Raftis, *Tenure and Mobility: Studies in the Social History of the Medieval Village* (Toronto, 1964); and R. H. Hilton, *A Medieval Society: The West Midlands at the End of the Thirteenth Century* (London, 1966). Emmanuel Le Roy Ladurie draws on Inquisition records to reconstruct French village life in *Montaillou: Promised Land of Error*, trans. by Barbara Bray (New York, 1978). Barbara Hanawalt uses criminal records to reveal the village social order in *Crime and Conflict in English Communities, 1300–1348* (Cambridge, MA, 1979).

Robert Chazan draws much of his material from the Responsa of the medieval rabbis, and a large selection of these judicial decisions has been translated by Irving Aguus in *Urban Civilization in Pre-Crusade Europe*, 2 vols. (New York, 1965). The most complete study of the medieval Jews is by Solo W. Baron, *A Social and Religious History of the Jews*, 2nd ed., vols. 3–8 (New York, 1957–58). See also, Cecil Roth and I. H. Levine, eds., *The Dark Ages: Jews in Christian Europe 711–1096* (New Brunswick, NJ, 1966). The Jewish view of the Crusades is represented in contemporary chronicles published in English by Schlomo Eidelberg, trans. and ed., *The Jews and the Crusaders* (Madison, WI, 1977). Connections with the Middle East made Jewish medical lore superior to Christians' in the West. See Joseph Shatzmiller, *Jews, Medicine, and Medieval Society* (Berkeley, 1994). Life in ethnically and religiously mixed medieval Spain is described by David Nirenberg in *Communities of Violence: Persecution of Minorities in the Middle Ages* (Princeton, 1996). Kenneth Stow reconstructs the Jewish family in "The Jewish Family in the Rhineland in the High Middle Ages: Form and Function," *American Historical Review*, 92:5 (1987):1085–1110.

A good general history of the Crusades is Steven Runciman, *A History of the Crusades*, 3 vols. (Cambridge, England, 1951–54). See also Riley-Smith, Jonathan, "State of Mind of Crusaders," and the other contributions to *The Oxford Illustrated History of the Crusades* (Oxford, 1997). On the Crusaders' kingdoms, see Dana C. Munro, *The Kingdom of the Crusaders* (New York, 1935); and Joshua Prawer, *The Crusaders' Kingdom: European Colonialism in the Middle Ages* (New York, 1973). Robert Bartlett widens the perspective on European expansion and colonization in his excellent study, *The Making of Europe: Conquest, Colonization and Cultural Change, 950–1350* (Princeton, 1993). For studies on colonial society in Spain, see Robert I. Burns, *Medieval Colonialism: Postcrusade Exploitation of Islamic Valencia* (Princeton, 1975); and Heath Dillard, *Daughters of the Reconquest* (New York, 1984).

THE EARLY MEDIEVAL HOUSEHOLD

DAVID HERLIHY

Investigating the culture of the barbarians who migrated into Europe poses special problems for the researcher. The Germanic and other peoples who invaded the empire were illiterate, and the earliest written sources we have about them are the descriptions that Romans such as Tacitus made. The information provided by the Roman sources is suspect for a number of reasons. First, the Romans who wrote about the barbarians were not trained ethnographers; they only understood the barbarians in terms of Roman values. Thus we can learn about what the Romans thought the barbarians were doing and the Roman reactions to these perceptions, but what the barbarians actually were doing, and why, often remains unknown. Second, the authors often had ulterior motives that throw doubt on the accuracy of their descriptions. Tacitus, for example, sought to criticize the sexual practices of the Romans by praising the barbarians for their monogamy. However, later legal and church records reveal that the barbarians actually were polygamous. Third, the Romans only described barbarian peoples who had come into contact with the empire or who were living within it. In both cases, they already had been influenced by Roman institutions and culture. As the barbarians settled in the empire or along its borders, they adopted Roman practices in agriculture, landownership, and trade, and modified their political forms in response to their dealings with the imperial government. What we see then is not unadulterated barbarian culture, but rather one cultural tradition in the process of assimilating another. Later, under the influence of churchmen and inspired by the example of Roman law, barbarian kings issued laws that provide a glimpse into their society. Again, however, historians must be careful to distinguish elements that were affected by contact with the Roman world and Christianity from those that seem to reflect what early barbarian society and culture were like.

From: David Herlihy, *Medieval Households* (Cambridge, MA: Harvard University Press, 1985), pp. 32–43.

Another source of information about barbarian culture is ar-
chaeology. Historians have turned to grave sites, the impressions
that houses have left on the ground, and even the remains of garbage
heaps to gain some clues about barbarian society both before and af-
ter the tribes came into contact with the Roman world. For Ireland,
an additional source exists: the early saints' lives. These stories
about Ireland's sixth- and seventh-century saints were written down
in the late eleventh or twelfth century, but they originated from an
oral tradition in the early medieval period. References in the saints'
lives to practices no longer common when they were recorded indi-
cate that the oral versions of the tales preserved much of the earlier
culture. In this selection, David Herlihy draws on the Irish saints'
lives to reconstruct the early medieval household. What the saints'
lives describe for Ireland corresponds very closely to what is known
about the marriage practices and families of the German tribes that
migrated into the Roman Empire. Thus they provide us with a
glimpse of what Germanic society was like before contact with the
empire and the Christian Church.

Information about the early medieval household also con-
tributes to efforts to determine women's status in the early Middle
Ages. Some historians argue that the early medieval period was a
golden age for women. They point out that early medieval marriage
practices and property rights seemed to give women far more inde-
pendence and personal value than they enjoyed either in late antiq-
uity or for much of the Middle Ages. For example, property rights
granted to wives under Germanic law enabled noble women to take
independent action in founding convents and monasteries and con-
sequently made them important and respected patrons of the church
during the early Middle Ages. Other historians doubt that a true
golden age existed for medieval women. They point out that
polygamy and concubinage would weaken a woman's position in
marriage, make her highly dependent on the whims of her husband,
and isolate her by forcing her into bitter competition with other
women.

Irish society was divided into tribes (*tuath*) and the tribes into kindreds
called septs, although the sources do not always differentiate with clarity one
from the other. The sept is exactly equivalent to the Germanic or Indo-
European sib, *Sippe* or *Geschlecht*. The sept appears frequently in the lives as
the *gens,* a kin group stemming from a named ancestor or founder. Its members are usually referred to as the "sons" or "grandsons" (*nepotes*) of the same
forefather. It is also called *cognatio* or simply *natio.*

The sources occasionally identify the founder of the sept and inform
us how distant he was in generational count from the present. Thus, in the

Old-Irish life of St. Abban, the head of the sept that produced the saint was Brian son of Eochaid, seven generations back; the founder of the sept of St. Mochua, named Lugo, was his *abavus* or great-great-grandfather, four generations into the past. It should be noted, however, that these short genealogies did not exhaust the lineage memory of the Irish. They were capable of pushing pedigrees back fifteen and more generations. The extended pedigrees showed the relationships of septs within the same territory and gave structure to tribes and nations, but did not define the functional kindred, that is, the sept itself.

Thus, within their seemingly interminable lineages, the sources identify some prominent figures as those who established existing kindreds. "This Lugo," reads the life of St. Mochua, "was the founder of the Lugic sept, which is not at all obscure among the Irish." The clear reference to the founding of a sept within human memory suggests that the septs within society were constantly dividing and reforming. Presumably, a member of an established sept, if he became wealthy, powerful, and prolific, could become the *auctor* of a new *gens*. If we assume that Lugo and his descendants all reared four children to adulthood (those marrying out would be replaced by those marrying in), then by Mochua's generation the sept would have included 32 households, about 160 persons. Abban's kindred would have had 256 households, more than 1250 persons—probably as large as the sept could be. These admittedly crude estimates at least give us a range of magnitude which the Irish septs probably attained.

Many historians of early law have maintained that the primitive Germanic and Indo-European *Sippe* or descent group was agnatic, that is, it recognized relationships only through males. Although all the founders of the Irish septs were indeed men, nonetheless the kin associated was emphatically not restricted to patrilineal relatives. King Echach tells St. Patrick that he hoped "to extend my lineage (*prosapia*) from the body of my daughter, by the procreation of grandchildren, for the strengthening of my kingdom." His wish would make no sense if matrilineal relationships were ignored. Descent through women was very important in Irish society. Among the works of the eighth-century Irish monk, poet, and hagiographer, Oengus, there are maternal genealogies of some 210 Irish saints, it is not known whether he ever traced the paternal lines of these holy people. . . .

HOUSEHOLDS

The sept was comprised of individual households, which, we have guessed, might number between 120 and 256. At the head of the household was the chief and his wife (or wives).

Most of the marriages in the lives are monogamous. But we hear of a "very rich man" who had two wives, "according to the law of that time." The life's unknown author finds no blame in such polygamy: "This man walked in the commandments of God, giving gifts and tithes in His honor." But his wives quarreled so much, that he eventually fled the household and entered the monastic life. And the apparent prevalence of monogamy did not, as we shall shortly see, preclude the formation of other forms of sexual liaison, with concubines and slaves.

The legal wife is the *domus domina,* the mistress of the household, as she is called in the life of St. Brigid. According to the *Cáin Adamnáin* or Law of Adamnan, all wives were at one time slaves. They were even forced to go to war, to slay and be slain, while their husbands, standing safely behind them, whipped them onward into the fray. St. Adamnan allegedly freed them; his was the first law made in heaven and on earth for women." Moreover, ". . . ever since Admamnan's time, one-half of your house is yours, and there is a place for your chair in the other half." It is hard to know what to make of his bizarre text, but clearly it celebrates the freedom of women and their authority within the Irish household.

The wife also performs certain critical services for her male kin. When the four half-brothers of Brigid try to force her into marriage, they complain that through her vow of virginity, "she avoids that for which God made her, and in her obstinacy so lives, and is determined to live, so as not to want to make her father a grandfather and her brothers uncles." She thus causes them "great shame and expense." Here, I believe, is an important insight. Brigid is the half-sister of these males, and indeed her mother is a slave. But their own mother—Brigid's stepmother—has become cursed with sterility and cannot produce another sister. Brigid offers her half-brothers their one possible link through a sister to the coming generation. (She also offers her father his last chance to have grandchildren through a daughter, and this may be the reason that he comes to regret his initially bad treatment of her.) Brigid's brothers seem to be unmarried, and no one of them is bothered by the celibacy of the others. Yet they strongly insist that Brigid marry. Their behavior highlights the capital importance of the relation of brother or sister's son (the "avunculate") in the early Irish kinship system, and indeed of all relationships running through women. To be sure, Irish chiefs certainly wanted male descendants, to uphold in a violent world the status of their lineages. But they also wanted the pedigree of male descendants certified through matrilineal connections.

In urging her to marry, Brigid's brothers further argue that her husband, who will surely be noble, will be for brothers and for father a *propugnator et amicus,* a champion and friend. The wife was thus of critical importance in defining the relations of her family of origin to other powerful persons and septs in the vicinity.

In keeping with the important services she renders, the legal wife seems also to have controlled important wealth. The brehon laws imposed strict limits on a woman's power to hold and to alienate property, especially land, but these restrictions have no trace in the hagiography. A woman named Flandnait holds from her father an "inheritance" in the town called Feic, along the banks of the Nem (Blackwater) river. And women often give themselves and their property to the saints.

One source of the wife's wealth was the dowry system. The groom, or his family, conveyed property to the bride, which she personally controlled. The reverse dowry, probably best called bridewealth, included even land. In the life of St. Mochteus, for example, a widow bestowed on the holy man a field she received as part of her dower, an *agrum dotalem*. Apparently some women accumulated wealth through gifts from their husbands, and even from other males, over the course of their marriages. In the life of St. Fursa, a nobleman of Gaul reminds his wife of the "riches I have given you." She had accumulated wealth "since youth." In the life of St. Aedh, a king gives a gold and silver brooch to a woman who is clearly not his wife. Other wealthy women are mentioned in the tales. St. Fursa, when passing through Arras in Gaul, seeks hospitality from a lady named Ermenfleda, who owns "many possessions and moneys." After the saint's death, his merits cure the illness of another rich lady, who holds "many riches and possessions." To be sure, some of these rich ladies live in Gaul and bear Germanic names (Leutisinda, Ermenfleda), but the lives give no hint that this in an Irish perspective was at all exceptional. As the Old Irish life of Berarch states, what valor is to the warrior, and learning to the clerk, so is prosperity or abundance to a woman.

The wives are likely to have wielded considerable influence, power even over decisions made within the household. They had the right to divorce their husbands and depart their households, taking their wealth with them. The stepmother of St. Brigid threatens to leave her husband Dubthach, if he does not sell his slave concubine, Brigid's mother, then pregnant with the saint. Her threat carries real force, as she bends her reluctant husband to her will, and later gains his acquiescence in her persecution of the young saint. So also, in Gaul, the lady Leutisinda berates her husband and threatens to abandon their marriage if he continues to bestow their properties on St. Fursa.

The legal wife in these elite households is rich and powerful, but her presence does not stop her husband from forming other sexual alliances. Concubines are frequently mentioned in the lives, and clearly not all of them are slaves. The life of St. Brigid offers a particularly lively picture of sexual relations, inside and outside of legal marriage. Dubthach, Brigid's father, is evidently a rich man, possessing large flocks and herds and extending the hospitality of his table to numerous guests. Perhaps he is also a Christian, at least he welcomes bishops to his table, with exultation and a smiling face, in the language of the life. Besides his legal wife, he cohabits with a slave girl, called *concubina* in the text. When the story of Brigid's life begins, Dubthach has made both women pregnant. The life utters not a hint of reproach against Dubthach for this violation of Christian marriage. On the contrary, the anonymous author rather reproaches the legal wife, for forcing her husband with threats of divorce to get rid of his concubine. The wife is depicted as stupid and mad; she lacks matronly modesty and fails to show proper respect for her husband, she has an evil mind, and she behaves like a raging beast. She draws all this abuse because she objects to the presence of a concubine in her household. Dubthach is exonerated from all guilt, even for driving his pregnant concubine from his home. "My wife prevents me," he explains, "from being liberal and humane toward my concubine." . . .

POLYGYNY

If these scattered references to early Irish households can be interpreted in terms of a single, coherent domestic system, it must be one that incorporates polygyny. According to the lives, the maintenance of several sexual liaisons is unmistakably the prerogative of the wealthy and the powerful. The man who lived with two wives "according to the old law" is expressly described as "very rich." Another rich man, Dubthach, Brigid's father, can afford to purchase a slave girl for a concubine and to support her in his household. The traffic in slave girls was so brisk that the word *cumalach* (female slave) serves as a standard measure of value in early Ireland. A petty king, such as Dimma, has the power to abduct the girl that he desires, and only a wonder-worker can retrieve her. The rescue of abducted girls gives frequent employment to the saints.

Those males who possess wealth and power use it to acquire women too. In anthropological terminology, the common name for such a system is "resource polygyny." Even in societies where polygyny is legal, only the richest and most powerful males will usually command the resources needed for the support of several sexual partners; this was the case in early Christian Ireland. But if some men claim several wives or concubines, then others will have none. The Irish lives do not reveal a great deal about the lower levels of society, which had to be marked by a shortage of women. Doubtlessly many males, unable to marry, worked as servants in the households of the powerful. Dubthach's own household employed shepherds, swineherds, cowherds, and cultivators. The lives give the further impression that the surrounding forests and wastes were infested with brigands; they waylay travelers, rustle sheep and cattle, and attack homesteads. Their ranks were doubtlessly filled by poor males unable to find mates.

The anthropological model of resource polygyny, applied to early Irish society, is suggestive, but still requires further refinements. Women were gathered into the households of the powerful not exclusively for sexual purposes. Even the households of the early Irish bishops, who were celebrated for their chastity, seem to have accumulated women. There is a curious passage on the "three orders of the saints of Ireland." The first, and indeed the holiest of the orders, flourished from the days of St. Patrick. It numbered some 350 bishops; founders of churches. "They did not," reads the passage, "spurn the administration of women, and their company." Presumably, these women directed the celibate bishops' households. Women were also involved in many productive activities. St. Brigid, when she labored under her stepmother's cruel dominance, was a jack of all trades, or a jill of all chores: she tended the sheep and pigs, milked the cows, and helped in the harvest, she cooked, baked, made butter and cheese, and brewed beer; she waited at table, and nursed the sick. Women dominated all phases of cloth manufacture, from spinning, to weaving, to dyeing, to the sewing of cloth. In the words of the *Cáin Adamnáin,* the woman "carries the spindle and . . . clothes everyone." The close association of women with cooking, brewing, and dyeing, with arts that men did not understand, may have given them prominence too in the practice of magic. The divorced wife of duke Colman murdered through incantations his offspring by his new wife, as soon as they were born; only the intervention of St. Coemghen finally broke her magic.

Among the arts considered appropriate for women—for religious women surely but perhaps lay as well—was reading. St. Ite was an extraordinarily learned woman. She tells her sister to send her son Mochoemog, Ite's nephew, known also by his Latin name Pulcherius. "Bring him here," she orders, "for it is fitting that I should nourish him." "And for twenty years the most blessed abbess Ite instructed him in honest morals and a knowledge of letters . . . so that he could become a priest and build a place for God." We should note the special relation here between a woman and her sister's son—an interesting variation of the avunculate tie.

Women thus tended to gather in the households of rich and powerful males, both for reasons of their sexual attraction and for reasons of service. A modified form of resource polygyny seems to have been a common model of aristocratic marriages and households in early Christian Ireland. The model allows us to draw certain inferences concerning the social life of the epoch. We can then judge whether such inferences find support in the period's scattered documentation.

One implication of resource polygyny is that it tends to raise the incidence of sexual promiscuity within the community, on the part of women as well as men. The rich man cohabiting with several women seeks to guard them from other men, but the task is difficult. Men without sexual partners will seek to overcome their deprivation through the purchase of a concubine, if they have the money; through abduction, if they have the power, or through seduction, if they have the charm. Moreover, the woman, like Dubthach's wife, may resent the fact that she shares her husband's attentions and look for satisfaction, or even retribution, in her own extra-marital affairs. And the disgruntled wife will have not trouble finding willing paramours.

Indeed, the women who appear in the Irish lives are not passive sexual objects, moved about without acquiescence or resistance among powerful males. Women sometimes initiate sexual liaisons. They repeatedly tempt the saints, although this may be only a hagiographical topos. St. Carthach was so handsome that "at various times during his youth thirty young women fell in love with him with great carnal passion, and did not conceal it." The beautiful daughter of king Echach seduces a soldier in her father's retinue, and becomes the mother of the great St. Tigernach. According to the life of St. Kieran, a queen named Ethnea, wife of Engus, comes with her husband to a feast sponsored by another king named Concraid. She falls in love with her host, and tries to seduce him. She is unable to consummate the adultery, but her failure does not indicate any lack, on her part, of desire and effort. One day, St. Columba asks a young monk whether his mother is a religious woman. The surprised young monk replies that his mother is certainly of good morals and reputation. The saint instructs him to inquire from her about a certain grave sin—unnamed, but surely sexual. The abashed mother admits her guilt. In the same story, a layman expresses the fear that his wife, out of love for a younger man, may murder him. Still another layman complains that his wife refuses to sleep with him, and only the saint's admonitions and power succeed in persuading her to fulfill her conjugal duties. In the life of St. Kentigern, bishop of Glasgow, a queen cultivates an adulterous relationship with one of her husband's knights, and gives him a ring, through which the affair is discovered. These are not passive women.

Even limited sexual promiscuity has the result of obscuring lines of descent through males. The issue of uncertain paternity emerges in the lives, and is a frequent occasion for miraculous enlightenment. St. Dimma is born out of an adulterous union, and no one knows what to call him. But St. Carthach has a vision of the past: "This baby is called Dimma, and he is the son of Cormac of the seed of Eathach." All present praise the saint, "who revealed the lineage of the holy baby Dimma, no one telling him except the Holy Spirit." In another incident, a woman commits adultery, bears a child, but refuses to identify the father; St. Ailbe summons all the men of her village, as if all were equally suspect. The baby at the saint's command names the father. In one of St. Brigid's miracles, the saint in comparable fashion instructs a three-year-old to identify its father; Brigid thereby refutes the allegations of his lying mother, who claims that a bishop is the father. A recently converted petty king named Brendan "begged St. Patrick that he should bless a certain pregnant woman, as he believed that his blessing would benefit her and her offspring." The saint was about to do so when, "the spirit revealing it to him," he recognized that the baby's father was of a lineage he had previously cursed, out of which, he had predicted, no king would come. Apparently, the woman—was she Brendan's wife?—was concealing the true paternity of her baby. The mother of St. Kentigern of Glasgow cannot tell him who his father is. "That which was born in her, she received by human intercourse. But she many times affirmed, and swore, that she did not have awareness by whom, or when, or how, she had conceived." Were it not for miracles, the paternity of all these babies would have remained uncertain.

Under such conditions, the male is likely to develop the most steadfast ties with persons related to him through women. He has good reason too for favoring them in the distribution of his properties through gifts and inheritance. The children of his sister are without doubt members of his kin and representatives of his stock—his *semen* in the terminology of the Irish lives. Indeed, they will usually be the sole members of the younger generation who can be so identified. And he can be more certain that his grandchildren through a daughter are his blood relatives than the grandchildren through a son.

The Irish lives make frequent mention of the avunculate tie, and of other forms of relationship running through women. In the life of St. Patrick written by the English Cistercian Jocelin of Furness (after about 1180), Patrick is represented as the great-nephew of St. Martin of Tours, his mother Conquessa is Martin's niece. Jocelin is the first to claim that the two saints were related, and significantly, he runs their blood tie through two women. Still according to Jocelin, to his *cognatus* Patrick, Martin gives the monastic habit and his rule. As a boy, Patrick had been reared in his aunt's house in a town called Nemphtor (presumably Clyde) in northern Britain. The aunt was his mother's sister. Patrick himself had three sisters, one of whom, Lupita, had seventeen sons and five daughters. They all become priests and nuns, and all come to help Patrick on his Irish mission; so also did his other nephews, sons of sisters. "Truly the offspring of these [sisters] appears blessed . . . and a holy inheritance was the nephews of St. Patrick." The embellishments, which Jocelin added to the ancient legends of Patrick, are extraordinarily rich in matrilineal allusions.

The maternal uncle of St. Alban, the bishop Ybar, is present at his birth and blessed both mother and baby. At age twelve, the nephew joins his uncle and remains with him "many years." The nephew of St. Braccan, again the son of a sister, is a thief. He accidentally kills his uncle, and the crime is represented as especially heinous. The three Irish saints, Cronan, Mobai, and Machonna, are parallel cousins whose mothers are sisters. Their spiritual relationship replicates the kinship tie running through women. In the life of St. Ruadanus, a man named Odo Guori flees for protection against an angered king to the bishop Senachus; the two are cousins, sons of sisters. Fraech, uncle of St. Berarch, takes the latter as a baby from his sister. The life in Old Irish relates: "And Berarch was the one person in all the world who was dearest to Presbyter Fraech of all who ever received human nature, save Christ alone." The Latin version adds a quaint touch: the uncle suckles his little nephew on his right ear.

The bond joins uncle and niece as well as nephew, but always through a woman. In the Old-Irish life of Brendan of Clonfert, "Brig, daughter of Findlug his sister, was with him there, and great was his love for her."

Under the system of Irish kinship, not only matrilineal relatives, but the women who served as linkages, and women generally, were held in high esteem. To St. Brendan, the face of his sister Briga, "whom he warmly loved," at times takes on "the look of the splendid moon." St. Cainnech finds "great joy" in visiting his sister Columba. And the *Cáin Adamnáin* is lyrical in its praise of mothers.

This modified form of resource polygyny also affected practices of child rearing. In the households of the powerful, the presence of several mothers and several sets of children inevitably invited jealousy and dispute. Dubthach's legal wife, herself pregnant, is incensed when she hears the bishop prophesy that the offspring of her husband's concubine is destined to be mistress over her sons, and indeed over all Ireland. Later she subjects the young Brigid to cruel persecutions. The wife of the king of Laigin, "like a faithless stepmother," tries to kill her husband's son, "for she feared that he would prevail over her own offspring." In part for their own protection, young children were frequently, even usually, sent to be reared in different, often distant households. The foster mother is called in the lives the *nutrix,* as she assumes the duty of nursing the young child. The foster father is the *nutritor.* The bonds linking foster child and parents were often close. In the life of St. Fintanus, a monk named Sinkellus tries to convert to the ways of righteousness both his natural father and his *nutritor.* He brings the two men to St. Fintanus. The saint utters the gloomy prophecy that the natural father will be numbered among the goats at the Last Judgment, and adds, rather anticlimactically, that kings will also confiscate his property. But the foster father will be saved, suggesting that the services of the foster father were more meritorious than those of the natural parent.

The household system of early Christian Ireland, in summary, was based on the descent groups, kindreds or septs, which traced their origins back to a named ancestor. The sept's founder was always male, but matrilineal ties retained a special importance. The sept's fortunes, especially in battle, depended upon men, but relations through women certified their membership and kindled their loyalties. The sept controlled a particular territory, and was in turn divided into households. The households were not, however, very similar or commensurable. Polygyny, concubinage, and a need for the services of women gathered females into the households of the rich and the powerful. At the other end of the social scale, bands of robbers—predominantly male, as far as we can judge—lurked in the forests and mountains and preyed upon the households of the *divites, duces,* and little kings, in quest of food, cattle, booty, and women. Between these two extremes, Irish households doubtless differed considerably in their size and the sex ratio of their members. And violence reigned, as some men sought to protect, and others to steal, these treasures.

The skewed distribution of women doubtlessly subjected them to high risks of rape and abduction. But the system also favored women, in marked ways. They played a major role in the administration of the great households, even those of the celibate bishops. They participated in, even dominated, many types of economic production, especially the manufacture of clothing. In religious life and perhaps in the secular world as well, women were repositories of literacy. The learned St. Ite "reared many of the saints of Ireland from their infancy." Within the kinship network, women served as signposts, indicating to ego his surest relatives.* This function made them important conduits for the flow of property, in the form of marital gifts and inheritances, down the generations. To pass on property through female relatives offered the best assurance that the wealth would benefit one's own lineage, one's *prosapia* and *semen.* . . .

---

*In cultures that trace descent from both the male and female lines, each individual has a unique descent pattern. The individual identifies his or her distinctive familial relations by starting with himself or herself ("ego") and then tracing the family links which radiate outwards from that point.—ed.

The Conversion of the Franks

J. M. WALLACE-HADRILL

In the fifth century, Christianity was only one of a number of religions that flourished within Europe's boundaries. Christianity had to compete for followers against the various pagan beliefs of the Celts, the Romans, and the barbarian tribes, as well as against Arianism, a heretical form of Christianity that denied the divinity of Christ. The conversion of Clovis, king of the Franks, to orthodox Christianity in the early years of the sixth century was a major watershed for the struggling Christian Church. Clovis's earlier military campaigns had united the separate Frankish tribes under his rule and had conquered the Arian Visigoths, Burgundians, and Alemans. Thus, with the baptism of Clovis, much of Gaul suddenly had a Christian king. After his conversion, Clovis continued his attacks on Arian territories, claiming he could not bear the thought of any part of Gaul being under the control of heretics.

What made Clovis's conversion so important to Christianity's success in Europe? The pagan barbarians believed that the king had a special relationship with the gods. It was the favor of the gods that qualified the king to rule and that gave him divine luck—what the Anglo-Saxons called mana. *The king served as intermediary between the gods and the tribe, his luck passing through him to his people in the form of good harvests and military victories. Successive defeats or a string of bad harvests were a sign that he had lost his divine luck and were cause to replace him with another man who seemed to enjoy the favor of the gods. It was the king's special role as intermediary between the gods and his people that made Clovis's conversion to Christianity such an important event in the history of the church. The king's gods were his people's gods, and when Clovis accepted the Christian god, so did his people. The participation of Clovis's most powerful supporters in his baptism symbolized both their acknowledgement of this fact and their acceptance of the new faith.*

From: J. M. Wallace-Hadrill, *The Frankish Church* (Oxford: The Clarendon Press, 1983), pp. 17, 19–24, 27–32, 35–36.

*Why did Clovis and other barbarian kings embrace a new reli-
gion? The king who converted to Christianity risked, according to
barbarian beliefs, offending the very gods whose favor had made
him king in the first place. Conversion could lead to the loss of his
royal luck and thus to the loss of the throne. Perhaps it is for this
reason that most of the voluntary conversions of barbarian kings, including that of Clovis, apparently followed military defeat and seem
to have been an effort to regain royal luck through the acquisition
of a powerful new divine supporter: Jesus Christ. The kings' conversions, then, were consistent with their traditional pagan beliefs
rather than with the principles of Christianity. The motivation behind a king's conversion and the automatic conversion of his entire
realm raises questions about the extent to which either the king or
his people were truly Christian. In this selection, J. M. Wallace-
Hadrill addresses this question by looking at the evidence for Christian belief among the Franks at three levels: the king, the aristocrats,
and the commoners. Because the Franks rarely wrote about their religious beliefs, Wallace-Hadrill must use indirect evidence such as archaeological finds, royal laws touching on religious matters, and the
accounts of Christian bishops and missionaries. Using these sources,
he is able to trace the slow process of the conversion of the hearts
and minds of the Franks, a conversion that in some cases occurred
centuries after Clovis's baptism.*

The time has gone, if it ever existed, when we could think of the Franks, or
any other Germanic people, as pagan one day and Christian the next. So hero-
ically simple a solution does no justice to the texts and is quite overthrown by
archaeology. We must move more cautiously, as did the Germans themselves.

Fifth-century Gaul was Christian and mostly Catholic in a formal sense.
But behind the forms lay a scarcely-converted countryside where Celtic and
other pagan beliefs still worried the clergy. These beliefs remained active in the
sixth and seventh centuries, and not only among the indigenous populations,
they affected the way the Franks accepted Christianity, as indeed they had already affected the way the Gallo-Romans themselves accepted it.

This is one side of the picture. The other is the nature of Germanic paganism. No sense can be made of Frankish Christianity, when it comes, unless
allowance is first made for the fact that all Germans were religious people.
Their lives, as individuals and as members of communities, were conditioned
by the sense they had of good and evil, life and death, gods and demons. This
can best be seen in the archaeological evidence from their remote homeland in
a yet more distant time. Much, too, can be inferred from later literary evidence. Recent work has shown what can be done for the religion of the
continental Saxons by collating the evidence of Scandinavian and Germanic
literature with that of the gold bracteates—medallions, once worn as amulets,

that have been found in Scandinavia and on the German mainland. From it emerges a picture of sixth-century paganism that has subsumed late Roman coin-material to make its own iconography of a conquering cult of Woden. Not nearly so much can be attempted for the Franks, for the sources scarcely lend themselves to this treatment. . . .

One pagan god to whom the Merovingians* certainly attached importance as their dynastic patron was a sea or river god, apparently represented with horns, as was customary among both Romans and Germans. This was the sea-beast, part man, part bull, and therefore like a Minotaur, from which Merovech was descended, as Fredegar reported in the seventh century. Gregory of Tours, more squeamish, omitted any mention of this background, though he betrayed knowledge of the legend by remarking that 'some hold that Merovech was of the race of Clodio'. He would not commit himself as to whether Merovech was the son of Clodio or of the Minotaur. It may well be, also, that he was confused, as we still are, about the identity of Merovech, who could have been either the eponymous founder of the family or the historical Merovech, son of Clodio. The likelihood is that the story had become attached to the wrong Merovech by Gregory's time. But in any case we are left with a legend commonly accepted by the Franks of the sixth and seventh centuries, and perhaps earlier, that their conquering dynasty had a respectable progenitor in a sea god. This does not mean that the Frankish people worshipped such a god nor that the Merovingians had no other god. He was rather a private acquisition for the Merovingian patheon, an ancestor peculiar to them. He does not help us to understand in what sense the Franks as a whole were a religious people. For this we must look at their grave-goods.

There is always a temptation to interpret any scene depicting warriors, birds and animals as representing specific Germanic heroes, gods or myths. This can be taken too far. On the other hand, when we look at such an object as the Franks Casket (Northumbrian work of about 700) we are reminded that quite elaborate stories could be depicted that contemporaries could interpret without difficulty, though we cannot. In the present state of knowledge, nothing is lost if we see Germanic gods depicted in plausible situations so long as we acknowledge that this is only a working hypothesis. For example, Woden may be intended by the naked figure armed with a spear on a seventh-century gravestone from Niederdollendorf. On his breast is a ring (as it might be, the ring Draupnir of the Eddas), a nimbus of rays surrounds his head and a snake or dragon lies beneath his feet. On the other side of the stone is a representation of the dead man, a singular pantalooned figure with a comb in his hair and a huge scramasax in his hand. Over his head is a two-headed bird-snake, while a third monster grips the hilt of the scramasax in its beak.

---

*Clovis was a member of the Merovingian dynasty, one of the most powerful of the ruling Frankish families. After Clovis brought all of the Frankish tribes under his control, the Merovingians ruled as kings of the Franks until the mid-eighth century.—ed.

Beneath it is an unidentified object rather like a plump money-bag with a symbolic coin in it that could signify booty, a wergild or an offering. It might be a cult-object. Altogether the impression is thoroughly pagan. Woden more certainly appears armed with a spear and mounted on his horse, Sleipnir, on a metal ring from Bräunlingen. And again we have him, accompanied by his ravens, Hugin and Munin, on a metal ring from Soest, and conceivably also in the bearded head between two birds on sword-chapes from Krefeld-Gellep and from the district of Namur. These witnesses to the cult come from the borders of Frankish settlement. But we have, plausibly, a Frankish Woden-like god nearer the centre of things Frankish on a late belt-buckle from a cemetery at Rouen, where he appears in an ecstatic pose, encircled by a great bird; and again, we may have a Germanic god in profile, facing a swastika, on a buckle from Monceau-le-Neuf. All this is little enough. But we must bear in mind that the Germans generally seem to have been unwilling to portray the human figure. A god may be represented by some token specially associated with him; as, for example, a swastika (often the sign on Thor), a bear (associated with Thor and Woden), a stag, a horse, an eagle, a serpent or, in the case of Frey, a boar. All these appear on Frankish grave-goods, on which scenes and symbols proliferate in hundreds. What, for example, should be made of the extraordinary representation on a buckle from Picardy of two mounted men whose horses drink from an urn? Or of a series of buckles showing horses covered with eyes and accompanied by birds? Or of the backward-looking monster on a buckle from Arnay-le-Duc? Or the naked figures on another Picard buckle? Or the face and inscription on a silver brooch from Liverdun? Or the two-headed dragon holding a magic ball on a buckle from Mont-sur-Lausanne? It is easy to be misled into a misreading; for instance, where we think we see an animal or bird attacking a man, the craftsman may have seen them communicating quite amicably with each other. To take an example, the two monstrous birds or griffins, whose beaks rest on the head of a man on a plaque from Combles, near Péronne, may be attacking the man, or they may not; and this is only one of a class of which the iconography remains to be interpreted. At present, at least, it would be unwarranted to assume that worship of the gods was not implied. And there is yet another way in which the gods may be present in a burial. A severed head in a grave (and there are not a few) may be a tribute to a god, drinking vessels buried with the dead may be not only for the use of the dead but also for ritual drinking; the looped or writhing dragons or snakes so common in Frankish iconography, whether singly or in groups, may hark back to serpents of northern myth; gods, the magicians *par excellence,* may be present in a number of guises we do not yet recognize; and they may also be present in the magic of runes. A runic message may be direct, such as that on a brooch from Kärlich, near Koblenz. It reads: 'I am consecrated to Woden: I have the power of good luck'. Or again, on a Scandinavian bracteate: 'I write runes', which signifies that the wearer is charmed and should be given a wide berth. But the message may be unintelligible, as with the runic inscription on the Charnay brooch. Secrecy could be the essence of runic protection to the illiterate. It was certainly so in the ninth century. In any case, runes are rare enough in Francia proper. There are only a few on metal and any on wood have long since perished. Two points need emphasis. The first—again—is that much of this must of necessity be conjecture. We have at present some, but very little, hard evidence of the worship of Woden, most powerful of the gods exported from Scandinavia; but there is this to add: he was not a god to travel in the baggage of an isolated warrior here or there. By the sixth century he was central to Germanic religion. Secondly, Woden was more than the spear god, the god of battle, though he was that to bands of young warriors advancing into fresh territory. Success in battle was a kind of magic. He was also the god of inspiration, regeneration and healing, the magician who could protect a kindred or a family just as well as a warband. This was how the continental Saxons regarded him. The Franks were physically and spiritually further from the seat of Woden's cult at Odense in Denmark than were the Saxons. But we are learning more of the ties, cultural and economic, that held these peoples together in the early middle ages. At present we can go so far as to say that by the sixth century Woden was worshipped by some Franks; and if Woden, then his colleagues; and if not Woden, then a god remarkably like him.

Frankish grave-goods witness in a more general way to the Germanic pagan view of the after-life and of the relationship of the dead to their surviving kindred. Religious feeling seems to have played some part in the choice of burial-sites. There was a preference for the slopes of hills, the proximity of running water and, as occasion afforded, old tumuli. More obviously suggestive is the filling-in of graves with soil brought from elsewhere; the evidence of ritual fires at the time of burial and later; the burying of three arrowheads with the body or the remains of animals and birds not meant for consumption hereafter by the dead—and of this a famous instance is the presence at the cemetery of Norion-sous-Gevrey of massive *sacrificia mortuorum,* sacrifices for the dead, a practice that continued to worry the Carolingians—placed in separate excavations; libations on a generous scale; human hair worn in belt-buckles, as at St Quentin; the presence of boars' tusks and bears' teeth. And to all this may be added, for good measure, the burying of parts of, or symbolic representations of, animals and birds of special religious significance, such as the stag (the conductor of the dead) and the horse, at once a means of travel and a source of strength. Of course it is easy to see symbolism where contemporaries would have seen none, or a different symbolism. Moreover, much of the symbolism that we associate with the Germanic peoples was common to the Celts and the peoples of the Steppe. Ideas and artefacts spread from East to West. However, we are left in the end with certain practices and beliefs of the Franks exemplified in a formidable number of graves. They were complex and deep-rooted and by no means suggestive of a people looking for a new religion.

But a new religion they found, and found it under their conqueror of northern Gaul, Clovis (or Chlodovech, to give him his right name). His father, Childeric, had been buried at Tournai, presumably by Clovis himself. Fragments of his grave-furniture can still be inspected in Paris and a valuable contemporary account of the discovery of his grave in 1653 can be read. The contents have often been described. They constitute much what one might expect for a well-established federate chieftain with wide contacts. The war-gear and jewellery and other paraphernalia (some of it, possibly, like the bull's head, symbolic of belief) betray a good pagan, to whom the gods have been kind. Under the same gods, one supposes, his son advanced south in force to take over control of northern Gaul and to establish his authority, as and when he could, over neighbouring Frankish chieftains. But he did more than this. He overcame neighbours who were not Franks; powerful neighbours, like the Rhenish Thuringians, the Alamans and the Visigoths. Whether he did so as a pagan or a Christian is keenly debated to this day. Much turns on whether one accepts the chronology established by Gregory of Tours, the historian of the Franks. It may well be that Gregory sometimes got his dates wrong but yet put events in the right order; which means that Clovis won his early victories as a pagan but the last at least as a Christian. Moreover, there was an intermediate stage between his decision to seek baptism and baptism itself. To Gregory of Tours, at least, what the victories as a whole proved was that Clovis belonged to the original, noblest, long-haired race of the royal Franks; and there was nothing Christian about that. Three aspects of the process are relevant here and call for comment: the nature of his conversion, the immediate implications of his baptism, and the effect of his baptism on his subsequent actions.

First, as to conversion. It was certainly not implied by his first foray into Gaul. The hard-headed bishop of Reims, Remigius, made no such assumption when he wrote to Clovis soon after his advance into Gaul, but merely congratulated him on taking over the administration of Belgica Secunda and loftily advised collaboration with the bishops. There is no word about conversion. In fact, the tradition recorded in some detail by Gregory of Tours suggests that the process was slow and difficult. For Gregory, it began with the marriage of Clovis to a Catholic Burgundian princess, Chrotechildis, and with her wish to have her two sons baptized. In the death of the first, just after baptism, the king saw the natural consequence of denying the pagan gods. It was a set-back. But the queen kept up the pressure until, at Tolbiac, Clovis faced defeat at the hands of the Alamans. Caught out, he tried the patronage of a new war god, Christ, and saw defeat turned into victory. . . . Clovis was not converted but he was impressed and readier to listen. At this stage the queen's efforts were supplemented by those of Bishop Remigius of Reims. The final stumbling-block for Clovis was how the Franks would take the news. But those whom the king consulted accepted his lead, and he was finally baptized with his following in arms—for this is the best interpretation of Gregory's statement that he was baptized with more than three thousand *de exercito*. In the end, it was not the Frankish people that was converted but the king and a warband that presumably recalled the story that got around after Tolbiac. The upper crust, or part of it, had accepted a new, perhaps an additional, war god, on approval, though some may have remained loyal to the old gods. The three thousand warriors (or whatever the number may really have been) comprised a high proportion of Clovis's leading men. It was to such, duly ensconced on their estates, that the earliest missionaries—often from Aquitaine—must have turned. Nor did they turn in vain. . . . But the real Clovis was more complex than he looks in the pages of Gregory. In his last years, for example, he exercised a controlling interest in the doings of the council of Orléans and yet at the same time sanctioned a barbarian law-book, *Lex Salica,* in which little if any Christian influence can be detected. He might no longer on his own account sacrifice to the gods but *Lex Salica* implies that he protects the sacrificial pigs of his still-unconverted subjects. He upholds the pagan practice of name-giving on the tenth day after birth; imposes a heavy fine on plunderers of corpses, buried or not; and makes a special case of the plundering of a body in a *tumba,* or the destruction of a *tumba. Tumba* has the sense of *tummulum,* which indeed is the reading preferred in two manuscripts of *Lex Salica.* The fact that the crime, glossed with a Frankish word, *tornechale,* is distinguished from similar sacrilege committed against a body laid in a Christian basilica or against a mere gravestone, indicates that the king meant to protect those who had been buried as pagans just as much as those buried as Christians. Perhaps this is why the grave of his father, Childeric, remained undisturbed at Tournai. Conversion, therefore, was a lengthy business.

The seventh century marks a big change in what is known of Frankish graves and grave-goods. There are more of them, and the iconography is more distinctively Christian. Rural cemeteries continue in use even though the big men now lie in churches, often of their own foundation and dedicated to the holy men whose relics protect them and their kindred.* The *locus classicus* is the monastery of St Denis, near Paris, where the saint's tomb was embellished in the late sixth century in the reign of Sigebert I, and still further embellished by Dagobert I a few years later. This ancient burying-place was above all others sacred to the Merovingian house. The graves of several of its members have been excavated. The church of Jouarre, east of Paris, is a good example of the burying-place of a nonroyal family that rose to prominence in the seventh century. In its crypt can still be seen the sarcophagi of some of them. At this social level and to some extent lower we can expect to find a grave-iconography that is no longer explicitly pagan. But it is from a pagan root that it has grown; a root that, like other strong roots, continues to send up suckers. Thus we find grave-goods and monuments incised with motifs that are Christian in intent though derived from pagan models, or are part-Christian, part-pagan, in such a way that the dominant factor is sometimes in doubt. Old habits persist, in religious iconography as in all else. There will be times when the maker of a brooch or the sculptor of a stone will be ignorant of the original meaning of a motif he adopts to a new purpose, and this may equally apply to the owner and to those who lay the object in his grave. In the early sixth century a Frankish chieftain was buried at Lavoye (Meuse) in an extensive cemetery. His

---

*Among the pagan Frankish aristocracy, families buried their dead in the countryside, near the family residence.—ed.

grave-goods (largely weapons) included a liturgical jug, presumably booty from a church. Its presence in the grave must suggest that those who buried him were either ignorant of its proper function or indifferent to it. Whether or not formally Christian, the warrior was not to be deprived of his loot because he was dead. We must also allow that the pagan tutelary intention persists in a general way. There are many examples. What are we to make of human masks, often of great ferocity and quite numerous in the seventh century, above which Christian crosses have been cut? Or how should one interpret a buckle from Marchélepot, on which two human heads seem to face a praying figure, the whole surmounted by a swastika? Even so commonplace a Christian scene as Daniel between his lions is not as straightforward as it appears, for reminiscence of a pagan solar cult is possible, if not probable. A pagan background is much more likely in the case of such a brooch as that from Précy-sur-Vrin. Extremely barbarized, it seems to portray Christ between St Peter and St Paul. At least it can be said in favour of the identification of Christ that he holds a cross of sorts, if nothing else can. Other brooches show a mixture of human figures, crosses and animals that cannot be understood at all, at least at present. If any of them were meant to be Christian, the pagan imagery is dominant enough to swamp the message. The prize exhibit is a funerary plaque of terracotta from Grésin in the Puy-de-Dôme. It shows Christ armed as a soldier, scramasax in belt and lance in hand, with other curious accoutrements. He has a long phallus, there are beasts round him and a snake under his feet, and he wears a head-dress not unworthy of a pagan god. Were it not for the presence of the Christian monogram with alpha and omega it would never occur to anyone to detect Christ here, and the figure could pass for that of a perfectly good pagan god. It has points of resemblance to the figure on a brooch from Finglesham in Kent, which is now thought to be Woden. What was made of it by those who nailed it as a phylactery inside a tomb? If they believed in Christ they had not got very far. Nor is the Grésin plaque unique. The same questions arise when one looks at the god on the Niederdollendorf gravestone. If he is Christian, as some hold, because of the nimbus, we have a parody of Christianity by and for men still essentially pagan. Iconographically at least, one must conclude that examples of this sort from the seventh century betray a Christianity that is largely an adaptation of paganism, and one would not care to say that the symbolic content of that paganism had disappeared from the minds of makers or users.

This view is reinforced by literary sources, which also leave a clear impression that there was a religion of the countryside that was not that of the cities. It was outside the city-walls that Germanic paganism met the still-active paganism of the Celts and to an undetermined extent fused with it. The official pagan cultus of Rome, as practised in the cities, had long since yielded to Christianity, but the countryside was another matter. Indeed, there may have been some resurgence of Celtic paganism once the grip of Rome had slackened upon Gaul. The *dii patrii* of the Celts, gods of rivers, springs, woods and hills, were certainly worshipped at rural cult-centres in the earlier fifth century, and it was with such, whether Celtic or Frankish, that the first missionaries had to wrestle. How they set about it is vividly illustrated in an incident related by Gregory of Tours in his *Liber in gloria confessorum*. It seems that a peasant community in the diocese of Javols, in the Lozère, observed a ceremony of throwing libations into a lake (probably the Lake of Saint-Andéol). These took the form of clothing, wool, cheeses, wax, bread and so on. The peasants came by carts, bringing picnics. They also sacrificed animals and then feasted for three days at a stretch. When the party was broken up by thunder and downpour, these were taken as omens—perhaps of the displeasure of a thunder-god like Thor. In due course the local bishop came to preach there, and got no reaction from the rustics. Learning of their ceremony, he dealt with the problem by building a church near the lake, which he dedicated to St Hilary of Poitiers and equipped with relics of the saint; and he admonished them to venerate the relics rather than the spirits of the lake: 'there is no religion in a pond!' This satisfied the rustics to the extent that thereafter they laid some offerings before the saint's relics, but almost within living memory they had not entirely abandoned their lake. Their conversion was neither from the purpose nor (sacrifice excepted) from the ritual of their former religion. They simply changed their patron and their venue. The line of demarcation between magic and prayer, an offering to a spirit of the countryside and to a local saint, remained sufficiently vague to haunt generations of clerics. The *Passio* of St Vincent of Agen betrays another peasant-community—that of Vernemet—up to its pranks in the sixth century. Annually, we are told, the peasants met on their hilltop under the leadership of their *praeses* to indulge in a specifically pagan ceremony. They rolled a flaming wheel downhill into the river, from which it emerged still flaming to make its ascent into the temple at the top. St Vincent put a stop to the practice by making the sign of the cross, whereupon the flames were extinguished and the wheel vanished. Vernemet was in southern Gaul, not in the Frankish north to which pagan practices were by no means confined. It was Caesarius, addressing his people of Arles and not the Franks, whose writings were to prove specially useful to missionaries of a later time, and no bishop of the ninth century was more worried about widespread belief in signs and other magic than Agobard of Lyon. There had to be a source of magic, some god to propitiate. 'A shadowy conception of power that by much persuasion can be induced to refrain from inflicting harm is the shape most easily taken by the sense of the Invisible in the minds of men who have always been pressed close by primitive wants.' . . .

If missionaries found the going hard, so too did the Merovingian kings on whose protection they counted. According to Gregory of Cologne, Theuderic I had to pacify a crowd of enraged peasants at Cologne, whose temple and idols had been burnt by a missionary. It had been an elaborate shrine, where offerings were made and feasts celebrated. Wooden images of injured human parts were suspended round it. The king took the best way out: 'he calmed them with smooth words and thus quenched their fury.' Not very far to the west was Nivelles—Niuwiala, the new place of sacrifice—in due course to be the site of a famous nunnery. It was a strongly pagan region. Yet further north, Frankish missionaries under Merovingian protection suffered serious set-backs in an area that has rightly been described as vibrantly pagan. The see of Tournai had to be moved south to Noyon in 577, while that of Arras was combined with Cambrai. The bishop of Tongres took refuge in the *castellum* of Maastricht and for a while his see was combined with Cologne. This retreat of the Church, even when backed by Frankish forces, may be connected with some renewal of pagan cremation in the Low Countries and western Germany in the sixth and seventh centuries. Theuderic's son, Theudebert I, while at a safe distance from his bishops, sacrificed Ostrogothic women and children to celebrate the winning of control by his army over a bridge at Pavia. 'These barbarians,' commented the Greek historian Procopius, 'though they have become Christians, preserve the greater part of their ancient religion, for they still make human sacrifices of an unholy nature, and it is in connection with these that they make their prophecies.' This same Theudebert was the recipient of the first known (but no longer extant) papal letter to a Frankish king, it came from Pope Vigilius and faced the issue of a barbarian's marriage with a sister-in-law. The popes were by no means to remain indifferent to the Merovingians, nor the Merovingians to them. Both Theuderic and Theudebert found themselves drawn into the affairs of pagan Germania as overlords of the southward-moving Saxons, and, with them, as implacable enemies of Thuringian power. It was not a propitious field for Christian missionaries and one must suppose that at this early stage the Merovingians were content to leave these important pagans to their own beliefs. . . .

It is not to be supposed that barbarian kings, let alone their peoples, would have accepted conversion unless they felt some sense of religious continuity. A spiritual revolution was never in question. On the other hand, neither were the serious implications first of paganism and then of Christianity to the barbarians ever in question. The business of national conversion was long and complex. Yet there is, even at so early a stage, some realignment of spiritual values of which some barbarians will have been dimly aware. Their Gallo-Roman mentors included men of intellectual and spiritual calibre, involved in theological issues of real moment, as, for example, the threat of Arianism, which preoccupied Caesarius of Arles at the beginning of the sixth century and was still preoccupying Gregory of Tours and his colleagues at its end. We do not have to wait very long before there are bishops of Frankish blood, and several members of the Merovingian family showed either an interest in theology or a practical concern for the spiritual life of the cloister. Nevertheless, the first stage of the transition to Christianity was, as we have seen, a matter related not to theology but to the substitution of one kind of folk-magic for another. It could not have been otherwise.

PEASANT LIFE IN THE MIDDLE AGES

EILEEN POWER

Medieval law placed the peasants and their families in formal sub-
jection to their lords, and some lived the poor and restricted life that
coincides with this legal status. But most peasants considered their
relationships with the aristocracy natural and advantageous. In the
chaotic conditions of the early Middle Ages, it may have been rather
more important to the peasants that the land was tied to them rather
than that they were tied to it. It was an age when farms needed pro-
tection both from marauders and from natural disasters. The lord
provided military security and, in times of famine, could reduce the
suffering of his villagers by buying grain and other foodstuffs in
neighboring districts.

Beside the minor fluctuations of agrarian prosperity, there was
a long-term improvement from the ninth to the thirteenth centuries.
This growth in prosperity stemmed both from the advance of agri-
cultural technology—an effective horse collar, the horseshoe, and the
heavy, wheeled plow—and from the expansion of arable land. Espe-
cially from the tenth century on, after the end of the Viking inva-
sions, lords and peasants put new lands into production. The recla-
mation of land provided the peasantry with a double reward. The
productivity of the group as a whole increased, and the peasants
were able to improve their status and living conditions by taking on
the risks of increasing the arable land.

Historians presume that the Romans kept records of the eco-
nomic activity on their estates, but the practice seems to have de-
clined sharply after the Germans assumed control of the western ter-
ritories. In the late eighth century, Charlemagne ordered that his
stewards make surveys of the royal estates and keep records of the
income that could be expected from each. The great ecclesiastical
corporations, which had accumulated large properties and which
had the educated personnel necessary, also made surveys at this time,
and we have a few of them still. These surveys reveal something
about the peasant families that worked the estates and paid the rent

From: Eileen Power, *Medieval People* (London: Methuen, 1924), pp. 19–38.

and other fees that constituted the income from the property, but historians have had difficulty using the documents for a statistical analysis of the peasant community. In this selection, Eileen Power uses the surveys and other sources to create a composite picture of a ninth-century peasant, whom she calls Bodo.

This [selection] is chiefly concerned with the kitchens of History, and the first which we shall visit is a country estate at the beginning of the ninth century. It so happens that we know a surprising amount about such an estate, partly because Charlemagne himself issued a set of orders instructing the Royal stewards how to manage his own lands, telling them everything it was necessary for them to know, down to the vegetables which they were to plant in the garden. But our chief source of knowledge is a wonderful estate book which Irminon, the Abbot of St. Germain des Prés near Paris, drew up so that the abbey might know exactly what lands belonged to it and who lived on those lands, very much as William I drew up an estate book of his whole kingdom and called it *Domesday Book*. In this estate book is set down the name of every little estate (or *fisc* as it was called) belonging to the abbey, with a description of the land which was worked under its steward to its own profit, and the land which was held by tenants, and the names of those tenants and of their wives and of their children, and the exact services and rents, down to a plank and an egg, which they had to do for their land. We know today the name of almost every man, woman, and child who was living on those little *fiscs* in the time of Charlemagne, and a great deal about their daily lives.

Consider for a moment how the estate upon which they lived was organized. The lands of the Abbey of St. Germain were divided into a number of estates, called *fiscs,* each of a convenient size to be administered by a steward. On each of these *fiscs* the land was divided into seigniorial and tributary lands; the first administered by the monks through a steward or some other officer, and the second possessed by various tenants, who received and held them from the abbey. These tributary lands were divided into numbers of little farms called manses, each occupied by one or more families. If you had paid a visit to the chief or seigniorial manse, which the monks kept in their own hands, you would have found a little house, with three or four rooms, probably built of stone, facing an inner court, and on one side of it you would have seen a special group of houses hedged round, where the women serfs belonging to the house lived and did their work, all round you would also have seen little wooden houses, where the household serfs lived, workrooms, a kitchen, a bakehouse, barns, stables, and other farm buildings, and round the whole a hedge carefully planted with trees, so as to make a kind of enclosure or court. Attached to this central manse was a considerable amount of land—ploughland, meadows, vineyards, orchards, and almost all the woods or forests on the estate. Clearly a great deal of labour would be needed to cultivate all these lands. Some of that labour was provided by servile workers who were attached to the chief manse and lived in the court. But these household serfs were not nearly enough to do all the work upon the monks' land, and far the greater part of it had to be done by services paid by the other land-owners on the estate.

Beside the seigniorial manse, there were a number of little dependent manses. These belonged to men and women who were in various stages of freedom, except for the fact that all had to do with the different classes, for in practice there was very little difference between them, and in a couple of centuries they were all merged into one common class of medieval villeins. The most important people were those called *coloni,* who were personally free (that is to say, counted as free men by the law), but bound to the soil, so that they could never leave their farms and were sold with the estate, if it were sold. Each of the dependent manses was held either by one family or by two or three families which clubbed together to do the work; it consisted of a house or houses, and farm buildings, like those of the chief manse, only poorer and made of wood, with ploughland and a meadow and perhaps a little piece of vineyard attached to it. In return for these holdings the owner or joint owners of every manse had to do work on the land of the chief manse for about three days in the week. The steward's chief business was to see that they did their work properly, and from every one he had the right to demand two kinds of labour. The first was *field work;* every year each man was bound to do a fixed amount of ploughing on the domain land (as it was called later on), and also to give what was called a *corvée,* that is to say, an unfixed amount of ploughing, which the steward could demand every week when it was needed, the distinction corresponds to the distinction between *week work* and *boon work* in the later Middle Ages. The second kind of labour which every owner of a farm had to do on the monks' land was called handwork, that is to say, he had to help repair buildings, or cut down trees, or gather fruit, or make ale, or carry loads—anything, in fact, which wanted doing and which the steward told him to do. It was by these services that the monks got their own seigniorial farm cultivated. On all the other days of the week these hard-worked tenants were free to cultivate their own little farms, and we may be sure that they put twice as much elbow grease into the business.

But their obligation did not end here, for not only had they to pay services, they also had to pay certain rents to the big house. There were no State taxes in those days, but every man had to pay an army due, which Charlemagne exacted from the abbey, and which the abbey exacted from its tenants; this took the form of an ox and a certain number of sheep, or the equivalent in money: 'He pays to the host two shillings of silver' comes first on every freeman's list of obligations. The farmers also had to pay in return for any special privileges granted to them by the monks; they had to carry a load of wood to the big house, in return for being allowed to gather firewood in the woods, which were jealously preserved for the use of the abbey; they had to pay some hogsheads of wine for the right to pasture their pigs in the same precious woods; every third year they had to give up one of their sheep for the right to graze upon the fields of the chief manse; they had to pay a sort of poll-tax of

4*d*. a head. In addition to these special rents every farmer had also to pay other rents in produce; every year he owed the big house three chickens and fifteen eggs and a large number of planks, to repair its buildings; often he had to give it a couple of pigs; sometimes corn, wine, honey, wax, soap, or oil. If the farmer were also an artisan and made things, he had to pay the produce of his craft; a smith would have to make lances for the abbey's contingent to the army, a carpenter had to make barrels and hoops and vine props, a wheelwright had to make a cart. Even the wives of the farmers were kept busy, if they happened to be serfs; for the servile women were obliged to spin cloth or to make a garment for the big house every year.

All those things were exacted and collected by the steward, whom they called *Villicus,* or *Major* (Mayor). He was a very hardworked man, and when one reads the seventy separate and particular injunctions which Charlemagne addressed to his stewards one cannot help feeling sorry for him. He had to get all the right services out of the tenants, and tell them what to do each week and see that they did it; he had to be careful that they brought the right number of eggs and pigs up to the house, and did not foist off warped or badly planed planks upon him. He had to look after the household serfs too, and set them to work. He had to see about storing, or selling, or sending off to the monastery the produce of the estate and of the tenants' rents; and every year he had to present a full and detailed account of his stewardship to the abbot. He had a manse of his own, with services and rents due from it, and Charlemagne exhorted his stewards to be prompt in their payments, so as to set a good example. Probably his official duties left him very little time to work on his own farm, and he would have to put in a man to work it for him, as Charlemagne bade his stewards do. Often, however, he had subordinate officials called *deans* under him, and sometimes the work of receiving and looking after the stores in the big house was done by a special cellarer.

That, in a few words, is the way in which the monks of St. Germain and the other Frankish landowners of the time of Charlemagne managed their estates. Let us try, now, to look at those estates from a more human point of view and see what life was like to a farmer who lived upon them. The abbey possessed a little estate called Villaris, near Paris, in the place now occupied by the park of Saint Cloud. When we turn up the pages in the estate book dealing with Villaris, we find that there was a man called Bodo living there. He had a wife called Ermentrude and three children called Wido and Gerbert and Hildegard; and he owned a little farm of arable and meadow land, with a few vines. And we know very nearly as much about Bodo's work as we know about that of a smallholder in France today. Let us try and imagine a day in his life. On a fine spring morning towards the end of Charlemagne's reign Bodo gets up early, because it is his day to go and work on the monks' farm, and he does not dare to be late, for fear of the steward. To be sure, he has probably given the steward a present of eggs and vegetables the week before, to keep him in a good temper; but the monks will not allow their stewards to take big bribes (as is sometimes done on other estates), and Bodo knows that he will not be allowed to go late to work. It is his day to plough so he takes his big ox with him and little Wido to run by its side with a goad, and he joins his friends from some of the farms near by, who are going to work at the big house too. They all assemble, some with horses and oxen, some with mattocks and hoes and spades and axes and scythes, and go off in gangs to work upon the fields and meadows and woods of the seigniorial manse, according as the steward orders them. The manse next door to Bodo is held by a group of families: Frambert and Ermoin and Ragenold, with their wives and children. Bodo bids them good morning as he passes. Frambert is going to make a fence round the wood, to prevent the rabbits from coming out and eating the young crops; Ermoin has been told off to cart a great load of firewood up to the house; and Ragenold is mending a hole in the roof of a barn. Bodo goes whistling off in the cold with his oxen and his little boy; and it is no use to follow him farther, because he ploughs all day and eats his meal under a tree with the other ploughmen, and it is very monotonous.

Let us go back and see what Bodo's wife, Ermentrude, is doing. She is busy too, it is the day on which the chicken-rent is due—a fat pullet and five eggs in all. She leaves her second son, aged nine, to look after the baby Hildegard and calls on one of her neighbours, who has to go up to the big house too. The neighbour is a serf and she has to take the steward a piece of woollen cloth, which will be sent away to St. Germain to make a habit for a monk. Her husband is working all day in the lord's vineyards, for on this estate the serfs generally tend the vines, while the freemen do most of the ploughing. Ermentrude and the serf's wife go together up to the house. There all is busy. In the men's workshop are several clever workmen—a shoemaker, a carpenter, a blacksmith, and two silversmiths; there are not more, because the best artisans on the estates of St. Germain live by the walls of the abbey, so that they can work for the monks on the spot and save the labour of carriage. But there were always some craftsmen on every estate, either attached as serfs to the big house, or living on manses of their own, and good landowners tried to have as many clever craftsmen as possible. Charlemagne ordered his stewards each to have in his district 'good workmen, namely, blacksmiths, goldsmiths, silversmiths, shoemakers, turners, carpenters, swordmakers, fishermen, foilers, soapmakers, men who know how to make beer, cider, perry [fermented pear juice], and all other kinds of beverages, bakers to make pasty for our table, netmakers who know how to make nets for hunting, fishing, and fowling, and others too many to be named'. And some of these workmen are to be found working for the monks in the estate of Villaris.

But Ermentrude does not stop at the men's workshop. She finds the steward, bobs her curtsy to him, and gives up her fowl and eggs, and then she hurries off to the women's part of the house, to gossip with the serfs there. The Franks used at this time to keep the women of their household in a separate quarter, where they did the work which was considered suitable for women, very much as the Greeks of antiquity used to do. If a Frankish noble had lived at the big house, his wife would have looked after their work, but as no one lived in the stone house at Villaris, the steward had to oversee the women. Their quarter consisted of a little group of houses, with a workroom, the whole surrounded by a thick hedge with a strong bolted gate, like a harem, so that no one could come in without leave. Their workrooms were comfortable places, warmed by stoves, and there Ermentrude (who, being a woman, was allowed to go in) found about a dozen servile women spinning and dyeing cloth and sewing garments. Every week the harassed steward brought them the raw materials for their work and took away what they made. Charlemagne gives his stewards several instructions about the women attached to his manses, and we may be sure that the monks of St. Germain did the same on their model estates. For our women's work,' says Charlemagne, 'they are to give at the proper time the materials, that is linen, wool, woad, vermilion, madder, wool combs, teasels, soap, grease, vessels, and other objects which are necessary. And let our women's quarters be well looked after, furnished with houses and rooms with stoves and cellars, and let them be surrounded by a good hedge, and let the doors be strong, so that the women can do our work properly.' Ermentrude, however, has to hurry away after her gossip, and so must we. She goes back to her own farm and sets to work in the little vineyard; then after an hour or two goes back to get the children's meal and to spend the rest of the day in weaving warm woollen clothes for them. All her friends are either working in the fields on their husbands' farms or else looking after the poultry, or the vegetables, or sewing at home; for the women have to work just as hard as the men on a country farm. In Charlemagne's time (for instance) they did nearly all the sheep shearing. Then at last Bodo comes back for his supper, and as soon as the sun goes down they go to bed; for their handmade candle gives only a flicker of light, and they both have to be up early in the morning. De Quincey once pointed out, in his inimitable manner, how the ancients everywhere went to bed, like good boys, from seven to nine o'clock'. 'Man went to bed early in those ages simply because his worthy mother earth could not afford him candles. She, good old lady . . . would certainly have shuddered to hear of any of her nations asking for candles. "Candles indeed" she would have said; "who ever heard of such a thing? and with so much excellent daylight running to waste, as I have provided *gratis!* What will the wretches want next?"' Something of the same situation prevailed even in Bodo's time.

This, then, is how Bodo and Ermentrude usually passed their working day. But, it may be complained, this is all very well. We know about the estates on which these peasants lived and about the rents which they had to pay, and the services which they had to do. But how did they feel and think and amuse themselves when they were not working? Rents and services are only outside things, an estate book only describes routine. It would be idle to try to picture the life of a university from a study of its lecture list, and it is equally idle to try and describe the life of Bodo from the estate book of his masters. It is no good taking your meals in the kitchen if you never talk to the servants. This is true, and to arrive at Bodo's thoughts and feelings and holiday amusements we must bid goodbye to Abbot Irminon's estate book, and peer into some very dark corners indeed; for though by the aid of Chaucer and Langland and a few Court Rolls it is possible to know a great deal about the feelings of a peasant six centuries later, material is scarce in the ninth century, and it is all the more necessary to remember the secret of the invisible ink.

Bodo certainly *had* plenty of feelings, and very strong ones. When he got up in the frost on a cold morning to drive the plough over the abbot's acres, when his own were calling out for work, he often shivered and shook the rime from his beard, and wished that the big house and all its land were at the bottom of the sea (which, as a matter of fact, he had never seen and could not imagine). Or else he wished he were the abbot's huntsman, hunting in the forest, or a monk of St. Germain, singing sweetly in the abbey church; or a merchant, taking bales of cloaks and girdles along the high road to Paris, anything, in fact, but a poor ploughman, ploughing other people's land. An Anglo-Saxon writer has imagined a dialogue with him.

> 'Well, ploughman, how do you do your work?' 'Oh, sir, I work very hard. I go out in the dawning, driving the oxen to the field and I yoke them to the plough. Be the winter never so stark, I dare not stay at home for fear of my lord, but every day I must plough a full acre or more, after having yoked the oxen and fastened the share and coulter to the plough!' 'Have you any mate?' 'I have a boy, who drives the oxen with a goad, who is now hoarse from cold and shouting.' (Poor little Wido!) 'Well, well, it is very hard work?' 'Yes, indeed it is very hard work.'

Nevertheless, hard as the work was, Bodo sang lustily to cheer himself and Wido; for is it not related that once, when a clerk was singing the 'Allelulia' in the emperor's presence, Charles turned to one of the bishops, saying, 'My clerk is singing very well,' whereat the rude bishop replied, 'Any clown in our countryside drones as well as that to his oxen at their ploughing'? It is certain too that Bodo agreed with the names which the great Charles gave to the months of the year in his own Frankish tongue; for he called January 'Winter-month', February 'Mud-month', March 'Spring-month', April 'Easter-month', May 'Joy-month', June 'Plough-month', July 'Hay-month', August 'Harvest-month', September 'Wind-month', October 'Vintage-month', November 'Autumn-month', and December 'Holy-month'.

And Bodo was a superstitious creature. The Franks had been Christian now for many years, but Christian though they were, the peasants clung to old beliefs and superstitions. On the estates of the holy monks of St. Germain you would have found the country people saying charms which were hoary with age, parts of the lay sung by the Frankish ploughman over his bewitched land long before he marched southwards into the Roman Empire, or parts of the spell which the bee-master performed when he swarmed his bees on the shores of the Baltic Sea. Christianity has coloured these charms, but it has not effaced their heathen origin; and because the tilling of the soil is the oldest and most unchanging of human occupations, old beliefs and superstitions cling to it and the old gods stalk up and down the brown furrows, when they have long vanished from houses and roads. So on Abbot Irminon's estates the peasant-farmers muttered charms over their sick cattle (and over their sick children too) and said incantations over the fields to make them fertile. If you had followed behind Bodo when he broke his first furrow you would have probably seen him take out of his jerkin a little cake, baked for him by Ermentrude out of different kinds of meal, and you would have seen him stoop and lay it under the furrow and sing:

Earth, Earth, Earth! O Earth, our mother!
May the All-Wielder, Ever-Lord grant thee
Acres a-waxing, upwards a-growing,
Pregnant with corn and plenteous in strength;
Hosts of grain shafts and of glittering plants!
Of broad barley the blossoms,
And of white wheat ears waxing,
Of the whole land the harvest. . . .
Acre, full-fed, bring forth fodder for men!
Blossoming brightly, blessed become!
And the God who wrought with earth grant us gift of growing
That each of all the corns may come unto our need.

Then he would drive his plough through the acre.

The Church wisely did not interfere with these old rites. It taught Bodo to pray to the Ever-Lord instead of the Father Heaven, and to the Virgin Mary instead of to Mother Earth, and with these changes let the old spell he had learned from his ancestors serve him still. It taught him, for instance, to call on Christ and Mary in his charm for bees. When Ermentrude heard her bees swarming, she stood outside her cottage and said this little charm over them:

Christ, there is a swarm of bees outside,
Fly hither, my little cattle,
In blest peace, in God's protection,
Come home and safe and sound.
Sit down, sit down, bee,
St Mary commanded thee.
Thou shalt not have leave,
Thou shalt not fly to the wood.
Thou shalt not escape me,
Nor go away from me.
Sit very still,
Wait God's will!

And if Bodo on his way home saw one of his bees caught in brier bush, he immediately stood still and wished—as some people wish today when they go under a ladder. It was the Church, too, which taught Bodo to add 'So be it, Lord', to the end of his charm against pain. Now, his ancestors for generations behind him had believed that if you had a stitch in your side, or a bad pain anywhere, it came from a worm in the marrow of your bones, which was eating you up, and that the only way to get rid of that worm was to put a knife, or an arrowhead, or some other piece of metal to the sore place, and then wheedle the worm out on to the blade by saying a charm. And this was the charm which Bodo's heathen ancestors had always said and which Bodo went on saying when little Wido had a pain: 'Come out, worm, with nine little worms, out from the marrow into the bone, from the bone into the flesh, from the flesh into the skin, from the skin into this arrow.' And then (in obedience to the Church) he added 'So be it, Lord'. But sometimes it was not possible to read a Christian meaning into Bodo's doings. Sometimes he paid visits to some man who was thought to have a wizard's powers, or superstitiously reverenced some twisted tree, about which there hung old stories never quite forgotten. Then the Church was stern. When he went to confession the priest would ask him: 'Have you consulted magicians and enchanters, have you made vows to trees and fountains, have you drunk any magic philtre?' And he would have to confess what he did last time his cow was sick. But the Church was kind as well as stern. 'When serfs come to you,' we find one bishop telling his priests, 'you must not give them as many fasts to perform as rich men. Put upon them only half the penance.' The Church knew well enough that Bodo could not drive his plough all day upon an empty stomach. The hunting, drinking, feasting Frankish nobles could afford to lose a meal.

It was from this stern and yet kind Church that Bodo got his holidays. For the Church made the pious emperor decree that on Sundays and saints' days no servile or other works should be done. Charlemagne's son repeated his decree in 827. It runs thus:

> We ordain according to the law of God and to the command of our father of blessed memory in his edicts, that no servile works shall be done on Sundays, neither shall men perform their rustic labours, tending vines, ploughing fields, reaping corn and mowing hay, setting up hedges or fencing woods, cutting trees, or working in quarries or building houses; nor shall they work in the garden, not come to the law courts, nor follow the chase. But three carrying-services it is lawful to do on Sunday, to wit carrying for the army, carrying food, or carrying (if need be) the body of a lord to its grave. Item, women shall not do their textile works, nor cut out clothes, nor stitch them together with the needle, nor card wool, nor beat hemp, nor wash clothes in public, nor shear sheep: so that there may be rest on the Lord's day. But let them come together from all sides to Mass in the Church and praise God for the good things He did for us on that day!

Unfortunately, however, Bodo and Ermentrude and their friends were not content to go quietly to church on saints' days and quietly home again. They used to spend their holidays in dancing and singing and buffoonery, as country folk have always done until our own gloomier, more self-conscious age. They were very merry and not at all refined, and the place they always chose for their dances was the churchyard; and unluckily the songs they sang as they danced in a ring were old pagan songs of their forefathers, left over from old Mayday festivities, which they could not forget, or ribald love-songs which the Church disliked. Over and over again we find the Church councils complaining that the peasants (and sometimes the priests too) were singing 'wicked songs with a chorus of dancing women,' or holding 'ballads and dancings and evil and wanton songs and such-like lures of the devil'; over and over again the bishops forbade these songs and dances; but in vain. In every country in Europe, right through the Middle Ages to the time of the Reformation, and after it, country folk continued to sing and dance in the churchyard. Two hundred years after Charlemagne's death there grew up the legend of the dancers of Kölbigk, who danced on Christmas Eve in the churchyard, in spite of the warning of the priest, and all got rooted to the spot for a year, till the Archbishop of Cologne released them. Some men say that they were not rooted standing to the spot, but that they had to go on dancing for the whole year; and that before they were released they had danced themselves waist-deep into the ground. People used to repeat the little Latin verse which they were singing.

Equitabat Bovo per silvam frondosam
Ducebat sibi Merswindem formosam.
  Quid stamus? Cur non imus?

Through the leafy forest, Bovo went a-riding
And his pretty Merswind trotted on beside him—
  Why are we standing still? Why can't we go away?

Another later story still is told about a priest in Worcestershire who was kept awake all night by the people dancing in his churchyard and singing a song with the refrain 'Sweetheart have pity', so that he could not get it out of his head, and the next morning at Mass, instead of saying 'Dominus vobiscum', he said 'Sweetheart have pity', and there was a dreadful scandal which got into a chronicle.

Sometimes our Bodo did not dance himself, but listened to the songs of wandering minstrels. The priests did not at all approve of these minstrels, who (they said) would certainly go to hell for singing profane secular songs, all about the great deeds of heathen heros of the Frankish race, instead of Christian hymns. But Bodo loved them, and so did Bodo's betters; the Church councils had sometimes even to rebuke abbots and abbesses for listening to their songs. And the worst of it was that the great emperor himself, the good Charlemagne, loved them too. He would always listen to a minstrel, and his biographer, Einhard, tells us that 'He wrote out the barbarous and ancient songs, in which the acts of the kings and their wars were sung, and committed them to memory'; and one at least of those old sagas, which he liked men to write down, has been preserved on the cover of a Latin manuscript, where a monk scribbled it in his spare time. His son, Louis the Pious, was very different; he rejected the national poems, which he had learnt in his youth, and would not have them read or recited or taught; he would not allow minstrels to have justice in the law courts, and he forbade idle dances and songs and tales in public places on Sundays; but then he also dragged down his father's kingdom into disgrace and ruin. The minstrels repaid Charlemagne for his kindness to them. They gave him everlasting fame; for all through the Middle Ages the legend of Charlemagne grew, and he shares with our King Arthur the honour of being the hero of one of the greatest romance-cycles of the Middle Ages. Every different century clad him anew in its own dress and sang new lays about him. What the monkish chroniclers in their cells could never do for Charlemagne, these despised and accursed minstrels did for him: they gave him what is perhaps more desirable and more lasting than a place in history—they gave him a place in legend. It is not every emperor who rules in those realms of gold of which Keats spoke, as well as the kingdoms of the world; and in the realms of gold Charlemagne reigns with King Arthur, and his peers joust with the Knights of the Round Table. Bodo, at any rate, benefited by Charles's love of minstrels, and it is probable that he heard in the lifetime of the emperor himself the first beginnings of those legends which afterwards clung to the name of Charlemagne. One can imagine him round-eyed in the churchyard, listening to fabulous stories of Charles's Iron March to Pavia, such as a gossiping old monk of St Gall afterwards wrote down in his chronicle.

It is likely enough that such legends were the nearest Bodo ever came to seeing the emperor, of whom even the poor serfs who never followed him to court or camp were proud. But Charles was a great traveller: like all the monarchs of the early Middle Ages he spent the time, when he was not warring, in treking round his kingdom, staying at one of his estates, until he and his household had literally eaten their way through it, and then passing on to another. And sometimes he varied the procedure by paying a visit to the estates of his bishops or nobles, who entertained him royally. It may be that one day he came on a visit to Bodo's masters and stopped at the big house on his way to Paris, and then Bodo saw him plain; for Charlemagne would come riding along the road in his jerkin of otter skin, and his plain blue Cloak (Einhard tells us that he hated grand clothes and on ordinary days dressed like the common people); and after him would come his three sons and his bodyguard, and then his five daughters. Einhard has also told us that

> He had such care of the upbringing of his sons and daughters that he never dined without them when he was at home and never travelled without them. His sons rode along with him and his daughters followed in the rear. Some of his guards, chosen for his very purpose, watched the end of the line of march where his daughters travelled. They were very beautiful and much beloved by their father, and, therefore, it is strange that he would give them in marriage

to no one, either among his own people or of a foreign state. But up to his death he kept them all at home saying he could not forgo their society.

Then, with luck, Bodo, quaking at the knees, might even behold a portent new to his experience, the emperor's elephant. Haroun El Raschid, the great Sultan of the 'Arabian Nights' had sent it to Charles, and it accompanied him on all his progresses. Its name was 'Abu-Lubabah', which is an Arabic word and means 'the father of intelligence', and it died a hero's death on an expedition against the Danes in 810. It is certain that even afterwards Ermentrude quelled little Gerbert, when he was naughty, with the threat, 'Abu-Lubabah will come with his long nose and carry you off.' But Wido, being aged eight and a bread-winner, professed to have felt no fear on being confronted with the elephant; but admitted when pressed, that he greatly preferred Haroun El Raschid's other present to the emperor, the friendly dog, who answered to the name of 'Becerillo'.

It would be a busy time for Bodo when all these great folk came, for everything would have to be cleaned before their arrival, the pastry cooks and sausage-makers summoned and a great feast prepared; and though the household serfs did most of the work, it is probable that he had to help. The gossipy old monk of St. Gall has given us some amusing pictures of the excitement when Charles suddenly paid a visit to his subjects:

There was a certain bishopric which lay full in Charles's path when he journeyed, and which indeed he could hardly avoid: and the bishop of this place, always anxious to give satisfaction, put everything that he had at Charles's disposal. But once the Emperor came quite unexpectedly and the bishop in great anxiety had to fly hither and thither like a swallow, and had not only the palaces and houses but also the courts and squares swept and cleaned: and then tired and irritated, came to meet him. The most pious Charles noticed this, and after examining all the various details, he said to the bishop: "My kind host, you always have everything splendidly cleaned for my arrival.' Then the bishop, as if divinely inspired, bowed his head and grasped the king's never-conquered right hand, and hiding his irritation, kissed it and said: 'It is but right, my lord, that, wherever you come, all things should be thoroughly cleansed.' Then Charles, of all kings the wisest, understanding the state of affairs said to him: 'If I empty I can also fill.' And he added: 'You may have that estate which lies close to your bisphoric, and all your successors may have it until the end of time.' In the same journey, too, he came to a bishop who lived in a place through which he must needs pass. Now on that day, being the sixth day of the week, he was not willing to eat the flesh of beast or bird; and the bishop, being by reason of the nature of the place unable to procure fish upon the sudden ordered some excellent cheese, rich and creamy, to be placed before him. And the most self-restrained Charles, with the readiness which he showed everywhere and on all occasions, spared the blushes of the bishop and required no better fare; but taking up his knife cut off the skin, which he thought unsavoury and fell to on the white of the cheese. Thereupon the bishop, who was standing near like a servant, drew closer and said: 'Why do you do that, lord emperor? You are throwing away the very best part.' Then

Charles, who deceived no one, and did not believe that anyone would deceive him, on the persuasion of the bishop put a piece of the skin in his mouth, and slowly ate it and swallowed it like butter. Then approving of the advice of the bishop, he said: 'Very true, my good host,' and he added: 'Be sure to send me every year to Aix two cartloads of just such cheeses.' And the bishop was alarmed at the impossibility of the task and, fearful of losing both his rank and his office, he rejoined: 'My lord, I can procure the cheese, but I cannot tell which are of this quality and which of another. Much I fear lest I fall under your censure.' Then Charles, from whose penetration and skill nothing could escape, however new or strange it might be, spoke thus to the bishop, who from childhood had known such cheeses and yet could not test them: 'Cut them in two,' he said, 'then fasten together with a skewer those that you find to be of the right quality and keep them in your cellar for a time and then send them to me. The rest you may keep for yourself and your clergy and your family.' This was done for two years, and the king ordered the present of cheeses to be taken in without remark: then in the third year the bishop brought in person his laboriously collected cheeses. But the most just Charles pitied his labour and anxiety and added to the bisphoric an excellent estate whence he and his successors might provide themselves with corn and wine.

We may feel sorry for the poor flustered bishop collecting his two cartloads of cheeses; but it is possible that our real sympathy ought to go to Bodo, who probably had to pay an extra rent in cheeses to satisfy the emperor's taste, and got no excellent estate to recompense him.

A visit from the emperor, however, would be a rare event in his life, to be talked about for years and told to his grandchildren. But there was one other event, which happened annually, and which was certainly looked for with excitement by Bodo and his friends. For once a year the king's itinerant justices, the *Missi Dominici,* came round to hold their court and to see if the local counts had been doing justice. Two of them would come, a bishop and a count, and they would perhaps stay a night at the big house as guests of the abbot, and the next day they would go on to Paris, and there they would sit and do justice in the open square before the church and from all the district round great men and small, nobles and freemen and *coloni,* would bring their grievances and demand redress. Bodo would go too, if anyone had injured or robbed him, and would make his complaint to the judges. But if he were canny he would not go to them empty-handed, trusting to justice alone. Charlemagne was very strict, but unless the *missi* were exceptionally honest and pious they would not be averse to taking bribes. . . .

Another treat Bodo had which happened once a year, for regularly on the ninth of October there began the great fair of St. Denys, which went on for a whole month, outside the gates of Paris. Then for a week before the fair little booths and sheds sprang up, with open fronts in which the merchants could display their wares, and the Abbey of St. Denys, which had the right to take a toll of all the merchants who came there to sell, saw to it that the fair was well enclosed with fences, and that all came in by the gates and paid their money, for wily merchants were sometimes known to burrow under fences or climb over them so as to avoid the toll. Then the streets of Paris were crowded with merchants bringing their goods, packed in carts and upon horses and oxen; and on the opening day all regular trade in Paris stopped for a month, and every Parisian shopkeeper was in a booth somewhere in the fair, exchanging the corn and wine and honey of the district for rarer goods from foreign parts. Bodo's abbey probably had a stall in the fair and sold some of those pieces of cloth woven by the serfs in the women's quarter, or cheeses and salted meat prepared on the estates, or wine paid in rent by Bodo and his fellow-farmers. Bodo would certainly take a holiday and go to the fair. In fact, the steward would probably have great difficulty in keeping his men at work during the month; Charlemagne had to give a special order to his stewards that they should 'be careful that our men do properly the work which it is unlawful to exact from them, and that they not waste their time in running about to markets and fairs'. Bodo and Ermentrude and the three children, all attired in their best, did not consider it waste of time to go to the fair even twice or three times. They pretended that they wanted to buy salt to salt down their winter meat, or some vermilion dye to colour a frock for the baby. What they really wanted was to wander along the little rows of booths and look at all the strange things assembled there; for merchants came to St. Denys to sell their rich goods from the distant East to Bodo's betters, and wealthy Frankish nobles bargained there for purple and silken robes with orange borders, stamped leather jerkins, peacock's feathers, and the scarlet plumage of flamingos (which they called 'phoenix skins'), scents and pearls and spices, almonds and raisins, and monkeys for their wives to play with. . . . Then there were always jugglers and tumblers, and men with performing bears, and minstrels to wheedle Bodo's few pence out of his pocket. And it would be a very tired and happy family that trundled home in the cart to bed. For it is not, after all, so dull in the kitchen, and when we have quite finished with the emperor, 'Charlemagne and all his peerage', it is really worth while to spend a few moments with Bodo in his little manse. History is largely made up of Bodos.

JEWS IN A CHRISTIAN SOCIETY

ROBERT CHAZAN

Histories of European Jews have focused on their role in economic and intellectual life. On the one hand, historians have been concerned with estimating the importance of Jewish merchant and moneylending activities. On the other, they have traced the textual traditions of important philosophical, theological, and medical works that came to Europe through the Jewish communities of Sicily and Spain. Neither of these approaches has revealed much about the nature of the Jewish communities in Europe. Actually, there were two groups of European Jews in the Middle Ages; today they still form distinct communities. In the south, centered in Italy and Spain, Sephardic Jews were an integral part of the society, a bridge between the Muslim and Christian communities. Prior to their expulsion by Ferdinand and Isabella in 1492, the Spanish Jews had participated in one of the most interesting social amalgams in history. In medieval Spain three religious and national groups produced a brilliant civilization. This harmony between the Jews and their neighbors contrasted strikingly to the relations between Jews and Christians in northern Europe.

The Ashkenazic Jews of northern Europe (Ashkenazim is the medieval Hebrew word for "Germans") were segregated in religious communities that formed the nuclei of the ghettos of the modern era. The Ashkenazim seem to have originated from groups of Jews brought north from Italy in the ninth century by the Carolingian emperors. It was later reported that one of the most famous communities, that of Mainz in Germany, was created when Emperor Charles the Fat brought Rabbi Moses of Lucca to the north about 887. The Rabbi naturally brought his congregation with him, and the little community expanded rapidly. Charles may have brought the Jews north in order to establish a skilled commercial group in his kingdom. In the ninth through eleventh centuries, the kings generally protected the Jews because of their importance in commerce.

From: Robert Chazan, *Medieval Jewry in Northern France* (Baltimore: The Johns Hopkins University Press, 1973), pp. 9–29.

The records of these Jewish communities, principally the Responsa, decisions of the rabbis in law suits, show that in the first three centuries of Ashkenazic life the Jews were borrowers of money, not lenders. The surplus capital produced on the great estates was lent to the Jews for their commercial enterprises at a time when Christians had almost no use for such capital. For example, the surplus production of the Archbishopric of Narbonne, managed by Jews, was lent to other Jews for their business operations. It was only in the twelfth century, as a result of two movements, that the Jews began to lend money to Christians and to establish the economic pattern that eventually led to the stereotype of the Jewish moneylender. The first of these movements was the crusades; the crusaders needed considerable liquid capital for the long journey to the Holy Land and borrowed against the future income of their estates. The second was the emergence of a Christian merchant class that could use business capital and sometimes turned to the Jews to get it.

The Responsa also demonstrate that although the Jews were not popular among Christians, they clung together in the medieval cities not so much because the Christians forced them to as for religious reasons. Adherence to the Talmudic laws demanded a close-knit community that could support and regulate the provisioning of the restricted diet and maintain the religious service. In some parts of Europe, the communities described by the Responsa continued to exist into this century, though the great age of the Responsa came to an end with the First Crusade.

In this selection, Robert Chazan uses the Responsa and other narrative sources to describe the life of the northern Jews in the "golden age," from the ninth through eleventh centuries.

During the tenth and eleventh centuries northern France slowly rose from its torpor. Population increased, the economy developed, and cities grew. This progress contributed to—and benefited from—the establishment of more effective political units. The dukes and counts of northern France carved out for themselves ever larger territories and began to control their domains with increasing authority. The most powerful of these magnates, William of Normandy, was able, during the 1060's, to muster sufficient force to conquer for himself a kingdom across the English Channel. Unobtrusively the king of France, overshadowed often by his mighty vassals, was subduing the Ile-de-France and bending it to his will, slowly laying the groundwork for the sudden expansion of royal power that materialized at the end of the twelfth century.

The revival of trade and of urban centers must have vitally affected the Jews of northern France; however, evidence from this period is sparse.

Documentary records, generally meager for this early age, shed no light whatsoever on the role and position of the Jews. The only non-Jewish materials available are the random observations of churchmen, in some instances enlightening, in others misleading. Jewish sources likewise are slim, consisting of a few brief chronicles, a substantial number of rabbinic responsa, and commentaries on the classics of Biblical and Talmudic literature. While the paucity of evidence precludes a detailed reconstruction of Jewish history during this period, enough remains to sketch in outline the condition of northern French Jewry prior to the First Crusade.

A precise geography of pre-Crusade northern French Jewry is impossible. There are, however, a number of locales for which Jewish settlement is attested: Auxerre, Blois, Châlons-sur-Marne, Le Mans, Orléans, Paris, Reims, Rouen, Sens, Troyes. These are major urban centers, all the seats of dioceses. Random evidence indicates Jewish presence in smaller towns as well. Thus, in the incident of 992, the villain, a convert from Judaism to Christianity, moved from Blois to Le Mans, visiting (and duping) a number of Jewish communities in western France along the way. Likewise the so-called Rashi ordinance, which dealt with taxation procedures in the Jewry of Troyes, reflects Jewish settlement in smaller towns. The ordinance was enacted by a major Jewish community surrounded by smaller satellites: "We the inhabitants of Troyes, along with the communities in its environs. . . ." By 1096 the Jews had begun to spread beyond the confines of the major cities of northern France.

Widespread insecurity had destroyed the centralized authority of the Carolingians and had brought to power the feudal barony of northern France. Endangered French society had reconstructed itself through a network of immediate personal ties; the unity embodied in Carolingian rule gave way to a host of localized principalities. The Jews, as perhaps the most exposed element in this society, had the deepest need for the protection that only these magnates could offer. They were thus cast into permanent dependence upon a plethora of seigneurs, ranging from king to petty noble.

It is difficult to trace the implications of this dependence in the pre-Crusade period. The political status of northern French Jewry was never specified in comprehensive charters, as was the case in Germany. It is only with the passage of time and the proliferation of records that a detailed picture of Jewish political circumstances emerges. In general it is obvious that even in this early period the political authorities were responsible for basic Jewish security. This included both protection of Jewish life and property and judicial jurisdiction over the Jews. In 992, when a serious charge was leveled at the Jews of Le Mans, the count not only constituted the court before which the Jews were to be tried; he in fact stipulated the procedure to be utilized. It is also possible that even at this early stage governmental support for the Jews included aid in Jewish business affairs. Detailed information on this comes only in the twelfth century, however.

Willingness to extend to the Jews protection and aid was contingent, of course, on significant advantage to be derived from these Jews. Governmental authorities anticipated two major benefits from Jewish presence: general stimulation of trade and urban life and, more tangible, the immediate profit to be realized from taxation. Tax records from the early period no longer exist, and information in the Jewish sources is fragmentary. There can be little doubt, however, that the flow of income from this taxation was the major factor in the protective stance taken by the barony of northern France.

The dangers inherent in this alliance with the ruling class were manifested early. While the authorities were relatively successful in protecting the Jews from others, there was no power that could effectively interpose itself between the Jews and their protectors. Only two incidents of any proportion mar the calm of Jewish life in northern France prior to 1096; in both cases it was rulers with unrestricted power over the Jews who were responsible for the persecutions.

The first crisis took place in 992 in the city of Le Mans. A convert from Judaism, one Sehok b. Esther, after earlier clashes with the Jews of Le Mans, deposited a waxen image in the synagogue ark and then unearthed it in the presence of the count of Maine, Hugh III, claiming that the Jews pierced the image regularly in hopes of destroying the count. In the face of adamant Jewish denials, Hugh of Maine ordered the Jews to be tried by combat with their accuser. The chronicle breaks off at this point, with the Jewish community seemingly on the brink of catastrophe. From the opening remarks of the communal letter which describes the incident, it is obvious that the community emerged unscathed. How this came about is unknown. Perfectly clear, however, is the danger stemming from the Jewish community's total reliance on the will of the governing authorities.

The second major incident was far more serious, both in scope and in consequences. According to a variety of extant sources, the years between 1007 and 1012 saw a series of edicts across northern Europe, posing to the Jews the alternatives of conversion to Christianity and expulsion or, on occasion, death. Most of the Jews seem to have chosen expulsion. In some cases, however, there was loss of life, the first instances of that readiness for martyrdom which became a significant characteristic of Ashkenazic Jewry. Although the factors in this persecution were of a religious nature, primarily a concern with the spread of heresy in northern Europe, the decision to convert or expel the Jews could only be made by those feudal lords who controlled Jewish fate—once more an important index of the potential dangers inhering in Jewish political status.

While the local lord exercised effective power over the Jews of his domain, there were other forces striving to make their influence felt. Chief among these was the Church. In some cases, churchmen were themselves feudal lords holding direct rights over Jews. Such overt control, however, was not so prominent in northern France as it was elsewhere. The normal channels of Church influence were twofold. The first was the Church's strong moral pressure on the barony. Clerics close to the feudal dignitaries would utilize this intimacy to further their views on the Jews. Thus, for example, in the 992 incident an anonymous church-man strongly bolstered the anti-Jewish animus by his inflammatory speech to the count of Maine. A more circuitous and less effective mode of influence was through the masses. This involved specifying the Jewish behavior which was unacceptable to the Church and threatening excommunication of those Christians having contact with recalcitrant Jews. According to Raoul Glaber, part of the early-eleventh-century program to eliminate Judaism entirely from sections of northern France was abetted by an episcopal decree outlawing all contact with Jews. The major problem with such boycotts was the difficulty of enforcement.

From the point of view of the Jews, ecclesiastical influence could be either beneficial or baneful. In the instance cited, the cleric of Le Mans much inflamed anti-Jewish passions. On the other hand, it was the awareness of potential Church protection that led a Jew of Rouen, Jacob b. Yekutiel, to deny the right of Richard II of Normandy forcibly to convert the Jews: "You lack the necessary jurisdiction over the Jews to force them from their faith or to harm them. This can only be done by the pope at Rome." The claim of Jacob was not a negation of the feudal rights of Richard over the Jews of Normandy; it was an assertion that the program undertaken ostensibly in the name of the Christian faith was in fact a perversion of Christian principles and had to be brought before the highest ecclesiastical officials for sanction or annulment. According to the Hebrew account, Jacob proceeded to Rome, pleaded his case, and secured a papal decree halting the program of forced conversion.

At this juncture the king exercised no special regalian rights over the Jews. He did, of course, possess normal baronial jurisdiction over the Jews of his own domain. Beyond this, he could on occasion exercise his prerogative as suzerain. It was on this basis that Robert the Pious intervened in the affairs of the county of Sens, deposing Count Raynaud on charges of Judaizing. In the incident of 1007–1012, the king exhibited strong moral leadership in the campaign of forced conversion. While the Hebrew chronicle emphasizes the king's central role in the affair, it also underscores the necessity of agreement by his vassals.

> Then the king and queen took counsel with his officers and his vassals throughout the limits of his kingdom. They charged: "There is one people dispersed throughout the various principalities which does not obey us. . . ." Then there was a perfect agreement between the king and his officers, and they concurred on this plan.

Thus the king could suggest action; its execution, however, depended on the consent and the support of the local authorities.

Yet another potential influence on the destiny of the Jews was the municipality and its burghers. In an early stage of development at this point, its lack of authority over the Jews was already manifest. For the Jews, this powerlessness was a boon. If to the princes the Jews promised economic advantage, to the burghers they offered primarily competition. It was all to the Jews' advantage to be removed from the jurisdiction of the growing communes. Yet this removal added political animosity to the religious and economic antipathies already harbored by the townsmen towards the Jews.

During this early period, the populace at large does not appear as a major instigating force in anti-Jewish activity. This was, to be sure, an epoch of substantial violence, and the Jews felt this lawlessness on occasion. The chronicle of 992 mentions in passing economic competition between the renegade Seḥok and a member of the Jewish community. This rivalry led eventually to assassination of the Jew by hired killers from Blois. The responsa literature reflects the same instability. There is, for example, an interesting responsum dealing with Jewish merchants captured and held for ransom. More striking, however, is the frequency with which governmental oppressions such as those of 992 and 1007–1012 were accompanied by outbursts of popular antipathy. This is attested by the Hebrew chronicle for 992 and by a number of the sources for 1007–1012. The breakdown of official protection allowed the overt expression of that popular hatred normally suppressed by the authorities.

The Jews of northern France were by the eleventh century already supporting themselves primarily by commerce, and, as the century progressed, this led them increasingly into moneylending. The reliance on commerce and usury is reflected in a most interesting responsum from the early eleventh century. The community had "levied on every man and woman, while under the ban, a fixed amount per pound of value of his or her *money, merchandise, and other saleable possessions*"; trade and banking were obviously primary. Despite the ordinance's orientation towards taxation of merchandise and money, the community attempted to levy taxes on a local Jewess' vineyard, demanding a portion of the value of both the land and its produce. The terms in which the issue was debated are revealing:

> They [the community] claimed that vineyards were in the same category as the capital of a loan, while the harvested crop was equivalent to the interest. One derived no benefit from the vineyard itself, nor from the capital of the loan, during the first half year or year of its investment. Since they paid taxes from both the capital and the interest of their money investments, from their merchandise as well as from its profit, they held that L should do likewise. L, on her part, pointed out that a vineyard could not be compared to the capital of a loan, nor even to merchandise. . . . Thus they argued back and forth.

What is plainly assumed by both sides in the dispute is the centrality of wares and capital in communal taxation. The reply of R. Joseph Bon Fils agreed with the position that *only* merchandise, money, and the profits from both are taxable.

The economic reliance on commerce and moneylending emerges also from the famous ordinance of Rashi, dating from the end of the eleventh century.

> We, the inhabitants of Troyes, along with the communities in its environs, have ordained—under threat of excommunication—upon every man and woman living here that they be forbidden to remove themselves from the yoke of communal responsibility. . . . Each one shall give per pound that which is enjoined by the members of the community, as has been practiced since the

very day of its founding. We have likewise received from our predecessors the practice of paying on all possessions, except household items, houses, vineyards, and fields.

A community which exempts "household items, houses, vineyards, and fields" from taxation is obviously heavily involved in mercantile pursuits.

Jewish commerce was probably largely local. As noted, evidence for settlement shows the Jews primarily in major urban centers. A number of responsa, however, indicate Jews traveling through northern France, trading at the fairs of this period. Insecurity made such travel hazardous on occasion; Jewish traders were seized and their goods confiscated. Sometimes the inherent dangers of commerce were magnified by involvement in shady dealings. An early-eleventh-century responsum deals with the legal complications arising from the disappearance and presumed death of an unscrupulous Jewish merchant. The questionable practices, which probably led to his violent demise, are described as follows:

> A was accustomed to travel to many places and to many towns situated within a day or two of his residence. He would sell to and buy from the overlords of these towns, his regular clientele. Whenever they were short of cash, he would sell to them on credit, against pledges of gold or silver, or exchange his merchandise for cattle (or horses) which they had robbed from their enemies. These cattle he would accept at a low price, bring them home and sell them for a much higher price. His activities aroused the anger and hatred of the plundered villagers, and of their feudal lords, who would say; "This Jew, by the very fact that he is always ready to buy looted goods, entices our enemies to attack and plunder us. . . ." Moreover, occasionally the overlords quarrelled with him on account of the pledges which A would eventually sell and because of the high interest he charged.

The normal hazards of eleventh-century trade were here much enhanced.

The same responsum reveals the very fluid transition which many Jews made from commerce to lending. When his customers lacked the necessary cash at hand to make their purchases, the Jewish merchant would extend credit. In fact, there is an indication of the mechanism utilized for safeguarding this investment. The debtors gained the necessary credit by depositing pledges, which were held as security for repayment of the obligation. In case of eventual nonpayment, these pledged objects could be sold. No litigation or third party was needed, and the creditor was amply protected from the moment that the loan was extended. Safeguarding loans through retention of a pledge is, of course, the simplest expedient available, and it was probably the most common method used during this period.

There are, nonetheless, fragmentary signs of more sophisticated arrangements. A responsum of Rashi deals with a dispute between a widow and her brother-in-law concerning gifts allegedly given to the widow and her deceased husband by his parents. Chief among these gifts was "the tithe collectible from a certain village, which tithe had been pledged with L and J [the parents] for a loan of seven rotl. L and J thus empowered R and A to collect the produce of that tithe and the principal of the loan in the event the original owner of the tithe should come to repay the loan and redeem his pledge." While this arrangement is also designated a pledge (mashkon), it is quite different from the pledges indicated earlier. The former were physical objects which were deposited at the time of the loan. When the debt was repaid, the pawn was returned; if the borrower defaulted, it would be kept or sold. In the case of the tithe, however, it was not a physical object that changed hands; it was a right. The difference in practical terms was twofold. First, there was constant revenue; the lender collected regular income, which was probably seen as the interest on the loan. More important, this was an arrangement that involved more than simply a creditor and a debtor; the implicit aid of a governmental agency was necessary. The creditor did not physically control the pledge; hence, should contention arise, he had to have the certainty of powerful support. Lending of the kind revealed in the responsum of Rashi is far more complex and generally more lucrative; it has as its result the further tightening of the crucial bond between Jew and baron. As Jews turned increasingly towards this kind of business operation, they began to depend on their overlords not only for physical protection but for buttressing their financial investments as well. Prior to the First Crusade this more complex method of lending may have remained rather uncommon. It was, however, destined to play an increasingly important role in Jewish economic life.

The aspect of pre-Crusade Jewish life that has attracted the most scholarly attention has been its communal organization. The Jewish communities of northern France were small, with a high level of internal cohesion and a broad range of activities. Yitzhak Baer has delineated three major functions in this community: the preservation of satisfactory relations with the ruling powers, the securing of internal discipline and order, and the establishment of necessary internal economic limitations and controls.

The alliance fashioned between the Jews and the barony was fueled by the tangible advantages realized by the feudal magnates. The most immediate expression of this was taxation. Collection of taxes was certainly one of the major functions assumed by the communal agencies. The responsum specifying those holdings open to taxation indicates that the purpose of the levy was "to collect the king's tax."

The methods for apportioning taxation were well-established and reflect the cohesiveness of the community. One method was that indicated in the above-noted responsum. This involved levying "on every man and woman, while under the ban, a fixed amount per pound of value of his or her money, merchandise, and other saleable possessions." This system depended for its effectiveness upon honest evaluation, by each member of the community, of his possessions. The likelihood of such honesty was enhanced by the religious sanctions mentioned and by the closeness of a small community, where the temptation to underevaluate would be tempered by the difficulty of concealing the truth. Occasionally, however, this arrangement broke down. R. Joseph

Bon Fils was asked to resolve a complicated issue that began with the following circumstance:

> The people of T came to pay the king's tax. They complained against one another, saying: "You lightened your own burden and made mine heavier." Whereupon they selected trustees, the noble and great of the town, the experts of the land, from the community, and (agreed) to abide by their decision, for they dealt faithfully.

The role of the Jewish community organization as a liaison between the Jews and the ruling authorities was not exhausted by the collection of taxes. On occasion the organized community had to make representation before the authorities on matters affecting the security of the Jews. Thus, in 992, when faced with the danger of trial by combat, the Jewish community made vehement protestations before the count of Maine. They appealed to precedent, on the one hand, and offered substantial material inducements, on the other. While in this instance there was large-scale community response, in periods of crisis a prominent individual could take the initiative, thrusting himself to the fore as the community's spokesman. It was in this manner that Jacob b. Yekutiel ventured to step forth before the duke of Normandy and ultimately before the pope himself.

In a community desperately anxious to preserve its insulation from the local municipality within whose boundaries it lived and to achieve a measure of distance from even the more favorably-disposed feudal authorities, there was an absolute necessity for maintaining inner discipline. While the small size of the Jewish community contributed to cohesiveness, close living could on occasion produce sharp conflicts between members of the community. In the face of such conflict, the community marshaled its forces and ordained limitations on intracommunal strife. The community's goal in such cases was the preservation of peace within the community, without the intervention of outside powers.

The economic outlets available to the Jews were not extensive. For this reason the community had to exercise significant control in the area of economics also. The two major thrusts of communal limitation were the granting of exclusive commercial privileges and the restriction of the right to settle. The former usually involved business dealings with important secular lords of ecclesiastical institutions. From the slim evidence available, it seems that the arrangement was not everywhere operative and that, even where the prerogative of the community to give such privileges was recognized, the rights of exclusive trade were not widely granted. Restriction of settlement was directly related to the economic situation of the Jews. The small towns of northern France could absorb only so many Jewish traders and moneylenders. Overpopulation would simply force the available income of the community below the subsistence level. Again it must be noted, however, that the right of the community to declare a total or even a partial ban on new settlement was far from universally recognized.

To the three major functions of the Jewish community delineated by Baer at least a fourth must be added. The Jewish community of necessity had to supply certain essential religious and social services to its membership. The centrality of the synagogue in the Jewish community of this period is undisputed. It was far more than a center of worship, serving as an educational and general communal center as well. Details of Jewish schooling at the time are almost nonexistent. The literacy demanded by the business pursuits of the Jews and the already high level of cultural achievement indicate a successful educational system. Within the medieval municipality there were of course no "neutral" social welfare agencies; such facilities as did exist were Church institutions and, as such, closed to the Jews; thus the Jews had to provide for their own indigent, ill, and unfortunate. The needs of the local community were often augmented by the requirements of Jews whose business took them from town to town. In the case of the central figure in the Le Mans letter, as he proceeded through the Jewish communities of northwestern France, the Jews "supported him, as is their custom, in every town to which he came." Perhaps the most striking evidence of such concern is revealed in the following responsum:

> Jews of Rheims, while on their way to the fair of Troyes, were attacked, plundered, and taken captive by "an adversary and an enemy." The charitable Jews of Troyes risked their own lives, (negotiated with the enemy,) and agreed to a redemption price of thirty pounds. The greater part of the ransom money was paid by the captives themselves; while in order to raise the remainder, the community of Troyes levied a tax of one *solidus* per pound on themselves, as well as on the neighboring communities of Sens and Auxerre, and on the Jews of Chalon-sur-Saône.

The locus of power in the Jewish community was the community membership itself. While the governing authorities benefited from the ability of the community to control its own affairs, particularly in the area of taxation, there was as yet no strong drive for more direct involvement in Jewish communal affairs or for more extensive exploitation of this useful and cohesive group. As noted, the community, for its part, was anxious to minimize outside interference.

The rhetoric of community enactments generally emphasized unanimous decision-making by the entire local Jewry: "The community of Troyes levied a tax . . ."; "the townspeople levied on every man and woman . . ."; "the community . . . heard about it and solemnly pronounced the ban. . . ." There was, in fact, even question as to the right of the majority to exercise its will over the minority.

At the same time, however, certain elements in the community did command special authority. Leadership was exercised by significant scholarly figures, such as Rashi, or by men of wealth and standing, such as Jacob b. Yekutiel. An interesting responsum indicates a more general tendency towards control by a segment of the community. In a conflict concerning the responsibility of individuals to accept the decisions of the majority, the following question was asked:

> We are a small community. The humble members among us have always abided by the leadership of our eminent members, dutifully obeyed their decrees, and never protested against their ordinances. Now, when we are about to enact a decree, must we ask each individual member whether or not he is in agreement with it?

Even at this early point a leadership class does seem to have emerged, although it certainly lacked the direct governmental support and the recognized religious authority that would later develop.

With the community itself as the fundamental authority, it is in no way surprising to find power highly localized. The question of the right of one Jewish settlement to legislate for others was raised a number of times. In general a distinction was drawn between daily administrative affairs—where each community was autonomous—and principles of Jewish religious behavior—where coercion could be exerted. One of a number of expressions of this distinction is phrased in the following way:

> As to your question whether the inhabitants of one town are competent to enact decrees binding on the inhabitants of another town, and to coerce the latter inhabitants while they are in their own town, the following ruling seems proper to us: If the decree that they are enacting deals with the needs of their place, such as taxation, weights, measures, and wages—in all such matters the inhabitants of one town are not competent to legislate for the inhabitants of another town. Thus we quoted above the Talmudic ruling: "The townspeople are permitted," which means that only the people of the town are competent to legislate in such matters but not outsiders. If, however, the inhabitants of a town transgressed a law of the Torah, committed a wrong, or decided a point of law or of ritual, not in accordance with the accepted usage—the inhabitants of another town might coerce them, and even pronounce the *herem* against them, in order to force them to mend their ways. In that case, the inhabitants of the former town may not say to the latter: "we are independent of you, we exercise authority among ourselves, as you do among yourselves." For all Israel is then enjoined to force them (to mend their ways); as we find in the case of the "rebellious sage," or "the condemned city," that the Sanhedrin coerces them and judges them.

Extensive authority was exercised by outstanding scholarly figures, whose enactments were generally considered binding over a wide number of settlements. Thus, Rashi affirms that the important edict of R. Gershom of Mayence would certainly be applicable in all Jewish communities.

> Should it become established through the testimony of reliable witnesses who are recognized authorities on this restrictive ordinance of the great teacher (R. Gershom), that he enacted this ordinance with greater rigor and strictness than all other anathemas and restrictive measures customarily enacted in the last generations; that in this enactment he used the awesome term *shamta;* and

that he solemnly prohibited to mention the disgrace (of temporary apostasy) not only to the culprits themselves who eventually returned to Judaism, but even to their descendants; and should it further become established that when A and his family were forewarned, the name of the great teacher (as author of the awesome ban) was mentioned to them—we cannot deal lightly with a ban of Rabbenu Gershom, since in our generation there is no scholar of his great eminence, capable to release a person from such a ban.

The sanctions at the disposal of the community were of course conditioned by the bases of its power. One possibility lay in the direction of the secular authority, but it was an avenue only sparingly utilized because of the danger inhering in such an approach. Thus, an early-eleventh-century Jewish community faced with the overt recalcitrance of two of its members and the support of a neighboring community for the rebels was "about to ask the king to order his constables to collect his tax directly from A and B. Upon further deliberation, however, they changed their minds and decided first to inquire whether their solemn decree was still valid, i.e., whether the cancellation thereof by the community of S was of any consequence." A turn to secular authorities was a step which most Jewish communities were reluctant to take.

Since the most tangible locus of power was the cohesive community self, the ultimate weapon at the disposal of the Jews was the ban of excommunication. Given the importance of the Jewish community and its facilities to the individual Jew, the power of exclusion was a formidable one. The ostracized Jew was in a hazardous position politically, economically, socially, and religiously. At the same time, excommunication was not an infallible tool in the hands of the Jewish community. The realities of power within the community often limited the effectiveness of the ban. In one case, for example, "since the members of the community feared that B and his friends, living so near the synagogue, would remove the scrolls of the Law and other community articles, and that no one would be able to stop them from taking these articles, they transgressed the law on several occasions—all on B's instructions." Another limitation on the effectiveness of excommunication was the localization of Jewish authority already noted. Thus two Jews excommunicated in community T "went to S and related there the whole incident. The people of S took A and B into their homes, wined and dined them, transacted business with them, lifted from them the ban of community T, and gave them a written release of such ban." While the action of community S was judged illegal, in fact the localization of power did weaken the impact of any such ban.

The Jewish community of northern France thus emerges, from earliest times, as a remarkably cohesive and comprehensive organization. The isolation of the Jews forced them to create for themselves all sorts of agencies—political, economic, social, educational, and religious. The small size of the individual Jewish settlements precluded the independence of each of these agencies. What emerged then was a total Jewish community responsible for filling every one of the vital needs of its constituents. Therein lies the secret of the wide range of powers and the effectiveness of the Jewish community organization even at its early stage of development.

Perhaps the most persuasive index of the level of maturity reached by northern French Jewry prior to the First Crusade is its intellectual creativity. It seems reasonable to conclude that a community capable of producing extensive scholarly achievement like that of R. Solomon b. Isaac of Troyes (Rashi) must have been well-established and effectively organized. Rashi, already noted as an outstanding communal authority—one of the few whose eminence was broadly recognized—wrote copiously. His works, which quickly became classics in Ashkenazic circles, included primarily extensive commentaries on the Bible and the Talmud. While he was always revered as the beginning—and not the culmination—of a brilliant series of northern French scholars, his creations indicate that, by the last years of the eleventh century, northern French Jewry had come of age.

At the end of the eleventh century many of the creative forces that had been germinating steadily throughout western Europe burst forth into the passion, vision, and violence of the First Crusade. The Crusade was an expression of the new militance of Christendom against its external foes; it revealed also new potential for internal upheaval and disruption. While the goal of the pope and of the great barons was a military expedition against Islam, the feelings unleashed by the call to the Crusade could hardly be contained within the particular channels delineated by its instigators. Thus the First Crusade brought more than the conquest of Jerusalem; it left a path of death and destruction within Christendom itself.

The dispossessed who took up the chant "Deus lo volt" savagely vented pent-up furies upon many of their long-despised neighbors. Given the pervasive religiosity of medieval civilization and the distinctly religious hatreds that animated the Crusaders, it comes as no surprise that the prime object of the internal violence associated with the First Crusade was European Jewry.

France, particularly northern France, played a major role in the great drama of 1095–1099. It was in the French city of Clermont that Urban II issued his appeal; French barons were conspicuous in their leadership of the crusading forces; it was in the French countryside that Peter the Hermit began his preaching for a humble army of the pious to free the holy places from Moslem hands. Yet France, despite its prominence, was spared the upheavals that followed in the wake of Crusade preaching. France's eastern neighbors bore the brunt of the devastation that crusading fervor unleashed.

The relative calm with which France weathered the Crusade is reflected in the fate of her Jews. The same Jewish and Christian sources that are so copious in their description of Jewish sufferings in the Rhineland area say almost nothing of Jewish fate in France. Although arguments from silence are always suspect, it is difficult to believe that this set of Jewish and Christian chroniclers and editors would have been unaware of, or uninterested in recounting, extensive Jewish tragedy in nearby France. The Rhineland Jews who compiled the Hebrew chronicles knew the reactions of the French Jews to the organization of the Crusade, and they detailed Jewish persecution over a broad area. It is inconceivable that large-scale catastrophe in France could have gone unknown or unreported. Moreover, the longest of the Hebrew Crusade chronicles is embedded in a late-twelfth-century communal history of Spires Jewry, which includes a series of letters detailing the Blois catastrophe of 1171 and its aftermath. The Spires editor would not have omitted information on Crusade tragedy in France had it been available.

There is satisfactory evidence for but one specific persecution of Jews within the area of northern France, an attack which took place in the Norman city of Rouen. The fullest description of this assault is given by Guibert of Nogent as a backdrop to his account of a monk of the monastery of Fly.

> At Rouen on a certain day, the people who had undertaken to go on that expedition [that is, the Crusade] under the badge of the Cross began to complain to one another, "After traversing great distances, we desire to attack the enemies of God in the East, although the Jews, of all races the worst foe of God, are before our eyes. That's doing our work backward." Saying this and seizing their weapons, they herded the Jews into a certain place of worship, rounding them up by either force or guile, and without distinction of sex or age put them to the sword. Those who accepted Christianity, however, escaped the impending slaughter.

The striking difference between the relative peace enjoyed by northern France and its Jews and the wholesale destruction, especially of Jewish life and property, further east can be accounted for in a number of ways. This difference is surely *not* a reflection of more benign French attitudes; as Norman Golb has argued, French Crusaders were deeply implicated in the wave of German atrocities associated with the First Crusade. In France, however, their antipathy was not translated into deed, partially because France was the very first area of organization. The problems of the undisciplined Crusader bands tended to multiply the further eastward they moved, the larger their numbers, and the slimmer their provisions. The initial rallying of these crusading groups in France and their speedy movement towards the East played a major role in the safety of French Jewry. A second factor was the protection afforded by the less pretentious, but more effective, French political authorities. While the emperor was the most exalted political dignitary of Europe, the base upon which his power rested was a shaky one. Thus, in town after town, the Jews found themselves separated from large and bloodthirsty mobs by the flimsy military and political power of the local bishop. Even the Hebrew chroniclers recognize that many of these bishops were sincere in their desire to protect their Jews; their failure resulted from a lack of the required force. In France, on the other hand, where the Capetian monarchy advanced none of the grandiose claims of the German empire, firm political power had been slowly crystallizing in a series of well-organized principalities. Within these principalities the count and his growing retinue of administrative officials exercised effective authority. It was this political stability also that aided in harnessing the violence of the Crusaders and in sparing the Jews.

Although the Jews of northern France suffered little during the tumultuous first months of the Crusade, they were hardly oblivious to the dangers. In fact they were far more aware of the impending threat than any of their fellow Jews, for it was in their land that the Crusade was called, that the first active preaching took place, and that the first crusading groups began to form. The same Hebrew chronicle that said nothing of overt persecution in France recorded faithfully the fears of the French Jews.

> At the time when the Jewish communities in France heard [of the beginning of the Crusade] they were seized with fear and trembling. They then resorted to the devices of their predecessors. They wrote letters and sent messengers to the Rhineland communities, that these communities fast and seek mercy on their behalf from the God who dwells on high, so that they might be spared.

The Hebrew chronicles also reported the more immediate steps taken by French Jewry to avert the threatened catastrophe. This information is contained in the brief description of the passage of Peter the Hermit through Trèves.

> When he came to Trèves—he and the multitude of men with him—to go forth on their pilgrimage to Jerusalem, he brought with him from France a letter from the Jews, indicating that, in all places where he would pass through Jewish communities, they should afford him provisions. He then would speak favorably on behalf of the Jews.

Given the lack of destructive violence against the Jews in northern France, we can readily understand the lack of a political aftermath parallel to that which took place in Germany. Guido Kisch has carefully chronicled the evolution in Germany of safeguards designed to protect the vulnerable Jewish communities. Jewish political status in France, however, underwent no significant development in the wake of the First Crusade. There had been, after all, no major calamity to arouse among the Jews themselves or among their baronial overlords a heightened sense of the urgent need for new protective devices.

Furthermore, French Jewry never viewed 1095–1096 as a watershed in its history, as did its German counterpart. While the works of Rashi represent an early high point of French Jewish religious creativity, his successors did not see themselves as mere compilers of his legacy; they considered their efforts a continuation, not a collection. When, much later on, the sense of a chain of giant figures emerges, this series runs from Rashi through R. Samson of Sens, from the late eleventh through the early thirteenth centuries. The years of the First Crusade are in no sense construed as a major dividing line. Interestingly enough, when in 1171 French Jewry suffered what it considered its first major catastrophe, the calamity at Blois, it very movingly expressed the feelings of horror evoked by the utterly senseless death of over thirty Jews. If ever one might expect French Jewish recollection of the First Crusade, this would surely be the point. Yet significantly there is no recall whatsoever of 1096. When old memories are summoned up, they are recollections of a much earlier period. Thus, according to Ephraim of Bonn, R. Jacob Tam ordained that the twentieth of Sivan, the day of the catastrophe itself, "is fit to be set as a fast day for all our people. Indeed the gravity of this fast will exceed that of the fast of Gedaliah b. Aḥikam, for this is a veritable Day of Atonement." The fateful year of the First Crusade in no way dominated the subsequent consciousness of northern French Jewry.

Through the late tenth and on through the eleventh century, then, northern French Jewry continued to develop, benefiting from the general progress of western European civilization and making its own contribution to that progress. Already tightly allied with the powerful feudal barony, the Jews were involving themselves ever more heavily in the burgeoning urban commerce and had begun to develop viable institutions of self-government. By the end of the eleventh century, northern French Jewry was sufficiently mature to produce its first figure of renown, R. Solomon b. Isaac of Troyes. Relatively unscathed by the anti-Jewish outbreaks of the First Crusade, French Jewry proceeded into the twelfth century in a spirit of continued growth.

THE WORLD OF THE CRUSADERS

JOSHUA PRAWER

Popular histories of the crusades dwell on the formation of the crusading armies, the trek across Asia Minor to the Levant, and the revival of trade between East and West. They also indulge in endless discussions concerning the motives of the crusaders. This selection by Joshua Prawer treats an important aspect of the crusading movement that receives scant attention in most histories—the experiences and everyday lives of the Europeans who settled the new Latin principalities in Palestine and Syria. The First Crusade was successful not only in driving the Saracens out of Jerusalem, but also in establishing a feudal principality there to protect the recovered holy places. Many of those who went with the first army were landless knights who stayed in the Holy Land to carve out baronies for themselves. Their good fortune, as well as the continual need for reinforcements to keep the new state strong against Muslim counterattack, brought in a steady steam of European knights.

What was this society of immigrants and, eventually, of second- and third-generation Levantines like? The Arabs of the region considered the new arrivals barbarians—brutes whose ability to fight had to be respected, but whose culture was shockingly primitive. The Europeans born in the Levant may well have had the same reaction to newcomers, but they were cultural hybrids themselves. Their kingdom produced a feudal charter, the Assizes of Jerusalem, that shows a faithful adherence to the social and political ideal of Europe. Their lifestyle, however, absorbed much from the surrounding Arab aristocracy with whom they learned to live during the uneasy truces.

From: Joshua Prawer, *The World of the Crusaders* (New York: Quadrangle Books, 1972), pp. 83–92, 92–96, 99.

The noble and knight brought with them from Europe notions and ideals of the seigniorial life-style and transplanted them in the soil of the newly conquered state. Western Europe perpetuated itself under oriental skies. The French language, fashions and customs struck roots in the Levant, and soon a second and a third generation of the original conquerors and settlers had grown up in the country for whom "home" meant the Holy Land, whereas Europe—the "old home"—was a place of their ancestors' far-removed origin. This was a new breed of men and women nicknamed *Poulains*, which should probably be translated or understood in the sense of "kids." Their home life, family relations and tutors were all reflections of Europe and, more specifically, France. Yet their environment—the physical conditions of life, the daily meetings in street and bazaar—was the Levant. Thus a scion of a noble, or even a knightly, family underwent the same process of upbringing and education as his European counterpart. He was raised under the mantle of the same religion, instructed in the same tenets of faith, drew his intellectual attitudes and images from the same legends, pious tales, heroic romances and courtly poetry. A *France d'Outremer,* a "France overseas," was created.

Yet the Syrian-born Frank was not wholly European. Mixed marriages with Armenian and Byzantine ladies were a common occurrence in the upper strata of the Frankish nobility. It was thus considered quite "normal" that one's mother, grandmother or aunt was an oriental Christian. This was true not only for the nobility but even for the royal and princely Crusader houses. Such a marriage brought with it the oriental servants and attendants— whether Christian or Moslem—which abounded in every wealthy Frankish household. Members of the lower strata of Frankish society, whether simple knights or burgesses, often intermarried with oriental Christians on their own social level. A Crusader chronicler reflected upon the resultant state of affairs:

> . . . Consider, I pray, and reflect how in our time God has transferred the West into the East. For we who were Occidentals now have been made Orientals. He who was a Roman or a Frank is now a Galilean or Palestinian. One who was a citizen of Rheims or of Chartres now has been made a citizen of Tyre or Antioch. We have already forgotten the places of our birth; they have become unknown to many of us or, at least, are unmentioned. Some already possess homes and servants here which they have received through inheritance. Some have taken wives not merely of their own people but Syrians, or Armenians or even Saracens who have received the grace of baptism. Some have with them a father-in-law, or daughter-in-law, or son-in-law, or stepson or stepfather. Here, too, are grandchildren and great-grandchildren. One cultivates vines, another fields. Both use the speech and the idioms of different languages. These languages, now made common, become known to both races; and faith unites those whose forefathers were strangers.

Thus a young Frank, a *Poulain,* was accustomed from childhood to meeting and living with the Occident in the Orient. The house or citadel which he inhabited in the city was usually an oriental building which had belonged to a Moslem before the Crusader conquest and was very different from European buildings and fortifications. Timber, the most common building material in the West, was almost unknown in the Holy Land. Stone was the common building material used in both the cities and villages. It was usually quarried not far from the cities themselves, like the stone cut out of the slopes of Mount Carmel for Caesarea, those of Chastel Pèlerin dug out of the nearby ridge which blocked the eastward-moving dunes, or the lovely pink-coloured stone brought to Jerusalem from Anathot.

Two- and three-story stone houses were the normal type of habitat, but even five-story houses were not unknown. Their flat roofs, often dotted with potted palms or evergreen trees and shrubs, were a place to enjoy the cool breezes after the hot sun had set. Inside, the thick walls preserved warmth in the winter, when the temperature in places like Jerusalem and Safed, as well as in the mountains east of Acre, Tripoli and Antioch, descended to the freezing point. In the summer, the walls and narrow windows kept the rooms cool, even during the scorching days of the *hamsin,* the Levantine first-cousin of the *sirocco.* The ceilings were very high, and the slightly pointed arches added to the feeling of height in the atmosphere, for the narrow windows restricted the entrance of light as well as heat. The windows were not boarded up by planks or covered with parchment, but glistened with locally fabricated glass. Pure, transparent glass was rather rare, but green- or blue-tinted, semi-opaque glass enclosing air bubbles was used, unless one preferred stained glass.

The ground-floor facade of Eastern houses was usually a solid wall except for the entrance-way. The windows on the upper floors let in some light, but basically the house opened onto the inner courtyard, where the precious, life-giving well, stored rain water or, in some places, a pit connected to one of the ancient aqueducts was normally situated. In some courtyards, as we know from a description of a marvellous Crusader palace in Beirut, a fountain cooled the air and its water-jets fell back into a mosaic-paved pool.

In some houses the staircase was located outside the building, allowing access from the street to each floor. The houses of the wealthy often had a kind of out-building composed of canvas- or plank-covered arches to protect the entrance from sun and rain, like the elaborate awnings in our luxury hotels. The shafts of the arches had holes drilled into them so that horses could be tethered.

The interiors of the better-endowed houses were decorated with mosaics of exquisite Byzantine-Moslem craftsmanship. In addition, rugs, draperies or tapestries covered the walls. Mosaics were an integral part of interior decoration and often displayed geometric designs, flowers and animals. In wealthier households, the ceiling arches may have rested on sculpted consoles, or a display of archvaults and simple arches might have added to the decor. Furniture was far more elaborate than that found in Europe. At their best, tables and chairs and the legs and posts of beds were of wood carved in lace-like patterns of bas-reliefs or small sculptures of flowers or human or animal heads. The chairs often looked like a rounded letter x, their upper part serving as a seat with handles. Oblong, cylindrical cushions covered with silk or samite that ended off in tassels were added for comfort. Mother of pearl, which became the glory of Bethlehem's craftsmanship, may already have been used in furniture decoration, as it was in some of the mosaics. Each noble household or ecclesiastical institution had a box-like writing table with accompanying chair. The writing was done on the inclined top, whereas the ink-pots, colours, quills and other paraphernalia of the scriptorium were kept on the table's lower shelves.

Kitchen utensils and tableware varied with the strata of society. Cooking was done in large earthenware pots in open ovens. Those preserved in several Crusader sites are huge pits over which meat could have been broiled or pots suspended or the pit was covered by a special iron grid to hold the pots and pans. Spoons and knives were the basic table utensils, the first normally of wood, the latter of iron or steel. One often used his dagger as a table knife (these sometimes had ornate handles of ivory or carved wood and blades of the famous Indian steel), although metal utensils were often imported from Europe. In noble households the younger squires or pages served the meal; but when the family was receiving honoured guests, the younger sons of the family would sometimes perform this duty. The carved meat was transferred on slices of round bread, which served as plates and sauce-sponges, or the bread was placed on earthenware plates which were often glazed and decorated with designs. The most common glazed crockery was a basic dark colour covered with geometrical designs of brown, green and yellow glaze. Sometimes these decorations were Christian symbols—such as crosses, fish, tiaras, mitres—but heads of animals, legendary griffons and the like were also used. The most elaborate plates would have drawings of knights or riders on their mounts.

Metal plates and goblets were part of the decor of the house. Some were purely ornamental, such as large, copper-brimmed plates engraved with verses or even scenes from the Scriptures. These seem to have been imported from Europe; but such decorative or ceremonial crockery as that on which the Crusader king's meal was served in the Mosque of al-Aqsa after the coronation must have been of precious metal designed and engraved in Syria and Palestine. Metal cups and goblets were in common use. Some were inlaid, usually with silver, in the lovely patterns of the oriental arabesque. The Arabic inscriptions which praised Allah were no impediments to their use among Christians, though they might have been used for wine-drinking (which was certainly not what their artisan-creator intended). Whereas metal cups and goblets were also in common use in Europe, glassware was far more common in the Orient. Some examples of glasses painted with scenes and inscriptions, probably made in Tyre, display excellent form and exquisite decorations. One bears the heraldic sign of its owner, which must have been a common custom.

The oriental house and its interior decoration found their complement in the cuisine. Whatever gastronomical tradition had been imported from Europe, it could hardly compete with the local menu. Not only was oriental cuisine better adapted to the local climatic conditions, but the tantalizing spices and their use in meat, fish and sauces easily got the upper hand in competition with the abundant but rather plain dishes known to the Europeans. The oriental servants, like vendors in streets and bazaars, had no difficulty introducing their specialties into both noble and lower households. We even know about Crusader old-timers who boasted about their Egyptian cuisine, as one would boast today of having a cook with a *cordon bleu*.

Fashion and dresses also left their mark on Crusader society, but in this sphere the Franks limited their adoption. The Frank was ready to take advantage of the sumptuous textiles of the Near or Far East. Textiles which in Europe could have been found in royal and princely households only or occasionally among the ceremonial wardrobe of prelates were within the range of people of even mediocre means in the Orient. Silk, taffeta, brocade, cotton, wool and gossamer muslins were all worn by the Franks and their ladies, but they resisted the adoption of oriental style. One would wear oriental fabrics, but the cut of the dresses remained European. A Frank never wore any oriental garb, at least not in public. Sometimes he would wind a short shawl or mantle over his helmet as protection against the sun's strong rays; he might even use a white cloak, as did the Orientals and members of the military orders. But his vestments were basically European and changed with European fashions. Articles of clothing which could not be found in the kingdom, like berets, were imported from Europe. And the Franks' sense of ethnic identity went so far that they prohibited non-Franks from wearing European-style garments. This keeping to the *mores Francorum* was also expressed by the resistance to the oriental custom of growing beards. Whereas the participants of the First Crusade were bearded, as was the custom in their homelands, when beards went out of fashion in Europe two generations later (middle of the twelfth century), the Franks in the Holy Land followed suit, and their clean-shaven faces and shoulder-length hair became as much a clearly distinguishable mark of their identity as the object of oriental disgust and ridicule.

Climate and environment had their influence in the realm of hygiene and cosmetics. A nineteenth-century historian described medieval Europe as a society which had forgone washing for a thousand years. This description certainly did not apply to the Franks in the East. Soap was produced locally and may even have been exported. The partiality of the *Poulains* for baths earned them the charge of the vice of "luxury." The austere Bernard of Clairvaux pointed out with pride that his protégés, the Templars, had no use for baths! Fifty years later, James of Vitry, the bishop of Acre, preached against this unholy institution which contaminated mores. He even hinted at some unsavoury goings on among the ladies of the Crusader upper class. The Genoese even allowed common bathing (albeit segregated by sex) in their *balneum* in Acre. Whatever the custom, Europeans who visited the kingdom returned to Europe with the impression that an effeminate society had succeeded the heroes of the First Crusade, who had since become legendary paragons of all chivalrous virtues. Today, one would probably describe such behaviour as subtlety, finesse or epicurean, but things looked different to the European newcomer. James of Vitry was rather vehement in his denunciation: "They were brought up in luxury, soft and effeminate, more used to baths than battles, addicted to unclean and riotous living, clad like women in soft robes." Beneath the heavy hand of the furious prelate, one detects a mode of life which a disgruntled contemporary observer would label as Levantine:

> They have so learned to disguise their meaning in cunning speeches, covered and bedecked with leaves, but no fruit, like barren willow-trees, that those who do not know them thoroughly by experience can scarcely understand their reservations and tricks of speech or avoid being deceived by them. They are suspicious and jealous of their wives, whom they lock up in close prison and guard in such strict and careful custody that even their brethren and nearest relatives can scarcely approach them; while they forbid them so utterly to attend churches, processions, the wholesome preaching of God's Word and other matters appertaining to their salvation, that they scarce suffer them to go to church once a year; howbeit some husbands allow their wives to go out to the bath three times a week, under strict guard.

As to crusader womenfolk:

> But the more strictly the *Pullani* lock up their wives, the more do they by a thousand arts and endless contrivances struggle and try to find their way out. They are wondrously and beyond belief learned in witchcraft and wickednesses innumerable, which they are taught by the Syrian women.

Despite almost chronic warfare, the amenities of the Holy Land made life less grim than it was under the grey, northern skies of Europe. Houses, dress, encounters in street or market-place, the gossip and politics in the baths recalled Hellenistic cities. The Frankish knight who grew up in such surroundings, despite his speech and dress, was not French but a Near Eastern Frank. One can hardly agree with the accusation of cowardice; they were good fighters. And while not always good diplomats, thirteenth-century Crusader nobles

were born politicians who loved to have a finger in every political pie and con-
spiracy, like the Renaissance Italians in their city-states.

The Frankish noble seldom lived in the countryside. Even the few nobles
who had castles as centres of seigniories would normally maintain a household
in the city (usually in Jerusalem and in the thirteenth century in Acre or Tyre).
Very few nobles lived in their manors. Basically they were a class of *rentiers*
who collected the income from their rural estates and spent it in their urban
residences. The countryside and its villages was a thing one lived off, supervised, but rarely inhabited. The squire-tenant or squire-serf relationship, typical in medieval Europe, was almost nonexistent in the Orient. The steward or
a similar official, often a scribe or *drugeman,* would supervise the village rents,
though he seldom intervened in the work itself. The Crusader noble did not go
into farming on his own, very seldom kept demesne land and was normally
satisfied with the third or quarter of the village crops, which were usually well
supplemented by income from urban taxation. As a matter of fact, a Crusader
noble's visit to his rural possessions was rather exceptional. One went out to
the countryside for hunting or fishing, but seldom for economic reasons. The
amenities of country life, without its burdens, were supplied by the beautiful
orchards, vineyards and olive groves which surrounded all the cities. Some
nobles maintained a kind of cottage or similar structure in these "suburbs"
where they passed the hot summer days and cooler evenings in the company
of others of their class, sometimes even Moslem nobles. From here they would
pursue the chase for fox or boar or hunt with falcons. A good part of time was
spent in riding and military exercises. Crusader nobles, like their Moslem antagonists, vied with each other over the beauty of their horses. A considerable
amount of money was spent acquiring horses and bedecking them with trappings of finery, expensive materials and precious metals. Pasture lands around
the cities were also parade grounds to display horses and horsemanship. During periods of peace, even Moslems would participate in such exercises. The
crowning glory of the mounted noble was, naturally, the tournament, a mock
battle of nobles or of single champions. On such occasions the ladies appeared
on city or castle battlements to participate in that most-cherished of medieval
shows. Here the young squire or the experienced knight could achieve prize
and renown for prowess and military skill. The horses, arms and armour of
the loser, often of considerable value, became the property of the winner. Still,
it seems that tournaments, which were often connected with festivities, were
rarer in the Crusader East than in contemporary Europe. Perhaps in a war-
ridden country mock battles were too close to everyday, grim reality to
exercise the attraction that was so strong in Europe, despite ecclesiastical
prohibitions.

The major part of a noble's or knight's time was spent in his normal habitat, the city. A simple knight's time-table was regulated by duties of service
in city garrison, manning the city's citadel, making the rounds of walls and

towers or guarding the lord's palace. Higher nobility would spend a good deal of time in attendance on their overlord, often sitting in his court as councillors or judges. As councillors they would advise on matters put before them for deliberation; as judges they performed the feudal obligations judging their peers.

A short treatise entitled "On the Four Ages of Men," written by a mid-thirteenth-century Frank and describing occupations fitting to each age, gives the impression that the Franks in the East were a noble, church-going society. Unfortunately, this picture clashes too strongly with other sources—albeit of ecclesiastical origin—which give a very different version of the nobles' behaviour. Whatever the truth, whether or not one really attended daily mass, there is no doubt that a noble would participate in the great church festivities which, in a city like Jerusalem, were not only religiously moving, but offered a rich pageantry to participant and spectator.

For other amusements and social contacts, one would meet friends at home, at the bath or even in a tavern. Chess—the king's game—was known, but dice was the most popular entertainment, and one ran the risk of losing both fortune and soul. Meals and drinking—heavy drinking—were part and parcel of entertainment, and many a tavern or private house had its quota of Western-style prostitutes or Eastern-style dancing girls, sometimes slaves of an oriental *souteneur*. Prostitution, common in all medieval cities and most accentuated in ports, was quite extensive in a port city like Acre, where the pope had to warn clergy about renting houses to prostitutes. We have a vivid description of this city, recorded by James of Vitry, who was bishop of Acre for some time:

> Among the *Poulains* there is hardly one in a thousand who takes his marriage seriously. They do not regard fornication to be a deadly sin. From childhood they are pampered and wholly given to carnal pleasures, whereas they are not accustomed to hear God's word, which they lightly disregard. I found here foreigners who fled in despair from their native countries because of various horrible sins. These people, who have no fear of God, are corrupting the whole city by their nefarious deeds and pernicious examples.
>
> Almost every day and every night people are openly or secretly murdered. At night men strangle their wives if they dislike them; women, using the ancient art of poison and potion, kill their husbands so as to be able to marry other men. There are in the city vendors of toxins and poisons, so that nobody can have confidence in anyone, and a man's foes shall be they of his own household.
>
> And the city is full of brothels, and as the rent of the prostitutes is higher, not only laymen, but even clergymen, nay even monks, rent their houses all over the city to public harlots.

It is difficult to ascertain the degree of literacy among the Frankish nobility. It seems that the higher nobility was literate, and the rather few works written by them, as well as other testimonies, indicate that their level of literacy was equal to that of their European counterparts. We know of festivities where episodes from the Arthurian cycle, as well as the fabliaux popular in Europe were performed. But it is doubtful whether the same degree of literacy was common among the lower nobility. Likewise, we know very little about the nobility's intellectual interests. Very few seem to have been interested in the rich oriental heritage around them, and few mastered Arabic, the common language of the Orient and the key to its treasures. On the whole, this breed of Europeans in the East does not strike one as being bent on an intellectual adventure.

The general lack of intellectual interests is stressed by the fact that no scholarly or intellectual centre, no university or school was ever created in the Crusader colonies—and this in an age when all major European centres were dotted with colleges or universities. A man bent on acquiring a wider education went to Europe, as did the only historian of the kingdom, William, bishop of Tyre, a *Poulain,* who easily ranks among the greatest historians in the Middle Ages. This phenomenon in itself explains why the Crusader colonies never became bridges between the Orient and Occident, despite the fact that for two hundred years they were the outposts of Europe in the Eastern Mediterranean. . . .

If Frankish nobility could usually trace their origin to a noble house in their European homeland—though not to the famous houses of Christendom—the burgesses, despite their title, were hardly descendants of European burghers or city dwellers. The lower strata of Frankish population were predominantly of peasant stock, villeins and serfs. They had left Europe either with one of the crusades or as part of a wave of migration. And it was these strata of society which made up the majority of the Frankish population. The transition from their basically rural life-style to the mastery of urban occupations was not an easy one. The native craftsmen, oriental Christians or Moslems, could offer far superior products which were better adapted to local needs and certainly more elegant than anything usually produced in the manorial worksheds of Europe. The burgesses, however, had the advantage of being able to produce goods according to European tastes and create fashions more easily acceptable to the new settlers. They also enjoyed the fact that the new immigrants preferred their own kin; but this advantage quickly disappeared—as it always does—in the face of the competitive prices of local talent.

It was these strata of immigrants which made up the new society's middle class of craftsmen and merchants, occupations which were seldom distinct. They filled the demand for tailors, shoemakers, goldsmiths, carpenters, smiths, millers, cooks, bakers, confectioners, and candle-makers. In the ports and anchorage places, the new profession of catering, to assure ships provisions for the three-week voyage to Europe, developed. And other new occupations appeared, like the muleteers and camel-drivers; porters of water; spice, incense and perfume vendors; and, naturally, guides, suppliers of holy relics, and publicans. The latter were notorious throughout Christendom.

Pilgrim and immigrant alike constantly complained of being cheated. Some taverns which served as hostelries in the ports and in centres of pilgrimage were often also bawdy houses. It was here that prostitution and dice games flourished to the outrage of those who were bent on penitence and spirituality.

On another plane, the burgesses filled the ranks of the kingdom's lower officialdom, whether in the city or in the lordship's rural administration. Some acquired enough Arabic to serve as dragomans; others, more literate, filled the office of scribes or petition-writers. We can visualise them squatting near the lord's or bishop's dwellings, with their portable tables, ink-pots, quills and strips of parchment, penning (for remuneration) the humble requests of the simple people. Then there were the administrative tasks proper. Both lordly and ecclesiastical institutions needed stewards to run their estates and their revenues, assure provisions for their households and to supervise their servants. At the gates of cities and entrances to the ports, a swarm of scribes, customs and tax collectors performed these duties in the din of haggling and recriminations.

The Crusader burgesses in the triple bazaars of Jerusalem or the *souks* of Antioch, Tripoli and Acre rented their nooks, stalls and benches from the city lord or an ecclesiastical institution. Here they sold their wares, the agricultural yield of their gardens and orchards or products purchased in the countryside to be resold to the city dwellers. Another typical burgess occupation was that of the money-changer. It was often connected with lending money and was the nearest the Frankish burgess ever came to the realm of high finance. Serious activities in high finance were beyond his reach because historical circumstances during the earliest period of conquest made the field a *de facto* monopoly of the Italian (later also Provençal and Catalan) merchants.

Beginning with the First Crusade, but especially during the following first decade of the kingdom, when the crusaders were fighting the Moslem powers from Cilicia to the Red Sea, the fleets of Venice, Pisa and Genoa—the great European emporia—were instrumental in the conquest of the maritime cities of Syria, Lebanon and the Holy Land. The Italians, whose participation in the Crusades was motivated by a mixture of religious ideals and material calculations, asked to be remunerated for their services. The pious declaration that they sailed to the East to fight the Holy Wars and in the service of Christianity did not prevent them from assuring themselves a share in the conquest—not only the immediate, tangible booty (which was not negligible), but more permanent gains in the form of streets or quarters in the cities, exemptions from tax and customs and privileges of immunity and autonomy in ruling their nationals and managing their possessions. Thus every major Frankish city in the Levant—and with the exception of Jerusalem, all of them were maritime cities—had at least one, but usually several streets or quarters which belonged to the various Italian communes. The Italians were the third distinctive class among the Franks (along with the nobles and burgesses), and their presence added to the variety of nations and to the Babel of languages.

The Italian settlements were not created immediately after the conquest. Few merchants settled during the early years of the kingdom, but the administrative nucleus sent from the Italian metropolis to safeguard its rights and privileges was a permanent fixture even then. It represented a foothold, but its future depended on the ability to use possessions in Antioch, Tyre or Acre as a basis for business. Realities never matched their expectations because even the great Crusader cities were not centres of production, or at least could not compare with Constantinople or Alexandria. Neither were they outlets for a rich hinterland. Consequently, European commerce could not forgo direct contacts with such Moslem or Byzantine centres. Nonetheless, the privileged position of the communes in the Crusader establishments counter-balances the obvious economic handicaps. For example, the customs exemptions enjoyed by the communes made the Crusader centres an ideal depot for merchandise imported from the Moslem hinterland—like medieval free ports on the Mediterranean. With the growing volume of trade and more daring penetration of the Moslem hinterland, Italian merchants who had used the Crusader ports only as way-stations began to prolong their stay in the Levant, and fairly sizeable Italian-merchant settlements were founded in all the major ports of the Crusader establishments in the East.

The communes, as such settlements were called, were a strange world—sort of colonies within colonies. A minority surrounded by a French-speaking majority, the Italians used and abused the "foreign language," as did every one else, in their contacts with their fellow Franks. But inside their quarters, in the precincts of the "*fondaco*," one was transported to beloved Italy. Once Byzantine or Moslem merchandise was acquired, business was often transacted between the Italian merchants themselves. Here each spoke his peculiar dialect of Venetian, Tuscan or Ligurian. Notaries wrote Latin, or sometimes thirteenth-century French, but thought in Italian. The Italians had all the conditions to preserve their identity. The commune overlord was not only of the quarter but also proprietor of all real estate within it. Large and often resplendent buildings—once the lodgings of a Moslem, Byzantine or Turkish governor or official—or houses which belonged to the Moslem merchant aristocracy of the city became *palazzi* in the Italian inventories and were taken over by the commune's administration. Buildings too large to serve any practical needs were divided into *camerae* (rooms rented for limited periods) and *magazini* (rooms to store merchandise). They often stood empty for the greater part of the year, but filled to overflowing when a *stola* (fleet of ships) arrived from Europe at around Easter time.

The main street or square of the quarter became the market-place, and the houses which surrounded it usually contained shops, stalls and magazines where the oriental merchandise waiting to be exported to Europe or imported European merchandise waiting for buyers were deposited. The merchants lodged in the upper floors. Taverns and hostelries catering to the Italian palate were to be found everywhere. In addition, *banci* (benches) were set up by money-changers and vendors of perishable foodstuffs. Besides shops and magazines, a market-place and usually a vaulted bazaar, each quarter had its bakeries, ovens and baths. Some Italian banking families even saw fit to open subsidiaries in the Crusader cities, and big business, still being family business, sent members of the trading class to Palestine.

The center of the quarter was the *palazzo* of the commune, which housed its administration. It housed the *vicomte* or consul, the governor sent from the mother-city. Supported by a council, he represented the commune's interest vis-à-vis the city's lord, ruler or king and was responsible for the management of the commune's possessions and privileges in the city. The notaries attached to him would draft agreements between merchants and marriage contracts; the jurors would sit in judgement or arbitration in cases regarding their own nationals, but in some cases they would also judge other inhabitants of the quarter. Crimes punishable by death, such as homicide or rape, were sometimes excepted from this system, and the guardians of peace— beadles or sergeants—would arrest the accused and turn him over to the seigniorial authorities. There was always some bickering in such cases as the Italians were naturally reluctant to hand over one of their own to external jurisdiction. The law of the communal courts was not that of the kingdom but that of the Italian mother-city. The proceedings were held in the merchants' native language, the procedure was familiar from homeland and the judgement was made by their peers. The head of the commune had his contingent of scribes and sergeants. The first were responsible for the inventory of the commune's property and for collecting rents, which were duly registered in "*quaterna*" (account books) and guarded in the community chest. The town crier and sergeants announced the ordinances of the commune's council and supervised their execution. Time and again ordinances prohibiting prostitution and gambling were issued, but in such communities of travelling salesmen, they were of doubtful effect. . . .

The degree to which the settlers of Italian origin mixed with the local Franks is rather difficult to ascertain. We know of Italians who looked for brides in Europe, but marriages with the local Frankish population were common. A Frankish family may well have seen it as advantageous to marry off their daughters to the Italian and Provençal merchants. Such a union was not considered a *mésalliance,* and it normally meant a step up on the social and economic ladder. The story of the wealthy merchant from Pisa who married a member of the Frankish aristocracy in Tripoli must have made the rounds of oriental *souks.* To receive the permission to marry the young lady, the merchant paid to the maiden's noble warden her weight in gold! A hundred and twenty or so pounds of pure gold could weigh down many barriers.

Some other families entered Frankish life not through marriage but through feudal positions. A Genoese family like the Embriaci, to whom the commune rented its property in the city of Gebal, severed its links with the mother-city and became part and parcel of the Frankish aristocracy. That they continued to favour their compatriots in the city, however, was to be expected. On a lower level, Italian families entered the Frankish *bourgeoisie* through marriage, which we know from documentation of the legal bickering over whether the marriage contract should follow local or Italian custom. Whatever the degree of assimilation through marriage, the Italians remained a power unto themselves, maintaining the customs, language and institution of the Rialto or Porto Vecchio in the Holy Land.

Thirteenth-century scholars studying the stars with an astrolabe. Figure on the left is reading out of an Arabic manuscript. Illustration from the Psalter of St. Louis and Blanche of Castille.

(SOURCE: Bibliothèque Nationale, Paris)

III

THE PEAK OF MEDIEVAL CIVILIZATION

12th–13th Centuries

The eleventh century was a turning point in the history of Europe. For the first time in more than a millennium, Europe was not attacked by outside invaders, and its social and political life was not disrupted by massive migrations. European monarchs now began the long process of consolidating their power, and the church succeeded in establishing its independence from secular control. In the same period, the various elements of medieval society reached a mature stage of development, marked by stability and increasing institutional consistency throughout Europe. This century of change was followed by one of cultural rebirth, the so-called twelfth-century renaissance. Scholastic philosophy, Gothic architecture, the revival of jurisprudence and medical studies—all are products of twelfth-century society and were carried over into the thirteenth century. Medieval civilization flowered in this period. The selections that follow reveal the character of the institutions and social conditions that underlay this flowering.

The selection by Sidney Painter recounts the youth of one of the most famous knights in the period. The knightly class dominated the noble society, which historians have traditionally called "feudal" because of the land tenure on which it was based. In this society, aristocrats held landed estates, called fiefs (*feudum* or *feodum* in Latin), in return for services. Fief-holders also owed loyalty to the lord from whom they held their estates. But by the twelfth century, the nobility had been expanded by the addition of armed retainers— trained soldiers who depended for their livelihoods on the great landowners. These soldiers were the knights. Not all knights joined the noble class, but they exerted a powerful influence on it. Whatever differences—and they could be vast—existed between the great baron and the average knight, both belonged to the order of knighthood, and they shared a common code of behavior and a common system of values. The first and second selections address knighthood and the nobility. William Marshall, the subject of Painter's piece, pursued his successful career in the second half of the twelfth century, the golden age of the knight. The means by which nobles defined and perpetuated themselves through marriage and the impact that changes in nobles' family strategies had upon their sons and daughters are the subject of investigation by Constance Brittain Bouchard.

During the twelfth and thirteenth centuries, people were increasingly attracted to depictions of Christ as a child. God's willingness to become not simply human, but a powerless baby for the sake of human beings spoke to the virtues of humility and of a God who made Himself accessible to all people. The image of the infant Jesus and the increasing veneration of the Virgin Mary in these centuries were part of a new emphasis on love that imbued both the spiritual and secular culture of Europe during the High Middle Ages. Did this new sentimentality have a parallel in the love that parents expressed for their children? It is one thing to idealize the infant Jesus as the incarnation of divine love and quite another thing to raise one's own child. The church taught that, unlike the infant Jesus, real-life babies were born tainted with original sin. Medieval parents also had more than sentimental reasons for raising a family. Among the nobility and wealthy city dwellers, children were crucial to dynastic strategies and to the devolution of the patrimony. They were an important source of labor and income to peasants and artisans, and could make the difference between poverty and some measure of comfort in their parents' old age. The selection by Shulamith Shahar describes the first moments when children joined the world of their parents and their early upbringing during those most dangerous years, from birth to five, when half would succumb to disease or accident.

In the fourth selection, C. H. Lawrence describes life in the monastery. Beginning in the tenth century with the foundation of Cluny and other reform monasteries, reformers had tried to maintain the independence of religious foundations against the influence of secular powers and to establish the observance of the Benedictine Rule. These reforms were extremely popular and spread throughout western and central Europe. The Benedictine Rule ordered the monk's day into periods of prayer, reading of religious works, and work. In most cases, the manual labor that Saint Benedict had prescribed was transmuted into intellectual work, such as copying manuscripts. The monks in these abbeys were individually poor in that they did not possess any private property. Monasteries grew rich on pious donations, however, and the monks began to enjoy luxuries that Benedict had not envisioned. The wealth and easy life of the monasteries inspired another wave of reforms at the end of the eleventh century, when the Cistercian and Carthusian orders were founded. The Cistercians and Carthusians practiced a rigorous asceticism and required that monks perform manual labor. In the thirteenth century, two other orders were founded: the Franciscans and Dominicans. The Franciscan and Dominican friars did not live out their lives behind cloister walls. As mendicants, they went about preaching and lived from day-to-day on the charity of others. Unlike the friars, Franciscan and Dominican nuns lived in convents, going out into the local community to teach and care for the sick.

The same religious trends that encouraged people to contemplate Jesus as an approachable child led them to desire a more personal and immediate contact with Jesus and the saints. People explored a more personal connection with the holy, one that was not necessarily mediated by the church. Pilgrimage was one such connection. The pilgrim could walk where Jesus had walked, visit the sites of famous miracles, or perhaps gaze upon a saint's relics. People visited pilgrimage sites for a number of reasons. Some sought inspiration. Some sought healing for themselves or a loved one. Some sought spiritual healing in the forgiveness of sins. Some had pilgrimage imposed upon them as part of a spiritual or secular sentence (cities sometimes ordered miscreants on long pilgrimages as a punishment). These travelers created a market for an extensive network of inns and for shipowners who ran tours to the Holy Land. They also created a literature about travel. By the middle of the twelfth century, there was a guidebook to Rome and its wonders, including the Colosseum, which was described as if it were the first domed arena. There were also travel accounts which served as manuals for the prospective pilgrim. From this literature, Jonathan Sumption draws an account of medieval land and sea travel.

BIBLIOGRAPHY

For the nobility, see Georges Duby, *The Three Orders: Feudal Society Imagined,* trans. Arthur Goldhammer (Chicago, 1980); and the essays in Thomas Bisson, ed., *Cultures of Power: Lordship, Status, and Process in Twelfth-Century Europe* (Philadelphia, 1995). For an introduction to the institutions of feudalism, see F. L. Ganshof, *Feudalism* (New York, 1961). For recent reconsiderations of feudalism, see Jean-Pierre Poly and Eric Bournazel, *The Feudal Transformation, 900–1200,* trans. by Caroline Higgitt (New York, 1991); and Susan Reynolds, *Fiefs and Vassals: The Medieval Evidence Reinterpreted* (Oxford, 1994). Richard Barber's *The Knight and Chivalry* (New York, 1974); George Duby's *The Chivalrous Society,* trans. Cynthia Postan (London, 1977); and Maurice Keen *Chivalry* (New Haven, CT, 1984) provide good surveys of the cultural milieu of the knights. Chivalry is explored by Stephen C. Jaeger in *The Origins of Courtliness: Civilizing Trends and the Formation of Courtly Ideals, 939–1210* (Philadelphia, 1994). For noble women, see Margaret Labarge, *A Small Sound of the Trumpet: Women in Medieval Life* (Boston, 1986); Penny Gold, *The Lady and the Virgin: Image, Attitude, and Experience in Twelfth-Century France* (Chicago, 1985); and the selections in Mary Erler and Maryanne Kowaleski, eds., *Women and Power in the Middle Ages* (Athens, Georgia, 1988).

See the bibliography for Part 2 for works on medieval marriage. See also Christopher Brooke's *The Medieval Idea of Marriage* (Oxford, 1989), and two books by Georges Duby, *Love and Marriage in the Middle Ages,* trans. by J. Dunnett (Chicago, 1994) and *Medieval Marriage: Two Models from Twelfth-Century France,* trans. by E. Forster (Baltimore, 1978). Philippe Ariès' controversial thesis in *Centuries of Childhood: A Social History of Family Life,* trans. by Robert Baldick (New York, 1962) has spurred much scholarship on the subject. Child mortality is treated in Hans-Werner Goetz's *Life in the Middle Ages: from the Seventh to the Thirteenth Century,* trans. by Albert Wimmer, ed. by Steven Rowan (Notre Dame and London, 1993; f.p. in German 1986). Barbara Hanawalt explores children's experiences in the city in *Growing Up in Medieval London* (Oxford, 1993), which provides a selection for Part 4. Toys, games, and schoolboy scribblings are described in Nicholas Orme "The Culture of Children in Medieval England," *Past and Present* 148 (1995):48–88.

The monastic outlook is evoked by Jean Leclerq in *The Love of Learning and the Desire for God: A Study of Monastic Culture,* trans. by Catherine Misrahi (New York, 1982, 1967). The popularity of the reform monastery of Cluny, as measured by the patronage it received from the nobility in its early years, is discussed by Barbara Rosenwein in *Rhinocerous Bound: Cluny in the Tenth Century* (Philadelphia, 1982). For a thorough treatment of English monasticism, see David Knowles, *The Monastic Order in England* (Cambridge, England, 1949); and Colin Platt, *The Abbeys and Priories of Medieval England* (New York, 1984). For women's monasticism, see Eileen Power's *Medieval English Nunneries, c. 1275–1535* (Cambridge, England, 1922), and Penelope Johnson's excellent study, *Equal in Monastic Profession: Religious Women in Medieval France* (Chicago and London, 1991). Not all those who professed monastic vows remained happy with their decision, and

Donald F. Logan investigates those who abandoned the religious life in *Runaway Religious in England, c. 1240–1540* (Cambridge, England, 1996).

For pilgrimage and travel in the Middle Ages, see E. L. Guilford, *Travel and Travellers in the Middle Ages* (New York, 1924); A. Kendall, *Medieval Pilgrims* (London, 1970); and Robert S. Lopez, "The Evolution of Land Transport in the Middle Ages," *Past and Present,* 19 (1956):17–29. Irving Agus, in *Urban Civilization in Pre-Crusade Europe* (New York, 1965), includes an entire section on travel. His material focuses on the activities of the Jews in the period from the ninth to the eleventh centuries, when political conditions made travel difficult and dangerous. For contemporary accounts of Jewish pilgrims and travellers, see Elken Adler, *Jewish Travellers in the Middle Ages* (New York, 1987).

The Training of a Knight

SIDNEY PAINTER

The knight in shining armor is mostly a figment created by medieval romance writers, refurbished and given new impetus by nineteenth-century authors. The real knight lived a life not so far removed in its material aspects from that of prosperous contemporary peasants. He was almost constantly on the move, living the hard life of a traveler and engaging in tournaments or real campaigns. The rules governing his life, so embellished by the romance poets, were largely responses to the demands of his existence and served to make its hardships bearable. Most of the rules evolved out of the conditions of feudal warfare; they regulated the treatment of prisoners taken in combat and the relations between the ranks in the feudal army. In the constant round of fighting, one week's victor might be next week's victim, and the economics of knightly life dictated a refined treatment of captured knights. A dead knight was not worth very much, but a live one might ransom himself at a considerable price. If a knight was one of the majority in his class who did not possess any landed estate and therefore had no stable income, collecting ransoms constituted a livelihood. Other aspects of the chivalric code, as the rules were called, were aimed at preserving the social and political structure of feudalism, although these too were related to military activities. The feudal system depended on the loyalty of vassals to their liege lords, and this loyalty was the cohesive element of the feudal army. Loyalty was won and kept by open-handedness, so generosity too was a knightly virtue.

It is important to study the training of a knight in order to understand the character of the class. In this selection, we observe the early training of William Marshal, a man who achieved the ideal of knighthood according to the writings of his time. He was born about 1146 in England, the fourth son of a petty baron, John, who was marshal for King Henry I. The marshal was originally in charge of the royal stables and the provisioning of the household, but by

From: Sidney Painter, *William Marshal* (Baltimore: The Johns Hopkins University Press, 1933), pp. 13–29.

John's day these duties had been delegated to others, and the marshal was a hereditary post in the king's entourage. William, as a younger son, had little chance of inheriting his father's position, but he was trained as a knight anyway, since he could make his way in the world as a feudal soldier. As it turned out, his talent won him one of the premier places in the feudal hierarchy of England.

There were several stages in the life of a successful knight. In his early youth, he was taught to ride and perhaps given the rudiments of his education in chivalry. His real training began around the age of thirteen, when he was sent to a relative's or lord's household as a squire. There he learned to handle a knight's weapons and to be part of a feudal army. He also learned the details of the life style he was expected to adopt. After the squire became a knight, he began an often long period of itinerancy, traveling from tournament to tournament and joining in real campaigns when the opportunity arose. Sometimes knights errant, as such men were called, joined the entourage of great lords or kings and became part of their "team" in the tournaments. William became a member of Prince Henry of England's (son of Henry II) entourage and quickly rose to a preeminent position within it. In William's time, the tournaments were not the controlled combats of the later Middle Ages so often described in popular literature. They were virtual free-for-alls in which knights teamed up and fought as armies. One of these mêlées is described in this selection.

For the knight who did not inherit a position within the feudal hierarchy, the period of errancy often lasted until he was past forty. At this point, if he was lucky, he would marry into the hierarchy. William achieved this goal in 1190 when Richard I of England (son and successor of Henry II) permitted him to marry the heiress of the great earldom of Pembroke. The marriage made William one of the first lords of England, and when Richard's successor, John, died in 1216, William became one of the regents of the realm. He himself died in 1219.

William's career demonstrates that there was mobility within the feudal ranks during the twelfth century. He was clearly the outstanding example of the possibilities that existed, but many others had similar if not so illustrious careers. In the later Middle Ages, the possibility of rising in the ranks became increasingly restricted as the feudal elite found its position challenged by the kings on one side and by the burghers on the other. In its heyday, the knightly class exhibited vitality and adaptability. Once it was forced to take a defensive stance, however, the knightly class became rigid and regressive in its social, economic, and political attitudes.

William Marshal was the fourth son of John fitz Gilbert and the second of those born to the castellan of Marlborough by the sister of Earl Patrick of

Salisbury. Our knowledge of William's youth is confined to a few brief glimpses through the fog of time—scenes which made so vivid an impression on his mind that he could recount them years later to his squire and biographer, John d'Erley. The earliest of these recollections concerned a comparatively unimportant incident in the contest between Stephen and Matilda.* In the year 1152 King Stephen at the head of a strong force suddenly swooped down on John Marshal's castle of Newbury at a time when it was inadequately garrisoned and poorly stocked with provisions. The constable, a man both brave and loyal, indignantly refused the King's demand for the immediate surrender of the fortress. When the garrison successfully repulsed an attempt to take the place by storm, Stephen prepared for a regular siege and swore that he would not leave until he had captured the castle and hanged its defenders. The constable, realizing that his lack of provisions made an extended resistance impossible, asked for and obtained a day's truce so that he might make known his plight to his lord, John Marshal. This was the customary procedure for a castellan who found himself in a hopeless position. Once granted a truce, he would inform his master that unless he were relieved by a certain day, he would be forced to surrender. If no assistance appeared within the specified time, the commander could surrender the castle without failing in his duty to his lord. The besieging force was usually willing to grant a truce in the hope of obtaining the castle without long, wearisome, and expensive siege operations. When John Marshal learned of the predicament of his garrison of Newbury, he was sadly perplexed. As he could not muster enough men to drive off Stephen's army, his only hope of saving his fortress lay in a resort to strategy. John asked Stephen to extend the truce while he sought aid from the Countess Matilda in whose name he held the castle. The king did not trust his turbulent marshal, but he finally agreed to give the garrison of Newbury a further respite if John would surrender one of his sons as a guarantee that he would observe the terms of the truce. John was to use the days of grace to communicate with Matilda—the hostage would be his pledge that he would not reinforce or provision the castle. Acceding to Stephen's demand, John gave the king his son William as a hostage. Then he promptly sent into Newbury a strong force of knights, serjeants, and archers with a plentiful supply of provisions. Newbury was prepared to withstand a siege—the cunning of John Marshal had saved his castle.

His father's clever stratagem left William in an extremely precarious position. By the customs of the time his life was forfeited by his father's breach of faith. Stephen's entourage urged him to hang William at once, but the king was unwilling to execute the child without giving his father a chance to save him

---

*In 1135, King Henry I died without a legitimate male heir to the throne. Henry had wanted his daughter Matilda to succeed him, but Stephen of Blois, Henry's nephew, seized the throne. Civil war raged in England for two decades between those who supported Matilda's claim to the throne and those who backed Stephen. Eventually, Stephen acknowledged Matilda's son, Henry of Anjou, as his heir.—ed.

by surrendering Newbury. But John Marshal, having four sons and a fruitful wife, considered the youngest of his sons of far less value than a strong castle. He cheerfully told the king's messenger that he cared little if William were hanged, for he had the anvils and hammers with which to forge still better sons. When he received this brutal reply, Stephen ordered his men to lead William to a convenient tree. Fearing that John planned a rescue, the king himself escorted the executioners with a strong force. William, who was only five or six years old, had no idea what this solemn parade portended. When he saw William, earl of Arundel, twirling a most enticing javelin, he asked him for the weapon. This reminder of William's youth and innocence was too much for King Stephen's resolution, and, taking the boy in his arms, he carried him back to the camp. A little later some of the royalists had the ingenious idea of throwing William over the castle walls from a siege engine, but Stephen vetoed that scheme as well. He had decided to spare his young prisoner.

For some two months William was the guest of King Stephen while the royal army lay before Newbury. One day as the king sat in a tent strewn with varicolored flowers William wandered about picking plantains. When the boy had gathered a fair number, he asked the king to play "knights" with him. Each of them would take a "knight" or plantain, and strike it against the one held by the other. The victory would go to the player who with his knight struck off the clump of leaves that represented the head of his opponent's champion. When Stephen readily agreed to play, William gave him a bunch of plantains and asked him to decide who should strike first. The amiable king gave William the first blow with the result that the royal champion lost his head. The boy was vastly pleased with his victory. While Stephen, king of England, was playing at knights with the young son of his rebellious marshal, a servitor whom Lady Sibile had sent to see how her son fared glanced into the tent. As war and enemies meant nothing to William, he loudly welcomed the familiar face. The man, utterly terrified, fled so hastily that the pursuit ordered by the king was fruitless.

The story of William and King Stephen is, no doubt, merely reminiscence recounted years later with the embellishments usual in such tales, but it bears all the ear-marks of veracity. It serves to confirm the statements of the chroniclers as to Stephen's character—that he was a man of gentle nature, far too mild to rule the barons of England. Furthermore the incidents of the tale are essentially probable. It was quite customary to give young children as hostages to guarantee an agreement and equally so to make them suffer for their parents' bad faith. When Eustace de Breteuil, the husband of a natural daughter of Henry I, put out the eyes of the son of one of his vassals, the king allowed the enraged father to mutilate in the same way Eustace's daughter whom Henry held as a hostage for his son-in-law's good behavior. Again in the year 1211 when Maelgwyn ap Rees, prince of South Wales, raided the marches, Robert de Vieuxpont hanged the prince's seven-year-old son who was in his hands as a pledge that Maelgwyn would keep the peace. The fact that Earl William of Arundel is known to have taken part in the siege of Newbury and might well have twirled his javelin before the fascinated William tends to confirm this story still further. Hence one can accept as essentially true this pleasant and very human picture of a dark age and an unfortunate king.

When peace was finally concluded between Stephen and Henry Plantagenet, William was returned to his parents who, according to the *History*, had been very unquiet about him. While John Marshal had probably counted to some extent on Stephen's notorious mildness, he had had plenty of justification for any fears he may have felt for his son's safety. Meanwhile the boy was growing rapidly. Within a few years the Marshal family would be forced to consider his future. If the romances of the time are to be believed, it was customary for a baron of any importance to entrust his sons' education to some friendly lord. John Marshal decided to send William to his cousin, William, lord of Tancarville and hereditary chamberlain of Normandy. The chamberlain was a powerful baron with a great castle on the lower Seine and ninety-four knights to follow his banner. Being himself a well known knight and a frequenter of tourneys, he was well fitted to supervise the military education of his young kinsman and to give him a good start on his chivalric career. When he was about thirteen years old, William started for Tancarville attended by a valet, or companion of gentle birth, and a servant. The fourth son of a minor English baron was setting forth to seek his fortune.

For eight years William served as a squire to the chamberlain of Tancarville. During this time his principal duty was to learn the trade of arms. The squire's body was hardened and his skill in the use of weapons developed by frequent and strenuous military exercises. While the chain mail of the twelfth century was far lighter and less cumbersome than the plate armor of later times, the mere wearing of it required considerable physical strength. To be able, as every squire must, to leap fully armed into the saddle without touching the stirrup, was a feat which must have required long and rigorous training. The effective use of the weapons of a knight—the spear, sword, and shield—was a highly intricate science which a squire was forced to master if he wished to excel in his chosen profession. In addition a knight should know how to care for his equipment. A squire spent long hours tending his master's horses and cleaning, polishing, and testing his arms and armor. William's success in battle and tourney will show how thoroughly he mastered these fundamentals of his profession. But while it was essential that a knight be brave and skillful in the use of his weapons, other quite different qualities were also expected of him. God and Woman, the church and the troubadour cult of Courtly Love, were beginning to soften and polish the manners of the feudal aristocracy. For a long time the church had demanded that a knight be pious, now ladies were insisting that he be courteous. If a squire hoped to be acceptable to such devotees of the new movement as Eleanor of Aquitaine and her daughter, Marie of Champagne, he must learn some more gentle art than that of smiting mighty blows. If he could not write songs, he could at least learn to sing them. Finally the professional creators and distributors of the literature which embodied these new ideas, the trouvères and the jongleurs, were formulating another knightly virtue—generosity. Their existence depended on the liberality of their patrons, and they did not fail to extol the generous and heap scorn on the penurious. Every time the squire confessed to a priest, he was instructed in the church's conception of the perfect knight. As he sat in the great hall of the castle while some trouvère or jongleur told of Tristan and Iseult or of Lancelot and Guenevere, he was imbued with the doctrines of romantic chivalry. The squire himself might be expected to while away the leisure hours of his lady and her damsels with one of the gentle songs of the troubadours. Possibly William owed his love for singing which remained with him to his death to the advanced taste of the lady of Tancarville.

By the spring of 1167 William was approaching his twenty-first year. As a squire he seems to have given little promise of future greatness. He gained a reputation for drinking, eating, and sleeping, but for little else. His companions, who were jealous of the favor shown him by the chamberlain, made fun of his appetite, but he was so gentle and debonnaire that he always kept silent and pretended not to hear the remarks. A hearty, healthy, good natured, and rather stupid youth was young William. The author of the *History* furnishes a personal description which probably belongs to this period of William's life. "His body was so well formed that if it had been fashioned by a sculptor, it would not have had such beautiful limbs. I saw them and remember them well. He had very beautiful feet and hands, but all these were minor details in the ensemble of his body. If anyone looked at him carefully, he seemed so well and straightly made that if one judged honestly, one would be forced to say that he had the best formed body in the world. He had brown hair. His face even more than his body resembled that of a man of high enough rank to be the Emperor of Rome. He had as long legs and as good a stature as a gentleman could. Whoever fashioned him was master." Is this a purely conventional portrait or a true one of William Marshal as he reached man's estate?

In a military society, be it that of the early Germans or the feudal aristocracy, the youth comes of age when he is accepted as a full-fledged warrior. Every squire burned to end his apprenticeship by receiving the insignia of knighthood. The squire followed his master to battles and tournaments, cared for his horse and armor, nursed him if he were wounded, and often guarded his prisoners, but he himself could not take an active part in the combat. Being simply an attendant, the squire had no opportunity to win renown. As eight years was, at least according to the testimony of contemporary romances, a rather long time to remain a squire, William must have been extremely impatient for the day when he would be admitted into the chivalric order. He longed for the time when the approach of a promising war or a great tourney would move the chamberlain to dub him a knight and give him a chance to show his worth.

The occasion for which William had hoped came in the summer of 1167. King Henry II was at war with his suzerain Louis VII of France. While Louis himself occupied Henry's attention by ravaging the Norman Vexin, the French king's allies, the counts of Flanders, Boulogne, and Ponthieu, invaded the county of Eu. Count John of Eu, unable to hold his own against the invaders, was forced to retire to Neufchatel-en-Bray, then called Drincourt. There he encountered a force of knights which Henry had sent to his assistance under the command of the constable of Normandy and the lord of Tancarville. The chamberlain decided that this was an auspicious time for knighting William. A goodly array of Norman barons was at hand to lend dignity to the occasion, and the future seemed to promise an opportunity for the young knight to prove his valor. William's induction into the order of chivalry was attended by little of the ceremony usually associated with the dubbing of a knight. Dressed in a new mantle, the young man stood before the chamberlain, who girt him with a sword, the principal emblem of knighthood, and gave him the ceremonial blow.

William had not long to wait for an opportunity to prove himself worthy of his new dignity. As Drincourt lay on the northern bank of the river Bethune at the southern extremity of the county of Eu, it was directly in the path of the army which had been ravaging that district. Count John of Eu and the constable of Normandy had no desire to await the advance of the enemy. On the morning following William's knighting they left Drincourt by the road which led south toward Rouen. Before they had gone very far, they were overtaken by a messenger with the news that the counts of Flanders, Boulogne, and Ponthieu, and the lord of St. Valery were marching on Drincourt at the head of a strong force of knights and serjeants. As the two barons halted their party to consider what they should do, they saw the chamberlain followed by twenty-eight knights of his household riding toward them from the direction of Drincourt. As soon as he was within speaking distance, the chamberlain addressed the constable, "Sire, it will be a great disgrace if we permit them to burn this town." "You speak truly, chamberlain," replied the constable, "and since it is your idea, do you go to its defence." When they saw that they could hope for no assistance from either the count of Eu or the constable, the chamberlain and his knights rode back toward Drincourt. Between them and the town ran the river Bethune. When they reached the bridge which spanned this stream, they found it occupied by a party of knights under the command of William de Mandeville, earl of Essex, who, lacking sufficient men to dispute the enemy's entrance into the town, had retired to hold the passage of the Bethune. The chamberlain hurried to join Earl William, and William Marshal, anxious to show his mettle, spurred forward at his leader's side. The chamberlain turned to the enthusiastic novice, "William, drop back; be not so impatient; let these knights pass." William, who considered himself most decidedly a knight, fell back, abashed. He let three others go ahead of him and then dashed forward again until he was in the front rank.

The combined forces of the chamberlain and the earl of Essex rode into Drincourt to meet the enemy who were entering the town from the northeast. The two parties met at full gallop with a thunderous shock. William's lance was broken, but drawing his sword, he rushed into the midst of the enemy. So fiercely did the Normans fight that they drove the French out of the town as

far as the bridge over the moat on the road to Eu. There the enemy was reinforced, and the Normans were pressed back through Drincourt to the bridge
over the Bethune. Once more the Normans charged, and once more they drove
the French before them. Just as their victory seemed certain, Count Matthew
of Boulogne came up with a fresh division. Four times the enemy beat their
way into the town, and each time the Normans drove them out again. Once
as William turned back from a charge, a Flemish serjeant caught him by the
shoulder with an iron hook. Although he was dragged from his horse in the
midst of hostile foot-soldiers, he managed to disengage the hook and cut his
way out, but his horse was killed. Meanwhile the good people of Drincourt
had been watching from their windows the fierce battle being waged up and
down the streets of the town. Hastily arming themselves, the burghers rushed
to the aid of the Norman knights, and the enemy was completely routed.

That night the lord of Tancarville held a great feast to celebrate the victory. The burghers of Drincourt were loud in their praises of the chamberlain
and his knights. While the constable and the count of Eu had deserted the
town, the chamberlain and his household had saved it from burning and pillage. As the revelers discussed the incidents of the battle, someone remarked
that William had fought to save the town rather than to take prisoners who
could pay him rich ransoms. With this in mind the earl of Essex addressed the
young knight—"Marshal, give me a gift, a crupper or an old horse collar."
"But I have never possessed one in all my life." "Marshal, what are you saying? Assuredly you had forty or sixty today." The hardened warrior was gently reminding the novice that war was a business as well as a path to fame.

The war was soon brought to an end by a truce between King Henry and
Louis of France. As their services were no longer needed, the chamberlain and
his entourage returned to Tancarville. Since no true knight would willingly rest
peacefully in a castle, the lord of Tancarville gave his followers leave to seek
adventure where they pleased. William now found himself in a most embar-
rassing position, for he had lost his war horse at Drincourt, and the cost of a
new one was far beyond his resources. While he still had his palfrey, this light
animal could not be expected to carry him in full armor through the shocks of
a battle or tourney. The chamberlain, who normally would have seen to it that
William as a member of his household was properly equipped, felt that the
young man should be taught to take advantage of his opportunities to capture
horses in battle and hence showed little sympathy for his predicament: By selling the rich mantle which he had worn when he was dubbed a knight, William
obtained twenty-two sous Angevin with which he purchased a baggage horse
to carry his armor, but while this arrangement allowed him to travel in comfort, it would not enable him to take part in a tourney. One day word came to
Tancarville that a great tournament was to be held near Le Mans in which the
knights of Anjou, Maine, Poitou, and Brittany would oppose those of France,
England, and Normandy. The chamberlain and his court received the news
with joy and prepared to take part in the sport, but William, who could not
go without a horse, was very sorrowful. The chamberlain, however, decided

that his young cousin had had enough of a lesson in knightly economy and promised to furnish him with a mount. After a night spent in making ready their arms and armor, the knights gathered in the castle court while their lord distributed the war horses. William received a splendid one, strong and fast. He never forgot the lesson taught him by the chamberlain and William de Mandeville. Never again did he neglect to capture good horses when he had the opportunity.

On the appointed day a fair sized company assembled to take part in the tournament. King William of Scotland was present with a numerous suite while the chamberlain himself took the field at the head of forty knights. This tourney was not to be one of those mild affairs in which everything was arranged beforehand even to the price of the ransoms, but a contest in which the vanquished would lose all they possessed. After the knights had armed in the refuges provided at each end of the field, the two parties advanced toward one another in serried, orderly ranks. William wasted no time in getting about the business of the day. Attacking Philip de Valognes, a knight of King William's household, he seized his horse by the rein and forced him out of the mêlée. Then after taking Philip's pledge that he would pay his ransom, William returned to the combat and captured two more knights. By his success in this tourney William not only demonstrated his prowess, but rehabilitated his finances as well. Each of the captured knights was forced to surrender all his equipment. William gained war horses, palfreys, arms, and armor for his own use, roncins for his servants, and sumpter horses for his baggage. His first tournament had been highly profitable.

This success sharpened William's appetite for knightly sports. When word came to Tancarville of another tourney to be held in Maine, he asked the chamberlain, who had decided to stay at home, to allow him to attend. He arrived at the appointed place just as the last of the contestants were arming in their refuges, and leaping from his palfrey hastened to put on his armor and mount his charger. In the first onslaught the young knight handled his lance so skillfully that he was able to unhorse one of his opponents, but before he could complete the capture of the fallen knight he was attacked by five others. Although by drawing his sword and smiting lusty blows on every side William managed to beat off his enemies, he received a stroke on his helmet which turned it around on his head so that he could no longer breathe through the holes provided for that purpose. While he was standing in the refuge repairing this damage, two well known knights rode past, Bon Abbé le Rouge and John de Subligni. "Sir John," said the first, "who is that knight who is so capable with his weapons?" "That is William Marshal," replied the other. "There is no man more true. The device on his shield shows that he hails from Tancarville." "Surely," said Bon Abbé, "the band which he leads should be the gainer in valor and hardiness." Much pleased by these words of praise, William put on his helmet again and reentered the contest. So well did he bear himself that he was awarded the prize of the tourney—a splendid war horse from Lombardy.

William now felt that he was well started on his chivalric career. He had achieved the dignity of knighthood and had shown his prowess in the combat at Drincourt and in two tournaments. It was high time that he visited England to parade his accomplishments before his admiring family. John fitz Gilbert had died in 1165 while William was still a squire at Tancarville. Of his two sons by his first wife the elder had outlived him but a year, the younger had predeceased him. Hence John, the eldest son by Sibile of Salisbury, had inherited the family lands and the office of marshal. When William sought the chamberlain's permission to go to England, the lord of Tancarville feared that his young cousin, being the heir presumptive to the family lands, might be tempted to settle down at home. He gave him leave to go, but urged him to return as soon as possible. While England was a good enough country for a man of mean spirit who had no desire to seek adventure, those who loved the life of a knight-errant and the excitement of the tourney should stay in Normandy and Brittany where such pastimes were appreciated. If one were to acquire the prizes of battle, one must live in a land of tourneys. England seemed to the chamberlain to be an orderly, dull, spiritless country. Carried across the channel by a fair wind, William traversed Sussex and Hampshire on his way to his Wiltshire home. At Salisbury he found his uncle, Earl Patrick, who received him joyfully as a gallant young knight and his own sister's son.

William's vacation in England was destined to be a short one. In December 1167 Earl Patrick was summoned to the continent to aid the king in suppressing a revolt of the nobles of Poitou led by the counts of La Marche and Angoulême and the house of Lusignan. Being in all probability heartily tired of his quiet life in England, William was only too willing to follow his uncle to Poitou. King Henry captured the castle of Lusignan, garrisoned it, and then turned north to keep an appointment with Louis VII in the Norman marches near Mantes. His wife, Eleanor, who was by right of her birth duchess of Aquitaine and countess of Poitou, stayed at Lusignan with Earl Patrick. Their position was far from comfortable. Of all the restless nobility of Poitou none were more turbulent than the five de Lusignan brothers, and none played so great a part in the history of their day. Two of the brothers, Hugh and Ralph, became respectively counts of La Marche and Eu, while Guy and Aimery, expelled from Poitou for their perpetual rebellions, both attained the throne of Jerusalem. Such a family was unlikely to stand by quietly while an enemy held their ancestral castle, even if that enemy was their liege lord. One day near Eastertide as the queen and Earl Patrick were riding outside the castle, they were suddenly confronted by a strong force under the command of Geoffrey and Guy de Lusignan. Although Patrick and his men were unarmed, the earl was unwilling to flee. Sending Eleanor to shelter in the castle, he called for his war horse and ordered his followers to prepare for battle. Unfortunately the de Lusignans were not sufficiently chivalrous to wait while their foes armed. Just as Earl Patrick was mounting his charger, a Poitevin knight killed him with a single blow at his unprotected back. Meanwhile William had donned his hauberk, but had not had time to put on his helmet. When he saw his uncle fall, he jumped on his horse and charged the enemy, sword in hand. The first man he met was cut down at a single stroke, but before he could satisfy his thirst for vengeance on the slayers of his uncle, a well directed thrust killed his horse. When he had freed himself from the saddle, William placed his back against a hedge to fight it out on foot as the loss of his horse made flight impossible. For some time he managed to hold his own by cutting down the chargers of his opponents, but at last a knight crossed the hedge, came up behind, and leaning over the barrier, thrust his sword into the young man's thigh. Disabled, William was easily made prisoner.

His captors mounted him on a mare and set off. No one paid any attention to William's wound, for according to the *History,* they wanted him to suffer as much as possible so that he might be the more anxious to ransom himself. William took the cords which bound his braies and tied up his wound as best he could. Dreading the king's vengeance, the rebel band kept to the wooded country and made its halts in secluded spots. Henry Plantagenet was not a monarch who would permit the slayers of his lieutenant to go unpunished. One night while they were resting at the castle of one of their partisans, a lady noticed the wounded prisoner. She cut the center out of a loaf of bread, filled the hole with flaxen bandages, and sent the loaf to William. Her kindness enabled him to dress his wound properly. Another evening William's captors amused themselves by casting a great stone. William joined in the game and defeated all the others, but the exertion reopened his wound, and as he was forced to ride night and day with little rest, he grew better very slowly. Finally Queen Eleanor came to his aid. She gave hostages to his captors to guarantee that his ransom would be paid, and he was delivered to her. To recompense him for his sufferings, she gave him money, horses, arms, and rich vestments.

The Poitevin campaign had a far-reaching effect on William's life. In it lay the origins of his intense hatred for the house of Lusignan and his close personal relationship with the Plantagenet family. To understand his bitter feud with the Lusignans one must realize that the killing of Earl Patrick, which seems to us a normal act of war, was in William's sight a dastardly crime. The author of the *History* calls the earl's slayer felon and assassin. Not only did he strike down an unarmed man, an unknightly act in itself, but he slew the lieutenant of his feudal suzerain. The first of these offenses probably did not trouble William greatly. Some years later when Richard Plantagenet was in rebellion against his father. William came on that prince when he was unarmed and slew his horse. William afterward insisted that it would have been no crime had he slain Richard himself. To attack an unarmed man was at worst merely a breach of knightly courtesy. But for a rebel to kill the representative of his suzerain was the most serious of feudal crimes—treason. William held Geoffrey de Lusignan responsible for his uncle's death. Whether he simply blamed Geoffrey as the leader of the party and responsible for his men or whether he believed him the actual slayer is not clear. Geoffrey himself denied his guilt, and one chronicler places the blame on his brother, Guy. One is inclined to believe that the two de Lusignan brothers were in command of the party, but had no intention of killing Earl Patrick. Some careless or over-enthusiastic subordinate struck down the earl whom the leaders were simply hoping to capture. This view is confirmed by the care exercised by the rebels to take William alive when, as he was fighting without his helmet, he could have been killed easily. But, rightly or wrongly, William never forgave the house of Lusignan.

The same brief combat which made William the mortal enemy of the de Lusignans brought him to the attention of Queen Eleanor, the ideal patroness for a young knight. The richest heiress of Europe by reason of the great duchy of Aquitaine which she had inherited from her father, Eleanor had at an early age married Louis VII of France. Divorced from him, she had promptly given her hand to Henry Plantagenet. As ruler of more than half of the homeland of the troubadours, as patroness of such artists as Bernard de Ventadour, and the mother of the countesses of Champagne and Blois whose courts were centers of romantic literature, Eleanor was the high priestess of the cult of courtly love. Unfortunately little is known of William's relations with this great lady. One cannot say whether she became interested in him because of his fondness for singing and his knightly courtesy, or simply because he had undergone hardships in her service. But whatever its origin, her favor was an invaluable asset. Normandy and England were full of brave young knights, but there were few who could say that they had suffered wounds and imprisonment in the service of Queen Eleanor and had been ransomed and reequipped by her.

When William Marshal left Poitou in the autumn of 1168, he may well have considered with satisfaction the accomplishments of his twenty-two years. While he had followed what the contemporary romances tell us was the usual course of a young man's education, he had done so with rare success. At the age of thirteen he had left home to seek his fortune in the service of William of Tancarville. At the chamberlain's court he had served his apprenticeship in the trade of arms and from his hand he had received the boon of knighthood. In the combat at Drincourt and in at least two tourneys he had shown himself a brave and capable warrior. The campaign in Poitou had not only given him a taste of the hardships of a soldier's life, but had gained him the favor of Eleanor of Aquitaine. William could with justice believe that he was on the high road to fame and fortune.

Noble Marriage

CONSTANCE BRITTAIN BOUCHARD

Wealth, power, and distinguished birth identified the noble. The aristocracy, with ancient bloodlines that often linked them to royalty and possessed of a public office such as count or duke, were indisputably members of the nobility. Below this exalted level, the exact qualifications for membership in the nobility remain unclear to the modern viewer. What is clear, however, is that from the eleventh century onward, the nobility received infusions from the strata below. In particular, knights—mounted military retainers in service to a lord—supplied fresh recruits. As central power waned and castles dotted the landscape, the exercise of power became definitive in determining nobility. Even possession of a castle or leadership of an armed retinue could be enough to qualify a man as noble in those unsettled times, and the boundaries of the noble class became more permeable than ever before.

The aristocracy was not always content with these developments. The twelfth-century Poem of the Cid *is the story of a humble Spanish knight who succeeds in winning for himself the city and lands of Muslim Valencia. His rise is viewed with hostility by the aristocratic heirs of the Counts of Carrión, who seek alternately to profit from his successes and to humiliate him through the abuse of his daughters. The Cid prevails in the* Poem, *and eventually marries his daughters to kings. The origins of the real-life Cid (c. 1043–1099) were not as humble as those of the* Poem's *hero, but the tale correctly portrays the rise of the knight and the knightly ideal in medieval Europe. By the thirteenth century, even the highest levels of the nobility described themselves as knights. In this selection, Constance Brittain Bouchard uses the marriage practices of the nobility to better understand how its members defined themselves.*

From: Constance Brittain Bouchard, *Strong of Body, Brave and Noble: Chivalry and Society in Medieval France* (Ithaca, NY: Cornell University Press, 1998), pp. 67–74, 86–91, 98–101.

Medieval nobles defined themselves by their families. Glorious ancestors were a key attribute of glorious aristocrats. Many of the decisions that modern society assumes are matters for the individual, such as choice of marriage partner, making a charitable donation, even buying and selling property, were carried out in the Middle Ages with the involvement and assistance of family members. Yet when discussing noble families it is important to keep in mind that these were not unchanging units, that the "family" varied in composition even for the same individuals at different times in their lives, and that however the nobles of the Middle Ages defined their families, it was never on the same basis as does modern society.

THE FAMILY AND FAMILY CONSCIOUSNESS

The term "family" must be used with some caution because of the multiple meanings attached to it. In modern usage, it usually means either the nuclear unit of father, mother, and children, or else a vague and rather unspecific collection of in-laws and more or less closely related people. Medieval Latin had no word for either of these meanings. People did indeed tend to live in nuclear units, but there was no single term to describe such a unit. The medieval Latin term *familia* meant not "family" but a household, including servants and attendants as well as actual relatives. A noble describing his relatives in unspecific terms might speak of his *consanguinei,* but these were people related to him strictly by blood, not his in-laws. For medieval nobles the important unit was the *stirps* or *gens,* a group of people related by blood, usually through the male line, existing in the dimension of time as well as space. It is to this group that I normally apply the term "family."

The way that the medieval noble family perceived and structured itself evolved over time, and even in a single period there was no one standard of "family structure" which individual lineages tried to match. Because family structures must be inferred from many sorts of evidence, including families' own memoirs and genealogies, donations to monasteries, and patterns of naming and inheritance, modern scholars have not always agreed on how medieval nobles conceived of the family groups to which they belonged.

There has been particular disagreement among historians concerning the extent to which noble families were patrilineal over the course of the Middle Ages. There is no doubt that in the High Middle Ages, the eleventh through thirteenth centuries, nobles preferred to identify themselves in terms of the male line of descent. What historians debate is whether this was a new development in the eleventh century, or whether nobles had always identified themselves patrilineally. The question is of course complicated by the lack of any fixed or broadly accepted kinship standard, external to individual families, which nobles purposely followed and which itself underwent change. It seems most likely that nobles, even in the early Middle Ages, gave the most significance to the men from whom they descended and inherited. In the turbulence of the ninth and tenth centuries, however, it was often very difficult to establish the male-line dynasties they would have preferred, since fathers often had no surviving sons, or at least no sons who went on to have sons of their own.

I should note that even though some scholars (including me) argue that male-line family consciousness had been the norm for at least several centuries before the year 1000, there can be no doubt that primogeniture, privileging the eldest son over all other sons (and certainly daughters), became the norm only in the eleventh and twelfth centuries. Even then, it was not an inflexible rule that the eldest son inherited nearly everything and his brothers little or nothing. The "Life" of Herluin, a knight who became a monk in the early eleventh century, says that the duke of Normandy assigned all his father's inheritance to him rather than to his younger brothers because he was more "eminent in true nobility," not because he was the eldest. William the Conqueror's eldest son succeeded him as duke of Normandy, but his second son succeeded him as king of England. Nevertheless, the expectation that all sons might earlier have had, of at least sharing in the family's patrilineal inheritance, was severely restricted in the High Middle Ages.

As one follows the history of nobles from the early Middle Ages into the eleventh century, it becomes easier to understand how they perceived their families because they defined them much more explicitly. In many cases, family gifts to local monasteries, which became much more common in the eleventh century than they had been earlier, seem to have encouraged identification with one's ancestors. Gifts had always been made for the souls of the donor's relatives, and as noble families began making repeated gifts over the generations to the same religious houses and, indeed, were often buried together at a particular monastery, their relationship with the monastery itself became a tool for making family identification more explicit.

One of the clearest signs of increasing male-line family consciousness was the gradual adoption of the *cognomen,* or second name (*cognomina* in the plural). Since the collapse of the Roman Empire a person had normally had only one name, but in the late eleventh century men whose fathers had witnessed charters simply as, for example, "Milo," might instead be inscribed as "Milo of Noyers." This phenomenon developed among the nobility well before the rest of society; peasants did not usually appear with last names until the fourteenth century.

In some cases, the *cognomen* might have its origins in a nickname; the lords of Brancion in the eleventh and twelfth centuries were all routinely called "Grossus." Most commonly it was a loconym, associated with the name of the family castle. When the castle became the key locus around which the newly powerful castellan families of the eleventh century organized themselves, the castle name became the clearest way to identify an individual. It should be stressed, however, that the *cognomen* was not, strictly speaking, a family name, even though relatives might all share the same one. Within a twelfth-century household, everyone from the serving knights up to the lord of the castle might take the same *cognomen,* whether they were related or not. Alternatively, a family member who moved to a different castle would generally change his *cognomen* to reflect his new home.

Cognomina became prevalent at the same time as the number of given names in use declined. In the ninth century, an enormous number of names had been in common usage, but by the end of the eleventh century the number had shrunk markedly. Thus the *cognomen,* as well as identifying a man with his castle and his relatives, was also important in distinguishing him from (for example) all the other men named Hugh. Earlier, although it was possible to be named for one's relatives, as kings were with some regularity, it was also common to take only one syllable of a parental name or to combine syllables from the names of several relatives. For example, among the children born to the noble couple Theoderic and Aldana at the end of the eighth century were two named Theodino and Albana. Families might go several generations without repeating a name, and this practice has proved intensely frustrating to modern scholars trying to establish family trees on the basis of name similarities. But from the eleventh century onward, aristocratic children were normally named for their relatives, their lords, or even such famous literary characters as Roland. This naming for people other than one's relatives, of course, poses different problems for the intrepid genealogist.

The spread of castles that were passed down from father to son—both the castles themselves and the castles' names—was accompanied by the spread of fief holding. Although far from universal, this institution did stress the importance of a single designated male heir, able to take up the vassal duties his father had exercised before him. Generally it was the eldest son who was most likely to be of age when his father died. In this way as well, the *cognomen* came to be associated with the male line.

Even with the adoption of the *cognomen,* however, the given name remained more important for a noble of the High Middle Ages, and it was generally chosen specifically to identify the child with relatives. Although there were no "rules" for parents to follow in choosing names, certain patterns may be discerned. Boys especially were named for their male-line relatives; the name of the paternal grandfather was the most obvious choice when naming a first son. The second son might be named for the father himself if his name was different from *his* father's.

One could thus end up with a family tree in which two names alternate for the lord of the castle, because each father named his eldest son for his own father. Or if father and son had the same name, then a single name might be given to each firstborn heir for generations, the name becoming so important to the family's sense of identify that a younger son might be renamed if his elder brother died. This happened to Duke William VIII of Aquitaine, who lived in the second half of the eleventh century. He was the younger brother of both

William VI and William VII and like William VII, had originally had a different name (in his case Gui) before taking both the duchy and the name William. The lords of Montpellier, routinely named William as well, did not want to take chances with renaming; the Lord William who died in 1178 named *both* his eldest sons William.

Because the people of the High Middle Ages did not regularly use numbers to distinguish different secular lords with the same name (most numbers attached to names, such as William VIII of Aquitaine, are modern), families had to find other ways to distinguish the generations. There was no consistent method of doing so. For example, two powerful families in which heirs were normally named William, the twelfth-century counts of Nevers and the aforementioned lords of Montpellier, followed quite different procedures. In the first case, individuals were distinguished by their descendants based on where they were buried, as in "William buried at Bethlehem," and in the second case by the names of their mothers, as in "William son of Sybil."

If a son were destined for the church, parents might name him for an uncle already in the church. Thus one can sometimes observe what are essentially parallel ecclesiastical and secular dynasties, only on the ecclesiastical side the position and the name descended uncle to nephew, rather than father to son. Whether naming a boy or a girl, in most cases parents chose a name that had belonged to someone they had known themselves, generally no ancestor further removed than their own grandparents or uncles and aunts.

New male names, however, could and did enter a lineage. If the eldest son died without heirs and the second son was not renamed, his might become the primary name for subsequent generations. If a man married a woman whose father was much more powerful than he was, then he might name even his first son and almost certainly his second for one of her relatives, rather than for his. In many areas, a powerful castellan's serving knights might all name a child for him, asking him to be godfather. Although some scholars have attempted to draw family trees based on name similarities within a region, such sharing of names between a lord and those who served him makes all such attempts suspect.

The family unit was in constant flux as births, deaths, and marriages took place, and only occasionally did it consist of individuals all sharing the same purpose. Indeed, because most noble wealth was inherited and brothers had to compete for the same inheritance, they often considered one another enemies. Even fathers and sons were at least potential rivals. Sons worried that their fathers would disperse the patrimony in pious gifts. Indeed, many young heirs in the eleventh and twelfth centuries immediately tried to reclaim what their fathers had given to monasteries on their deathbeds. Fathers, for their part, saw their sons as possible rebels. The Carolingian kings, for example, had routinely discouraged their sons from marrying while they were still alive themselves, because such marriages would make the sons into established figures with powerful allies in their in-laws. Even in the twelfth century, a son often did not marry until his father died, unless he married an heiress with substantial property of her own.

Membership in the family varied both over the generations and in the relatively short term, as new family members were born. Here the position of women is especially interesting, because they went during their lifetimes from membership in the family into which they were born to membership (or at least association) in the family into which they married. Because the *gens* or *stirps* was male oriented, a wife always remained something of an outsider to her husband.

This status can be seen most vividly in the names noblemen chose for their daughters; because the given name, even after the adoption of the *cognomen*, was such an important part of someone's identity, these names were never chosen lightly. It was common to name the first daughter for the husband's mother and very unusual to name her for her own mother. If a woman gave her name to any of her daughters, it might well be only the youngest of a sizable family. The relative infrequency with which daughters (as compared to sons) are found in the charters makes it more difficult to trace their names, but several sources provide insights into naming patterns. When Lord William of Montpellier made his testament in 1172 he mentioned all his children, and it is interesting to note that his eldest daughter was named Sybil for his own mother, his second daughter Willelma for his sister, and none of the five girls then living for his wife. If a wife was so foreign to her husband's family that he was slow to name a daughter after her, then it is not surprising that her own relatives, for example, her mother, were almost never sources for the names of a couple's girls. The main exceptions were found when the wife came from a much more exalted background than her husband.

And yet wives underwent an important transformation in status during their lifetimes as married women, from being considered outsiders to the family by their husbands and in-laws, to being considered integral members of the family by their sons. A son, as already noted, frequently named his first daughter for his mother. Thus women's names often skipped a generation; a woman would not give her name to any of her daughters but might have several granddaughters, by several sons, all named for her. . . .

The choice of marriage partner throughout the Middle Ages (and for that matter in antiquity as well) was a matter of political maneuvering and expediency for the aristocracy. The interests of the families took precedence over the particular desires of the couple, who might barely have met each other before the wedding. One castellan, for example, married his daughter to the illegitimate son of King Philip I at the beginning of the twelfth century, thus satisfying both Philip, who had found that particular castle a thorn in his side for years, and the castellan himself, who could thus be assured that his family would not lose it.

During the twelfth century, however, the modern concept of falling in love and getting married began to appear in the chivalric romances. Of course, in these romances people usually fall in love with people whom it was entirely appropriate for them to marry anyway. In *Raoul de Cambrai* Lord Guerri's daughter conveniently falls passionately in love with the man with whom her father needs to make peace in order to avoid a new outbreak of war. "If you marry me, generous, true-hearted knight, then the peace might last, and the war be put aside for ever," she tells him. In actual practice, young people were considered much less capable of judging whom it was suitable to marry than were their older relatives (especially older male relatives), but at least after marriage it was considered appropriate to love one's spouse.

One of the key elements in the arrangement of a marriage was the transfer of property from one family to the other or from one or both families to the new couple. Early Germanic law had emphasized the bride-price, the money the groom's family gave to the bride's relatives. Roman law, on the other hand, had stressed the importance of a dowry, the money and property a woman brought to her husband, which remained his when she died or even if he divorced her for adultery or another suitably heinous crime. While a dowry was not absolutely necessary under Roman law, it was the normal practice, and if there was a question whether a man had merely taken a woman as his concubine or actually married her (a question that might arise, for example, if a wealthy Roman contracted a liaison with a woman of substantially lower status), the payment of a dowry could indicate unequivocally that a real marriage had taken place.

The Roman dowry system predominated along the Mediterranean in the Middle Ages, and in northern Europe the Germanic bride-price was more important, but in France in the High Middle Ages *both* were often found, although the dower, property a husband would fix on his wife for her lifetime if he predeceased her, came to replace the old Germanic bride-price. Given the dual system of dowry and dower, negotiations over who was to pay what to whom and when could understandably occupy the male relatives of an espoused couple for months.

An example of such negotiations is found in the agreement reached in 1201 between the count of Boulogne and King Philip II of France. These two agreed that the count's daughter Mathilda would marry the king's young son within forty days of when she reached "marriageable age." The count announced that she would bring as her dowry one-third of the county of Boulogne, or one-half if her mother had died before the marriage took place, indicating that the count had fixed a sixth of his county on his wife as dower. Here, as doubtless in most important marriages, the political and financial dealings took precedence over any notions of love derived from the romances.

As this example suggests, an aristocratic bride's dowry, the property that she brought to her husband, could be fairly substantial in France in this period. It essentially constituted her inheritance in advance, so that ordinarily she received nothing more when her father died—not that the sons-in-law of wealthy men refrained from trying. During her marriage, a noblewoman had a fair amount of control over her dowry property, but her authority was still commonly exercised through her husband, and she could certainly not alienate it without his consent. In some cases, the husband might even control and receive income from his wife's dowry just as from his own property during her lifetime. Still, it was not his own property. It passed at once to a couple's children upon a woman's death, even if her husband were still alive, for under medieval law couples did not normally inherit anything from each other beyond the wife's life interest in her dower.

In some families, dowry property was treated as something special and separate which arrived with a wife and left again with a daughter as *her* dowry, serving as nothing more than a temporary source of extra family income, if that, in the meantime. When one young noble girl was made a nun by her parents at the house of St.-Jean-le-Grand of Autun, the entry gift her parents made, the sum total of all of their property that she would receive, was said explicitly to be "that land which her mother had received as her own marriage portion." Since the mother's family—and hence the mother's dowry— might be located some distance from the possessions of the male-line family, a dowry that came into the family with a marriage might be more useful as something to leave with a daughter, as dowry or nunnery entry gift, than as income-producing property.

The dower property a husband fixed on his wife functioned a little differently from the dowry—or, for that matter, the old Germanic bride-price— because it never actually left the (patrilinear) family. It was ceded not to the relatives of the woman joining her new family but to the woman herself. By the thirteenth century a prenuptial agreement might specify what part of a man's property a wife would be entitled to after his death; a third of his assets was common. In addition to fixing a dower on her, a noble might also make his wife a "morning gift" *(Morgengabe)* after their first night together; this would be substantially smaller.

Whereas the rest of a husband's property could be given away by testament or passed directly to his heirs, the dower was his wife's as long as she lived. A castellan's widow whose dower consisted of some land and a manor house might retreat there when her son took over the castle, maintaining her own autonomous household during her lifetime. In *Raoul de Cambrai,* the hero's widowed mother is advised to "keep house on her dowerland" after her husband dies, "for she will have no legal concerns with, or income from" anything else of his.

When a widow died, the dower passed to the children she and her husband had produced. Again it should be noted that husband and wife did not inherit from each other in the sense of acquiring full control over any property, beyond small gifts made when both were alive. Children would inherit from both their parents, but neither spouse obtained full rights to the other's property (at most a life interest) when he or she died. The marriage contract drawn up in 1178 between the noble couple Rudolph and Adelaide spelled out the property she would bring to the marriage as a dowry, *in dotem,* and specified that as a dower or marriage gift, a *donatio propter nuptias,* he had fixed half his property on her. If the couple had children, the contract noted, this dower property would pass to them after the wife's death; otherwise, it would return to his close relatives.

Among the aristocracy, women generally married substantially younger than did men. Once a girl reached puberty, she was considered ready for marriage, and in some cases parents who had found an appropriate bridegroom might not even wait for that. Boys might sometimes marry equally early. Guibert of Nogent, whose autobiography tells of family life at the end of the eleventh century, records that his parents got married when his mother was perhaps eleven and his father only a few years older; not surprisingly, they were then unable to consummate their marriage for several years. But for the most part men seem to have married substantially later, in their thirties or even forties, after they had inherited or made their fortunes. The romances are full of young wives married to old husbands—and inevitably more attracted to men their own age than to the men they were supposed to love.

Because noblewomen frequently married men perhaps twice their age—who had had more opportunities to die unmarried in tournament, war, Crusade, or from disease—there were substantially more noblewomen in the High Middle Ages looking for husbands than noblemen looking for wives. The imbalance was further magnified because boys entered the church in much greater numbers than girls. Men were therefore able to pick and choose their spouses much more easily than could women. As a result, men could reasonably hope to marry women of higher social standing than their own or, at worst, settle for wives of a comparable situation. The knight Aucassin in "Aucassin and Nicolette" is urged to seek the daughter of a count or even a king as a rational alternative to the girl he loves. Women, on the other hand, could at best hope to marry their social equals and often had to settle for husbands beneath them in status.

Marriages were thus an excellent opportunity for social advancement among the male aristocracy. Sometimes a castellan might tie his knights to him more tightly by making them his sons-in-law as well as his sworn warriors and vassals. Because of such marriages, nobles who could boast of glorious noble ancestors also had ancestors whose nobility and glory were at best dubious. At the beginning of the twelfth century the king of England found the marriage he was trying to arrange for one of his daughters thwarted when it turned out that she was a distant cousin of the chosen bridegroom; both were descended from a certain forester whose name was not even remembered.

Of course a knight like Aucassin could not really marry a king's daughter. But as knights married castellans' daughters, castellans married counts' daughters, counts dukes' daughters, and dukes kings' daughters, the entire aristocracy was tied together into a network of blood and alliance in which women formed a key connection. By the thirteenth century, even while nobles were desperately trying to reestablish the rapidly shrinking gap between the aristocracy and everyone else, knights' daughters might indeed find it expedient to marry young men of the wealthy urban classes. . . .

LIFE IN THE CASTLE

Once a couple was married, if the husband was the lord of a castle they also became the symbolic parents of all the people in that castle. Indeed, before the thirteenth century there was rarely more than one married couple in a castle at a time, since the heir usually did not marry until his father died. There were also usually no women other than the lady herself, perhaps a few female attendants, and her daughters. Perhaps the lord's mother, aunt, or sisters might live with him as well. All the staff in the castle, from the kitchen to the stables to the battlements, were men.

The lady of the castle had the responsibility of overseeing all these people. Because women married substantially younger than men, often in their early teens, and because when a girl did marry she might at once become the lady of a castle, responsible for all its functions, girls had to be trained in castle management from the time they were big enough to tag along behind their mothers, from the kitchen to the treasury to the grain storage bins. As well as making sure there was enough food for everyone in the castle, a lady's duties might even, if her husband was away, include commanding the castle's defense. Juliana, an illegitimate daughter of King Henry I of England, defended her castle against the king when she and her husband tried to rebel and went so far as to try to shoot him with a crossbow during a parley in which she had feigned repentence as a dutiful daughter. The king, to punish her, had her jump off the castle wall into the moat with nothing on but a shift; she was pulled out wet and freezing but still impenitent.

Most castles' ladies were not as active or warlike as Juliana, but they were still expected to be knowledgeable, skillful, and full of initiative. The lady carried the only set of the castle's keys on her belt, including the keys to the treasury and to the spice chest (nearly as valuable). When Christina of Markyate ran away from home to become a recluse, her last act was to give the keys to her younger sister. With the responsibility for the welfare of everyone within the walls, the lady was the busiest person in the castle.

The whole castle's population, lord and lady included, originally lived like one big family, eating and sleeping in one large room. The present-day distinction between public and private space (for example, in such buildings as the American White House) would have made no more sense to a twelfth-century castellan than the distinction between public and private rights and income. Since the early Middle Ages, as is evident in such poems as *Beowulf*, aristocratic life had centered around a large hall, the center of a complex of ancillary buildings, a room where people ate, slept, entertained, and received justice. The original castles of the eleventh and early twelfth centuries kept this focus on the great hall, the center of castle life. Often the hall filled the entire second floor of the keep, the large square tower that was the center of a castle's defense, although it might also be contained in an adjoining structure. Here in the hall trestle tables were set up for meals, and the castle staff stretched out to sleep at night. Individual private bedrooms were not customary, even in the homes of the mighty, until the end of the Middle Ages.

This retreat toward privacy evolved gradually. Originally the lord and lady's bed was in the middle of the hall, separated from everyone else only by curtains. During the course of the twelfth and thirteenth centuries, however, their bed was gradually moved, first to a dais at the end of the room, then to a great chamber reached by stairs from the end of the great hall. By the late Middle Ages, even the great chamber was no longer private enough for the lord and lady. They might eat here in great formality and relative isolation, but they slept in a smaller room beyond it, called the closet (a word which has since lost all its original importance, being now only a place to keep the clothes or the mop). The retreat of the bedroom—accompanied by increasing formality—continued in the postmedieval period, until in eighteenth-century France one's status at the royal court could be determined by how far down the long corridors to the royal bedchamber one was allowed to go.

The most important activity to animate the great hall throughout the Middle Ages, the event around which chivalric activity revolved, was the feast. Entertainment, gifts, fine clothing, and even tournaments were all aspects of feasts. The food served would be a combination of meat and vegetables produced by the lord's peasants with wild birds and animals caught in the hunt—the whole flavored with imported spices. Many an Arthurian romance begins with a banquet at which something unexpected happens—someone, say, whether Perceval or the Green Knight, rides his horse into the middle of the hall. The feast also symbolized the unity of all the castle's inhabitants, in that they ate together rather than having the lord retreat for special, private meals.

Such feasts, which might go on for hours, were an opportunity to display elegant table manners, joke and flirt (in a refined and courtly way, of course), and revel in conspicuous consumption. Unusual, even imaginary birds and beasts show up on platters in the romances, and even in real banquets hard-to-produce foods were a source of pride for the host, as were enthusiastically used expensive spices, fine and expensive tableware, and the host of servants that really personal dinner service required.

The feast was the emblem of the court, the place where the model of "courtly" behavior developed. But there is another key aspect of the feast: it took place within someone's family home. The greatest display of wealth and social skill took place in the heart of a lord's family, where the guests became almost extensions of that family. It is not accidental that the High Middle Ages had a perfectly good word for the household, the *familia*, whereas it had none for the nuclear family.

And yet a noble's broader kin group, the "extended family" in modern usage, was enormously influential, its consensus more important for many decisions than the wishes of the individual. In difficult times, one needs a group to which to belong, and the medieval patrilineal kin was the preeminent group of that sort. Blood ties had been important far before feudal ties or the sense of belonging to a specific kingdom, and they did not lessen in importance in the High Middle Ages.

In fact, during the course of the eleventh and twelfth centuries aristocrats defined their kin more and more clearly and precisely, all taking a shared *cognomen*, often based on a family castle, as well as continuing the earlier practice of virtually always giving a child the Christian name of an older relative. Kinship was especially oriented around the male line of descent and, increasingly over this period, around the eldest son, as symbolizing in himself the entire family. But even while men thought of their families in this way, they always found themselves in constant competition with other male members of the same family; being related did not mean a shared purpose but rather, in many cases, rivalry for the same inheritance. . . .

Child-Rearing in the Middle Ages

SHULAMITH SHAHAR

No more than half of the children born in the Middle Ages lived to see their fifth birthday. How did parents cope with this simple, brutal fact? Did they distance themselves from their children in order to protect themselves from the agony of their possible, indeed likely, deaths? Did they put all their energies into the survival of the family as a unit and into the preservation of the patrimony rather than in nurturing and loving individual children? The Catholic Church exalted virginity and saw all sexual behavior as inherently sinful. How did this position shape people's attitudes toward the products of sexual intercourse, children? In a seminal work on the history of children and child-rearing in Europe, Philippe Ariès argued that the concept of childhood as a special phase in human development did not exist in the Middle Ages. Children wore clothing that looked like adults' clothing, they frequented the same places as adults—the tavern, the church—and they worked alongside adults. In this hard world of heartbreaking mortality, adults devoted few resources and little emotion to the raising of their children.

Not surprisingly, Ariès' thesis has been subjected to considerable testing and retesting. Critics point out that, at least for infancy and the early stages of childhood, there could never have been a society that did not recognize and accommodate in some way children's extreme physical and intellectual dependence. Moreover, saints' lives and a handful of autobiographies from the Middle Ages indicate that medieval parents loved their children. Yet there is disturbing evidence that seems to confirm Ariès' position: parents who could afford it were likely to send their babies to wet nurses, despite the fact that they knew that infants nursed by their own mothers and raised at home stood a better chance of survival. The preponderance of male names in early manorial records and variable rates of survival for young girls and boys in orphanages suggest that adults sometimes fought harder for the lives of some children than for others.

From: Shulamith Shahar, *Childhood in the Middle Ages*, (London: Routledge, 1990), pp. 32–39, 34–44, 77, 92–93, 97–108.

In this selection, Shulamith Shahar uses a range of sources—
saints' lives, chronicles, confessors' manuals, sermons, and medical
and educational treatises—to investigate how people raised children
during those early, dangerous years.

From the twelfth century, with the burgeoning of the worship of the Holy Mother and Child, certain images became universally familiar: Mary heavy with child, and St Elizabeth, pregnant with John the Baptist; Mary immediately after the birth of Christ, Mary and Elizabeth holding their infants and smiling at them. Through popular literature and drama, and mainly through painting and sculpture, these sacred maternal archetypes were known to all strata of society. At the same time, it was well known that childbirth was hazardous for both mother and child. The authors of medieval medical works were aware of the difficulties and risks of childbirth and attended to them in their writings. Preachers who exhorted offspring to honour their parents referred to the sufferings and dangers to which mothers were exposed in pregnancy and delivery. Those writers who advocated virginity and scrupulously warned young girls of the tribulations of marriage and raising children elaborated on the uncleanness of conception, the suffering and ugliness of pregnancy, and the agonies and mortal risk of childbirth. The priests were instructed to ensure that the pregnant women in their parishes attended confession and received the Eucharist before giving birth. A number of saints, like Antony of Padua, St Margaret, and St Dorothy, were regarded as the patron saints of pregnant women, and midwives encouraged women in labour to pray to them or to the Holy Mother to help them in their delivery. There were special benedictions in the Church for the 'pregnant woman' and 'the foetus in her womb'. Mention is sometimes made in literature of pregnancy and the hazards of childbirth, and the actual delivery is sometimes the tragic or positive dramatic peak of the narrative. According to Wolfram of Eschenbach's epic poem in German, *Parzival,* for example, word of the death of her husband reached Parzival's mother in the eighteenth week of her pregnancy when the foetus was already moving in her womb. It is her unborn child, 'seed of his [the husband's] life, which our mutual love gave and received', who deters her from killing herself in her grief. When her time comes, she gives birth surrounded by her female companions. Because of the size of the infant, the delivery is difficult and she has a brush with death. Another heroine of the same poem, Parzival's maternal aunt, Schoysiane, dies in giving birth to her daughter. The Danish ballad 'Redselille og Medelvold' ('Birth in the Grove') tells of two lovers who flee after the girl's parents learn of her pregnancy. The birth-pangs begin while they are *en route,* and the girl dies in childbirth. Conversely, one finds in the sources reflections of the joy and hopes of the couple during the wife's pregnancy. In the fourteenth century Giovanni Morelli recorded in his diary that he had preserved in his memory the date, place, and way in which his son was conceived, and describes the joy he experienced in touching his wife's belly and feeling the movements of the foetus, and their anticipation and hopes as the birth approaches.

BIRTH

In writing of birth and midwifery, and in discussing gynaecology and other medical issues, the authors of Latin medical treatises in the Central Middle Ages cited Greek and Roman medical scholars: Hippocrates, Galen, and Soranos of Ephesus, as well as the Moslem medical scholars of the ninth to twelfth centuries, such as Albuckasis, Hali Abbas, Rhazes, and Ibn Sina, and, in particular, the writings of Arib ibn Saïd of Cordova. They discussed female diseases, conception, pregnancy, barrenness, and its causes, miscarriages, infant care, and birth itself. However, there are very few instructions aimed at guiding the midwife in her task. Although some of the encyclopedias devote relatively extensive space to gynaecology, they include no discussion of birth itself. The work called *De Passionibus Mulierum Curandarum* (On the Cure of Women's Ailments), which for a long time was attributed by scholars erroneously to a woman author, Trotula of Salerno, discusses at length irregular menstruation, cessation of menses as a cause of failure to conceive, barrenness in general, symptoms of pregnancy, difficult deliveries, physical problems arising after childbirth, pain and diseases of the vagina and the womb, and methods of infant care, and treatment of diseases unconnected with gynaecology. But, even in this work, instructions on delivery are also limited. This failure to discuss childbirth itself stems from the fact that the authors had no personal experience of the subject, and found little data in the works of Greek, Roman, and Moslem writers. According to the classical and Moslem medical tradition, physicians were not trained in obstetrics, and deliveries were carried out only by midwives. One guidance on the subject, for example, is confined to the statement that if the birth is natural—that is to say, if the infant is born head first—there is no need for manual intervention. If it is in any other presentation, however, the midwife must try to turn it by hand. Moreover, the vagina and cervix of the woman in childbirth should be rubbed with oil to expedite the delivery. Another author, who knows that in a natural delivery the infant should emerge head first and face down, confines himself to advising that the mother be made to sneeze and that an agrimony plant be tied to her thigh to expedite the delivery. The view of medical sages that childbirth was a matter for women and hence should be discussed only in very general terms is clearly reflected in the remarks of one of the Late Medieval writers. After very brief mention of the difficulties of delivering twins or triplets, he adds 'and since this matter requires attention on the part of the woman there is no point to studying it at length'. Bartholomaeus Anglicus writes 'This is the skill of women to help the mother to deliver as easily as possible.' At the same time, we learn from the sources of some scholars who discussed proper delivery methods. From the statements by Albertus Magnus (thirteenth century), who stressed the need to train midwives, we learn that he acknowledged their professional skills if not from actually being present at deliveries, then from contact with midwives and talks with them about their profession. From the Late Middle Ages, there was a gradual increase in works in the vernaculars dealing with women's diseases and with obstetrics. Some were translated from Latin (or at least contained texts translated from Latin—usually one of Trotula's versions or Musico's text); others were composed in the vernacular, apparently also by women. They were aimed at midwives, healers, and literate women in general, to enable them to treat themselves and their companions without recourse to the help of a male physician. In some of these writings, which were also based on observation and experience, one finds more detailed guidance on childbirth itself than in the Latin writings. The work known as *An English Trotula,* for example, mentions sixteen possible complications and unnatural presentations such as a large head presented forward which does not pass through the birth canal, commencement of emergence before full opening of the cervix, width presentation, breech presentation, etc. Apart from instructions to shift the child or turn it over in order to return it to the proper presentation, and to oil the vagina and cervix, the authors also propose producing vapour by boiling a herb near these parts of the body, and placing on the genitals bandages soaked in liquids extracted from various plants, or preparing a bath in which various herbs have been steeped. If the head of the infant was too large to pass, the midwife was instructed to endeavour to expand the cervix. The authors also listed indications that the foetus had died *in utero:* lack of movement in the uterus, contraction of the nipples, chills, bad breath, sunken eyes, lack of sensation in the lips and the face as a whole. In order to cause expulsion of the dead foetus, the authors propose use of vapours, introduction of liquids into the uterus, baths of various herbs, and various potions. If all these efforts failed, the midwife was instructed to extract the dead foetus from the uterus with a hook with the aid of a mirror. If it could not be extracted whole she was to remove it in parts. If the mother died and the foetus was still alive, it was the obligation of the midwife, according to both the authors of medical works and the synodal decrees, to make an incision in the left side of the corpse with a razor and to extract the living infant. In one of the manuals for priests, advising them to instruct midwives to carry out this operation in order to save the life of the child, the author adds that, if the midwife lacks the courage to do this herself, she should summon a man to her aid lest the child be lost through her fault.

If the delivery was spontaneous without special difficulties, so much the better, but, in the event of any complication, the midwife could do very little, even if she was a townswoman who had been well trained. Manual intervention might, at times, help to shift the child into a normal position for delivery, but, to the same degree, there was a chance that it might be twisted further out of position, creating the risk of detachment of the placenta from the wall of the uterus or pressure on the umbilical cord, which could prove fatal. There was also a strong danger of infection for the mother in cases of manual intervention, particularly when a hook was used to extract the dead child, not to mention the immediate danger of haemorrhage in these cases. Caesarean operations were apparently only carried out when the mother had died during delivery and an attempt (as outlined above) was made to save the child. Means of easing the suffering of a woman during a protracted delivery were almost non-existent. Many mothers died in childbirth and many infants died in the course of delivery. Some 20 per cent of all married women who died in Florence in the years 1424, 1425, and 1430 died in childbirth. In English ducal families in 1330–1479, some 36 per cent of boys and some 29 per cent of girls died before the age of five. There are no figures to indicate how many died during the delivery or immediately *post partum,* but the number was undoubtedly high. Since it is highly feasible to assume that the mortality rate among infants in the Middle Ages was no lower than in the sixteenth to eighteenth centuries, and perhaps even higher, the more accurate demographic data extant from the later period can serve as a guideline to the mortality rate among both mothers and infants in the Middle Ages. The demographers estimate that some 25 out of every 1,000 women died in childbirth in England in the sixteenth and seventeenth centuries, and some 200–300 out of every 1,000 infants died before the age of 5. According to a study by Lebrun, out of every 1,000 infants in eighteenth-century France, 280 died before the age of 1, and only 574 out of every 1,000 reached the age of 5. In periods of famine and plague, the number was even higher in all countries. From an additional study of several English parishes in the sixteenth century, we learn that some 50–60 per cent of all infants who died before their first birthday died in their first month and some 30 per cent during delivery.

In view of the high mortality rate and the limited medical means in that period, it was only natural that women in childbirth, midwives, husbands, and relatives appealed to divine aid through special prayers, or vows to visit the shrines of saints and bring offerings to the churches in which they were buried, and also relied on charms and incantations. Apprehensive pregnant women often went on pilgrimages to the shrines of saints before the anticipated delivery date, or asked to be anointed with consecrated oil, and amulets were prepared for the event itself. The risks of pregnancy were particularly high in the case of women who suffered from some disease, particularly deformities of the spine, and what was known at the time as ydropsis—a general swelling of the tissues—or anaemia. One of the prayers customarily recited three times at the bedside of the woman in labour was the opening of the Athanasian creed ('quicumque vult'). Also popular was the incantation 'O infant, whether living or dead, come forth because Christ calls you to the light.' If the woman in labour was a member of the high nobility, the local priest sometimes recited a special prayer for her well-being. Among the most popular talismans were 'birth girdles' and precious stones. The origin of the custom of using belts lay in the pre-Christian era, and in England it was known from the time of the Druids. Some of these girdles were handed down in families from generation to generation. Some were acquired as relics of saints. And many religious houses kept such girdles for use in childbirth. As for precious stones, Jews, Moslems, and Christians alike believed that the eaglestone *(aetities)*, attached to the thigh of a woman in labour, would draw out the child, whether alive or lifeless. The use of amulets and incantations during childbirth did not disappear from Western Europe and both Catholics and Protestants continued to use them until the nineteenth century, when significant changes occurred in standards of hygiene and in medical science, and obstetrics became one of the branches of academic medicine. In the Late Middle Ages (and later as well), midwives were sometimes accused of causing the death of the child. Midwives were also considered likely to engage in witchcraft, and, of the women charged with witchcraft, some were midwives who had failed in their efforts.

We have mentioned the appeals to the aid of saints. Since people tended to seek their help in order to cure or banish afflictions which they were powerless to deal with alone, very many of the miraculous acts attributed to saints related to opening the womb of barren women or saving mothers and children during delivery. One can find very few saints whose recorded miracles do not include response to the appeal of childless couples and the saving of mother and infant. Just as special prayers were said for pregnant women and their unborn children, there were special incantations and masses for barren women. Childlessness was quite common. According to a study of English ducal families in the fourteenth to fifteenth centuries, some 16 per cent of the males and 17 per cent of the females in these families whose marriages lasted throughout the age of fertility of the couple had no progeny. Among the labouring classes, it seems that in many cases women suffered from temporary infertility as a result of the cessation of menses caused by a starvation trauma or due to malnutrition or strenuous work. Those who appealed to saints for succour (childless couples, midwives, pregnant women, and their families) made a vow to go on pilgrimages to the shrines of saints and to give offerings if the woman conceived or if the mother and child were saved. Of the childless couples, some vowed that any son or daughter born to them would be dedicated to the religious life. It would appear, therefore, that, although certain reservations were expressed with regard to procreation (mainly by churchmen, but sometimes by laymen as well), people who married wanted children of their own. Apart from the yearning for children, nobles wanted to continue their line; prosperous town-dwellers wanted an heir to their property and peasants wanted additional labour for their farms. If people had not wanted children, they would not have sought the aid of physicians and various kinds of healers, and employed amulets, incantations, and other means (including stealing the Host from the altar in order to bring it to the barren woman), nor would they have appealed to the saints to cure barrenness and to save new-born infants. Failure to procreate could disrupt the marital life of a couple, and the misery and the helplessness which childlessness caused sometimes led to the levelling of charges of witchcraft against people, particularly women, believed to have caused impotence or infertility. In literature, we often find descriptions of the desire of a childless couple for a child, their prayer, their suffering, and their eventual joy when a child is born to them.

The authors of medical works acknowledged that a man too might be infertile, but, in theological writings and popular belief, infertility was considered, primarily, to be the failure of the woman. A woman who did not take the veil but never gave birth had failed in the central function assigned to her by nature according to Divine will. According to Thomas Aquinas, a woman who was spared the penalty of 'In sorrow shalt thou bring forth sons', imposed on all women because of the Original Sin, suffered from the flaw of barrenness more heavily than did other women from the pangs of childbirth.

The few women who gave birth in hospitals included the most poverty-stricken, who were widowed while pregnant, and, in particular, women who conceived outside wedlock (just as with the sick in general, it was only the poorest and the homeless who were treated in these institutions, which were houses of refuge rather than hospitals in the modern sense of the word). In some hospitals in various European countries in the thirteenth to fifteenth centuries, beds were allotted for deliveries. Most women, however, gave birth at home. Some did so without a midwife with the help of female relatives and neighbours, and assistance to a newly delivered mother, like despatch of food to poor mothers, was considered an act of charity. Other women, particularly in towns, were assisted by midwives. In the tale of the good deeds committed by a certain saint in his lifetime, it is related how he passed by the house of a woman in labour who was alone and heard her cries. He hastened to bring her a midwife, and she was delivered safely. Women of the nobility or the prosperous middle class, in all the countries of Europe from England and Germany to Italy and Spain, were often attended by several midwives. One of the authors of tracts in praise of virginity considered it contemptible even to require the 'indelicate skills of old women' (namely, midwives) whose aid the woman in childbirth could not forgo. During many deliveries the father was in the vicinity. It was he who made a vow to the saint when the situation was desperate, and it seemed that mother or child or both were close to death, and expressed his deep concern for the fate of the two, or pain and sorrow at their death. In rural areas, in families living in isolated hovels with neither midwives nor even neighbours nearby, it was the husband who assisted his wife during the delivery. Childbirth was undoubtedly considered a most important event, and, within the limitations of the means and the know-how at their disposal, people did all they could for the mother and child.

An illustration in an English fifteenth-century manuscript depicts a woman in labour pulling on a rope tied to a beam above her bed. Women also apparently gave birth while seated on a stool known as the 'birth-stool', which had been recommended by Soranos of Ephesus. The authors cautioned as to the size of the empty space at its bottom which should be neither too wide nor too narrow. In the fourteenth century, the stool apparently evolved into a chair with back and armrests. What were the characteristic situations in which the aid of the saints was evoked? Many women ceased to feel the movement of the foetus *in utero* and, fearing that it was lifeless, appealed to saints. Many other appeals were made when a delivery was difficult and protracted—2, 3, 6, 7, 9, 15, and even 25 days—or so, at least, the writers claim. The mother was sometimes so weakened by labour that she was unable to summon the strength required for the final effort. If she was a young girl, the authors sometimes attributed her difficulties to her age, in line with contemporary medical beliefs. The authors of medical works believed that sexual intercourse at too early an age not only caused the birth of deformed infants, but also placed the young mother at particular risk. In breech deliveries, which were particularly dangerous, appeals were also made to saints. If the infants survived such a delivery or were 'restored to life' this was attributed to miracles. Surgeons were summoned only when there was no alternative but to operate, when the foetus died, or when the mother had died or was dying. People greatly feared surgery, rejected it whenever possible, and preferred to seek the aid of saints. In one case in which the foetus was lying in horizontal position in the uterus, and only one of its arms had emerged while the rest of the body was unable to advance, a surgeon was summoned by the father, to be ready to extract the child by surgery *(incisio)* in the event that the mother died. In another case, the infant died *in utero* and the surgeon was called to extract it 'with an iron instrument'. The fact that it was eventually extracted without surgical intervention (after a relic of the saint was placed on the mother's body) was considered a miracle. The mother of one of the saints died while giving birth to him, and he was removed from her womb by incision by the midwife alone, no surgeon being available. Only very rarely were academic physicians *(medici, physici)* summoned to the aid of the women from the nobility during difficult confinements. They were undoubtedly capable of doing no more than were the midwives and surgeons.

Medical supervision during pregnancy was non-existent, and, even if it had been available, it is unlikely that physicians would have been capable of diagnosing complications. Many women miscarried. In the labouring classes, the miscarriage was often caused by strenuous work in general and the carrying of heavy loads in particular. It was not only the authors of medical works who discussed the precautions the pregnant woman should adopt to prevent a miscarriage. The priests were also instructed to inform the women in their flock of the risk of miscarriage through over-strenuous work during pregnancy, and the men of the hazards of sexual intercourse during pregnancy. It is to be doubted whether women of the labouring class could, in fact, abstain from hard work during pregnancy (and one of the authors of didactic works comments on how poor women continued to work hard during pregnancy), but they wanted their children and feared miscarrying. The records of the Inquisition tribunal at Pamiers refer to two women, one a noblewoman and the other a peasant, who expressed concern as to the fate of the infants in their wombs: the noblewoman when she was urged to leave her home and join the Cathars; the peasant woman when she crossed the river by boat. According to the latter, everyone feared drowning, 'and I particularly, since at the time I was with child'. Among the women who miscarried, some appealed to saints during the next pregnancy to forestall another miscarriage. In one case, a woman appealed to a saint in his lifetime. He did not perform a miracle but gave her spiritual support. This woman miscarried or gave birth to dead infants five times and considered this a punishment for some sin she had committed. The saint heard her story, offered her some of his food and drink, and ordered her to go to the priest and confess her sin. When her time came, she was delivered of a healthy son. In cases where the survival of the child is attributed to a miracle or its 'restoration to life' is described, the descriptions are sometimes realistic and touching. Thus, for example, one tale relates how a certain woman, for six years, gave birth to dead infants. When she again experienced a difficult confinement, the midwives feared that this time as well the new-born child would die, but, after prayers were recited and vows made, he was seen to move, his tiny chest rose, his tiny mouth opened, and he began to breathe, and after half an hour or so began to cry like all new-born babies. . . .

SONS AND DAUGHTERS

Did men and women express the wish for the birth of a son rather than a daughter? Did parents respond with disappointment to the birth of a girl? Like the writers of ancient Greece and Rome, the authors of medieval medical and didactic works listed signs which, they claimed, made it possible to establish whether a woman was carrying a male or a female foetus. And, together with general advice as to the ideal conditions (such as the alignment of the celestial bodies) for the conception of healthy children with noble qualities, we find words of instruction on how to act in order to ensure the birth of a son or a daughter. Clear and fresh complexion in the pregnant woman, for example, was regarded as a sign that she was carrying a boy—the implication being that the male was superior to the female. A clearer indication of belief in the superiority of the male is reflected in the superstition that the male child lay on the right side of the womb and the female on the left. Thus greater swelling of the left breast or stronger movement of the foetus on the right side of the uterus were also considered signs that the child was male. Some authors believed that over-ardent intercourse between husband and wife could cause the birth of deformed and weak males or of females. This was a direct return to the Aristotelian and medieval theory that a female was an incomplete male. Aegidius Romanus held that the most suitable season for conceiving males was the winter. The midwives suggested to women who wanted sons that they pray mainly to Saint Felicitas. There were, of course, also various potions which allegedly guaranteed the conception of a male. The authors of manuals of guidance apparently conceded that it was possible to desire a daughter. But, since the advice on how to ensure the conception of a girl is directed solely at women, it was evidently assumed that only women could want daughters. The woman who wanted a daughter was instructed to dry the testicles of a hare, and, at the end of her monthly cycle, to ground them into a powder and prepare a potion, which she was to drink before retiring to her bed 'and then go to play with her mate'. Preachers like Bernardino of Siena, who exhorted children to honour their parents as commanded in the Scriptures, promised them many offspring, mainly sons who would some day resemble their fathers. At the same time Bernardino reprimanded fathers who did not welcome the birth of daughters. Giovanni Morelli writes in his memoirs that he was particularly happy when his first child was born, since it was a son. And one of the interlocutors in *I Libri della Famiglia* (The Books of the Family) by Alberti describes how, immediately after their marriage, he and his wife prayed for sons. In the event of the birth of a daughter in urban Late Medieval Italy, relatives and friends would endeavour to console the parents by saying that the girl would certainly be a beauty so that they would not be obliged to give her a large dowry which would be a burden to them. As for royalty, it was not only necessary to comfort and encourage Louis IX of France on the birth of a daughter, but his courtiers were afraid to give him the news; some members of his Capetian dynasty even divorced their wives for bearing only daughters. Wolfram of Eschenbach describes how, when Parzival's mother regained consciousness after the delivery, she and her female companions carefully scrutinized 'the tiny pizzle' between the legs of the infant. And, the author adds, 'He could not be other than fondled and cherished, for he was possessed of the organ of a man.' The saints also sympathized with those women who wanted male children. One woman poured out her heart to a living saint and told him that her husband had begun to hate her. The saint promised her that she would be delivered of a handsome and good son and that then her husband would like her again, and this indeed happened. A woman in Spain, who adored St Dominic and his order, prayed to him for a son, who would some day join the order. When she heard from the midwives that she had borne a daughter, she continued to pray, to complain, and to weep, and a miracle occurred—the female became a male! However, a woman who had been delivered of dead infants several times prayed to a female saint and took a vow to go on a pilgrimage to her shrine and to make an offering, irrespective of whether the living child born to her would be a son or a daughter. A noblewoman who underwent a difficult confinement, and bore a healthy daughter after fifteen days of labour, thanked the saint with all her heart. When a girl-child was in mortal danger immediately after birth, or when her parents thought her dead, both often expressed their sorrow and grief and appealed to the saints, as in the case of a male infant. In the Late Middle Ages in Italy, some heads of families proclaimed that daughters brought them no less joy than sons, despite the problem of the dowry, and even though it was customarily said that daughters, unlike sons, did not set up families but disbanded them. . . .

THE FIRST STAGE OF CHILDHOOD

The term 'paediatrics' came into existence only in 1872. However, books devoted to paediatric medicine and including guidance on methods of childraising were composed from the sixteenth century onward. Some of these works were based on the writings of medieval medical scholars who did not usually devote separate works to the medical problems of children, but discussed them within the framework of general treatises (such as manuals on obstetrics). In composing those chapters devoted to paediatrics and to the rearing of infants and children in general, the medieval experts had recourse to Greek, Roman, and Moslem medical sources. The authors of didactic works and of encyclopedias also discussed proper methods of infant-care and childrearing (and they too cite the works of the classical authors, particularly Aristotle). Hence, they provide a picture of contemporary—or, to be more exact, expert—views on proper rearing and education. It is, of course, harder to know to what extent the manuals of guidance were known in wider circles and to what degree people followed their advice. We shall return to this issue below. . . .

The authors of medical works acknowledged that children developed at different paces. Their explanations of this phenomenon were erroneous, but their awareness that the infant should not be forced to sit, stand, or walk before it was ready, but should be allowed to develop at its own pace, was in itself valid. As regards sitting, parents were exhorted to take care to ensure that the child's seat was not too hard and had no protrusions. From a will written in the first half of the fifteenth century, we learn that there were small seats for children. A man bequeathed to his godchild 'a joint stool for a child and another joint stool large for to sit on when he comes to man's state'. The paterfamilias in Alberti's book says that the infant who still finds it hard to sit or stand at length requires rest and long intervals without activity. If he is over-tired, this can only weaken him. A detailed description of ways of encouraging a toddler can be found in a work by the mid-fifteenth-century Paduan, Michele Savonarola, directed at wetnurses. When the child begins to walk, he should be stood near a bench. He should always stand in front of the wetnurse so that they can see one another. (Therefore, it should be a round bench.) The sight of the wetnurse enhances the child's self-confidence, and she will be able to encourage him from time to time. He should not be led by the hand since an incautious movement could cause dislocation. After having acquired confidence, the child should be placed in a walker—'a chair with wheels on the legs'. When his steps become more certain, he should be placed beside a wall, and the wetnurse should stand at a certain distance and throw him a box or purse or apple, thus luring him to walk while fixing his gaze on the object. When he feels confident when walking this distance, the wetnurse can increase it gradually. The walker, as contemporary illustrations show, was known from the thirteenth century. Its infrequent appearance in illuminations indicates that it was only used in prosperous families. We also learn from this source that, as is customary today, the infant was not put into shoes until he began to walk. Authors warn the wetnurse to take particular care of the child from the moment he begins to walk, and to make sure that his first steps are taken on a straight, flat surface. Since toddlers fall constantly, they should be dressed in padded bonnets. Contemporary illustrations show such bonnets.

Most authors saw a connection between emergence of teeth and the commencement of speech, and believed that toothlessness hampered speech. Accordingly, they held that at the age of 2 approximately, after all the teeth had appeared, the child should be able to speak. Discussing the different pace of development in different children, they specify the beginning of walking and the beginning of speech as distinct indications of the child's pace of development. They did not consider speech to be the outcome of systematic instruction, but rather the realization of human potential through imitation. At the same time, they declared that a child should be assisted in this process of social acquisition. He should be encouraged to utter various words and praised when he succeeded; he should be shown an object he covets and told 'You can have it if you repeat what I say', and encouraged first to utter 'words which do not require the tongue to move much, such as "father" and "mother"'. According to Francesco of Barbaro, if a child had difficulty in talking, the wetnurse should take a large mirror, and place behind it a child who could speak already, and whose voice resembled that of her charge. The child behind the mirror should repeat various words on the instruction of the wetnurse, and her charge, believing it to be his own voice, would undoubtedly repeat them, and begin to speak like the child behind the mirror. This advice is probably based on Francesco of Barbaro's awareness that older children tend to talk to themselves. (The general view is that this habit of talking to himself fosters both the child's ability to control his external actions and helps him in the process of learning to integrate language and thought.) As was also the case with regard to advice on treatment of various ailments, expert views on the commencement of speech include both sound advice and groundless nonsense. Thus some writers proposed treating the mouth in order to induce the child to speak: his tongue should be rubbed with honey, salt, frankincense, and a touch of liquorice. Those who advocate assisting the child at this stage direct their advice at the wetnurse, or state in general that women have the most experience in this sphere. . . .

FROM 2 TO 7

In some cases, it is difficult to establish to which age the advice of medical manuals refers: 2, 3, or 4. Generally speaking, however, it can be said that they go into greater detail about the infant from birth to 2 years of age than about ages 2–7. This was because the risk of mortality gradually dropped from this age on, and because physical care from the age of 2 onward is simpler. The authors recommend continuing to bathe the child daily, or at least several times a week, and activating him through gymnastic exercises. These are conducive to health since they assist the digestive process and make him light-footed. However, up to the age of 7 care should be taken to avoid overstraining the child, since his limbs are still weak, and the exercises should be simple and pleasant. Heavy food and wine are not suited for small children.

I have found no reference to toilet training. This may be due to the con-viction that there was no need for special instruction since the child would learn habits of cleanliness gradually and of his own free will through imitat-ing adults. It will be recalled that, according to Erikson, the most important achievement at the age of 15 months to $2\frac{1}{2}$ years is the development of a sense of the self as a separate personality, so that education must aspire to maintain suitable equilibrium between freedom and supervision. In contemporary west-ern society one of the tests is toilet training; it is part of society's indispensable demand for adaptation, but, in the course of the process of habituating the child, it must be ensured that he does not forfeit his trust and his self-respect. We have no way of ascertaining how parents and wetnurses acted in the Middle Ages. We can only deduce from the fact that the medical writers do not relate to this issue that they did not consider it a problem requiring instruction such as was given in other spheres. The fact that, from the age of about 1 year, the infant was dressed in a shirt without underpants, enabling the escape of the bodily secretions without soiling the garment or the body, undoubtedly made life easier for the mother or nurse until the child was toilet trained. It is also known that contemporary adults were not over-modest about biological functions and were not bound by the restrictions on bodily movements and ac-tivities which govern modern western conduct in public. It is, therefore, highly feasible that children learned gradually and at their own pace through imitat-ing adults, without specific 'toilet training'.

Some of the authors of medical works deliberately confine their discussion to physical nurturing, stating, in the wake of the Greek and Moslem authori-ties, that education is a matter for moral philosophers and not for physicians. The author of the work attributed to Arnold of Villanova following Aristotle's conception of the body-mind unity, adds only that there is a connection be-tween the physical and the spiritual: distortions of the soul affect the state of the humours, and hence the temperament and the body as a whole. A corrupt soul corrupts the body. Since fear and dread cause melancholy, one should re-frain, when rearing a child, from angering or saddening him. Nor should one act with excessive merriment. Everything should be done with moderation and in the proper proportion. Other authors devote slightly more space to educa-tion at this age, and all, like most didactic writers, favour essentially lenient education and granting the child freedom to act in accordance with his natural tendencies.

Francesco of Barbaro, in his advice to wetnurses or nurses, prescribes di-version instead of head-on clashes with the child. A small child should not be shown something which cannot be given to him; and, if he happens to glimpse it, his attention should be diverted through offering him some other object. If he asks for something which is permissible and is not harmful, it should be given to him. If he receives an injury, the wetnurse, when binding his wound, should pretend to be taking revenge against the object which hurt him and should console him with small gifts. When the child is a little older, he should be allowed to go out to play with his peers. Konrad of Megenberg counsels parents to employ a young nursemaid in addition to the nurse. (It is not clear if he is referring to a relative or a young servantgirl.) Her conversation will enrich the child's vocabulary; she will entertain him with various games and carry him in her arms when the adult nurse is occupied with other matters. Raymond Lull writes that up to the age of 7 or 8 the child should be allowed to behave in accordance with his nature, permitted to play with his peers, and not forced to begin studying. The mother of the eponymous hero of Lull's book *Blanquerna* acted in this fashion. When he was old enough to go out to play with children of his own age she allowed him to do so, and he began to study only at the age of 8. Konrad of Megenberg, who also emphasizes the importance of play for the physical and spiritual development of the child, also prescribes play in the open air, and notes that a child who is still capable of marvelling at small things will rejoice even in the simplest objects while at play. However, a wise nurse should know when the child is fatigued and ready for bed. When a child cries without knowing why and refuses to accept food and drink or anything else offered him, this is a sign that he is tired and should be taken to his bed. These remarks are undoubtedly the fruit of observation of small children. Even the writers who asserted that everything should be done in moderation, and that a child should not be allowed to play too much, considered play to be a natural need: 'Children should be allowed to play since nature demands it,' writes Philip of Novare. According to Aegidius Romanus, games arouse a positive competitive instinct. He also recommends telling children stories with an educational message, conversing with them about great events of the past, and even singing them songs. Like the author of the work attributed to Arnold of Villanova, Aegidius and Aldebrandin of Siena also stress that the child should not be saddened. It was generally accepted that a child, like a tender shoot, needed suitable conditions for growth, differing from those required by an adult, and that a child could not endure certain things which an adult could suffer. A light blow to a tender branch causes it more damage than a deep cut to a mighty tree-trunk, says one of the interlocutors in Alberti's book. In view of the conviction that strict instruction in Christian morals and in obedience to parents and those in authority should commence only at a later age, parents were essentially exhorted by parish priests only to guard their children against various accidents, and to ensure that they were baptized and that they learned the three most important prayers (Paternoster, Ave Maria, and Credo) and how to cross themselves morning and evening. Some authors of didactic works added that small children should also be taught the two first commandments (love of God and love of one's neighbour). Those preachers who reprimanded parents for not giving their children a Christian education and for pampering them were referring, almost without exception, to children over the age of 7.

This lenient and freedom-oriented educational outlook was inspired by the prevailing theory on the pattern of child development and by both the positive and the negative images of childhood. The small child was considered weak, tender, and vulnerable. He was perceived as innocent and incapable of committing an unpardonable sin on the one hand, and as lacking the understanding and capacity for choice between good and evil, on the other. According to Konrad of Megenberg, children under 7 are blessed with only a sliver of reason, and Aegidíus Romanus writes that, up to the age of 7, the child is almost totally incapable of using his reason. He can be taught neither science nor morals. He can be taught only the vernacular language *(ydeomata vulgaria)*, and, apart from baptism and the sacraments of the church (he was apparently referring to confirmation), attention should be focused primarily on good physical condition or, in other words, on keeping him alive. These comments confirm Levine's view that, in societies in which infant and child mortality are high, parents concentrate in the first years of childhood primarily on ensuring the survival and physical well-being of their child. The stimuli for social and cognitive development are postponed to a later stage, when the child's survival appears more or less certain. In the second stage of childhood, Aegidius writes, in addition to concern for physical health, the educator should strive to ensure that the child's urges are balanced and coordinated *(ordinatio appetitus)* and he can already receive instruction. But only from the age of 14 onward, when the intellect is mature, can he engage in all types of academic study. The same belief that small children should not yet be educated and that not everything can be taught even in the second stage of childhood is also reflected in the response of Anselm of Canterbury to the question why he devoted most of his time and efforts to teaching and educating the young *(adolescentes, juvenes)*. He cited the image of wax, this time in the context not of the tender body but of spiritual and intellectual development. Tender children are like too-soft wax, which is almost liquid and cannot take the shape of the mould. Their understanding is slight, they find it difficult to distinguish between good and evil, and, when one discusses a moral issue with them, they do not understand. The old are like overhard wax, and also cannot be moulded. Between the two stages lie the young, who are like wax which is neither soft nor hard, and hence can be instructed and educated.

The author of a manual for priests clearly expresses the view that a child under 7 is innocent and free of sinful lust. He writes that priests should inform their flock that boys and girls who have reached the age of 7 should no longer sleep in the same bed, lest they develop desires for the 'fouwle dede'. In other words, children under 7 can sleep together without being tempted to sin. At the same time, priests should also caution godparents against sleeping in the same bed as their godchildren while the latter are small, lest they smother them under the weight of their bodies. From this, as well, it is clear that no objections were voiced to the accepted custom of sleeping in the same bed with small children if they had reached an age at which this no longer posed a risk.

Conflicting opinions were also expressed. The opposite extreme was represented in the early fifteenth century by Giovanni Dominici, who appears not only to have thought that a child's innocence should be protected from a very early age, but also to have questioned the very essence of this innocence. He writes that the sexual modesty of the child should be protected from the age of 5, and preferably even from the age of 3. From 3 on, it is not desirable for him to see naked people, and care should be taken to ensure that he distinguish between the sexes only according to clothing and hairstyle. From 3 to 25, neither the mother nor any other person should hug or kiss him. Although no 'natural' thought or movement will be roused in a child under 5, none the less from 3 on he should be dressed modestly (as should girls) by day and night. From this age on, brothers and sisters should not sleep in the same bed. In the same spirit, and counter to the accepted view that only older children should be whipped for purposes of education and moral instruction, Dominici asserted that three-year-olds could be whipped, albeit not severely and in proper proportion to the scope of the sin. If the child repents and confesses his sin, he should be treated leniently. Like Dominici, Jean Gerson warns, in one of his sermons, against the corruption of innocent children by men- and maidservants, and he was apparently also referring to small children. Unlike Dominici, Gerson does not deny the existence of infantile innocence, but he fears that it may be corrupted. Konrad of Megenberg also believed that children under the age of 7 should be whipped for mendacity. He rebukes parents who are amused by childish profanity, and admonishes those who teach girls to stimulate their genitalia, thereby rousing the sexual instinct. But he too observes that, since the child does not know what it is doing, it is the adults who are committing the sin.

There were doubtless conflicting theories, just as there were two conflicting images of childhood. However, not only did the 'positive' image of the small child predominate, but in everyday life, with the exception of those who were placed in monasteries at a very early age, children up to the age of 7 generally enjoyed freedom. Few restrictions were imposed on them, nor were they kept at a distance from adults, for better or worse, according to our conceptions. Throughout society, boys and girls were not separated up to the age of 7, even in the prosperous urban households and the castles of the nobility. They were a part of a society in which people of all classes were crowded densely together. Everything was more open, and western man had not yet begun to seek privacy. Even masters and servants, whose class differences were emphasized by different clothing and forms of address, lived in close proximity. The problem of the harm liable to be done to children from nearness to servants concerned educators in the next few centuries as well. Ariès has described these issues vividly, and he was, of course, correct in claiming that children were involved in adult society. Clothing was not particularly modest, since both boys and girls wore shirts with very little under them. (After the period in which infants wore nothing under their shirts, they were dressed in drawers held closed with a string. These 'peeped out' when the shirt was short or when it was long and was rolled up for comfort during play or other activities.) It was customary for several members of a family to sleep in the same bed; brothers and sisters, parents and their child or an uncle and his nephew. There is a tale of a boy of 8 who at night 'was carefully laid by his mother by her side'. Even a preacher such as Stephen of Bourbon describes as natural the fact that three young boys shared a bed. To quote Jean Flandrin: in the labouring classes the shared bed was one of the expressions of 'the spirit of communality in family life'. Often adults and children slept naked. Not only was adult nudity no secret to children but, as a result of their nocturnal propinquity, sexual relations were also no mystery to them, for those either in towns or in villages. Nor, apparently, were manifestations of sexuality in children suppressed, as can be seen from the reprimands of the authors of didactic books. In short, adult sensuality was overt, and infantile sexuality was considered innocent and perhaps even amusing. Parents appear not to have taken a strict view of the use of profanity, but were rather diverted by the 'wit' of the child. Not only Konrad of Megenberg reprimanded them for this. According to a certain preacher, once a child has learned to walk and talk, the Devil takes the trouble to teach him coarse words and profanity. And parents, instead of fighting this phenomenon, consider it amusing and a sign of 'cleverness' in the child. It seems abundantly clear that people did not internalize the exhortations of the preachers and didactic writers. But neither this fact nor the failure to keep children at a distance from adult society should be regarded as indications that childhood was not recognized as a separate phase of life, with its own characteristics and privileges. The proximity to servants did not obliterate awareness of the differences between servants and masters, and did not bestow on the former similar rights. It is typical that in fourteenth-century Venice, where sexual morals were remote from the norms which the church wished to sustain, the legal authorities of the town imposed penalties severalfold harsher for the rape of a female minor *(puella)* than for the rape of an adult woman. The authors of confessors' manuals imposed heavy penances on churchmen or monks who seduced minors. They also proclaim that a man who has committed this sin should never again be permitted to speak to a child.

There is no question but that children were allowed the opportunity of playing, as writers recommended. From the sources we learn of outdoor group-games, of games played with natural objects and materials both indoors and out, and even of toys. In the tales of the miracles attributed to saints or in descriptions of boys or girls cured of ailments or injuries after accidents the expression 'went out to play with the children of his [or 'her'] age' is often reiterated; or, after the saint has performed the miracle, the father finds his daughter 'completely healthy, laughing and playing'. It is only the future (male or female) saint, who differs from all other children, being as serious as an old man and shunning the company of his peers, who does not play. And, from the description of his conduct, we can ascertain what was considered typical childish behaviour. Some of the accidents mentioned occurred in the course of play, while a small child was playing outdoors without supervision or when his older siblings, who were supposed to watch him, neglected their task. Jean Froissart, in his work *L'Espinette amoureuse* (The Cage of Love), lists fifty-one children's games, individual games and, in particular, group-games. Most of the games he describes, particularly the group-games, are for older boys from

7 on who are already attending town-schools, and he distinguishes between the games of the under-twelves and those of children over that age. But some of the games are also suitable for small boys and girls, who were in the habit of imitating the older children. Out of earth, water, strips of wood and of cloth they build a dam, a boat, a mill, and an oven. From a shell they make a sieve, two sticks become a harrow; one stick is a hobby-horse, and a duel can be conducted with two blocks of wood. The child is unwilling to give up his treasures at any price and, however tired, will not cease his play. One of the English preachers also describes a child at play at home with everyday objects and materials, transforming them into whatever he chooses with his hands and with the aid of his imagination. A stick becomes a white horse, crumbs of bread are kneaded into a boat, chips of wood become a castle, and a stick a sword. In these games, as in some of the outdoor games which Froissart describes, there was a mimetic element, as in many children's games throughout the ages, and the writers who depicted these games were aware of this. Hence, when they write of a future saint who, unlike most of his kind, plays with damp sand, they attribute to him the desire to build churches and monasteries, altars and crucilixes, while they attribute to ordinary children the desire to construct houses, fortresses, and horses and riders. Another future saint loved only one game—to imitate the mass ceremony with which he was acquainted from church. Giovanni Dominici, who was opposed to giving expensive toys to children, also acknowledged children's predilection for imitation and the importance of play for the child, and proposed methods of exploiting it as an educational tool. He suggests that parents playing with children deliberately lose the game and then hasten to the household chapel to pray. In this way, the child would learn to appeal to God when in distress, and would also realize that God also loves the losers. He also proposed that a kind of psychodrama be conducted: the child should deliver a sermon to the household (to which all would listen attentively without laughing), and on the next occasion the parent would preach. Instructors of the children in the 'children's confraternities' in Florence in the first decades of the fifteenth century, recognizing the predilection of children for imitation and their fondness for dramatic play, instructed them not only to observe the precepts of Christian morality and to ensure that their parents did the same, to pray, and to attend religious processions, but also to act in plays with an educational-religious message. And smaller children, who were not yet members of the confraternity, also took part in these performances. (These confraternities were established in a spirit of ambivalence: apprehension with regard to children and recognition of the need to restrain them and to guide them into paths of action desirable to adults, and a kind of worship of childhood—an extreme expression of belief in its redeeming power, stemming from its innocence.)

There were some medieval games of which modern western mothers would not have approved. For example, a chick fell into a pit and drowned. The mother took it out and gave it to her child as a plaything. (The child then summoned the aid of a saint who revived the chick.) Toys also existed. The generosity of a future saint, the child of noble parents, was manifested when he was only 5. He not only invited the poor children of the neighbourhood to meals, but also divided up his toys among them. Medieval children are known to have played with rattles, hobby-horses, rocking-horses, blocks, bones, balls, hoops, dolls, spinning tops, see-saws, small windmills, little wooden boats, whistles, clay birds, miniature cooking utensils, marionettes, with which adults played as well, glass rings, which were also worn as jewellery by little girls, and drums and cymbals. A wood carving from the fifteenth century shows a mother teaching her son to ride a bicycle-like toy. Her expression is concentrated, and her hand rests gently on his head. As is the habit of children everywhere, medieval children tried to play with the possessions of adults and were sometimes granted permission to do so. In a domestic scene described by a preacher, a child asks to play with his mother's jewellery. She tells him that he must first wash his hands and then she will give them to him. The writers clearly distinguished between the form of play of older and younger children. In the German literary work, *King of Tyrol*, a child is depicted imitating older children playing peek-a-boo, and understanding the game in his own way: he covers his eyes with his hands and believes that nobody can see him.

Psychologists have noted the importance of play for the intellectual and social development of the child. According to Erikson, in the third stage of life (from 2½ to 6) language is enriched, motor skills improve, inquisitiveness increases, and the development of the self as a separate entity continues. The most important aim at this stage is the development of initiative, which is made possible through the ability to move about freely and to try out new experiences with great energy. According to medieval sources, children appear to have been allowed the opportunity of achieving this aim. Socialization proceeded at a gradual pace and without too much pressure. Norbert Elias has noted the differences in the code of conduct in medieval western society as compared to later periods. It seems that, in the Middle Ages, people were not expected to restrain themselves or, as has been noted above, to keep their physical distance from one another or to act discreetly with regard to biological functions (defecation and urination, nose-wiping, spitting, etc.). The threshold of embarrassment was much higher than in later periods. The manuals of etiquette for adults (in the nobility) deal with the most basic matters, which in modern times are taught to small children: one should not belch during meals, should not cram large hunks of food into one's mouth, a hunk of food which has been chewed should not be put back on the communal plate, the eyes and nose should not be wiped with a table-napkin, etc. This suggests that these issues were not stressed in early education, and that only limited pressure was brought to bear on small children to learn elementary manners.

Children who received an education did not usually attend school before the age of 7. Some, however, were taught at home from the age of 5 or 6, by their father or a private tutor. The authors who recommended beginning to teach reading at this age stressed that study should be gradual, that the child should not be forced to study long hours each day, and that the instruction should be gentle and pleasant. Peter Damian lists several 'literary games', known by various names, which were intended to teach proper speech and apparently reading as well. Others advocated giving small prizes with the aim of encouraging the pupil. For example, letters could be formed from fruit and sweets. If the child succeeded in deciphering the letters, he should be given the fruit or sweet. Giovanni Dominici also recommends giving the child who has done well at reading a small gift, such as new shoes, an inkwell, or a slate. Greater pressure was sometimes brought to bear on five- or six-year-olds who studied at home, when they were earmarked for service in the secular church or for the monastic life. Gilbert of Nogent began his studies with a private tutor in his mother's home before he was 5. Describing this period in his autobiography, he writes that the tutor was very pious and well-intentioned. However, his education was limited and he lacked any talent for teaching. Although he loved the child, 'his love was cruel'. He restricted Gilbert stringently: he did not permit him to play with his peers, forced him to study long hours, did not allow him to take a step without permission, and beat him severely. Of those designated for ecclesiastical service or the monastic life, some began studying at 5 or 6 in small local schools. There were isolated cases of children who were not earmarked for the church, like Giovanni Morelli and his son, who began studying at this age. In one case, the writer, who was aware that the five-year-old boy had begun his studies at an earlier age than usual, and that the other children were older than him, described him as 'short in stature and delicate'. Other boys and girls, designated for the monastic life, were placed in monasteries and convents at the age of 5, and, in exceptional cases, even younger. Their lives undoubtedly differed drastically from those of most other children, and we shall discuss them in a separate chapter. Generally speaking, it should be recalled that only a small minority of children learned to read. An even smaller proportion learned to read and write, and even fewer received a proper education.

In the written sources, we encounter displays of affection for small children, expressions of understanding of their conduct and the workings of their imagination, and even tolerance, approaching permissiveness, towards mischief. In feudal literature, the mischievous conduct of the small heroes sometimes bordered on wildness, without being punished. The biographer of Catherine of Siena, who learned of the saint's childhood from her mother, wrote that 'When she was weaned, she began to eat bread dishes and to walk by herself. She then began to please all those who saw her.' He relates that relatives and neighbours loved to listen to her childish and charming speech and enjoyed her cheerfulness. Her mother had difficulty in keeping her at home since neighbours and relatives continuously came to beg to take the child to their homes. When she was 5 or so, after having learned the Ave Maria, she would halt at every step, when going up or down stairs, kneel, and recite a sentence from the prayer. This description is not a *topos;* it is based on observation of the conduct of a small girl engaged in ritual repetition, as is often the case with children. Understanding of the ways in which a child's perception differs from that of an adult, and of the workings of the childish imagination, is revealed in the tale of the English Franciscan Thomas of Eccleston. He relates that the minister of the order in England often visited the home of the noble, Geoffrey Despenser, and that, each time he came, the host's small son, John, would greet him with great friendliness. One day the child saw him conducting mass in the chapel. The next time he visited the house, the child ran away from him, and all his mother's persuasion could not bring him to approach the visitor as in the past. When she eventually asked him why he had run away and what had frightened him, he replied that he had seen the Franciscan friar eating a child on the altar of the chapel, and he was afraid that he too would be eaten. The story sounds authentic, but even if it did not occur, and was only the projection of the author's own remembered childhood fears of the host, it still reflects acknowledgement of the fact that a child thinks and sees differently from an adult. It is not the fact that the child is described as having imagined that he saw an infant in the host which reveals the author's understanding of the childish mind, since there was a lengthy literary and artistic tradition of the revelation of Christ in the form of a little child in the host. The author's perception of the child's view is unique in that the child is said to fear that he too will be eaten by the priest.

The biographer of Anselm of Canterbury writes of a childhood memory which Anselm related to him. Having been bred in the mountains, and having lent a ready ear to his mother's conversation,

> he imagined that heaven rested on the mountains, that the court of God was there, and that the approach to it was through the mountains . . . One night he saw a vision, in which he was bidden to climb to the top of the mountain, and hasten to the court of the great king, God . . . He saw in the plain through which he was approaching the foot of the mountain, women—serfs of the king . . . who were reaping the corn, but doing so carelessly and idly. The boy was grieved and indignant at their laziness, and resolved to accuse them before their lord the king. Then he climbed the mountain and came to the royal court, where he found God alone with his steward. For, as he imagined, since it was autumn he had sent his household to collect the harvest . . . The Lord asked him in a pleasant and friendly way who he was, where he came from, and what he wanted . . . Then at God's command the whitest of bread was brought him by the steward and he refreshed himself with it in God's presence. The next day, therefore, when he recalled to his mind's eye all that he had seen, like a simple and innocent boy he believed that he had been in heaven and that he had been fed with the bread of God, and he asserted as much to others in public.

This story, like the preceding ones, was certainly anchored in medieval culture, with its values and images, but also reveals awareness of the unique perceptions of childhood.

The child who senses both the beauty and the pain of being, but cannot express his sensations, has been described by Wolfrain of Eschenbach.

> Of sorrow he knew nothing, unless it was the birdsong above him, for the sweetness of it pierced his heart and made his little bosom swell. Weeping, he ran to the queen, and she said 'Who has hurt you? You were out on the meadow.' He could tell her nothing, as is still the way with children.

The written sources teach us about children in the towns and the nobility as well as about those who were destined for the secular church or the monastic life. There is almost no direct evidence on small children from the peasantry. It is hard to believe that in the first phase of childhood they were more restricted and enjoyed less freedom than children in higher social strata. They certainly did not receive either the gymnastic exercises recommended by medical scholars (it is doubtful that these were practised in the upper classes either) or the delicate food they prescribed, nor did they suffer the overfeeding criticized by didactic writers. They ate the same food as their parents. (A study of the nutrition of peasants in the Late Middle Ages reveals that prosperous peasants ate wheat-bread, soups, gruel, pork, and (in certain areas) fish. They ate more vegetables and dairy products than the nobility, in whose diet meat played a more important part. The middling peasants enjoyed meat, cheese, and beer more rarely than the more prosperous peasants, and soup and gruels from pulses and oats played a more major part in their diet. Poor peasants and hired labourers did not always have enough grain, so that they did not always receive sufficient calories, and only rarely did they consume animal protein and beer.) It is known that the average number of offspring in prosperous families was greater than in middle-income families, and in the latter was higher than in poor families in the same time and place. There were several reasons for this. The well-to-do married younger than the poor, and the fertility span of the couple was exploited more fully than in the case of poor couples. The fact that women of the labouring class nursed their own infants increased the interval between pregnancies. At the same time, it is highly likely that more of the children of the rich survived because of better nutrition and environmental conditions. One should not deduce from this that the children of peasants received less affection or were less valued than those of the rich. Contemporary authors who wrote about the peasants did not assert that in this social stratum there was no material and emotional investment in children. According to a thirteenth-century preacher, peasants praised their children when small, and dressed them in many-coloured shirts, and, when they grew up, set them behind the plough. Noblemen, on the other hand, 'set their children under their feet' and force them to eat with the servants, and laud and glorify them when they grow to adulthood. It is not clear whom the preacher is admonishing and whom he is praising in this statement. Nor should one take the statement literally. It seems reasonable to assume that he identifies with the spartan education he attributes to the nobility, but we also learn something of the contemporary view of the way in which peasants reared their children. A carving in the Church of the Magdalen in Vézelay shows a barefoot peasant woman affectionately combing the hair of her small son. In a ballad in which the peasant and his wife exchange roles for one day the husband is given the task—amongst others—of wiping away the tears of his small children and consoling them. The author apparently considered this to be part of the day-to-day activities of the peasant woman. . . .

LIFE IN A MONASTERY

C. H. LAWRENCE

Of all of the ways of life—those of the laity, the secular clergy, and the monks—monasticism was considered the best spiritually, morally, and intellectually. Only monasticism allowed a complete withdrawal from the distractions and temptations of the secular world, so that the individual could concentrate all energies on prayer and the salvation of his or her soul. Monks and nuns renounced all ties and obligations to the outside world and withdrew into the world of the monastery. Entrants gave up the family of their birth for the spiritual family of the convent. They gave up all claim to property in order to grow rich on the spiritual blessings of a life in which everything was shared in common. Throughout the Middle Ages, monasticism was extremely attractive, and a significant number of people were willing and able to renounce their responsibilities to family and lord and devote themselves to the religious life.

Monastic life was a withdrawal of the individual from the secular world, but monasteries themselves were very much engaged in secular affairs and performed a number of important functions for the world outside their walls. Monasteries served as a connection between the material and spiritual worlds. The prayers of monks, who had devoted themselves to a lifetime of prayer and worship, were thought to be specially efficacious. They could encourage God to look on a community with favor and to protect it from the scourges of famine, sickness, and war. Their prayers could protect a soul from the demons who waited like vultures to drag it to Hell at the moment of death and could help speed its passage through Purgatory. The wealthy donated land to monasteries in order to win these spiritual champions to their side, and many arranged to spend their final days in a monastery, dying in the habit of a monk or nun. These gifts of land created another link between the monastic and secular worlds by turning monasteries into landlords who rented land to peasants and, like any seigneur, had rights to labor dues, taxes, and

---

From: C. H. Lawrence, *Medieval Monasticism: Forms of Religious Life in Western Europe in the Middle Ages* (New York: Longman, 1989; 1984), pp. 111–27.

jurisdiction. Monasteries also received gifts of urban properties, which they rented out, and sometimes had the right to hold markets and fairs. In this way, monasteries were very much involved supervising their properties, collecting fines and payments, negotiating with their tenants, resolving disputes, and punishing malefactors.

Another connection with the outside world was the monasteries' role in education. Most monasteries followed some version of the Benedictine rule, which required that each monk or nun devote a part of every day to the study of religious works. Since many of their entrants were children, monasteries had to provide basic education. From time to time, they also educated children who were not destined for the religious life. This was especially the case for convents. Religious foundations for women did not receive as many or as generous gifts as did those for men, and consequently, some took on children boarders and students to help ease financial pressures. Church reformers were suspicious of such arrangements, though, and regularly forbade nuns from taking these young members of the outside world into their midst. The fact that the prohibitions were routinely repeated suggests that they were not always obeyed.

Another function that monasteries performed for the secular world was charity. Charity became increasingly important in the thirteenth century, as gradually worsening weather led to more and more crop failures and as the growing European population began to strain the limited capacities of medieval agriculture. During the thirteenth century, many monasteries established officers in charge of distributing alms and devoted more and more of their resources to feeding and clothing the poor who gathered outside their gates. In this selection, C. H. Lawrence uses monastic regulations and financial records to reconstruct what daily life was like inside the monastery, and how its officers conducted its business.

Bare ruined choirs and empty cloisters kindle the imagination of the modern visitor but cannot satisfy it. Standing on the floor of the dormitory at Fontenay and glancing down the night-stairs into the transept of the great church, it is easy to visualise the cowled figures, hands hidden in the voluminous white sleeves, scurrying down for the night office. From the stone pulpit high up in the wall of the roofless refectory of Fountains one can look down upon a ghostly multitude of bowed heads. But it is hard to recapture the experience and atmosphere of daily life in a medieval cloister. Our documents can conjure up for us the exterior acts of the monastic routine; but at the end, the inwardness of it eludes us. Our sources cannot penetrate the interior experience of the individual that energised and gave meaning to a pattern of life built round a belief in the omnipresence of the supernatural and the power and necessity of constant prayer, and to which the modern secular world offers us no key.

How exactly did monks spend their day? Here we have to make distinctions of time and place. Although the Rule of St. Benedict constituted a thread of continuity through the centuries, the domestic arrangements and assumptions of a monastic community were no more static than those of the society that surrounded it. The experience and mental furniture of a Benedictine monk living in the fifteenth century would have been different from those of a monk of the twelfth century, and the life-style and expectations of both would have differed from those of a monk living in a Carolingian abbey of the eighth century. Let us try to reconstruct the daily round in a Benedictine establishment towards the close of the eleventh century.

There is much to be said for selecting this point in time. Letters and monastic chronicles provide us with occasional glimpses over the walls of the enclosure; but the most systematic information about the occupations that filled the monk's day comes from the customaries, and these survive in substantial numbers from the two centuries between 1050 and 1250. These were treatises recording the established practices of particular monasteries. They were compiled to supplement the general instructions of the Rule and contained detailed regulations for the celebration of the divine office and for every activity that occupied the monastic day. One of the primary objects of these compilations was to secure uniformity of observance in houses belonging to the same congregation, and so they were widely circulated, carefully preserved and periodically amended. Uniformity of practice was the avowed motive for the composition of the *Regularis Concordia*—the common customary agreed by the monks of tenth-century England; and a similar intention must have underlain the customary, or so-called statutes, that Archbishop Lanfranc gave to the cathedral priory of Christ Church, Canterbury, soon after 1070, for they were copied in other cathedral monasteries of Norman England.

Some of the fullest of these rule-books are those written in the eleventh century as a guide to the customs of Cluny. One of them was compiled by a monk of the Italian abbey of Farfa, who had been sent to Cluny by his abbot to learn the usages and report back home. Another was compiled by Ulrich, himself a monk of Cluny. He had been on a visit to the Swabian abbey of Hirsau about the year 1075, and during his stay his host, Abbot William, had plied him with questions about Cluniac practice. So on returning home Ulrich wrote up the customs of his abbey for William's benefit and also, unforeseeably, for ours. Together these two treatises provide us with a fairly detailed guide to the pattern of life at Cluny under the regime of Odilo and St Hugh. We have already drawn upon them in describing some of the features of Cluniac observance. All the customaries give elaborate instructions for the celebration of the divine office at the various seasons of the year and omit much else that we should like to know. Nevertheless they do enable us to reconstruct in some detail the routine of daily life in a Benedictine abbey of the eleventh century.

Both the brethren and the children slept in the common dormitory fully clothed in their habits except for cowl and scapular. This may have been no hardship on winter nights in an unheated stone building, but it must have been uncomfortable in summer. It was the rule at Cluny that even on the hottest nights no more than feet or arms might be uncovered. At some time between 2 and 3 a.m., depending upon the time of year, the community was roused by the bell. They rose, pulled the covers over their beds, put on night-shoes and cowl—a monk, explains Ulrich, must not enter the lavatory (which connected with the far end of the dormitory) with head uncovered, for the cowl conferred anonymity—and then, while the bell continued to ring, they made their way down the stairs which led directly into the church and assembled in choir to sing the night offices of Nocturns (now called Matins) and Lauds. A monk who is not in choir in time for the preliminary prayers, which are said when the bell ceases to ring, must confess his fault and ask pardon in chapter. The adult monks were followed into the choir by the boys shepherded by their master. And after them came the novices, who slept in their own quarters. When they had arrived the service could start. Engulfed in a cavern of darkness that was only intermittently broken by the pools of light shed by lanterns and candelabra, the cantors began their chant.

Staying awake during the lengthy readings of Nocturns was evidently a problem. The Cluny customary provides for a lantern-bearer to perambulate the choir to make sure that everybody is awake. If he comes upon a monk who has fallen asleep during the lessons, he does not speak, but gently moves the lantern to and fro close to his face until he wakes. Although the day began in the early hours of the morning, it was not unduly long as the community retired for the night at dusk. The longer summer days were punctuated by a siesta that was allowed in the afternoon. At some periods of the year the community would go back to bed after singing the Lauds of the Dead and rest until the bell woke them again at first light. They then returned to the church to sing Prime—the first service of the day. After this there was an interval, which in summer might last a couple of hours or more, before the bell rang for the short office of Terce, the service of the third hour sung towards 9 a.m. During this period the monks changed into their day-shoes and washed hands and face at the lavabo, which was situated in the cloister, and occupied themselves with reading or tasks about the house.

As St Benedict had intended, vocal prayer at the canonical hours formed the framework of the monastic day. There were the three short services of Terce, Sext, and None, the last two sung respectively at about midday and three in the afternoon, and the rather longer evening office of Vespers. And the day concluded at dusk with the brief service of Compline. But as we have seen, by the eleventh century the relatively simple liturgical scheme of the Rule had been greatly enlarged by the addition of further services—the offices of the Dead and of All Saints—and by additional psalms. The community now attended two masses daily, the 'morning mass' celebrated immediately after Terce, and the high mass that followed the office of Sext at about midday. Besides these, there were the private masses murmured at the many side-altars in the early hours before daybreak, for by this period it had become the practice to ordain a high proportion of monks to the priesthood.

At major festivals the rituals of the liturgy were enriched with added magnificence. On the vigils of Christmas, Easter, and Pentecost, the church and cloister were decorated, and the brethren were woken for the night office by the pealing of all the bells. The high altar was illuminated by hundreds of candles, the cantors wore gorgeous copes, and during the Nocturns two priests circulated incensing the altars and the members of the community. When Matins was finished, the solemn mass of the feast was celebrated, heralded by a peal of bells, and following this the night services were completed by the singing of Lauds. The brethren could then return to bed to snatch what sleep they could before daybreak. It is impossible for the modern student to assess the psychological impact upon the individual of these interminable hours spent daily in vocal prayer and liturgical rituals. How much of the participation was simply mechanical? It is significant that some of the most reflective minds of the period rejected the Cluniac pattern of observance and that the new orders of the twelfth century drastically pruned the traditional monastic liturgy.

Outside choir, the most important assembly point of the day was the chapter. Following the morning mass, the community processed out of the church into the chapter-house. The brethren sat on the gradines—the tiered seats around the walls—and the abbot or prior presided. After the reading of a lesson and a chapter of the Rule, the head of the house delivered a conference or sermon. Business matters concerning the community might then be discussed. This was also the occasion when individuals who had committed breaches of the Rule confessed their faults or were accused by others, and were assigned penances. The boys met in a chapter of their own. There, Ulrich explains, those who have blundered in singing the psalmody, misbehaved in any way, or simply fallen asleep during the services, are stripped of cowl and frock and beaten by their master with willow rods. Harsh, but no harsher than the treatment children expected to receive in the outside world. It was a general conviction in medieval society that constant beating was indispensable for the proper education of the young.

After chapter, which would have ended towards 10 a.m., there was a clear period that could be devoted to work or study, lasting until the bell rang for Sext, about midday. Work was a part of the monk's routine expressly enjoined by St Benedict. There were always tasks to be performed in the offices and workshops of the monastery. But the abbeys of the eleventh century employed servants for the menial jobs. In a major establishment such as Cluny, or the cathedral priory of Canterbury, which contained perhaps upwards of a hundred monks, as much as half of the community might be occupied with administrative duties either inside or outside the enclosure. Those who were not involved in administration spent the hours outside choir in reading, copying books in the scriptorium, or in artistic work. The manual labour prescribed by the Rule had by now become largely ritualised. 'To tell the truth,' says the maestro in Ulrich's *customary*, 'it amounts to nothing more than shelling the new beans or rooting out weeds that choke the good plants in the garden; sometimes making loaves in the bakery. On the days when it is done, after holding a shorter chapter than usual, the abbot says, "Let us proceed to manual labour". All then process out, the boys leading, to the garden. Psalms are sung, and after a spell of weeding, the procession re-forms and returns to the cloister'.

The virtual elimination of manual work in favour of intellectual activities was partly the result of the great elaboration of the monk's liturgical duties. Far more of his day was spent in choir than St Benedict had envisaged; and choir duties were physically exhausting as well as time-consuming. The change also reflected changing social assumptions. Tilling and hewing were work for peasants. Peter the Venerable argued that the delicate hands of his monks, who came from a social milieu unfamiliar with toil, were more suitably employed furrowing parchment with pens than ploughing furrows in fields. It was one of the objects of the Cistercian reform to reinstate manual labour and assert its spiritual value. But it was a reversal of the prevailing trend, in which the Benedictine houses did not follow the reformers.

The importance of reading in the life of the monk was underlined by the generous amount of time allocated to it in the Rule; and it was symbolised by the annual issue of books for private reading at the beginning of Lent. At Cluny, the keeper of the book-store, in accordance with the Rule, had the books laid out on a carpet spread on the floor of the chapter-house. A list of the books issued the previous year and their recipients is read out. Each monk, on hearing his name, hands back his book and receives another. Anyone who has not finished his book confesses his fault and asks pardon. Lanfranc's constitutions describe an identical ritual at Canterbury. A chance survival in the Farfa abbey customary of a list of sixty-three books issued to the monks one Lent in the mid-eleventh century gives us a momentary glimpse of the reading tastes of one community. Most of the books fall into the expected categories of works of devotion and ascetical theology—Cassian, Smaragdus's commentary on the Rule, Lives of the Saints, and the Scriptural commentaries of the Fathers from Jerome to Gregory the Great, as well as the later commentators like Bede, Alcuin, and Rhabanus Maurus. But the list also contains an interesting selection of historical works, the *History* of Josephus, the *Ecclesiastical History* of Eusebius, an anonymous *History of the English,* which must be Bede, and, more surprisingly, the secular Roman history of Livy, not a work that was widely known at this period. The reading of history was regarded as an improving spiritual exercise. As John of Salisbury observed in the twelfth century, through studying the chronicles of the past, men came to perceive the invisible working of God.

A significant part of the book-holdings in a Benedictine library was likely to come from donations. When Odo became a monk at Baume he took with him a hundred books, which were probably transported in due course to Cluny. Medieval library catalogues, like the great catalogue of Canterbury cathedral priory which was compiled in the thirteenth century, sometimes list the books under the names of donors. Nevertheless, a proportion of the librarian's stock had to be supplied by the monastery's own scriptorium.

The work that went on in the scriptorium or writing-room was vital to the internal life of the monastery and it also provided an important service to the outside world. At any given time several monks were likely to be engaged in copying texts or composing books of their own. Sometimes they worked in the northern walk of the cloister alongside the church, but often a separate room off the cloister was allocated to the task. The ninth-century plan of Saint Gall provides for a spacious scriptorium above the library with seven writing-desks. The first charge on the workers in the scriptorium was the reproduction of the books needed for the services in choir and the readings in the refectory—the antiphoners, tropers, missals and lectionaries. An equally important task was the provision of grammars for the education of the boys in the cloister and the multiplication of books to stock the library. Most of the energies of the monks engaged in writing would be devoted to making copies of approved texts. If exemplars were needed, they could be borrowed from other monasteries. Since pen, ink, and parchment were the sole materials of production, books took long to make and they were rare and costly objects in the medieval world. Men used them as security for loans, and they were often passed on by pious bequest. A complete Old Testament might cost more than the total annual stipend of a country curate. A whole flock of sheep would be needed to provide the parchment for it. Understandably, therefore, some abbeys demanded a deposit before lending books. 'Send by the bearer of these present letters', writes Peter the Venerable to the monks of the Grande Chartreuse, 'or by some other trustworthy person securities for the books I have sent—not as a pledge for their better preservation, but so that the orders of our father St Hugh relating to such loans may be observed.'

It was not only the humble copyists of texts who worked in the scriptorium of course. The regulated leisure of the cloister provided the ideal conditions for authorship. The evidence lies in the product. The monastic writing-office was the factory that, until the twelfth century, produced the great bulk of the literary works, secular as well as sacred, that filled the libraries of the Middle Ages. Abbo of Fleury (d. 1004), grammarian, mathematician, historian and hagiographer, to Fulbert of Chartres 'the most famous master of all France', held that, after prayer and fasting, the practice of literary composition did most to bridle the lusts of the flesh.

Although the community itself had first call upon the resources of its scriptorium, monastic scribes also provided important services to the outside world. Both in France and pre-Conquest England, early rulers who possessed no organised chanceries of their own made use of the scriptoria of the abbeys to write their letters and diplomas. Abbot Hilduin of Saint-Denis was archchaplain to Louis the Pious, and the abbey supplied the emperor with a writing-office. But besides such periodic help to princes the monasteries performed an essential service for the world of letters by reproducing books to order for scholars or secular patrons. Some houses acquired a reputation for the technical excellence of their calligraphy and the beauty of the illumination and miniature painting with which they decorated their manuscripts. It was of course a source of income to the monastery. The person who ordered the book paid for the labour, and it was quite common for him to supply the necessary parchment. Canon Hillin of Cologne, when he commissioned a text of the four Gospels from the tenth-century workshop of Reichenau, apparently sent the monks the parchment already cut and made up into quires. Reichenau in the tenth-century, like St Augustine's Canterbury in the twelfth, was famous for the sumptuous quality of its painted manuscripts. But the monks produced utilitarian copies of texts as well as display books. In fact, until the rise of the university stationers in the thirteenth century, who specialised in the rapid reproduction of cheap scholastic texts, the monasteries had a virtual monopoly of book production. As time went on, however, the pressure of demand made it necessary to supplement the efforts of the monk copyists by employing professional scribes, who were paid a salary out of the monastic coffers.

The monastic timetable allocated two periods of the day to reading or writing, one in the morning before the midday office, and the second between the main meal of the day and Vespers. The hour of dinner—the main meal—varied according to the season. In the summer months, beginning with Easter, it was eaten soon after midday following the high mass; and there was a second meal in the evening after Vespers. In the shorter days of winter the timetable allowed for only a single meal, which was taken rather later in the afternoon, but some other form of solid refreshment or a drink of wine was given before Compline and departure to bed. Meals, like other activities, had their ritual. After washing their hands, all entered the refectory, where places were allocated by strict rules of seniority, and remained standing until the arrival of the abbot or prior, who pronounced the blessing. The meal was served and eaten in silence except for the voice of the lector who read to the community from a lectern or pulpit.

The preservation of silence in which prayer and reflection could flourish was one of the primary aims of all strict monastic observance. After the morning chapter and after dinner in the afternoon there were periods of the day when conversation was permitted in the cloister. But in church, refectory, and dormitory, silence was perpetually observed, save for the chant and the public readings of the lectors. Some latitude was allowed to individual officers engaged in business or to the head of the house who might be entertaining guests in his own quarters, but with Compline all talking had to cease. The silence of Cluny in the early days was proverbial. An elaborate sign language, a kind of deaf-and-dumb alphabet, was developed so that the monk could express his needs without speaking. 'The novice must needs learn the signs with diligence,' explains Ulrich, 'for after he has joined the community he is very rarely allowed to speak.' A request for bread was indicated by a circular motion made with the thumbs and first two fingers of both hands; fish was signified by a motion of the hand simulating the tail of a fish moving through water; trout was the same, but in addition the finger was drawn from eyebrow to eyebrow—a sign indicating that even if no flesh-meat was eaten at Cluny, the table did not lack some variety; for milk, the lips were touched with the little finger, 'because thus does an infant suck'. A monk who wanted to make confession approached a priest of his choice and standing before him indicated his wish by drawing his right hand from his scapular and placing it on his chest; whereupon the priest rose and led him into the chapter-house to hear his confession.

The rules of silence did something to mitigate what strikes a modern student as one of the most oppressive aspects of life in a medieval monastery—the total lack of privacy. It was not only that the individual slept, ate, and moved about in the constant company of others; even such humdrum personal activities as shaving and taking baths were closely supervised communal exercises. Shaving was reserved for the eve of major festivals, so that by the end of Lent the community must have presented an exceedingly shaggy appearance. At Cluny the razors were locked away in a cupboard beside the entrance to the dormitory, to be produced when a general shave took place. The brethren sat in lines along the cloister wall and passed round the razors and bowls. The operation was preceded by the recitation of psalms and collects. At St Augustine's, Canterbury, the monks shaved one another but, as the chronicler explained, the wounds they inflicted by their inexpert hands were so bad that Abbot Roger of Chichester imported lay barbers to do the job.

The Benedictine Rule urged that bathing was a practice to be discouraged except for those who were sick; and the customaries commonly ordained baths three times a year, before the festivals of Christmas, Easter, and Pentecost, but always with the proviso that those who did not wish to participate need not do so. Lanfranc's constitutions for Canterbury lay down an elaborate procedure for the provision of baths before Christmas. The brethren assemble in the cloister and wait until the senior monk in charge of the operation calls them in groups to the bath-house. There each monk undresses and enters a cubicle shielded by a curtain and takes his bath in silence. And even this moment of solitude was not to be prolonged; 'when he has sufficiently washed, he shall not stay for pleasure, but shall rise, dress and return to the cloister'. An unmistakable air of anxiety hangs over the whole proceeding.

It would be a mistake, of course, to suppose that the monks themselves felt oppressed by the lack of solitude. Medieval society did not afford the individual much opportunity to be alone, unless he retreated to the desert. Peasant families occupied one-room dwellings separated in many cases from their livestock by only a partition; townsmen lived in small congested houses; and rural knights lived and ate in halls surrounded by family, bailiffs, neighbours, and servants. Continuous company was the normal lot. The privacy we take for granted is the product of a more affluent society. As Héloise reminded Abelard when she was trying to dissuade him from marriage, only the very rich had houses with many rooms, and scholars were not usually wealthy.

The customaries set out an orderly routine covering every hour of the day and night. They make it clear what everyone has to do and when he is required to do it. What they cannot tell us, however, is the extent to which the rules were observed at any given time. The history of most monasteries that were long-lived reveals alternating periods of strict observance and relaxation. Much depended upon the quality of the superior. Under an easy-going or senile abbot discipline tended to disintegrate. There were always those in a community who were ready to take advantage of such a situation. For, as long as the practice of child-oblation continued, a fair proportion of monks in the Benedictine houses had been drafted. Some, when they reached adulthood, were able to rise to the ideal that had been wished upon them; others obviously sought to create a comfortable life for themselves in a predicament from which medieval society offered no escape. Nor were all adult postulants motivated by a simple enthusiasm for the ascetical life. Many sought admission because the monastic habit offered them the best prospect of status and security.

Apart from the question of lax observance, the customaries by their very nature convey a deceptive impression of peaceful and undisturbed routine. But this was a condition few communities can have enjoyed for very long. The erection of monastic buildings, which look homogeneous to the casual eye of the modern visitor, often took several generations. And in a thriving establishment there was a constant process of rebuilding and enlargement. During the eleventh century there can have been few periods when the claustral peace of Cluny was not disturbed by the sound of hammer and chisel, the creaking of hoists and the clatter of workmen. The even tenor of monastic life was often disrupted, too, by natural mishaps and by the violent intrusion of the outside world. A wealthy landed corporation could not hope to insulate itself entirely from the turmoils of war and political upheaval. Canterbury cathedral priory, like other English monasteries, suffered disturbance of its internal harmony after the Norman Conquest by the forcible importation of an alien prior and a group of Norman monks; and for some years racial animosity kept the two sections of the community apart. The life of the priory was also disrupted by the wholesale building operations that followed the Conquest. Its church was twice rebuilt in the course of the next sixty years, only to be devastated in 1174 by a fire which left the monks without a usable choir for more than a decade. Such mishaps were almost commonplace. But the quiet erosion of community life was less the consequence of catastrophes like this than of forces that sprang from the internal administration of the monastery itself.

MONASTIC OFFICIALDOM

As St Benedict had envisaged, the abbot found it necessary to appoint a number of subordinate officers from among the brethren to assist in the management of the monastery's affairs. By the eleventh century a fairly elaborate chain of officialdom had been evolved in the greater Benedictine houses. The special task to which each official was assigned was called an 'obedience' and he himself was referred to as an 'obedientiary'. In the first place there was the prior. Although the abbot appointed all his subordinates, the head of a great abbey was a prominent person with public responsibilities that frequently took him away from the monastery. He might be absent for long periods in the service of king or pope or on the business of his own congregation. When he was at home, he was expected to entertain important visitors at his table. All this tended to separate him from the routine life of his monks; and during the twelfth century it became normal practice for the abbot to have his own house, with hall, kitchen, and chapel, within the enclosure. This development meant that the responsibility for maintaining regular life and discipline in the cloister fell increasingly to the abbot's second-in-command, the claustral prior. The bigger houses had more than one prior. At Cluny, where the abbot was constantly on his travels visiting his far-flung dependencies, there was a grand prior, charged with the general management of the abbey's properties and its relations with the external world, a claustral prior to oversee the internal life of the community, and second and third priors to help him. There were also roundsmen, called *circatores,* whose role was to tour the premises during periods of work and reading and ensure that there was no disorder or idle gossiping.

The various administrative departments of the establishment were entrusted to a lengthening chain of obedientiaries. The precentor, or cantor, was responsible for training the monks in the chant and the proper celebration of the liturgy and also, since he had to ensure a supply of service books, for supervision of the scriptorium. The sacrist had the duty of looking after the fabric of the church, the altars, and sacred vessels, and he had care of the shrines—a heavy duty in abbeys that boasted famous relics and attracted a large number of pilgrims. The novice-master had the care and training of the novices. The almoner was entrusted with the task of dispensing food and other forms of relief to the poor. It was an evangelical obligation that was reiterated in the Rule, and most monasteries took it seriously. Monastic alms-giving was in fact the only regular form of poor relief that existed in medieval society. The almoner of Cluny was assigned a portion of the tithes from the churches in the abbey's possession to enable him to meet the demands on his charity. There was a daily distribution of bread and wine and twelve pies, weighing three pounds each, from the monks' kitchen. On Quinquagesima Sunday all the poor who cared to come were fed with a meal of salt pork. Besides giving food to those who begged at the abbey gates, the almoner also provided hospitality for the poorer pilgrims and clerks who arrived on foot. And his charity was not confined to callers. According to Ulrich, he was expected to make a weekly tour of the township to seek out any who were sick and in need of food or medicaments. It was a practice that Lanfranc enjoined upon the almoner of Canterbury.

The monk-chamberlain saw to the provision and laundering of clothing for the brethren. The supply of food, drink, and fuel for the community and its guests was the business of the cellarer. 'He should be sober and no great eater', urges St Benedict with understandable anxiety. Much of his time was taken up with the transport, checking, and storage of provisions from the abbey's estates. It was common practice to allocate to his use the buildings off the west range of the cloister for storage purposes.

Another sensitive appointment was that of the infirmarian. He had charge of what was in effect a parallel establishment, usually situated a little to the east of the main complex, containing its own dormitory, hall, chapel, and suites of private rooms. It was a monastery in cameo. This was because it had not only to house and nurse monks who were sick, but also to provide a permanent rest-home for those who were too old and infirm to take full part in the routine of the monastery. It might also be called upon sometimes to furnish quarters for the head of the house if he retired on account of age or bad health. As the Rule restricted the eating of meat to the sick, in times of strict observance the refectory in the infirmary was the only place in the monastery where meat was served.

In a great abbey like Cluny one of the heaviest tasks was that of the guest-master. He was in fact running what, by eleventh-century standards, was a first-class hotel, providing accommodation, meals, and stabling facilities, for a continual stream of visitors which included prelates and princes and members of the higher nobility. The guest-house built by Odilo was a palace with a frontage of one hundred and thirty-five feet, containing forty-five beds for male guests and, in another wing, thirty beds for their ladies; but it was reserved for visitors who came on horses; those arriving on foot were assigned to a less grand establishment under the infirmarian's jurisdiction. As time went on, the senior obedientiaries, who had the heaviest responsibilities, delegated part of their task to subordinate officers, so that it came about that an ever larger proportion of the community was involved in administrative or supervisory duties. Thus the sacrist was assisted by a subsacrist and in some cases by a separate warden of the shrine, and some of the cellarer's duties were distributed among a kitchener in charge of the catering, a refectorer, a gardener, and a woodward.

Although all the obedientiaries owed their appointment to the abbot, in practice they acquired a large degree of independence in the administration of their offices. This was the outcome of a growing tendency to divide the properties of the abbey in such a way that a proportion of lands, tithes, and offerings was allocated to maintaining each of the offices. This subdivision was encouraged by the habits of benefactors, who often made pious bequests expressly earmarked to support specific departments such as the almonry—a favorite object for charitable bequests—the infirmary, or the guesthouse. It gave each of the major obedientiaries control over a portion of the monastery's income and over the property from which the income came. It was a practice fraught with dangerous implications both for regular observance and for financial stability. It meant that a group of monks were not only preoccupied with internal administration but were also involved in managerial responsibilities which frequently took them away from the monastery, for estate management necessitated inspecting distant properties, interviewing bailiffs, hearing accounts, and attending courts. It was thus necessary to exonerate obedientiaries from regular attendance in choir, a duty that St Benedict had insisted was the first priority in the life of a monk: 'Let nothing take precedence over the Divine Office.'

The devolution of authority and economic decision-making could also have damaging financial consequences. In the course of the twelfth century bad housekeeping or financial adventurism by individual monastic officers got some abbeys into serious debt. Cluny, whose estates were under the control of twenty-three monk-deans, was in financial difficulties when Peter the Venerable was elected abbot in 1122. Excessive expenditure and mismanagement of the demesne manors had made it difficult to keep the abbey supplied with regular provisions. It had to be rescued from this predicament by a reorganisation of the abbey's farms and by generous financial help from one of its former monks, Henry of Blois, the brother of King Stephen and now bishop of Winchester. Crises like this were common among the Benedictine houses. In the thirteenth century there was a general move by ecclesiastical authorities to improve the situation by reestablishing central control over monastic finances. This was done by pressing each house to appoint a monk-treasurer and to set up a central exchequer, through which all income and disbursements had to pass, and by requiring an annual audit of accounts.

RECRUITMENT

Although monks had in principle withdrawn from the world, the monastery was an organism whose roots were deeply embedded in the social landscape. Many of the older Benedictine houses were situated in, or on the fringe of towns, and were intimately involved in civic life. At Bologna, the ancient abbey of Santo Stefano still carries on its twelfth-century façade an open-air brick pulpit, the outward and visible sign of the pastoral role it discharged towards the surrounding city. Those richly endowed abbeys that were founded in the countryside usually became the nuclei of new townships, created by the need of a large monastic community for goods and services.

The most obvious and immediate link between the cloister and the world outside it lay in its sources of recruitment. Throughout the eleventh and twelfth centuries new monasteries were founded and the monastic population continued to increase. The rising number of monks and nuns was a dimension of the general population increase that most parts of Western Europe experienced during this period. In the latter end of the period, growth was most conspicuous among the new orders, particularly the Cistercians. Firm figures for the Benedictines are hard to come by before the thirteenth century and have been variously interpreted. Some abbeys suffered a marked decline in numbers after the eleventh century; others, after a phase of rapid expansion which was often the result of local circumstances, settled down to a steady level of recruitment which continued with little change for the next two hundred years. Canterbury cathedral priory, for instance, experienced a boom in applicants in the two generations that followed the Norman Conquest, which can be explained by the dispossession of many English landed families and the destruction of their worldly prospects. Thus by 1120 the number of monks at the priory had risen from about sixty in Lanfranc's time to something like one hundred and twenty. Thereafter numbers declined to about eighty and remained at about this level during the thirteenth century. Here, as elsewhere, the relative constancy of numbers over a long period of time indicates not so much a shortage of recruits as a determination of monastic chapters to match numbers to material resources. With this end in view, both Cluny and Cîteux in the thirteenth century assigned a fixed quota of monks—a *numerus clausus*—to each house of their order, which was not to be exceeded. Numbers at Cluny touched their maximum of about three hundred by the death of St Hugh. He seems to have admitted all who applied, without much regard to their character or suitability; but his successors found it necessary to adopt a more discriminating policy over admissions. By 1250 the community contained two hundred monks, and it seems to have remained at roughly that level for the next hundred years.

Who were these people and where did they come from? As we have seen, the children donated by their parents formed one section of the monastic population. But the new orders generally declined to accept child-oblates, and although the Benedictines continued to take them, the children formed a declining proportion of black-monk communities in the twelfth century. Peter the Venerable regarded them as a potential source of trouble and he reduced the number of boys at Cluny to six. The surge of new recruits to the cloister thus consisted largely of adult postulants, both clerical and lay.

The scarcity of systematic records makes it difficult to generalise about their social origins. Some establishments, like the Swabian abbey of Reichenau, boasted of their social exclusiveness, but this was far from being the general situation. The requirement of noble birth as a qualification for entry was commoner in the monasteries and cathedral chapters of Germany than it was elsewhere. The leading figures in the Cluniac empire were men of aristocratic birth, but the rank and file were trawled from a more varied background. Most Benedictine houses appear to have recruited from their own locality and to have admitted men without distinction of birth, provided they could bring some form of endowment with them. The only class debarred was that of the unfree. But the property requirement, even if it was small, obviously meant that most recruits came from the ranks of middling landowners and better-off townspeople. One reservoir of recruits, about which we know too little in this early period, may have been provided by the local schools in monastic ownership. The chronicler of Bury St Edmund's tells us that his hero, Abbot Samson of Bury, got his early education at the abbey's school in the borough, where he was taught by Master William of Diss, a secular clerk. We have no means of telling how many others made their first and most decisive contacts with the cloister through this channel.

Canterbury cathedral priory provides an illuminating case history of a large and wealthy Benedictine establishment which drew a significant number of recruits from the local township. The surviving rent-rolls reveal that in the twelfth century many Canterbury families gave a relative to the cathedral monastery. Those monks who can be identified, including some of the senior obedientiaries, were children of the more substantial families—those of the borough reeves and the wealthier tradespeople, such as goldsmiths and mercers. The endowment they brought with them when they took the habit consisted in many cases of quite modest properties—a house or a plot of land within the city walls. Some of these recruits were evidently late converts to the monastic life. One of them, a monk named Henry, was the father of Hamo, the Reeve of Canterbury. Another late convert, a leading citizen named John Calderun, retired to the cloister about the year 1176, while his wife was still living: he arranged for her maintenance by contracting the priory to supply her with a daily corrody or pension of food from the monastic kitchen and a periodic provision of clothes. Thus many of the monks had relatives among the townspeople including, in some cases, sons as well as brothers and sisters.

Pilgrimage and Medieval Travel

JONATHAN SUMPTION

Beginning in late imperial times, pilgrims traveled to shrines throughout Europe. The churches of St. Martin at Tours and of Santiago de Compostella in northwestern Spain were two of the most popular destinations, and the latter became particularly important after the beginning of the reconquest of Spain in the eleventh century. Pilgrimage to Jerusalem and the holy places in its vicinity also became popular in the eleventh century, and the establishment of the Latin kingdom of Jerusalem in 1099 facilitated the movement of pilgrims to that region.

In early times, pilgrims were probably the most numerous travelers in Europe—along with some of the Jewish merchants whose activities Robert Chazan described in "Jews in a Christian Society." By the later Middle Ages, commercial travelers were by far the most important group, although the number of pilgrims had also increased drastically. The pilgrims followed the trade routes and in fact became an important part of the traffic going through the great Italian commercial centers. The seriousness with which city fathers regarded the pilgrim trade is indicated by the steps taken by the Venetian doges. They created elaborate regulations to govern sea captains who transported pilgrims to the Holy Land, and who even seem to have offered "packaged tours." The pilgrims have left many accounts of their journeys across Europe and the Mediterranean; these travel diaries are the principal source of our knowledge of the conditions of transport and travel during the medieval and early modern periods. In the following selection, Jonathan Sumption uses these accounts to create a picture of pilgrimage and of travel on land and sea during this long period.

From: Jonathan Sumption, *Pilgrimage* (Totowa, NJ: Rowman & Littlefield, 1975), pp. 168–70, 171–74, 175–83, 184–87, 188–90, 192–96.

PREPARATIONS

'He that be a pilgrim,' declared the London preacher Richard Alkerton in 1406, 'oweth first to pay his debts, afterwards to set his house in governance, and afterwards to array himself and take leave of his neighbours, and so go forth.'

His first act, if he was a man of substance, was to make his will. Pilgrims enjoyed the special privilege of disposing of their property by will, a privilege which, until the late middle ages, was accorded to very few. As well as naming his heirs, the will would deal with such matters as the administration of his property in his absence and the length of time which was to elapse before he should be presumed dead. In Normandy local custom required every landowner to make a will which would automatically be executed if he did not announce his return within a year and a day. Some pilgrims also made private agreements with their wives as to how long they should leave before remarrying. The Church did what it could to ensure that the terms of a pilgrim's will were respected. In Spain, for instance, it made his companions responsible for looking after his personal effects. Failing companions, the local clergy were expected to keep them for a year and a day and, if they remained unclaimed, to sell them and apply the money to endowing masses for the repose of the dead pilgrim's soul.

In his absence, a pilgrim's property was immune from all civil claims in a court of law. The service which he owed to his feudal lord was usually suspended during the pilgrimage, and in northern France, according to Beaumanoir, pilgrims were exempt from the obligation to take part in family vendettas. In effect, there was no legal remedy to be had against a bona fide pilgrim, so long as he returned home to face his adversaries within a reasonable time. Illegal remedies were *a fortiori* forbidden, and those who had recourse to them faced both civil and ecclesiastical sanctions. In the bull *Quantum Praedecessores* of December 1145, Eugenius III proclaimed that the wife and children, goods and chattels of every pilgrim or crusader were 'placed under the protection of the Holy See and of all the prelates of the Church of God. By our apostolic authority we absolutely forbid anyone to disturb them until their return or death.' Before the first crusade this principle had probably been honoured chiefly in the breach. But effective protection was essential if crusaders were to be recruited for the defence of the Holy Land, and by the end of the twelfth century, flagrant violations of a pilgrim's rights never failed to arouse indignant protest. The invasion of Normandy by Philip Augustus of France while Richard Coeur-de-Lion was in the Holy Land was bitterly criticized, and some of Philip's own vassals refused to follow him. When, at the beginning of the thirteenth century, it seemed that the entire Angevin empire in France must shortly fall into the hands of the French king, loyal vassals of John were afraid that Philip would seize their lands. Some of them regarded a pilgrim's privileges as the best guarantee of the rights of their heirs. This, at any rate, was the reason given by Archambert de Monluc when he joined the fourth crusade, appointing as trustees of his property a formidable list of ecclesiastical personages.

Although few pilgrims went to the extremes recommended by the preacher of the sermon *Veneranda Dies,* most of them made some concession to the principle that a pilgrimage should be accomplished in poverty. Rich pilgrims often made generous donations to the poor before leaving. The cartularies of monasteries, from the eleventh century onwards, are full of deeds recording the gifts made by departing pilgrim and crusaders. A donor could have the best of both worlds by making his gift conditional on his not returning alive. Then, when he returned home, he could demand the usufruct of his property for the rest of his life, after which it would become the unencumbered possession of the Church. When Aimeric II, count of Fézensac, gave some windmills to the canons of Auch in 1088 as he was about to leave for the Holy Land, he insisted that 'if I come back alive from Jerusalem, I can have them back until my death.' If the knight never returned, the monks were often required to give a pension to his widow and sometimes even to his children. In fact, even if no such conditions were explicitly mentioned, they were almost certainly implied by both parties. When Leteric de Chatillon died in Palestine in 1100, the monks of La Charité allowed his widow half the revenues of his estates, although no such arrangement is found in the deed whereby Leteric had made the monks his heirs. Hughes de Lurcy, on returning from the Holy Land in the 1080s, claimed back his lands from the monks, promising to leave it [sic] to them on his death. Pilgrims probably adopted this roundabout procedure in order to ensure that their lands were safe in their absence. Some of them may also have borrowed the cost of the journey from the monks and left the lands with them as a pledge.

The true pilgrim, urged the preacher of the sermon *Venerenda* [sic] *Dies,* ought before his departure to make amends to all those whom he has offended, and to ask the permission of his wife, his parish priest, and anyone else to whom he owed obligations. The most important of these, for a layman, was his feudal lord, whose consent would be necessary if the pilgrim wished to nominate his heir or safeguard the position of his wife. Even the kings of France, Louis VII in 1146 and Philip Augustus in 1190, sought formal permission to leave with the crusade from St. Denis, whose vassals they recognized themselves to be. A cleric was required to ask the permission of his superior before making a pilgrimage, and until the fourteenth century this obligation was enforced with vigour. The German annalist Lambert of Hersfeld recalled how he had set out for Jerusalem in 1058, immediately after his ordination, without asking his abbot:

> 'I was afraid that since I had set out without his blessing, I might have given him offence. If he had died in my absence I would have remained forever unreconciled to him and would thus have committed a terrible sin in the eyes of God. But God's favour was with me, . . . for I returned in safety, confessed my sin, and was received with kindness. I felt as if I had just escaped alive from the fires of Hell.'

He was, in fact, only just in time, for the abbot became feverish that very evening and died a week later. . . .

When his enemies had been placated and his creditors satisfied, the pilgrim sought out his parish priest or, occasionally, his bishop, and received a formal blessing. Texts of these blessings for travellers survive from the early eighth century, though they did not pass into general use until the eleventh. Blessing ceremonies reflected the growing feeling among pilgrims that they belonged to an 'order' of the Church, distinguished from other men by a uniform and by a solemn ritual of initiation. Mass departures to the Holy Land or Santiago were marked by public ceremonies in the cathedrals. But most pilgrims received their blessing privately from their parish priest, or else from a monk whose sanctity they respected. The hermit St. Godric of Finchale was said to have performed the ceremony regularly. Joinville, in 1248 sought out the Cistercian abbot of Cheminon on account of his saintly reputation, and then, after receiving his blessing, made his way on foot without shoes or coat to the embarkation point of the crusade at Marseilles.

PILGRIM'S DRESS

Once initiated into the 'order' of pilgrims, he signified his attachment to a new way of life by wearing a uniform, as distinctive in its own way as the tonsure of a priest. 'When the debts be thus paid and the meine is thus set in governance', continued Richard Alkerton in 1406, 'the pilgrim shall array himself. And then he oweth first to make himself be marked with a cross, as men be wont to do that shall pass to the Holy Land. . . . Afterwards the pilgrim shall have a staff, a sclavein, and a scrip'. The staff, a tough wooden stick with a metal toe, was the most distinctive as well as the most useful part of the pilgrim's attire. The 'sclavein' was a long, coarse tunic. The scrip was a soft pouch, usually made of leather, strapped to the pilgrim's waist; in it he kept his food, mess-cans, and money. Such was the attire of every serious pilgrim after the end of the eleventh century. Much later, probably in the middle of the thirteenth century, pilgrims began to wear a great broad-brimmed hat, turned up at the front, and attached at the back to a long scarf which was wound round the body as far as the waist.

The origin of this curious garb is not at all clear. The staff and pouch were used by the migrant monks of Egypt in the fourth century, but they were obvious and sensible accessories for any traveller on foot, not only for pilgrims and not only in the middle ages. The tunic, on the other hand, whose practical usefulness is not as readily apparent, seems to make its first appearance at the beginning of the twelfth century. Canute, setting out for Rome in 1027, 'took up the scrip and staff as did all his companions', but there is no mention of the tunic. St. Anselm, in 1097, 'took his scrip and staff like a pilgrim', but again, no tunic. Orderic Vitalis, writing in about 1135, said that he could remember a time when pilgrims were indistinguishable from other travellers, except by their unshaven faces. Indeed it is probably about this time that the normal clothing of the traveller took on a sudden rigidity and became peculiarly the garb of the spiritual traveller.

This was almost certainly due to the fact that at the end of the eleventh century the Church began to bless the pilgrim's clothes and sanctify them as the uniform of his order. A special order of ceremony for pilgrims, as opposed to ordinary travellers, was now coming into existence. This usually took the form of blessing the pilgrim's pouch and mantle and presenting him with his staff from the altar. The ceremony has its origin in the blessing conferred on knights departing with the first crusade, and it is referred to in 1099 as a 'novel rite'. Behind the 'novel rite' is the pronounced tendency of the Church in the eleventh and twelfth centuries to stimulate lay piety by assigning to laymen certain defined spiritual functions. Those who fulfilled these functions were clothed with a special, almost ecclesiastical, status; they enjoyed spiritual privileges and ultimately secular ones as well. Hence the religious ceremony which now almost invariably accompanied the dubbing of a knight. Indeed, the ritual presentation of the pilgrim's staff bears a striking resemblance both to the dubbing of a knight and to the ordination of a priest. To the more austere pilgrim, the act of putting on his travelling clothes might have the same significance as taking the monastic habit. One such pilgrim was Rayner Pisani, an Italian merchant who experienced a sudden conversion during a business visit to Tyre in about 1140. Rayner took his pilgrim's tunic under his arm to the Golgotha chapel in Jerusalem and, in full view of an astonished crowd, removed all his old clothes and gave them to beggars. He then placed his tunic on the altar and asked the priest serving the chapel to invest him with it. This the priest did, and Rayner passed the remaining twenty years of his life as a hermit in Palestine.

In the course of time the Church invested the pilgrim's uniform with a rich and elaborate symbolism. Already in c. 1125 the author of the sermon *Vereranda Dies* is found explaining that the pilgrim's pouch is the symbol of almsgiving, because it is too small to hold much money and the pilgrim who wears it must therefore depend on charity. The pilgrim's staff is used for driving off wolves and dogs, who symbolize the snares of the Devil; the staff is the pilgrim's third leg, and three is the number of the Trinity; the staff therefore stands for the conflict of the Holy Trinity with the forces of evil, etc. This kind of imagery became very popular in the fourteenth and fifteenth centuries and it provided the theme for most of the sermons delivered to congregations of pilgrims before their departure. To Franco Sacchetti, the pilgrim's tunic stood for the humanity of Christ. The staff recalled the wood of the Cross in which lay the pilgrim's hope of salvation. Perhaps the most involved as well as the most popular of these allegories was the work of Thomas of London, a Dominican who taught in France and who wrote, in c. 1430, an *Instructorium Peregrinorum*. Here the staff, pouch, and tunic stand for faith, hope and charity, respectively, for reasons which are pursued as far as scholastic subtlety will permit. These arid academic exercises make dull reading today, but at the close of the middle ages they were much enjoyed.

On his way home, the pilgrim usually wore a badge or token showing where he had been. The best known and probably the earliest of these souvenirs was the palm of Jericho which pilgrims customarily brought back from Jerusalem. It is the origin of the English word 'palmer'. Like so many of the rituals associated with the pilgrimage to the Holy land, this seems to have had its origin in the eleventh century. The palms, which were collected in the plain between Jericho and the Jordan, were regarded as a symbol of regeneration, of the victory of faith over sin. Peter Damian refers to the picking of palm leaves as 'customary' in c. 1050, and the soldiers of the first crusade all travelled *en masse* to the Jordan in July 1099 to baptize themselves in the river and collect their palms. William of Tyre, writing in c. 1180, remarks that the palm of Jericho was 'the formal sign that the pilgrim's vow has been fulfilled'. And so it remained throughout the middle ages, though later generations did not have to travel as far as the Jordan for their palms. After the twelfth century palm-vendors carried on a thriving trade in the market of the 'Rue des Herbes' in Jerusalem and stalls piled high with palms could be seen beneath the walls of the Tower of David. . . .

TRAVEL OVERLAND

A long journey in the middle ages was not a thing to be lightly undertaken. The great sanctuaries were separated by hundreds of miles of unmade, ill-marked roads, many of them running through unpopulated tracts of Europe infested with bandits. 'O Lord, heavenly father', ran a blessing commonly conferred on pilgrims in the twelfth century, 'let the angels watch over thy servants N.N. that they may reach their destination in safety, . . . that no enemy may attack them on the road, nor evil overcome them. Protect them from the perils of fast rivers, thieves, or wild beasts.' The outbreak of a war could interrupt the flow of pilgrims to an important sanctuary or even choke it altogether. Thus the disordered state of central Italy brought about the serious decline of the Roman pilgrimage in the tenth century and again in the thirteenth. The Hundred Years War ruined the abbey of St.-Gilles and many other shrines of southern France, and significantly affected the prosperity of Santiago itself. In the fifteenth century a sudden Arab or Turkish descent on Rhodes might prevent all travel to the Holy Land for a year.

The condition of the roads was the first obstacle. Europe relied throughout the middle ages, on the network of roads bequeathed to it by the Roman empire. This network was far from comprehensive, but new roads did appear from time to time in response to changing needs. Thus the Roman road from Lyon to the south-west was diverted in the eleventh century through the hard granite mountains of the Ségalas to take it past the abbey of Conques; when the pilgrimage to Conques was forgotten, in the fourteenth century travellers returned to the old road. In France, the roads were never allowed to fall into complete disrepair, as they were in parts of England. Nevertheless travel was not easy and even an experienced rider could not expect to cover more than thirty miles in a day. The seigneur de Caumont, who rode from Caumont to Santiago in 1418, was reduced to six miles a day in the Pyrenees and Astruias, but he was capable of doing twenty-seven miles when the terrain was good.

The manor was responsible for the upkeep of the roads, but too often it had few resources and little enthusiasm for the work. Important roads, particularly if they were used by pilgrims, were frequently maintained by volunteers. For the maintenance of roads was regarded as a work of charity equivalent, for example, to alms-giving. Bridge-building was particularly meritorious, 'a service to posterity and therefore pleasing to God', declares a charter of 1031 concerning the construction of a bridge over the Loire at Tours. French hermits in northern Spain were active road-builders at the time when the great road to Santiago was being rebuilt by the Castilian kings. Their names are preserved in the *Guide for Pilgrims to Santiago*, 'and may their souls and those of their companions rest in everlasting peace.' The bridge over the river Miño at Puerto Marin was rebuilt after a civil war by Peter the Pilgrim. St. Domingo 'de la Calzada', another French immigrant, founded a celebrated hospice on the site of his hut by the river Oja, and spanned the stream with a wooden bridge; he built the first cobbled road across the marshy expanse between Nájera and Redecilla. Several medieval roads and bridges still survive in Spain and southern France, built under the impulsion of the pilgrimage to Santiago. At St.-Chély d'Aubrac and St.-Michel Pied-de-Port the old track, its stones worn or displaced, can still be followed for a few hundred yards. The fine stone bridges which span the river at Orthez and Oloron in Gascony date from the fourteenth century and replaced older, wooden ones. At Puente la Reina one can still see the great five-arched bridge where the two roads from southern France to Santiago came together.

The *Guide for Pilgrims to Santiago* catalogues the full range of catastrophes which could overcome the traveller on the roads in the twelfth century. It is both a historical guide and a route-book, offering its readers information about towns and hospices, a few useful words of the Basque language, an architectural description of Santiago cathedral, and precise directions on how to get there. The pilgrim is warned that the eight-mile ascent of the Port de Cize, the principal pass over the Pyrenees, is a steep climb; that in Galicia there are thick forests and few towns; that mosquitoes infest the marshy plain south of Bordeaux where the traveller who strays from the road can sink up to his knees in mud. Some of the rivers are impassable. Several pilgrims had been drowned at Sorde, where travellers and their horses were ferried across the river on hollowed-out tree trunks. Other rivers were undrinkable, like the salt stream at Lorca, where the author of the *Guide* found two Basques earning their living by skinning the horses who had died after drinking from it. Pilgrims were in theory exempt from the payment of tolls, but nevertheless the

Guide reports that the local lords exacted payment from every traveller in the Béarn. At the foot of the Port de Cize, pilgrims were searched and beaten with sticks if they could not pay the toll. The author demanded immediate action by the bishop and the king of Aragon, but it was more than half a century before the extortionist suffered retribution at the hands of Richard Coeur-de-Lion.

The supply of food and fodder is a constantly recurring theme in the *Guide,* and an important one at a time when it dictated the beginning and end of the travelling season much more effectively than the weather. There was no fodder to be had in the Landes south of Bordeaux, and the horseman was well-advised to bring three days' supply with him. There were parts of the route where the pilgrim would find it hard to buy a good meal for himself, even in summer. The food and wine were excellent in Gascony but dreadful in the Basque country. Fish caught in the river Ebro were disgusting, even poisonous. In general, concludes the *Guide,* Spanish meat should be avoided by those who are unused to it, 'and if any one can eat their fish without feeling sick, then he must have a stronger constitution than most of us.'

Against wild animals, bad roads, and natural catastrophes, the traveller had no protection. But, in theory, he enjoyed a measure of protection against man-made hazards. Every criminal code imposed special penalties on those who molested travellers, and synods of bishops regularly threatened them with the severest ecclesiastical censures. In 1096 a steward of the king of France was excommunicated for seizing a vassal of his on the road to Véze-lay during Lent. 'But you should know', the archbishop of Lyon pointed out, 'that all those who travel to the shrines of the saints are protected against attack at all times, and not only in Lent. Those who disturb their journey will suffer the harshest penalties of the Church, so that the fear of God may remain for ever in their eyes.' From 1303 onwards, molesters of pilgrims were included in the annual bull *In Coena Domini,* in which the pope solemnly anathematized an ever-lengthening list of obnoxious persons. But although it is true that pilgrims were marginally safer from attack than other travellers, they can never have felt secure. In the eleventh century the Tuscan nobleman Gerard of Galeria supported himself in part by attacking rich pilgrims on the roads north of Rome. King Harold's brother Tostig was one of his victims. The French robber-baron Thomas de Marle owed much of his notoriety to his practice of holding pilgrims to ransom and mutilating them if the ransom was not paid. He terrorized the roads of northern France for many years before Louis VI mounted a military expedition against him in 1128. From the constant complaints of the ecclesiastical authorities, it is clear that Thomas had many imitators. We are better informed, however, of the bandits of the fourteenth and fifteenth centuries, most of whom were never brought to justice. The Roman Jubilee of 1350 brought considerable prosperity to one Berthold von Eberstein, who descended daily on the long processions of pilgrims winding through the Rhine valley. The German *routier* Werner von Urslinger was another bandit who enriched himself in 1350. His hunting-ground was Tuscany, where several of the main routes to Rome met. Jacopo Gabrielli, the papal rector of the Patrimony, was allowed 14,000 florins to raise mercenaries against him, the cost to be defrayed from the offerings at the Roman basilicas. The banditry of the latter middle ages is remarkable for its international quality. The roads of northern Italy were infested with German robbers. On the roads which crossed northern Spain to Santiago, many of the bandits seem to have been Englishmen. In 1318 the provost of Estella spent several weeks in pursuit of one John of London, who had robbed pilgrims as they slept in a local hospice. In the following year a number of English bandits were captured at Pamplona. It was the same in the middle east. After the disappearance, in 1187, of the crusading kingdom of Jerusalem, the hills of Palestine were terrorized by brigands from every western nation, Englishmen, Frenchmen, and Germans, common criminals and former knights Templar, living side by side with Arabs for whom brigandage had been a way of life for centuries.

To the depredation of professional robber bands were added those of innkeepers and villagers, who found the constant stream of pilgrims passing their doors a temptation too great to resist. The inhabitants of the coastal villages of southern Normandy repeatedly waylaid pilgrims bound for Mont-St.-Michel. Those of northern Italy were said, in 1049, to be murdering Norman pilgrims 'daily'. Rather later, the villages of Navarre and the Basque country took to preying on pilgrims passing on the roads to Santiago; at the border towns of Sorde and Lespéron this was even described as 'customary'. Lawlessness on this scale was a familiar problem whenever the rise of a great sanctuary drew its seasonal flux of pilgrims onto the roads. The anarchic state of Italy in 1350 encouraged whole villages to seize and despoil pilgrims travelling to the Roman Jubilee. Peter, bishop of Rodez, and his companion were ambushed outside the village of Sant' Adriano in Sabina and were saved only [by] the timely arrival of Napoleone Orsini. The Romans themselves were reported to be mounting expeditions to rob pilgrims on the roads north of the city. One observer believed that half the pilgrims who set out for Rome in 1350 were robbed or killed on the way.

Innkeepers, never the most popular of men, were blamed for many thefts and murders. The most celebrated of all the miracles of St. James told of a man wrongly hanged for stealing money from the pockets of some wealthy German pilgrims as they slept in an inn at Toulouse. The true culprit, it transpired, was the innkeeper, 'wherefore it is clear that pilgrims should take great care before staying at an inn lest a similar fraud be perpetrated on them.' German pilgrims were notoriously the victims of these frauds, probably because they travelled in a somewhat more showy style than others. Tales of gruesome murders of pilgrims in lonely inns were commonplace. In the forest of Châtenay, near Mâcon, there lived, at the beginning of the eleventh century, an innkeeper who used to accommodate travellers at night and murder them as they slept. According to Radulph Glaber, an investigation by the authorities revealed eighty-eight bodies hidden in his hut.

No one doubted that the journey to Jerusalem was by far the most dangerous that a pilgrim could undertake. Every hazard which a mediaeval traveller could encounter is exemplified in the experiences of those who walked three thousand miles or endured six weeks in a tiny, unstable boat, in order to visit the Holy Places.

At the beginning of the eleventh century the conversion of Hungary and the revival of Byzantium had brought most of the overland route to Jerusalem under nominal Christian rule. Latin pilgrims learned how nominal that rule was in 1053, when the Irish pilgrim, Colman, was battered to death at Stockerau outside Vienna, after an angry mob had taken him for a government spy. Although travellers now passed the frontier of the Byzantine empire at Belgrade, behind that frontier lay tracts of untamed territory which never recognized Byzantine rule. Lietbert, bishop of Cambrai, found Christian slaves being sold here in the summer of 1054. The valley of the Danube was so insecure in 1053 that travellers were being turned back by border guards at Belgrade. Pilgrims passed the southern extremity of the Byzantine empire at the coastal town of Lattakieh in northern Syria. Here again, they encountered a deeply hostile and suspicious population. Gerald of Saumur was battered to death by Syrian peasants in 1021, while others, like Anselm of Ardres, fell into the hands of Moslem fanatics and were lucky to escape by renouncing their faith. . . .

The eleventh century had been the heyday of the overland route to the Holy Land, but the growing instability of eastern Europe sharply reduced its popularity in the twelfth. Wealthy pilgrims with large escorts might fight their way through the Balkans as Henry the Lion, duke of Saxony, did 'cum magna gloria' in 1172. But for most men, a pilgrimage to the Holy Land involved a long and expensive journey by sea. After the final disappearance of the crusading states at the end of the thirteenth century, there is scarcely a single case on record of an overland pilgrimage to Jerusalem.

TRAVEL BY SEA

A voyage by sea in the middle ages was an uncomfortable experience. Pilgrims were crowded like grains of corn into small, unstable boats where, for six weeks or more, they endured stale food and water, boredom, disease, and intense discomfort.

Men may leve alle games
That saylen to seynt James.

sang an Englishman of the fifteenth century with bitter memories of a voyage to Santiago. The seamen shouted at him and rushed to and fro, continually ordering him out of their way. The bark swayed and tossed, so violently that he did not feel like eating and could not hold a tankard to his lips. The poorest pilgrims, stowed in the most uncomfortable part of the ship, slept next to the bilge-pump, and had to make do with bread and salt and water.

The well-to-do pilgrim could mitigate the discomfort of the journey by paying a little more for his passage. Two types of ship were available at Venice. There were large, oared galleys which were safe, comfortable, and expensive; and small ships for the use of the poor, which were crammed to overflowing. Sebald Rieter, the opulent merchant of Nurnberg, paid sixty-seven ducats for his fare to the Holy Land in 1479 and shared the ship with only sixty-three other passengers. On the other hand an anonymous German pilgrim who travelled in the cheap ship paid only thirty ducats. The Florentine, Lionardo Frescobaldi, took the expensive ship to Alexandria in 1384 and watched the cheap one foundering in the first storm with two hundred pilgrims on board. When the demand for places fell, both rich and poor would share the same ship but occupied different parts of it. 'Chose yow a place in the sayd gallery in the overest stage', advised William Wey, 'for in the lowest under hyt is ryght smoulderyng hote and stynkyng.' When Hans von Mergenthal sailed to the Holy Places in 1476, the place alloted to poor pilgrims was so narrow that it was impossible to turn over in one's sleep. Sleepers were bitten by insects and trampled over by large rats. The animals penned up on the deck to be slaughtered for food broke out from time to time and trod on the sleeping bodies. When the sea was rough, passengers could not stand upright for fear of being struck by swinging booms and ropes.

Pilgrims were advised to bring mattresses and warm clothes with them. Frescobaldi, Gucci, and Sigoli, the three Italians who travelled together in 1384, brought several mattresses, a large number of shirts, a barrel of Malmsey wine, a Bible in several volumes, a copy of the *Moralia* of St. Gregory, a silver cup, 'and other delicate things'. Santo Brasca, who did the journey in 1480, recommended a long thick coat, and also suggested some provisions which every pilgrim would need to supplement the ship's meagre diet: a good supply of Lombard cheese, sausages, salted meat, white biscuits, sugar loaves, and sweetmeats. He should also bring some strong spices for curing indigestion and sea-sickness, 'and above all a great quantity of fruit syrup, for this is what keeps a man alive in hot climates.' William Wey agreed that the prudent pilgrim should arm himself with laxatives, restoratives, ginger, flour, figs, pepper, saffron, cloves, and other 'confections and comfortaciouns': it was essential to have half a dozen chickens in a cage 'for ye schal have need of them many tymes.' All travellers were agreed on the appalling quality of ship's food. 'Sum tymes', declared William Wey, 'ye schal have swych feble bred, wyne, and stynkyng water, that ye schal be ful fayne to eate of yowre owne.'

The manner in which the food was served was not calculated to stimulate the appetite. At the sound of a trumpet the passengers separated into two groups, those whose fare included food, and those who were seeing to their own wants. Members of the first group then scrambled for a place at one of three small tables in the poop. After dinner another trumpet signalled for the diners to retire, while their place was taken by the ship's officers and crew.

Their food was even more frugal than that of the pilgrims, but it was served with great pomp on silver dishes, and their wine was tasted before it was offered to them. The galley was a scene of unending chaos. 'Three or four hot-tempered cooks struggle with the food in a narrow passage lined with pots and pans and provisions, while a fire crackles away in the middle. Sounds of angry shouting issue forth from the room while, outside, crowds of passengers shout each other down in the effort to order special meals from the cooks.'

After hunger and sleeplessness, boredom was the principal problem of the passengers. 'Unless a man knows how to occupy himself, he will find the hours very long and tedious', Felix Faber observed. Saxons and Flemings, 'and other men of low class', usually passed the days drinking. Others playing dice or cards. Chess was very common. Communal singing went on in the background all the time. A small group of contemplative pilgrims gathered in a corner to read or pray. Others slept day and night. Many wrote travel diaries. A number of pilgrims, Faber remarked with contempt, amused themselves by running up and down the rigging, jumping up and down on the spot, or weight-lifting. 'But most people simply sit about looking on blankly, passing their eyes from one group to another, and thence to the open sea.' During Faber's first pilgrimage, in 1480, the news of Turkish naval activity in the eastern Mediterranean caused the passengers to agree on measures of moral reform which would preserve them from capture. All games were forbidden, together with quarrels, oaths, and blasphemies. Disputes between the French and the Germans were to cease, and the bishop of Orléans promised to give up gambling. Extra litanies were added to the daily service.

Sermons were the only organized recreation. The company who travelled with canon Casola in 1494 were fortunate enough to have amongst them one Francesco Tivulzio, 'a holy friar with a wonderful library in his head'. Whenever the ship was becalmed, he would rise and deliver an elaborate and learned sermon, many hours in length. On the eve of the feast of St. John, he delivered a sermon on the merits of that saint in nine parts which lasted from 5 p.m. to sunset, and promised to deliver the rest of it on the following day. While waiting for permission to disembark at Joppa, the pilgrims listened to another sermon from friar Tivulzio on the allegorical significance of sailing ships, followed, a few hours later, by 'a beautiful sermon on trade'. Such discourses, however, were not always received in rapturous silence. On Faber's first pilgrimage his preaching was repeatedly interrupted by inane laughter, after which he refused to utter again. On his second pilgrimage the company was more polite, and he favoured them with regular sermons. Even so, a number of noblemen disliked his preaching, which Faber attributed to the fact that they practised the vices that he castigated, 'and truth ever begets hatred.'

The tedious serenity of a long sea voyage was occasionally disturbed by the appearance of pirates. The law of the sea required all passengers to assist in defending the ship, and although pilgrims were exempt from this obligation on account of their religious calling, they usually fought as hard as any. In 1408, a Venetian galley returning from the Holy Land was attacked by a

Turkish pirate in the gulf of Satalia. The captain was found to have no cross-bows on board, and it was only after the pilgrims had beaten off their assailants in fierce hand-to-hand fighting that the ship escaped capture. In consequence, the Venetian senate enacted that a proper supply of bows, arrows, and lances was to be carried on every pilgrimship. . . .

The fact that pilgrims continued to visit the Holy land in large numbers, in spite of the obstacles in their way, was largely due to the enterprise of the Venetians. The ship-owners of Venice provided the earliest all-inclusive package tours. Galleys licensed by the republic left for Joppa every year as soon as possible after Ascension Day and returned in the autumn. When the demand for passages was high, two fleets sailed from Venice, one in March and one in September. The fare included food and board throughout the journey as well as in the Holy Land itself; the ship-owner, who was generally the master as well, paid all tolls and taxes, and met the cost of donkeys and pack-horses, guided tours of Jerusalem, and special expeditions to the Jordan. The popularity of these tours was entirely due to the high reputation of Venetian ship-owners. The stiff regulations of the serene republic enforced on them standards of safety and commercial morality which were uncommon in other ports. The anonymous English pilgrim of 1345 was advised by the inhabitants of Brindisi that it was unsafe to travel in any ship but a Venetian one. If he entrusted his life to a Sicilian or a Catalan master 'he would undoubtedly enjoy eternal rest at the bottom of the sea.' The ship-owners of Genoa and Pisa were suspected of selling their passengers into slavery at Arab ports. Francesco da Suriano gave four reasons for sailing from Venice in the latter half of the fifteenth century. It was so busy that a traveller never had to wait more than a few days before a ship sailed for his destination; the port was safe from pirates; the Venetian navy patrolled much of the route; and Venetian sailors were 'the finest travelling companions in Christendom'. He might have added that the Venetian currency was among the most stable in the west, and it was the only one which passed for legal tender in Arab territories. 'And so', counselled Santo Brasca, 'travel via Venice, for it is the most convenient embarkation point in the world.'

The Venetian republic began to license and regulate the traffic of pilgrims at the beginning of the thirteenth century. The maritime statutes of 1229 laid down the maximum number of pilgrims which one ship could carry and the date of sailing. At that time there were two fleets per year. The first, which reached the Holy Land in time for Easter, was to return not later than 8th May, while the second was to leave Joppa before 8th November. Further regulations, in 1255, enjoined officers of the republic throughout the eastern Mediterranean to inspect every pilgrim ship calling at their ports and to impose heavy fines if they were overloaded. Mariners were required to swear an oath not to steal more than five shillings from the passengers. The rights and duties of the pilgrim were set out in a lengthy contract, which was signed by both parties. Some of these contracts have survived. The contract between Jan Aerts and the shipowner Agostino Contarini, signed in April 1484, is in every way typical. It permits the pilgrim to go ashore whenever the ship is in port, and to visit Mount Sinai instead of returning with the ship, in which case Contarini will refund ten ducats of his fare. Contarini undertakes not to take on too many passengers or too few crewmen and not to appropriate the pilgrim's chattels if he dies during the journey; he promises to supply enough arms for twenty-five men in case of attack, and to accompany his passengers wherever they go in Jerusalem. The passengers may elect two of their number to oversee him. But there were no standard forms of contract, and pilgrims occasionally insisted on a special term. A contract dating from 1440 provides for a four-day stop at Nicosia, in Cyprus. William Wey advised English pilgrims to insist on a clause forbidding the owner to call at Famagusta on account of its unhealthy air. Once signed, the contract was lodged with a magistrate in Venice who would hear any dispute that arose. In 1497, for example, pilgrims protested that the space allotted to them was too small; port officials boarded the ship and resolved that each passenger should have one and a half feet of deck on which to sleep. On another occasion, pilgrims complained on their return to Venice that they had been manhandled and ill-fed and that their sleeping-quarters had been filled with cargo. Some of them had refused to return with the ship and had instead taken a passage from Beyrut in a Genoese vessel. The rest returned to Venice in an exceedingly hostile mood and, as they included a number of 'great lords', the Senate hastily sequestered the vessel and ordered the owners to refund the fares. . . .

STRANGE CUSTOMS AND FOREIGN LANGUAGES

It would be pleasant to learn that pilgrims returned from their travels with minds broadened by the experience of strange people and unfamiliar customs. But it would be the reverse of the truth. Such exchange of ideas as had occurred in the 'dark ages' of the west did not survive the onset of an age of mass-pilgrimage. All too often, those who lived on the pilgrimage roads regarded pilgrims as fair game to be plundered at will. The pilgrims in turn had little incentive to understand their hosts, and viewed them with that uncomprehending contempt which uneducated people commonly accord to foreigners. The impressions of French pilgrims in Spain are a case in point. So loathsome a race as the Basques, thought the author of the *Guide for Pilgrims to Santiago,* could only have originated in Scotland. After describing their national dress, he goes on to comment on their food and language in the following terms:

'Not only are they badly dressed, but they eat and drink in the most disgusting way. The entire household, including servants, eat out of the same pot and drink from the same cup. Far from using spoons, they eat with their hands, slobbering over the food like any dog or pig. To hear them speaking, you would think they were a pack of hounds barking, for their language is absolutely barbarous. They call God *Urcia;* bread is *orgui* and wine *ardum,* while meat is referred to as *aragui* and fish *araign*. . . . They are in fact a most uncouth race whose customs are quite different from those of any other people. They have dark, evil, ugly faces. They are debauched, perverse, treacherous and disloyal, corrupt and sensual drunkards. They are like fierce savages, dishonest and untrustworthy, impious, common, cruel and quarrelsome people, brought up in vice and iniquity, totally devoid of human feeling. . . . They will kill you for a penny. Men and women alike warm themselves by the fire, revealing those parts which are better hidden. They fornicate unceasingly, and not only with humans. . . . That is why they are held in contempt by all decent folk.'

In the *Chanson de Roland* the Basques appear in an extremely sinister light, and the influence of this celebrated poem may well be responsible for the contempt which many pilgrims expressed for them. But this alone will not explain the venom of the *Guide,* which entertains a remarkably similar opinion of the Gascons, characterizing their way of life as impious, immoral, and 'in every way detestable'.

If a Poitevin could write thus of the Gascons, he was unlikely to feel closer in spirit to the Greeks and oriental Christians, let alone to the Arabs. Throughout this period, relations with the Greeks were marked by a bitterness which can only be understood in the light of the tortuous relations of Byzantium with the crusaders. Most Latin Christians despised the Greeks as effeminate schismatics and believed with immovable conviction that they had betrayed the twelfth-century crusades. A guide-book written at the end of the century refers to them characteristically as 'cunning men who do not bear arms and who err from the true faith. . . . They also use leaven bread in the Eucharist and do other strange things. They even have an alphabet of their own.' This mood of suspicion was aggravated by the widespread belief that the Byzantine authorities deliberately obstructed pilgrims passing through Constantinople. The emperor Alexius Comenus was once described by an eminently sane Latin writer as 'that great oppressor of pilgrims to Jerusalem who hinders their progress by guile or by force.' Indeed, it never struck western pilgrims that their habit of helping themselves to whatever they required, and of insulting and attacking local people, might arouse justifiable resentment on the part of their hosts. The importance which Greeks attached to their own traditions was regarded by some Latin pilgrims as nothing less than a calculated insult. Jacques de Vitry denounced them as 'foul schismatics moved by sinful pride', and then went on to consider the Jacobite and Armenian Christians, 'barbarous nations who differ from both Greeks and Latins . . . and use a peculiar language understood only by the learned.'

Language was indeed the principal barrier. Few mediaeval men, however cultivated they were, understood more than a few words of any language but their own or Latin. Travelling through regions such as eastern Europe or Egypt, where pilgrims were rare and Latin unknown, was a difficult and dangerous undertaking. Lietbert, bishop of Cambrai, who passed through the Danube valley on the way to Jerusalem in 1054, listed 'the strange and foreign language of the Huns' amongst the perils which he had encountered, together with mountains, swamps, and impenetrable forests. During the twelfth century, French was the language of Jerusalem, and this is said to have made difficulties for the Germans. At any rate, one of the reasons given for the foundation of the German hospice in Jerusalem was that 'in such a place Germans might talk in a language they can understand.' In Venice the authorities were constantly embarrassed by the activities of sharp traders or shipowners who took advantage of foreigners bound for the Holy Land. 'It is well known that many scandalous mistakes have been made of late, on account of the great number of pilgrims boarding ships at Venice', the senate noted in 1398; 'for the said pilgrims are of divers tongues . . . and unless a remedy is found, still greater scandals will follow.'

It is worth following the Burgundian pilgrim Bertrandon de la Brocquière in his efforts to learn a few words of Turkish. Bertrandon visited the Holy Land in 1432–3, but he avoided the Venetian package tour because he wished to spy out the land at leisure, with a view to planning a crusade. In Damascus he made the acquaintance of a Turk who spoke Arabic, Hebrew, Turkish, and Greek. Bertrandon spoke none of these languages, but he had a working knowledge of Italian, and the Turk found a Jew who knew a little Italian and some Turkish. The Jew compiled a list of everything that Bertrandon would require on his journey, in parallel columns of Turkish and Italian. In the first day after leaving Damascus, Bertrandon had occasion to ask a group of peasants for some fodder for his horse. He consulted his piece of paper and made his request, but there was no reaction. He showed the paper to the leading peasant, who began to roar with laughter. The group then gave him an impromptu lesson in Turkish, picking up various articles and pronouncing their names very carefully several times. 'And when I left them I knew how to ask in Turkish for almost everything I wanted.'

Italian was the only European language known to a significant number of Arabs. Pilgrims who visited Mount Sinai via Egypt could usually find an Italian-speaking interpreter at Alexandria or Cairo, but this was an expensive luxury of which few travellers availed themselves. In 1384 Lionardo Frescobaldi's party spent more than forty-nine ducats on interpreters between Alexandria and Damascus. In addition, one of their interpreters stole eight ducats from them, and another was in league with a group of Bedouin bandits. More than a hundred ducats was spent on bribing the personal interpreters of various Arab officials to present their requests for safe-conducts in a favourable way.

Phrase-books, then as now, were the simplest way to overcome the language difficulty. As early as the ninth century, we find a phrase-book entitled *Old High-German Conversations (Altdeutsche Gespräche)* being used by Franks travelling in Germany. It consists of orders to servants, requests for information, and demands for hospitality such as 'I want a drink':

'Erro, e guille trenchen; id est, ego volo bibere.'

A number of early phrase-books of Greek and Hebrew survive, most of which were clearly intended for the use of pilgrims to the Holy land. The abbey of Mont-St.-Michel had, in the eleventh century, a Greek phrase-book containing useful demands like

'Da mihi panem: DOS ME PSOMI.' ['Give me bread.']

An interesting manual for crusaders, dating from the twelfth century, includes such tactful requests as 'What is the news about the Greek emperor? What is he doing? He is being kind to the Franks. What good things does he give them? Much money and weapons.' During the period of mass-pilgrimages in the late middle ages, an immense number of phrase-books was available, some of them very comprehensive. The library of Charles V of France contained a manual for pilgrims entitled *How to ask in Arabic for the necessities of life.* Another French-Arabic phrase-book, preserved in the Swiss abbey of St.-Gall, has a long section on how to ask one's way in a strange town.

Some pilgrims found oriental alphabets a source of limitless fascination. *Mandeville's Travels,* that strange mixture of fact and fantasy, sets out the Greek, Hebrew, Arabic, and Persian alphabets, though they contain many mistakes and the Hebrew one is incomprehensible. Johann Schiltberger appended to the account of his travels the *Pater Noster* in Armenian and Turkish. But the most proficient linguist amongst the pilgrims of the fifteenth century was certainly Arnold von Harff, a wealthy young nobleman of Cologne who, between 1496 and 1499, travelled through Italy, Syria, Egypt, Arabia, Ethiopia, Nubia, Palestine, Turkey, and Spain. He was a worldly pilgrim of the type mocked in the *Canterbury Tales* and the *Quinze Joies de Mariage,* but he took a genuine interest in the people of each country and particularly in their languages. Von Harff collected alphabets. His memoirs contain many oriental alphabets (some of them are undecipherable), as well as useful phrases in nine different languages, Croatian, Albanian, Greek, Arabic, Hebrew, Turkish, Hungarian, Basque, and Breton. He was a cultivated man, a gallant knight and an aristocrat whose range of phrases was broader than that of most conventional pilgrims. Thus, 'Wash my shirt for me—I do not understand—Will you sell me that?—How much is this?—Madam shall I marry you?—Madam shall I sleep with you?—Good woman, I am already in your bed.'

But Arnold von Harff was scarcely typical even of his own worldly age. He was an acute observer who was interested in such diverse matters as wild animals in the Nile valley, and the Mamluk system of government. He doubted the authenticity of the body of St. James at Santiago, and openly disputed the claims of several Roman relics. He considered the Turks closer to the spirit of Christianity than the Spanish. A more faithful reflection of the mentality of pilgrims is found in the account of the Arab way of life in the travel diary of one of Frescobaldi's companions, which begins, 'now let me tell you of their bestial habits.'

Selling bread from a side-street bakery, c. 1385, Italy. From Tacuinum Sanitatus.

IV

THE LATE MIDDLE AGES
14th–15th Centuries

Medieval folk prayed that God would deliver them from what they called the three scourges: war, famine, and disease. During the eleventh and twelfth centuries, and much of the thirteenth century, their prayers were answered for the most part. By the fourteenth century, however, all this changed, and the three scourges returned with a vengeance. Particularly devastating for France was the Hundred Years' War, which was fought almost entirely on French soil. The war touched even French and English communities situated far from the fighting, as taxes were levied and men were recruited into the armies. The first selection brings us to the battlefield of one of the decisive contests of the Hundred Years' War: Agincourt.

The destruction caused by war often brought famine and disease in its wake, but these two scourges were far more widespread than any damage that a medieval army could do. By the second half of the thirteenth century, the weather became cooler and wetter than it had been in the previous centuries, resulting in an increased number of failed and poor harvests. Famines followed, and the population of Europe had already begun to decline well before the bubonic plague pandemic of 1348–1351 struck, killing some 30 percent of Europe's inhabitants. Subsequent epidemics, though less devastating than the first, continued the downward trend in population size. The rapid loss of a substantial portion of Europe's population altered the circumstances in which medieval society had evolved. Governments faced fiscal crises as tax revenues fell precipitously. Landlords had difficulty renting out their lands. The scarcity of labor trapped employers in a double bind by pushing wages and the prices of manufactured goods upward and forcing profits down.

Yet the fourteenth and fifteenth centuries were not simply a period of contraction; they were also a time of positive change. High mortality led to a redistribution of wealth that opened up new possibilities for social change, although it did not eradicate poverty. City governments began to take on some of the functions previously performed by the church and the nobility. For example, municipal governments began to introduce new forms of charitable assistance when the monasteries, faced with shrinking revenues, were no longer capable of performing this role. Moreover, the late Middle Ages were full of innovation and experimentation. Artisans tinkered with clocks and rudimentary automata and put the Chinese technologies of gunpowder and printing to new uses by inventing guns and moveable type.

The second and third selections treat medieval cities. Cities had benefited from the general prosperity of the high Middle Ages, growing in number and size during that time. Their prosperity lasted well after the rural economy began to decline, and even withstood the first shocks of the bubonic plague. Migration to cities remained at pre-plague levels until the mid-fifteenth century when Europe's late medieval population reached its lowest point. In the second selection Barbara Hanawalt describes the environment and society of London.

The economic and social dislocations of the later Middle Ages reverberated throughout medieval society. Paradoxically, while farms sometimes were idle for want of hands to work them, vagabonds and beggars flocked to the cities in unprecedented numbers. Governments in England, France, and Spain passed regulations requiring unemployed men either to find work or leave the cities, threatening them with forced labor, imprisonment, or even corporal punishment. Early movements toward the replacement of private, unregulated charity with civic charity directed at providing only for the "deserving poor" emerged in many cities during the late Middle Ages. The goal of the charitable reforms was to limit begging; many people suspected that at least some beggars were nothing more than con artists mimicking illnesses or injuries. Beggars were also a visible and disturbing expression of what Bronisław Geremek describes as the social disorganization brought on by warfare, economic crises, and the mobility of particular groups. Living on the margins and slipping easily into crime, beggars and vagabonds posed a threat to the public order. In the third selection, Geremek describes the criminal element in late medieval Paris.

The fourth selection explores public life in the village. Most villages cooperated with their lords in carrying out local government. In England, for example, tithing groups were responsible for reporting newcomers. Village jurors were responsible for reporting crimes, naming suspects, providing information pertinent to their trial, and either acquitting or convicting them. Additionally, all landholders were obliged to attend the proceedings of the manorial court. Not all villagers participated equally in the public life of the village; some served as jurors and appeared in the courts with frequency, some hardly if ever did. Those who were most active in these public functions exercised considerable influence over their fellow villagers. Women participated less frequently and less significantly than men, but there were times when women were active in public life. Judith Bennett explores the patterns of both male and female participation in public life and in doing so reveals the relationships between property, gender, and power.

In the fifth selection, Barbara Hanawalt investigates the provisions that peasants made for their old age. The problems of growing old in a society with few institutional provisions for the elderly clearly emerge from her sources. Additionally, Hanawalt's study touches on the question of the family's and the community's responsibilities for the care of those who could not care for themselves.

BIBLIOGRAPHY

For a general history of war in medieval Europe, see the classic book by Charles Oman, *A History of War in the Middle Ages* (London, 1924). See also Philippe Contamine, *War in the Middle Ages* (Oxford, 1984); John Beeler, *Warfare in Feudal Europe, 730–1200* (Ithaca, NY, 1971); J. R. Hale, *War and Society in Renaissance Europe, 1450–1620* (Leicester, England, 1985); and William McNeill, *The Pursuit of Power: Technology, Armed Force, and Society since A.D. 1000* (Chicago, 1982). For a general history of the Hundred Years' War see the short history of Anne Curry, *The Hundred Years War* (New York, 1993); or the detailed account provided by Jonathan Sumption in *The Hundred Years War, Vol. 1: Trial by Battle* (London, 1990). See also H. J. Hewitt, *The Organization of War Under Edward III* (Manchester, England, 1966), where traditional ideas about the limited destructiveness of medieval armies and strategy are put to rest. See the bibliography of Part 3 for works on chivalry and knightly behavior. See also Arno Borst, *Medieval Worlds: Barbarians, Heretics, and Artists in the Middle Ages* (Chicago, 1997); and B. Norman, *The Medieval Soldier* (New York, 1971).

The study of medieval cities has flourished in recent decades. David Nicholas provides a general survey of cities of the Middle Ages in *The Growth of the Medieval City: From Late Antiquity to the Early Fourteenth Century* (London, 1997) and *The Later Medieval City, 1300–1500* (London, 1997). See also Fritz Rorig, *The Medieval Town* (Berkeley, 1967) and Edith Ennen, *The Medieval Town* trans. by Natalie Fryde (New York, 1979). For a description of city life and city houses see Georges Duby and Philippe Ariès, eds., *History of Private Life. vol. 2: Revelations of the Medieval World* (Cambridge, MA, 1988). For criminal behavior in the Middle Ages, see John G. Bellamy's important work, *Crime and Public Order in England in the Later Middle Ages* (London, 1973). Natalie Zemon Davis reconstructs convicted criminals' accounts of their crimes in *Fiction in the Archives* (Stanford, CA, 1987). Barbara Hanawalt's *Crime and Conflict in English Communities* (Cambridge, MA, 1979) treats rural crime and the rural justice system. Sexual crime is explored in Guido Ruggiero's excellent *The Boundaries of Eros* (Oxford, 1989). See also his *Violence in Early Renaissance Venice* (New Brunswick, NJ, 1980).

For the late medieval family, see David Herlihy, *Medieval Households* (New Haven, CT, 1985), from which the selection "The Early Medieval Household" in Part 2 was taken; see also the readings cited in the bibliography of Part 3. The care of orphans is the subject of John Boswell's *The Kindness of Strangers: The Abandonment of Children in Western Europe from Late Antiquity to the Renaissance* (New York, 1990); it is also treated in David Nicholas, *The Domestic Life of a City: Women, Children, and the Family in Fourteenth-Century Ghent* (Lincoln, NE, 1985). Michel Mollat provides an excellent study of poverty and charity in *The Poor in the Middle Ages,* trans. by A. Goldhammer (New Haven, CT, 1986). For a charitable tradition that helped the poor help themselves, see Judith Bennett, "Conviviality and Charity in Medieval and Early Modern England," *Past and Present* 134 (Feb. 1992):19–41. For women's exercise of power, see Mary Erler and Maryanne Kowaleski, eds., *Women and Power in the Middle Ages,* cited in the bibliography for Part 3; Georges Duby, *Women in the Twelfth Century,* trans. by Jean Birrell (Chicago, 1997). Margaret Wade Labarge gives an account of the role of a baron's wife in *A Baronial Household of the Thirteenth Century* (London, 1965) and discusses noble women in *A Small Sound of the Trumpet: Women in Medieval Life* (Boston, 1986). Shulamith Shahar provides a general history in *The Fourth Estate: A History of Women in the Middle Ages* (London, 1983); as do Susan Mosher Stuard, ed., *Women in Medieval Society* (Philadelphia, 1976); and Edith Ennen, *The Medieval Woman,* trans. by Edmund Jephcott (New Haven, CT, 1989).

FEUDAL WAR IN PRACTICE

JOHN KEEGAN

Many books and articles have been devoted to the study of warfare in the Middle Ages and to individual battles and campaigns, but the great majority of these works focus on the art of war rather than on the actual conduct of operations. The military predominance of the heavily armed knight, and the great body of contemporary literature promulgating the ideal of knightly life have influenced the historiography of warfare so as to emphasize the role of the knight. Medieval chroniclers, too, focused on the aristocratic mounted soldiers, but recent studies show that the major portion of most medieval armies was an infantry force.

Recognition of the composite nature of medieval armies, with its attendant appreciation for the tactics of such forces, does not, however, satisfy the British historian John Keegan. He asserts that historians of modern wars and armies, where the composition of the troops has not been in question, nonetheless give a distorted history of campaigns and battles because they see them from the standpoint of generals and politicians. Keegan points out the defects of this sort of military history and suggests that we will not get a fair view of war unless we look at battles and campaigns against the background of the societies in which they occurred. How violent or sacrificial was the society that produced the army and its generals? What impact did contemporary ideas of mortality have? Questions such as these would enlarge the field of military history and make it part of the general historiography on any period of society. Keegan himself wants to do something more specific, however. He wants to focus on battle itself, but to see it from the standpoint of the common soldier. He asks: What was the common experience of war in medieval and modern Europe? He explains his approach this way: "I do not intend to write about generals or generalship, except to discuss how a commander's physical presence on the field may have influenced his subordinates' will to combat. I do not intend to say anything of logistics or strategy and very little of tactics in the formal sense. And I

From: John Keegan, *The Face of Battle* (New York: Viking Press, 1976), pp. 81–116.

*do not intend to offer a two-sided picture of events, since what hap-
pened to one side in any battle I describe will be enough to convey
the features I think are salient. On the other hand, I do intend to
discuss wounds and their treatment, the mechanics of being taken
prisoner, the nature of leadership at the most junior level, the role of
compulsion in getting men to stand their ground, the incidence of accidents as a cause of death in war and, above all, the dimensions of
the danger which different varieties of weapons offer to the soldier
on the battlefield. . . . [M]y purpose [is] . . . to suggest how and why
the men who have had (and do have) to face these weapons control
their fears, staunch their wounds, go to their deaths. It is a personal
attempt to catch a glimpse of the face of battle."* (The Face of
Battle, p. 78). *What follows is Keegan's description and explanation
of the battle of Agincourt, October 25, 1415, one of the principal
battles of the Hundred Years' War.*

The army embarked in the second week of August at Portsmouth and set sail
on August 11th. It had been gathering since April, while Henry conducted deliberately inconclusive negotiations with Charles VI, and now numbered about
ten thousand in all, eight thousand archers and two thousand men-at-arms,
exclusive of camp followers. A good deal of the space in the ships, of which
there were about 1,500, was given over to impedimenta and a great deal to the
expedition's horses: at least one for each man-at-arms, and others for the baggage train and wagon teams. The crossing took a little over two days and on
the morning of August 14th the army began to disembark, unopposed by the
French, on a beach three miles west of Harfleur. Three days were taken to
pitch camp and on August 18th the investment of the town began. It was not
strongly garrisoned but its man-made and natural defences were strong, the
Seine, the River Lézarde and a belt of marshes protecting it on the south, north
and east. An attempt at mining under the moat on the western front was
checked by French counter-mines so the small siege train, which contained at
least three heavy guns, undertook a bombardment of that section of the walls.
It lasted for nearly a month, until the collapse of an important gate-defence,
the repulse of a succession of sorties and the failure of a French relieving army
to appear, convinced the garrison that they must surrender. After parleys, the
town opened its gates to Henry on Sunday, September 22nd.

He now had his base, but was left with neither time nor force enough to
develop much of a campaign that year; at least a third of his army was dead
or disabled, chiefly through disease, and the autumnal rains were due. Earlier
in September he had set to paper his intention of marching down the Seine to
Paris and thence to Bordeaux as soon as Harfleur fell; that had clearly become
unfeasible, but honour demanded that he should not leave France without
making a traverse, however much more circumspect, of the lands he claimed.
At a long Council of War, held on October 5th, he convinced his followers that

they could both appear to seek battle with the French armies which were known to be gathering and yet safely out-distance them by a march to the haven of Calais. On October 8th he led the army out.

His direct route was about 120 miles and lay cross a succession of rivers of which only the Somme formed a major obstacle. He began following the coast as far as the Béthune, which he crossed on October 11th, revictualling his army at Arques. The following day he crossed the Bresle, near Eu, having made eighty miles in five days, and on October 13th swung inland to cross the Somme above its estuary. On approaching, however, he got his first news of the enemy and it was grave; the nearest crossing was blocked and defended by a force of six thousand. After discussion, he rejected a retreat and turned south-east to follow the line of the river until he found an unguarded ford. For the next five days, while his army grew hungrier, the French kept pace with him on the northern bank until on the sixth, by a forced march across the plain of the Santerre (scene of the great British tank battle on August 8th, 1918), he got ahead of them and found a pair of unguarded though damaged causeways at Bethencourt and Voyennes. Some hasty sappering made them fit for traffic and that evening, October 19th, the army slept on the far bank. Henry declared October 20th a day of rest, which his men badly needed, having marched over two hundred miles in twelve days, but the arrival of French heralds with a challenge to fight was a reminder that they could not linger. On October 21st they marched eighteen miles, crossing the tracks of a major French army and, during the three following days, another fifty-three. They were now within two, at most three, marches of safety. All were aware, however, that the French eventually stood down and withdrew a little to the north where they camped astride the road to Calais.

The English army found what shelter it could for the night in and around the village of Maisoncelles, ate its skimpy rations, confessed its sins, heard Mass and armed for battle. At first light knights and archers marched out and took up their positions between two woods. The French army, composed almost exclusively of mounted and dismounted men-at-arms, had deployed to meet them and was in similar positions about a thousand yards distant. For four hours both armies held their ground. Henry apparently hoped that the French would attack him; they, who knew that sooner or later he would have to move—either to the attack, which suited their book, or to retreat, which suited them even better—stood or sat idle, eating their breakfasts and calling about cheerfully to each other. Eventually Henry decided to up sticks (literally: his archers had been carrying pointed stakes to defend their lines for the last week) and advance on the French line. Arrived within three hundred yards—extreme bowshot—of the army, the English archers replanted their stakes and loosed off their first flights of arrows. The French, provoked by these arrow strikes, as Henry intended, into attacking, launched charges by the mounted men-at-arms from the wings of the main body. Before they had crossed the intervening space they were followed by the dismounted men-at-arms who, like them, were wearing full armour. The cavalry failed to break the English line, suffered losses from the fire of the archers and turned about. Heading back for their own lines, many riders and loose horses crashed into the advancing line of dismounted men-at-arms. They, though shaken, continued to crowd forward and to mass their attack against the English men-at-arms, who were drawn up in three groups, with archers between them and on the right and left flank. Apparently disdaining battle with the archers, although they were suffering losses from their fire, the French quickened their steps over the last few yards and crashed into the middle of the English line. For a moment it gave way. But the French were so tightly bunched that they could not use their weapons to widen the breach they had made. The English men-at-arms recovered their balance, struck back and were now joined by numbers of the archers who, dropping their bows, ran against the French with axes, mallets and swords, or with weapons abandoned by the French they picked up from the ground. There followed a short but very bloody episode of hand-to-hand combat, in which freedom of action lay almost wholly with the English. Many of the French armoured infantrymen lost their footing and were killed as they lay sprawling; others who remained upright could not defend themselves and were killed by thrusts between their armour-joints or stunned by hammerblows. The French second line which came up, got embroiled in this fighting without being able to turn the advantage to their side, despite the addition they brought to the very great superiority of numbers the French already enjoyed. Eventually, those Frenchmen who could disentangle themselves from the mêlée made their way back to where the rest of their army, composed of a third line of mounted men-at-arms, stood watching. The English who faced them did so in several places, over heaps of dead, dying or disabled French men-at-arms, heaps said by one chronicler to be taller than a man's height. Others were rounding up disarmed and lightly wounded Frenchmen and leading them to the rear, where they were collected under guard.

While this went on, a French nobleman, the Duke of Brabant, who had arrived late for the battle from a christening party, led forward an improvised charge; but it was broken up without denting the English line, which was still drawn up. Henry had prudently kept it under arms because the French third line—of mounted men—had not dispersed and he must presumably have feared that it would ride down on them if the whole English army gave itself up to taking and looting prisoners. At some time in the afternoon, there were detected signs that the French were nerving themselves to charge anyhow; and more or less simultaneously, a body of armed peasants, led by three mounted knights, suddenly appeared at the baggage park, inflicted some loss of life and stole some objects of value, including one of the King's crowns, before being driven off.

Either that incident or the continued menace of the French third line now prompted Henry to order that all the prisoners instantly be killed. The order was not at once obeyed, and for comprehensible reasons. Even discounting any moral or physical repugnance on the part of their captors, or a misunderstanding of the reason behind the order—that the prisoners might attack the English from the rear with weapons retrieved from the ground if the French cavalry were suddenly to attack their front—the poorer English soldiers, and perhaps not only the poorer, would have been very reluctant to pass up the prospects of ransom which killing the prisoners would entail. Henry was nevertheless adamant; he detailed an esquire and two hundred archers to set about the execution, and stopped them only when it became clear that the French third line was packing up and withdrawing from the field. Meantime very many of the French had been killed; some of the English apparently even incinerated wounded prisoners in cottages where they had been taken for shelter.

The noblest and richest of the prisoners were, nevertheless, spared and dined that evening with the King at Maisoncelles, his base of the previous evening, to which he now returned. En route he summoned the heralds of the two armies who had watched the battle together from a vantage point, and settled with the principal French herald a name for the battle: Agincourt, after the nearest fortified place. Next morning, after collecting the army, marshalling the prisoners and distributing the wounded and the loads of loot among the transport, he marched the army off across the battlefield towards Calais. Numbers of the French wounded had made their way or been helped from the field during the night; those still living, unless thought ransomable, were now killed. On October 29th, the English, with two thousand prisoners, reached Calais. The King left for England at once, to be escorted into London by an enormous party of rejoicing citizens.

These are the bare outlines of the battle, as recorded by seven or eight chroniclers, who do not materially disagree over the sequence, character or significance of events. Of course, even though three of them were present at the scene, none was an eye-witness of everything, or even of very much, that happened. An army on the morrow of a battle, particularly an army as small as that of Agincourt, must nevertheless, be a fairly efficient clearing-house of information, and it seems probable that a broadly accurate view of what had happened—though not necessarily why and how it had happened—would quickly crystallize in the mind of any diligent interrogator, while a popularly agreed version, not dissimilar from it, would soon circulate within, and outside, the ranks. It would seem reasonable therefore to believe that the narrative of Agincourt handed down to us is a good one; it would in any case be profitless to look for a better.

THE BATTLE

What we almost completely lack, though, is the sort of picture and understanding of the practicalities of the fighting and of the mood, outlook and skills of the fighters which were themselves part of the eyewitness chroniclers' vision. We simply cannot visualize, as they were able to do, what the Agincourt arrow-cloud can have looked, or sounded, like; what the armoured men-at-arms sought to do to each other at the moment of the first clash; at what speed and in what density the French cavalry charged down; how the mêlée—the densely packed mass of men in hand-to-hand combat—can have appeared to a detached onlooker, say to men in the French third line; what level the noise of the battle can have reached and how the leaders made themselves heard—if they did so—above it. These questions lead on to less tangible inquiries; how did leadership operate once the fighting had been joined—by exhortation or by example? Or did concerted action depend upon previously rehearsed tactics and corporate feeling alone? Or was there, in fact, no leadership, merely every man—or every brave man—for himself? Less tangible still, what did "bravery" mean in the context of a medieval fight? How did men mentally order the risks which they faced, as we know it is human to do? Were the foot more likely to be frightened of the horses, or of the men on them? Were the armoured men-at-arms more or less frightened of the arrows than of meeting their similarly clad opponents at a weapon's length? Did it seem safer to go on fighting once hard pressed than to surrender? Was running away more hazardous than staying within the press of the fighting?

The answers to some of these questions must be highly conjectural, interesting though the conjectures may be. But to others, we can certainly offer answers which fall within a fairly narrow bracket of probability, because the parameters of the questions are technical. Where speed of movement, density of formations, effect of weapons, for example, are concerned, we can test our suppositions against the known defensive qualities of armour plate, penetrative power of arrows, dimensions and capacities of the human body, carrying power and speed of the horse. And from reasonable probabilities about these military mechanics, we may be able to leap towards an understanding of the dynamics of the battle itself and the spirit of the armies which fought it.

Let us, to begin with, and however artificially, break the battle down into a sequence of separate events. It opened, as we know, with the armies forming up in the light of early morning: whether that meant just after first light, or at the rather later hour of dawn itself—about 6:40 a.m.—is a point of detail over which we cannot expect the chroniclers to meet Staff College standards of precision. Nor do they. They are even more imprecise about numbers, particularly as they concern the French. For though there is agreement, supported by other evidence, that Henry's army had dwindled to about five or six thousand archers and a thousand men-at-arms, the French are variously counted between 10,000 and 200,000. Colonel Burne convincingly reconciles the differences to produce a figure of 25,000, a very large proportion of which represented armoured men-at-arms. Of these, about a thousand brought their horses to the battlefield; the rest were to fight on foot.

The two armies initially formed up at a distance of some thousand yards from each other; at either end of a long, open and almost flat expanse of ploughland, bordered on each side by woodland. The width of the field, which had recently been sown with winter wheat, was about twelve hundred yards at the French end. The woods converged slightly on the English and, at the point where the armies were eventually to meet, stood about nine hundred to a thousand yards apart. (These measurements suppose—as seems reasonable, field boundaries remaining remarkably stable over centuries—that the outlines of the woods have not much changed.)

The English men-at-arms, most of whom were on foot, took station in three blocks, under the command of the Duke of York, to the right, the King, in the centre, and Lord Camoys, on the left. The archers were disposed between them and also on the flanks; the whole line was about four or five deep. The archer flanks may have been thrown a little forward, and the archers of the two inner groups may have adopted a wedge-like formation. This would have made it appear as if the men-at-arms were deployed a little to their rear. Opposite them, the French were drawn up in three lines, of which the third was mounted, as were two groups, each about five hundred strong, on the flanks. The two forward lines, with a filling of crossbowmen between and some ineffectual cannon on the flanks were each, perhaps, eight thousand strong, and so ranked some eight deep. On both sides, the leaders of the various contingents—nobles, bannerets and knights—displayed armorial banners, under which they and their men would fight, and among the French there was a great deal of tiresome struggling, during the period of deployment, to get these banners into the leading rank.

Deployed, the armies were ready for the battle, which, as we have seen, resolved itself into twelve main episodes: a period of waiting; an English advance; an English arrow strike; a French cavalry charge; a French infantry advance; a mêlée between the French and English men-at-arms; an intervention in the mêlée by the English archers; the flight of the French survivors from the scene of the mêlée; a second period of waiting, during which the French third line threatened, and a small party delivered, another charge; a French raid on the baggage park; a massacre of the French prisoners; finally, mutual departure from the battlefield. What was each of these episodes like, and what impetus did it give to the course of events?

The period of waiting—three or four hours long, and so lasting probably from about seven to eleven o-'clock—must have been very trying. Two chroniclers mention that the soldiers in the front ranks sat down and ate and drank and that there was a good deal of shouting, chaffing and noisy reconciliation of old quarrels among the French. But that was after they had settled, by pushing and shoving, who was to stand in the forward rank; not a real argument, one may surmise, but a process which put the grander and the braver in front of the more humble and timid. There is no mention of the English imitating them, but given their very real predicament, and their much thinner line of battle, they can have felt little need to dispute the place of honour among themselves. It is also improbable that they did much eating or drinking, for the army had been short of food for nine days and the archers are said to have been subsisting on nuts and berries on the last marches. Waiting, certainly for the English, must then have been a cold, miserable and squalid business. It had been raining, the ground was recently ploughed, many in the army were suffering from diarrhoea. Since none would presumably have been allowed to leave the ranks while the army was deployed for action, sufferers would have had to relieve themselves where they stood. For any afflicted man-at-arms wearing mail leggings laced to his plate armour, even that may not have been possible.

The King's order to advance, which he gave after the veterans had endorsed his guess that the French would not be drawn, may therefore have been generally genuinely welcome. Movement at least meant an opportunity to generate body heat, of which the metal-clad men-at-arms would have dissipated an unnatural amount during the morning. Note, however, when the moment came, that they would have moved forward very fast. An advance in line, particularly by men unequally equipped and burdened, has to be taken slowly if order is to be preserved. The manoeuvres, moreover, was a change of position, not a charge, and the King and his subordinate leaders would presumably have recognized the additional danger of losing cohesion in the face of the enemy who, if alert, would seize on the eventuality as an opportune moment to launch an attack. Several chroniclers indeed mention that on the King's orders a knight, Sir Thomas Erpingham, inspected the archers before they marched off in order to "check their dressing," as a modern drill sergeant would put it and to ensure that they had their bows strung. The much smaller group of men-at-arms would have moved as did the banners of their lords, which in turn would have followed the King's.

The army had about seven hundred yards of rain-soaked ploughland to cover. At a slow walk (no medieval army marched in step, and no modern army would have done so over such ground—the "cadenced pace" followed from the hardening and smoothing of the surface of roads), with halts to correct dressing, it would have reached its new position in ten minutes or so, though one may guess that the pace slackened a good deal as they drew nearer the French army and the leaders made mental reckoning of the range. "Extreme bowshot," which is the distance at which Henry presumably planned to take ground, is traditionally calculated at three hundred yards. That is a tremendous carry for a bow, however, and two hundred and fifty yards would be a more realistic judgment of the distance at which he finally halted his line from the French. If, however, his archer flanks were thrown a little forward, his centre would have been farther away; and if, as one chronicler suggests, he had infiltrated parties of bowmen into the woods, the gap between the two armies might have been greater still. Something between two hundred and fifty and three hundred yards is a reasonable bracket therefore.

There must now have ensued another pause, even though a short one. For the archers, who had each been carrying a stout double-pointed wooden stake since the tenth day of the march, had now to hammer these into the ground, at an angle calculated to catch a warhorse in the chest. Once hammered, moreover, the points would have had to be hastily resharpened. Henry had ordered these stakes to be cut as a precaution against the army being surprised by cavalry on the line of march. But it was a sensible improvisation to have them planted on the pitched battlefield, even if not a wholly original one. The Scots at Bannockburn, the English themselves at Crécy and the Flemings at Courtrai had narrowed their fronts by digging patterns of holes which would break the leg of a charging horse; the principle was the same as that which underlay the planting of the Agincourt archers' fence. Though it is not, indeed, possible to guess whether a fence was what the archers constructed. If they hammered their stakes to form a single row, it supposes them standing for some time on the wrong side of it with their backs to the enemy. Is it not more probable that each drove his in where he stood, so forming a kind of thicket, too dangerous for horses to penetrate but roomy enough for the defenders to move about within? That would explain the chronicler Monstrelet's otherwise puzzling statement that "each archer placed before himself a stake." It would also make sense of the rough mathematics we can apply to the problem. Colonel Burne, whose appreciation has not been challenged, estimates the width of the English position at 950 yards. Given that there were a thousand men-at-arms in the line of battle, ranked shoulder to shoulder four deep, they would have occupied, at a yard of front per man, 250 yards. If the five thousand archers, on the remaining seven hundred yards, planted their stakes side by side, they would have formed a fence at five-inch intervals. That obstacle would have been impenetrable to the French—but also to the English archers;* and *their* freedom of movement was, as we shall see, latterly an essential element in the winning of the battle. If we want to picture the formation the archers adopted, therefore, it would be most realistic to think of them standing a yard apart, in six or seven rows, with a yard between them, also disposed chequerboard fashion so that the men could see and shoot more easily over the heads of those in front: the whole forming a loose belt twenty or thirty feet deep, with the stakes standing obliquely among them.

What we do not know—and it leaves a serious gap in our understanding of the mechanics of the battle—is how the archers were commanded. The men-at-arms stood beneath the banners of their leaders, who had anyhow mustered them and brought them to the war, and the larger retinues, those of noblemen like the Earl of Suffolk, also contained knighted men-at-arms, who must have acted as subordinate leaders. There is thus no difficulty in visualizing how command was exercised within these fairly small and compact groups—providing one makes allowances for what a modern officer would regard as the unsoldierly habit in the man-at-arms of seeking to engage in "single combat" and of otherwise drawing attention to his individual prowess and skill-at-arms. But if the "officer class," even though the expression has a very doubtful meaning in the medieval military context, was wholly committed to the leadership of a single component of the army, who led the rest? For it is not naive, indeed quite the contrary, to suppose some sort of control over and discipline within the archers' ranks. Had the groupings into twenties under a

---

*Indeed, they could not have got back *behind* it after they had driven their stakes in.

double-pay "vintenar" and of the twenties into hundreds, under a mounted and armoured "centenar," which we know prevailed in the reign of Edward I, at the beginning of the fourteenth century, persisted into the fifteenth? That would be probable, but we cannot tell to whom the "centenars" were immediately answerable, nor how the chain of command led to the King. We can only feel sure that it did.

ARCHERS VERSUS INFANTRY AND CAVALRY

The archers were now in position to open fire (an inappropriate expression, belonging to the gunpowder age, which was barely beginning). Each man disposed his arrows as convenient. He would have had a sheaf, perhaps two, of twenty-four arrows and probably struck them point down into the ground by his feet. The men in the front two ranks would have a clear view of the enemy, those behind only sporadic glimpses: there must therefore have been some sort of ranging order passed by word of mouth. For the archers' task at this opening moment of the battle was to provoke the French into attacking, and it was therefore essential that their arrows should "group" as closely as possible on the target. To translate their purpose into modern artillery language, they had to achieve a very narrow 100° zone (i.e., that belt of territory into which *all* missiles fell) and a Time on Target effect (i.e. all their missiles had to arrive simultaneously).

To speculate about their feelings at this moment is otiose. They were experienced soldiers in a desperate spot; and their fire, moreover, was to be "indirect," in that their arrows would not depart straight into the enemy's faces but at a fairly steeply angled trajectory. They need have had no sense of initiating an act of killing, therefore; it was probably their technical and professional sense which was most actively engaged in an activity which was still preliminary to any "real" fighting that might come.

They must have received at least two orders; the first to draw their bows, the second to loose their strings. How the orders were synchronized between different groups of archers is an unanswerable question, but when the shout went up or the banner down, four clouds of arrows would have streaked out of the English line to reach a height of a hundred feet before turning in flight to plunge at a steeper angle on and among the French men-at-arms opposite. These arrows cannot, however, given their terminal velocity and angle of impact, have done a great deal of harm, at least to the men-at-arms. For armour, by the early fifteenth century, was composed almost completely of steel sheet, in place of the iron mail which had been worn on the body until fifty years before but now only covered the awkward points of movement around the shoulder and groin. It was deliberately designed, moreover, to offer a glancing surface, and the contemporary helmet, a wide-brimmed "bascinet," was particularly adapted to deflect blows away from the head and the shoulders. We can suppose that the armour served its purpose effectively in this, the opening moment of Agincourt. But one should not dismiss the moral effect of the arrow strike. The singing of the arrows would not have moved ahead of their flight, but the sound of their impact must have been extraordinarily cacophonous, a weird clanking and banging on the bowed heads and backs of the French men-at-arms. If any of the horses in the flanking squadrons were hit, they were likely to have been hurt, however, even at this extreme range, for they were armoured only on their faces and chests, and the chisel-pointed head of the clothyard arrow would have penetrated the padded cloth hangings which covered the rest of their bodies. Animal cries of pain and fear would have risen above the metallic clatter.

CAVALRY VERSUS INFANTRY

We can also imagine oaths and shouted threats from the French. For the arrow strike achieved its object. How quickly, the chroniclers do not tell us; but as a trained archer could loose a shaft every ten seconds we can guess that it took at most a few minutes to trigger the French attack. The French, as we know, were certain of victory. What they had been waiting for was a tactical pretext; either that of the Englishmen showing them their backs or, on the contrary, cocking a snook. One or two volleys would have been insult enough. On the arrival of the first arrows the two large squadrons of horse on either flank mounted—or had they mounted when the English line advanced?—walked their horses clear of the line and broke into a charge.

A charge at what? The two chroniclers who are specific about this point make it clear that the two groups of cavalry, each five or six hundred strong, of which that on the left hand was led by Clignet de Brébant and Guillaume de Saveuse, made the English archer flanks their target. Their aim, doubtless, was to clear these, the largest blocks of the enemy which immediately threatened them, off the field, leaving the numerically much inferior centre of English men-at-arms, with the smaller groups of their attendant archers, to be overwhelmed by the French infantry. It was nevertheless a strange and dangerous decision, unless, that is, we work on the supposition that the archers had planted their stakes among their own ranks, so concealing that array of obstacles from the French. We may then visualize the French bearing down on the archers in ignorance of the hedgehog their ranks concealed; and of the English giving ground just before the moment of impact, to reveal it.

For "the moment of impact" otherwise begs an important, indeed a vital question. It is not difficult to picture the beginning of the charge; the horsemen booting their mounts to form line, probably two or three rows deep, so that, riding knee to knee, they would have presented a front of two or three hundred lances, more or less equalling in width the line of the archers opposite, say three hundred yards. We can imagine them setting off, sitting (really standing) "long" in their high-backed, padded saddles, legs straight and thrust forward, toes down in the heavy stirrups, lance under right arm, left free to manage the reins (wearing plate armour obviated the need to carry a shield); and we can see them in motion, riding at a pace which took them across all but the last fifty of the two or three hundred yards they had to cover in forty seconds or so and then spurring their horses to ride down on the archers at the best speed they could manage—twelve or fifteen miles an hour.*

So far so good. The distance between horses and archers narrows. The archers, who have delivered three of four volleys at the bowed heads and shoulders of their attackers, get off one more flight. More horses—some have already gone down or broken back with screams of pain—stumble and fall, tripping their neighbours, but the mass drive on and . . . and what? It is at this moment that we have to make a judgment about the difference between what happens in a battle and what happens in a violent accident. A horse, in the normal course of events, will not gallop at an obstacle it cannot jump or see a way through, and it cannot jump or see a way through a solid line of men. Even less will it go at the sort of obviously dangerous obstacle which the archers' stakes presented. Equally, a man will not stand in the path of a running horse; he will run himself, or seek shelter, and only if exceptionally strong-nerved and knowing in its ways, stand his ground. Nevertheless, accidents happen. Men, miscalculating or slow-footed, and horses, confused or maddened, do collide, with results almost exclusively unpleasant for the man. We cannot therefore say, however unnatural and exceptional we recognize collisions between man and horse to be, that nothing of that nature occurred between the archers and the French cavalry at Agincourt. For the archers were trained to "receive cavalry," the horses trained to charge home, while it was the principal function of the riders to insist on the horses doing that against which their nature rebelled. Moreover, two of the eyewitness chroniclers, St. Remy and the Priest of the Cottonian MS, are adamant that some of the French cavalry did get in among the archers.

The two opposed "weapon principles" which military theorists recognize had, in short, both failed; the "missile" principle, personified by the archers, had failed to stop or drive off the cavalry; they, embodying the "shock" principle, had failed to crush the infantry—or, more particularly, to make them run away, for the "shock" which cavalry seek to inflict is really moral, not physical in character. It was the stakes which must have effected the compromise. The French, coming on fast, and in great numbers over a short distance, had escaped the deaths and falls which should have toppled their charge over on itself; the English, emboldened by the physical security the hedgehog of stakes lent their formation, had given ground only a little before the onset; the horses had then found themselves on top of the stakes too late to refuse the obstacle; and a short, violent and noisy collision had resulted.

Some of the men-at-arms' horses "ran out" round the flanks of the archers and into the woods. Those in the rear ranks turned their horses, or were turned by them, and rode back. But three at least, including Guillaume de

---

*The horses were probably a big hunter type, not the carthorse of popular belief, and the weight they had to carry some 250 lbs (man 150 lbs, armour 60 lbs, saddle and trappings 40 lbs).

Saveuse, had their horses impaled on the stakes, thumped to the ground and were killed where they lay, either by mallet blows or by stabs between their armour-joints. The charge, momentarily terrifying for the English, from many of whom French men-at-arms, twice their height from the ground, and moving at ten or fifteen miles an hour on steel-shod and grotesquely caparisoned war-horses, had stopped only a few feet distant, had been a disaster for the enemy. And as they rode off, the archers, with all the violent anger that comes with release from sudden danger, bent their bows and sent fresh flights of arrows after them, bringing down more horses and maddening others into uncontrolled flight.

INFANTRY VERSUS INFANTRY

But the results of the rout went beyond the demoralization of the survivors. For, as their horses galloped back, they met the first division of dismounted men-at-arms marching out to attack the English centre. Perhaps eight thousand strong, and filling the space between the woods eight or ten deep, they could not easily or quickly open their ranks to let the fugitives through. Of what happened in consequence we can get a clear idea, curiously, from a cinema newsreel of the Grosvenor Square demonstration against the Vietnam war in 1968. There, a frightened police horse, fleeing the demonstrators, charged a line of constables on foot. Those directly in its path, barging sideways and backwards to open a gap and seizing their neighbours, set up a curious and violent ripple which ran along the ranks on each side, reaching policemen some good distance away who, tightly packed, clutched at each other for support, and stumbled clumsily backwards and then forwards to keep their balance. The sensations of that ripple are known to anyone who has been a member of a dense, mobile and boisterous crowd and it was certainly what was felt, to a sudden and exaggerated degree, by the French men-at-arms in the face of that involuntary cavalry charge. As in that which had just failed against the archers, many of the horses would have shied off at the moment of impact. But those that barged in, an occurrence to which the chroniclers testify, broke up the rhythm of the advance and knocked some men to the ground, an unpleasant experience when the soil is wet and trampled and one is wearing sixty or seventy pounds of sheet metal on the body.

This interruption in an advance which should have brought the French first division to within weapon's length of the English in three or four minutes at most gave Henry's men-at-arms ample time to brace themselves for the encounter. It also gave the archers, both those in the large groups on the wings and the two smaller groups in the central wedges, the chance to prolong their volleying of arrows into the French ranks. The range was progressively shortened by the advance, and the arrows, coming in on a flat trajectory in sets of five thousand at ten-second intervals, must have begun to cause casualties among the French foot. For though they bowed their heads and hunched their shoulders, presenting a continuous front of deflecting surface (bascinet top, breast-plate, "taces"—the overlapping bands across the stomach and genitals—and leg-pieces) to the storm, some of the arrows must have found the weak spots in the visor and at the shoulders and, as the range dropped right down, might even have penetrated armour itself. The "bodkinpoint" was designed to do so, and its terminal velocity, sufficient to drive it through an inch of oak from a short distance, could also, at the right angle of impact, make a hole in sheet steel.

The archers failed nevertheless to halt the French advance. But they succeeded in channelling it—or helping to channel it—on to a narrower front of attack. For the French foot, unlike the cavalry, apparently did not make the archers' positions their objective. As their great mass came on, their front ranks "either from fear of the arrows . . . or that they might more speedily penetrate our ranks to the banners (of the King, the Duke of York and Lord Camoys) . . . divided themselves into three . . . charging our lines in the three places where the banners were." We may also presume that the return of their own cavalry on the flanks would have helped to compress the infantry mass towards the centre, a tendency perhaps reinforced (we really cannot judge) by the alleged unwillingness of men-at-arms to cross weapons with archers, their social inferiors, when the chance to win glory, and prisoners, in combat with other men-at-arms presented itself. Whatever the play of forces at work on the movement of the French first division, several narrators testify to the outcome. The leading ranks bunched into three assaulting columns and drove into what Colonel Burne, in a topographical analogy, calls the three "re-entrants" of the English line, where the men-at-arms were massed a little in rear of the archers' staked-out enclosures.

Their charge won an initial success, for before it the English men-at-arms fell back "a spear's length." What distance the chronicler means by that traditional phrase we cannot judge, and all the less because the French had cut down their lances in anticipation of fighting on foot. It probably implies "just enough to take the impetus out of the onset of the French," for we must imagine them, although puffed by the effort of a jostling tramp across three hundred yards of wet ploughland, accelerating over the last few feet into a run calculated to drive the points of their spears hard on to the enemy's chests and stomachs. The object would have been to knock over as many of them as possible, and so to open gaps in the ranks and isolate individuals who could then be killed or forced back on to the weapons of their own comrades; "sowing disorder" is a short-hand description of the aim. To avoid its achievement, the English, had they been more numerous, might have started forward to meet the French before they developed impulsion; since they were so outnumbered, it was individually prudent and tactically sound for the men most exposed to trot backwards before the French spearpoints, thus "wrong-footing" their opponents (a spearman times his thrust to coincide with the forward step of his left foot) and setting up those surges and undulations along the face of the French mass which momentarily rob a crowd's onrush of its full impact. The English, at the same time, would have been thrusting their spears at the French and, as movement died out of the two hosts, we can visualize them divided, at a distance of ten or fifteen feet, by a horizontal fence of waving and stabbing spear shafts, the noise of their clattering like that of a bully-off at hockey magnified several hundred times.

In this fashion the clash of the men-at-arms might have petered out, as it did on so many medieval battlefields, without a great deal more hurt to either side—though the French would have continued to suffer casualties from the fire of the archers, as long as they remained within range and the English had arrows to shoot at them (the evidence implies they must now have been running short). We can guess that three factors deterred the antagonists from drawing off from each other. One was the English fear of quitting their solid position between the woods and behind the archers' stakes for the greater dangers of the open field; the second was the French certainty of victory; the third was their enormous press of numbers. For if we accept that they had now divided into three *ad hoc* columns and that the head of each matched in width that of the English opposite—say eighty yards—with intervals between of about the same distance we are compelled to visualize, taking a bird's-eye viewpoint, a roughly trident-shaped formation, the Frenchmen in the prongs ranking twenty deep and numbering some five thousand in all, those in the base a shapeless and unordered mass amounting to, perhaps, another three thousand—and all of them, except for the seven or eight hundred in the leading ranks, unable to see or hear what was happening, yet certain that the English were done for, and anxious to take a hand in finishing them off.

No one, moreover, had overall authority in this press, nor a chain of command through which to impose it. The consequence was inevitable: the development of an unrelenting pressure from the rear on the backs of those in the line of battle, driving them steadily into the weapon-strokes of the English, or at least denying them that margin of room for individual manoeuvre which is essential if men are to defend themselves—or attack—effectively. This was disastrous, for it is vital to recognize, if we are to understand Agincourt, that all infantry actions, even those fought in the closest of close order, are not, in the last resort, combats of mass against mass, but the sum of many combats of individuals—one against one, one against two, three against five. This must be so, for the very simple reason that the weapons which individuals wield are of very limited range and effect, as they remain ever since missile weapons have become the universal equipment of the infantryman. At Agincourt, where the man-at-arms bore lance, sword, dagger, mace or battleaxe,* his ability to kill or wound was restricted to the circle centred on his own body, within which his reach allowed him to club, slash or stab. Prevented by the throng at their backs from dodging, sidestepping or retreating from the blows and thrusts directed at them by their English opponents, the individual French men-at-arms must shortly have begun to lose their man-to-man fights, collecting blows on

---

*A category which includes glaive, bill, and similar weapons.

the head or limbs which, even through armour, were sufficiently bruising or stunning to make them drop their weapons or lose their balance or footing. Within minutes, perhaps seconds, of hand-to-hand fighting being joined, some of them would have fallen, their bodies lying at the feet of their comrades, further impeding the movement of individuals and thus offering an obstacle to the advance of the whole column.

This was the crucial factor in the development of the battle. Had most of the French first line kept their feet, the crowd pressure of their vastly superior numbers, transmitted through their levelled lances, would shortly have forced the English back. Once men began to go down, however—and perhaps also because the French had shortened their lances, while the English had apparently not—those in the next rank would have found that they could get within reach of the English only by stepping over or on to the bodies of the fallen. Supposing continuing pressure from the rear, moreover, they would have had no choice but to do so; yet in so doing, would have rendered themselves even more vulnerable to a tumble than those already felled, a human body making either an unstable fighting platform or a very effective stumbling block to the heels of a man trying to defend himself from a savage attack to his front. In short, once the French column had become stationary, its front impeded by fallen bodies and its ranks animated by heavy pressure from the rear, the "tumbling effect" along its forward edge would have become cumulative.

Cumulative, but sudden and of short duration: for pressure of numbers and desperation must eventually have caused the French to spill out from their columns and lumber down upon the archers who, it appears, were now beginning to run short of arrows. They could almost certainly not have withstood a charge by armoured men-at-arms, would have broken and, running, have left their own men-at-arms to be surrounded and hacked down. That did not happen. The chroniclers are specific that, on the contrary, it was the archers who moved to the attack. Seeing the French falling at the heads of the columns, while those on the flanks still flinched away from the final flights of arrows, the archers seized the chance that confusion and irresolution offered. Drawing swords, swinging heavier weapons—axes, bills or the mallets they used to hammer in their stakes—they left their staked-out positions and ran down to assault the men in armour.

This is a very difficult episode to visualize convincingly. They cannot have attacked the heads of the French columns, for it was there that the English men-at-arms stood, leaving no room for reinforcements to join. On the flanks, however, the French cannot yet have suffered many casualties, would have had fairly unencumbered ground to fight on and ought to have had no difficulty in dealing with any unarmoured man foolish enough to come within reach of their weapons. The observation offered by two chroniclers that they were too tightly packed to raise their arms, though very probably true of those in the heart of the crowd, cannot apply to those on its fringes. If the archers did inflict injury on the men-at-arms, and there is unanimous evidence that they did, it must have been in some other way than by direct assault on the close-ordered ranks of the columns.

The most likely explanation is that small groups of archers began by attacking individual men-at-arms, infantry isolated by the scattering of the French first line in the "reverse charge" of their own cavalry or riders unhorsed in the charge itself. The charges had occurred on either flank; so that in front of the main bodies of archers and at a distance of between fifty and two hundred yards from them, must have been seen, in the two or three minutes after the cavalry had ridden back, numbers of Frenchmen, prone, supine, half-risen or shakily upright, who were plainly in no state to offer concerted resistance and scarcely able to defend themselves individually. Those who were down would indeed have had difficulty getting up again from slithery ground under the weight of sixty or seventy pounds of armour; and the same hindrances would have slowed those who regained or had kept their feet in getting back to the protection of the closed columns. Certainly they could not have outdistanced the archers if, as we may surmise, and St Remy, a combatant, implies, some of the latter now took the risk of running forward from their stakes to set about them.*

"Setting about them" probably meant two or three against one, so that while an archer swung or lunged at a man-at-arms' front, another dodged his sword-arm to land him a mallet-blow on the back of the head or an axe-stroke behind the knee. Either would have toppled him and, once sprawling, he would have been helpless; a thrust into his face, if he were wearing a bascinet, into the slits of his visor, if he were wearing a closed helmet, or through the mail of his armpit or groin, would have killed him outright or left him to bleed to death. Each act of execution need have taken only a few seconds; time enough for a flurry of thrusts clumsily parried, a fall, two or three figures to kneel over another on the ground, a few butcher's blows, a cry *in extremis*. "Two thousand pounds of education drops to a ten rupee. . . ." (Kipling, "Arithmetic on the Frontier"). Little scenes of this sort must have been happening all over the two narrow tracts between the woods and the fringes of the French main body within the first minutes of the main battle being joined. The only way for stranded Frenchmen to avoid such a death at the hands of the archers was to ask for quarter, which at this early stage they may not have been willing to grant, despite prospects of ransom. A surrendered enemy, to be put *hors de combat*, had to be escorted off the field, a waste of time and manpower the English could not afford when still at such an apparent disadvantage.

But the check in the front line and the butchery on the flanks appear fairly quickly to have swung the advantage in their favour. The "return charge" of

---

*Soon afterwards, the English archers perceiving this disorder of the advance guard . . . and *hastening to the place where the fugitives came from,* killed and disabled the French. (Author's italics.) Nicolas, *The History of the Battle of Agincourt,* p. 268.

the French cavalry had, according to St Remy, caused some of the French to retreat in panic, and it is possible that panic now broke out again along the flanks and at the front.* If that were so—and it is difficult otherwise to make sense of subsequent events—we must imagine a new tide of movement within the French mass: continued forward pressure from those at the back who could not see, a rearward drift along the flanks of the columns by those who had seen all too clearly what work the archers were at, and a reverse pressure by men-at-arms in the front line seeking, if not escape, at least room to fight without fear of falling, or being pushed, over the bodies of those who had already gone down. These movements would have altered the shape of the French mass, widening the gaps between its flanks and the woods, and so offering the archers room to make an "enveloping" attack. Emboldened by the easy killings achieved by some of their number, we must now imagine the rest, perhaps at the King's command, perhaps by spontaneous decision, massing outside their stakes and then running down in formation to attack the French flanks.

"Flank," of course, is only the military word for "side" (in French, from which we take it, the distinction does not exist) and the advantage attackers enjoy in a flank attack is precisely that of hitting at men half turned away from them. But presumably the state in which the archers found the French flanks was even more to their advantage than that. On the edge of the crowd, men-at-arms were walking or running to the rear. As they went, accelerating no doubt at the sight of the English charging down on them, they exposed men deeper within the crowd who would not until then have had sight of the archers, who were not indeed expecting yet to use their arms and whose attention was wholly directed towards the banging and shouting from their front, where they anticipated doing their fighting. Assaulted suddenly at their right or left shoulders, they can have had little chance to face front and point their weapons before some of them, like those already killed by the English men-at-arms, were struck down at the feet of their neighbours.

If the archers were now able to reproduce along the flanks of the French mass the same "tumbling effect" which had encumbered its front, its destruction must have been imminent. For most death in battle takes place within well-defined and fairly narrow "killing zones," of which the "no-man's-land" of trench warfare is the best known and most comprehensible example. The depth of the killing zone is determined by the effective range of the most prevalent weapon, which, in infantry battles, is always comparatively short, and, in hand-to-hand fighting, very short—only a few feet. That being so, the *longer* the winning side can make the killing zone, the more casualties can it inflict. If the English were now able to extend the killing zone from along the face to

---

*The sight of archers killing men-at-arms might either have provoked a counter-attack from the Frenchmen on the flanks *or* persuaded them individually that Agincourt had become no sort of battle to get killed in. There was no reputation to be won in fighting archers.

down the sides of the French mass (an "enveloping" attack), they threatened to kill very large numbers of Frenchmen indeed.

Given the horror of their situation, the sense of which must now have been transmitted to the whole mass, the French ought at this point to have broken and run. That they did not was the consequence, once again, of their own su-periority of numbers. For heretofore it had only been the first division of their army which had been engaged. The second and the third had stood passive, but as the first began to give way, its collapse heralded by the return of fugi-tives from the flanks, the second walked forward across the wet and trampled ground to lend it support. This was exactly *not* the help needed at that mo-ment. Had the cavalry, in third line, been brought forward to make a second charge against the archers, now that they were outside the protection of their stakes and without their bows, they might well have achieved a rescue. But they were left where they were, for reasons impossible to reconstruct.* In-stead, the second division of infantry men arrived and, thrusting against the backs of their tired and desperate compatriots, held them firmly in place to suffer further butchery.

From what the chroniclers say, we can suppose most of those in the French first line now to be either dead, wounded, prisoner or ready to sur-render, if they could not escape. Many had made their surrender (the Priest of the Cottonian MS cattily reports that "some, even of the more noble . . . that day surrendered themselves more than ten times"); some had not had it accepted: the Duke of Alençon, finding himself cut off and surrounded in a dash to attack the Duke of Gloucester, shouted his submission over the heads of his attackers to the King, who was coming to his brother's rescue, but was killed before Henry could extricate him. Nevertheless, very large numbers of Frenchmen had, on promise of ransom, been taken captive, presumably from the moment when the English sensed that the battle was going their way. Their removal from the field, the deaths of others, and the moral and by now no doubt incipient physical collapse of those left had opened up sufficient space for the English to abandon their close order and penetrate their enemy's ranks.

This advance brought them eventually—we are talking of an elapsed time of perhaps only half an hour since the first blows were exchanged—into con-tact with the second line. They must themselves have been tiring by this time. For the excitement, fear and physical exertion of fighting hand-to-hand with heavy weapons in plate armour quickly drained the body of its energy, despite the surge of energy released under stress by glandular activity. Even so, they were not repulsed by the onset of the second line. Indeed its intervention seems to have made no appreciable impact on the fighting. There is a modern

---

*But probably having to do a) with the lack of effective overall command in the French army, b) with the difficulty of seeing from the third line (c. 500 yards from the "killing zone") what was happening at the front.

military cliché, "Never reinforce failure," which means broadly that to thrust reinforcements in among soldiers who have failed in an attack, feel themselves beaten and are trying to run away is merely to waste the newcomers' energies in a struggle against the thrust of the crowd and to risk infecting them with its despair. And it was indeed in congestion and desperation that the second line appear to have met the English. The chroniclers do not specify exactly what passed between them, presumably because it was so similar to what had gone on before during the defeat of the first line. Though we may guess that a large number of the second line, as soon as they became aware of the disaster, turned their backs and ran off the way they had come, some were dragged out by their pages or servants.

What facts the chroniclers do provide about this, the culmination of the hand-to-hand phase, are difficult to reconcile. The English appear to have had considerable freedom of movement, for they were taking hundreds prisoner and the King and his entourage are reported to have cut their way into the second line (it may have been then that he took the blow which dented the helmet which is still to be seen above his tomb in Westminster Abbey). And yet in at least three places, suggested by the priest's narrative to have been where the enemy columns initially charged the English men-at-arms, the bodies of the French lay piled "higher than a man." Indeed the English are said to have climbed these heaps "and butchered the adversaries below with swords, axes and other weapons."

This "building of the wall of dead" is perhaps the best known incident of the battle. If it had occurred, however, we cannot accept that the King and his armoured followers were able to range freely about the field in the latter stages, since the heaps would have confined them within their own positions. Brief reflection will, moreover, demonstrate that the "heap higher than a man" is a chronicler's exaggeration. Human bodies, even when pushed about by bulldozers, do not, as one can observe if able to keep one's eyes open during film of the mass-burials at Belsen, pile into walls, but lie in shapeless sprawling hummocks. When stiffened by rigor mortis, they can be laid in stacks, as one can see in film of the burial parties of a French regiment carting its dead from the field after an attack in the Second Battle of Champagne (September 1915). But men falling to weaponstrokes in the front line, or tripping over those already down, will lie at most two or three deep. For the heaps to rise higher, they must be climbed by the next victims: and the "six-foot heaps" of Agincourt could have been topped-out only if men on either side had been ready and able to duel together while balancing on the corpses of twenty or thirty others. The notion is ludicrous rather than grisly.

The dead undoubtedly lay thick at Agincourt, and quite probably, at the three places where fighting had been heaviest, in piles. But what probably happened at those spots, as we have seen, is that men-at-arms and archers achieved an envelopment of the heads of the French columns, hemmed in and perhaps completely surrounded groups of the enemy, toppled them over on top of each other with lance thrusts and killed them on the ground. The mounds thus raised were big and hideous enough to justify some priestly rhetoric—but not to deny the English entry into the French position.

THE KILLING OF THE PRISONERS

Indeed, soon after midday, the English men were "in possession of the field"— by which soldiers would understand that they were able to move freely over the ground earlier occupied by the French, of whom only dead, wounded, and fugitives were now to be seen. Fugitives too slow-footed to reach hiding in the woods, or sanctuary among the cavalry of the still uncommitted third division, were chased and tackled by bounty-hunters; others, greedy for ransom, were sorting through the recumbent bodies and pulling "down the heaps . . . to separate the living from the dead, proposing to keep the living as slaves, to be ransomed." At the back of the battlefield the most valuable prisoners were massed together under guard. They were still wearing their armour but had surrendered their right gauntlets to their captors, as a token of submission (and subsequent reidentification), and taken off their helmets, without which they could not fight.

Henry could not allow each captor individually to sequester his prisoners because of the need to keep the army together as long as the French third division threatened a charge. So while small parties, acting both on their own behalf and that of others still in the ranks, reaped the rewards of the fight, the main bodies of men-at-arms and archers stood their ground—now about two or three hundred yards forward of the line on which they had received the French charge. Henry's caution was justified. Soon after midday, the Duke of Brabant, arriving late, half-equipped, and with a tiny following, charged into these ranks. He was overpowered and led to the rear. But this gallant intervention inspired at least two French noblemen in the third division, the Counts of Masle and Fauquemberghes, to marshal some six hundred of their followers for a concerted charge. They could clearly be seen massing, two or three hundred yards from the English line, and their intentions were obvious. At about the same time, moreover, shouting from the rear informed the English of a raid by the enemy on the baggage park, which had been left almost unguarded.

It was these events which precipitated Henry's notorious order to kill the prisoners. As it turned out, the charge was not delivered and the raid was later revealed to have been a mere rampage by the local peasantry, under the Lord of Agincourt. The signs were enough, however, to convince Henry that his victory, in which he can scarcely have yet believed, was about to be snatched from him. For if the French third division attacked the English where they stood, the archers without arrows or stakes, the men-at-arms weary after a morning of hacking and banging in full armour, all of them hungry, cold, and depressed by the reaction from the intense fears and elations of combat, they might easily have been swept from the field. They could certainly not have withstood the simultaneous assault on their rear, to which, with so many inadequately guarded French prisoners standing about behind them on ground littered with discarded weapons, they were likely also to have been subjected. In these circumstances, his order is comprehensible.

Comprehensible in harsh tactical logic; in ethical, human, and practical terms much more difficult to understand. Henry, a Christian king, was also an experienced soldier and versed in the elaborate code of international law governing relations between a prisoner and his captor. Its most important provision was that which guaranteed the prisoner his life—the only return, after all, for which he would enter into anything so costly and humiliating as a ransom bargain. And while his treachery broke that immunity, the mere suspicion, even if well-founded, that he was about to commit treason could not justify his killing. At a more fundamental level, moreover, the prisoner's life was guaranteed by the Christian commandment against murder, however much more loosely that commandment was interpreted in the fifteenth century. If Henry could give the order and, as he did, subsequently escape the reproval of his peers, of the Church, and of the chroniclers, we must presume it was because the battlefield itself was still regarded as a sort of moral no-man's-land and the hour of battle as a legal *dies non*.

His subordinates nevertheless refused to obey. Was this because they felt a more tender conscience? The notion is usually dismissed by medieval specialists, who insist that, at best, the captors objected to the King's interference in what was a personal relationship, the prisoners being not the King's or the army's but the vassals of those who had accepted their surrender; that, at worst, they refused to forgo the prospect of so much ransom money (there being almost no way for a man of the times to make a quick fortune except on the battlefield). But it is significant that the King eventually got his order obeyed only by detailing two hundred archers, under the command of an esquire, to carry out the task. This may suggest that, among the captors, the men-at-arms at any rate felt something more than a financially motivated reluctance. There is, after all, an important difference between fighting with lethal weapons, even if it ends in killing, and mere butchery, and we may expect it to have been all the stronger when the act of fighting was as glorified as it was in the Middle Ages. To meet a similarly equipped opponent was the occasion for which the armoured soldier trained perhaps every day of this life from the onset of manhood. To meet and beat him was a triumph, the highest form which self-expression could take in the medieval nobleman's way of life. The events of the late morning at Agincourt, when men had leapt and grunted and hacked at each other's bodies, behaving in a way which seems grotesque and horrifying to us, was for them, therefore, a sort of apotheosis, giving point to their existence, and perhaps assuring them of commemoration after death (since more chroniclers were principally concerned to celebrate individual feats of arms). But there was certainly no honour to be won in killing one's social equal after he had surrendered and been disarmed. On the contrary, there was a considerable risk of incurring dishonour, which may alone have been strong enough to deter the men-at-arms from obeying Henry's order.

Archers stood outside the chivalric system; nor is there much to the idea that they personified the yeoman virtues. The bowmen of Henry's army were not only tough professional soldiers. There is also evidence that many had enlisted in the first place to avoid punishment for civil acts of violence, including murder. The chroniclers also make clear that, in the heat of combat, and during the more leisurely taking of prisoners after the rout of the French second division, there had been a good deal of killing, principally by the archers, of those too poor or too badly hurt to be worth keeping captive. The question of how more or less reluctant they were to carry out the King's command need not therefore delay us.

But the mechanics of the execution do demand a pause. Between one and two thousand prisoners accompanied Henry to England after the battle, of whom most must have been captured before he issued his order to kill. The chroniclers record that the killers spared the most valuable prisoners and were called off as soon as Henry assured himself that the French third division was not going to attack after all. We may take it therefore that the two hundred archers whom he detailed were heavily outnumbered by their victims, probably by about ten to one. The reason for wanting them killed, however, was that they were liable to re-arm themselves from the jetsam of battle if it were renewed. Why did they not do so when they saw themselves threatened with death, for the announcement of the King's order "by trumpet" and the refusal of their captors to carry it out can have left them in no doubt of the fate he planned for them? And how were the archers able to offer them a match? It may have been that they were roughly pinioned (some contemporary pictures of battle show prisoners being led away with their hands bound); but in that case they offered no proper—or a very much reduced—menace to the army's rear, which in turn diminishes the justification for Henry's order. And even if they were tied, their actual killing is an operation difficult to depict for oneself. The act of surrender is notably accompanied by the onset of lassitude and self-reproach. Is it realistic to imagine, however, these proud and warlike men passively awaiting the arrival of a gang of their social inferiors to do them to death—standing like cattle in groups of ten for a single archer to break their skulls with an axe?

It does seem very improbable, and all the more because what we know of twentieth-century mass-killing suggests that it is very difficult for small numbers of executioners, even when armed with machine-guns, to kill people much more defenceless than armoured knights quickly and in large numbers. What seems altogether more likely, therefore, is that Henry's order, rather than bring about the prisoner's massacre, was intended by its threat to terrorize them into abject inactivity. We may imagine something much less clinical than a *Sonderkommando* at work: the captors loudly announcing their refusal to obey the proclamation and perhaps assuring their prisoners that they would see them come to no harm; argument and even scuffling between them and members of the execution squad; and then a noisy and bloody cattle-drive to the rear, the archers harrying round the flanks of the crowd of armoured Frenchmen as they stumbled away from the scene of fighting and its dangerous debris to a spot nearer the baggage park, whence they could offer no serious threat at all. Some would have been killed in the process, and quite deliberately, but we need not reckon their number in thousands, perhaps not even in hundreds.

The killing, moreover, had a definite term, for Henry ordered it to end when he saw the French third division abandon their attack formation and begin to leave the battlefield. The time was about three o'clock in the afternoon, leaving some two hours more of daylight. The English began at once to spread out over the field looking for prisoners and spoil in places not yet visited. The King made a circuit and, on turning back for his quarters at Maisoncelles, summoned to him the French and English heralds.

THE WOUNDED

The heralds had watched the battle in a group together and, though the French army had left, the French heralds had not yet followed them. For the heralds belonged not to the armies but to the international corporation of experts who regulated civilized warfare. Henry was anxious to hear their verdict on the day's fighting and to fix a name for the battle, so that its outcome and the army's exploits could be readily identified when chroniclers came to record it. Montjoie, the principal French herald, confirmed that the English were the victors and provided Henry with the name of the nearest castle—Agincourt—to serve as eponym.

That decision ended the battle as a military and historical episode. The English drove their prisoners and carried their own wounded back to Maisoncelles for the night, where the twenty surgeons of the army set to work. English casualties had been few: The Duke of York, who was pulled from under a heap of corpses, dead either from suffocation or a heart-attack, and the Earl of Suffolk were the only notable fatalities. The wounded numbered only some hundreds. What were their prospects? In the main, probably quite good. The English had not undergone an arrow attack, so most of the wounds would have been lacerations rather than penetrations, clean even if deep cuts which, if bound up and left, would heal quickly. There would also have been some fractures; depressed fractures of the skull could not be treated—the secret of trepanning awaited rediscovery—but breaks of the arm and lower leg could have been successfully set and splinted. The French wounded enjoyed a much graver prognosis. Many would have suffered penetrating wounds, either from arrows or from thrusts through the weak spots of their armour. Those which had pierced the intestines, emptying its contents into the abdomen, were fatal: peritonitis was inevitable. Penetrations of the chest cavity, which had probably carried in fragments of dirty clothing, were almost as certain to lead to sepsis. Many of the French would have suffered depressed fractures of the skull, and there would have been broken backs caused by falls from horses in armour at speed. Almost all of these injuries we may regard as fatal, the contemporary surgeons being unable to treat them. Many of the French, of course, had not been collected from the battlefield and, if they did not bleed to death, would have succumbed to the combined effects of exposure and shock during the night, when temperatures might have descended into the middle-30s Fahrenheit. It was, therefore, not arbitrary brutality when, in crossing the battlefield next morning, the English killed those whom they found alive. They were almost certain to have died, in any case, when their bodies would have gone to join those which the local peasants, under the supervision of the Bishop of Arras, drug into pits on the site. They are said to have buried about six thousand altogether.

THE WILL TO COMBAT

What sustained men in a combat like Agincourt, when the penalty of defeat, or of one's own lack of skill or nimbleness was so final and unpleasant? Some factors, either general to battle—as will appear—or more or less particular to this one are relatively easy to isolate. Of the general factors, drink is the most obvious to mention. The English, who were on short rations, presumably had less to drink than the French, but there was drinking in the ranks on both sides during the period of waiting and it is quite probable that many soldiers in both armies went into the mêlée less than sober, if not indeed fighting drunk. For the English, the presence of the King would also have provided what present-day soldiers call a "moral factor" of great importance. The personal bond between leader and follower lies at the root of all explanations of what does and does not happen in battle: and that bond is always strongest in martial societies, of which fifteenth-century England is one type and the warrior states of India, which the British harnessed so successfully to their imperial purpose, are another. The nature of the bond is more complex, and certainly more materialistic than modern ethologists would like to have us believe. But its importance must not be underestimated. And though the late-medieval soldier's immediate loyalty lay towards his captain, the presence on the field of his own and his captain's anointed king, visible to all and ostentatiously risking his life in the heart of the mêlée, must have greatly strengthened his resolve.

Serving to strengthen it further was the endorsement of religion. The morality of killing is not something with which the professional soldier is usually thought to trouble himself, but the Christian knight, whether we mean by that the ideal type as seen by the chroniclers or some at least of the historical figures of whom we have knowledge, was nevertheless exercised by it. What constituted unlawful killing in time of war was well-defined, and carried penalties under civil, military, and religious law. Lawful killing, on the other hand, was an act which religious precept specifically endorsed, within the circumscription of the just war; and however dimly or marginally religious doctrine impinged on the consciousness of the simple soldier or more un-thinking knight, the religious preparations which all in the English army underwent before Agincourt must be counted among the most important factors affecting its mood. Henry himself heard Mass three times in succession before the battle, and took Communion, as presumably did most of his followers; there was a small army of priests in the expedition. The soldiers ritually entreated blessing before entering the ranks, going down on their knees, making the sign of the cross and taking earth into their mouths as a symbolic gesture of the death and burial they were thereby accepting.

Drink and prayer must be seen, however, as last-minute and short-term reinforcements of the medieval soldier's (though, we shall see, not only his) will to combat. Far more important, and, given the disparity of their stations, more important still for the common soldier than the men-at-arms, was the prospect of enrichment. Medieval warfare, like all warfare, was about many things, but medieval battle, at the personal level, was about only three: victory first, of course, because the personal consequences of defeat could be so disagreeable; personal distinction in single combat—something of which the man-at-arms would think a great deal more than the bowman; but, ultimately and most important, ransom and loot. Agincourt was untypical of medieval battle in yielding, and then snatching back from the victors the bonanza of wealth that it did; but it is the gold-strike and gold-fever character of medieval battle which we should keep foremost in mind when seeking to understand it.

We should balance it, at the same time, against two other factors. The first of these is the pressure of compulsion. The role which physical coercion or force of unavoidable circumstance plays in bringing men into, and often through, the ordeal of battle is one which almost all military historians consistently underplay, or ignore. Yet we can clearly see that the force of unavoidable circumstances was among the most powerful of the drives to combat at work on the field of Agincourt. The English had sought by every means to avoid battle throughout their long march from Harfleur and, though accepting it on October 25th as a necessary alternative to capitulation and perhaps lifelong captivity, were finally driven to attack by the pains of hunger and cold. The French had also hoped to avoid bringing their confrontation with the English to a fight; and we may convincingly surmise that many of those who went down under the swords or mallet-blows of the English had been drawn into the battle with all the free-will of a man who finds himself going the wrong way on a moving-staircase.

The second factor confounds the former just examined. It concerns the commonplace character of violence in medieval life. What went on at Agincourt appals and horrifies the modern imagination which, vicariously accustomed though it is to the idea of violence, rarely encounters it in actuality and is outraged when it does. The sense of outrage was no doubt as keenly felt by the individual victim of violence five hundred years ago. But the victim of assault, in a world where the rights of lordship were imposed and the quarrels of neighbors settled by sword or knife as a matter of course, was likely to have been a good deal less surprised by it when it occurred. As the language of English law, which we owe to the Middle Ages, reveals, through its references to "putting in fear," "making an affray," and "keeping the Queen's peace," the medieval world was one in which the distinction between private, civil, and foreign war, though recognized, could only be irregularly enforced. Thus battle, though an extreme on the spectrum of experience, was not something unimaginable, something wholly beyond the peace-loving individual's ken. It offered the soldier risk in a particularly concentrated form; but it was treatment to which his upbringing and experience would already have partially inured him.

LONDON AND ITS NEIGHBORHOODS

BARBARA A. HANAWALT

One of the most noticeable results of the economic and demographic expansion of the tenth through the thirteenth centuries was the disappearance of much of Europe's forests, as growing numbers of peasants put previously uncultivated soil under the plow. Just as noticeable was the growth in the number and size of Europe's cities. With the growth of productivity and trade, hundreds of new cities were established and pre-existing ones outgrew the walls that encircled them. Most of the cities in present-day Europe were founded at this time.

The two most highly urbanized regions in Western Europe were Italy and Flanders. Parts of Italy had been urban since antiquity, but had experienced a long period of stagnation and decay during the early Middle Ages. Beginning in the eleventh century, Italian merchants brought the goods of northern Europe to the Mediterranean and the silks and spices of north Africa and the Middle East to Europe. Most cities in Flanders were more recent. Their prosperity was based largely on the manufacture of woolen cloth. Flemish merchants would bring their cities' cloth to the fairs of Champagne, where Italian merchants would buy it and transport it south and east. London, one of England's principal ports and a residence of the king, benefited from the general economic expansion as well as from England's special commercial relationship with Flanders.

Premodern cities depended on immigration from the countryside to maintain their populations. The relationship of cities to the medieval society and culture out of which they arose is a topic of considerable debate. Were cities with their communal liberties and their commercial economy profoundly different in outlook than a rural society populated by peasants and dominated by a landowning nobility? The makeup of the population of a city like London might help answer that question. In this selection Barbara

From: Barbara Hanawalt, *Growing Up In Medieval London: The Experience of Childhood in History* (New York: Oxford University Press, 1993), pp. 23–39.

Hanawalt recreates London as it might have been seen through the eyes of its children and young people. She takes us through the streets of medieval London and into the homes and workshops of its residents. It is a description that the city's adult residents would have recognized too. Who were the residents of a medieval city, particularly one like London, which grew so rapidly during the High Middle Ages? How might they have shaped London's street life and neighborhoods?

Glowing descriptions of medieval London abound, beginning with Fitzstephen's from the twelfth century. But looking at the city through the eyes of its children and youth gives a different perspective on the city and on the material conditions within it. The London that most children knew was an intimate one that included their house or tenement rooms, their street (which was also their play area), and their parish. This microcosm must be our first vantage point as we investigate the London of young children. As the children, particularly the boys, grew, their perambulations could take them farther afield, as they went to school or began to be useful for errands. The city walls extended for 2 miles and 608 feet and enclosed only a little more than 1 square mile. One has a sense of an intimate environment in which one could walk from the Tower to Ludgate in about half an hour.

Most of the young people inhabiting the city, however, did not grow up in it, and their initial view of the city was quite different from that of people who had been born there. London, like the other cities of medieval Europe, did not replace its own population as a result of the prevalence of disease, delayed marriage, and high infant mortality. It relied on recruits from the countryside for its servants and apprentices. In the view of these young people, London must have looked vast. They could enter London through one of the seven gates, gates so huge that two of them, Newgate and Ludgate, had prisons in them; the others served as dwellings. If they came from the south, they would have seen a panorama as they approached the city, with St. Paul's dominating the skyline. They would have crossed London Bridge, with its 138 shops. Once in the city, they might well have found it oppressively and confusingly crowded. (In the years before the plague of 1348, London had an estimated population of between 40,000 and 60,000, or higher. After the plague, the population dropped and remained low, reaching perhaps 50,000 in 1485.) Most of the young men and women who came to London were from villages of perhaps 200 people, and even if they came from York or Norwich, they would have left towns with populations of only about 12,000.

As we describe the material environment of youth in fourteenth- and fifteenth-century London, we must keep both perspectives in mind: that of the neighborhood and that of the larger metropolis. Throughout this [paper], we will try to see London through the eyes of its young people.

HOUSING

The size of young Londoners' houses or tenements and the amenities in them varied considerably, depending on the wealth of the youths' parents, guardians, or master. In the beginning of the fourteenth century, houses were arranged on plots in essentially three different configurations. The large houses of prosperous merchants had courtyards. The front of the property (perhaps 30 or 40 feet of street frontage) had a range of buildings containing shops and other rental units. The proprietor might use one of these shops, but he or she could rent out the others at considerable profit. As a visitor entered the courtyard, he or she would find the large hall and other buildings of the owner or renter directly ahead. The second configuration, typically used for narrower properties, was an L shape, with the frontage use being similar to that for larger properties, but with the hall placed at a right angle and extending back along the property line. The courtyard occupied the other part of the property. The third configuration, used for the smallest properties, included street frontage with a shop, a room behind, and a kitchen in a small courtyard; there might be no courtyard at all.

Record sources give us considerable information about living arrangements. For instance, in 1384 a lease for a group of houses on the Thames specified that the lessee would build a range of buildings along the street that would be three stories high, with the individual stories measuring 12 feet by 10 feet and reaching 7 feet in height. Behind this street frontage, he was to build a hall measuring 40 feet by 23 feet, a parlor, a kitchen, and a buttery. Underneath the structures would be cellars 7 feet high for storage of merchandise. Three-story houses, especially on the main streets, were typical in the fourteenth and fifteenth centuries. Another lease for 100 years at £12 a year required the tenant to build new housing 40 feet high facing the street, with three stories measuring 12, 10, and 8 feet high, respectively. In addition, he was to build a chief dwelling place with a hall measuring 40 feet by 24 feet, a parlor, a kitchen, and a buttery. All these buildings were to be made of heart of oak (the most durable building material) and to have cellars to the depth of 12 feet. Wattle and daub filled the space between the timber framing, although, by the fifteenth century, brick had come into use. For a more luxurious appearance, some houses had façades of stone.

Concern about fire, obstruction of public passages, nuisances, and the tempers of the citizens prompted the first mayor of London to issue what amounted to a building code in 1189. The walls between adjoining buildings were to be 3 feet thick and were to extend up to the gables which were to point toward the street. Aumbries (arches in the wall for larders) could be only 1 foot in depth. Roofs were to be made of slate, stone, or, later, tile, because thatching posed a fire hazard. Outside stairways and ladders were used to reach the various levels of the houses because each level could be used as a freehold or an independent tenement. To prevent disagreements between neighbors over waste water, latrines, and windows overlooking one another's property, Fitzalwyne's assize set regulations that the city enforced through the Assize of Nuisance.

An apprentice arriving in London from the countryside would have been struck by the height and density of the houses. To someone used to low buildings scattered about closes in peasant villages, the London streets must have felt like canyons, with their overhanging buildings and a forest of signs spreading over them horizontally like tree branches. A contemporary poem described the "[d]yvers sygnys hih and lowe/Wher-by that men ther crafft mak knowe." Lions, eagles, griffins, and other painted animal motifs were common on signs. Taverns put out boughs of green or fresh bunches of straw. The city finally had to regulate the length of the poles supporting the signs, decreeing that they could be no more than 7 feet long. To gain extra room in the upper stories, projections called penthouses started 9 feet up from street level (high enough so that a man on horseback could ride under them). The shops on the ground floor also projected into the streets when their horizontally shuttered windows were opened for business. Stalls for exposing wares could extend no more than 2½ feet into the street and were supposed to be movable.

A few preserved inventories from the end of the fifteenth century permit us to form an intimate view of the halled houses, with their parlors, chambers, kitchens, butteries, shops, and storehouses. The new apprentice, passing through an entrance between the shops facing the street, would have seen his master's hall directly across the courtyard. If the apprentice had arrived at Richard Bele's house in the 1480s, he would have been ushered into the hall, which probably had a raised eating area at one end furnished with benches made comfortable with six luxurious Flemish-tapestry cushions. The walls were hung with cloth painted with designs and, as was typical in these halls, with old weaponry. Furniture was sparse, consisting of a few chairs and stools and a folding table made in London. A container for holy water hung by the door. A fireplace, burning either wood or coal, heated the room. The apprentice's tour of his new surroundings would have included a look at the shop, with its axes, cleavers, knives, tubs, scales, and weights. This type of shop was typical and—be it a butcher's, baker's, or candlestick maker's—could be managed by a master and one or two apprentices. A journeyman might also work with them if demand was high enough. The buttery and the kitchen contained such luxuries as candlesticks, pewter pots, and a chafing dish. Most of the valuables in Bele's house were kept in the chief chamber (master bedroom) in chests and cupboards. The house also included a sparsely furnished room for a maid and, finally, the garret, where the apprentice might sleep and which was also sparsely furnished, with old and broken furnishings.

Bele's estate was modest (amounting to 65s. 8d.) compared with that of Sir Matthew Phyllyp, who was an alderman. Phyllyp had a richly furnished and tapestried hall and a parlor for more intimate conversation. This private room contained such pleasant amenities as two cupboards for displaying plate, a bird cage, a looking glass, and a book, *The Chronicles of London*. Phyllyp had at least three chambers in addition to the chief chamber. But the grandest housing for the merchant princes of London resembled palaces, such as that of the grocer Crosby, who built Crosby Hall.

Many types of more modest living arrangements were available, including shops with living quarters, rented rooms (particularly garrets), and impermanent shacks erected against walls and buildings. By the time of Edward II, annual rents were 40s. or less. Parish churches rented various properties that had been left to them in pious bequests. The churchwardens' accounts for one church from the late fifteenth century indicate that annual rents varied from 8s. to £4 in that period. The houses ranged from one with eighteen rooms to some with one or two rooms.

The drama of life (and death) in one of the solar or garret rooms comes through clearly in a coroners' inquest. Robert de Keng, a cordwainer, his wife, Matilda, and their two sons, William and John, had gone to bed "in a certain high solar." Matilda had fixed a lighted candle to the wall; a little before midnight, the candle fell on the bed of Robert and Matilda and set the whole house afire. Robert and William were caught immediately in the fire and perished, and Matilda and John escaped with great difficulty. One can imagine the problems of being caught in a fire on the third floor, with a steep stairway or a ladder as the only exit. Straw was the normal sleeping pallet for the poor who inhabited the solars, and the floors might also be covered with straw or rushes.

Rent of a room, since the room did not contain a kitchen, usually included board as well. In the mid-fourteenth century, a landlord complained that a man and his wife had "lived at his table" for three months and owed him 34s., or about 11s. a month for room and board. An inn room in the same period could cost as little as 1½d. a day. In a fifteenth-century suit, a woman paid 6d. a week for room and board.

As in modern cities, the homeless were also a presence. Children learned early the custom of giving alms to the poor who stood at church doors. The poor paid for these privileged positions. Margaret Kind, who occupied a bench at St. Andrew Hubbard, paid 2s. a year to the churchwardens for the privilege. Alice de Goldenlant, a pauper and beggar, had a lean-to by the wall of a chapel and died of disability in this makeshift abode. Squatters were also a problem, breaking into unoccupied property and staying there against the will of the owner.

Such living arrangements had a number of social implications for the growing child. First, it meant that the rich, middling, and poor might all live on the same property or on the same street. From early in life, children mixed with a varied population. Second, although some children were reared in commodious surroundings akin to palaces, the majority grew up in two rooms and a kitchen, or perhaps even less space. Apprentices, family, and servants shared the space. Probably few children had rooms of their own. Thomas Cowper, a stockfishmonger whose probate is dated 1488, apparently had his children with him in the chief chamber, in which there was a little feather bed with a bolster and a cradle with an old pillow.

The crowded living conditions also presented their share of tensions in which children, apprentices, and servants might well become embroiled. In 1473, the Goldsmiths' guild had a difficult time mediating a quarrel between Edward of Bowden and David Panter. Their living arrangements were partly to blame, since one disputant and his family lived above the other. Finally, the wardens of the Goldsmiths' decreed that in the future neither man should stop up the other's gutters or drains or cause his wife or servants to do so:

> And because the house of the said Davy is over the shop of the said Edward . . . and the said Davy shall not willfully of malice, he or his servants cast or pour on his floor any water or other liquor to run or drop down into the said Edward's shop, not make a dunning [loud noise] with hewing wood. Nor cast down water or dust out of the window upon the said Edward's stall.

Each was to have a key to the front door, and the door was not to be bolted against the other household. Furthermore, the guild would install in each dwelling a bell hanging in a convenient place so that the disputants could summon the members of the guild if one or the other started the affray again. If a dispute broke out again, the one injured was "to suffer and keep silence, whatever be said or done, except bodily hurt" and to report the incident to the warden.

The closely packed housing and the shared space also reflects on the sanitary conditions in which the children grew up and explains why so many of them did not survive childhood. While the city ordinances regulated the placement of latrines and stipulated that their walls be lined with stone, too often the latrines proved to be a nuisance to neighbors or were placed too close to wells.

Children probably received their initial toilet training either in the freedom of yards or streets or, for the more refined, on chamber pots ("jakes," as they are called in the probate inventories). Privies constituted the second phase of toilet training. Cesspits with their privies might be located in yards, or under houses in cellar floors. These latrines could be terrifying to a young child because the holes revealed a dark, smelly pit. One can imagine children sitting on the edge of the bench, worried about falling in. Even adults occasionally fell in. Poor Richard le Rakiere, who, according to his surname, must have made his living pushing the muck down London streets, died by his trade. He was seated on a latrine in his house when the planks, being rotten, gave way, and he fell in and drowned. Some houses had privies located in or off the solars, with wooden chutes (called pipes) connecting them to the cesspit. Some of these privies were cleansed with runoff water from roofs. Alice Wade had an illegal arrangement in which she connected the seat of a privy in her solar to a gutter that ran under the house of a neighbor, who was bothered by the stench.

Londoners felt strongly that their privies should afford them privacy. When some of their neighbors removed parts of the roof of a shared privy, Andrew de Aubrey and his wife complained that the extremities of those seated on the privy could now be seen, "a thing which is abominable and altogether intolerable."

Stench from privies was a continual problem. Privies had to be cleaned about every two years; "gong farmers" did the job at night. The cost of cleaning a privy in the late fifteenth century was 2s. a ton, and for the cleaning of one privy the churchwardens recorded a 10s. expense plus 16d. to have the muck carted off in a dung boat. If one adds the dirt of poultry, pigs, dogs, and horses, as well as kitchen waste, the filth generated by London's households was considerable.

NEIGHBORHOODS: STREETS, PARISHES, AND WARDS

With living space cramped, one would expect that children and adults alike would spend time in the streets. As we discuss the activities of youth, we will find that, indeed, this was so. Playing, carousing, soliciting, pimping, working, and carrying on business deals were often done in the streets. The next most common place of public encounter was a tavern or church, of which the city boasted many. During the day, therefore, the streets were crowded. But were they clean?

For the most part, refuse from the households found its way into the streets. The wider streets had gutters running down each side that were to carry away the runoff rainwater from roofs, as well as the contents of chamberpots, kitchen refuse, and other waste. Narrower streets had only one gutter. Streets also served as an alternative to latrines, although the city provided public latrines. Richard Whittington, of storybook fame, left money for a latrine that provided two rows of sixty-four seats each, one for men and one for women. The latrines were located where they would be flushed out by the tide.

In spite of municipal provisions, people found it inconvenient to climb down the ladders from upper stories to go to the latrines. We have [elsewhere] related . . . the story of the servant who "rose naked from his bed and stood at a window of the solar 30 ft. high to relieve himself towards the High Street" and fell to his death.

The city of London went to considerable efforts to keep its streets clean, not relying on rainwater alone to wash away the filth. Rakers regularly cleaned the streets, and the city provided carts and rented "gong boats" for removing the refuse. Londoners took an active role in city cleanliness. In 1299, two citizens reprimanded a groom of the prince for relieving himself in a lane rather than going to a public privy, which would have been "more decent." For the most part, the system seems to have worked well, but in the period following the Black Death, the streets apparently did become dirtier. Although not clean by our standards, the streets that children played in were perhaps not as filthy as modern mythology about medieval times would have them.

While the city and its citizens tried to manage the refuse and the filth, rats, mice, and bacteria could not be eradicated. One of the churchwardens' accounts tells of the problem of rats eating holes in prayer books and even in the altar cloth. To try to control the rodents, the wardens paid 4*d.* to the rat taker for milk and "rattisbane." It is no wonder that the plague in 1348 was so devastating.

To better preserve order in its crowded streets, London had a curfew at night and provided for the wards to patrol the streets to see that it was enforced. Curfew was rung on the bells of St. Mary-le-Bow, All Hallows Barking, St. Bride in Fleet Street, and St. Giles Cripplegate at perhaps nine or ten o'clock. All city gates closed, and taverns were also to close. People wandering on the streets were challenged by the ward patrols. But some people, apprentices and servants among them, often defied the curfew in pursuit of revelry. Thus about midnight on February 2, 1322, a group of fourteen revelers came up Bradstrete "singing and shouting, as they often did at night." When a shopkeeper asked them to be quiet so he and his neighbors could get some rest, they responded by taunting him and daring him to come out. When he finally did, he was armed with a staff and killed one of the revelers.

People knew one another well within their street, parish, and ward. London had 107 parish churches by the late Middle Ages. The large number of parishes indicates a preference for neighborhood worship, a place to be baptized, married, and buried among close friends. Wills and surviving churchwardens' accounts reflect the strong attachment of parishioners to their parish churches and their clergy. Our investigation of youth begins at the parish church with the baptism of the infant and ends there with the marriage ceremony that, for many Londoners, marked the end of adolescence.

The largest neighborhood unit was the ward. London had twenty-four wards until 1394, when Farringdon was divided into that Within and that Without, making the number twenty-five. The wards, the basic governmental and peacekeeping units of London, had initially functioned like the hundred courts under their head men or aldermen. Each ward had an alderman and other officials, including a beadle and his sergeants. It was at this level that the daily squabbles of inhabitants and other irritants could be brought up in the wardmoot. The alderman presided over the moot, which, in addition to listening to charges and complaints, registered freemen, examined hostlers and victualers, and appointed such officials as rakers, scavengers, and ale-conners. Those wards located by the city gates also had the responsibility of protecting the gates and of regulating traffic. All wards had a watch that enforced the curfew, pursued suspected felons, and policed the streets. Apprentices and servants wandering at night would come to know the night watch.

The surviving wardmoots indicate that neighborhoods contained a wide social mix. Aldermen lived side by side with craftsmen and prostitutes. For instance, Lymstrete reported on January 10, 1423:

Mawde Sheppyster keeps open shop, retails and is not a freewoman; also she is a strumpet to more than one and a bawd also. Thomas Brid is a forestaller and regrater of victuals coming to the market. John Cool is a sustainer of them in his shop. Anneys Edward, Gass Furneys, Cateryn Sprynger and Julian Blyndale are regraters of poultry and wildfowl.

In addition, the prior of Wenlok had a garden that extended 3 feet into the highway and stopped the dung and water flowing in the gutter, making it hard to walk in that part of the street. In Cripplegate Without, a stewhouse, or brothel, in Grub Street was attracting a bad sort of clientele, including priests and their concubines. Not only the stews' privies but also those of grocers and goldsmiths (high-status occupations) were common nuisances.

Children, therefore, grew up in an environment that provided sharp contrasts of luxury and poverty; pious morality and drunken, depraved immorality; exhortations to cleanliness and order and surroundings full of filth and noise. Providing a "sheltered" environment for children would have taken a major effort. Instead, children were instructed on the behavior that was appropriate to their place in the social hierarchy or to that position to which their parents aspired.

THE LARGER CITY: FORAYS OUTSIDE THE NEIGHBORHOOD

London had two major centers that drew youth outside their own neighborhoods. St. Paul's Cathedral was the center of much of London life. Since it dominated the London skyline, it was an obvious place for people to meet. It played a prominent role for those conducting business deals, partly because there were taverns nearby and partly because the altars provided a convenient place for swearing to contracts. The Folkmoot for London citizens was also located near St. Paul's. On major feast days and days of celebration, the citizens came in procession to the cathedral to hear Mass. Disputes among the guilds over the most prestigious locations in processions and in St. Paul's were heated enough to cause major fights. The Mercers, for instance, took great exception to the upstart Grocers taking the Mercers' place in St. Paul's on Halloween; finally, the mayor had to arbitrate the dispute.

The other focus of general civic business was Cheapside, a wide market street, and the nearby Guildhall. Children went to St. Paul's for religious processions and to Cheapside and the Guildhall for the mayor's show and for various political processions, such as the entrance of a new king or queen into London.

The Guildhall, the seat of London's government, also entered into the lives of youths when they enrolled their apprenticeship. Enrolling required that the apprentice and the master go together with the apprenticeship contract to the mayor. When a London citizen with minor children died, his orphans became wards of the mayor and might appear in person to have their goods and persons assigned to guardians. When an apprentice became a citizen or an orphan came of age, he or she again went to the Guildhall to receive the symbols of his or her maturity. The mayor and the aldermen held their many courts at the Guildhall, so youths suing or being sued would appear there as well.

Other features of the city with which apprentices and servants would be familiar were the various districts in which specialized shops were located. West Cheap was the center for traders in luxury goods, such as those found in goldsmiths' shops. East Cheap was also a market center, with chandlers and other services. The quern at St. Paul's was the major corn market. Names such as Bread Street, Milk Street, the Poultry, Wood Street, Friday Street, Ironmonger Lane, Fish Market, and the Stocks Market (source of dried and fresh fish) all indicate the location of major markets for various goods. Because the slaughter of animals gave rise to problems of waste disposal, the butchers were segregated to the Shambles, located initially near Newgate but eventually moved to Smithfield. Since medieval artisans and traders tended to live in or behind the shops in which they practiced their trade, the street names also indicated a concentration of residents working in particular crafts and trades.

By the fifteenth century, artisans and traders also had their own guildhalls in or close to their districts, so that they had a common meeting place and perhaps also some almshouses for elderly members. Apprentices and journeymen knew these halls well because they took their oaths in them before the guild wardens and because disputes with their masters came to the wardens for arbitration before they went to the mayor.

Pursuit of pleasure took the young people not only to the local taverns, but also across the river to Southwark for bear baiting and prostitution. For some of the young women . . . the taverns and stews of London and Southwark led to a life of prostitution instead of the honest service positions they undoubtedly sought when they first arrived from the countryside. Smithfield, the horse and cattle market, was also a center for horse racing, to which youths came to watch, bet, and act as jockeys. Judicial punishments might lead them to go to Tyburn to witness the hanging of felons or to the Tun on Cornhill to watch the pillorying of false traders or the shaving of prostitutes' heads. To be sure that no one missed such events of public humiliation, musicians played rough music as the miscreants were paraded through the streets. The meeting of Parliament in Westminster drew crowds of young people looking for diversion. The Tower of London provided a constant parade of political prisoners (including the king of France), nobles and courtiers, soldiers, judges, and high church officials.

The Thames and London Bridge were places of both work and pleasure. Many youths worked at the wharves or on London Bridge. In the fifteenth century, the mayors began to take a barge upriver to receive their office from the king, and their fine and colorful boat processions drew crowds. Of course, there was also the diversion of viewing traitors' heads on poles at the entrance to London Bridge.

Monasteries and hospitals played a large role in some London youths' lives. For sons and daughters of wealthy citizens who aspired to a religious life, they were appropriate establishments with which to affiliate. They were close to town and well endowed by London citizens; one almost surely had a relative among the monks and nuns. For the poor, including children, they were a source of alms. Large, extramural monasteries and hospitals—such as Clerkenwell Nunnery, Charter House, and St. Bartholomew's Priory and Hospital, northwest of Aldgate—drew considerable patronage. In addition, a few of the more urban-oriented orders established themselves in the city proper during the thirteenth century. The Franciscan (Gray) friars, Whitefriars (Carmelites), and Augustinian (Austin) friars all acquired property within the city for chapels, cloisters, and other monastic buildings. The Franciscan establishment was very grand and became the preferred burial place of the nobility and of wealthy Londoners in the thirteenth century. The Blackfriars (Dominicans) acquired the site of Castle Baynard and built such a large monastery that they had to tear down the city wall on the west to accommodate it.

The crowded conditions within the walls did not preclude large gardens, nor did they drive Londoners to create extensive suburbs. The roads leading into London had bars, and because some development occurred near the bars, five of the city's wards—Farringdon Without, Aldersgate, Cripplegate, Bishopsgate, and Portsoken—were outside the walls. To the west of the city, the presence of royal government in Westminster encouraged both business and residences. Bishops and nobles built their palaces along the Strand, and today the Savoy still lends its medieval name to grandeur. The presence of the Inns of Court, Fleet Prison, and the seat of royal justice fostered considerable residential development in the Holborn and Temple sections outside the walls. The presence of the Inns of Court also attracted a number of apprentice clerks, who, lacking the supervision common to other apprentices, frequently caused riots in the city. But the ring of suburban development was shallow, and city inhabitants, with their children and apprentices, often went to the country outside the walls for recreation.

THE MATERIAL STANDARD OF LIVING

We now move from the larger outside world back into the homes that young people occupied with their families or surrogates for them (masters and guardians).

Obviously, the degree of comfort in a home varied considerably with the wealth of the proprietor. It also varied with the time in which the home's occupants lived. In general, the quality of the houses, diets, and dress of all groups improved during the course of the fourteenth and fifteenth centuries. As terrifying as the plague was to London's population, the market response to depopulation was to increase wages for survivors and thereby encourage more investment in food, housing, and luxury goods. Thus youth coming of age in late-fourteenth- or fifteenth-century London could look forward to a much better provisioned environment than could those growing up in the early fourteenth century.

A 1332 subsidy roll gives us some idea of the relative wealth of the different wards in London and the distribution of trades in which wealth resided. Roughly speaking, the three wards on the river in east London contained the largest concentration of the wealthy mercantile class. These included vintners, fishmongers, and other long-distance traders who needed access to the quays. The shopkeepers along the Cheap to their rear formed a prosperous center, with the goldsmiths heading their ranks. To the west, workers in the trades involving butchering, tanning, and so on inhabited wards of moderate wealth. The poor tended to be on the northern and eastern fringes of the city.

To be subject to tax in 1332, a man had to have more than 10s. of movable wealth, so taxpayers came from only the well-to-do class of citizens. Considerable status differences existed within this group. Only 16 citizens had property worth more than £60; 172 had property worth between £15 and £60; and 141 had property worth between £7 10s. and £15. Members of the wealthiest group are referred to as "merchants of England"—that is, those engaged in long-distance trading. The next two groups contained some merchants, but also had a considerable number of shopkeepers, including fishmongers, goldsmiths, skinners, and practitioners of various crafts related to leatherworking. The 253 people paying on goods valued at from £3 15s. to £7 10s., the 502 with possessions valued at between £1 and £3 15s., and the 543 with possessions worth from 10s. to £1 also included butchers, ironmongers, plumbers, and other crafts people. The lower two groups also included a number of victualers and brewers.

Much of the untaxed population must have had wealth below the 10s. limit, but was not poverty-stricken. In addition, for every adult male citizen, there were perhaps three Londoners who were not freemen. They were not necessarily poor people, although many of them were probably servants, street vendors, and laborers. A writ refers to them as *mediocris populi,* or people of middle condition, in the city.

The number of very poor is hard to assess and probably varied with conditions. For instance, in the famines of the early fourteenth century, people seeking charity probably flocked to the city. It was during one of the famine years, 1318, that Robert de Lincoln left a bequest of 1d. for each of 2,000 poor people.

Wills and the few extant probate inventories help us to form some picture of the living conditions that a child or youth might experience as a member of these different economic groups. Since the more descriptive of these documents come largely from the late fourteenth and fifteenth centuries, they help to show the change that had taken place as a result of depopulation.

The poor are, of course, the most difficult to describe. While it is easy to think of them as single, old, and decrepit and as strangers to their community, in fact, . . . some . . . were well integrated into their parish and their guild and . . . managed to raise children to adulthood. Some glimpse of their economic and social position comes from wills. As part of their attempt to provide all Christians with an opportunity to make a will, the London ecclesiastical courts recorded those of a few people that they labeled as beggars. One such woman, called simply Alice, was a beggar. Her estate, which she asked the chaplain to administer, included a bequest of 29s. to the parish church, 6s. 8d. to be distributed to paupers. Hers was the largest estate of any of the paupers. If we recall Margaret Kind, who paid 2s. a year to beg at the parish church, we can see that begging had some rewards. Another woman, the widow of a minstrel, was described as a pauper. She left the residue of her estate to another minstrel and asked to be buried next to her husband. Of the seven women and eight men who were listed as paupers, most seem to have had some tie to a parish and even to have some living kin, whether spouse, children, or siblings. Two of the men had practiced a trade; one was a carpenter and the other, a goldsmith. One widow had a house and garden (in dower) but an estate worth only 14s. 4d., and another had kept the amenity of one silver spoon. These examples come from the late fourteenth and early fifteenth centuries, when the standard of living, even for the poor, had improved considerably compared with the conditions evident from the earlier tax records.

Laborers and servants also had very modest estates, but missed the label of pauper because they had an assured living with room and board. Many of those in low-paid occupations made simple wills that left the residue to a wife or an executor; the value of the estate was not given. A laborer left the residue of his estate to his wife, but also gave his parents 40s. and a surgeon and his wife, 6s. 8d. The estates of most people in this group consisted of movable goods, such as clothing, bedding, perhaps some kitchen equipment, and maybe silver spoons or a fine girdle, or belt. People might also bequeath the residue of a lease on a tenement. Although many of the testators in this group were not married, a few had wives and children.

Craftsmen appear in great numbers in all the will collections, but their estates often were not recorded beyond mentioning the residue and specific bequests. All the testastors appearing in the Husting Court wills had real property, although some were simply craftsmen. A twice-widowed lighterman and shipwright left his married daughter a house, and his son, a boat, a tenement, and a house. A 1495 probate of the will of Richard Leman, a tailor, revealed goods worth £115 in his house. The house included a hall, a parlor, two butteries, a kitchen and bake house, three chambers (including one for a maid), a counting house, a garden by the waterside, and a white boat. His was a modest establishment, but his trade gave him access to rather fine fabrics. Red silk hangings in the hall and stained ones in the parlor and tapestry cushions stuffed with flock stood in contrast to the few tables, one chair, and some stools. His cupboards contained not silver, but pewter and latten objects that amounted to only 66s. in value. He indulged in green silk hangings in the master chamber, along with feather beds and bolsters. Despite his being a tailor, his clothing was rather ordinary and came to only 8s. 6d. in value.

Wealthy citizens such as Sir Matthew Phyllyp, mentioned earlier in this chapter, had considerably more furniture and bedding, as well as chests and cupboards to display their plate. Phyllyp's clothing included numerous gowns and cloaks lined with a variety of furs. Henry Barton, a skinner whose will dates from 1436, had jugs, basins, platters, cups, and crosses, all of gold and silver. Salt cellars provided an opportunity to display considerable wealth, and some appear in the records described in elaborate detail. The alderman Stephen Forster pledged a silver-gilt one in 1448 that weighed twelve pounds troy. The base was embattled, and within these mock battlements was a hedge in silver gilt enclosing a landscape dotted with silver sheep. A shepherd and shepherdess in white silver were pictured driving a wolf away from the sheep. Also part of the scene were a bloodhound and a bear. The bowl of the salt cellar rose out of this relief work and was itself chased like bark. The cover, attached by a silver chain, repeated the theme of the base and included seven silver-gilt banners with coats of arms. A child growing up in such a household, surrounded by luxury and beautiful objects, must have imbibed a strong sense of social privilege. Girls knew that a part of this plate was reserved for their dowry and would grace their own tables when they were married. Indeed, wealthy families had a tendency to establish themselves as country gentry within a few generations.

The inventories indicate colorful dress for inhabitants of London: violets, greens, scarlet, crimson, russet, red, murrey, blues, and mixed colors describe outer garments, gowns, hats, and hoods. Linings were of wool fleece or of various furs, depending on the wealth and status of the owner. Doublets were a bit more subdued, often tawny or black. Bright colors were not necessarily the preserve of the upper classes. A thriving trade in frippery (secondhand clothes, shoes, and furniture) took place in evening markets at Cornhill and Cheapside. Because the city tried to force merchants of past finery to sell only during daylight hours, we can form some idea of the nature of those selling and buying. The sellers seem to have been small-scale merchants who came under suspicion partly because they obviously could defraud their customers better in poor light and partly because they were suspected of buying stolen property. Londoners of the lower orders, then, might be seen in faded and frayed secondhand garments.

Clothes given in alms, however, were almost always subdued in color, because they were given to paupers who took part in funeral processions. Henry Barton ordered gowns and hoods of the best Welsh gray cloth for paupers. Thus it seems that only paupers, the clergy, and perhaps widows routinely wore dark-colored clothing, in contrast to the rest of the population. . . .

Diet was as varied as were living accommodations and clothing. Part of the conspicuous consumption of wealthy Londoners was grand feasts. Guild banquets were affairs of many courses, mostly protein of various sorts, and quantities of ale and wine. Even the weekly expenses of running a large household seem overwhelming. Robert Basset, an alderman, had his house supplied with beer at a rate of seven barrels a week, paying from 3s. to 1s. 8d.

a barrel, depending on the quality of the beer. Laborers demanded meals along with their wages, so that three carpenters and two plumbers lunched on a shoulder and brisket of mutton, bread, and ale for working on a church porch. The churchwardens would have found payment in ale perfectly normal, for they went out to a tavern every time they hired a priest, sexton, or bell ringer. Food and drink were part of the enjoyment of life.

The government of London continually tried to regulate the quantity, quality, price, and distribution of basic victuals so that no one would make an undue profit and all would have access to the necessities of life. An assize regulating bread and ale guaranteed the quality of these items, and by the end of the fourteenth century, the mayor even introduced a farthing ($\frac{1}{4}$ $d.$) loaf of bread and measure of ale so that the poor would have ready access to these necessities of life. The city had installed conduits for water so that all citizens could have water, even if they did not have wells. The prices of meat, poultry, eggs, fish, shellfish, cheese, candles, and charcoal were also regulated.

Provisions were available either at markets or from local vendors and hucksters, so much of the daily shopping could be done in the neighborhood. The cries of London street vendors were legendary even then. Cooks and their knaves cried, "Hote pies, hote! Gode gris [pigs] and gees, gowe dyne, gowe!" And taverners cried, "White wyn of Oseye [Alsace] and red wyne of Gascoigne,/Of the Ryne and the Rochel [Rochelle] the doste to defye."

We . . . cite many cases that give a sense of this active street market because vending was one of the occupations available to youth. William Routh, a fruiterer, said that he was walking along the street with a basket of fruit when he was called into the house of John Douning outside Cripplegate. He went in at the residents' request, but they wanted to pay him 1$d.$ less than he could afford to accept for his fruit. When he tried to leave the house, they dumped out his fruit and kept his basket and cloak, thus inhibiting his chances of earning a living.

Remembering that London streets and neighborhoods contained a mix of people from very different circumstances, we can end the discussion of the material environment with the annual celebration of Midsummer Eve (St. John's Day). The wealthier inhabitants set out tables in the streets to feed their neighbors. Bonfires burned in the street, carefully watched to avoid disaster. All houses were decked out with flowers, boughs of leaves, and branches of herbs, and some houses also hung lanterns. All men of the wards turned out in bright harness for the Midsummer Watch and formed a procession, led by the giants Gog and Magog, through the city. Young children must have been awed by the giants, and one can imagine the fun had by the apprentices and servants who found the occasion one for drink and possible riot.

DOWN AND OUT IN PARIS: CRIMINALS AND THEIR MILIEU

BRONISŁAW GEREMEK

What acts are deemed criminal and their perceived severity vary dra-matically from society to society and over time. For example, rape was not classified as a felony in England until the fourteenth century. As a category of crime, it included acts as different as forced sexual intercourse and elopement with a willing partner. An individual's predisposition to commit crimes is also highly dependent on time, place, and circumstances. In Italian cities during the late Middle Ages and Renaissance, young noblemen were considered most likely to commit crimes of violence, primarily against men and women of lesser status. In English villages at about the same time, the most prosperous and publicly active men were similarly inclined toward violence and property crimes. The crimes rural women committed reflected their family responsibilities. They tended to steal household goods and food, and almost always in amounts so small as to con-stitute only petty theft. In villages, thefts increased whenever grain prices rose, revealing a direct relationship between hard times and crime. Similarly, the distinctive elements of the urban economy and society were revealed in the types of crimes committed in cities and the kinds of people who perpetrated them.

In the following selection, Bronisław Geremek constructs a "collective biography" of criminals in Paris by combing through the records of the criminal court of the Châtelet. As a consequence of the recent introduction of Roman law into the French judicial sys-tem, criminals were regularly "put to the question," in other words, subjected to judicial torture. Judges were well aware that individ-uals subjected to torture would eventually confess to anything their interrogators asked, so defendants were required to repeat their confessions voluntarily outside the interrogation room. Their con-fessions to priests just before execution can provide much-needed

From: Bronisław Geremek, *The Margins of Society in Late Medieval Paris* (Cambridge, England: Cambridge University Press, 1987), pp. 96–105, 106–117, 118–121.

confirmation of their courtroom confessions and sometimes provide information on additional criminal activity.

Who was most likely to commit crime in fourteenth- and fifteenth-century Paris? Geremek explores the social circumstances that predisposed certain individuals to a life of crime. He pays special attention to the social disruptions of late medieval France, when bubonic plague and the Hundred Years' War created demographic and economic crises.

One theft does not make a thief, and, besides, there is theft and theft. But the harsh repression which theft encountered in the social judgement of the Middle Ages meant that one single slip could have serious consequences, and entail the loss of social position.

Severity of repression extended even to trivial cases. Snatching a bunch of grapes, for example, was enough to have an apprentice charcoal-burner imprisoned. The theft of registers of Parlement and their subsequent sale to paper-makers took Etienne le Gay, called Courtequeu, to the gallows; it is true that this was hardly a trivial case.

Theft often had an accidental character, and the courts took this into account, recognising that the offence had been committed in a moment of weakness, 'at the instigation of the devil'. For example, a young carpenter, 'a poor young man', who owned a house near the church of Saint-André-des-Arts, set off one Sunday for the house of the Duc d'Orléans to see a play about the Annunciation and the Birth of Christ; he went into a house where he had once worked, and finding that the master was absent, stole the table silver. In another case, Colin Jourdain, who probably came from a background that was far from poor, instead of repaying his creditor the 9 francs he owed him, plied him with drink till he was blind drunk, then escorted him back home, and, once there, extracted the record of his debt from a chest; as he was unable to read, he pocketed all the debts in the chest, subsequently destroying his own, and returning the others, for a consideration, of course, to the other debtors. Even representatives of the militia failed to resist temptation; early one morning, an archer from Fort-l'Evêque broke into a house where, with the aid of a knife, he forced a chest, in which he found two bags of money, a cup, a small bag of silver thread, and precious fabrics.

Theft was often the consequence of a temporary need—no money in the house, no wine to continue a drinking session, no honest way of earning a living. The difficulties of life in Paris in the first half of the fifteenth century multiplied such circumstances. The petitions of the families of offenders introducing appeals for mercy always cited the argument of the misfortunes of war as an attenuating circumstance. Etienne Hervy, before stealing old scrap-iron from a derelict mill near Paris, had had to leave Montrouge, where he was born, hide in Paris, buy his freedom four times over from the Armagnacs, and had lost the cart which was his means of livelihood. A draper, 'tempted by the devil and poverty' stole the tiles from the roof of the Hôtel de Nesle. Jean Husson, a poor working docker handling wine and bread from Corbeil, slipped one night into one of the grain stores of the Hôtel de Ville and stole wheat to sell to a baker; he was constrained to this by his poverty and the high price of food in Paris at the time.

Most cases of theft were the work of domestic servants, wage-earners, or the employees of artisans. When a woman silk-spinner, on trial for stealing raw material from her employers, identified a woman to whom all her cronies took their stolen thread, it was emphasised how common this procedure was. The thefts committed by apprentices and journeymen typically consisted of the raw or finished product, or else cash or objects of value from their masters' chests. The unscrupulousness of domestic servants, a literary convention, is amply illustrated in judicial records. Menservants and maidservants regularly stole the silver tableware from the houses of their masters. Where circumstances were more modest, they stole the dresses of the mistress, the linen from the chest, the money from the bag, or the precious objects and jewels from the casket.

Such thefts often attained considerable importance. The case of Marion le Dioyne, a native of Bonneuil, is recorded in a pardon. Engaged two months earlier for a year as a chambermaid at the house of Geuffroy Robin 'in the old Rue du Temple, at the sign of the crescent', she left her employer just before Christmas, carrying off from his chest a long list of items including a cloak and a fur-lined coat, gilded silver belts, two purses, two keys, two knives—one with a sheath of silver, the other of ivory—and two gold rings, one set with an emerald. Having concealed these objects under a shawl, she fled with her booty to Bonneuil, where she hid at the house of a tailor who was to marry her. She presented the stolen goods to her fiancé as her dowry 'so that he would be more inclined to take her as his wife', but Geuffroy Robin tracked her down, and she was quickly locked up in the Châtelet. In this particular case, the value of the haul was estimated at 28 livres; in a similar theft, committed by a nursery-maid, the value of the goods taken was as high as 50 francs *tournois*.

Hostelries and inns were the scene of many crimes. Communal bed-chambers shared by people who were strangers offered ample opportunities for theft, at the expense of the property of the innkeeper or, more often, the luggage of the guests. For example, in June 1460, at the Hôtel 'de l'Amour-de-Dieu', Rue de la Barillerie (near the royal palace, in the Cité) one communal bedroom brought together: Jean Beffine, a native of Dijou, Bertran de Chisse, a native of Normandy, Alain Robert, a native of Nantes in Brittany and two unidentified 'journeymen' (Jean Beffine shared a bed with the two journeymen, and the other two were in a second bed). Alain Robert was caught in the act of stealing money from the bag of the man next to him in bed. It is characteristic that this Breton should be described in the records as *demourant par tout*, that is without fixed abode. Thefts committed by prostitutes have a similar character; they took advantage of the opportunities which were offered during the exercise of their profession.

In the cases mentioned above, the robbery was a sporadic act, performed in the normal course of life, or in a specific professional situation. It is difficult on this basis to tell whether the offence inevitably meant that the stigma of delinquency was attached to the culprit, and whether it excluded him once and for all from the 'society of honest people'. These seem, in fact, rather to be borderline situations which demonstrate the fluctuating nature of the division into the world of work and the world of crime. Poverty, bad luck or the temptation to improve their material situation impelled artisans, wage-earning servants or peasants to steal. The situation is not so different if we turn to notorious criminals, or those who were treated as such by the courts.

The robbery committed by Ernoul le Barbier in August 1390 in the vicinity of Paris was fairly minor. Hired by a 'labourer and thatcher' for a daily wage of 12 deniers plus food, and left unsupervised, he stole the tools entrusted to his care, and went off and sold them in Paris, on the Petit Pont, for which he got 8 deniers. Imprisoned in the Châtelet, he stated that he came from Guise in Thiérache, where he had lived for a long time and learned the trade of carter. He had then carried wine and other goods to Bourges, Flanders, Picardy and Germany. He swore that this was his first theft, but the judges, bearing in mind the circumstances of the theft, and the fact that the accused was a vagabond, decided to put him to torture. In the torture chamber he confessed several other thefts: at Valenciennes, five years before; at Guise, three years before; at Vieurin, where he served as an 'inn-boy', eight years earlier; and at Montcornet six years before that, and a week later, at Chouy, a quarter of a mile away. He had spent the money he stole on amusements and debauchery. He was proclaimed a *très fort larron,* and three days later he was hanged. The theft of tools which had led Ernoul le Barbier to the Châtelet was only one episode in his life in Paris, and we may suppose that he had previously lived from his work, hiring himself out for various jobs in the surrounding villages or on the property of Paris burgesses.

A Parisian baker and pastry-cook, Guillaume Yvoire, earned his living honestly for twenty years by the practice of his trade. However, he was forced to engage in a law-suit and, unable to meet the cost, he broke into a tavern at night and stole some pewter vessels. Under torture, he confessed to another serious burglary from a house belonging to the Duc de Bourgogne. These two thefts had been committed several months apart. Just before his execution, at the foot of the gallows, he also confessed to a burglary carried out three years earlier at a house in Les Halles, left empty during the wine harvest. Once again, we have an example of a craftsman who carried on his trade, but committed three significant robberies in three years. He never let his wife into the secret, but slipped out at night, a candle in his hand, and if he failed to find an open window, he forced the latch of the door with his knife; he carried his booty back home, and went back to bed. At daybreak, before his wife woke up, he carried the stolen goods to a friend who was a receiver and who hid them in his house. All this shady activity seems not to have disturbed the course of his bourgeois existence.

The tortures of the episcopal prison of Fort-l'Evéque forced Jean Cousin, whose occupation is not stated, to reveal that he had carried out his first theft in the house of his parents, a theft which was by no means negligible: first 120 francs from his father's chest, then 100 écus which his father had buried for greater security. He had committed these crimes five years earlier, before setting up a family; he was now twenty-five years old, married, and had two children, the elder of whom was three. Judging by the value of the sums stolen from his father, he came from a well-off family. But he continued to steal. He got into various houses and stole money and valuables from chests. He obtained a royal pardon, probably thanks to the activities and bribes of his father, since we read in the document that he restored to his father everything he had stolen. We lack information about the earlier style of life of this prisoner, but the number of his thefts, and the time which elapsed between each of them, makes it impossible to see them as a passing, youthful phase.

Whilst on the subject of young men of rich family, we may note the case of an eighteen-year-old squire, Colin de Sales. This son of a knight from the Beaujolais accompanied his brother to the battle of Agincourt. The brother died fighting, and Colin de Sales set off for Paris with his dead brother's equipment, which was worth about 600 livres; but he got into debt, and soon found himself without money. At this point, 'as a result of his youth, and the temptation of the devil' he turned to theft. The petition, repeated, according to the custom of the chancellery, in the royal document, lists a long series of thefts committed by Colin de Sales: three at the Port Baudet, three at the church of the Holy Innocents, one in the vicinity of the Châtelet, and one at the Hôtel de Ville. The sites of these robberies are very characteristic; these were busy districts where cutting the thongs of a purse was easy. The thefts of which he was accused are of precisely this kind. The most important was the last, the one which resulted in his imprisonment in the Châtelet. He had stolen at random from the banker Pierre Marado a money pouch containing 27 English nobles, a gold signet ring and several small coins. This is all we know about the life of this knight's son in Paris. If he arrived soon after the battle (when he was sixteen), he had spent nearly two years in Paris, up to the autumn of 1417. Nor do we know how and when he came to be stealing purses for a living. We can only guess at the hazards of fortune for a survivor of Agincourt in these years of crisis for chivalric values. On his way back to his native Beaujolais he tarried in Paris, where it was easy to squander money, and equally easy to acquire it.

The examples quoted, notwithstanding the frequency, number and importance of the offences, do not concern people who were in practice excluded from the social community. In the case of Adenet le Brioys, the element of marginality is much clearer. This Breton, 'a manual labourer and cleaner of latrines' was imprisoned for stealing the bridle of a mule from the stable of the Comte de Dammartin. He claimed at first that the bridle had been given to him by a journeyman at Les Halles; under torture, he confessed his theft, and admitted that he had sold the bridle for 10 sous parisis, and committed several other crimes. One year earlier, when he was working with two other cesspool-cleaners at the Hôtel du Cheval Blanc, Place Maubert, he had stolen wooden plates and dishes worth 20 sous. Two years before, while spending the night with several comrades at the Port au Foin, on the banks of the Seine, he joined in a brawl which ended in murder. Six years earlier, taking cover in the Petit Bois de Paris, between Paris and Melun, he had murdered one of his comrades, but found on him only 10 sous; finally, in August 1383, he left on an expedition to Flanders with a group of Bretons, and, near Arras, they murdered four people—this time, he got 20 francs. These confessions were enough for him to be proclaimed a criminal and a thief. At the foot of the gallows, he freely confessed to several other crimes: returning from Melun to Paris, with Perrin Petit, also a cleaner of cesspools, he stopped on the way at the Hôtel-Dieu of la Ferté-Gaucher, where his comrade stole 40 sous parisis; two years earlier, when he was working with the said Perrin and a third thief on the drains of the Bishop of Paris, Perrin pushed a workmate with whom he was quarrelling into the ditch; this crime had cost him and Adenet a long incarceration in the palace and at Saint-Eloi. And finally, they had both been beaten on another occasion because they were suspected of a theft in the house where they were working, but the theft had been committed by one of their workmates, Adenet le Brioys himself having taken only what was due to him for his night's work (4 sous).

Adenet le Brioys was suspect from the start, and the theft of the bridle was merely the revelation of his criminal nature. He was a Breton, and, like many of his compatriots, he exercised a profession which was naturally despised; both his origin and his occupation attracted social repulsion. But the proposition can equally well be turned on its head; this Breton cesspool-cleaner nourished a sentiment of repulsion, and felt himself a stranger in the society of urban property-owners amongst whom he lived. Theft was both the expression and the consequence of this state of affairs, although not yet a profession.

It seems that the common characteristic of this category of people was the exercise of several occupations in succession, all the while on the look-out for opportunities to steal. This was carried to the point where the occupation declared to the court appears to be a cover for criminal activity.

Henriet Testart, a native of Senlis, said he was a 'labouring man and mason's assistant'. He was accused of stealing money from the bag of a man who, like him, was spending the night in the church of Saint-Laurent, outside the walls of Paris. Arrested by the militia, he tried to explain that the money found on him came from his work as a harvester at Frêt, near Lagny. However, he had already been in the Châtelet prison for dicing and embezzlement, so the judges had no hesitation in putting him to torture. He then confessed to this and some fifteen other thefts; these crimes had been committed in small towns in the environs of Paris—Poissy, Montmirail-en-Brie, La Verrière—and some towns further away—Sens and Amiens—but most of all, however, in Paris. It was there that, two years earlier, in the company of several cronies, he had entered the attic of a prostitute at Glatigny, from where they stole a fur-lined cloak, which they sold next day at Les Halles for 2 francs. In the evening, they robbed a peasant returning home from Paris. During the course of the previous week, Henriet Testart had worked as a porter in the company of 'Jehannin Porte-Pennier', 'Jehannin au Court-Bras' and 'someone called Symonnet' at the gates of Paris. But every day they stole something. Their victims were the people who slept under the bridges, at the Port au Foin, or under the ramparts. One of them had tried to resist; they stripped the unfortunate wretch naked and threw him into the river, where he drowned. Testart's mobility was remarkable. He was to be found along all the principal thoroughfares connecting Paris to its hinterland. The reason for this mobility was the search for work as much as the 'inclination to steal'. He was, besides, a married man; his wife lived in the Rue de Franc-Noyer, where she sold cheese.

The list of Testart's thefts is long. One of the accomplices he cited had already been arrested, and this man added extra information. Jehannin Machin, called Court-Bras, first stated that he was born in Paris, and that he had carried on his trade there as baker and pastry-cook until he took part in the royal expedition to Germany, from which he returned with a crippled arm. From this point he could no longer practise his trade, and he started to work as a porter at the gates of Paris. We do not know, however, how much of this story is true, because when, as a vagabond he was submitted to torture, he stated that he was born in Louviers, in Normandy. It is only after a second, and more severe, session of torture (and being transferred from the *petit trestau* to the *grand trestau*), that he decided to make a complete confession: with Testart and other 'fellow vagabonds', he had held up for ransom ten or a dozen people in the course of the last three weeks just outside the walls of the town. During the previous year, he had carried out many minor thefts in Paris and its vicinity (in the region of Multien and in Brie) where he had begged for a living. In Machin's case, the permanent disablement was perhaps the cause of his social exclusion; it permitted him to live by begging, but, as we have seen, he did not give up work, or, above all, stealing. . . .

Amongst the cases cited as examples above, burglary is treated with greater severity. There appeared at the end of the fourteenth century an aggravating circumstance: burglary with a picklock. We can be fairly sure that the use of the picklock has a much longer history, all sorts of iron objects being capable of serving this purpose. This type of theft is even dignified by a special name: lock-picking, and its perpetrator is called a lock-picker. Whilst the very fact of entering a house was a crime, the discovery that a picklock had been used in the theft assumed enormous importance in the judicial practice of the fifteenth century; it was considered as a more serious charge, because it increased the vile and deceitful element in the theft itself. The records of accusations of theft began to emphasise this particular procedure, and the question whether a picklock had been used cropped up regularly in the course of interrogations. The fact that a thief had got into a house without making use of one was worth noting, because it mitigated the offence. On the other hand, the use of a picklock was the mark of the regular and professional practice of the trade of thief. Even if theft was not his sole occupation, the burglar had to be equipped with numerous and varied tools of the trade. These small arsenals, kept in a small box or bundle, sometimes fell into the hands of the authorities, and turned out to be quite considerable. In most cases, however, a few rudimentary tools must have been sufficient for the burglar.

The type of theft which occurs with the greatest frequency in the pages of the judicial registers was the 'pickpocket' type. The medieval pickpocket in fact had an easy job, because of the absence of pockets in the clothes of the period. Normal practice was to carry a small money-bag hanging from the belt; while travelling, or as a precaution against theft, it was sometimes hung from the neck. Parisian pickpockets took ingenuous new arrivals to Notre-Dame, showed them Pépin and Charlemagne in the gallery of kings, and sneaked away their purses from behind. Opportunities for stealing were also provided by the influx of faithful into the church—with a little experience, cutting the thong of a purse was easy. Any large gathering facilitated this activity. Even the pomp and solemnity of ceremonies failed to discourage robbers. At the reception given at the coronation of Henri VI in 1421 at the royal palace, to which the common people were admitted, there were thieves all over the place. Pickpockets also operated at the law-courts, where they took advantage of the large audience.

Adam Charretier will serve as an example of these 'cut-purses'. Imprisoned at the Châtelet in 1391, he declared at the beginning of his hearing that he was a pastry-cook, but the rest of his statement shows that he was a pimp (which deprived him of the advantage of clerical privileges). He was no longer young; he began by claiming to have practised his trade for twenty-three years. However in the last five years he had been stealing constantly, cutting the purses of all and sundry, both in Paris and in places near by. At Les Halles alone he had stolen about fifty purses. He had so many thefts to his credit that he was unable to count them all up.

Markets provided plenty of opportunity to pinch purses, which explains why Les Halles was a favourite haunt of those attracted by easy gains. The fair of Saint-Denis was another such place, and attempts to deter pickpockets by public executions in the middle of the fair were in vain.

Thieves also operated wherever humble people gathered: inns and hostelries, hospices and hospitals, and, in summer, the town ramparts, the banks of the Seine, and the fields surrounding the ramparts. Theft did not only affect the rich. There are degrees and differences in poverty; the purse of one poor fellow might hold what his neighbour's lacked. We must bear in mind, also, that robbing a poor wretch was less risky. A poor man was weak before the law, he hesitated to appeal to the authorities, indeed, he might well prefer not to remind the town sergeants of his existence. This explains why bands of dockers, passing themselves off as sergeants, stole from those unfortunates spending the night in the hay, or under the bridges, or rolled in a cloak on the banks of the Seine, or why the cesspit-cleaner insinuated his hand into the bag of his neighbour in the shelter for the poor; their booty consisted of a day's wages, or the small savings of their victim.

The outskirts of the town offered just as many opportunities for theft. Outside the agglomerations and town walls there was no need to fear attracting the attention of passers-by, and the risk of being caught unawares was reduced. Frequent movement and travel in search of work, repeatedly alluded to in the confessions made by our heroes before the courts, often turned into pillage on the roads, on the paths, and in the woods. All that was needed, in general, was to go out into the immediate vicinity of Paris, take cover in the forests or scrub, and lie in wait for someone going to or returning from the town. Another option was to travel to villages further away from Paris; either the vagrant found some temporary work, or he stole whatever he could find: a piece of cloth, a dinner service, some clothes.

CRIMINAL TIES

In the examples given above, we have presented the criminal milieu by means of the individual life histories of its members. But if only through the recurrence of similar criminal scenarios, and the repeated appearance of the same locations—cemeteries, markets, inns, ramparts—it has been possible to guess at the connections which existed between the people of this milieu. The notoriety of thefts and other offences led to the establishment of certain social ties, to the formation of relationships and friendships, and to the birth of partnerships in crime and criminal bands. The examples above showed us, for the most part, occasional offenders who cannot be excluded from a general picture of the milieu, but who did not become part—or had not yet become part—of groups within it. If we now turn our attention to the true criminal groups, we will be dealing with people whose lives were more consistently led on the margins of society.

A large section of the urban population was composed of people whose way of life lacked stability. The preconditions of a stable life were possession of a family, a house and a workshop. The streets and squares of Paris were full of young men looking for work who had not yet acquired the rights of mastership. Those who were bound by a long-term contract of employment entered, if only temporarily, into the family of the master, and lived under his supervision. The rest constituted the very large group 'of no fixed abode', who cropped up so often in court cases. It was altogether natural for them to forge ties of friendship; they met each other at hiring-places, in church (or in front of churches), in the tavern, or in the less frequented streets. They set off together to enjoy themselves, and together plotted more or less innocent breaches of the peace.

This sort of contact is often discovered behind crimes. The plans for many a burglary, swindle and sortie were hatched round a jug of wine at an inn. It is altogether typical that when, in 1481, Jean Augot, called Paris, sought pardon from the king after numerous robberies, his story began with an encounter at the inn with a very mixed bunch of comrades. One of them, albeit a priest, incited him to burgle the house of a prostitute; this profitable venture was followed by others. He picked up accomplices wherever he could, and the booty was sold by the servant of the priest. Meetings in taverns were also the scene of much boasting about crimes; in one of them, no doubt well-known for its shady clientele, a competition was organised as to who had committed the most, the finest, the most profitable, and the cleverest crimes.

As is generally the case with enterprises involving risk, people frequently banded together to commit robberies. Let us take as an example the case of two workmen, the older more experienced, the younger only a beginner. They decided to leave Dun, near Troyes, for Paris, in the hope of easy gains. They made a mutual pledge to share whatever they managed to steal (theft was, however, their secondary occupation, as, at the same time, they hired themselves out as servants). This agreement between two servants setting out for Paris is particularly significant; it shows the timidity and fear felt about life in the big city, but also the hope that, once there, they would strike lucky.

An association formed by three Parisian comrades with theft in mind in 1417 displays an entirely different character. They got to know each other through the agency of a goldsmith, to whom they delivered silver and gold. Jean Cuignet, called d'Arcys, and Robin du Chesne, a cloth-shearer by trade, met at the tavern of La Coquille, beyond the Porte Saint-Honoré. Robin du Chesne was accompanied by his cousin, Jean de Villers, a *curé*. All three swore on the bread and the wine, in the presence of the goldsmith (and perhaps at his instigation) that they would always act in concert, in the utmost secrecy, and that they would bring all their booty to the said goldsmith (who also swore to keep the secret), at the tavern where the oath was sworn. Situated outside the town, probably frequented by pilgrims, and perhaps also by beggars, who often used a pilgrim's staff to pass unobserved, this tavern was no doubt a well-chosen spot for this type of meeting and business. And metal began to flow, in the form of holy vessels pinched from churches in Paris. Luck, in the end, deserted them. They did not manage to leave Paris as they had planned, and all three found themselves in the bishop's prison. The goldsmith was locked up in the Châtelet, from which he escaped, thanks to a royal pardon, paid for, no doubt, in gold.

Associations of criminals were an objective necessity. When thieving assumed a more regular character, and a larger scale, collective action became possible. This was the case, as we saw above, with Testart, who, when he grew short of cash, left for the countryside with three companions.

Another example of a criminal association comes from the juridical conflict between the bishop of Rouen and the bailiff of Caux in the criminal chamber of Parlement in 1406. The subject of the dispute was Jehan des Haies, called le Decier. This is his life story. He was born into a poor family, left home early, and got to know a profligate trickster who made dice. The latter taught him to load dice, after which he spent his time in taverns and brothels. While a pimp in Rouen, he was often in prison for brawls and disputes. During one of these, he killed his opponent, and spent some time in prison in Louviers. He had money, so he had a fairly easy time, then managed to get out. From there, he took to the road, joined a band of brigands, and acquired a reputation as a mighty thief. After long and complicated travels in Brittany, he arrived in Paris, and joined up with three accomplices; they stole horses, money, precious objects, and linen. One of them was arrested, and gave the others away. When they were arrested in a tavern in Caux, a bag of instruments used for burglary was found in their baggage. Before their arrest, they defended themselves with drawn swords, and stolen horses were found in the stable, so it is reasonable to assume that Jehan des Haies and his accomplices also engaged in armed brigandage on the roads.

The list of thefts committed in Paris by three young ruffians, described below, is much more modest. They committed their robberies at night; they got into houses by concealed doors, often with the assistance of the servants, or used a rope to climb up to the windows, and stole whatever they could find, from food to precious objects. They confessed to thirteen thefts. The thieves decided on their objective during the day, then, after midnight, armed with daggers and picklocks, they set off for their targets, their success uncertain because the bars on the windows often proved an effective barrier. They broke open chests with a special tool called a 'turquoise'.

A series of trials which took place in the late autumn of 1389 at the Châtelet, following the confessions of Jehan Le Brun, reveals an extensive network of criminal relationships. At the end of September, an apprentice furrier by the name of Jehannin la Greue, who was accused of having made away with furs and skins, was locked up in the Châtelet. He had committed one of these thefts in the Rue Sainte-Croix-de-la-Bretonnerie, with the connivance of an accomplice, Jehan Le Brun. The latter had been captured at Bobigny, near Saint-Denis, where he was attempting to sell a fur-lined cloak, and he was shut up in the local prison. Taken to the Châtelet to be confronted with la Greue, he became talkative, and as he was convicted of treason with regard to the king, his case was soon transferred to the jurisdiction of the provost. At the Châtelet, he made a statement which implicated nearly forty persons as well as himself; he gave their names and described their crimes. At the foot of the scaffold, the condemned man withdrew the accusations against sixteen of the people he had named, saying that he had only given their names to prolong the enquiry, and thus delay the execution of the verdict (this execution was in fact put back for five months). We do not know what exactly were the reasons which drove Le Brun to make these confessions, because, exceptionally and remarkably in the practice of the Châtelet, he was not subjected to any torture. On the other hand, we do not know how the enquiry at Bobigny was conducted. When he was brought from there the first time, the Parisian authorities already knew that he could provide plenty of information. Did Le Brun make his first confession in the prison of the seigneur of la Mire, holder of the fief of Bobigny and, knowing only too well that he was condemned to the scaffold, decide not to spare his accomplices? The fact remains that the confessions of Le Brun and the people he consorted with and betrayed make possible a fascinating excursion into the criminal milieus of the late fourteenth century.

Let us look first at the principal character in the drama, the informer himself. Successive statements describe Le Brun's life in great detail. He was a bastard. His father was a soldier in the companies of the king of Navarre, and his mother, a girl from Normandy, accompanied him on his expeditions. Still very young, the child was apprenticed by his father to a blacksmith in Harfleur. After that he left, probably as a journeyman, for Rouen (he stated that this happened eight years earlier, that is about 1381). He worked there in a forge, but not for long, because Jacquet le Bastart, called Damiens, a twenty-eight-year-old squire who lodged in the same house, offered to take him into his service, promising to equip him with arms, and to take him to the Limousin. He then served for six years as an archer in the English garrison of La Souterraine, in the Limousin, with Jacquet Damiens, who was *mouche des Englois contre les François,* that is, a spy; also with Blanche-barbe, the English captain of the stronghold of Corbesin. He took part in military expeditions, he pillaged, he ransomed subjects of the king of France, he raped, he captured—all everyday activities during the Hundred Years War. His military service did not provide him with a fixed income; he was content with what he was given by his leaders, but, in time, he conceived a strong aversion for this service. He said that he became convinced that Blanche-barbe was not paying him as much as he deserved and was not allowing him to benefit from the profits of the war. So he decided to give him the slip and quit this occupation. He fled to Paris, taking with him a charger which belonged to Blanche-barbe and was worth nearly 30 francs. In Paris, which he had reached two years before the trial, he sold the horse, which added to the fifteen gold francs he had saved. This enabled him to dress decently and to survive for a while playing dice and frequenting taverns and brothels. When his money ran out he had to find some way of getting more.

Three possibilities presented themselves: going back to being a smith, a soldier, or a bandit; occupations he had previously practised. He chose the last two. Having run through his money, he re-entered the service of the constable, then, whilst staying in Rouen, he joined the royal army, which was leaving for a campaign in Germany (July to September 1388). The rest of the time he stole and pillaged with chance companions. He also recorded in the course of his story visits to girls, tavern friendships, and trips outside Paris; Saint-Cloud, Mantes, Brie-Comte-Robert, Meaux, Saint-Denis. These expeditions took him well away from Paris, but he always came back, along with his accomplices. Each trip left bloody traces. These ruffians took a prostitute from the brothel in the Rue Tiron into the wood of Vincennes, and, by way of payment, cut her throat and sold her dress on the way back. On another occasion, Le Brun killed a salt merchant, took his horse (which he later sold for 3 francs) and found 7 *blancs* in his bag; he also killed a traveller on foot, in whose bag he found a mere 12 sous. In towns, he stole merchandise from stalls. At Mantes, taking advantage of the fair, which was held in mid-May, he stole hose, knives and cauldrons; in Paris, he stole silver rings, silk head-dresses and furs; in Saint-Denis, linen left out to dry. The fruits of these thefts were disposed of through second-hand clothes dealers, or served as pledges for tavern accounts, or bought him the favours of Guillemette, a *fille de péché* of Saint-Denis, who had been his mistress and fiancée for the last year. For this man of war, life had little importance and murder was a trifling matter. So much so that when one of his accomplices returned to Paris better dressed than him, he was beaten and stoned to death, stripped, and his money squandered in the tavern.

Out of the dozens of names revealed by Le Brun to the Parisian authorities, a small group of fifteen people were caught. On 26 October 1389, Le Brun was condemned to be dragged to the scaffold and beheaded as a 'traitor to the king', but the execution of the sentence was postponed in the expectation of the services he could render as witness; ten days later, a verdict of death was pronounced on seven other accomplices (two, as thieves and murderers, were condemned to be dragged to the gallows and hanged, four were doomed to the rope, and the last, who admitted to being guilty of sodomy, was to be burnt at the stake). Two offenders in this first group of accused did not belong to the circle of Le Brun's friends and accomplices; they had been associated with them because their cases were similar, and occurred at the same time, and also because, like the cronies of Le Brun, they claimed the right to *privilegium fori*. There remain from this first haul six other accomplices; their six trials are to be found in the criminal register of the Châtelet, staggered over two and a half years (the document stops in May 1382), and some were late in being captured. All ended up on the gallows, the two who were murderers being first dragged through the streets. . . .

All were accused of theft. Under torture they confessed to between two or three and twenty robberies. As a general rule, a first theft from the house of their employer was succeeded by others committed elsewhere and ever more widely. One of Le Brun's comrades, Raoulet de Laon, was even unable to list all the thefts he had committed since his first exploit at Chartres, in the workshop of the furrier where he was employed. He declared simply that 'since then, he had always been a thief'. The thefts were of very different types: for example, a barrow-boy's purse was cut in the throng of customers; a neighbour at the inn was robbed; poultry was pinched from a henhouse; a horse was seized, or linen, clothes or dishes were stolen from houses; a dress or a piece of cloth was sneaked from a stall. On one occasion, fire broke out in a house and the hue and cry was raised next door; a throng of bystanders assembled to watch a wounded man carried out, and immediately this provided a chance for one of them to steal a dish or some clothes. Or it could be brigandage on the main road accompanied by murder; five out of twelve confessed to murders. Some of them, like Le Brun, had found the opportunity for an easy life in military campaigns. They acted as the instruments of private vengeance by turning themselves into hired thugs, and the same elements recur: the inn, the tavern, prostitutes. These last were not only companions in pleasure, but also a source of profit; accusations of 'protecting' girls and acting as pimps were repeated over and over again.

Seven of those who appeared before the court were tonsured, the visible sign of belonging to the *ordo clericorum*. Like Le Brun, and following his denunciations, they admitted, freely or under torture, that this sign was false, that they had had it done on the advice of comrades experienced in the art of escaping lay jurisdiction and the rope. The tonsure gave robbers a greater feeling of security. It enabled them to hang on to their heads even after imprisonment. These men were hardly novices before the court or in prison; at least six of them had already been punished, two of them many times, and two others had even been banished. We may, therefore, assume that the circle in which Le Brun moved was composed of professional criminals. Moreover the false tonsure was the characteristic sign of belonging to the criminal milieu. This is not only because it arose from experience of law-breaking (personal or second-hand), but also because it was the result of choosing a particular way of life and was the guarantee of being able to follow it.

Evidence about the social origin of these people is lacking in the confessions (with the exception of Le Brun, who we know was a bastard, only one of his accomplices recorded his origin). On the other hand we know their occupations; they were mostly artisans. The occupations claimed by the accused are as follows: there were three tailors, two agricultural workers, two navvies, and one each from the following trades: smith, furrier, hose-maker, tanner and joiner.

Eight out of twelve, then, had some qualification as artisans; they were obviously servants, who had probably not always completed their apprenticeship. The navvies and agricultural workers might be considered to be lacking any professional qualification. But whatever trade had been learned (at least if their statements are to be believed), they engaged in a very wide range of activities. Thus we see a tailor's servant stating that he was also a navvy and dug ditches, and a farm-worker who was also a carter in the town and assistant to a mason. Many of them did seasonal work on the wine or corn harvests, in the period when wages were high.

Everything also suggests that they were young. Only two were married. They did not state their own age to the court, but gave information about that of their accomplices (which the authorities needed to start proceedings). Their ages were usually between twenty and thirty. On the basis of the biographical information contained in their own confessions (date of false tonsure, of leaving the workshop or of the first theft), we may conclude with some confidence that they were themselves young, that none—with one exception—was more than thirty and that most were about twenty-five.

POWER, PROPERTY AND GENDER IN VILLAGE LIFE

JUDITH M. BENNETT

Did women enjoy a "golden age" in the Middle Ages? Historians who chart the discouraging succession of detrimental changes in women's status in the early modern and modern periods have postulated that these mark a decline from an earlier, happier time when women enjoyed more control over their lives and greater respect from their society. Proponents of the theory of a medieval golden age for women can point to courtly romances, which describe a relationship between the sexes in which women are men's social and moral superiors. They can also appeal to the example of a few great women—queens and noblewomen—who exercised an important influence on culture and politics. The vast majority of men and women, however, were not those depicted in courtly romances or playing key parts on Europe's international stage. Currently, historians have attempted to lower their sights to the less exalted, yet far more common experiences of the rest of Europe's women, who came from the lower nobility or who lived in cities and villages.

By far the greatest proportion of Europe's women—and men—lived out their lives in the countryside, yet they are also the most inaccessible to the historian. Few left their own accounts of what life was like for them. In this selection, Judith Bennett turns to the voluminous records of the English manorial courts in an effort to reconstruct the public lives and social networks of men and women in the late-thirteenth- and early-fourteenth-century village of Brigstock. There she finds evidence that for both men and women, the exercise of public power was shaped by property and marital status. Exactly how property and marital status combined to affect an individual's position in village life, however, differed profoundly according to gender.

From: Judith M. Bennett, "Public Power and Authority in the Medieval English Countryside," in Mary Erler and Maryanne Kowaleski, eds., *Women and Power in the Middle Ages* (Athens, GA: University of Georgia Press, 1988), pp. 18–29.

How did women's and men's roles in the village differ? Is it correct to conclude that their roles differed because women's sphere of action and authority was private while the men's sphere was public? What does the changing nature of men's and women's roles, as they passed through their life stages, suggest about relationships between women and men, wives and husbands, in the later Middle Ages?

Villagers in medieval England lived in a very public world. Bound together by nucleated settlements, common fields, and shared lordships, medieval villagers cooperated with their neighbors in coordinating work and government, monitoring courtship and marriage, and exchanging land and labor. Community interest and control extended even to the most private of acts—sexual relations and marriage. As a result, the notion of a public sphere for males and a private sphere for females was much less important to medieval peasants than it was to the middle class of the nineteenth century. A dichotomy between private wives and public husbands was certainly embedded in the households of the medieval countryside, but it was an ideal, not a real dichotomy. Women were never thoroughly isolated from the public life of medieval villages because their daily activities brought them into regular contact with neighbors, officers, laborers, traders, and the like.

A clear but relatively fluid sexual division of labor also promoted the public activity of medieval countrywomen. Skilled or heavy work away from the domestic croft was usually undertaken by men, and women took responsibility for a wide variety of smaller tasks centered on the household. Household duties did not, however, isolate peasant women. On the one hand, women regularly assisted men in planting and harvesting. Whenever agricultural work required additional laborers, women left their tasks around the croft and joined their fathers, husbands, and brothers in the fields. On the other hand, women's work around the croft was often more public than private. As dairymaids, poulterers, gardeners, bakers, and brewers, medieval countrywomen not only supplied the needs of their own households but also produced marketable surpluses. The enforcement records of the assize of bread and ale leave no doubt, for example, that women were some of the most active of commercial bakers and brewers in the countryside. Rural women and men worked with equal vigor to support their households and relied with equal intensity upon each other's labor. The private idealization of the economically inactive "angel in the house" that so strongly characterized the Victorian middle class had no place in the rural household economy of the Middle Ages.

Neither the public nature of life in the medieval countryside nor the economic importance of women's work, however, assured that public power and authority were shared equally by the sexes. Power, defined as "the ability to act effectively on persons or things . . . [in ways] not of right allocated to individuals," can be best assessed for medieval countrypeople through their landholding, legal, and social activities. All medieval peasants did not hold land, were not treated equivalently by their courts, and were not socially active to the same extent and degree. Still, the most effective members of rural communities were legally competent and socially active landholders. Defined in these terms, power was most readily acquired by men, but it was not denied to women. In contrast, authority, defined as "recognized and legitimized power," was strictly reserved for males. Women never served as rural officers and were also excluded from the formal associations that bound men together into a political community. In the villages of medieval England, political action brought sanctioned power, social prestige, and personal profit, benefits available only to men.

The experiences of the medieval peasantry are set forth in the records of courts held by manorial lords. Manorial courts usually required the attendance of all tenants at meetings every three weeks and oversaw a wide variety of local matters, including inheritances, land conveyances, trespasses, assaults, disputes, and petty thefts. These courts were rural as well as seigneurial institutions. Convened by a lord's authority but managed by peasant officers, manorial courts blended the seigneurial need for control with the local need for community regulation and mingled the lord's law with local custom. These local forums differed from modern courts in familiarity (most peasants probably knew their courts as well as they knew their churches), use (most contacts in manorial courts involved cooperation rather than the conflict we associate with modern legal action), and form (business was conducted by laypeople who normally acted without the aid of lawyers). Where manorial court rolls survive in long and complete series, they provide unparalleled insights into the public affairs of preindustrial rural communities.

The use of such records to study the access of rural women to public power and authority presents, however, two basic problems. First, private influence cannot be traced in court records, and no other sources survive to counterbalance the public focus of court rolls with information about private ideals, aspirations, and actions. Because both male and female peasants were illiterate, they have left no diaries or memoirs that describe their personal hopes and visions. The peasantry was generally despised by the literate minority, and its portrayal in contemporary literature is, at best, highly suspect. The private attitudes and activities of medieval countryfolk are, as a result, hidden from historical view. Still, given the public nature of life in the medieval countryside, there can be no doubt that public activities were important in medieval villages and that the ability of women to act publicly was one significant component of their lives. Neighborliness was vital to rural living, and those whose public options enabled them to be better neighbors accrued not only power but possibly also authority. Manorial court rolls offer only a partial view of medieval rural society, but it is a view focused on essential activities.

Second, since court rolls are best used in studies of specific localities, their findings can be extended to other areas and times only with the greatest care and caution. This essay uses the 549 courts extant for the manor of Brigstock (in Rockingham Forest, Northamptonshire) between 1287 and 1348 to

examine the access of women in that community to public power and authority. Were the experiences of women in Brigstock typical of all English countrywomen? Because no single community can represent fully the extraordinary
diversity of economy, settlement, and custom found in the English medieval
countryside, none was "typical" of all others. And because the history of rural
women is a relatively new field in medieval studies, little comparable research
is available. Nevertheless, comparison of the Brigstock data with information
drawn from the archives of two other manors—Iver, a pastoral community in
Buckinghamshire, and Houghton-cum-Wyton, an open-field, mixed farming
manor in Huntingdonshire—suggests that gender relations in Brigstock followed a pattern broadly characteristic of most rural communities before the
plague.

In these communities, then, public power was less available to women
than to men, and public authority was, essentially, a male preserve. No matter
what private pressures and influences countrywomen might have mustered to
influence events in their communities, they were less able than men to exert
formal and public power. This finding is, perhaps, unsurprising, since women
have been observed in many societies—urban as well as rural, modern as well
as medieval—to be excluded from the formal exercise of power. What distinguishes the experiences of medieval countrywomen, however, is that their
gender only indirectly affected access to many types of public power but de-
finitively determined the extent of their participation in public authority. Although rural women, under certain circumstances, acquired many attributes
commonly associated with the public power of men, they never attained public authority. Women held land, pursued legal pleas, and forged complex networks of friendship with fellow villagers, but politics remained a male affair.

Access to public power in Brigstock was determined as much by household position as by gender. Because of their sex, all women faced obstacles to landholding, legal competency, and social activity that were unknown to men, but
these obstacles reflected a presumption of household dependency more than
gender distinctions. In rural communities such as Brigstock, the full range of
landholding, legal, and social options was reserved for householders (including most males) and was less available to their dependents (including most females). Those men, however, who were not full householders (adolescent sons,
bachelors, and retired fathers) were less publicly powerful than male householders, just as those women who were freed of household dependency (widows and, in some measure, adolescent daughters) more nearly emulated the
public activities of men. Public power, in short, was most available to heads of
households. Since most households were headed by males, an assumption of
publicly powerful males (i.e., householders) and publicly passive females (i.e.,
wives and daughters) underlay the distribution of power in the countryside.
These gender distinctions, however, not only were secondary to household status but also were moderated by the many household positions that fit poorly
the presumption of male power and female dependency.

Because of the influence of household position upon access to public power in Brigstock, women's power waxed, waned, and waxed again over the course of the female life cycle. During adolescence, as young people of both sexes gradually detached themselves from parental authority in anticipation of marriage, the public opportunities of young women roughly matched those of young men. Consider the adolescent experiences of Cristina Penifader and her future brother-in-law, Henry Kroyl junior. Cristina Penifader first appeared in the court of Brigstock in 1312 when she began to accumulate property, while she was still unmarried, from her father. In 1312, he gave her future control of a plot and croft that he had purchased; in 1314 he granted her the use of a full virgate of meadow; in 1316, he gave her four butts of land valuable enough to merit the high entry fine of two shillings. When she needed a personal pledge or legal assistor during these years, Cristina Penifader turned sometimes to her father, but she was sufficiently well connected in the community to seek such aid, as she usually did, from other men to whom she was presumably not related. She was also, by virtue of her propertied status, a suitor of the Brigstock court, obliged to attend all its meetings unless properly excused. By the time Cristina Penifader married Richard Power in 1317, she was a competent landholder, an experienced court suitor, and a socially active member of her community. The experiences of Henry Kroyl junior during his unmarried years were quite similar. In the three years that preceded his marriage to Agnes Penifader in 1319, he accumulated property through gifts from his parents (acquiring parcels of land in six separate transactions), relied often, but not exclusively, upon his father for legal assistance, and paid suit to the Brigstock court.

Cristina Penifader and Henry Kroyl junior belonged to the more privileged sector of a heterogeneous rural community, but their experiences indicate the many ways in which young people—of both sexes and from both relatively rich and relatively poor households—enjoyed access to public power in early fourteenth-century Brigstock. Young people often established independent economic reserves by acquiring land or saving wages, and daughters, like sons, could hold, sell, and buy land without restriction. Adolescents of both sexes were also treated by the Brigstock court as legally responsible adults who could be trusted as landholders, were liable as criminals, and were competent as suitors. Social experiences were similarly parallel, as both young women and young men slowly expanded their horizons while still maintaining close ties with their parents. The public powers of adolescent daughters and sons were certainly distinguishable; sons came to court more readily than daughters, their economic privileges (including preference in inheritance and better wages) assured them of greater success in establishing economic autonomy, and their networks of friends and associates were usually larger and more diverse than the networks of their sisters. Still, adolescent daughters and sons in Brigstock enjoyed fundamentally similar access to public power even if sons more quickly and more easily exploited the options available to them.

Marriage sharply divided the public power of the sexes. It dramatically expanded men's access to power derived through landholding, legal competency, and social action, and it just as dramatically limited the access of women to the same activities. When such women as Cristina Penifader married, they lost many opportunities they had known as adolescents. A wife no longer enjoyed economic independence; her lands were merged into the conjugal property and could not be conveyed or sold without her husband's concurrence (a husband's lands were not similarly encumbered). A wife also lost legal competency; she no longer owed court suit (her husband did it for her), and she no longer invariably took personal responsibility for her own actions (her husband could be implicated for her crimes and pleas). And whereas marriage brought men an expansion of social opportunities and decreased reliance upon family, it had the opposite effect upon women; the court associations of wives were distinguished from those of all other adults (whether male or female) by their small size and heavy focus upon kin. The public powers of women and men were most distinct when they lived together as wives and husbands.

Widowhood and old age brought a new equivalency in the public power of the sexes in Brigstock. The extant records preclude the study of male widowhood, but many men clearly began to exercise their public options less vigorously as they aged. Without formally retiring, they dispersed some landed property among their grown children, they less frequently attended court or brought matters to the court's attention, and they associated less intensely and less widely with others in the community. The means of exercising public power were not closed to aging men, but they nevertheless seem to have activated those means much less commonly than they had done when they were younger. For women, however, the later years of life often brought an expansion, rather than a contraction, in both the availability and the exercise of public power. When widows took over the households left by their husbands, they acquired public opportunities that surpassed those of all other women. Widows freely traded and sold their personal properties, and many managed in addition to circumvent the custodial restrictions placed upon the "free bench" lands assigned, from the conjugal property, for their use. More than daughters or wives, widows most emulated the participation of men in the Brigstock land market—independently trading, exchanging, and selling small parcels of property. Widows were also distinguished by their legal actions. They, like daughters, owed suit to the Brigstock court and answered complaints and pursued litigation without the *couverture* of a male. In addition, they, like husbands, could be legally liable for the actions and problems of their dependents. The social experiences of widows betray a similar breadth of social activity and power. Although the court associations of most women were characterized by a strong focus upon kin, the associations of widows more closely matched the male pattern of wide and varied reliance upon neighbors as well as kin.

As an adolescent daughter or widow, then, a woman in early fourteenth-century Brigstock faced many more public opportunities and responsibilities than she encountered as a married woman. Her experiences suggest that the conjugal households of the medieval countryside had a contradictory effect upon the sexual distribution of power. Conjugality, by creating an expectation of powerful male householders and powerless female dependents, certainly played a crucial role in defining gender. Norms of female and male behavior in the medieval countryside drew heavily upon the private subordination of wives to their husbands. Femaleness was defined by the submissiveness of wives who were expected to defer to their husbands in both private and public. A popular saying advised, "Let not the hen crow before the rooster." Maleness was defined by the private authority of husbands who, as householders, controlled most domestic and community matters. The distinction between a private, female sphere and a public, male sphere received its fullest elaboration in the nineteenth century, but a dichotomy of private wives and public husbands was already firmly established in the households of medieval communities such as Brigstock.

The public-private distinction in the medieval countryside, however, applied more to husbands and wives than to men and women. At the same time that conjugality defined gender, it also moderated the severity of gender distinctions by sustaining many domestic circumstances that did not accord with the expectation of male power and female powerlessness. As long as adolescent daughters had to prepare for independent marriage and widows had to take over the households left by their husbands, power wielded by women, no matter how anomalous, had to be tolerated. Despite the public reticence expected of wives, the access of women to public power varied enormously, according to whether "be she mayde or wydwe or elles wyf."

In contrast to the relatively fluid and wide dispersion of public power in medieval rural communities, public authority, or legitimated power, was more rigidly and more narrowly distributed. Medieval communities like Brigstock were, perhaps, overorganized and overgoverned. Local order was preserved through peace-keeping groups whose members were mutually responsible for each others' behavior. Legal judgments were enforced through a system of sureties or pledges, who guaranteed that persons would meet court-ordered obligations. Governance was maintained through a wide variety of officers who served either manor or village. In Brigstock, reeves and bailiffs supervised manorial operations, affeerors determined the fines assessed against offenders, jurors judged disputes and claims, chief pledges managed the tithings, messors oversaw harvest operations, and aletasters ensured that ale sold in the community was sound, well measured, and properly priced. The authority that could be obtained through political action—as tithing members, as pledges, and as officers—was available only to men.

The basic peace-keeping system of medieval England, the frankpledge or tithing, never included women. These groups, originally containing only ten persons each, were responsible for bringing their members to court to answer for crimes or offenses. If a tithing, headed by a chief pledge, failed to produce an errant member, it was fined. This system of mutual responsibility was carefully maintained through most of the English countryside. In Brigstock, annual views of frankpledge fined those illegally outside tithings, inducted new members, and considered the chief pledges' presentments of offenses against the peace. With very few exceptions, all men in England, both free and unfree, were expected to join tithings at twelve years of age, but women, considered to be legal dependents of their householders, never joined these groups.

Women were also barred from a variety of legal actions that enabled men to solidify friendships and to enlarge political influence. Men frequently assisted one another in court, acting as attorneys who stood in for absent litigants, as essoiners who brought other suitors' excuses for failing to attend court, and especially as pledges who guaranteed that a person would fulfill a stipulated legal obligation. Almost all persons judged liable by the Brigstock court to pay a fine, perform an assigned task, or answer a specific plea had to produce a personal pledge, who promised that the legal obligation would be met. If such persons defaulted, their pledges were liable for a fine or other punishment. The private arrangements that accompanied pledging are unknown, but most people probably pledged not for remuneration in cash or goods but for ties of friendship and mutuality. The political ramifications of pledging are best illustrated by the fact that the people who most actively served as pledges in Brigstock were, as in most medieval villages, among the wealthiest and most influential members of the community. Although men of all social ranks and ages were accepted as pledges by the Brigstock court, women were rarely allowed to act in this capacity; of the thousands of pledges recorded in the rolls of the court, only forty-six were women. Brigstock was unusual in this respect; on most medieval manors, no female pledges were ever accepted by the court. In Brigstock, as elsewhere, women never served their neighbors as either attorneys or essoiners.

The Brigstock court yielded the right of pledging to women only in unusual and restricted circumstances. Most female pledges were widows; of the twenty-four women accepted by the court as pledges, at least fourteen were widows, and the unknown marital status of the others raises the strong possibility that they were also widowed heads of households. Indeed, the major status requirement for acceptance of a female pledge was widowhood; women from the various social strata of Brigstock (as shown by the activities of their husbands or other males presumably related to them) acted in this capacity. Most female pledges also acted within a restricted sphere, pledging only for the petty liabilities of kin. The extremely high rate of familial pledging by female pledges (twenty-six cases of forty-six, or 57 percent) was matched by a tendency for such sureties to guarantee the payment of the small fines levied for minor crimes (thirty-eight cases) or baking infractions (two cases). The few women who served as pledges in other, more momentous legal transactions were personally involved in other aspects of the case. Clearly the occasional pledging privileges extended to women in Brigstock responded to the practical reality that widows, as heads of households, had to accept responsibility for their dependents.

In the end, female pledging was so limited that it lacked the political ram-ifications that it carried for men. Any man could serve as a pledge—adolescent sons as well as householders, laborers as well as landholders. Furthermore, men used pledging both to aid family members in minor distress and to form political alliances. Standing as a surety not only for petty matters but also for the weightier obligations involved in land transactions, contracts, and inheri-tances, Henry Kroyl junior built up a complex political network of obligation and reciprocity that involved literally hundreds of his neighbors. He was un-usually active, but most of his brothers and brothers-in-law also pledged on a fair number of occasions for their friends and neighbors in the Brigstock court. Of the seven women in their familial generation, only one ever acted as a pledge; Alice Kroyl pledged once, for a child guilty of a minor field infraction. For Henry Kroyl junior, pledging was an important and commonly used po-litical tool. For his female kin, pledging was a rare obligation that offered no political benefit.

The public authority of women was severely restricted by their inability to form political associations with others through tithings, pledgings, or other forms of legal assistance. The exclusion of women from public office, however, constituted the major obstacle to female authority in medieval rural commu-nities. The method of selecting bailiffs, reeves, messors, aletasters, affeerors, and jurors is unknown. Court records simply note that a particular person was chosen (*electi est*) to a particular office, without specifying either electors or selection procedures. The criteria for selection, however, are much clearer; most rural officials were married males who possessed substantial landhold-ings. Not all men served their communities as officers, but only men did so.

The official career of Henry Kroyl junior of Brigstock again provides a pertinent example. During his adolescent years, Henry Kroyl junior began to build a political network both through his tithing and through assisting others in court as a pledger, essoiner, and attorney. He did not embark upon a dis-tinguished career of official service, however, until after his marriage. Active in the local court since 1316, Henry Kroyl junior first served as an officer in Sep-tember 1319, just a few months after his marriage to Agnes Penifader. As ado-lescents, young men participated in the basic political organizations of rural communities such as Brigstock; as married householders, they gained the ad-ditional opportunity of controlling political processes through local offices. Those men who were most able to seize this opportunity came from the elite of their communities. Both Henry Kroyl junior and his brother John Kroyl held extensive properties in Brigstock, and both served often as officers. Their brothers, Robert and William, possessed much more modest landholdings and never served as local officers. The normal prerequisites for officeholding in-cluded not only male sex but also married status and comparative wealth.

Official service was not an unmitigated benefit. In addition to time lost from other pursuits, officers in Brigstock were liable for fines for dereliction of duty and attacks from disgruntled villagers. As a result, some attempted to avoid official duties, as did William ad Stagnum, who paid two shillings in 1314 to be excused from serving as reeve. Attempts to avoid office were rare, however, because official activity not only signaled privileged status but also enhanced privilege. On the one hand, officers used their authority to personal advantage, taking gifts, arranging lucrative contracts, and using the lord's labor services to work private lands. On the other hand, officers also worked together to control the poorer and more marginal members of their communities. Rural officers decided what pleas would be disallowed, what crimes would be ignored, and what customs would govern land use and devolution. Their decisions on such matters reflected the concerns of a male elite working to control marginal males, poorer households, and women.

The clerks of manorial courts never noted any protests by women about their lack of political opportunity or any formal efforts by men to exclude women from political matters. Instead, the relegation of politics to men was likely accepted as natural by both sexes. Just as medieval people expected wives to be submissive and husbands to be dominant, so they expected women to accept the government of men. Although it is reasonable to suppose that countrywomen exercised some informal say over political processes, such influence cannot belie the basic power held by the men who controlled rural politics. Informal influence is, of course, inherently limited. It usually exists only to compensate for a lack of formal authority and not only lacks authority but also easily erodes. Moreover, public institutions in the medieval countryside were so highly articulated that the ability of women to influence public matters informally was necessarily curtailed. In communities where all adult males belonged to tithings, where community matters were regulated with numerous by-laws enforced by numerous officers, and where triweekly seigneurial courts required the attendance of all tenants, political life was so active and varied that informal influence was correspondingly limited. Indeed, even in the highly unlikely event that some sort of equilibrium existed in rural communities between male political authority and female informal influence, that balance would have been destroyed by the advantages that those men who wielded formal authority exercised in the world beyond the village. The same men who helped govern a community and run its court also acted as brokers with the outside world—dealing with manorial officials, negotiating with royal tax collectors, and testifying at county courts. Because they lacked political authority, medieval women stood in relation to the men of their villages as those men stood to their manorial lords; the medieval world was a hierarchical world with peasant women at the bottom.

The experiences of medieval countrywomen suggest that political authority was the first sector of public action to be denied to women. Rural women were, under certain circumstances, permitted to hold land, pursue legal claims, and form public associations with neighbors and friends, but they were not allowed to participate in matters political. Such patterns indicate that women were, for convenience's sake, allowed to exercise certain forms of power but that such power was under no circumstances allowed to become sanctioned authority.

Women's exclusion from political authority was strictly maintained despite its legal inconsistencies and practical inconveniences. Unmarried or widowed tenants were as obliged as male tenants to attend all sessions of the manorial court and to observe local by-laws, but they were never—despite their acceptance of the legal responsibilities of landholders—eligible for political authority. Because some of these female landholders were as wealthy as the males who served as reeves, aletasters, jurors, and the like, it seems that their sex was the major barrier to political authority. Unmarried and widowed women also often lived outside the control of a male householder who could be trusted to bring them to court for petty crimes and offenses. Such spinsters and widows, however, were never inducted into tithings to ensure that they kept the peace; again, their sex seems to have been the excluding factor. Similarly, the acceptance of some female pledges demonstrates the legal sufficiency of such actions, but custom limited the political impact of female pledging by only infrequently allowing widows to pledge for their dependents. Moreover, the exclusion of women from the office of aletaster—despite the fact that they, as brewers, were the most knowledgeable and skilled candidates—again illustrates the importance of barring women from authoritative positions. When it came to extending political authority to women, legal precedents and practical requirements had no importance; politics was the business of men.

F. W. Maitland's summary of the public functions of women under the common law in the thirteenth century applies just as well to women under the customary law of communities like Brigstock: "In the camp, at the council board, on the bench, in the jury box there is no place for them." Indeed, the extension of public power to women when convenient, and their exclusion from political authority no matter how inconvenient, might apply to medieval Englishwomen generally. All women, regardless of rank or class, were effectively excluded from formal political activity in medieval England. Countrywomen never served as reeves, townswomen never acted as mayors, and gentlewomen never went to Parliament to advise their king. All these women, however, especially when widowed, could aspire to public power, not only as heads of households, but also as controllers of the economic resources left by their husbands. Medieval Englishwomen, in short, were often powerful, but they were never authoritative.

GROWING OLD IN AN ENGLISH VILLAGE

BARBARA A. HANAWALT

Critics of urban, industrial society tend to romanticize life in the medieval village. They argue that, in contrast to the atomistic, self-centered society of the industrial city, where relations are reduced to cash transactions, the preindustrial village created a nurturing environment in which everyone had his or her special place and people took care of each other. In contrast to the individualistic and competitive values of modern industrial society, the values of the preindustrial village were communal and cooperative. Historian Marc Bloch's work on the medieval economy supports this view of village life. The very nature of medieval agricultural production, he argued, necessitated the development of communal and cooperative values. The heavy plow that peasants used north of the Alps required several oxen to pull, more oxen than most peasants owned individually. Bloch reasoned that peasants must have shared each other's oxen to get the plowing done. Similarly, the open field system made cooperation in the sowing and harvesting of crops absolutely necessary. Use of common pastures also must have called for cooperation and sharing. Proponents of this view of preindustrial village society further reason that a society with communal and cooperative values will take care of its poor, weak, old, and orphaned members through charity and a wide network of family and friends. In contrast, Barbara Hanawalt's study of crime in fourteenth-century English villages indicates that those aspects of rural life that required cooperation, such as harvesting, were a source of considerable and sometimes homicidal conflict. Moreover, petty theft rather than charity was often the recourse of the very poor. Which view most accurately describes medieval village society? Unfortunately, nearly all medieval peasants were illiterate and left us no personal accounts of what village society was like. Often we are forced, like Bloch, to make educated guesses based on what we know about landholding patterns, cultivation practices, and manorial customs.

From: Barbara A. Hanawalt, *The Ties That Bound: Peasant Families in Medieval England* (New York: Oxford University Press, 1986), pp. 227–36, 242.

*Another romanticization of rural life in medieval Europe is that
the family was extended, rather than nuclear. Three and even four
generations of people, it was thought, lived and worked together, the
very young and very old looked after by the rest of the family. Peter
Laslett's study of England and subsequent studies of much of Western Europe reveal that this was not usually the case in the early modern period. Western European families rarely had more than two
generations living together at once and rarely did more than one
married couple live under a single roof. At least as far back as the
early modern period, then, the majority of Western European households resemble modern nuclear families more closely than they do
the extended families found in Russia and central Europe. Which
type of household predominated in the West in the Middle Ages, and
what does this tell us about how medieval villagers took care of
those who could not take care of themselves?*

*In this selection, Barbara Hanawalt sheds light on the nature of
both the medieval peasant household and the village community. By
studying coroners' reports and the provisions that English villagers
made for their old age and death, Hanawalt provides us with a rare
glimpse of family relations among medieval peasants. These provisions also reveal the extent to which individuals could expect a communal response in their times of need.*

Concern about aging is not new. Both literary remains and court records speak
of problems that are all too familiar to us: the physical decline of the body, the
lack of dignity and respect that advanced age brings, and the anxiety of guaranteeing continued care when one cannot provide for oneself and when the society in which one lives does not venerate the aged. The harsh reality of the
problem is succinctly summed up in the medieval story of the divided horse
blanket. The son has inherited the family house and land and is raising his own
family, but his old father lives on as another mouth to feed. It is winter and the
old man, shivering with cold, asks his son for a blanket. The son directs his son
to get the horse blanket and give it to his grandfather. The grandson returns
with half the blanket, and when asked why he cut the blanket in two, he replies,
"I will keep the other half until I am a man, and then use it to cover you."

Care of the aged produces a far greater variety of societal adaptations and
solutions than do other stages of life. While childrearing must take into consideration such biological imperatives as feeding, clothing, and teaching children the rudiments of survival, and marriage is, in most preindustrial societies,
an institution of economic and biological perpetuation, aging brings about
such culturally extreme responses as veneration and parricide. Anthropologist
Jack Goody, in "Aging in Non Industrial Societies," has surveyed, cross-
culturally, the basic problems that the aged face in securing their material survival and respect in their social milieu. Concerns with shelter, clothing, and

food dominate the list of needs, but participation in household decisions, assurances of political and religious inclusion, and the guarantee of a "decent" burial are important psychologically as well. Above all, the older generations must have cultural institutions that will ensure that provisions for their old age will be maintained even when they become impotent.

If the war between the sexes was cause for comment, so too was the clash between young and old. Moralists not only repeated homilies about the callousness of children toward aged parents, but also warned fathers not to use their children as executors, for, as Robert Mannyng observed, children would not carry out the provisions of a will because they would stand to lose the most from bequests not directed to them. He shrewdly comments that you should make neither your heir nor your doctor an executor. A persistent tension existed between the possessors of land, goods, and power and their heirs. Once the old person retired and passed on these accoutrements of adult life, he or she could be left at the mercy of the younger generation. From the younger generation's viewpoint, the aged pose problems. They no longer worked equivalent to the amount they consumed; they stood in the way of the young adult's advancement; their appearance offended the aesthetics of their juniors. A young man might have to wait until his father died or retired before he could marry and set up his own household. If old men married younger women, then they were taking potential wives of young men in the community. A young man might marry an older widow to get her rights in dower and thereby deprive a village girl of a desirable marriage partner. The young, therefore, had ample reason for not regarding old people as benign, and their prudent elders sought legal safeguards for retirement rather than relying on cultural precepts about honoring father and mother and respecting the aged.

But how serious was the problem of coping with old people in late-medieval England? To answer that question we must know how large the problem was and the ways in which the aged functioned in society. The age at which people were specified as old in the Statute of Labourers was sixty. Beyond that age the statute's provisions did not apply. Ecclesiastical sources indicated that anyone aged fifty or more could be called *senex* (old), but peasants would not necessarily have been aware of the ecclesiastical divisions of life stages and even the scribes in manorial and royal courts did not use the word *senex* to describe the elderly. Indeed, neither the statute nor the ecclesiastical descriptions could have had practical application, for people had only a vague idea of their ages since they never recorded births and were seldom called upon to give their age. When an adult's age was given in the coroners' inquests, it was always rounded off with the statement *et amplis* (and more). The description of a person as aged was based on his or her physical appearance and general health, not simply on calendar years.

We may never know the percentage of old people in the medieval English population, but we must not be misled into thinking that because life expectancy was about thirty-three years of age there were few old people. High infant mortality rather than adult deaths was the chief contributor to the low life expectancy. Analysis of bones from medieval English burials indicates that 10 percent of the people were over fifty. Late sixteenth- and seventeenth-century parish registers show that roughly 8 to 16 percent of the population was over sixty. And in fourteenth- and fifteenth-century Tuscany 6 to 15 percent of the rural population was over sixty.

Although 10 percent or more of its population was over fifty and conflicts between the needs of the old and the aspirations of the young could produce tension, parricide in medieval England was extremely rare. Instead, either the old people themselves, their families, or the community made arrangements for the aging. These accommodations varied considerably in the material comfort and satisfaction they provided, but there was a range of options open to the aged.

Retirement contracts are one of the most apparent of these arrangements because they appear frequently in manorial court rolls. In essence, these contracts provided that the retiring peasant would relinquish the use of his buildings and lands in exchange for food, shelter, and clothing from the person, whether a kinsman or not, who took up the contract. While wills mostly describe arrangements men made for their aging wives, manorial records are a rich source on the lot of both sexes.

The historian Elaine Clark has studied 200 maintenance cases largely from fourteenth-century East Anglia and has provided an insightful discussion on retirement. Her conclusions may be extended back to the late thirteenth century and to other regions of England as well. Maintenance contracts could be made in three ways. First, the lord and the community could impose a contract on a tenant who became too old and impotent to work the land and pay the rent. In such cases the community leaders met in manorial court and made arrangements for someone else to take the land in exchange for providing for the person. By so acting, the community made way for a younger person to establish him or herself while still guaranteeing care for an aged neighbor. The lord encouraged such arrangements so that he could get rents from the land. Thus, for example, in Chertsey Abbey court John Atte Wyle's mother was described as "of great age and *non compos mentis* and it seems useful to the court that John shall be admitted." The court could settle the senile or impotent person's affairs with a neighbor, if there was no kin or if the kin were not interested in taking over the tenement.

In most cases the retiring tenant made his or her own arrangement through a contract. A father might make such an agreement with a son when he relinquished the family land to him or with a daughter at the time of marriage. Richard Loverd of Northamptonshire put his cottage with appurtenances into the lord's hands, and Emma, his heir, did the same. Her prospective husband paid the lord 5s. to enter the tenement, agreeing at that time that he would marry Emma and provide her father with food and clothing. In another case, a kinsman of Ralph Beamonds took over the tenement because Ralph was impotent. The kinsman promised Ralph that he would have a cottage and a curtilage along with, yearly, a garment valued at 2s. 6d., a pair of linen hose, a pair of shoes worth 6d., a pair of woolen hose worth 6d., four bushels of fine white wheat, and four bushels of barley. As in court-dictated settlements, the agreement could be reached with someone not related to the pensioner. When Hugh took over Simon's tenement, he agreed to recondition the property and "to look sufficiently after Simon's wife Alice, his son and all his children and Simon was to have food and drink when Hugh acts as host to his wife."

And third, the dying tenant or peasant proprietor could make provision for his wife and family by recording his provisions or will in the manor court. These were often deathbed scenes with the bailiff coming to record the final arrangement or, as in one case, the whole manorial court came. On his deathbed John Whytyng surrendered his messuage and land to Simon Wellyng with the provision that Simon provide John's widow with food, drink, and sixteen bushels of barley. He also had to maintain for her use one cow, six hens, and one goose and cultivate and seed an acre of arable in every season of the year. He was to provide 3s. for clothing annually as well as a pair of shoes each Easter. She was to be allowed to continue to live in her late husband's house, although she was only guaranteed entry, a place by the fire, and a bed.

In the cases that we have looked at so far, the retirees have all been sufficiently well off that they exchanged only their land and buildings in return for specific arrangements for their comfort. But what of cottars who might find it hard to get good terms because they had so little with which to bargain? With two to three acres being considered necessary for the support of one person, these people found it difficult to attract a caretaker. Cottars often made further concessions in order to ensure care, such as promising the caretaker not only the use of the land but also making him or her the chief beneficiary of the will. In practice this meant that all of their household equipment, clothing, and other movables would go to the person who agreed to provide for them in their old age.

The retirement contracts show great care in planning and indicate that the individual making them tried to cover all possible contingencies. Rather than leaving to chance the food, clothing, and shelter that they would receive, the pensioners spelled it out in detail. Modifications in the house plan might be specified so that a solar, hall, or chamber be added for the retiree. Sometimes separate houses were built. In 1281 Thomas Brid agreed to build for his mother a house thirty feet long and fourteen feet wide and having three doors and two windows. In addition, some asked for the regular laundering of clothing, horses for riding, gardens, fuel, tools of their trade, and other such benefits. Psychological needs were also stipulated in the contracts. Provisions were made for regular visits from friends when the pensioners were on their sickbeds and for funeral processions and prayers for their soul when they died.

To protect the agreement and ensure that the terms of the contract would be met, the pensioner always transferred the land conditionally. If the terms were not met, the land reverted to the pensioners. Custom as well as the binding nature of the contract protected them, for the community or the lord could insist on the reversion to the pensioner if the contract was broken. Furthermore, when the contracts were recorded in the manorial court, the son or other contractee swore he would uphold its obligations. He had to produce kin and friends who were to act as surety or guarantors that he would abide by his oath or they would be personally responsible.

The reversion clause served another purpose as well. The contractee might die before the pensioner. In the century and more following the Black Death, this eventuality was a real risk because mortality from disease was so high. The contract could specify that heirs of the original caretaker would have to take up the tenement along with the continued support of the pensioner. Sometimes the original caretaker decided to sell his or her rights in the land and the contract changed hands. The person taking up the land had to agree to the old terms and continue to provide for the pensioner in order to hold the land.

Clark's study permits some generalizations about the preferences and concerns that retiring peasants shared. Whether married or widowed, they wished to continue living on their own property. In the manorial cases the norm was for coresidence with their contractee; only one in twelve had the luxury of a private residence. Second, even after the population decline of the late fourteenth and fifteenth centuries made land readily available, 50 percent of the retirees had small holdings of less than 5 acres. While few pensioners mention the issue of how long they expected to live, those who did anticipated that they would live another six to nine years. All sought the most binding legal protections in making their contracts so that their comfort would be ensured. Perhaps the most interesting of Clark's findings is that only one-third of the pensioners negotiated contracts with their own children.

These conclusions are provocative and deserving of further analysis. Should there have been a census taken in the fourteenth century it would have shown that households with old people present would not necessarily be stem families, but, rather, the old person could be a pensioner unrelated to the current head of the house. Manorial records, however, may tend to overrepresent this type of nonkin arrangement. One may assume that some parents and children had amicable agreements that did not have to be guaranteed in manorial court. More well-to-do peasants, as we shall see, chose to make their arrangements by will or established their children in separate holdings before their death. The manorial cases, therefore, may represent people with fewer resources or without close kin. An alternative hypothesis is that the contracts with nonkin were second retirements, that is, peasants who had already distributed their land to their children but had retained a cottage and a few acres. They were thus making arrangements for final illness. In any case, these households probably did not constitute a large percentage of the population, if we may infer from later studies where population information is available.

The position of aging single people was not necessarily worse than that of married people with family, provided they had some land that they could negotiate into a maintenance contract. In Clark's figures only 36 percent of the pensioners were married, while 43 percent were women alone and 21 percent were men alone. The predominance of single people suggests that retirement contracts were normally negotiated when the person or persons felt that they could no longer cope with providing for their own living, particularly after the loss of a spouse.

It is curious that a cottage and a few acres encumbered with the care of an old and sick person was in demand at all, since land was readily available following the Black Death. One can easily imagine that such an arrangement would be much sought after in the land hunger of the early fourteenth century, but it would appear to be undesirable if one could get land free of an aged tenant. Unfortunately, manorial records do not permit a comparison between the number of contracts recorded before the plague of 1349 and those afterward. One might conclude, looking at Clark's study, that the incidence increased following the depopulation, but her data were not collected in such a way as to permit a comparison. Missing records from the early part of the century could easily explain the disparity. Nevertheless, the continued popularity of the retirement contract from the contractee's viewpoint needs further investigation.

An unpleasant explanation is that entrepreneurs bought up these retirement contracts simply to get the land and might even have hastened the death of the pensioner through neglect. A breakdown of those taking land with pensioners on it suggests a different motive: 44 percent were couples, 5 percent were single women, and 51 percent were single men. While entrepreneurs cannot be ruled out completely, it appears that some of these may have been young people whose families had not yet provided for them, or could not, and who were planning to set up households on their own. Even in the land glut of the early fifteenth century, people put a premium on land that had traditionally belonged to a family. The people taking up the contracts were, therefore, being "adopted" by the retiring peasant and could enter the land with the same claims to it that the old person had. The cottage and few acres became "family land" rather than rented lands and gave the contractee a secure tenure on it.

Simply knowing the provisions of the maintenance contracts, however, does not indicate the standard of living and treatment of the aged. Did all of the legal ploys at least safeguard the promised material standards? Complaints of contract violations indicate that the unscrupulousness suggested in the story of the divided horse blanket did occur. A Wakefield manor court case underscores the problems entrepreneurial caretakers created. The community charged in 1286 that William Wodemous drove out Molle de Mora and her son from her house, killed her dog, and carried off ten ells of linen. He also took a cloak of hers and did not meet his obligations to repair her house. When the community had to intervene in these cases, they meted out suitable punishment to the offender. When John Catelyne evicted Elena Martyn from her house and tore it down, the jurors of Wistowe ordered him to rebuild the house and find a suitable residence for her until it was done. When a son failed to honor the terms of his contract with his aged mother, the jurors fined him and gave the land back to her, banning him from holding it during her lifetime.

A complication related to contracts was that they could be sold by one contractee to another. Such a transfer of a contract must have been a great disruption to the elderly. For instance, a cottar died in 1415 and made provision that his wife should have the cottage and acre conditional to her caring for his enfeebled sister for her life. After six months the widow left, making arrangements with a local man that he take up the obligations and live in the house. After a year he too moved out, selling the contract to another villager. Once a person was unable to cope with the courts, the village community would have to be the watchdog on broken contracts, and in all likelihood neighbors would only intervene in cases of flagrant neglect and maltreatment.

Wills present a somewhat different picture of retirement than do the contracts arranged in manorial courts. People at the upper end of the village social scale were more likely to make wills, and thus they represent the arrangements of people who are more likely to be well off. Furthermore, unlike retirement contracts, wills usually entrusted the care of the old person to close kin rather than to strangers.

When wives were aged, husbands might make provisions in wills similar to those made in manorial courts, spelling out in detail the care for the old woman. In such cases a son was the most frequent person assigned to carry out the terms of the will. Again, the careful peasants tried to anticipate failures to honor the arrangements. One man expressed his suspicion of his son and stated explicitly that his wife should have one-half of the crops for the first year and three acres of grain the following years along with an old horse to carry her grain sacks to the mill. Other times the husband made contingency plans. The mother and son should live together, but if they were not able to get along, the mother would be given a separate house or be guaranteed a room in the house. Another man worried that his son might sell the property and instructed that whoever holds the property left to his son John shall provide a chamber in the house for the testator's wife to dwell in, and also meat and drink such as he "ettythe and drynkes" for life.

One foresightful husband tried to cover all the possible contingencies in providing for his widow and his mother. He left his eldest son, John, the family holding with the provision that "he pay the testator's mother £4 per year for life and to find her meat and drink if she wants to live with him." His wife was to have a place with the second son and receive 20s. from each of the three younger sons when they reached the age of majority. If the wife was not satisfied with the annual payment, she could have her dower as provided by law. Husbands also appealed to finer sentiments in wills. One stepfather provided for the daughter of his wife and instructed his own son to keep his wife "during her lifetime, as he would have kept his own mother."

The men leaving provision for widows in wills had, for the most part, lived a comfortable life. Those who lived their span to the fullest had already distributed the family tenement to a son but had retained a house, some land, and possessions for themselves. The majority of men leaving wills (72 percent) had wives and their own homes. But Thomas Smyth intended to sojourn at his son's hearth and rewarded the kindness of his son and daughter-in-law. His will was, in fact, a retirement contract. He left his daughter-in-law all the goods in the house that still belonged to him and two bushels of malt. As long as he lived he would give his son 40s. at Christmas for board and "for his good attention to him and his labours" another 40s.

The extent to which kin were relied on for care in age is difficult to determine. If we may again use later studies as an inference, it would appear that living with children, other kin, or strangers was not the preferred arrangement for retirement. In rural Austria, where there were legal and customary mechanisms for stem families, they were still rare in the seventeenth through nineteenth centuries. In early modern England only when all else failed did an aged parent live with an offspring. All medieval evidence suggests that this was already an established pattern: People lived on their own as long as they could manage (usually as long as they had a spouse alive and were healthy), and even when they were driven to maintenance contracts only a third made them with kin.

Another solution that the aging person might pursue was hiring a caretaker to come and live in the house. Thomas Cyne, for instance, had become very prosperous, as had his two brothers and a sister whom he mentioned in his will. He appeared to have no wife or children but left money to a woman whom he described as his "keeper." Katherine Vyncent, a widow, had no children but remembered her "wench" and her "keeper" in her will. Aging parish priests often hired caretakers for their old age, although there were hospitals that specialized in the care of aged clergy.

For the most part, peasants would not have had access to hospitals or monasteries for their retirement and final sickness. They did, however, form voluntary associations of their own that provided some benefits to the aged and impotent. Of the 507 gilds that returned descriptions of their charters in 1389, about a third of them (154) provided their members with benefits during disaster or old age. In a fifth of the gilds the benefits were a weekly allowance and perhaps clothing in the event of disaster. The average weekly allowance was 7d., only enough to buy a loaf of bread a day. An additional 7 percent offered to bury a brother or sister who was too impoverished to pay for interment. Since the time of payment was limited to a few months or a couple of years, the dole from the gild was obviously not meant to support a prolonged retirement and may only have helped the indigent members or those terminally ill.

The gilds were significant, however, in providing psychological comfort to aged brothers and sisters, one of those important aspects in the treatment of the aged that Goody has identified. Testators (48 of the 389 Bedfordshire wills) left money, malt, and sometimes land to their gilds. The gilds were in some respects an extension of family, for they provided gild feasts, visitors to the sickbed, and a chaplain, or at least prayers, for their members.

The people we have considered so far had some property with which to negotiate care and perhaps respect. But what of those who had little or no land and had lived on wages earned by the sweat of their brow or those whose ungrateful children actually threw them into the streets? These people often appear, as is the case today, in a coroner's inquest where they are described as having died of exposure or some accident relating to their poverty. Alice Berdholf of Donyngton, a beggar seventy years of age, was drunk and near a well in the highway. She saw a straw and fell in the well trying to get it. Alice was known and died near her home, but often the person is simply described as an old stranger such as one who was found dead of cold and exposure in a cowshed in December 1362. The impoverished elderly were sometimes forced to beg even when they had adult children living in the village:

> On 14 January 1267 Sabina, an old woman, went into Colmworth to beg bread. At twilight she wished to go to her house and fell in a stream and died by misadventure. The next day her son Henry searched for her, and found her drowned.

This was not an isolated incident, so that the warning of the homilies to beware of children mistreating their parents was not entirely misplaced.

Wanderers were dependent on community charity for their meals, food, and space in the cowshed. If the person was known in the community, he or she might fare moderately well at begging; but strangers were regarded with suspicion. The village bylaws permitted the very young, the old, and the impotent to glean in fields after harvest. But as we have observed, gleaning could only provide grain for several weeks and assumed that the old person was still sufficiently able-bodied to do the arduous, backbreaking labor of gleaning. Religious houses and parish priests were expected to give charitable contributions of food and perhaps clothing for the poor, including the aged poor, and gilds and private individuals often made alms part of the burial ceremony. Such aid, however, was sporadic and could not be counted on every day. . . .

The evidence from a broad range of fourteenth- and fifteenth-century English sources indicates a considerable tension between the young and the old. The young were desirous of gaining control of the family resources while the old wished to secure care and comfort. In the absence of a binding cultural norm of devoting family resources to caring for the aged, such as is found in China, English peasants resorted to contracts and wills when they doubted that their families would provide adequate care. How one fared in such contract negotiations depended then, as now, on the personal resources one had amassed in a lifetime. Peasants with land and goods could negotiate for their care either with kin or with other parties. Those with nothing depended on private charity. Retirement arrangements were flexible. The aged persons showed a marked preference for staying in their own homes even if it meant that they would have to share it with nonkin. But sharing a home was a choice imposed by economics and not by preference.

Ostade: Farm Cottage Dooryard, seventeenth century.

(SOURCE: National Gallery of Art, Washington DC)

V

THE RENAISSANCE AND REFORMATION

16th–17th Centuries

The cultural and religious movements that gave their names to the Renaissance–Reformation period occurred against a social background that has become familiar through many historical studies. In Italy, urbanization combined with a rediscovery of classical Greek and Roman literature to create a new view of history and a new sense of national and human identity. Whereas medieval scholars and rulers had extolled the virtues of the Roman Empire and its autocratic government because they saw themselves as its continuators, the Italian humanists, some of whom were both scholars and political figures, rediscovered the Roman Republic and made it their ideal. This shift of political consciousness necessitated a change in historical consciousness, because it made humanists aware of historical discontinuity. For them, the study of Roman history could not be, as it had been for their medieval predecessors, a study of an earlier stage of their own development. Instead, it was the study of a civilization wholly separate from theirs. On the one hand, this historical consciousness led them to attempt a revival of ancient culture. On the other hand, the rediscovery of the Republic brought into vogue republican political values, which were at odds with Roman and medieval imperialist ideals, and a new appreciation for urban life. In the first selection, Dana Thornton turns our attention away from the public world of city councils and princely courts, and approaches the humanist ideal from the perspective of the scholar's home with the emergence of a separate room devoted to study.

The image of the sorcerer surrounded by books and astronomical instruments, who summoned demons at will and forced them to do his bidding, is the counterpart of the scholar in his study. The study of ancient languages and writings led some scholars to ancient mystical and magical texts that claimed to impart knowledge of—and control over—the spiritual and natural worlds. The fear behind the witch trials of the sixteenth and seventeenth centuries, however, was not of a powerful man controlling the elements but a weak female in the service of Satan. In the second selection, Guido Ruggiero explores the story of a young woman abandoned by her lover and her efforts to use magic and the law to win him back.

Sixteenth-century Europe experienced not one but two reformations, the Protestant Reformation, represented by Luther's publication of his Ninety-Five Theses in 1517, and the Catholic Reformation, represented by the Council of Trent (1545–63). Both transformed the role that the Church had played in the local community. Medieval churches had served to integrate the spiritual and secular lives of their parishioners. Worshippers could gaze at statues of the Virgin Mary and the saints, assured that these would intercede with Christ on their behalf on Judgement Day. Looking upward, they might have seen the heavens depicted as stars painted against a dark blue background on the church's ceiling. The very walls of the church were covered with religious images. Sacraments marked the stages of their lives, and religious rituals and festivals marked the passage of the year. These events helped unite the community spiritually. They also helped unify it in secular ways. People gathered, feasted, and relaxed and played together. The parish priest might tolerate a good deal of play, especially on days of misrule, when boys and young men turned the world upside down for a day, appointing one of their number as abbot of misrule, conducting mock masses and making fun of local authorities. The priest was present also at communal celebrations and rituals, some with origins that predated Christianity. With luck and a bit of diplomacy, he might keep these manifestations of popular culture within the bounds of Christian propriety.

In the name of reform, Protestants (and, later, Catholic reformers) abolished many rituals and festivals. They looked askance at community gatherings and celebrations. At best, these were invitations to gluttony, drunkenness, and lascivious dancing. At worst, they were superstitious and unchristian. Far from tolerating popular celebrations, local religious leaders were exhorted to stamp them out. Although reformers hoped to forge a new, godly community united in Christ, a number of historians have argued that the attack on popular culture severed the link between church and community. In the third selection, Tessa Watt investigates the local inn, which in many ways took over the parish church's secular functions. At a time when Reformed churches were whitewashed and any hint of iconography stamped out, the English decorated the walls of inns and their homes with images and words. These decorations provide insight into ordinary people's religious sensibilities. They also reveal the ways in which popular culture and piety continued to interact during the English Reformation.

Under Luther's influence Protestants elevated the status of marriage from a way of life inferior to the virginity (or at least celibacy) of the priests, monks and nuns to one that embodied the complete fulfillment of divine will and natural law. The Protestant emphasis on marriage has led historians to explore changes in the family and childhood in sixteenth-and seventeenth-century Europe. The readings in the fourth selection treat adolescence in the years following the Reformation. Ilana Krausman Ben-Amos describes apprenticeship and the social networks that helped teenagers gradually move toward independence. Steven Ozment explores the emotional ups and downs of a Protestant teenager a long way from home and living in a Catholic city.

The fifth selection describes women's contribution to the early modern urban economy. Europe's economy underwent an unprecedented inflation as American silver dramatically increased the money supply and Europe's growing population led to steadily rising food and housing prices. Wages tended to fall behind prices, leading to increasing hardship for wage earners. These trends sped up changes in the organization of guilds. Beginning in the fifteenth century, guilds became increasingly restrictive. It became harder and harder to become a master and some journeymen effectively became lifelong wage earners. Journeymen responded by forming guilds of their own, and they stridently insisted that women be banished from the workshop. Other kinds of economic enterprise sprang up outside of guild control, offering opportunities to those excluded from the traditional guild organizations. Natalie Davis discusses the ways in which women's work differed from that of men's.

BIBLIOGRAPHY

The classic work on Renaissance humanism is Jacob Burkhardt, *The Civilization of the Renaissance in Italy,* 2 vols. (New York, 1951 [originally published in German in 1860]). The more recent classic of Hans Baron, *The Crisis of the Early Italian Renaissance,* rev. ed. (Princeton, NJ, 1966), treats specifically the relationship between trends in humanist thought and politics. Lauro Martines, *Power and Imagination* (Baltimore, 1979, 1988) is an important analysis of the relationship between humanist ideals, art, architecture, and the changing political landscape of the Renaissance Italian city. See also Peter Burke, *The Italian Renaissance: Culture and Society in Italy* (Princeton, NJ, 1987) and Denis Hay, *The Italian Renaissance in Its Historical Background,* 2nd ed. (Cambridge, England, 1977). For changes in households and growing emphasis on privacy, see Georges Duby and Philippe Ariès, eds., *History of Private Life, Vol. 3: Passions of the Renaissance* (Cambridge, England, 1988). Karen Neuschel provides a fascinating account of the use of rooms, location of beds, and who got to use them in "Noble Households in the Sixteenth Century: Material Settings and Human Communities," *French Historical Studies,* 15:4 (1988):595–622. See also Kate Mertes, *The English Noble Household, 1260–1600* (Oxford, 1988).

The scholarship on the witch craze of the sixteenth and seventeenth centuries is vast. See Keith Thomas' seminal work *Religion and the Decline of Magic* (New York, 1971). Carlo Ginzburg explores the evidence for the survival of pre-Christian beliefs in magic in *Night Battles: Witchcraft and Agrarian Cults in the Sixteenth and Seventeenth Centuries* (London, 1983). See also Richard Kieckhefer, *European Witch Trials, Their Foundations in Popular and Learned Culture, 1300–1500* (Berkeley, 1976). Robin Briggs's *Witches and Neighbors: The Social and Cultural Context of European Witchcraft* (New York, 1996) locates the origins of accusations of witchcraft in daily interactions and conflicts. Some important regional studies are Alan McFarlane, *Witchcraft in Tudor and Stuart England* (New York, 1970); Christina Larner, *Enemies of God: The Witchhunt in Scotland* (Baltimore, 1981); H. C. Middelfort, *Witch-hunting in Southwestern Germany, 1562–1684; The Social and Intellectual Foundations* (Stanford, CA, 1972); and Michael Kunze, *Highroad to the Stake* (Chicago and London, 1987; f.p. in German 1982).

Elizabeth Eisenstein discusses the revolutionary impact that the introduction of printing had on scholarship and the communication of ideas in *The Printing Press as an Agent of Change* (Cambridge, England, 1979); *The Printing Revolution in Early Modern Europe* (Cambridge, England, 1983) is a shorter version of her argument. The role of print in the German Reformation, and the question of how it functioned in a largely illiterate society are explored by Robert Scribner in *For the Sake of the Simple Folk: Popular Propaganda for the German Reformation* (Cambridge University Press, 1981). Rudolf Hirsch describes the early developments in the German printing industry in *Printing, Selling, and Reading* (Westbaden, Germany, 1974, 1967), and S. H. Steinberg provides a survey of the history of printing in *Five Hundred Years of Printing,* rev. ed., (Bristol, England, 1961). For debate concerning the relationship between literate high culture and popular oral culture, see Roger Chartier, *The Cultural Uses of Printing in Early Modern France,* trans. Lydia C. Cochrane (Princeton, 1987) and Peter Burke, *Popular Culture in Early Modern Europe* (New York, 1978). Carlo Ginzburg explores the relationship between high and popular culture by following the inquisition trial of a village miller in *The Cheese and the Worms: The Cosmos of a Sixteenth-Century Miller,* trans. by John and Anne Tedeschi (New York, 1983).

The effect of the Reformation on family life is explored in Steven Ozment, *When Fathers Ruled* (Cambridge, MA, 1983). A different perspective on the public nature of marriage in Reformation Europe is provided by Lyndal Roper's *The Holy Household* (Oxford, 1989). The differences in boys' and girls' adolescence in Italy is discussed by Stanley Chojnacki in "Measures of Adulthood: Adolescence and Gender in Renaissance Venice," in the *Journal of Family History* 17:4 (1992):371–96. Youth and Reformation are the subject of Gerald Strauss' *Luther's House of Learning: Indoctrination of the Young in the German Reformation* (Baltimore, 1978), and are treated in David Sabean's *Power in the Blood: Popular Culture and Village Discourse in Early Modern Germany* (Cambridge, 1985). Steven Ozment follows three teenagers into adulthood in *The Three Behaim Boys* (New Haven, 1990), and explores the troubled relations between a father and daughter in *The Burgermeister's Daughter* (New York, 1996). The adolescent years of Felix Platter and his son, Thomas, are described by Emmanuel Le Roy Ladurie in *The Beggar and the Professor: A Sixteenth-Century Family Saga,* trans. by Arthur Goldhammer (Chicago, 1997).

Discussions of apprenticeship can be found in Steven Epstein, *Wage Labor and Guild in Medieval Europe* (Chapel Hill, 1991); and James Farr, *Hands of Honor: Artisans and Their World in Dijon, 1550–1650* (Ithaca, NY, 1988). Gender proves a fruitful tool of analysis in Carol Loats, "Gender, Guilds, and Work Identity: Perspectives from Sixteenth-Century Paris," *French Historical Studies* 20:1 (1997):15–30 and in the important argument that Merry Wiesner makes regarding the growing hostility of journeymen to women in the workshop in *Gender, Church and State in Early Modern Germany* (London, 1998). For women's work see the articles in Barbara Hanawalt, ed., *Women and Work in the Pre-industrial Economy* (Bloomington, IN, 1986); and David Herlihy *Opera Muliebria: Women and Work in Medieval Europe* (New York, 1990). The erosion of women's dominating role in brewing in the early modern era is discussed in Judith Bennett, *Ale, Beer and Brewsters in England: Women's Work in a Changing World 1300–1600* (New York, 1996). Concerning whether women suffered a decline in the status of their work and in their opportunities to work, see Martha Howell, *Women, Production, and Patriarchy in Late Medieval Cities* (Chicago, 1986). Also see Merry Wiesner, *Working Women in Renaissance Germany* (New Brunswick, NJ, 1986). On the social life and culture of early modern France, see Natalie Z. Davis, *Society and Culture in Early Modern France* (Palo Alto, CA, 1975).

THE SCHOLAR IN HIS STUDY

DORA THORNTON

The Renaissance was profoundly shaped by the political evolution of the Italian cities. The rise of communes and the emergence of republics led scholars to explore the history and political treatises of ancient Rome. Humanists prescribed an educational program for citizens who might serve in government. Those who sought to hold public office or influence the deliberation of government councils should study of the history of Rome and their own city, ancient examples of rhetoric and oratory, and to counterbalance the pagan influence of ancient Roman culture, morality. This sort of education was feasible for only the few: men who could afford to educate their sons and with the leisure to continue to devote time to study. Scholarship and the life that made it possible became deeply entrenched as a social ideal for members of the prosperous classes and a goal for those who strove to join their ranks. This ideal survived and continued to evolve as many republics gave way to despots and princes, and then as Italy was wracked by foreign invasions beginning in 1494. Less and less able to participate in governments, well-to-do city folk might find personal and intellectual refuge among their books and papers.

Historians agree on the relationship of Italian humanism to trends in public life, but little consideration has been given as to how the ideal of the well educated citizen was realized. The medieval homes of prosperous folk afforded little privacy. In the eleventh century, Heloise remarked on this fact when she told her new husband, the great logician Abelard, that a family household was no place for a scholar. It was too noisy and busy. Early Renaissance households offered little improvement over their medieval counterparts in this regard. Even large, prosperous households had only a few rooms and offered little privacy.

A scholar needed a place to withdraw from the distractions of the world as well as the leisure time do so. He needed books, a

From: Dora Thornton, *The Scholar in His Study: Ownership and Experience in Renaissance Italy* (New Haven: Yale University Press, 1997), pp. 27–29, 29–30, 31–33, 35–36, 36, 176–178.

writing desk, and a secure place to store important papers. In a pri-
vate little room set off from the public space of the rest of the house,
the scholar could surround himself with his books, perhaps some
pieces of art or some scientific object of interest, and the fruits of his
own intellectual labors. There its possessor was free to express his
own individuality. In this selection, Dora Thornton traces the devel-
opment of the study.

The role of the study in the planning and construction of the Italian Renaissance apartment was determined by its status in the eyes of its owner. During
the fifteenth century demands for greater privacy were combined with a concern for regularity and symmetry in the planning and distribution of rooms.
Studies were one of a variety of smaller, more intimate spaces which came into
common use as the concept of the apartment developed. The word 'apartment'
does not appear to have been used in this sense until the early seventeenth century, when the French took the initiative from the Italians as leaders of fashion and etiquette in formal planning. Since it has already been analysed elsewhere by architectural historians, the role of the apartment is discussed here
only with specific reference to the location and use of studies in the fifteenth
and sixteenth centuries.

The nucleus of the fifteenth- and sixteenth-century Italian palace (using
the word in its widest and most inclusive sense) was the principal bedchamber
or master bedroom (*camera principale*). It served as an informal reception
room at the time of a wedding or after the birth of a child. During the fifteenth
century a number of small rooms used as studies, lavatories (*agiamenti* or *de-
stri*), bath or bathing-rooms (*stufe, stufette* or *bagni*) and storerooms came to
be grouped near the *camera,* and closely associated with it. The idea of the
apartment was to provide a linear sequence of rooms for the use of an individual, which would lead from the more public rooms at the entrance of the
house to the more withdrawn ones at its core: this is the scheme of organisation which Alberti and Francesco di Giorgio prescribed in their treatises on architecture. The most public room in the Florentine house throughout this period was the hall (*sala,* derived from the Latin *aula*). Anton Francesco Doni
described its functions in his book *I marmi* (1552). The women of the house
would sit in the window seats to work at their sewing and look out of the window, while 'one eats at the high table; to that side one plays board games; and
so there is space for everyone'. The importance of the *sala,* and the fact that it
was situated near the entrance of the house, made it the first room to be described in the majority of sixteenth-century Florentine inventories. The Venetian equivalent was the *portego* (dialect spelling for *portico*) which, like the
sala, would have other less public rooms opening off it, leading towards the
principal bedchamber. The order of progression through the house is best described by Scamozzi in his treatise on architecture, printed in Venice in 1615:

Let the principal parts of the palace be the *sale, salotti,* and large rooms, followed by the medium sized ones, and the smaller ones; so that people who accompany the owner may remain in the first type of room; and his intimate friends in the second. Those who come to negotiate with him may go into the more withdrawn rooms. Let this disposition of rooms be observed not only in Princes' palaces, but adapted in accordance with proportion in the well-governed houses of private gentlemen.

The more withdrawn rooms which Scamozzi mentions were the *anticamera, camera, studio* and possibly a number of other small spaces. Architectural theorists had little to say about the uses of this complex of rooms, including the *studio* and the *camerini* which were sometimes adjacent to it. A *camerino* might serve the same function as a *studio:* when Ulisse Aldrovandi described the collection of Giovanni Gaddi in Rome he listed 'the most distinguished, but also the smallest things' in 'the *camerino,* which serves as a *studio'*. Both *camerini* and *studii* were forerunners of the seventeenth-century French *cabinet* and the English closet, although the Italian word *cabinetto* or *gabinetto* was rarely used in the sixteenth century. It appears however in Bartoli's translation of 1550 (from Latin into Italian) of Alberti's treatise on architecture, in which the order of rooms in an apartment in a villa is described as leading from the portico 'through the *sale,* and then through the *camere,* and finally through the *cabinetti'*.

The role of the study in the planning of a Renaissance apartment is analogous to that of the bathroom, as described by Nancy Edwards in her classic study. Both room-types were Renaissance creations, based on classical precept and practice as deduced from the interpretation of ancient texts, and both were adapted to modern usage. The aim was to provide greater intimacy and privacy in relatively withdrawn rooms, and to give an elegant, antique form to one's leisure. Studies and bathrooms, it was recognised, had in ancient times been painted with the same kinds of wall decoration. Cellini, railing against the inaccuracy of his contemporaries in referring to this repertory of playful, frivolous ornament as 'grotesques' since they were associated with 'grottoes' (rooms which had long been buried underground), commented how bedchambers, bathing-rooms, studies and drawing-rooms had been decorated alike with what he preferred to call *mostri:* monsters and mythical beasts. His comment applied as much to Renaissance Rome as to the ancient city, as he knew. Like studies, bathing-rooms tended to be close to the principal bedchamber if not adjacent to it. Both rooms gained from this proximity and interdependence; bathing-rooms acquired an atmosphere of literary leisure from studies, while the latter gained useful warmth—always important for sedentary readers and writers—and associations with sensuous pleasure from the bath. These qualities can be found in a house designed by Antonio da Sangallo the Younger between 1537 and 1546 for a certain Messer Sebastiano Gandolfo in the ideal city of Castro, which Pier Luigi Farnese had made the centre of his duchy. Both the study and the bathroom were on the ground floor at the back of the house; the study . . . measured 6 by 12 palms (1.34 by 2.68

metres). The room would have been heated by the boilers for the bath next door. Sangallo's plan not only illustrates a useful way of heating a study, but also enables a man of scholarly interests to integrate the pleasures of bathing and study into his daily life; an individual's ideal which was in accordance with Castro's planned role as an ideal state.

A close relationship between the functions of the study and the bathroom is also implied in another Sangallo design, the Roman palace of Melchiorre Baldassini, which was admired by Pietro Bembo and later by Vasari. Like the mysterious Messer Sebastiano Gandolfo, Baldassini was a man of scholarly interests (he taught civil law in Rome) rather than great wealth or status. On the first floor was a bedchamber, bearing a frieze depicting scenes from ancient Roman history, appropriate to Baldassini's career as an advocate and orator. Next to this was a study—it has been identified as such on account of its small dimensions—with painted decoration incorporating the Baldassini arms supported by putti, and an acanthus leaf frieze. Interestingly, we know the date by which Baldassini was using his study from the fact that land contracts were drawn up there in May 1521.

Studies were also closely associated with staircases and the landings leading off them; that in Bartolo di Tura's house in Siena is a good example. Another scholar, Cristoforo Barzizza, had a study 'in a small room, situated in the middle of the staircase' in his Paduan house, which was inventoried in 1444. Similarly, the Venetian poet Andrea Pasqualigo had a 'study next to the staircase which leads up from the ground floor'. Some Venetians kept their most treasured possessions in rooms at the tops of their houses, as did the Milanese merchant-collector Andrea Odoni. These far-flung locations tested the stamina of visitors, as Torquato Tasso described in one of his dialogues. On a hot afternoon, he negotiated the stairs to the study of a Roman collector, only to collapse, breathless, on a leather-covered chair at the entrance of the room. Having seen the room, however, he concluded that the collection was so impressive and well organised that it had been well worth the effort.

Felix Platter, a Swiss medical student, enjoyed the fact that his landlord let him use a room at the top of his house in Montpellier as a study. In the summer of 1553 he wrote in his journal:

> I had to move my lodging to another of his [his master's] houses, a veritable palace, which he had inherited from a Doctor Falcon, a Spaniard and a Maran [*Marrano*: a converted Jew] also. At first I was given a vast chamber, but afterwards I installed myself in a little boarded study on the upper floor. I decorated it with my pictures, and my master put in a gilded armchair—for he showed me all sorts of kindness now that his two sons were with my father. At the top of the house there was a fine terrace, or platform, reached by a stone stair. It commanded the whole town, and one could see as far as the sea, the sound of which could be heard when the wind was in the right quarter. This was where I liked to study. I grew an Indian fig-tree there in a vase—my master had been sent a leaf of it from Spain.

There were close links between the study and gardens, particularly in the context of the villa, for it was the villa which offered the greatest potential for making the pleasures of reading, writing and working continuous with the rest of one's existence. The idealised literary perception of the villa had a long history, reaching as far back as the eighth century BC. The fact that real villas of the Roman empire had been celebrated in letters, which were in themselves literary models for Renaissance writers, made the theme yet more fascinating to them. In his treatise on *The Solitary Life* Petrarch articulates the ideal of creative leisure and literary-minded solitude which he saw the villa as providing. This could be a matter of pursuing a systematic programme of study, as envisaged by Petrarch, and suggested by Cardinal Pietro Bembo in a letter of 1505 to a fellow cardinal:

> It has always been my first and most intense desire to be able to live in easy and not dishonourable liberty, in order to advance the study of letters, which has at all times been the vital food for my thinking.

Perhaps this was one reason for Bembo's particular interest in the development of his villa at Santa Maria di Non outside Padua as a place uniquely suitable for study.

Petrarch pictured the solitary man as one who shuttles constantly back and forth between a busy city life and learned rural retreat. Similarly, when Alberti came to write about the villa, he stipulated that it should be situated within walking distance of one's town house. As Richard Goldthwaite has commented, 'the fetish made of *otium* (rural leisure) presupposes an urban point of view'. The tone of Renaissance Italians when writing about life in their villas is one of sophisticated and above all literary nostalgia; a Renaissance humanist was unlikely to forget that Pliny the Younger had written a letter describing his villa, with its study and garden, in some detail. Writing to Bernardo Leoncino, the Vicentine humanist Bartolomeo Pagello described the villa he intended to build at Monticelli di Lonigo, mentioning a garden, portico and courtyard on to which the rooms were to open. The villa would be just large enough to contain his things, and fitted for 'honest pleasure':

> It would be quite sufficient for me to have only one single portico running from the house into the nearby garden, raised above the level of the courtyard by two little steps. On both sides there should be rooms suited for general use, and not luxurious. There should be quite an elegant library, my sole ornament [*unica mia suppellettile*], annexed to the bedchamber.

He added that the gardens should contain many fruit trees and vines, a laurel, trimmed box trees and 'a fountain, clearer than glass itself, sacred to the Muses'. All this provided an appropriate literary and pastoral setting for reflection; a place where you could be 'in good humour with yourself', as one of Petrarch's friends wrote.

Scholars liked to turn from their studies to the sensuous delight and relaxation of a garden. A scholar could share figs from the tree outside his study with his friends, as recounted by Angelo Decembrio in his dialogue about literary culture in Ferrara at the time of Leonello d'Este. Decembrio described a delightful, carefully orchestrated outing to the house in Ferrara of one of Leonello's senior courtiers, Giovanni Gualengo. Having demolished the figs in Gualengo's walled garden as a kind of pagan sacrifice, the friends climb a covered staircase to his library. The room is described by Gualengo later in Decembrio's dialogue:

> At my suburban estate there is daily conversation about books, and in this house there is a library—as you see, looking out over the greenest little plot—not perhaps one fortified with such an abundance of books as our Leonello determined ought to be possessed by the most refined owner (nor was I ever as familiar with Greek literature as I am with Latin), but furnished nonetheless with many useful books.

The connection between the delights of a garden and the treasures of the study was worked into a literary topos by Anton Francesco Doni in a dedicatory letter to one of his books, in which he presents his work as 'fruit from my garden, and jewels from my study'.

NIGHT-TIME STUDY

Night-time study was a literary ideal with impeccable classical precedent, and its popularity as a topos in Renaissance letters illustrates one way in which, building on classical models, writers sought to emphasise the continuity—even the dialogue—between ancient Roman and Renaissance worlds, a continuity which was best expressed through the study. One of the greatest Roman scholars, Pliny the Elder, had been extolled by his nephew for habits of study to be emulated by all scholars:

> He always began to work at midnight when the August festival of Vulcan came round, not for the good omen's sake, but for the sake of study; in Winter generally at one in the morning, but never later than two, and often at midnight. No man ever slept more readily, in as much that he would sometimes, without retiring from his book, take a short sleep, and then pursue his studies.

Hence Juan Ludovicus Vives, in his Latin dialogue *The Bedchamber and Studies by Night,* names the main speaker Pliny to make the character fully recognisable to his readers and to identify the classical source on which his playful exercise in colloquial Latin is based. Vives shows Pliny settling down to work at a desk set up in his bedchamber, so that he can best make use of the quiet hours in the night 'when everything rests and is silent'. Erasmus made fun of just this kind of scholarly zeal and its impeccable literary precedent in his dialogue, *The Ciceronian:*

NOSOPONUS: I have a shrine of the Muses in the innermost part of the house, with thick walls, doors and windows, and all the cracks carefully sealed up with plaster and pitch, so that hardly any light or sound can penetrate even by day, unless it's a very loud one, like quarrelling women or blacksmiths at work.

BULEPHORUS: True, the sudden boom of human voices and workshop crashes destroy one's concentration.

NOSOPONUS: I won't allow anyone to use any of the nearby rooms as a bedroom, because I don't want the voices even of sleepers, or their snorts, breaking in on the sanctuary of my thoughts. Some people talk in their sleep, and a good many snore so loudly that they can be heard quite a long way off.

HYPOLOGUS: When I'm trying to write at night I'm often troubled by mice as well.

NOSOPONUS: In my house there's no place even for a fly.

Formal retreat into the study is often described in a self-consciously rhetorical way. Machiavelli, writing to a friend, contrasted the days spent working on his villa estate at San Casciano with the evenings, when he would change his clothes and enter his study in order to read classical texts.

> When evening comes, I return home and go into my study. On the threshold I strip off my muddy, sweaty, workday clothes, and put on the robes of court and palace, and in this graver dress I enter the antique courts of the ancients and am welcomed by them, and there I taste the food that alone is mine, for which I was born. There I make bold to speak to them and ask the motives for their actions, and they, in their humanity, reply to me. And for the space of four hours I forget the world, remember no vexations, fear poverty no more, tremble no more at death: I pass into their world.

On a more practical note (while still recalling classical literature at several removes), Benedetto Cotrugli, author of a fifteenth-century treatise on the business and conduct of merchants, suggested that those who had an interest in books should have a study near their bedchamber, which would be accessible and quiet whenever they had a few moments' leisure. He explained that this was likely to be at night, or in the early hours of the morning before the working day began:

> You ought to have a *scrittoio* in the *solar* on the first floor, suitable for your needs [. . .] which should be separate [from the rest of the house] without causing disturbance to your family on account of the strangers who come to the house to contract business with you. He who delights in letters should not keep his books in the common *scrittoio*, but should have a *studiolo*, set apart in the most remote part of the house. Should it be close to the room in which one sleeps, it is an excellent and most salubrious thing, for it allows one to study with greater ease whenever time allows.

To Cotrugli, the office (*scrittoio*) is obviously the essential public room, while the study is a luxurious extra—a room in which the gains of mercantile activity are evident, rather than the activity itself. He presents the study as a private space in which to pursue leisure interests whenever time permits, hence the importance of its location. He is concerned with literary pursuits, rather than with the study as a repository for works of art or other small ornaments, perhaps because he saw book-ownership as evident proof of culture. This is a definition of the study which is more characteristic of the fifteenth than the sixteenth century, and it has to be remembered that not only was Cotrugli's treatise written a century before it was finally published (in Venice in 1569), but that his book is an amalgam of advice which was for the most part derived from other manuals. His recommendation to place a study next to one's bedchamber may have been derived from a health handbook, the *Tacuinum sanitatis*, which had been translated from Arabic into Latin in the thirteenth century and had consequently enjoyed great popularity. The author, who was an Arabic physician, advocated night-time study to prevent oversleeping, which he considered injurious to the health, since it dehydrates the body. A copy of the *Tacuinum* which was illuminated in Venice around 1480 illustrates how the fifteenth-century Italian reader would have visualised the way in which such precepts were to be applied. The ink drawings in this manuscript were left unfinished. The text on this folio lists the advantages and disadvantages to the human body of particular seasons in the year, and the four illustrations place these comments in a contemporary context. Men are shown chopping firewood in 'Winter', and the companion piece to this activity is '*Somnus*', represented by a bedchamber in which a couple sleep while a maid sits in a nursing-chair minding the baby in its cradle. 'Summer' is suggested by an airy house in a landscape; its neighbouring piece, '*Vigiliae*', shows a man in his study at dead of night. The implication is that this man has gone into his study next to his bedchamber to read his books by the light of the oil-lamp suspended from his rotating lectern. The drawing gives the viewer the sense of being in a pleasant, panelled room, enclosed and private; this scholar is evidently delighted to be there.

Secrecy is the emphasis in Paolo Cortesi's treatise on the ideal Cardinal's palace, in which it is recommended that:

> the room used for study at night and the bedroom [. . .] should be very near to one another; because they serve closely-related activities. Both these rooms should be especially safe from intrusion and so we see why they should be placed in the inner parts of the house. There should be listening devices through which the disputants in the auditorium can be heard, as well as a spiral staircase which provides an inside passage down into the library.

Despite the fact that Cortesi's treatise deals with the needs and neuroses of a princely household, including a range of specialised rooms complete with eavesdropping devices, the essential nature of a cardinal's study is envisaged as being much the same as that of an ordinary householder.

THE STUDY-BEDCHAMBER

Some collectors chose to live with their collections in close proximity, even to the extent of sleeping in the same room. This may have been as much a question of security as possessiveness, which would explain why many merchants and patricians in sixteenth-century Venice did the same, according to the evidence of inventories. The pattern was established well before 1600 however, as can be deduced from Carpaccio's *Vision of St Ursula*. The saint is shown asleep in her bedchamber, in the corner of which is a table with a writing-desk upon it in front of an open bookchest.

Two Venetian incunabula show similar arrangements. A woodcut from the Malermi Bible of 1490 shows the learned King Solomon in his audience chamber, which is also fitted up as a study. The room would have been immediately recognisable to a late fifteenth-century viewer. Solomon is shown reclining on an elaborate daybed with a carved cornice, where he will receive visitors who are entering through the door on the right. He is also shown at work on his books in the study in the left-hand corner of the room. Solomon's study-corner consists of a desk with a table-carpet, a lectern, a convex mirror above to refresh his eyes in writing, and a bookshelf above that. The second is also a late fifteenth-century Venetian woodcut, from the *Hypnerotomachia Poliphili*, which illustrates a man sitting at a desk in a corner of his bedchamber regarding his quill pen critically as he writes a letter. The arrangement is very similar to that in Carpaccio's *St Ursula*. The combination of these illustrations and the later inventory evidence suggests that living like this was relatively common, not just reserved for impecunious scholars and teachers or obsessive unworldly collectors. It could demonstrate good taste in living with one's antiquities; things which were not to be appreciated by the uninitiated. This seems to have been the spirit in which the humanist Poggio Bracciolini set up a study in his bedchamber: he wrote to his friend Niccolò Niccoli explaining how he had had his chamber 'furnished with marble heads' and that though some of these were damaged, they were yet of sufficient quality to 'delight a good artist'. In another letter he described how Donatello had done just that.

Sharing one's daily life with one's collection could also be an elegant arrangement, as it must have been for Cardinal Pietro Bembo. Raphael advised Bembo to write to Cardinal Bibbiena to request the loan of a statuette of Venus which had originally been intended for Bibbiena's famous bathroom. In his letter, Bembo pleaded that he wished to place the Venus in the study in the 'corner of my *camerino*'. The statuette would be placed:

> between Jove and Mercury, her father and brother, so that I may gaze on her ever more pleasurably day by day, which you, because of your unceasing commitments are unable to do. [. . .] I have already prepared that part, that corner of my bedchamber where I can set up the Venus.

Lorenzo Lotto's portrait drawing of a young ecclesiastic in his study-bedchamber, dating to about 1530, demonstrates just how a collector such as Bembo could live with his collection. Berenson's description of the sitter as 'so contented with his possessions' aptly sums up the ecclesiastic's demonstrative gesture as he invites the viewer into his *camerino*. Berenson seems almost to have identified himself with the sitter, as did Philip Pouncey in commenting on the drawing 'we are in the presence of a man who is cultivated and well-to-do, who likes books, tasteful furnishing and comfort'. People have strong responses to Lotto's drawing for just these reasons—the sense of someone at ease with himself, living untidily and harmoniously with his possessions.

One part of his bedchamber is dedicated to his collection. The drawing shows the influence of Flemish depictions of interiors, as a remarkable evocation of a particular way of life. There are spilled coins on the table and large ancient vases and vessels on shelves, rather like scaffolding, which project from the foot of the bed. There is a bust of the Roman Imperial period on the table (possibly an artist's prop belonging to Lotto, since it appears in other paintings) and large folio volumes behind, leaning against the foot of the bed and against the wall. By the cleric's bed on the wall is a devotional painting with folding wooden covers, beneath which hangs a holy water stoup, exactly as in Carpaccio's *Vision of St Ursula*. Made of metal, this is a type mentioned in inventories: one Venetian inventory of 1591 mentions 'two small bronze buckets for holy water'. While the X-frame chair alone indicates that the sitter is someone of consequence so does the fact that he has a Near Eastern carpet on the floor by his bed (such a luxury would normally be displayed on a table—indeed, the word 'carpeta' in Italian meant a table-carpet). Similarly, the table bell for calling servants is an accessory listed in the inventories of cardinals and represented in portraits of high-ranking prelates, as well as patricians. . . .

It was the quest for greater comfort, privacy and commodity (*commodità*, a fusion of convenience and elegance perfectly adapted to one's needs) that characterised the development of Italian thinking about domestic arrangements from the fifteenth century onwards. Italians themselves believed that they had made considerable advances in this direction, and within a few generations. Something of these processes can be seen at work in the recorded comments of the aged Isabella d'Este, when she made a visit to the Palazzina constructed by her son Federico Gonzaga for his bride, Margerita Paleologo, in 1531. Federico clearly sought Isabella's approval, for he had had a special handrail constructed along a difficult staircase for her, though she proved unable to use it. Federico's act was not only one of filial piety, for Isabella's discriminating taste in creating and furnishing her own rooms was renowned. Her comments are therefore fascinating in revealing her own sense of the building's comfort, as being superior to anything which she herself had been able to create in her thirty years in Mantua. She admired the distribution of rooms in the new apartments, their comfort, privacy and elegance, seeing them as superior to her own. Elegant, urbane architectural planning was considered to be a feature of modernity: in the second edition of his *Vite* Vasari praised Michelozzo for his advanced distribution plan in the Medici palace as providing for 'utility' and 'commodity'; for comfort 'in the modern manner'. Here again, in the words of a recent commentator, the study had a key role, for

> it was in such small rooms [as the study] that personal comfort in many guises was first evolved, as those who owned a study tended to spend long hours there.

Much of this book, in elaborating the idea and nature of the study in Renaissance Italy, has centred on the room as a virtuous space of unique moral and aesthetic worth. This property resided in the room itself as much as in its owner, and did not therefore necessarily depend on the rank or social status of the person who created it. The study rooms of the urban élites which are the subject of the book had a dignity in the minds of their owners which could stand comparison with the grandest examples: a belief exemplified by Vieri's comments on the quality of his small but select library in his villa study, or Fra Sabba's delight in his collection and his discriminating tastes. Vieri explicitly compares his library with that of the Medici and Sassetti, with a just sense of its quality and proper standing. The way in which Fra Sabba situates his own collection modestly but firmly within his discussion of contemporary collecting habits and artistic achievement is a clear indication of how he rated it: as something built up with limited means, but with taste and discrimination. He intended his audience to read from the study to the man, and in doing so, he set himself up as a model of those qualities he most admired: wit, politeness, civility and good manners (*ingegno, politezza, civiltà, cortigianeria*).

The concept of *virtù* residing in a collection of select antiquities and works of art, or in a library, is a Renaissance topos, one which is implicit in Fra Sabba's account of his study, but which is developed by a number of Renaissance writers. It was not however just through its contents, as proofs of urbanity or good taste, that the study derived its virtue, but also through its nature as a philosophical space. The Renaissance debate about the proper uses of solitude focused on the need for a private space, a need uniquely fulfilled by the study. In his essay 'On Solitude', Montaigne advised that we should

> choose treasures which no harm can corrupt and [. . .] hide them in a place which no one can enter, no one betray, save we ourselves. We should have wives, children, property and above all, good health [. . .] if we can: but we should not become so attached to them that our happiness depends on them. We should set aside a room, just for ourselves, at the back of the shop, keeping it entirely free and establishing there our true liberty, our principal solitude and asylum. Within it our normal conversation should be of ourselves, with ourselves, so privy that no commerce or communication with the outside world should find a place there; there we should talk and laugh as though we had no wife or children, no possessions, no followers, no menservants, so that when the occasion arises that we must lose them it should not be a new experience to do without them. We have a soul able to turn in on herself; she can keep herself company; she has the werewithal to attack, to defend, to receive and to give.

Much of Montaigne's argument derives from the moral epistles of his beloved Seneca: a source used by other Renaissance writers in advocating the physical demarcation of personal space within the household. What was new in this Renaissance elaboration of classical ideas was the wish to map this plea for what was essentially an inner sanctuary onto a particular room, the study.

While Pliny the Younger had referred to his study-library at his villa, as all Italian Renaissance letter-writers knew and echoed in their own letters written to like-minded friends from their villas, the emphasis on the study-room as a dedicated space for managing one's affairs and the practice of reflection was essentially an emphasis of their own, and it was distinctly modern. Significantly, when the Authorised Version of the Bible came to translate the injunction from the Sermon on the Mount to construct an inner sanctuary in the soul, the word 'closet'—one of the English equivalents of the Italian *studio*—was used to denote it: 'When thou prayest, enter into thy closet, and when thou hast shut thy door, pray to thy Father which is in secret; and thy Father which seeth in secret shall reward thee openly' (Matthew, 6:6). Doni, Cotrugli and Montaigne, to name just a few of the writers on the theme, imply that this 'room [. . .] at the back of the shop' or near one's bedchamber was not reserved for the few, but should be—and was—available to a wide range of people in their daily lives. Both the room, and the demands which it was uniquely qualified to answer, were familiar to their readers.

While the French royal model of the fourteenth century was undoubtedly important in the history of the study, it was Renaissance Italians who gave the room-type its associations with civility, learned leisure and urbane culture. In doing so, they made it available to a wider social group, subtly and permanently changing its character. It was as an important feature of a well-appointed, gentlemanly residence that the Italian Renaissance study was to be exported to the rest of Europe in the course of the sixteenth century. . . .

LOVE AND MAGIC IN THE RENAISSANCE

GUIDO RUGGIERO

Europe's reformations brought with them an accentuated sense of the power of both God and Satan. They fueled a growing fear of demonic witchcraft that had been slowly mounting since the later Middle Ages. Over the course of the sixteenth and seventeenth centuries, the fear of witches coalesced into mass trials and executions. An estimated 100,000 people lost their lives in the witch trials. About 80 percent of these were women. Theologians, secular authorities and common folk seem to have had little fear of witches in the Middle Ages. Why, then, were witches persecuted with such ferocity in the sixteenth and seventeenth centuries? Was the fear and persecution of witches something imposed on society by governments and theologians? Was it the product of folk beliefs? Was witchcraft something new? Historians investigating the origins of the witch craze, the course that the persecution took, and the identities of the accusers and the accused have discovered a bewildering variety of circumstances, possible causes and contributing factors.

The victims of witchcraft accusations were often older women, typically widows, who begged from their neighbors and sometimes cursed them when no charity was forthcoming. Reputation, too, was a determining factor. Long-standing suspicions and animosities provided fertile ground for accusations of witchcraft. Historians link both to economic trends—growing poverty and the social tensions caused by a new market-oriented outlook—to explain why accusations mounted in the sixteenth and seventeenth centuries. Some historians posit that the persecution of witchcraft was the consequence of a growing hostility of elite, reformed, culture toward a popular culture that was in many ways still pagan. Other historians examine changes in government and justice. While these probably were not the reason for an initial accusation of witchcraft, judicial and governmental institutions could have profound effects on what happened to the accused and whether a single accusation escalated into a witch craze.

From: Guido Ruggiero, *Binding Passions: Tales of Magic, Marriage, and Power at the End of the Renaissance* (Oxford: Oxford University Press, 1993), pp. 57–64, 66–75, 76–78, 85–86, 86–87.

In the following selection, Guido Ruggiero reconstructs the events around an accusation of witchcraft in an Italian town. Why did people resort to magic? Who was likely to be blamed for maleficia (harm done through witchcraft)? The story of Elena and Lucretia provides some clues.

In early May 1588, three priests were celebrating Mass in the Cathedral Church of the small Alpine town of Feltre when, just before the *Lavabo*, the subdeacon, Andrea da Canal, noticed hidden near the altar "a small figure of a child." Quietly he nudged the deacon, Geronimo Lusa, whispering to him, "Look there, it's a small child." Geronimo motioned to him that they should finish the service, and the Mass continued as it had presumably done since the Council of Trent in the sleepy little town of the northern Veneto, lying just over the front range of the Alps on one of the pass roads connecting Venice and northeastern Italy with Austria and southern Germany.

After the Mass, Andrea and his fellow priests took a closer look at the figure and found it a very troubling little package indeed. They discovered wrapped in a white veil not the figure of a child, as Andrea had assumed, but rather a detailed wax figure of a nude man with "many needles stuck all over it, especially the eyes, temple, heart, and phallus. Then the statue was wrapped in three places, with a piece of fabric around the eyes, a second around the stomach, and a third black sash around the genitals full of bent needles." All three clerics were troubled. What the figure meant, what it was doing hidden near the altar of San Prosdecimo, who had put it there, and what should be done all were unclear. On the last point—what should be done—they were of two minds: destroy it as a work of the Devil and forget it or turn it over to the Bishop of Feltre for investigation.

Perhaps as little as a generation earlier, the matter would have been allowed to drop, but by the late sixteenth century the reformed Church was not only busily working to bring the large urban centers of Italy under its more aggressive discipline, it was reaching out to the smaller centers as well. Not that Feltre was that small. The chief Venetian official there at the time, the Podestà, Vicenzo Capello, reported upon the return from his posting: "The site of this city [is] hilly and blocked in by mountains although it has some level land lying over towards Belluno. The territory extends in length 25 miles and in breadth seven and has in all about 22,000 souls [in the town itself there were only about 8700]. . . . But what is most important is that it has several difficult and mountainous passes that mark the border with the territories of the Duke of Austria . . . which make the place most significant." As it was a border area with Austria, the peace and stability of this little town were more important to Venice than its size or wealth might seem to warrant. Even apparently minor disruptions of the status quo could be viewed as threatening. Thus this small wax figure, caught between the Church's drive to discipline Catholic society and Venice's desire to maintain the stability of its border territories, was saved to create a little ruffle in the quiet flow of provincial life, a ruffle that slowly circled outward to involve the hierarchy of the Church, the courts of Venice, and ultimately us as well.

Quickly, however, gossip and rumors spread through Feltre, and the local bishop began an investigation to determine who was responsible. Both the rumors and the investigation focused on a rather unlikely group of women. Foremost among them were Elena Cumano, the eighteen-year-old older daughter of an important local lawyer; her mother and their household women; and finally, Lucretia Marescaldo, a woman in her early fifties reputed to be a witch. After the investigation had gone on for a couple of weeks in Feltre, a denunciation sent to the Venetian Holy Office by a powerful local family, the Faceno clan, outlined one case that was being built on these rumors—theirs: "In the city of Feltre there is a woman named Giulia Cumano, wife of Messer Zuan Cumano doctor of law, who has several children, among them a daughter of about eighteen. This mother decided to have Gian Battista Faceno, a young citizen of Feltre of about twenty-two, take as his wife her daughter. Not able to secure her ends legitimately, she turned to evil ways and witchcraft. With the aid and instruction of other women knowledgeable in these arts she had specially made at a workshop . . . a figure of white wax about one foot high in the form of a naked man. . . . Then with the help of these women, witches and evildoers, she inserted many needles in all the parts of the said statue."

The recourse to magic and a group of women knowledgeable in witchcraft by the wife of a prominent lawyer to secure a match for her daughter with the son of a major local noble family does not square well with received notions about how marriages were arranged in Renaissance Italy, even if it echoes in many ways the accusations made against Andriana Savorgnan and anticipates similar accusations that we will discuss later. Marriage, especially upper-class marriage, was normally a carefully negotiated joining of families contracted by their leaders primarily for dynastic, economic, and political motives. And, as we have seen, at midcentury, the Council of Trent attempted to clarify doctrine in this area. The earlier position, which held that only the consent of the couple involved was required, had created myriad problems. Most significantly for family marriage strategies, it allowed young couples to subvert privately the most careful plans of families and clans with clandestine marriages. Trent attempted to clarify marriage in part so that consent would remain central, but also so that broader dynastic interests would be respected. The new requirements of published bans and clerical participation ideally made marriages more public and gave families more opportunity to intervene before consent could be given against their wishes. But legal niceties and family interference aside, our needle-pierced doll and the recourse to magic it reveals open a perspective on a different range of problems that grew up around marriage and sex, at least in part, in response to the reforms of Trent and, in addition, to a continuing range of problems with premarital sex that Trent did not address.

Society, however, had not ignored these problems. Crucial was the disciplining power of a complex web of concepts that turned on honor and reputation and their association with female sexuality. Broadly sketched, while male honor was variously determined given the intricacies of public and private behavioral expectations for men, for women public and, to a degree, private expectations were more limited. As a result, female honor focused more narrowly on sexual concerns—chastity and fidelity in marriage and virginity before it or at least before a promise of marriage. Sexual honor, however, was not limited to women. With a nice irony in this patriarchal society, men found that their honor was intimately intertwined with that of the women they claimed to control; thus, the chastity and fidelity of wives, the virginity of daughters, and even the sexual conduct of female dependents reflected on the honor of men and, in turn, on the family as a whole. Strikingly, a female's sexual honor was not solely or even perhaps primarily her own; it was bound up in a much more convoluted calculus of honor that involved her family and the males who dominated it.

Yet even in this patriarchal society, the sexual component of a woman's honor did not come close to exhausting the standards that measured her life. Beyond honor, but closely related to it, stood more nebulous concepts of public reputation (*fama*) that for women went well beyond the sexual. *Fama* was constantly evaluated in late Renaissance life by means of public evaluation and gossip. Significantly, women played a central role in this in theory, as gossip was widely recognized as a woman's prerogative. Certainly men participated in gossip evaluation also, and ultimately it may have been their evaluation that mattered; but gossip, even women's gossip in a patriarchal society, should not be underrated. For what was often labeled idle words, in an environment so finely attuned to reputation, actually was a potent form of power. Power, because the world of gossip evaluation had the ability to create crucial realities: honor, reputation, and, of course, at times even husbands, wives, and witches.

THE MARRIAGE AND REPUTATION OF ELENA CUMANO

Which brings us back to the plight of Elena Cumano. For her much more than marriage was involved. At age eighteen in 1588, she found herself seduced, abandoned, and pregnant and her life relentlessly laid out before the courts of Feltre, the Church, Venice, and the public of her community in ways that allowed the complex web of honor, reputation, and gossip in which she was entangled to be evaluated by all. At the very moment that she and her mother were being accused of using witchcraft to win a husband, her father was suing the family of her erstwhile husband to force them to accept her as his wife. Testifying before the Podestà of Feltre, Vicenzo Capello, Elena laid out her vision of her situation, a vision that, self-servingly or not, excused her behavior and sought to save her reputation. She claimed that Gian Battista Faceno was already her husband and, in fact, had been so long enough to make her legitimately pregnant before deserting her. "I wish to say concerning my husband signor Gian Battista Faceno that having promised to make me his wife, he insisted even before he knew me [sexually] that I ought to say in confession to my confessor at Easter a year ago that he was my husband."

Apparently here we have a traditional secret exchange of consent that Elena suggested Gian Battista was anxious to formalize to a degree even before sexual intercourse began by having it reported to a priest. While not quite up to the standards of Trent for marriage, consent and a priest's involvement came close, and it may have been hoped that this would win a certain sympathy for Elena's plight. It was at least a promise of marriage, which for many was adequate for initiating honorable sexual contact between future spouses. Of course, before Trent, if Elena could have proven her assertions, she would have had her husband and her honor and the case would have been closed. By 1587, when this promise was given, things were more problematic, and Elena went on to try to demonstrate more effectively that Gian Battista had married her. "He continued always to pledge that I was his wife and that he did not intend to have any other woman but me. . . . I said that I wished two witnesses to the marriage promise. He asked me if I wanted a greater witness than our Lord God. Thus we called upon him for our witness with very great oaths."

Duped by Gian Battista, Elena nonetheless presented a case that went a long way to reestablish her honor and reputation even if it did not meet the legal requirements for marriage. She portrayed herself as accepting an apparently honorable man's word, with God as her witness. Soon Gian Battista began visiting her at home under the pretext of being a suitor and a friend of the family. Unfortunately for her, however, he did not visit merely to talk, and shortly she found herself pregnant. Elena reported the strains this put on their relationship in a manner that again added to her reputation and continued undermining that of Gian Battista. "Thus I became pregnant. He began to say, then, that he wanted me to have an abortion, but I did not want that at all. He said to me that he had spoken with the physician Rizzardo, but that he did not want to give him any medicine [for an abortion] and that he had gone to Venice for advice. . . . But I said that I did not want to lose my body and my soul. He replied that he had had other women abort and that they had not died." A good Christian operating in good faith found that her presumed husband was neither; clearly, honor and reputation fell on her side in her telling of the tale.

It is interesting to note that Gian Battista turned to a male doctor for advice on abortion. Apparently men used male networks for such things, just as they used male networks to hire wet nurses for "their" children—almost as if the aspects of the female body and reproduction that concerned men and their honor directly had to be controlled by other males. This is not to suggest, however, that women's networks did not also deal with abortion. Rather, it appears that women turned to other women more in the context of acting against the wishes of the males who were responsible for them, whether that meant husbands, fathers, or brothers. It also seems that among women the lack of a period was often construed as an illness, rather than as a sign of pregnancy—an illness that could be treated. And, of course, the cure for such an illness was to invoke menstruation.

A woman healer named Elena reported one such remedy to the Holy Office in 1571: "To cure a woman whose period [*fior*] has not come, I take some sage and I grind it very fine for three mornings and I give some of the paste of it to her for three mornings and she will be freed." It appears that in concentrated enough form, sage is a poison that can induce abortion; as such, it is a remedy with a long tradition. But suggestively, by treating a late period as an illness rather than as a pregnancy, women healers conceptualized the problem and women's bodies in a radically different and less threatening way than male networks. Only more systematic research will confirm if this apparent distinction was a consistent one; but if so, it would be a significant break between a male culture and vision of birth and a female one.

During their discussion about abortion, Elena reported yet another admission by Gian Battista. "He said that there was no question that I was his wife, but that he had suggested an abortion because at that time he had other business to do before making the marriage public." Elena, deeply troubled, continued to follow the reputable path. She visited her confessor to ask his counsel. He suggested another meeting between the couple; thus Elena claimed to have summoned Gian Battista to one more secret meeting in her bed. But the events of that encounter, which occurred on December 7, 1598, even in her testimony engender suspicion. Undressed together in bed, she reported, "he said that he wanted to keep the promise that he had made me." Apparently a moment of warm reconciliation that fulfilled her confessor's optimistic hopes and hers as well, the scene rapidly degenerated. "At that moment Gian Battista was discovered . . . by chance by my father, two of my brothers and two of my uncles . . . they were lamenting the situation when he said to them that I had been his wife for four months. . . . Then my father called two witnesses and said 'In confirmation of this contract made give her here this ring in pledge.' This he did putting on my finger this ring." At this point in the transcript the scribe inserted in Latin that Elena displayed to those present "a gold ring on her ring finger adorned with a pearl." Again with her ring and its display, Elena was building her reputation in a public forum before the Podestà of Feltre.

She continued undermining the honesty and, in turn, the honor of Gian Battista, "My father also wished to call a priest, but Gian Battista said, 'Sir, don't bother because tomorrow I will return with my brothers to do what is necessary . . .' and he added, 'Do not believe that I have been forced to do this, because I have wanted to do this for months.'" After numerous apologies again reflecting on his dishonorable treatment of the Cumano family, he left, taking with him the accoutrements that presumably many a young rake took to a tryst—a stiletto, pistol, and a rope ladder used to gain entrance to Elena's room. Gian Battista, however, did not keep his word, or at least the words Elena put in his mouth. That night was the last time Elena was to see him.

As soon as he escaped from her bedroom and the hands of her father, brothers, and relatives, in fact, he began trying to escape from his problematic marriage, claiming that it had been forced on him. That night he waylaid one of the witnesses and tried to convince him, mainly with threats, that he had been forced to agree to the ceremony. The next day his family took up the case, also trying to press witnesses to portray the events of that evening as a trap and Gian Battista as a victim rather than as a happy husband relieved at last to have his marriage finalized and public as the Cumano telling of the tale would have had it. Thus, for a time, a war of words and tales raged in Feltre until finally, after a month of public claims and counterclaims, the city's bishop, Giacomo Revelli, ruled that the marriage was not valid because the forms of Trent had not been followed. In addition, he ordered that Elena must stop claiming that she was Gian Battista's wife and defaming him. Theoretically the war of words was over.

What for an evening had appeared to have been a triumph for the Cumano family—Gian Battista's "willing" confession of marriage before witnesses and the exchange of a ring—thus collapsed before the new requirements of the Church. As Zuan Cumano, Elena's father and a lawyer, must have been uncomfortably aware, he and his family lacked the canon law prerequisites to have a binding marriage. Nonetheless, as a lawyer, he was well aware that the Venetian government had become increasingly concerned about young men taking advantage of women by consenting to marriage; convincing them that that alone constituted a marriage; then robbing them of their honor and occasionally of their dowries as well; and finally, deserting them with the unwitting support of the Church, which declared such presumed marriages null because they had not followed the new forms of Trent, just as Bishop Revelli had done. Already in 1577, Venetian authorities had begun to pass legislation to limit such practices, legislation that Zuan cited in his case against Gian Battista. Clearly, he hoped to win support for his and his family's plight from those concerned authorities.

In a formal complaint written to the Podestà of Feltre, Zuan Cumano summed up the situation after that night nicely from a male perspective: "Thus I expected that shortly there would be done what should have been done before the Church [*in faciem Ecclesia*] but that wicked and most evil man thinking to increase his honor and reputation with his new addition of this evil wickedness began to refuse, making the claim that he violated my daughter without any promise of marriage and to have fooled and made a joke of me [*burlato*]." After admitting bitterly Gian Battista's treachery, Cumano's testimony swung to a more evaluative mood that says much about a masculine vision of the double standard of honor and reputation involved in premarital sex for women and men. "He burned to make himself renowned for his great and evil betrayal, holding for himself as a signal trophy the prostitution of the honesty of my house and the awful violence to his given and obligated pledge [of marriage]. He hoped also to make himself glorious for having scaled the walls [of my home] with a rope ladder and at the same time for having violated the security of my house and the honor of all my family preserved forever intact by my ancestors. And surpassing all iniquities . . . he has gone to the reverend vicar of our most reverend Bishop and secured a formal admonition against my daughter that she must desist from claiming this marriage."

Cumano's perspective is instructive. Clearly he was laying out his problems in terms designed to play on the concerns of Venetian authorities about such matters; yet his words struck deeper chords by playing on references to his family's honor and reputation in terms of the marital and sexual problems of his daughter. From Cumano's perspective as the male head of his family, a predatory Gian Battista had created serious difficulties for his daughter's honor, his own honor, and that of his family. Significantly, even the issue of the unwed pregnancy tended to be evaluated in terms of family honor. Equally suggestive was the strong appeal Cumano made to a double standard of honor. He assumed that the very same events that had dishonored his house, as Gian Battista presented them to the public, would bring honor and glory to the young man. For Cumano even the violation of the walls of his house had been given a heroic twist that added to the culprit's honor. It should be noted, however, that this double standard was not perfectly symmetrical here. All agreed that Gian Battista, to gain fame and reputation at the expense of the honor of a woman and her family, had to claim that he had violated both her house and her body "without a promise of marriage" or at least a serious promise of marriage. The breaking of one's word seriously given undercut even a rake's *fama,* changing him from the fantasy of many a Renaissance male to the feared predator of family honor that haunted the worst nightmares of those same men. . . .

Perhaps Cumano hoped that by going on the offensive, drawing out the honor dimension of the conflict, and demonstrating that potentially dangerous tensions were being exacerbated by it, pressure might be brought to bear on the nobility and the Podestà to back down on the issue of the wax statue and perhaps even support the marriage of the young couple as a way to defuse the situation.

In the light of this complex calculus of reputation and honor, the Cumano family's stress on Gian Battista's frequent admissions of marriage and intention to marry take on additional meaning as well. As noted earlier, while that marriage could not be established before the Podestà of Feltre, his court provided an ideal public forum to try the honor and reputation of Gian Battista Faceno. And while no formal verdict could be given on that, a less heroic view of the rake's progress could be publicly presented—one that stressed that with false promises he had led astray an innocent Christian girl and a trusting father who had had faith in the binding honor of his word and pledge. The Cumano family may have even hoped that whatever the outcome of the case, making public this vision of events (whether they were true or not) might have forced the Faceno family to reconsider their own honor and reputation and decide on marriage.

This, of course, was the perspective of the Cumano family, a perspective that, given a modern sensitivity to the evident plight of Elena, deceived, abandoned, and pregnant, may miss the way the Faceno could read the same tale. A healthy corrective is provided by the literature of the period. For while Shakespeare might at times show sympathy for his star-crossed lovers, other perspectives on star-crossed love, especially when it involved class, were well represented. Bandello, in novella 31 of part II of his *Novelle,* tells the tale of a Milanese nobleman who fell in love with the daughter of a substantial commoner, much as young Gian Battista seems to have done with Elena. He, however, did do the correct and honorable thing. After courting his love from a suitable distance, he approached the girl's father for her hand. Bandello reports that the father, in turn, did the honorable thing, going to the young man's mother (his father was dead) to warn her of the unwise love across class lines. Together the parents plotted to send the young man away and marry his love to someone of her own station while he was gone; they plotted, that is, to respect the normal imperatives of family and social order that the unbound passions of love had blinded their children to.

The successful outcome of the tale for Bandello, and presumably for his readers as well, was underscored by the clever metaphoric ending he provided. When the young man returned, learning of her marriage, he rushed to see her. But he was surprised to find her less beautiful than he remembered and blind in one eye as well. Once more, however, the young noble behaved correctly, congratulating his ex-love on her marriage and expressing his condolences for the accident that he assumed must have caused her to lose the sight of one eye while he was away. She replied warmly, "And I say from my heart to you that I am happy that you have recovered the sight of both your eyes." Her remark, and his moral, Bandello explained as follows: "She had been blind in that one eye ever since she was a small child. . . . Thus love often blinds incautious lovers." And thus, from the patriarchal perspective of the late sixteenth century, Gian Battista's timely withdrawal to the wars of Flanders may have prevented blind love from doing harm. In such a reading, Zuan Cumano becomes the person who acted dishonorably, and the Faceno family, Gian Battista, and his own daughter were the victims.

Be that as it may, it is Zuan Cumano's complaint that we have on the broken pledge. And that complaint is also eloquently evocative in its metaphors of sexual victimization and honor that figure so prominently in the description of Gian Battista's deeds. Again, it was not so much Elena's victimization that was central, but rather a form of familial reputation expressed in sexual terms. Gian Battista had "violated" [*violata*] the walls of Zuan's home by physically scaling them. "Violated" was used in just this sense to describe in criminal records the taking of a woman's virginity. In the process, Faceno destroyed the honor of Zuan's family, "always conserved intact" [*conservato sempre intacto*] by his ancestors. Again, "intact" was the usual way of referring to honorable unmarried women still virgins [*vergine intacto*], and "conserving" that virginity intact was a central goal of the family. In sum, Cumano was describing literally the sexual desecration of his family's honor, and it is not at all surprising that he concluded that Gian Battista had gloried in the "prostitution of the honor of my house." Cumano was not only clever in this use of metaphor, he was following a normal pattern of language found in many such cases. Regularly there was a metaphorical wedding of the sexual and the honorable that saw a woman's body and honor being bound up with the tradition/body of a family and its honor.

That symmetry of vision could hardly be better exemplified than in the opening lines of Zuan Cumano's written complaint: "Giovan Battista Faceno . . . a youth most arrogant and audacious, destroyer and prostitutor of the honesty of families had the desire under a false and wicked promise of matrimony to *violate* the security of my house in order to wickedly betray and deflower Elena my daughter . . . carrying off [*levando*] her virginity and carrying off [*levando*] eternally the honor of myself and my entire family which has always been *more dear to me than life itself.*" Again Zuan's house is portrayed as violated in conjunction with his daughter's "deflowering." The parallel is reinforced by the repetition of "carrying off," which is explicitly used to describe the loss of Elena's virginity and the loss of his and his family's honor. As a result, as Zuan makes absolutely clear, he finds himself facing in the loss of his daughter's virginity a loss of personal and familiar (*sic*) honor more dear to him than life itself.

Such rhetoric may have been overblown, but it suggests a central perspective on why such tight control of a daughter's sexuality was deemed necessary, especially by upper-class fathers. Not only was a daughter's honor and, in turn, her marriageability crucially colored by perceptions of her sexual purity; in much more complex and subtle ways, a family and the men responsible for it found the honor of all of them turning on the intactness of a daughter's virginity. As has been well documented, upper-class daughters were expensive to marry and difficult to place well in the Renaissance; in addition, when not bound by marriage and unplaced, their passions were very dangerous for the honor of father and family as long as they remained so.

One might well ask if daughters and women in general saw their situation as equally perilous. Did young women see that they had honor to lose, and did they evaluate it from the perspective of their virginity before marriage and their chastity thereafter? Could it be that that intactness that meant honor in a male world was less significant for women; that women did not evaluate themselves by the codes evolved for them by men, and that Elena and many other young women like her were less concerned about their virginity than their fathers and brothers? Perhaps. But the answer to that question is a complex one that requires more extensive research. Nonetheless Elena's case and its broader context provide some suggestive insights on the matter. First, Elena's sacrifice of that which her father held more dear than life itself needs to be more carefully considered. It might well be argued that, in fact, Elena only put her honor at risk in sexual intercourse in return for Gian Battista's putting his own honor at risk by giving her his word even before God "with very great oaths."

Throughout her testimony before both the civil and ecclesiastical authorities, Elena was most concerned to demonstrate that she had given herself only after a promise of marriage reinforced by oaths to God and discussions with her confessor. Without mentioning her honor, as noted earlier, such testimony reinforced her honor by demonstrating that she had given her virginity with the assumption that she was acting correctly as a wife in the eyes of her

Church and community. Suggestively, however, Elena seemed to imply that her vision of her reputation and honor went beyond the sexual. For example, when referring to a conversation that she had heard about between Gian Battista and several local notables, she reported a telling detail. One of those notables, responding to Gian Battista's proclamation that he was leaving for the wars in Flanders, objected, according to Elena: "it is not well to run off to Flanders when you have taken for a wife that woman *who is well-born, intending by this me.*" Elena implied, using the words of another, that she was honorable on more than one level in the eyes of the community. First, of course, she reinforced her primary line of attack by revealing that members of the community perceived her as Gian Battista's wife. But in addition, she was an honorable woman because she was well born into that family whose tradition her father was anxious to defend. And finally, of course, that honor would be secured by a marriage tie to another prominent family of Feltre, Gian Battista's, and perhaps even increased, as his family was a noble one. In fact, this goal may come closer to explaining the risk she took in exchanging her honor with his: if the risk had succeeded, she would have secured for herself and her family the correct place in society for a well-born woman—marriage into another important family.

MAGIC, MARRIAGE, AND REPUTATION

Honor, status, and family power, however, were not enough to secure Elena's marriage. For that matter, neither was the entrapment of Gian Battista, apparently engineered by her father, or even the public pressure reported from the community. But Elena, disappointed, still did not see herself as without hope, which brings us back to the wax figure found hidden near the altar in the Cathedral Church and eventually to a larger circle of the residents of Feltre and their perceptions of reputation and honor. When her case was brought before the Holy Office of Venice, Elena provided an explanation for the statue: "sleeping with my husband [Gian Battista] one night, he said to me that many times he had heard that men made women come to them with a statue. They bound the statue and needles were stuck in it to give the hammer [*martello*] to those women whom they wished to have come. . . . The next day my husband left after he had been found in my house and I did not see him again."

Elena had begun to set the stage for the dangerous admissions that were to come. Her husband, before he deserted her, had described a magical way men used to bind women to themselves. But again, nicely, she demonstrated to the Holy Office that she had at first avoided such questionable tactics, adopting instead the correct Christian approach—prayers, Masses, and a good life to win the support of God, Mary, and the Church: "I was pregnant by him so I hoped to make him return with prayers and I sent a woman . . . to light eleven candles, have a Mass said and ask for the grace to see the road to be reunited [with my husband]. I also had a Mass said to the Holy Spirit and sent alms to the Monastery of the Angels and Santa Chiara. Moreover I had us inscribed in the school of the rosary so that I could say the rosary for us both. I also had a prayer said at the chapel at the door of San Lorenzo where there is a Christ, a Madonna, and a Santa Lucianna that have done many miracles in order to ask the grace that things be made right and my husband return."

Thus, following the correct Christian path with candles, masses, prayers, alms, and even the new fashion of the rosary, Elena demonstrated her faith in the power of the Church. And for a moment it seemed that the path of the good Christian would work. Just before Easter, Gian Battista's brothers were reported to be talking in public about how Gian Battista had confessed, been forgiven, and, having taken advantage of a special general indulgence offered by the Pope, was planning to return to Feltre. Elena saw this as a sign that her prayers had been answered. She explained to the court that it had seemed clear to her that if he had confessed and been forgiven, he must have certainly been convinced by his confessor to honor his promise of marriage. Once again with an apparent artlessness in her testimony, Elena had suggested that the Church's power should have been adequate to bring her husband back and properly bind their passions. If candles, Masses, prayers, and alms were not adequate, surely the Church's control over confession and the central mystery of the faith that it provided access to—the Eucharistic Ceremony—should have carried the day and secured her husband's return.

Gian Battista did return, but not to Elena. Rather, he slipped in and out of town on his way to the wars in Flanders. The Church had failed her. But there was another range of binding powers available to Elena, powers that often were not so distant from Christianity as it was commonly practiced as the Church might have hoped. "Having learned this [that Gian Battista had fled to Flanders], I resolved to try to make him return using the statue that I had heard him speak of himself." Thus she began to reveal the love magic used to try to force her husband's return. "I gave four *soldi* . . . to Lucia my maid, so that she would buy a statue of wax." From the beginning, however, the plan did not go smoothly. The first statues delivered were rejected. And when an adequate statue was brought, Elena reported that there was an extra two-*soldi* charge, which wisely she did not explain to the Holy Office. It seems that she had sent her servant to buy the wax statue from a local craftsman, Pietro Grevo, who specialized in wax figures as *ex voto* and funerary ornaments. Normally, these were dressed and hung in the churches of the city as a memorial, a request for divine aid, or an expression of gratitude for aid received. As such they lacked an element essential to the magic at hand; thus the first statues sent had been unacceptable because they lacked "a virile member and testicles." As a proud craftsman, Pietro, when called to testify, even explained how he modified his regular molds for making the statues, using beans to achieve the desired additional physical details, and noted that when he delivered his revised work, Elena's servant had informed him that "the statue was pleasing to her mistress."

Elena admitted to the Holy Office that the evening the correct statue was delivered, "after dinner while the rest of the house rested, I wrapped my white veil that I wear on my head at night around the statue in order to tie it up and stuck a needle into it so that it would stay bound. Then I stuck eight or ten needles in diverse places as seemed fitting to me all over the statue. But as I was doing this the leg broke off, so I used a bit of taffeta to put the pieces back together and tie them back in place. Then I gave it to my maid and told her to carry it to the cathedral and leave it at the head of the altar behind the altar cloth . . . because this would make my husband return either tomorrow or shortly. But he never did return."

Although Elena's story put the blame for her actions squarely on her own shoulders, exculpating her mother and the other women accused of complicity, it also placed her actions in the best possible light. Having failed to win back her husband as a good Christian with the aid of the Church, she had in a way tried the next best avenue open to her as a good woman: as a good wife, she had tried to win her husband back following the advice of that very husband! Gian Battista had explained to her the magic of the wax statue, which apparently worked as a *martello*, or hammer, to force a person to return. The *martello* was a widely used form of magic, as we shall see, often adopted to punish enemies—to hammer them or, as in this case, to force them to act to avoid the pain and suffering that the hammer created for its victim. Usually the hammer was activated by prayerlike language that used Christian imagery to call on God or his heavenly supporters to punish/hammer the victim until they fulfilled the hammerer's desires. Elena, however, did not admit to using such language; rather, she turned to the Church to trigger her hammer in a more formal way. Her hammer was to have been activated by the Masses said over the statue, and it was in that context that the statue had been discovered near the altar in the Cathedral Church of Feltre.

Her interrogators in the Holy Office were particularly troubled by her use of the Church in conjunction with the hammering magical wax figure. They noted that seeking the aid of the Church "for good things is licit and laudable, but evil with illicit means." Then they asked, "Could you clear up whether or not you understood that you were doing evil?" Elena admitted, "At the time I believed that I had done a good thing, but later when I confessed during the Jubilee to an Observant Friar he told me that I had sinned . . . thus at first I believed it was not a sin, but after the friar explained I believed it was." Once again Elena was putting her case in the best possible light, but her examiners were suspicious about her account of the magic and how she had come to know about it. In part they were suspicious because another woman reputed to be a witch had been implicated in the case by the investigation in Feltre, but in part they were troubled by Elena's claim that her husband had provided the idea for the magic used. Statistically speaking, that claim was unlikely; in this period, most of the people tried for the use of love magic were women and, more important, the cases themselves, as we shall see, suggest an underlying assumption common at several levels in society: that women were the masters of such magic. In turn, those few men prosecuted were usually priests, not husbands. This is not to argue that men did not practice such magic, but merely to point out that Elena's examiners were predisposed to be suspicious about her claim that a man had taught her the rather complex magical program that she had followed. In fact, they were quite concerned to discover the women's networks that they assumed lay behind the wax figure.

WITCHCRAFT, REPUTATION, AND THE POWER OF WORDS

Significantly it was a woman's reputation that forced the direction of the original inquiry by the Bishop of Feltre. Lucretia, a woman of about fifty and married to a builder known as Giorgio Marescalio, immediately became the focus of the investigation there, in large part because she had the public *fama* of being a witch capable of such magic and also of being particularly adept at securing marriages between unwilling partners. A large group of neighbors and local ecclesiastics testified to her evil *fama* in disturbing detail, claiming not only that she knew and used binding love magic, but also that she destroyed children, hammered her enemies, and knew what people said about her in secret. A neighbor, Bartolomeo Bressano, gave a typical account of her activities. He claimed that Lucretia had put a spell on [*fatturato*] one of his children. Moreover he reported that "while visiting my house Lucretia's daughter told my wife that once she had given birth to a badly deformed child which no one dared to touch except her mother. She [Lucretia] killed the child and said that it had a blessed cowl which her husband wore thereafter. It had the power to protect one from enemies."

Such destruction of deformed children was apparently common, often done by the midwife who oversaw the birth. But Lucretia's interference seemed to imply several things to her neighbors and to the ecclesiastics who heard the case as well. First, monstrous births threatened the regular order of life in a community. They suggested that things were radically out of joint in the family involved and also in the larger community; hence, their frequent association with other portents and God's judgment. The reported reluctance to touch the child seemed to reflect a deeper fear of its significance as well. In turn, Lucretia's lack of fear suggested that she was familiar with the powers that stood behind such things. With a familiarity and a coolness that impressed, she killed the child and, in addition, demonstrated enough understanding to draw out the magical implications of the baby's cowl to benefit her husband. Bartolomeo continued: "And moreover I heard from Zuan Battista Galletto that if it had not been for this Lucretia, messer Piero Sandi would never have married his wife and also that Francesco Ochies one time was ready to strike her because she had made a male child of his die. He brought a case against her, but because he was poor, he could not prove what was being said publicly. Concerning her evil *fama* one may question all our neighborhood in which there are Vicenzo Busiga, Antonio Gallot, Michael Forner, messer Zan Vettor Capra the barber, Francesco the apothecary and many women whose names I do not know."

Clearly, we have in Lucretia another woman whose reputation was evaluated by her neighbors on broader criteria than her sexual behavior or chastity.

As Bartolomeo had promised, those neighbors called before the court confirmed that they viewed her as an evil woman and a witch. The widow Giacoma Patugalla provided an account of a damning incident of a type often associated with witches. Lucretia had visited her house one day about five years earlier and, seeing her young son, had placed her hand on his head, saying, "Oh, what a pretty child." Shortly thereafter the child became sick, and Giacoma began to suspect Lucretia of being a witch and of having made her child sick. Witches were, of course, well known for destroying children; the frequent wasting diseases of childhood were regularly assumed to be the result of their spells. Giacoma tried an experiment, however, to test her hypothesis; she was no credulous victim of superstition. She had learned that there was a way to determine if a witch had cast a spell over a child: "I had been taught that one had to beat the clothing of the child and that the person who had given the sickness/evil [*male*] to him would come. Thus I tried it and the day following the said donna Lucretia came to my house and told me that my child would no longer have the sickness/evil. Nonetheless the child died and I had the impression that the child died because of her."

While Giacoma's account is clear and virtually stereotypical, right down to her experiment to determine if Lucretia was a witch, one thing in her account is less clear: why did Lucretia want to destroy her child? In some regions, witches were reputed to destroy children by sucking their blood and causing them to waste away simply for the malicious pleasure of destruction or as a mark of their full commitment to evil. Lucretia's neighbors, although ready to accuse her of heinous crimes aplenty, were silent on her reasons for killing children. But a hint to their perception of her motives, and perhaps to their deeper fears of her as well, is provided by the testimony of another neighbor named Giacoma, Giacoma dal Cumo. She reported that Paolina, the daughter of Lucretia, had asked her to do a favor for her and keep it a secret from her mother, apparently because her mother would have disapproved. Somehow, however, Lucretia found out. As a result, Lucretia came right to her and, after giving her a punch or two, "she put a hand on me . . . which made a tremor and fear come over me and I shook so much that I did not know what I was doing." Giacoma was so frightened that she confessed the secret favor, and Lucretia then "made the sign of the cross over me and said, 'Go and be blessed. Go in the name of God.' Immediately that fear went away and I went home without feeling any more pain." Here Lucretia was punishing a neighbor for acting against her interests and implicitly against her wishes. In other words, her spells gave her a power over her neighbors, a power that could punish them for acting against her or even her desires. It may well be that neighborhood babies were seen as having been destroyed in much the same context. Rather than mere evil, their destruction was evil to an end.

Perhaps the best example of Lucretia's use of her punishing powers is also the most apparently banal. Orsola, wife of Vettor Buziga, had gotten into an argument with Lucretia while washing clothes almost a decade earlier, perhaps about who was first. The discussion passed from words to deeds, and water was splashed by each woman on the other. After Lucretia left, however,

Orsola was suddenly paralyzed and unable to move for two days. A number of people still remembered this incident years later, perhaps because it epitomized the power and danger of Lucretia's reputed use of punishing witchcraft. It may be that Orsola's splashing and public argument with Lucretia should be read as well as a public affront to the latter's honor. In that light, Orsola's punishment could be seen as a form of vendetta, as well as a demonstration of Lucretia's power. And neighbors remembered the incident, if that interpretation is correct, because even a minimal dishonoring of Lucretia carried with it a threat of vendetta in the form of witchcraft. It may be that given the brief accounts of Lucretia's magic, most of it could be explained in simple terms of power, but it is worth considering in this late Renaissance society so rife with concepts of honor and vendetta that the power of witches could serve as a significant tool in the vendetta side of the honor dialectic. The person who dishonored a witch could expect the treatment that Orsola received or perhaps something worse, like the death of a child. If this were true, then the honor of witches had to be treated with unusual care by those who associated with them either voluntarily or involuntarily as neighbors—and one can see another possible reason why Lucretia's neighbors were so troubled by her. . . .

. . . [N]eighbors feared [Lucretia] as a witch, but her reputation had spread more widely and even local clerics were convinced that she was one. Perhaps the most revealing testimony came from the cleric Zuan Victor, who reported spying on Lucretia in the cathedral shortly after the discovery of the wax statue. In a long testimony he described her movements around the church, movements that an innocent eye could easily have read as those of a devout woman involved in her private devotion. But lurking in the choir, the cleric watched with a suspicion that layered her every movement and glance with dangerous implications. Reading his testimony, one sees how a woman with the reputation of being a witch, whether she was one or not, underwent a scrutiny that made it almost certain that she would become one in the public eye at least.

"I put myself to walking there in the church," he reported, "and while I strolled through the chapel of San Zuane, there entered four or five women whose names I do not remember. Also there entered Lucretia wife of messer Georgio, the builder, who is reputed to be a witch and who has been given the nickname Circe. . . . Lucretia kneeled on the first step of the steps that go into the choir from the side that overlooks the altar of San Prosdecimo [near which the wax figure had been found] . . . seeing her there I moved back very slowly behind the altar painting of San Rocco in order to clearly see the woman and not be seen. After all the other women left, remaining alone in the church. . . . This Lucretia began to make the sign of the Cross. . . . Then she began to kiss the floor and for this reason I knelt down [in order not to be seen]. But at that moment some people arrived . . . and donna Lucretia stopped right where she was. After those women had left for a time, this woman returned to making the sign of the cross and kissing the floor. She repeated these things four times because when she began to make the sign and kiss the floor people came in.

Finally after the fourth time, I believe that was after about three quarters of an hour . . . there arrived messer Vettor Guslin and a peasant. And this time Lucretia got up from where she had been and it appeared to me that she was trying to look over towards the principal altar of San Prosdecimo. She went towards the part of the church that is towards the Church of San Lorenzo near which again lies the altar of San Prosdecimo. When she arrived at the font for Holy Water she turned giving a quick glance [un occhiata] as they say around the Church and then slowly left walking over to San Lorenzo."

Lurking in that silent church with the cleric Zuan Victor, one gets a sense not only of how his suspicions magnified the significance of Lucretia's every action, but how the Church was for at least some women in the late Renaissance a special and familiar space. Witch or merely good Christian, Lucretia had her own sense of the Church and used it for her own programs with a familiarity that comes through even Victor's suspicions. In many ways the churches of the late Renaissance were a special place for women. First, of course, women operated there in an environment where in theory they were the equals of men. Both were ultimately involved in the same battle for salvation. But beyond that much circumscribed and overlooked point, in many ways it appears that church space had been appropriated quite aggressively by some women. It was one of the few public spaces where women could move freely with a certain lack of suspicion. Perhaps this is one reason why public officials had been worried for a long time about the potential for illicit sexual contacts in church.

Clearly, church space had an important social dimension for women, and it may have been more significant than for men, who had a wider range of social spaces to frequent. In some ways, we might even conjecture that the church played a role for women similar to the role that the bar and later the coffee house would play for men. More significantly for understanding Lucretia and her reputation, however, there is much evidence in the cases heard by the Inquisition in Italy that certain women, struck by the deeper meanings that they perceived as underlying the special space and objects of their churches, had attempted to use those powers for their own programs of magic and witchcraft. The same was true for domestic space and objects, as we shall see. Altars, the Mass, holy oil, holy water, the Host, blessed candles, and the very geography of specific churches, as well as domestic doorsills, hearths, stairways, beds, hearth chains, pans, beans, salt—together they make an unlikely list, but all shared the status of familiar yet special places and things where women moved and that women used. And certain women discovered in and around these places and things a world of deeper meanings that created a special culture and a range of deeper powers that they drew upon at times most effectively to bind people and their passions. Victor's suspicions and his testimony were probably designed to play on fears of just that, fears that were shared more broadly. When we read of Lucretia's movements about the church from that perspective, they become rich with meaning and threat. . . .

Among all the accusations leveled against her, one significant one emerges: that she magically forced people to marry against their will. Her daughter put this accusation in a different light, claiming that her mother was called "a witch in Feltre because she labors to make marriages, as she did with messer Bartolomeo Sandi who married madonna Marieta daughter of messer Vettor Scalladria and she arranged also the marriage of donna Pellegrina del Zas with messer Bernardo in Zas. These marriages she arranged with deliberations between one side and the other." Every town had its marriage brokers, people who arranged marriages between families and either collected a small fee for their services or the more nebulous good will of the families involved. At times, however, such good offices could backfire on the marriage broker, especially when the match did not work well or the partners crossed social or age boundaries in ways that troubled society.

In such instances, it was not hard to assume that some magic or witchcraft was involved in creating the binding emotions that had led to marriage . . . [I]t might be more accurate to say that when everyone was happy with a match made using magic, there were no complaints and the good witch/matchmaker was a popular and powerful person. When the matches were seen as incorrect, crossing class lines, thwarting the wishes of the powerful, or even merely creating unhappy marriages, the same magic could quickly become evil in the eyes of the community and was much more likely to come to the attention of the authorities.

Lucretia's neighbors' complaints about her witchly ways, when read in this light, take on additional meaning. We see from their perspective a potentially positive and useful service to the community that had gotten out of hand and become literally destructive. Giacomo Cambrucio remembered perhaps the most damning incident. It appears his eighteen-year-old daughter had been courted by a young man whose attentions she did not appreciate. The young man turned to Lucretia for help. As a result, according to Giacomo, one day she came to his house and called his daughter to the door, saying, "If you do not make love with that man, I would tell you to repent and you will be unhappy with your life." He continued, "As far as I can remember she [Lucretia] touched her on the shoulder. The child after that began to cry and complain that her heart ached. She remained like that slowly dying for twenty months and neither medicine nor doctors could aid her, until she became like a statue and died. Before she was always healthy and full of life."

Rather than making a positive match that would have served the community and its desire to see young women successfully married and families continued, Lucretia's magic had caused death. Clearly, this undercut Lucretia's daughter's claim that her mother was performing a useful and necessary social function, but it does not undercut her contention that such a service could be positive if used judiciously. And as we shall see, whether it was used judiciously or not, it was used extensively both in the urban environment of Venice and in the countryside of the Veneto. From a slightly different perspective, however, it should also be noted that once again Lucretia appears to have been trying to use words here to control the future. With or without magic, she had subtly threatened Giacomo's daughter, warning her that she should accept the attentions of her suitor or her life would turn out badly. Given her reputation, the young girl might well have heeded her warning, accepted her suitor, and married him. If that had occurred, presumably Lucretia's magic would have worked again, and if the marriage had worked out her words would have brought a better future, binding passions to continue family and community.

That was not the case, however, and the failure was compounded by the young girl's suspicious death. The testimony of Lucretia's neighbors reveals that this failure and others like it, read negatively, had slowly built into the conviction that she was a dangerous and evil witch. Thus the discovery of Elena Cumano's magical quest to regain her lost husband once again focused suspicions on her. While Elena's father followed more regular masculine paths to regain her husband, it was logical in the eyes of the community that Elena and perhaps her mother would turn to another source of power available especially to women—the marriage broker/witch Lucretia. According to her *fama*, she had forced other marriages; the wax figure under the cathedral altar was just another instance of her powers.

Witch or victim of her reputation, wife or victim of a rake's progress, both Lucretia and Elena remain enigmas. The many-layered tales that they, their supporters, and their enemies constructed create a web of words behind which it is almost impossible to uncover the truth of their deeds. But that web, much like a spider's web, both disguises and builds; in this case, it builds a complex vision of the interrelationship between marriage, honor, and reputation in the lives of women and men in late-sixteenth-century Italy. Moreover, it suggests how some women could use elements of that vision to their advantage, building realities out of certain strands of the social fabric such as honor and reputation to bind their opponents and advance their own causes. Neither Lucretia nor Elena was completely successful in this; both leave the court records still more victims than winners. Lucretia escaped being prosecuted as a witch but undoubtedly was still reputed to be one by her neighbors. Elena remained unmarried, although she did eventually gain money from Gian Battista's family for a dowry and maintenance. But neither woman was a passive victim; each in her own way chose a strategy that attempted to turn the calculus of honor and reputation that society applied to women to her advantage. And in the end, they realized that what the patriarchs of their world held to be "more dear . . . than life itself" could give them a certain leverage even in what appeared to be largely hopeless situations.

PICTURES, PRINT AND PIETY

TESSA WATT

The advent of the printing press with moveable type changed forever the way that ideas could be communicated as well as the possibilities for repressing them. Before printing, ideas were communicated only through the spoken word, individual works of art, or through manuscripts, which were produced slowly and in small numbers. Printing allowed the rapid dissemination of ideas over a wide area. Moreover, once a message was in print, it became virtually impossible to stamp out all traces of it. The Church might burn a critic or an unconventional thinker at the stake, but his words could continue to spread in printed form. Just as important, printing ensured that the idea could be transmitted unchanged. Inevitably, ideas were changed in oral transmission. If the ideas were unfamiliar to people, they changed even more during transmission and could be distorted beyond recognition. In contrast, people could pass a printed book or a broadside among themselves and receive exactly the same message (how the individual reader understood it is another matter).

The Protestant Reformation, print, and literacy were closely intertwined. The printed word helped spread Luther's message with unprecedented speed and accuracy. It also had a part to play in his understanding of the good Christian life. Luther railed against the monopoly that priests exercised in the interpretation of Scripture and called on people to read and consider God's word for themselves. The proliferation of printed editions of the Bible made Luther's command all the more possible. In principle, the Reformation was linked to its converts' ability to read. Books, however, were expensive, and many people were illiterate. Male literacy in England in the 1640s, for example, ranged from 30% in the countryside to 78% in London. Women's literacy rates were even lower.

Print's impact was far greater than literacy rates indicate. Illiterate folk might listen to someone read a tract. They could look at the illustrations on broadsides and memorize their captions. In this selection,

From: Tessa Watt, *Cheap Print and Popular Piety 1550–1640* (Cambridge University Press, 1991), pp. 193–205, 208–216.

Tessa Watt demonstrates that printed images and words had spread throughout English society by the early years of the seventeenth century. The cheapest form of print—the single-sheet broadside—could be found even in humble inns and farmhouses. How did ordinary folk use print? How might they have "read" a picture? Many scholars believe that with print the flow of ideas went in only one direction, from elite culture to popular culture. Tessa Watt argues that the themes and images that people preferred and the uses to which they put print indicate that ideas flowed in both directions in Reformation England.

In 1564, William Bullein wrote *A dialogue . . . wherein is a goodly regimente against the fever pestilence,* in which he used the journey of a London citizen and his wife into the countryside as an excuse for a literary rag-bag of fables, jests, allegories and word-emblems. 'Civis' and 'Uxor' arrive in a town several hours' ride past Barnet, where they find an inn for the night. It has 'a comlie parlour, verie netlie and trimlie apparelled, London like, the windowes are well glased, & faire clothes with pleasaunte borders aboute the same, with many wise saiynges painted upon them'. Painted on these cloths, on the walls, on the chimney and on individual 'pictures' or 'tables' are both proverbial inscriptions (in Latin) and pictorial emblems. Civis reads and interprets the paintings at his wife's request:

UXOR. I pray you housband what is that writyng in those golden letters.
CIVIS. Meius est claudus in via quam cursor preter viam. That is, better an halting ma[n] whiche kepeth the right waie, then yᵉ swift ronner besides, that wandereth a straie.

UXOR. What beaste is that, havyng many colours, one bodie, and seven horrible heddes.
CIVIS. The bodie of sinne, with many infernall heddes: Wickednesse in every place under the Sonne. . . .

An ordinary inn may not have had painted Latin inscriptions and grand religio-political emblems as Civis described them, but wall paintings with moral sayings or figure subjects were a common feature of inns and taverns. Even mean alehouses were expected to provide decoration for their customers as Wye Saltonstall commented in 1631: 'A Country Alehouse. Is the center of the Towns good fellowship, or some humble roof't cottage licens'd to sell Ale. The inward hangings is a painted cloath, with a row of Balletts [ballads] pasted on it'. This standard decor is confirmed by Izaak Walton, who in 1653 described a visit to 'an honest Alehouse, where we shall find a cleanly room, Lavender in the windowes, and twenty Ballads stuck about the walls'. According to Donald Lupton's account of 1632, the more substantial country alehouse-keepers arranged for a more permanent form of decoration:

> If these houses have a Boxe-Bush, or an old Post, it is enough to show their
> Profeshion. But if they bee graced with a Signe compleat, it is a signe of good
> custome: In these houses you shall see the History of Iudeth [Judith], Susanna,
> Daniel in the Lyons Den, or Dives & Lazarus painted upon the Wall.

Wall paintings of biblical stories, some illustrating the very episodes Lupton
mentions, have been found in former victualling houses of this period. Although the chances of survival have favoured the larger establishments we
would call inns, contemporary descriptions suggest that these 'histories' were
found in one medium or another (wall painting, cloth or paper) right through
the victualling hierarchy.

This victualling hierarchy formed a national network of communications:
in a census of 1577, over 14,000 alehouses, 2,000 inns and 300 taverns were
listed in 27 counties, with 3,700 alehouses and 239 inns in Yorkshire alone.
With the growth of private marketing in the early seventeenth century, the inn
became the most important meeting place for a 'community of wayfaring merchants'; it functioned as 'the hotel, the bank, the warehouse, the exchange, the
scrivener's office, and the market-place'. Bargains were drawn up here, grain
bought and sold, carriers hired; some of the larger inns provided facilities for
drovers or were used as wool marts, operating outside the regulations of the
official market. Lesser wayfarers stayed at the ubiquitous alehouses, located
along all the main trading routes, in woodland hamlets, and in all but the
smallest villages. A Hertfordshire tippler* lodged 'all baggage people such as
rogues, tinkers, pedlars and such like'; in 1640 an Essex alehouse harboured
petty chapmen† from Norfolk, Ely and Sherborne in Yorkshire. Ballad sellers
sold their wares at the alehouse; minstrels like Richard Sheale sang their songs
of Chevy Chase, Bevis and Sir Guy; companies like the Yorkshire weavers and
shoemakers performed their interludes. Printed texts, oral songs and stories,
and (as we see in this chapter) visual imagery were disseminated here.

The victualling house was the point of intersection between this nation-
wide network of communications and the local community, of which it was
also an important focus. The increasingly grand 'county inns' were used by the
gentry, merchant and professional classes for administrative and political business; the small village alehouse was a social centre for husbandmen, labourers,
poor craftsmen and servants. Peter Clark has suggested that an upsurge of
victualling in the century before the Civil War was partly a result of the alehouse taking over much of the 'communal and ritual life' which had formerly
centred on the parish church. Such a transfer may also have been reflected in
the visual environment, as inns and alehouses were decorated with the narrative wall paintings formerly found in churches.

During Mary's reign, Protestant activists used alehouses for their conven-
ticles. In 1553, one Thomas Cundale of Orwell, Cambridgeshire, spent an

---

*Tipplers sold ale or beer.

†Chapmen were itinerant peddlars.

evening in the alehouse offering to show his friends an anti-Catholic ballad entitled 'maistres masse'. A group of puritan farmers who marketed in Royston in the 1630s used to meet afterwards at a local victualling house to 'talk freely of the things of God'. Some tipplers were proselytizers for the opposite cause, like the bold Richard Brock of Bunbury in the 1630s, who brought out 'one great Crucifix of brasse' and set it up in front of the drinkers. Even if alehouses were more often centres for 'popular irreligion', encouraging rowdiness and drinking during Sunday service time, the news of political events and religious change was transmitted and discussed here. The country alehouse described by Lupton in 1632 included 'tinkers and poor souldiers' among the drinkers, but at the same time 'either the parson, Churchwarden, or Clark, or all; are doing some Church or Court-businesse usually in this place'. The evidence of ballads and wall paintings suggests that 'religious' song and imagery had a place in the victualling houses, belying any simple polarity between a godless 'alternative society' and the church-going 'elite'.

Even the labourer who lived in a flimsy shack that 'blew away', if he could not afford ballads to decorate his own walls, was likely to come into some contact with printed or painted 'stories' at the local alehouse. However, painting on cloths and even walls was also surprisingly common in humble domestic interiors. Before looking at specific 'stories' we need to examine the general evidence for the use of decorative painting.

The real poor man's picture was the painted cloth. Almost none survive: like the clothing of the lower orders, they fell apart through use. They served a practical purpose of keeping out the draughts in the walls of timber frame houses, as the fillings of wattle and daub were prone to shrink. For the second half of the sixteenth century, 56% of inventories in Nottinghamshire (to pick a county at random) mentioned painted cloths or hangings. Husbandmen worth only £20 in total might own 3s. worth of painted cloths. Nicholas Chapman was worth just over £5 after his debts were paid, but still had 'wolle and paynted clothes' worth 4s. A 'halling' (painted cloth for the hall) could be worth as little as 4d.; while four 'queschens [cushions] with pentyd clothes' were valued at 4d. in total. The wealthy John Bagaley who left an estate of £232 owned twenty-two painted cloths valued at £1.10s or an average of 16d. each. Unfortunately subjects are rarely listed. . . .

. . . The Elizabethans regarded every part of the interior of a room, including timber beams and supports, as an appropriate surface for painting. When wall painting did begin to die out in the second quarter of the seventeenth century, it was partly because painting on timber frame was no longer considered acceptable: a smooth surface was desired. The extant examples are often found behind wainscot, or covered over with a continuous lath and plaster skin. Perhaps the growing ownership of paintings and prints as we now know them changed ideas about what 'art' should be, and made the use of every odd surface for painting seem old-fashioned and inferior.

For the half-century before this, wall painting has been found in every size and standard of house still standing. Of course the chances of survival have favoured larger houses rather than cottages, especially for dwellings built before the late seventeenth century. Margaret Spufford describes the latter as the crucial period of 'rebuilding' for agricultural labourers and cottagers, when they 'might expect to move into a house which had at least a chance of standing up for more than a generation'. Surviving wall paintings are most typically found in a yeoman's house, consisting of hall, parlour and service-end, with three chambers above; but paintings are sometimes uncovered in dwellings of less than four rooms. In a modest cottage in Chalfont St Peter, Buckinghamshire, there is a panel framed in strap-work with a black-letter text: 'When any thinge thou takest in hand to do or Enterpryse fyrst markewell the fynall end there of that may Aryse. Feare God.' Another cottage at North Warnborough, Hampshire has some very crude stick-men which may represent the journey of the Magi to Bethlehem. Paintings in 'farmhouses' include a series on the prodigal son and a crude Adam and Eve with a black-letter placard: 'As by the disobedience of one mane many weare made sinners so by the obedience of one shall many be made righteous.'

The greater number of wall paintings are to be found in manor houses, in substantial town houses once belonging to tradesmen and in former inns—which are, of course, the dwellings most likely to survive intact. But paintings like the Adam and Eve suggest that the themes executed by professional painter-stainers in inns and manor houses might have been copied at a lower social level by unskilled locals. Even the simplest Adam and Eve were not created from a blank slate, but took up the conventional pose used in the woodcuts of the 'Biblia Pauperum' [Paupers' Bible], illustrating again the importance of printed pictures as a medium for dissemination of visual themes.

The most common form of domestic wall painting was the ornamental pattern; sometimes imitating panelling or textile hangings; sometimes incorporating animals, mythical figures, flowers and texts. But of figure subjects, biblical themes were possibly more frequent than any other. Although the survivals do not lend themselves to precise dating, we can roughly trace a slide of decorative painting, during the second half of the sixteenth century, down the 'ladder of sanctity', on the same route taken by biblical drama and printed pictures.

The evidence of inventories suggests that the balance shifted from New Testament to Old in the years soon after Elizabeth came to the throne. The iconoclasm of the later Henrician and Edwardian years did not prevent people from having on their walls 'a clothe of christ', 'a table of s. barbara & ecce homo', 'a story of saynt mathewe in bords' and even 'a story of ower [our] lady in bords oylled'. But from the mid-sixteenth century, the narrative Old Testament picture was also becoming common. In the 1560s and 70s the old devotional images were almost entirely replaced by items like a picture of 'Solomon', another of 'Barsaba', 'one painted storie of Adam and Eva framed', and 'a table of pictures of thold testament'. Towards the end of Elizabeth's reign, in painting as in prints, allegorical subjects and portraits became more common than religious themes. By the end of the century, gospel scenes in domestic wall painting seem to have been genuine grounds for suspicion. When figures of the Evangelists have been found from the late Elizabethan period, they turn out to be from the house of a recusant,* in an attic chamber reached by a ladder and trap-door, which was probably used as a secret chapel.

The four most popular biblical subjects of the late sixteenth century (based on surviving wall painting and contemporary remarks) come below the Old Testament on the bottom 'rungs' of the ladder of sanctity. Two were from the Apocrypha:† the stories of Susanna and of Tobias. The other two were parables: Dives and Lazarus, and the prodigal son. Although these latter were from the Gospels, they were apparently safe to depict because they were only stories, containing no historical holy figures.

These four themes appeared on walls, on cloths and on paper. The prodigal son was one of Godet's series of six prints; the other episodes were illustrated in the woodcuts on the broadside ballads. Thus, not only did they cross over various visual media, but into oral culture as well. Susanna, Tobias and the prodigal son were all among the long-enduring 'stock' of godly ballads, and Dives and Lazarus was one of the 'traditional' songs collected by Francis Child. These stories, which are mentioned more frequently than any others, illustrate the fusion of various cultural strands: the Protestant impetus for popularization of the Scriptures, the iconophobic tendency to avoid the more sacred figures of Christianity and the traditional demand for narrative pictures.

The story of the prodigal son was a particularly popular one in taverns and inns during the 1590s, if Shakespeare is to be believed, and a favourite theme of Falstaff's. At the Boar's Head Tavern, Eastcheap, Hostess Quickly fears she will have to pawn 'both my plate and the tapestry of my dining chambers' because of Prince Harry's visit. Falstaff suggests that her tapestries are out of fashion: 'Glasses, glasses, is the only drinking, and for thy walls, a pretty slight drollery, or the story of the Prodigal, or the German hunting in waterwork, is worth a thousand of these bed-hangers and these fly-bitten tapestries.' A few years later, Falstaff's bedroom at the Garter Inn, Windsor, has been decorated to his taste: 'There's his chamber, his house, his castle, his standing-bed and truckle-bed; 'tis painted about with the story of the Prodigal, fresh and new.'

Pictorial fashions like this may have spread along the network of inns and alehouses, and from these nodal points outward to the manor houses and cottages of the local communities. . . .

The Knightsland Farm wall paintings preserve a subject commonly depicted on other materials which have disintegrated. The prodigal theme was told in painted cloths, such as the ones owned by a butcher of St. Helen's, Worcester. The 1605 inventory of Christopher Coxe records a series of hangings 'in the hall about the said rome conteyninge the storye of the progigall childe'. At Owlpen Manor in Gloucestershire, the prodigal son appears on a

---

*Recusants were Roman Catholics who refused to attend the worship services of the Church of England.

†Apocrypha are non-canonical, semi-scriptural books of doubtful authorship and authority.

rare extant painted cloth: an imitation tapestry, probably much more expensive than our butcher's hangings, and apparently imported 'from some unknown foreign source'.

This popular story appears to have been flexible in the purposes it served. Like the broadside ballad on the theme, the painting could be taken as a warning to youth not to waste away their money with riotous living. As a lesson on the vanity of worldly pleasures and the importance of filial piety, it was an appropriate accompaniment to the moral texts which were considered suitable for domestic walls. The godly viewer might read the picture on another level, according to the original meaning, as a parable of God's mercy. But for a hardened sinner like Falstaff, the forgiveness extended to the returned prodigal might be taken as a good excuse for debauchery in the meantime. Visually, the tale could be a pretext for a lively scene of loose women, feasting and merry-making.

The parable of 'Dives and Lazarus' offered a similar pictorial opportunity to portray the rich man in his fine clothes at his sumptuous table. At Pittleworth Manor, Hampshire, the story was painted in 1580 in two panels: one of Dives and three other figures banqueting, the other of Lazarus outside the house with the dogs licking his sores. Above is a black-letter inscription:

> of Dives and poore Lazarus the Scripture telleth us playne the one lived in wealth the other . . . payne. Dyves was well clothed and fared of the best but Lazarus for hunger lying at [hy]s [g]ate/coulde have no rest. Lazarus dyed for lacke of foode: so did the rich glutton for all his worldly good: in hell fyer for ever shall burne because his [remainder of text destroyed].

Depicted in contemporary Elizabethan costume, the banqueting scene must have presented a self-image to the manor house inhabitants, reminding them in their relative luxury of their duty to the poor. The image of the poor beggar functioned much like a skull on the desk, which warned one in the fullness of life to be thinking of death. In fact, such a *memento mori* appears as a moral text on another wall in the same room, amidst a brocade pattern of pomegranates: 'Thus lyving all waye dred wee death and diing life wee doughte.'

The 'Dives and Lazarus' parable was also a standard theme of painted cloth. Again Falstaff is our informant, describing his soldiers as 'slaves as ragged as Lazarus in the painted cloth, where the glutton's dogs lick'd his sores'. If the viewers at Pittleworth Manor identified with Dives, perhaps there were some who saw the story painted on rough brown hemp in an alehouse, for whom the meaning was rather different: a message of encouragement that the poor would go to heaven and the rich would get their just deserts.

The popular stories of Susanna and Tobias were probably (like their ballad versions) more entertaining than didactic in purpose. . . .

The schemes of story-painting on late Elizabethan walls seem to follow a common pattern: they are told in a horizontal series of panels (sometimes in the frieze), accompanied by black-letter texts; they use bold black outlines, with bright colouring, and their biblical characters are always dressed in contemporary costume. The custom of reinforcing the story in a text may have arisen partly from the need to establish good Protestant credentials: the Elizabethan homily distinguishes an idol from 'a process of a story, painted with the gestures and actions of many persons, and commonly the sum of the story written withal'. At the White Swan Hotel in Stratford-on-Avon, formerly a tavern, are painted scenes from the story of Tobit dated *c.* 1570–80. The scenes are separated and framed by classical columns, as in the prodigal son scheme at Knightsland Farm. Scrolls with black-letter texts summarize the story: 'Heare tobit tobyas sent to ye sitte of rages for mone that was [lent]', and so on. A less prosperous alehouse-keeper might have stuck the same story on the wall in broadside ballad form. With the strong black lines and stunted figures, the effect of these woodcuts is not unlike that of the painted series at the White Swan. Once again, the same theme spread to private houses: a 1575 inventory of Wassell Wessells (in the Prerogative Court of Canterbury) included 'a storie of Tobias'; while in Essex a mercer who died in 1584 owned 'a little story of Tobias' with other stained cloths.

While these parables and Apocrypha were most common, a few Old Testament themes do survive. At the Black Lion Inn, Hereford, a series of biblical scenes illustrated the breaking of the Ten Commandments. This is a post-Reformation adaptation of the medieval 'morality' paintings, where the warning against ungodly behaviour had usually been presented in the format of the seven deadly sins. Jonah and the whale, a popular story in the pamphlet and ballad press, had obvious pictorial possibilities; as did 'Daniel in the Lyons Den', mentioned by Lupton as a popular alehouse theme. The story of Joseph (one of Godet's woodcut series) was depicted on painted cloths, and on a mural in Hadleigh, Suffolk. . . .

A number of factors must have encouraged the repetition of the same stories in various different media. On the practical side was the availability of prints as models, and (one suspects) the habits of travelling painters who found it easiest to repeat the same themes. Meanwhile, the more a subject occurred in ballads and plays, and on the walls of inns and alehouses, the more fashionable it became. This recurrence presumably acted as insurance that a given theme was safe from criticism.

The need for a post-Reformation iconography was met partly by the 'safe' narrative biblical paintings we have been looking at, and also by secular and allegorical themes based on the new developments in printed pictures. The wall paintings at Knole in Kent (*c.* 1605) followed the lead of the up-market copper engravings: they depicted figures in elaborate feigned architectural settings, such as the six virtues, and the four ages of man after engravings by Crispin Van de Passe. A tantalizing reference to 'A painted cloth of Robin Hood that hangeth in the hall' in an Essex inventory of 1589 suggests that stories from popular ballads, chapbooks and jest-books may have been transmitted visually on the painted cloths.

One theme which did cut across many forms of oral and visual culture was 'the nine worthies', of medieval French origin. Traditionally this pantheon was made up of three pagans (Hector of Troye, Alexander the Great, Julius Caesar), three Jews (Joshua, King David, Judas Maccabeus) and three Christians (Charlemagne, King Arthur and Godfrey of Boulogne). In England the lesser-known of these figures were sometimes deposed by more popular heroes like Guy of Warwicke, Pompey and Hercules. The worthies may have been popularized, like St George, by way of mummers' plays and pageantry. The homely performance Shakespeare gives us in *Love's Labours Lost* also contains a clue about the familiarity of the heroes as a visual theme. Costard chastises Sir Nathaniel after his faulty performance as Alexander the Great: 'O sir, you have overthrown Alisander the conqueror! You will be scraped out of the painted cloth for this. Your lion, that holds his poll-axe sitting on a close-stool, will be given to Ajax; he will be the ninth Worthy.' One of the worthies, Hercules, is in fact the subject of a rare surviving painted cloth, now hanging in the Ipswich Museum. Late sixteenth-century wall paintings of the entire nine worthies theme have been found in Amersham, Buckinghamshire, in a timber frame house which probably belonged to a prosperous tradesman at the time. The heroes, who stand about 4 feet high on nine panels around the room, have idiosyncratic faces which suggest the possibility that they commemorate a local pageant of townsmen. A life-size version was painted at Harvington Hall, Worcestershire (*c.* 1576–8), while the lone figure of Hercules in another substantial Amersham house (early seventeenth century) may once have been part of the series.

The great appeal of the worthies can be explained by the way they integrated various cultural strands of the period: the medieval chivalry of the popular printed romances, the 'Renaissance' interest in classical mythology and the Protestant focus on the historical figures of the Old Testament and Judaic history. They were entertaining and heroic, while at the same time permeated with a nationalistic sort of religiosity. The moralizing possibilities were brought out in a woodcut book printed in 1584 which was structured in the emblem-book formula of picture, explanation or history of each character, and 'motto' or moral. An account of the worthies' adventures could be obtained more cheaply in a broadside ballad of *c.* 1626: 'A brave warlike song . . . ' to the tune of 'List Lusty Gallants'. Here the nine worthies mingle with 'other brave Warriors' including recent explorers like Drake and Frobisher, and the 'seven champions of Christendome' whose names are repeated in the refrain:

> Saint George for England
> Saint Denis for France
> Saint Patricke for Ireland,
> whome Irishmen advance,
> Saint Anthonie for Italie
> Saint Iames was borne in Cales [Calais]
> Saint Andrew is for Scotland
> and Saint David is for Wales.

These 'saints' have been secularized through their assimilation to the military spirit of chivalric romance. They were reproduced with stereotyped heroic physiognomies in an octavo book of copper engravings published in 1623. However, unlike the worthies, they do not appear in wall paintings: apparently the early seventeenth-century public was not ready for saints on the walls, even when stripped of most of their miraculous and talismanic power.

One of the results of Protestant constraints on the presentation of sacred figures seems to have been to elevate classical and English heroes, which then became confused with Old Testament figures and medieval saints in the popular imagination. The nine worthies theme in balladry, pageantry, painted cloth, wall painting and woodcut presents a striking instance of wide familiarity with classical legends. The influence of 'Renaissance' classical tastes can also be seen in the ornamental schemes which were one of the most common forms of wall painting, found even in modest farmhouses. 'Antique work', incorporating armorini, mythical creatures, flowers and so on, was the English interpretation of the Renaissance grotesque. It was also used for the borders of printed books and broadsides, and for hangings: an Essex inventory of 1589 lists a painted cloth 'of antique work'.

Iconoclasm was only one factor encouraging the dominance of ornamental painting. Another may have been the practicality of a simple repetitive pattern for covering large spaces of wall. And the more positive demand for Italianate fashion, which began at the upper social echelons, could trickle down as it translated into the desire for a house that looked like that of one's wealthier neighbours. Were the mythical creatures and foliage only background decoration, or did they actually mean something to the inhabitants? The appearance of florid antique work together on the same wall with religious inscriptions indicates that classical aesthetics and Protestant piety were considered to be compatible. However, some qualms over the juxtaposition of pagan and sacred images in this period are apparent in the alterations made by the printer Henry Middleton to his woodblock device of Christ as the Good Shepherd. Originally cut in 1567 for Henry Wykes, the image of Christ was framed by an oval border with several tiny faces, a rampant lion and an elephant. In 1579 Middleton had these creatures carefully cut out of the block and replaced with inanimate scroll-like decorations. Here the pagan images were removed; but in the decoration of contemporary houses, Protestant opinion ensured that it was Christ who had no place on the walls, while the faces of the grotesque reigned triumphant.

A house decorated with 'antique work' could happily be inhabited by a mainstream English Protestant of 1600, who might equally happily purchase prints of the Ages of Man and books adorned with figures of Justice and Charity. Yet unless he were an extremely 'iconophobic' ancestor of William Dowsing, he would probably also approve of the wall painting of the prodigal son or Jonah and the Whale at his local inn. This tradition of biblical 'stories', found in inns and even alehouses (the supposed centres of 'irreligion'), seems to represent an aspect of shared culture between the more Protestantized and more traditional groups in society. The same stories recurred on the walls of the manor houses owned by the gentry and yeomanry, in the town houses of substantial tradesmen, and in the lowly broadside ballad. The same iconographical universe was inhabited by 'elite' and 'popular' classes, both rural and urban. The medium of print may have been an instrument of this shared visual culture, as ballads, woodcut prints and engravings influenced the themes portrayed in other crafts, from the mural paintings at Hill Hall to the roughest painted cloth. . . .

ON THE THRESHOLD OF
INDEPENDENCE: ADOLESCENCE

Our biological rhythms vary little from those of early modern Europeans. We reach sexual maturity somewhat earlier and we generally live longer now than they did, but our bodies develop much the same way as theirs. How we understand those biological rhythms and how we divide them up into distinct phases of life, however, is quite different. Preindustrial children were expected to work from an early age. Initially, they might perform simple tasks under supervision; gradually they would take on jobs calling for more skill, strength, and responsibility. By the time they reached their teens, they were ready to work for and perhaps live with an employer. This pattern of early entry into the work place suggests that preindustrial Europeans grew up fast, and that there was little in what adolescents did (or did not do) that would distinguish them from adults.

While preindustrial children apparently grew up fast in terms of work, the nature of family life suggests a very different pattern of maturation. Male heads of household exercised considerable authority over their families, including their servants and apprentices. Since apprentices might be in service to a master well into their twenties, their "childhood" could be very long indeed. For girls, adolescence ended abruptly with marriage. In Italy, upper-class girls tended to marry much earlier than boys, and their "youth" was quite short.

From the legal and economic standpoints, youth and adulthood were blurred, but historians can find examples of ways in which adolescents in early modern Europe did act as a distinct group. In French cities, groups of young unmarried men formed "youth abbeys" or "kingdoms" during festival times. Their mock role-playing of authority figures gloried in the ridiculous, but could also deliver criticisms of local authorities and recent events. Young men in the Spanish

From: Ilana Krausman Ben-Amos, *Adolescence and Youth in Early Modern England* (New Haven: Yale University Press, 1994), pp. 100–108, 170–75; and Steven Ozment, "The Private Life of an Early Modern Teenager: A Nuremberg Lutheran Visits Catholic Louvain (1577)," in *Journal of Family History* 21:1 (1996):22–32, 36–37, 37–38.

and French countryside also could serve as informal regulators of sexual propriety. Widowers or widows who remarried to someone much younger than themselves, for example, would be subjected to a charivari, *in which young men from the village would gather at night outside the home of the newlyweds, making "rough music" and shouting rude comments.*

What were the experiences of adolescents who, either as apprentices or students, had left home to acquire the skills necessary to advance to adulthood? Did their society recognize adolescence as a distinctive phase in the life cycle? Did adults make certain concessions for these young people? How did adolescents negotiate between the responsibilities of work and their subordination to masters and other adults? In the following selections, Ilana Krausman Ben-Amos and Steven Ozment explore some of these questions.

APPRENTICES AND MASTERS

ILANA KRAUSMAN BEN-AMOS

A few young people had known their masters before their apprenticeships began. Lodowick Muggleton, who was born and reared in London, was about 15 years old when apprenticed to a tailor who lived in the same 'walnut-tree-yard' as he. The tailor knew his parents well, and Lodowick also wrote that the tailor 'liked me very well'. In every town there were a few young people who were apprenticed to their own fathers, as well as to cousins, brothers, uncles and grandparents. But overall, the evidence suggests that most apprentices barely knew the people to whom they were apprenticed, and that the masters, their wives and children (if there were any) were strangers to the young apprentice, even when his apprenticeship had been arranged well in advance. For example, Richard Oxinden, the son of a Kentish gentleman, was placed as an apprentice in London with the assistance of one of his kin, Valentine Pettit. Yet there is no indication that Pettit had been acquainted with the master at all. As for the Oxinden parents, it is clear that they had never met the master, Mr Newman, while Richard was introduced to him only after arriving in London, when part of the premium had already been paid and when Richard began a trial period to see what his master and his profession were like. George Bewley was also sent to Dublin on the basis of an arrangement his parents had made; the master was a linen-draper neither young Bewley—who was then 14 years old—nor his parents had known or even met.

Even when parents were acquainted with the master in some way or another—a business associate, a friend they had known—this did not mean that their son had known or met the master prior to the signing of the indenture. For example, the parents of John Croker from Plymouth arranged an apprenticeship for their son with a sergemaker who lived in the colonies, whence young John was sent in the company of his parents' friends. The parents themselves may have known the master before his migration—the parents, their friends and the master were bound by ties of religion and mutual friendship—but clearly young Croker himself had never seen his master. Even when the master was related to the youth by ties of kinship, this did not necessarily mean that the master would have been an acquaintance or a person with whom the youth had been in any kind of contact before. James Fretwell had, on occasion during his childhood, met his uncle, a London attorney. Nevertheless he appears to have known little about his character, or his business and dealings, before he came to London for a trial period as his apprentice. To some migrant apprentices, especially those arriving from great distances, uncles or cousins in the large town were complete strangers. Edward Barlow had probably never even seen his uncle before he arrived in London at about the age of 14. It is when we realise how strange nearly all masters were to young-sters who came to learn and live under their roofs that we can begin to ap-preciate the difficulty involved in adapting to apprenticeship.

That difficulty was compounded by the necessity to adjust to life as a young apprentice. During the early part of their training, and sometimes well after, apprentices were required to do a wide range of demeaning tasks: clean-ing, carrying, dusting, washing, sweeping, fetching coal, making up fires, and doing errands of a variety of sorts. Complaints to the effect that apprentices were required to do household tasks instead of being properly trained in their trade reached the local courts, in London as well as in Bristol. Some young-sters, who were bound at a relatively young age, were employed in doing er-rands for one or two years, and only then began their proper instruction. Overall, meaner tasks were particularly likely to be imposed on the newly ar-rived youth, whatever his precise age. Simon Forman remembered that 'being the youngest apprentice of four' in his master's shop in Salisbury, he was put to do 'all the worst', and that 'everyone did triumph over me'—fellow ap-prentices, and also the kitchen maid, Mary Roberts. That sense of humiliation involved in the age hierarchy of the small shop was also conveyed in Francis Kirkman's account of his life as a London scrivener's apprentice, who was not only required to do the dirtiest and most burdensome tasks, but 'being the youngest apprentice was to be commanded by everyone'.

In some shops there were no fellow apprentices or even journeymen, and the youngster confronted only his master. In every town there was a large group of such craftsmen who did not have more than a single trainee or ap-prentice in their shop. In London in 1566, 13 out of 42 cloth finishers had a single assistant—apprentice or a journeyman—in their shop. And in Bristol in the first decade of the seventeenth century, more than half of the masters who hired apprentices took only one apprentice in the space of eight years. In some occupations this was even more pronounced. Among Bristol woodworkers—coopers, joiners, carpenters, turners, shipwrights and so on—who took ap-prentices in the years between 1532 and 1658, nearly two-thirds employed no more than a single apprentice in their entire career as masters in the town. In addition, not a few employed two apprentices, and they hired the second ap-prentice only after seven years, that is, after the previous one had left. Some of these carpenters and joiners probably died relatively young, and others possi-bly left Bristol after a few years of working there; but not a few among these many woodworkers had only one apprentice in their shop, and so the young-ster entered a small shop with only a single master, a stranger with whom he was to begin an intimate routine of hard work.

Some smoothing of the process of adjustment to a master and to the rou-tine of the shop could be obtained through a period of trial during which a youngster could evaluate the character of his master and what life as an ap-prentice entailed. Edward Coxere, an apprentice on a ship, Richard Davies, apprenticed in Welshpool in Wales, William Stout, apprenticed in Lancaster, and John Coggs, apprenticed to a London printer, all began their apprenticeship with a trial period—to be 'upon liking,' as some called it—of a few weeks. Some youths were able to withdraw from their contracts following a trial period, as the case of Adam Martindale, who returned home to his parents, suggests. But a period of trial was too short to reveal the full extent to which an apprentice could accommodate to his master and the new demands of assistance and work in the shop and the house; a proper alternative, especially for poorer apprentices, was not always available. There was something impractical about this procedure of a trial period, for when the apprenticeship had taken long to arrange, a youth could well find it hard to change his mind. This is clear in the case of Richard Oxinden, who, at the end of his trial period in London, decided to leave his master. Although Valentine Pettit, the kinsman who had arranged his apprenticeship, complied with his feelings and reasoning, and tried to look for another master, the whole process was not without difficulties. Although the apprenticeship was not as yet registered, part of the premium had already been paid to the master and the indentures had been signed, so there was the question of how to make sure the master would return the money. It is clear from Pettit's letter to the Oxinden parents that he and others were of the opinion that even if the master would let his apprentice depart, he would keep at least part of the money paid as a premium. Some time later, after young Oxinden had gone back to the country when he became ill, he decided to return to London. Another kinsman now informed his mother that he would try to persuade his old master to take him back, because to find a new master 'will cost a good summe of mony and a longe time of treatinge, both with his old master to gett in his Indentures and to settle him with the new'.

There were also formal ways to ensure reasonable behaviour of masters, by demanding that they signed on bonds of security. When Richard Risby, a Bristol shoemaker, took Robert White as an apprentice in 1616, he agreed 'that if he put away the boy within two years or cause him to run away through his default', then he would pay back the full £3 he had received as premium. John Davis, a tiler, also signed a bond of the value of £4: 'that if he shall put him away or misuse him whereby he shall run away' then he would repay the premium of £2; and Anthony Bazar, a metalworker, was bound to repay 40sh. 'if the boy departe through his master's default'. Similar bonds were signed by Richard Coulston, a wiredrawer, John Spratt, a haberdasher, Roger Stevens, a lighterman, John Allin, a weaver, Thomas Taylor, a pinmaker, and John Room, a mason. In other cases two bonds were signed: one for the apprentice's 'service and truth', and a counter-bond for the youth's safety and well-being. Still other masters promised, without signing a bond but putting it in writing along with the record of the apprenticeship, that if apprentices or their parents were dissatisfied, the contract would be annulled.

Whatever the safeguards, many youths found the adjustment to apprenticeship quite difficult, as the case of John Nutt, a Bristol cooper apprentice in the 1650s, shows. A year after his apprenticeship had been enrolled, his mistress, Ann Nutt, appeared in Quarter Sessions to ask for the release of her apprentice, because of his 'weakness of body'. Ann Nutt was a widow and probably related by kinship ties to John. There is no indication that she was unable to continue to employ the youth, for she was immediately allowed to take another apprentice for a period of trial; in fact she appears to have been diligent in teaching the youth her art, for the court also ordered that a bond of no less than £100 be signed, to ensure that John would not 'exercise the trade of a cooper'. This order also casts some doubt on the description of young Nutt as being weak and unable to work, for obviously the mistress, the apprentice and his parents, who appeared on his behalf, all agreed that there was a real possibility that he would soon begin to practise the trade of a cooper on his own. The youth also consented to depart from his mistress, even though the departure cost his parents a great deal of money in compensation to his mistress. What remains from the whole episode is that, as it was plainly put by the justices, 'he [the apprentice] having served the space of a year [is] praying that hee might bee released of his apprenticeship'.

Some youths reacted to their masters and the new circumstances they encountered quite violently. In April 1627 John Morgan, a migrant from Wales, was apprenticed to John Godman, a Bristol baker, and after several months the master complained at court that young Morgan had 'behaved himself in very insolent sort' and threatened him with a knife. Unlike other cases in which an unruly apprentice was sent to Bridewell, the court only discharged John Morgan, with his own consent. And Thomas Watkins, apprenticed in the early 1660s to Abraham Edward, a Bristol mercer, was said to have been 'very disorderly', to have assaulted and beaten his master and mistress, absented himself from work and committed several other misdemeanours. Again the court only discharged the apprentice, and it even ordered that he be compensated: the master had to return part of the premium (£10) paid to him before the apprenticeship had begun. The court also ordered that the master should take care of his apprentice and find someone else in his place. In both of these cases the court appears to have acknowledged, probably after some sort of investigation, that the fault was not only in the behaviour of youths like Morgan and Watkins, that John Godman and Abraham Edward and their apprentices were in some way incompatible, and that different masters might well prove more suitable and successful.

Other youths were less violent, but still failed to adjust to their apprenticeship, as is suggested by the appearance in Bristol's Register of Apprentices of many entries that have been crossed out. Most of these were apprenticeships which ended in some sort of informal agreement between the apprentice and his master rather than by an order of a court. For example, Thomas Brown, the son of a husbandman in Gloucestershire, was bound in Bristol with a house carpenter called Robert Price, in June 1615. Five months later, on 15 November, his indentures were cancelled, his record of apprenticeship in the apprentice register crossed out, and in the margin it was written that he was released with the consent of his master. Examples like these are scattered throughout the volumes of the Register of Apprentices. Between five and ten indentures were cancelled every year, and in a sample of apprenticeships in the period between 1600 and 1645, 5.1 per cent were crossed out, a proportion which fluctuated only slightly from year to year. In none of these cases was there any indication of a serious dispute—of the kind recorded in some detail in Quarter Sessions and other courts—which involved some sort of breach of the conditions of the contract on the part of the master or his apprentice. The more or less even distribution of these cases over time also suggests that these dismissals were not affected by conditions that might force masters to dismiss their apprentices, such as an economic depression. Occasionally the clerk recorded in the margin of the entry that the master or mistress had died, and this led to the annulment of the contract. But in most cases all the clerk wrote down was that the apprentice was 'released' or 'exonerated', and that this was done with the consent of his master, or with the consent of the apprentice and other parties involved. By far the largest number of these cases were crossed out within the first months or within two years following the beginning of the apprenticeship.

Getting on with a new, unfamiliar master, in what immediately became an intimate routine of hard, sometimes humiliating, labour and life, was not devoid of strain and tension. Some masters turned out to be exceptionally brutal, but many more were probably simply difficult, stubborn or hard to please. Still others had burdens and responsibilities of their own, and a few were quite young, not altogether experienced in handling apprentices not much younger than themselves. To all of this, an apprentice, a youth in his mid- or late teens and not infrequently with definite ideas about his apprenticeship, had to adjust. Some youngsters were frustrated in their expectations, like James Fretwell, who in the course of the first weeks of his apprenticeship found out that his master was 'not unkind', but he was still apprehensive about not being 'so thoroughly instructed in my business as I could wish,' as he put it later. And John Nashe, a young apprentice, obtained a bond of security from his master, a Bristol pinmaker, to repay 'if his boy goe away through [the master's] default'. John's father, Thomas Nashe, was himself a Bristol pinmaker who was probably acquainted with the future master of his son; but this did not prevent them both from agreeing to sign a bond in which they took it for granted that Thomas Tayler, the master, might fail to fulfil his obligations, and that young Nashe might become dissatisfied. In the case of the apprentice William Middleton, a Bristol native bound to a saddler, his master signed a bond promising to repay the premium in the course of the first three years of the apprenticeship if 'any complaint . . . or dislike . . . shall be between them'. Apprehension about the misunderstandings, complaints and dislike that might arise in the course of the early stage of an apprenticeship must have been prevalent, among young trainees no less than among those acting on their behalf.

There was also the mistress of the house. In some towns, such as in Bristol, the wife was an equal party to the contract and her name was entered along with that of her husband in the Register of Apprentices. Even in places where this was not the custom, a mistress would have been in charge of the apprentice as soon as he entered the household. Some autobiographies convey a sense of strain, if not outright animosity, between male apprentices and their mistresses. Richard Oxinden and his fellow apprentices attributed everything that went wrong with their master to his new wife. 'Hee always telld mee that hee liked his master well,' his kinsman wrote in a letter to his parents, 'but his Mistris was somthinge a strange kynde of wooman.' His kinsman also thought that 'moste of London mistrisses ar strange kynde of woomen'. Edward Barlow also appears to have had greater difficulties with his mistresses than with his masters. When he first came to London he was a servant in the house of his uncle and aunt. While he had little to say about his uncle's character in his autobiography, he recalled that he was displeased with his aunt, for she 'was a woman very hard to please and very mistrustful'. Later on he became apprenticed on a ship, and his recollections also convey the differences between his relations with his master and those with the mistress, with whom he lived in between voyages to the sea. From the start, his master appeared to him a 'very loving and honest person', and so he remained 'for the most part'. His relations with his mistress, by contrast, were more sour. They scolded each other, had many disputes and 'fallings out' whenever he came back on shore and was required to do household tasks. These accounts remind us that there was someone else besides the master to whom the apprentice had to adjust, and that the relationship with new mistresses could be tenuous. If the master himself was a stranger to the new apprentice, the mistress was not only that, but also a woman, sometimes not much older than the apprentice himself.

Some accounts also suggest that it was not simply the mistress but the strain in the relationship between the master and his wife which aggravated the situation. William Lilly remembered that when he began his service in London his life was 'more uncomfortable, it being very difficult to please two such opposite natures' as those of his master and mistress. Simon Forman, who had been apprenticed in the late 1560s in Salisbury, recalled many controversies he had with his mistress, who often turned to his master and incited him to 'beat Simon for it'. But Simon was of the opinion that the master did this 'against his will', and that he 'knew his wife to be a wicked, headstrong, and proud fantastical woman, a consumer and spender of his wealth'. In fact most of the controversies in the house were between the master and his wife; 'oftentimes they two were also at square—insomuch that twice he had like to have killed her by casting a pair of tailor's shears at her'. Forman's account suggests not only that he was exposed to the strain in the relationship, but that he somehow became part of it, for often he and his master used to walk outside the shop and complain to one another about her, and his master would say to him, 'Simon, thou must suffer as well as I myself. Thou seest we cannot remedy it as yet; but God will send a remedy one day.'

Some apprentices failed to adjust to their masters and so they left, but most others persevered, hoping for a remedy for whatever it was that continued to cause them unease or dissatisfaction. Some adjusted with greater ease than others, and became satisfied with their masters and their new home. Some were quite fortunate in finding exceptionally suitable masters to whom they took an immediate liking. Strange and unfamiliar as most masters were, some did show genuine kindness to their apprentices from the outset. We have already mentioned that the master of Edward Barlow commanded his trust from the moment he saw him. Barlow deposited whatever monies he had saved with his master, who turned out to be generous, even though he was a total stranger, an officer on a ship with some 500 men and youths, amongst whom young Barlow felt 'a stranger'.

Individual circumstances and fortunes apart, the adjustment to a new master and mistress was quite demanding, above all because a young apprentice was on his own in confronting his new circumstances. We have discussed the cases that were crossed out in Bristol's Register of Apprentices—some 5 per cent of all apprenticeships—which apparently ended in agreement between the master and his apprentice to part ways. Some time in the early 1620s these entries begin to include the marks or signatures of those involved in the decision to dissolve the contract and who were present when the record of apprenticeship was crossed out. Often there was the signature or mark of the master, the clerk or some other magistrate present, the father or someone else on behalf of the apprentice, the new master in case it was decided an apprentice would be bound again, as well as the apprentice himself. But often it is clear that the only people present were the master and his apprentice. In February 1622 Thomas Elliott was released with the consent of his master, a gunmaker to whom he had been bound only three months earlier. Elliott had come to Bristol from a village in Gloucestershire, and the record of his apprenticeship suggests that his father was still alive. Nevertheless, the only people who appeared when the apprenticeship was crossed out were the gunmaker and young Elliott; the master left his mark, and Thomas Elliott left his signature. In 1634 Edward Gill, apprenticed to a Bristol pewterer, was discharged; only the mark of the master and the signature of the apprentice appear in the margin.

Not all those who left their masters were completely on their own, . . . but the consequences of the poor adjustment of some youths to their masters and their apprenticeships may perhaps be captured from a case which appeared in Bristol's Quarter Sessions in 1672. From the description of the justices, we learn that Thomas Burgess was the apprentice of John Bryant, a Bristol pinmaker, and that he departed from his service several times without his master's permission. It is uncertain what led to Burgess's decision to leave; there is no mention of exceptionally harsh treatment, and it is clear that the master wanted his apprentice to come back, for he 'had made enquiry after him [and] could not hear any news of him'. The case also indicates that the magistrates, having heard the complaint of the master, made some enquiries regarding his whereabouts and notified the mother about her son. Thomas's mother was aware of the previous times when her son had run away, but she 'did confess . . . that she did not then know what was become of him'. Young Thomas

Burgess, who took 'all his clothes' when he left his master, probably with the intention never to return, was quite evidently on his own. . . .

MASTERS

There is some difficulty in capturing the nature of the norms governing the support and assistance of masters to their servants and apprentices, for there was some ambiguity in these norms. That ambiguity had to do with the fact that the interaction involved in any service or apprenticeship arrangement—whether made for a short or long period, in writing or not—was, in addition to being an interaction based on a contract, something akin to the special obligations associated with kin and even parents. The master provided his servant or apprentice with food, lodging, clothing, skills and small wages in return for labour, and sometimes for premium money he had paid. But given the intimacy in which the master and his servant worked and lived, and given the fact that servants were young, special commitments and obligations were attached to these ties as well. This lack of clear boundaries between the contractual and the moral aspects of the arrangement of service could lead to many expectations, but at the same time to frustrations and disappointments. And there were always those who failed to fulfil even their basic contractual obligations, because they were too harsh, incompetent, or simply too poor. So, implied in this arrangement was great scope for variation in types of interaction between masters and their servants, possibly more than the variation one could observe in interactions with kin, or in relationships between parents and their offspring.

Despite ambiguity and variation, there were several types of aid and benefit a youth could reasonably hope to obtain on entering a service contract—aids and benefits which were not made explicit in the terms of employment agreed upon in the contract, whether orally or in writing. The first and most distinct benefit was that an apprentice was guaranteed his basic needs for the whole term of the contract, including periods when his master had little or no work on his farm or shop. Agricultural servants were normally hired to do the least seasonal tasks (especially in animal husbandry); but in corn-growing areas the burden of work during the winter slackened and the wages of a farm servant had to be paid whether or not there was daily work to be done. In small shops and domestic industries, an apprentice was likewise guaranteed his basic needs for the whole term of his contract, including the periods when his master had little or no employment. . . . [S]ome craftsmen sent their apprentices out to work for wages when they could give them no employment themselves; others were forced to send their apprentices away when they became destitute or unemployed. But many more continued to support their servants and apprentices even in difficult circumstances. For example, Benjamin Bangs, whose master, a Norfolk shoemaker, was forced to migrate because of debts he was unable to repay, told him that 'if I would go along with him, he would take as much care of me as of himself', and so the master and his apprentice travelled and found temporary employment together in a nearby town. During periods of depression, bad harvests and other hardship some masters discharged their servants or apprentices, but most did not. For example, while a number of apprentices in Bristol were dismissed from service during the depression of 1622, there is no evidence that any massive firing of apprentices occurred.

Support could also be expected when an apprentice became ill or injured and was unable to work. Evidence from court records in towns like Norwich and Bristol makes abundantly clear that to send an apprentice away when he became ill was considered a violation of the norm. When apprentices were discharged because of illness, the master was legally required to cover the cost of maintaining the disabled youth. This requirement also included the costs of special medical treatment and medications. Lucinda McCray Beier has shown that among the patients treated by Joseph Binn, a seventeenth-century London surgeon, nearly a fifth were servants and apprentices, both male and female. Binn's treatments were quite expensive, but there is some reason to believe that the masters of these servants covered at least part of the costs. A case in Chancery, in which a London apprentice demanded that his master repay the costs of a rather luxurious treatment he took in the natural springs of Bath, suggests that masters were expected to pay the costs of whatever treatment the apprentice, or his parents or kin, felt was necessary.

Other types of assistance were also quite common, although they were more varied and flexible, and were likely to depend on the type of relationship between the master and his servant. These might include small gifts and benefits, casual wages and pocket money, and legacies. Bristol's merchants and traders left legacies to female servants, and to male apprentices and servants, occasionally naming as many as four, five or six servants in their wills. Among wealthier merchants these legacies could sometimes be quite large. In 1571 Alderman William Pepwall left his servant, Mary Roche, £20 towards 'the preferment of her marriage'. Some 10 per cent of kin mentioned in the wills of yeomen and traders in Essex and Wiltshire were servants.

Direct financial benefits and rewards were likely to be gained when a servant stayed with his or her master for a number of years, or when an apprentice remained the full length of his term of seven and more years. Edward Nelson, a Bristol sherman, promised to pay his apprentice 12d. a week 'for half a year service', after six years of his term; and Francis Eaton, a Bristol carpenter, promised to give his apprentice, a Bristol orphaned youth, 25 acres of land in New England, and 15 bushels of wheat, if he served him 'truly' the full term of seven years. In many crafts masters promised to give their apprentices £1, £2, and sometimes £3 at the end of their terms towards buying tools and material or stock to help them start a shop of their own. In Bristol, nearly half the apprentices registered between 1605 and 1609 were promised financial assistance and tools if they stayed the full length of their terms.

Youths who served long enough in the distributive trades could expect exceptional benefits. Bristol's apprentices who acted as their masters' factors, sometimes after three or four years, were given a commission of 2 per cent or more on transactions they handled overseas. Roger Lowe, apprenticed in a grocer's shop, also received commissions on commodities he bought on his own; and some Chancery cases show that merchant apprentices were not only promised that they would be taught the profession but that they would be employed as factors for the master and for 'others in that professon'. Others were allowed to trade on their own. John Prickman, apprenticed in 1601 to Ann Dyes, a Bristol grocer, was permitted to buy and sell his own stock 'to his own profitt and comoditie' in his last year of apprenticeship. Other contracts guaranteed youths special permission to trade on their own in the final year of their long terms of apprenticeship. Apprentices who had served their full terms could hope to be given a great deal of advice and special concessions by their masters: credit, raw materials, various moveable goods in the shop, and occasionally even the shop itself, as was the case with William Stout, who offered his apprentice the opportunity to buy his shop on good terms when the latter finished his term.

Some servants developed particularly strong attachments to their masters, establishing relationships based on emotional support, friendship and companionship. A few examples will serve to illustrate the quality of these bonds and the circumstances in which they could develop. Simon Forman's master had continuous rows with his wife, so he confided in Simon, and the two used to talk together and complain about her. Roger Lowe recorded in his diary that very early one morning, when his master was still in bed, they 'talked of every thing, [and] something about his [i.e. the master's] marige'. Benjamin Bangs, forced to join his master in his migration in search for work, remembered that when they finally arrived in London they 'dwelt together in the name of brothers'. Some masters became companions to their servants, not only in times of hardship, but when the two sought relaxation from work. Joseph Oxley described how his master took him as a 'companion' to places of 'diversion' where he 'learned to sing what they called a good song'. From court evidence it is also apparent that youths sometimes frequented ale-houses under the influence of a master who was inclined to spend a great deal of his time there rather than in his shop.

Some masters and servants referred to each other as 'friends', which implies that at a certain point their relationship had taken on the quality and obligations involved in ties of kin. Benjamin Bangs referred to his master as a 'brother', and John Smythe, a Bristol merchant, left in his will a dowry for an illegitimate daughter in London 'whom my friend Hugh Hammon[d] [his apprentice] do know'. References in wills to servants as 'friends' were not uncommon either. Youths often described their masters as 'friends', but the connotation was less of kin than of friendships based on voluntary support and reciprocity. Joseph Oxley remembered that he and his master parted 'good friends, continuing a correspondence as occasion required'; and Thomas Chubb also preserved with the family of his master, a glover in Salisbury, 'a particular friendship the remainder of his life'. These examples suggest that, when attachments were formed between masters and their servants, they were modelled on the interactions of brothers or friends rather than on those between a father and his son, and that they involved elements of parity and reciprocity rather than hierarchy, authority and control. Given that servants and apprentices were sometimes not much younger than their masters, such references are perhaps not altogether surprising.

Even when no companionship or special commitment between the master and his apprentice formed, and even when an apprentice served his master only a short while, casual assistance could still be hoped for. In the countryside, servants sometimes moved from one master to the next on the basis of information given by their old masters, or of connections formed through them. Apprentices could be given advice and information about lodging and shops to rent, regardless of whether they stayed their full terms. Even when an apprentice left before his contract came to an end and against his master's will, he could still hope to benefit from the master's connections, or obtain a letter of recommendation to assist him with another master. For example, John Woodhouse had obtained a letter of recommendation from his old master before he left and he became an apprentice with another.

It is true that, given the strong contractual element in any arrangement of service, and given that many masters themselves lived quite perilously, a degree of precariousness was built into all types of interaction between masters and their servants. There are examples of apprentices who were discharged not only when their masters were on the verge of total deprivation, but simply when they decided to improve their lot, or migrate elsewhere; and there were also servants and apprentices who were discharged during a depression. In the countryside, too, servants were sometimes turned away or denied treatment when they were ill. In general, servants and apprentices of small craftsmen and husbandmen were less likely to obtain legacies from their masters. In a collection of 103 wills approved by the Consistory Court of Bristol in the period 1546–93, in which the vast majority were those of widows, small craftsmen (farriers, wiredrawers, glovers, weavers, tanners, etc.), there was not a single reference to servants or apprentices. Even among wealthier merchants and craftsmen, the leaving of legacies to servants and apprentices was by no means a normal rule. In addition, the pressures created by a growing population, especially in the late sixteenth and the first half of the seventeenth centuries, reduced the opportunities for annual service; in the countryside many masters preferred to take labour on a seasonal or daily basis rather than for longer periods. In towns, too, such pressures could have an effect on the conditions of apprenticeship and the benefits youths were likely to obtain even if they served the full length of their terms.

Nevertheless, the assistance masters provided their servants was usually quite substantial, first and foremost because it included critical support; that is, support when an apprentice or servant was unemployed or unable to work. Although by comparison with the parental bond the support of masters was less predictable and much less durable, masters could still provide assistance in times of hardship and, especially in services which lasted a long time, they provided a wide range of valuable benefits and supports, both practical and non-practical.

THE PRIVATE LIFE OF AN EARLY MODERN TEENAGER

STEVEN OZMENT

Most of us have found ourselves from time to time in situations that both excite and distress us. Often these occasions involve activities or associations that threaten to betray the expectations others may have of us and perhaps we of ourselves. At the same time, however, we find ourselves caught up in an adventure or an indulgence in which we choose to engage. On such occasions, we simply give in to one set of emotions against another and allow one side of our nature, not necessarily the worst, to get the better of the other.

In the fourth quarter of the sixteenth century, the setting of this story, people went to great lengths to keep their private thoughts and behavior secret. In the fragile societies of early modern Europe, betrayals of public expectations unsettled neighbors and threatened public order and for these reasons, could bring a family shame and harm. When episodes of conflicted emotion are discovered in the distant past, they are almost always in written private communications intended to be kept under lock and key or, if shared with another, to be destroyed immediately upon reading. Such episodes also remain hidden from public view, however, because people then did not think it either true or fair to treat random acts of private behavior as embodiments of their entire lives. If one were not exactly what one appeared to be in public, neither was one entirely one's private life.

By the mid-fifteenth century, the private lives of growing numbers of European townspeople, both high and middling, began to be recorded in well-preserved diaries, house books, chronicles, and letters. These new family archives were made possible by rapidly expanding lay education and travel, the availability of cheap paper, and the desires of ordinary men and women to write the histories of their families and to be remembered themselves. Here we find the fullest expressions of that "self-fashioning" after which a generation of modern historians has hunted, but without having to go through the intellectual contrivances and question begging required when the sources consulted are impersonal and oblique.

The story that follows is about the ordinary experiences of an extraordinary young man, who was born to money and power but, sadly, not to good health and long life. His name is Sebald Welser (1557–1589), eldest son of Nuremberg patrician Sebastian Welser (1527–1559) and an equally prominent mother, Maria Haller (1534–1583), whose own father, Sebald Haller (1500–1578), was one of Nuremberg's chief financial officers and young Sebald's namesake and later guardian. Sebald's paternal uncles Hans (d. 1601) and Jakob (d. 1591) Welser ran the Nuremberg branch of the Augsburgbased Welser banking and mercantile empire. His father died prematurely at thirty-two, the age at which Sebald, too would later die. At his father's death, the boy was not much more than a year old and, in the words of his eulogist written many years later, was left without "a guide for his life, the protector and pride of his youth," as fathers then were kindly described.

The widowed mother soon married again (in 1561), and no less well than on her first try. The new stepfather, Julius Geuder (d. 1594), was a member of the city council's powerful executive body, the "Seven," and a high-ranking member of the board of governors at the nearby prestigious Altdorf Academy. Fortunately for the then toddling Sebald, the marriage was also his stepfather's first, and he embraced Sebald from the start as his very own son.

Between the ages of eight and seventeen, Sebald was educated in the best available schools, spending seven years at Nuremberg's church school of St. Aegridius (1565–1572) and two at the internationally famous humanistic gymnasium of Johann Sturm (1572–1574) in Strasbourg, which was already then becoming the model for the emerging Protestant world, both Lutheran and Calvinist. By his midteens, Sebald had chosen a career in law, the most fitting preparation for the position he would inherit in the family business and for a youth destined to govern. In Sebald's social circle, the study of the law was not only held in high regard but hallowed. At his funeral oration in 1589, his eulogist proclaimed of his profession: "The lawyers dispense justice and have knowledge of what is right and fair, and for this reason, they are the ones closest to God and to divinity . . . who deserve no less praise than those who proclaim God's word."

It was in the continuing pursuit of his legal education, already begun in Strasbourg, that Sebald, at seventeen, accompanied by a tutor, traveled to Venice and Padua in September 1574. His studies there were cut short, however, by his failing health, which forced him to return to Nuremberg in the spring of 1576 and convalesce in his parents' home. More than a year passed before he was able to resume his legal education, this time not in Padua but in the Belgian city of Louvain. On June 1, 1577, Sebald, now nineteen, set out for the university there. In his escort were his prominent stepfather, his two famous uncles, and two extremely well-to-do Nuremberg peers: Wolfgang Harstörffer (1560–1624) and Carl Imhof (1555–1619). The latter were childhood friends with whom Sebald had traveled before and who now became his classmates for a semester in Louvain.

Arriving in Louvain on June 17, Sebald devoted the next six months to his law books and the exploration of the region's then very exciting history and culture. Eight months before his arrival, the ten largely Catholic southern provinces had formed an unprecedented union with the seven largely Calvinist northern provinces to drive out the Spanish, who, since the 1560s, had attempted to render the Netherlands a politically docile and solidly Catholic part of the Habsburg empire. Five months before Sebald's arrival, the Spanish had agreed to withdraw their forces with dispatch and at the same time had recognized William of Orange (1533–1584), the Catholic turned Lutheran turned Calvinist ruler of the northern provinces, as the leader of the unified

Netherlands resistance. In addition to witnessing the political and military turmoil occurring in the great cities of the Netherlands at this time, Sebald, a Lutheran, also found himself in the midst of a lethal struggle between Catholic and Calvinist extremists for control of the religious life there.

We know about Sebald's semester in Louvain because of the survival of a diary he kept for that year. Typical of the age, it is actually an almanac of thirty-two pages created by the locally famous Nuremberg astronomer Johann Pretorius, to which, happily, one hundred eighty-four pages of writing paper were appended. On many of those pages, Sebald briefly entered, in chopped Latin and German sentences that are often mixed, his observations and thoughts for the day. With the exception of the month of December, his activities for the entire year are covered there, the first five months on scene in Nuremberg, the next six months (June through November) traveling and studying in the Netherlands.

While in Louvain, this young visitor from the first city of German Protestantism had frequent opportunity to observe the region's rich religious culture. To say that he was no bashful tourist in the Roman Catholic world of the Spanish Netherlands would be an understatement. He immersed himself in that world to a degree that startles the modern reader of his diary, particularly in light of his Lutheran beliefs. In mid-July, four weeks after their arrival in Louvain, Sebald and his companions traveled to Brussels to witness the famous procession of the Holy Sacrament. This grand spectacle dated from the fourteenth century (1369) and had originally commemorated the punishment of a Jew who had allegedly stolen and desecrated a host. Revived in 1529 after a plague miraculously disappeared from the city, the procession had become an annual event.

The celebration in 1577 was both a political and a religious statement. Brussels at this time was much contested, with union and Spanish forces alternately occupying the city, while its religious life seesawed back and forth between Catholic and Calvinist radicals. This year's procession indicated that the Spanish had the upper hand; when union forces controlled the city, as they would soon do again in September with William of Orange's triumphant return, the Calvinists made the most of their opportunity to display their confessional colors.

At the center of the procession was a golden monstrance containing three consecrated hosts. If Sebald and his friends followed the parade with mixed emotions at first, those emotions soon clarified, because before the procession had ended, Sebald behaved in a way that could not have been foreseen at the start: "I kissed the artifice [i.e., the monstrance]," he writes. The derogatory German term he uses to describe it, *gauckelwerk*, connotes drivel, twaddle, foolishness, trickery. That he uses that term suggests at least ambivalence on his part. It does not, however, explain so great a loss of self-discipline and seeming hypocrisy. A week later, startling the modern reader of his diary even more, he announces that he bought an indulgence at St. Michael's Church in Louvain.

How are these actions to be explained? Had Sebald been so emotionally unprepared for the spectacular forms of traditional piety he now witnessed that he simply fell under their spell? Was he perhaps a closet Catholic, compromised by his earlier visit to Italy? Or were these actions less the compulsive behavior of an innocent, and more the mockery of one who knew far better than he acted?

Sebald's religious devotion is the subject of constant commentary in the diary. At the beginning of the year, long before he departed for Louvain, he established for himself "an order of prayer and [Bible] reading," designed to take him systematically through the greater part of the Old Testament by year's end. He read in a circuitous, but steady fashion through the books of Daniel and Ecclesiasticus into Proverbs and Ecclesiastes, digressing briefly and without explanation into selected New Testament letters. On eighteen different occasions, he records his progress, most of which occurred during the six months he was in the Netherlands, often accompanied by occasional outbursts of relief ("happily finished!" "completed, thank God!"), as he reached the end of the more difficult, or less interesting, biblical books.

He also arrived in Louvain fully armored with Lutheran prayer books. At the beginning of the year, while still at home, he bought a copy of the Latin edition of the prayer book of Andreas Musculus (*Prayers from the Old Orthodox Doctors, the Hymns and Songs of the Church, and the Psalms of David* [1575; 2d ed., 1577]), to which two other devotional books were added by March. The diary is full of quotations and references to these prayers and is also peppered with invocations of divine aid, which Sebald makes as readily to accomplish a routine chore as to see himself through some great task. So frequent are such appeals that he resorts to abbreviations. Together with the Old Testament, the *Institutes* of Emperor Justinian was his priority reading for the year, the first book of which he set out to memorize "A.S.T." (*Auxilio Sanctae Trinitatis*: "with the aid of the Holy Trinity"). He looks forward to finishing the book of Tobias and beginning that of Judith "A.S.T." (*Annuente Sanctissima Trinitate*: "with the concurrence of the most Holy Trinity"). He hopes that his next posing for his portrait will be his last, "G.G.G." (*Gott geb Glück*: "if God grants good fortune"). On one occasion, he invokes God's help with a novel expression, pledging to memorize the second book of Justinian's *Institutes* (as he claims to have done with the first), *Deus Fax*: "if God sends the 'Fax,' [*Fax* = *Fackel* = torch]," if God provides the light.

The bona fides of Sebald's Lutheran devotion is further documented by his youthful philanthropy. Thanks to his paternal and grandpaternal inheritances (he received a whopping 26,329 gulden from his grandfather Sebastian Welser alone), he was a very rich man already in his early twenties. In 1581, he endowed both a library and a scholarship at his alma mater, St. Aegridius's, and his generosity also built an auditorium for the study of law and public policy at the Altdorf Academy, known then, as it still is today, as the "Welserianum." At the time of his donations, he described his gifts as both an obligation of Christian charity and the best way to keep the light of the Reformation burning, "because before all other people, the true, gracious God has caused the light of the Holy Gospel to shine pure and clear upon us Germans, for the preservation of which, nothing is more fitting than the building and maintenance of Christian schools."

Like many of his fellow Nurembergers, Sebald also had intimate Catholic associations. In his boyhood, he had been a regular visitor to the city's longest surviving Catholic cloister, St. Katherine's. That opportunity came about because for almost thirty years, from 1550 until his death in 1579, his maternal grandfather, Sebald Haller, supervised that cloister on behalf of the city council. With the triumph of the Reformation, new Protestant governments dissolved local cloisters and banned the religious life, turning the physical plants over to secular use or transforming them into public hospices or educational institutions with a still strong, but now distinctly Protestant, religious aura. In large cities like Nuremberg, with a rich Catholic heritage and prominent families with centuries-long attachments to the old faith, it was customary to keep at least one nunnery and one monastery open lifelong for those religious who either could not or would not be pensioned off with the majority of their peers and wanted to die in the religious life. St. Katherine's was such a cloister for the sisters of Nuremberg, with powerful patrons in the persons of the Catholic emperors Charles V and Maximilian II. Like the contemporary queens Mary Tudor and Mary, Queen of Scots, the Holy Roman Emperors looked on the surviving cloisters as footholds for the restoration of Catholicism in Protestant lands, and they pressured the city council of Nuremberg to protect St. Katherine's and to permit it to recruit new sisters. As a rule, Protestant cities did not allow the recruitment of new members into such cloisters, which ceased to exist as traditional religious institutions upon the death of their last surviving member, as happened with St. Katherine's in 1598.

During his visits to the cloister with his grandfather, Sebald became friends with the sisters there and enjoyed their company. On those occasions, he took his meals with them, once banqueting into Walpurgis night (the eve of May Day). Before going to Louvain, he donated some of the legal skills he had acquired in Padua to the cloister by twice balancing their books. While in Louvain, he twice wrote to "the worthy women of St. Katherine's," as he describes them, and on one of those occasions, he sent the prioress a sketch of a great fish, "fifty-two shoes long, forty-three around," caught off Antwerp in July.

Sebald's most explicit comments on his own spiritual life occur when he confronts traditional religious practices that are not his own. Prior to his departure for the Netherlands, he witnessed the annual Annunciation festival in the neighboring village of Dormitz, a spectacle he derides in his diary as "a few foolish people bringing offerings to St. Mary." He reacted in a similar fashion when he encountered the new, aggressive Counter-Reformation piety on the streets of Mainz while en route to Louvain. After observing the open air performances put on there by the Jesuits, he wrote in his diary: "On the streets of the city, the Jesuits performed their deceit with the Eucharist and showbread in monstrances."

Notwithstanding such confessional sentiments, which never disappear from the diary, the deeper Sebald penetrated into Catholic Germany and the Catholic Netherlands as he traveled north to Louvain, the more ambivalent his attitude toward the old religious culture became. Amazement displaced criticism as he beheld the visible feast of medieval Catholic art and architecture and witnessed the great festivals of the old Church. He was not totally unprepared for the sights he now saw, for even reformed Nuremberg had splendid churches and religious processions, and he had also visited Venice and Padua. But unlike the rituals and institutions he had grown up with, those he now beheld were not treated by the population as mere memorials or monuments to the past. They rather embodied the sacred in the present life, and spectacularly so—a palpable, sensual divine presence against which a teenager, even one from the first city of the Lutheran world, had few sophisticated defenses.

In Cologne, another stop along the way to Louvain, Sebald beheld the elaborately ornamented shrine of the three kings of the Orient who had visited Jesus at his birth, glimpsing their relics, with difficulty, through a narrow grate—a composition whose very awkwardness in viewing, probably by design, must have enhanced the mystery of the subjects. During a tour of Cologne's Rathaus, Sebald credulously imbibed the ancient story, preserved in white stone, of some angry priests who had tried to kill the city's burgomaster by locking him in a room with a starved lion—an attempt that backfired when the suspecting burgomaster killed the lion with a knife he had concealed on his person and escaped to accuse the priests and see them hung. Sebald describes the tower across from a church where the murderous priests were executed. Then, in the Dominican cloister, he viewed the glassed-in remains of Albertus Magnus, the famed teacher of St. Thomas Aquinas, whose head nestled on a silk and gold-gilded pillow, a haunting presence of the brain trust of medieval Catholicism.

Stopping next in Aachen, Sebald beheld for the first time some of Germany's most famous relics, among them, the sword of Charlemagne, a piece of Christ's cross, the blood of St. Stephen, and the remains of numerous martyrs. The longest and most detailed entry in the diary during the journey to Louvain describes in stunned admiration the beauty and craftsmanship of the Celestinian cloister at Heuren.

It was not only the young man's eyes that were being captivated. He also debated religious subjects that had not preoccupied his mind before. He argued with Carl Imhof over whether the Dominicans wore only white in choir—a matter weighty enough for the two of them to wager a bottle of wine on the outcome. Carl harbored Catholic beliefs and would later be arrested in Nuremberg with other citizens for covertly attending masses held in the city's continuing cloisters strictly for the religious within. On another occasion, Sebald spent an evening discussing the imperial relics stored in Nuremberg, particularly one known as the "lance of the Lord," a spear dating back to Charlemagne and allegedly containing a nail from the cross of Christ.

Some of the subjects that preoccupied the boys late into the evening appear bizarre and even contrived. One night, when the subject of debate was God's love of humankind, Sebald posed the question of whether the human race could continue if either all the men or all the women in the world were killed. He concluded that the extermination of men would have no effect, since there would always be pregnant women able to continue the species. Apparently, he did believe that the absence of womankind would end the human race.

The success of the Reformation and the ongoing Protestant-Catholic conflict in the Netherlands also posed topics for debate. One hot question was whether children who die unbaptized go straight to hell. Belief that they did had earlier moved the Church to console concerned parents by permitting midwives to baptize premature and nonviable infants immediately upon birth, which in difficult deliveries might occur as soon as the head or a limb of the child could be reached within the birth canal. Protestant stress on original sin and salvation by faith alone had revived this ancient issue. The Reformation also made the propriety of closing cloisters a topic for debate among the boys.

For the international body of students in Louvain, these were not academic questions but personal and "national" ones as well. Their discussion kept students at table late into the night and could occasion a brawl. Once, when debating why Sunday rather than the Sabbath was a Christian holy day, Sebald found himself confronted by an angry student from Westphalia, who interpreted the Bible literally. "I had my Bible on the table," Sebald writes, "and [he] was completely enraged." Another argument that invited mayhem was the question of whether anyone had ever seen God the Father. Contrary to everyone else, the same Westphalian youth insisted that Moses had done so, because it was written in the Bible that Moses spoke to God face to face. Despite his biblical literalism and extremely short temper, this Westphalian lad must have had a kinder and gentler side, because Sebald also reports that he learned how to knit from him.

Sebald understood well both the destructive and the edifying power of religious emotion. Six months earlier, while still in Nuremberg, he had visited an aging and badly injured assistant of his grandfather, a man depressed by religious worry, who four days before the visit had tried to jump to his death. Although obsession with religion was not a new experience for Sebald, he appears not to have encountered it before in quite the alternating grandeur, pettiness, and danger with which it now surrounded him in Louvain and Brussels.

His fascination with the Catholic culture of the Netherlands did not, however, prevent him from expressing his misgivings about it while there. Privately, he continued his Lutheran devotions, especially on the anniversaries of important days in his life. He commemorated his first visit to his beloved physician, Dr. Melchior Ayrer, for example, by reading a Christocentric prayer from the collection of Musculus. On his twentieth birthday (September 11), he spent the entire day immersed in that same prayer book, recording in his diary the first lines of each prayer he said, and he then repeated those same prayers twice in the following week. He also prayed for the Protestants he met. Learning over breakfast one morning that two of the duchess of Aerschot's daughters were Protestant, he expressed to one of her ladies-in-waiting his wish that

God might give them the strength to remain such. And whereas in Nuremberg, he mentions the days he took the sacrament with his friends and attended Easter service in his finest clothes, at the end of his first week in Louvain, he and his companions skipped church and feasted the morning away at the inn where they lodged.

How could so apparently devout a Lutheran surrender himself seemingly so completely to a religious culture he did not share and on occasion even scorned? One possible explanation is suggested by his reaction to the discovery that a strongly worded oath of allegiance to the Roman Catholic Church was required of all matriculating students at the university. The oath was actually an enhanced version of a more perfunctory one normally required of entering students. However, in the new religious climate, with Dutch Calvinism triumphantly on the march, university authorities, who were deeply Catholic and loyal to the king of Spain, deemed that milder version insufficient. The new oath required each student to "deny [Martin] Luther and all other heretics," and swear allegiance to the Catholic church "under the absolute authority of the pope in Rome."

The requirement did not please Sebald, who complained about it to his stepfather and grandfather. In response, his stepfather and uncle contacted the Welsers' Antwerp agent (Daniel Rindfleisch), who had been entrusted with Sebald's financial and official affairs while he was in the Netherlands. Despite learning from him that the oath could not be avoided, the senior Welsers nonetheless sought legal counsel in Louvain in a futile attempt to find a way for Sebald to skirt it—an indication of the seriousness with which the family looked on an oath of allegiance to the pope. Unlike numerous other German students who refused to take it and returned home, Sebald by all accounts complied, and apparently without any amelioration of the conditions. Two years later, he would take a similar, well-documented oath as a student at the papal university of Bologna.

In the sixteenth century, it was not unusual for German merchants and students abroad to defer to foreign religious practice in the interest of their businesses and programs of study. And host governments, too, insisted that foreign visitors respect local customs for the safety of all. Neither merchants nor students liked to be harassed by foreign governments in such personal matters and protested when the pressure became extreme. But short of such coercion; public compliance with the host community's practices did not seem either unreasonable or hypocritical, and Protestants in Catholic lands, as Catholics in Protestant lands, could console themselves privately with the knowledge that in the fortresses of their hearts and consciences, they remained immune from the sacrileges they were obliged to observe in public.

Although Sebald was not the only Nuremberger to take the oath in 1577, such pragmatism may have been more incumbent upon a young Welser than upon other youths, for Sebald represented a trans-European financial empire, in whose debt even the reigning king of Spain then stood. So loyalty to his family, a body to which he was no less beholden for his life and well-being than to his church may conceivably have dictated his compliance.

When, however, Sebald kissed the monstrance in Brussels and bought an indulgence in Louvain, he was not simply acting expediently. There was no expectation or coercion either from peers or Catholic authorities requiring him to do either. Nor were these the acts of an enthusiastic tourist in search of a good story or souvenir to impress friends with upon his return home. Sebald appears on these two occasions to have been carried away by irresistible new experiences—and such experiences were occurring not only in the spiritual realm. His religious behavior in Louvain and Brussels is of one piece with his pursuit of new intellectual and political interests at the same time. He read with genuine interest the writings of a Catholic moralist, and when he visited Antwerp, he joined with citizens there to demolish a citadel the Spanish had used to besiege the city, boasting of having thrown "three shovels full" of rubble down the hill, while keeping a stone from the pile as a relic of his participation. The episode so absorbed his interest that he sent a charcoal sketch of it to a friend, replete with the toppling of a statue of the Duke of Alva that had stood at the top.

In such behavior, we witness the eruption of emotions that are larger than religion, and that thus seek an outlet in other actions as well. It is telling that Sebald was just as fascinated by the region's contemporary politics as he was by its old religious culture. He is as much in awe of the men who led the resistance to the Spanish occupation as he is of the saints and martyrs he has seen. Here, too, he readily plays the "idolater." In Brussels, he twice visited the homes of the count of Egmont (d. 1568) and Ernst von Mansfeld (d. 1604). On the second visit, he points out that ball was being played in front of Egmont's house, apparently thinking it disrespectful of the man, who had been publicly executed nine years earlier during the duke of Alva's reign of terror in the southern provinces.

During their second visit to Brussels, Sebald and his companions caught sight of William, Prince of Orange, as the great leader of the resistance rode past the inn where they lodged. The next morning, the boys followed him as he entered the city council. When he left an hour later, at noon, Sebald followed after him again and quietly watched from a distance as he entered a tavern and ate lunch. Smitten, he writes of his brief contact with "this completely good prince, one worthy of every praise," and a week after the sighting, he composed an essay praising William's promotion to commander-and-chief of all Netherlands' forces.

Contemporary political symbols and debates captivated Sebald almost as much as the living heroes of the conflict. He sent his grandfather running accounts of the major events, along with the latest political relics, such as copies of the capitulation articles presented to the resistance leaders by the famous Austrian Don John, victor over the Turks at Lepanto six years earlier (1571) but now the unhappy commander of the humiliated and retreating Spanish army of occupation. Although he mentions them less often, Sebald also joined in civic debates as readily as he did in those over religion, citing, for example, one on whether a citizen who had been coerced against his will by the state could continue to be a citizen of that state.

Sebald lived in an age of conflicted emotions not only in regard to religion and politics but also in the more elemental sphere of youthful sexuality, which also holds a clue to his behavior in the Netherlands. No group in the sixteenth century experienced sexual feelings with more ambivalence than youth in their late teens and early twenties, and not just because of their blossoming sexuality. By virtue of their own experience, city governments were pessimistic about the moral strength of their citizens and kept them under close surveillance. Local churches and schools assisted in these efforts by attempting to instill a strict ethic of self-denial in new generations.

In molding young consciences, the moralists of the age attacked the actual temptations to which the young were then most immediately prey, the ever-threatening three horsemen of adolescence: sex, alcohol, and the theater. Such badgering did not necessarily demoralize the young, even though the clergy went to great lengths to persuade twelve- to fourteen-year-olds of their dormant bestiality and subsequent need for constant vigilance and self-restraint. Beset by the adult world's well-intentioned pleading and constant scrutiny of their lives, Sebald's generation grew up in heightened awareness of the tension between their public and their private selves. Their well-drilled consciences commanded self-denial, while their innermost desires begged them to let go.

Sebald was no stranger to moral temptation. While still in Nuremberg, he declined two invitations to "spinning bees" (also known as spinning parties, spinning rooms, and maidens' courts (*Spinnstuben, Jungfrauenhöfe*). These were informal gatherings, in both private homes and public places, of unmarried youth of similar age and social standing—the sixteenth-century equivalent of "hanging out" and "partying." They provided single men and women the opportunity to meet privately in the evening and pass the time together in the apparently wholesome atmosphere of a woman's sewing circle. Concerned parents and suspicious officials knew that such gatherings were also "[occasions] for the unfolding of sexuality, sensuality, and emotionally anchored outside the family," and feared them as potential "sowing" circles. In 1572, the Nuremberg city council forbade them on moral grounds.

Sebald's first-mentioned invitation to such a gathering came from a male friend, evidently designated to round up an appropriate male cohort. Sebald says the invitation was "declined on his behalf," because the person extending it "had a meeting with girls [in mind]." The next day, he received a second invitation to another such party, which he personally declined. That the first invitation was declined for him by an unidentified third party suggests that an alert adult authority may have thwarted Sebald's own plans to go. The question is a fair one, because six weeks later he did attend a spinning bee with his friend Carl Imhof and stayed until midnight. And on two other occasions, Sebald attended dances with a similar ambivalence about joining in. At one, a wedding party, he says he did not dance at all, while at the other, he claims to have danced until midnight.

Despite the impression left by the excesses of a Rabelais or a Bosch, it was not characteristic of Sebald's contemporaries to talk publicly about sexual matters. Even when spouses and secret lovers discussed sexual desire, pregnancy, and infidelity in private correspondence, they did so, as a rule, with oblique language, deferring to contemporary norms of propriety and good taste. Fear also encouraged such restraint, for there was always the danger that a messenger might open a letter and read it, or that a letter might fall into the wrong hands at its destination, or that the intended recipient might carelessly leave a letter lying about for others to read, thereby permitting intimacies to become grist for the rumor mills.

Although the entries are extremely rare and not profound, Sebald does talk about sexual matters and can even joke about them in a fashion. He reports, for example, the burning of holes in the facial cheeks of "five sluts" who had continued to solicit customers on the streets of Neuenwald after the closing of the public house there. In a lighter vein, he mentions a playful agreement between himself and another Nuremberg friend in Louvain (Sigmund Oertel), as they promised to give each other appropriate gifts on their wedding days—Sebald pledging the customary seven pounds of silver, but computed at thirty pfennig a pound (not a great sum), his friend promising him a woman's undergarment and a bridal crown.

Such information as is provided in the diary does not permit any conclusions to be drawn about Sebald's own sexual feelings or conflicts. It does, however, suggest the lengths to which the adult world was then prepared to go to impress upon his generation the difference between private and public behavior and the importance of appearances at all times. The diary does a better job of documenting Sebald's losing battle with drink, a major health and social problem at the time for young and old alike. Sebald and his companions knew that too much liquor, like too much religion, could kill. He remembered the ignominious death of a debauched man, who was found one day at noon behind a table in a Nuremberg tavern, where he had collapsed unnoticed, dead on the spot. "Here pertain the words of St. Paul, the words of Wisdom, and divine punishment," Sebald observes.

If there was an eternal lesson in this sad story, Sebald was not yet ready to learn it. He reports numerous occasions on which he and his companions drank to excess, suggesting that sobriety was the first to retire from their table as the evening progressed. He remembers the night in August when his French teacher got completely drunk and demanded a vacation. On another late night, in September, after much wine had been consumed, he bet his companions that they could not walk upright into the great tower that dominated Louvain's fortified walls—an error in judgment that cost him two additional rounds. A week later, the fencing master, whom one might have expected to be a steadying influence, joined a few of them at dinner, and the boys again drank "uncommonly well." Then, there was the evening they "drank heartily" with Master Hans, the shoemaker, in the course of which they relieved him of his knife, evidently for the safety of all. On three occasions, Sebald confesses to having gotten "completely" or "extraordinarily" drunk, on one of them (a visit to Heuren) becoming so intoxicated that he could not remember the next day what he had done the previous night.

The final great temptation of Sebald's youth was one to which he succumbed without any hesitation or conflict, and even proudly. Here, again, he was at odds with the clergy and magistrates of his youth, for whom theatrical productions were a morally gray area at best. In January 1577, Nuremberg's city council ordered the play masters at St. Martha's Pilgrim-Hospice Church, whose performances Sebald frequently attended, to seek official approval before performing any more plays in the future—this in reaction to their alleged staging of "shameless and undisciplined epilogues." Unlike sex and alcohol, Sebald deemed the theater to be a pure pleasure, one to which he gave himself completely and in good conscience, attending in February and March, among others, a play by Terence (*Adelphoi*), a biblical drama (*Ahab and Jezebel*), an unnamed comedy, and three pieces by Nuremberg's famous poet and playwright Hans Sachs, on the staging of one of which Sebald himself apparently worked. . . .

On first hearing a story about a devout Lutheran youth who kisses a monstrance and buys an indulgence, a modern reader might be inclined to conclude that the Protestant Reformation was something of a spiritual failure. Any who would draw such a conclusion will find himself in the company of a great many historians today. For despite the Reformation's obvious and enduring success in rewriting the laws governing traditional Christian practice and in restructuring the institutions that housed it, there exists today a near scholarly consensus that the Reformation had little effect on most ordinary folk, who vastly preferred tradition and folklore to Luther's new gospel. If young Sebald's example is now to be taken as a test of its success, it would appear that the Reformation did not have much effect on extraordinary people either.

There are two large lessons to be drawn from Sebald's story, each of which is a truism, yet in the present cultural climate, each must be pointed out and argued. The first is that consistency is not the watchword of the emotions and the inner life. Always embattled, the inner life was never more so than in the sixteenth century. At that time, the weapon of choice for besieged hearts and minds was religious faith, and not just any religious faith but one capable of numerous spiritual maneuvers, able not only to attack, dig in, and retreat but also to innovate, live off the land, and rig new defenses from spent or discarded materials. The seeming irrationality of that faith was actually a way of seeing and knowing in situations where one literally could not see and know: thus a sense of direction when one was mystified or threatened, a leap out of indecision when one's present situation clearly could not be survived.

In late medieval and early modern Europe, reliance on religious faith was commonplace and ordinary, something foundational and constant, not exceptional or instrumental. It was always prominently there: in, with, around, and under all of one's individual and social experience. Hence Sebald's seemingly confused behavior: the prayers of Musculus on his lips at night in the privacy of his room, his lips on a monstrance at the procession of the Holy Eucharist in Brussels; three Lutheran prayer books at the ready on his bed stand, yet an indulgence in hand when he shopped the streets of Louvain—the fog of faith, a path to health, the resolution of passive suffering.

In Sebald's case, the seeming contradictions between his professed belief and his actual behavior need not necessarily mean that the one was false or the other disingenuous. Core beliefs are the bedrock to which both reckless and principled behavior return, and they are arguably as fixed as behavior is fickle. Sebald was no less a Lutheran for having kissed a monstrance and obtained an indulgence, nor did the fact that these acts logically contradicted his Lutheran faith render them either unpleasant or useless to him at the time. . . .

When dealing with human emotions, hard and fast rules are likely to disappoint and possibly tyrannize. That is because the inner life is prey to the forces of circumstance and the power of the moment. Any canonical belief or principle that would sit in judgment here had best be flexible and forgiving, prepared to base reward and punishment not on consistent behavior but on an honest recognition of the likelihood of capricious behavior. Here the formula cannot be an eye for an eye or a tooth for a tooth, or an offer of heaven in exchange for a lifetime of good works. It must rather be an open door for anyone willing to respond in good faith. . . .

The second lesson to be drawn from Sebald's story is less obvious, but may be the larger explanation of his behavior in Louvain: the most formative experiences in a person's life are familial. We are primarily the creatures of the small families into which we are born and within whose circles we do most of our growing up. That young Sebald could derive strength and meaning from the religious culture of the Netherlands, and immerse himself freely and easily in the society and politics surrounding it, is not explained solely by the fluidity of contemporary religious belief. His actions were deeply informed by the habits and values inculcated in youth at this time in both Catholic and Protestant homes.

The one thing Philippe Ariès admired in the traditional family and bemoaned the loss of in its modern counterpart was the ease with which the former could live beyond the household and lead a public life. The erection of barriers between private and public life, he believed, had been the terrible price paid for the creation of the child-centered, sentimental family of modern times. As the last two decades of historical research on the family have demonstrated, however, Ariès and his many followers failed to appreciate the degree to which the traditional family was both a private and a public institution: on the one hand, an intimate, tightly knit, parent-child unit, on the other, a porous household open to and comfortable with society at large. The traditional family sought safety and success for its members not by retreating behind closed doors but by diffusing itself as widely as possible into the world outside. It did this most strikingly by placing its children, between roughly the ages of ten and fifteen (not seven, as Ariès imagined), in the homes, shops, and schools of others to be educated for life. Initially, this was done locally, within the hometown, and later beyond its walls and in foreign lands, where the young continued an education and socialization begun in the home, as they prepared themselves vocationally and culturally for a life independent of their parents.

Before Sebald arrived in Louvain, he had already studied for two years in Strasbourg and a little over a year in Padua. Even then, he departed home for the first time at a later age (fifteen) than other youth in Nuremberg, a circumstance for which Nuremberg's excellent primary schools may be blamed. Both in and out of his peer group, others began foreign apprenticeships as early as twelve and university study at fourteen. In contemporary England, rural youth as a rule did not live and work away from home until thirteen, while their urban counterparts began apprenticeships at fourteen and university study at sixteen. An appreciable number of urban youths, however, "boarded out" for periods up to several years before departing home for apprenticeships or schooling elsewhere.

Living in new households with new masters and often far away from home, the young learned by their midteens that theirs was a world of many languages and cultures, in which solitary lives and exclusive behavior were both rare and frowned upon. This experience hastened their maturity and independence and endowed them with an indelible public self. The formation of the latter actually began in earnest in the parental home, whose lessons were not replaced or overridden by life-cycle service, apprenticeship, and boarding school but were complemented, extended, and completed there.

Away from home, a youth's first duty was to accommodate: to adapt to a new household, socialize with new peers and superiors, learn new customs and languages, and acquire new skills. These adjustments did not come easily, and the complaints are frequent. For while apprentices and students might have contractual guarantees of fair treatment and expert vocational training from their masters, there was never any expectation that the host household and culture would or should accommodate the beliefs and customs of visiting youth. The visitors, after all, were not there to enlighten, much less to challenge, the natives but to learn everything they could from and about them.

A good part of the rationale behind such studied docility was its prophylactic and disciplinary qualities; in a foreign land, the accommodating child was a safer and more successful child, more likely to learn the necessary skills, make important contacts, even gain admiring friends. There were also intrinsic reasons for accommodating the religion of the host household and culture. By attending generically Christian services, the Protestant child exercised his faith and kept his own religious devotion strong, thereby growing in favor with both men and God. But not to be lost amid its protective, career-advancing, and devotional benefits, the ability of early modern youth to live, work, and study abroad in foreign lands and cultures was the fullest expression of the extroverted and gregarious traditional family, which from the start conscientiously reared its children to live comfortably and independently beyond the doors of their houses and the gates of their cities.

WOMEN AND WORK

NATALIE ZEMON DAVIS

In the premodern domestic economy, women played an important part in providing for their families. Although the care of young children often kept women close to home, the scope of their activities was not restricted to the hearth. Most women devoted their energies to contributing to the domestic economy. The fact that production often took place in and around the home meant that women could combine child raising and productive activities.

In the countryside, the peasant woman tended the livestock, grew vegetables and fruits to supplement her family's simple diet of bread, and preserved milk by making it into cheese and butter. She gathered wool from the family's few head of sheep, spun it into thread and made her family's clothing. During times of peak demand for agricultural labor, such as the harvest, she worked alongside the men in the fields. Additionally, once the needs of her family were satisfied, she would increase its cash reserves by selling fruit, vegetables, eggs, chickens, butter, cheese, and thread at the local market. The importance of women's contribution to the peasant family is witnessed by the speed with which men remarried when their wives died. In the city, women also participated in their husband's work. As widows, they often continued to practice their husband's trade.

Daughters also contributed to the domestic economy. They learned how to spin and sew from their mothers, and daughters of craftsmen usually received an informal apprenticeship at the side of their fathers. The young woman who was trained in a craft could be an important asset to a prospective husband, although women frequently married men who practiced trades different than the one in which they were trained. These women then had to learn the trade of their husbands. However, not all wives contributed to their family's support by sharing in their husband's work. For example, the wife of a craftsman or a merchant might spend her days in the

---

From: Natalie Zemon Davis, "Women in the Crafts in Sixteenth-Century Lyon," *Feminist Studies,* Vol. 8, (1982): 49, 53–72.

market selling food or spices, or she might be engaged in a craft of her own, as mistress in one of the crafts thought to belong to the feminine domain, such as the manufacture of wimples or lace. In such a case, it is likely that she would employ a few female apprentices. Some women pursued occupations that were different from, but complementary to, their husband's interests. In the countryside, the wives of some prosperous peasants became ale-wives, brewing the family's excess grain into ale and selling it to fellow villagers. In the city of Cologne, the wives of some international merchants made silk, which their husbands then sold at distant markets.

During the fifteenth and sixteenth centuries, women's place in the work force seems to have suffered a downturn. The fifteenth century was a period of economic decline, and the number of craftsmen a city could sustain fell. Guilds tried to ensure that their members could earn a decent living by restricting the number of masters they admitted. Guilds also began to exclude women from membership and from participating in their husbands' and fathers' work and chipped away at widows' rights to continue their husbands' trade. At first glance, there seems to be little doubt that the guilds were sacrificing women's economic well-being in an effort to protect the economic well-being of the men who were their members. However, the exclusion of women also was linked to the changing functions of guilds and the changing political landscape of premodern cities. Guilds began to take on political functions, and often guild membership became a criterion for holding political office. Women had always been excluded from the exercise of political power in premodern European cities, and the growing political role of the guilds consequently made female membership increasingly inappropriate. Thus part of the erosion of women's status in the work place may have been the indirect result of the changing function of the guilds.

What was the status of women's work in the fifteenth and sixteenth centuries, and how did it differ from men's work? In this section, Natalie Zemon Davis describes the work that women did and the place it held in sixteenth-century Lyon.

Women's production in the crafts was of two kinds: that which they did as unpaid helpers to a father, a husband, or a son; and that which they did for wages or fees paid directly to themselves. In both cases, their strictly occupational identity was thinner than that of the men in their milieu, the women's energies available to be shifted into other work channels if the situation demanded it. (By the widely held humoral theory of sexual temperament, men were hot and dry, and therefore firm and stable, while women were cold and wet, and therefore changeable and slippery. Our artisan women have some cold and wet characteristics.) Much of the time, female work was seen as a necessary complement to male work; but on occasion, it could be perceived as dangerous, if not to the woman's own kin, then at least to the established masters in a threatened trade. I will try to see what, if any, consciousness women developed of themselves as actors under these conditions. . . .

When a young woman of the *menu peuple* changed her status from "the daughter of so-and-so" to "the wife of so-and-so," she ordinarily left the household of her family, or the family she had served, to move into rooms or part of a house with her husband. Other arrangements were possible, of course: Odette de Luire, daughter of a whitewasher, married the printer's journeyman, Jean de Tournes, and they lived in the house of Odette's widowed mother. Years later in 1545, their daughter Nicole married Guillaume Gazeau, and the newlyweds stayed on in the same house, where Jean, then a proud master (and considered today one of France's finest printers), printed with his son-in-law. Only in 1551 did Jean move into an establishment of his own on the nearby rue Raisin, leaving Nicole mistress of the house that once belonged to her maternal grandmother.

Although the varieties of work that the wife did in her new household—childbearing, marketing, cooking, washing, and helping her husband—were not paid, the notion that they could be assigned a rough cash value was not wholly foreign to the cultural assumptions of the *menu peuple* in the sixteenth century. Husbands making large testamentary bequests to wives—that is, beyond the return of the dowry and the *augmentation de dot* ("increase in the dowry") agreed on in the marriage contract—would sometimes use the formula "And this for the good and agreeable services which she has done for him during their marriage." Families accounting their household and workshop expenses together could conceive of the *idea* of a salary for wives, even if it were not used. Thus in 1559, two silk merchants set up both a partnership and a joint household, to be run by their wives, and agreed that the women would take "no salary," but would be supported at the expense of the partnership.

The wife's ability to help her husband in his craft was a function of several things: location and character of the work; social life and customs in the atelier; and physical state of the wife and the amount of time she had free from other tasks. As for the location, work regularly performed on sites away from the house, as in the building or transport trades, rarely seems to have involved wives as "helpers." (When women have jobs in these areas, they are usually employed on their own.) The wives of journeymen would not be in a position to help their husbands at work either.

As for the character of the work, the crafts of the weaponmaker, of the smith and the caster, which by cultural definition had a marked masculine quality about them, probably drew little on wifely aid for the technical processes. Such artisans may not have agreed with the judgement of the town lawyer Claude de Rubys, who (citing Aristotle) called them "vile, sordid and dishonest," but they may well have followed the view of a current metallurgical manual that the "fire arts" (hot and dry!) were not for those with a "gentle spirit." Here the craftsmen had to be very strong; here they looked brutish, with their faces full of powder and half-burned; here they were plagued with worries till the work was done, "by reason of which they are called Fantasmes."

The nature of social relationships and mores in the atelier might also set limits to the wife's assistance. Imagine a printing shop with an apprentice or two and a few journeymen. If the master's wife tried to order the men about, they might resent this violation of nature's order or at least of their contract, which bound them only to serve their master in his art. So in 1549 in Geneva, the proofreader Guillaume Guéroult, soon to be working in the Lyon shop of Balthazar Arnoullet, complained bitterly of his master's wife: she refused to comply with her husband's rulings, would not unlock the cabinet for his *vin de compagnon* ("journeyman's wine") when he started proofreading at 2 A.M. and in fact "that she would rather the printing house be ruined so that she could live better according to her voluptuous tastes." And then, what of the sexual excitement that a wife could cause in the shop? Anne de Noyer, the spouse of printer Claude de Huchin, was said to have committed lewd acts with her husband's tall apprentice René and to have been unduly familiar with his journeyman Gabriel Challiot. Challiot had to admit "that he would like to have a wife as beautiful as she."

Finally, the wife's participation in the work of the atelier was affected by how much time she had free, even with the help of the inevitable servant, from other household tasks (including preparing food for journeymen and apprentices), and from childbirth and nursing. In Catholic artisanal families, the "state of pollution" which clung to a new mother may have kept her out of the shop until she had her churching ceremony, the *relevailles,* lest her glance bring everybody bad luck. And popular beliefs about the dangers of menstruating women to technical and natural processes, which we know were current in the sixteenth century, may have barred the wife from some workshops at certain times of the month, lest she rust iron and brass, dull cutting instruments, jeopardize the already hazardous process of casting, and so forth.

Wifely help, then, was bound to be periodic, affected by custom, and more readily drawn upon by some crafts than by others. But it was needed for the survival of the family and could sometimes involve the woman so much that she took on a joint work identity with her husband. The evidence we have on this comes primarily from the provisioning and textile trades, with some interesting examples from barber-surgery and printing.

Among the provisioning trades, the households of butchers, hotelkeepers, and tavernkeepers show much joint work by husband and wife. For instance, Benoîte Penet, a butcher's daughter and herself a mother of four girls, aided her husband at his trade, and after he died in the 1540's, went on selling meat to hostelers and private individuals. Presumably her husband bought the cattle over at the Croix de Colle market on the Fourvière Hill and did the slaughtering with his journeymen, while Benoîte Penet helped with preparing the meat and with sales. One of her clients was the nearby Bear Inn, a hotel catering to Germans at the northern end of the peninsula. It was kept by Michel Hiberlin and his wife, Katherine Fichet, natives of Nimburg in Breisgau, who together sought letters of naturalization from the king in 1536. Several years later, Hiberlin married a local woman for his second wife, and she bought meat and took out small loans from Benoîte Penet. Meanwhile, the keeper of the Popinjay Inn was so grateful to his wife "for all the trouble she had taken to help him earn and amass his goods" that he donated one-half of them to her.

Among the textile trades, silkmaking emerges as a family enterprise, even when apprentices and journeymen were also in the shop. Certain tasks assisting at the loom were ordinarily done by girls, either a daughter or a hired worker. The wife of a silkthrower, a taffetamaker, or a velvetmaker might specialize in unwinding the cocoons and preparing the thread for bobbins, so we learn from the records of the orphan girls farmed out by the Aumône Générale: indeed, Estiennette Léonarde, wife of a silkthrower on the rue Grôlée, took on six girls for unwinding during a nine-month period in 1557. If these were to be characteristically female tasks until the nineteenth century, in the sixteenth century we can also find wives who spelled their husbands weaving at the looms. The 1561 agreement among the male silk manufacturers and silkweavers took it as a matter of course that the wives of masters were working the looms if they knew how. Sometimes this is even given recognition in notarized acts, as in 1561 when Etienne Buffin and his wife, Gabrielle Fourestz, involved in a donation, are both described as "silkweavers (*tissotiers*), inhabitants of Lyon."

Joint activity can be found in trades like pinmaking, where we know women were apprenticed, but it is perhaps more surprising to find it among printers and barbers, where the formally trained and hired labor force was exclusively male. Barber-surgery was, in addition, one of the sworn trades in Lyon, and that meant that the masters of the guild were especially vigilant lest "incapable persons" set up shop and practice. Yet in 1537, King François I granted "letters of mastership in barbering" both to Benoit Fanilhon and to his wife, Anne Casset. (The young couple may well have gone over the heads of the local sworn masters and purchased these letters without examination.) It is significant that approval seems to have been given only for the simple tasks of barbering—shaving, bleeding, and similar jobs—rather than for surgery, which Fanilhon was to add himself later on. His wife helped him over the years, although she remained unlettered, signing her daughters' marriage contracts only with an X. The number of widows of barber-surgeons who tried to run a practice with the aid of journeymen after their husband's death suggests that if Anne Casset's royal letters were unusual, her working experience was not.

In printing shops, pulling the press was "men's work," and only a small percentage of artisanal women could read well enough to help with typesetting and proofreading. But there are, nonetheless, a few examples of wives who went beyond the occasional tasks to associate themselves more directly in running the atelier. One is Louise Giraud, wife of the well-known humanist master Etienne Dolet and a formal partner in a "printing company" with her husband and their backer, the financial officer Hélouin Dulin. Because at least thirteen editions came out under Dolet's name and mark in 1542–44, while he was in prison on charges of heresy or in hiding, Louise Giraud must have had considerable familiarity with the business and good relations with the journeymen at the shop at the Sign of the Hatchet.

Another example is Mie Roybet, wife of Barthélemy Frein, alias Rapallus, journeyman printer and one of the leaders of the workers' Company of the Griffarins (as they called their secret union) during and after the strike of 1539, keeper of a small tavern which was a favorite journeymen's haunt, and finally master printer from 1545 until his death in October 1556. Mie Roybet helped with the tavern, but must also have had a full knowledge of the shop, if we may judge by the printing activity into which she was plunged right after her husband's demise. By August 1557, she was in the royal prisons in Lyon together with Michel Chastillon, "governor of the printing house," for having printed "certain books in the French language touching matters of the Christian Religion, without privilege and permission of the Faculty of Theology of Paris." Chastillon was, of course, the brother of the liberal Protestant of Basel, Sébastien Castellion, early advocate of religious tolerance. Roybet was literate enough to write her brother-in-law letters in French and surely knew what she and Chastillon had been printing. Hearing about the arrests, Pastor Theodore Beza was to say from Geneva, "Castellion's brother has been seized at Lyon and thrown into prison with an abominable libel by his brother on predestination, which he has just printed there." Beza did not bother to mention Mie Roybet, but without her collaboration, Castellion's plea for the liberty of the will would not have seen the light of day.

Released from prison, Roybet and Chastillon married in September, and then he died a few months later. Roybet immediately married another printer and kept on as she had been, helping with printing and running her first husband's little tavern. Many women in Lyon did not have this continuity in their work lives. Of all the widows contracting marriage in an artisanal milieu in the years 1553–60, only 25 percent married men in the same trade as their first husbands. If we add marriages to men in allied trades (such as a clockmaker's widow marrying a goldsmith), the number rises to only 34 percent. Some wives may then have carried on a trade of their own. Some may have tried to influence the course of their new husband's career through the money, equipment, contacts, and skills they brought from the past. But for most it was a matter, as it had been when they first married, of accommodating their work abilities and energies to a new family setting.

THE WOMAN AS WAGE-EARNING ARTISAN

At whatever stage of her life cycle, a Lyon woman who hired herself out for wage labor in a craft was likely to be poor and needy. In the years between their first "training" and marriage. Most girls of the *menu peuple* were either in domestic service or helping father, mother, or brother with a craft in the household. If a girl had no such resources—her parents were themselves wage-earners or were dead or widowed—then she provided for herself as best she could. She might try prostitution in rooms in the Saint George quarter, near the Rhône Bridge Hospital, on the rue Mercière, or elsewhere. But if she had some craft skill, she might look for a mistress with whom she could make lace, wimples, buttons, cords, hats, or gloves; with whom she could unwind silk from cocoons or weave linen cloth. She might find a tavernkeeper who would take her on to serve the customers. She might find a master silkworker who would hire her to pull the cords for the large looms that made the fanciest silks. Indeed, in 1561 the master silkweavers were still talking about *compaignonnes,* as well as *compaignons,* in their shops, which means that some trained females were weaving for wages.

Married women who fell upon hard times or widows with children might leap into any kind of short-term paid work to support themselves and their families. The wife of an urban gardener helps a shoemaker's wife travel to Romans in Dauphiné; the wife of a printer's journeyman leaves her own daughter at home to take care of a surgeon's daughter during her illness; the wife of an unskilled day laborer wetnurses the triplets of a weaver's wife; over at the cathedral a woman comes in from time to time to change the straw for the choirboy's pallets. Some adult women unwound cocoons together with the girls at the silk centers; and adults were evidently the main source of semi-skilled female labor at construction sites, doing road repair and other building along with the male hod carriers. So the royal architect Philibert Delorme, the son of a Lyon mason, asked "can anything be found which can employ and busy more people of either sex than building? . . . poor people, who otherwise would have to go beg for their bread?" On the other hand, I have found no sign of Lyon women at this stage of life farming themselves out for a year or two to a master or mistress in a craft, an arrangement probably incompatible with their family responsibilities. Rather than live in such dependence, some of the women would try to get inscribed on the rolls of the welfare organization for a weekly handout of bread and cash, or even try to keep out of sight of the beadles of the Aumône and beg for a few hours each day.

What about the wages of female workers in the crafts? The evidence is very scanty, but it confirms the usual picture of lower compensation for females than for males. Of the masons working for the *ingénieur* Olivier Roland widening a street up near the Church of Saint Vincent in 1562, masters were paid five *sous* a day, and journeymen and hod carriers were paid variously at four, three, and two *sous,* and one *sou* and six *deniers* per day. The women were clustered at two *sous* and at one *sou* and six *deniers,* although it should be noted that some men were remunerated at this low level as well. In 1567, Marie Darmère paid a young woman making lace for her three *livres* a year, together with room and board, while in 1557 the wages of the girls hired out by the Aumône Générale to unwind cocoons ranged from one *livre* and ten *sous* to four *livres* and two *sous* per year. Although we have no exactly comparable wages for males (unwinding silk was a female task, as we have seen), the lowest salary for a male in silk manufacture that I have found for this decade is ten *livres* per year *avec bouche, couche et chausse* ("with board, room, and pants")—and this for a young velvetmaker from Avignon early in his work career. To find male wages approximating those of women, we have to look over to the poorer leather trades, where shoemakers' journeymen in 1555 were being paid as little as three *livres* per year with board, room and pants, and in 1560–63 they were paid four *livres* and sixteen *sous* per year, with room and board.

When male workers were unhappy with their wages, they sometimes organized to get higher ones. Over decades, the consulate complained of "the monopolies of the masons, carpenters, hod carriers and mortar-mixers, who every day raise the price of their day's work," "who make themselves be paid more for their day's work than is customary." The dyers' journeymen had a company and a captain; insisted that hiring take place only on Mondays in front of the Church of Saint Nizier, where they appeared armed and made "resolutions pernicious to the good of the dyers' estate"; and maintained a "jurisdiction" over the apprentices so as to keep down the labor supply. The printers' journeymen had a *compagnonnage*, a full-fledged journeymen's organization, with rites of initiation and techniques for work stoppages, for punishing Forfants (as they called those not in their Company of the Griffarins), and for bringing suits against their masters.

Now there is no sign whatsoever of women workers in sixteenth-century Lyon participating in such activities. The men made no effort to include them in the brotherhood of their "assemblies" and organizations, where rowdy banquets were held, lascivious songs sung, and secret oaths were sworn over daggers. Indeed, one wonders how *compagnonnes* and serving-girls fit into the predominantly male culture of the mixed shop: What was it like when the men collected grumbling at 4:30 A.M. (as they did in dyeing); when they argued every noon with the mistress about whether their customary "journeyman's wine" was of the same quality and amount as that drunk by the master? Interestingly enough, despite the low wages of the women, the journeymen did not seek "jurisdiction" over them as they did over apprentices and over journeymen coming in from other towns, nor did they use sanctions against them as they did against Forfants, willing "to work for beggar's pay." Relatively few in number, less highly skilled or in their own vocational niche, the women did not appear a threat. How could they carry on work at the construction site if the men walked off?

But even in the all-female shops and larger centers for unwinding silk, the girls do not seem to have organized protests. This is not because the modesty of their sex prevented them from ever being disobedient: the individual serving-girl was sometimes saucy and recalcitrant; wives and mothers were prominent actors in the Grande Rebeine, the grain riot of 1529, and their voices were to be heard again in the streets during the religious struggles of mid-century. Rather, it was because the sphere of work, unlike that of food and religious protection for their families, was one in which most women—and especially young women—did not believe they had primary rights. With little to bolster their work identity, who were they to argue, as the journeymen did, for the "ancient customs" of their craft? And with little active involvement in organizational structures, like confraternities, who were they to institute secret societies and clandestine rituals? By the midsixteenth century, stories of witches' sabbaths were arousing fear on all sides. Although no group trials took place in Lyon, individual women among the *menu peuple* were being accused by their neighbors of sorcery and maleficent harm. Under these circumstances, a female *compagnonnage* might look like a witches' coven and bring down upon itself much more wrath than the company of the Griffarins.

The girls unwinding cocoons for Dame Lucresse and Dame Estiennette Léonarde, making lace for Marie Darmère, and making gloves and wimples or pins for other mistresses must have had customs and a shop culture of their own, however. From the glimpses we can get of them from early texts, such as *The Gospels of the Distaffs (Les Evangiles des Quenouilles),* they connected female work and its timing with love, magic, and Christian practice. The events of a spinning day could be used to foretell the future: a broken thread meant a quarrel; a man crossing a thread stretched at the doorsill (it must be the first thread spun that day) bore the same name as one's future husband. A good day's work could be helped by spinning a thread first thing in the morning, before praying and with unwashed hands (still part of the magic of the night), and throwing it over one's shoulders. Washing one's thread, one must not say to one's gossip, "Ha, commère, the water's boiling," but rather "the water's laughing," or else the thread would turn to straw. The women's workplace was itself open to fairies. At best they came when everyone was asleep and finished the spinning. More often they were mischievous, and would take a spindle as their right if all the week's thread had not been properly wound on the reel on Saturday. Saturday was, however, an unlucky day to work. A Franciscan in Lyon condemned those "women who don't want to spin on Saturday out of superstition and who apply themselves instead to other vain activities," while he approved "the devotion of the good dames who on Saturday after [mid-day] dinner turn aside from spinning, sewing or other mechanical work in honor of the Virgin Mary, to whom Saturday is voluntarily dedicated."

What we seem to have here is a domestic work culture, hidden from the streets, eliciting comment not from city councils, but from storytellers. It drew on certain general features of a woman's life, as adaptable to spinning as to any other setting where women were working together, in contrast to "ancient customs," connected with the technology of a particular craft, which one might find in a shop dominated by men. The domestic work culture provided a kind of vertical identity between mistress and female worker, which could sometimes be used by the former to hurry along the work process and sometimes by the latter to slow it down. It was available to any woman—at least to any Catholic woman—who wanted to impose a rhythm on her work life.

THE WOMAN AS INDEPENDENT ARTISAN

Unlike mere wage earners, independent women artisans in Lyon elicited respect and even apprehension and could sometimes defend openly their economic turf. They were ordinarily married women or widows and were likely to have (or have had) husbands also prospering in a craft. And they appear in quite a variety of trades—at least as many as Epistémon told Pantagruel he saw being performed in Hell by Melusine, Cleopatra, Dido, and other classical ladies. If we know of no "verdigris grater" at Lyon—one of the amusing female trades Rabelais refers to in this episode—we do hear about *les bastelières de Lyon* ("the boatwomen of Lyon"), of whom Epistémon was reminded when he saw the knights of the Round Table rowing devils across the Styx. As the student Felix Platter reported during his visit to the city in 1552, "there are always small boats in the charge of women along the length of the quay, ready to transport you to the other shore [of the Saône]." There was no shyness about them: his boatwoman threatened to throw him in the river unless he paid his fare immediately, and then refused to give him change. The young man got his revenge by throwing stones at her from a safe distance.

In the building and construction trades, there were few, if any, women carpenters or fully trained masons, but we do find Catherine Fromment, "cabinetmaker," in the local prison for some kind of crime in 1548. Similarly, in the metal trades, only pin-making had women operating on their own. Thoine Riniere and a certain Jehanne, *espinglières de Lyon,* were among the poor sick at the Rhône Bridge Hospital in 1560. More successful in their trade were the widows of two pinmakers, carrying on the craft in their own right after their husbands died: Dame Ysabeau de Seure worked with her son, but was also able to hire a journeyman in 1565, while the next year, Jehanne Tutilly was buying 170 *livres* worth of brass wire for her pins from German merchants. Dame Anne Durtin made gold thread with at least one female apprentice at her side, while her husband busied himself with gold objects.

Many more women had independent artisanal status in the textile and clothing trades. Languishing at the hospital in 1560 were Thoine Baton, the cordmaker, Claude Cousande, the hatmaker, and Marie Odette, a dressmaker from the Saint George quarter. Monette, the glovemaker, headed a household on the rue Mercière in 1557 and was expected to provide a man for the urban militia. Wimplemaking by females was common enough for the ordinances of the trade to envisage *maistresses* as well as *maistres.* Such a one was Pernette Morilier, a goldsmith's wife, who took on a female apprentice for a goodly fee in 1564 (clearly a busy household, for her husband accepted a male apprentice the same month). Lacingmakers also had their mistresses, appropriate perhaps, because the witch who knotted trouser lacing to make bridegrooms impotent (*nouer l'aiguillette*) was characteristically a female. In weaving linen, women were a familiar sight, and pattern books printed in Lyon had pictures of them at work. In silkmaking, in addition to the women running shops for unwinding cocoons, we can find Françoise la Regnarde, a silkthrower, and

Germaine Clément, a silkweaver, both taxed in their own right in 1571. In fact, the independence of *maistresses* like Clément had begun to trouble the *maitres tissotiers,* as we will see.

On the other hand, the enthusiasm of Benoîte Larchier for the linen trade did not worry her husband, the merchant-shoemaker Jean Pierre, alias Pichier. He had come to Lyon as a young man from the Piedmont, had married Larchier around 1536, and received the astonishingly high dowry of 1,000 *livres.* For twenty-five years, they pursued their trades "separately," he with his shoes, she in "linenmaking and commerce in linen cloth." So great had been her profits, Pierre admitted in 1561, that they had paid for most of his purchases of real estate. In recognition of this, he changed the initial arrangements of their marriage contract to a community of goods, so as to reward her more amply if he predeceased her. Possibly the husband of the linenmaker Barbe de Valle had similar reasons to be grateful to his wife. She appears on the tax rolls in her own name, assessed "for her movables and craft." Indeed, on a 1567 list of Huguenots reconverted to Catholicism, he is characterized simply as *"le mary de La Barbe, lingère"* ("the husband of La Barbe, linenmaker"), without any name of his own.

The provisioning trades also afforded scope for female economic activity. Among millers and bakers, we find only the occasional widow continuing on her own ("La vefve de Champaignon" is the sole member of her sex on a list of forty-eight bakers compiled by the consulate in 1564). There were several other fishmongers like Michelette Godet, a boatman's wife, and especially there were females running butcher shops. Some *bouchières* were poor, such as Monde Bazare, who entered the hospital in 1560 having "nothing," and some "marchandes-bouchières" were well off, such as widow Estiennette Moyne, official purveyor of meat to the hospital a few years later. Quarrels among women in the craft even came to the attention of the courts: in 1549 three butcher-women, all married and at least one the mother of six or seven little children, were accused of hurling a duck in the face of a fourth woman, perhaps a case of economic rivalry. One might have expected the missile to be a piece of liver, for selling *la triperie* ("innards") seems to have had special attraction for members of the so-called weaker sex.

As for the world of the tavern and the inn, the role of the female was so pronounced that a book for the traveling merchant, published in Lyon around 1515, promised in its title to teach what to do "to speak to the hostess to ask how much one has spent." A few years later, Erasmus's *Colloquy on Inns* maintained that guests stayed extra days at Lyon because of the graciousness of the *hôstesses* and their daughters. They might be simple women like "La Loyse," at whose inn a fight broke out in 1531, or like Jane, hostess at the Sign of the Broken Lupine on the rue Grôlée, whose last name could not be remembered by a neighboring widow when she left her a bequest of ten *livres.* The women might come from more substantial families: Catherine Berthaud, daughter of a paper manufacturer and widow of a pewterer, hostess in 1573 at the Sign of Our Lady, rue de Bourgneuf; Claudine Dumas, daughter of a notary, hostess at the Golden Chariot at the Fossés de la Lanterne.

Dumas was one of the most interesting women of her day in the city. In the 1520s she had married the proprietor of the Golden Chariot, Pierre Peraton, who was also a merchant and financial officer. By 1551 he had died, and she continued to administer the inn and went on to buy properties in the Dauphiné and Lyonnais. And La Dame du Chariot, as she was called, had connections. As a young bride she had served as a godmother to the sons of the learned Cornelius Agrippa of Nettesheim, then living in Lyon (and author of a book on *The Nobility of the Female Sex*). She was also kin to Hélouin Dulin, financier of the evangelical publications of the ill-fated printer Etienne Dolet and his wife, Louise, and of the vernacular Bibles of publisher Guillaume Rouillé. In her mature years, La Dame du Chariot was to let her inn be used as a place of Protestant worship.

Finally, one can even find independent artisanal women in unusual trades like the manufacturer of tennis rackets. Such a woman was Widow Estiennette Gonter, who assured her labor supply by marrying off her orphaned goddaughter to a racketmaker. The young couple would live with her; she would give them board if "they would obey her," and Gilles would make rackets for her at forty *sous* a racket, "as she was accustomed to pay other workers in the said craft."

What can we say of the work identity—as perceived by themselves and by others—of La Loyse; La Dame du Chariot; Widow Estiennette, the tennis racket maker; Monette, the glovemaker; and Dame Anne Durtin? It did not grow out of the experience and rituals of apprenticeship, for, as we have seen, female training was often informal, and some of these women struck out on their own only as widows. It was hardly buttressed by organizational structures and formal public or political recognition in Lyon. The females did not march in their craft's parades; the few sworn guilds had no women as officers or in any significant role; the city council never selected women to be *maîtres de métier,* that is, the two persons from each craft who ratified the new consuls and attended meetings of notables. Mistresses were expected to pay dues to a painters' confraternity in 1496 and to a confraternity of lacingmakers in 1580, but they were never officers of any craft confraternity, played no part in confraternity drama, and may not always have been invited to the banquets. In any case, confraternities were much weakened during the years 1550–65 by the Reformed movement, and no self-respecting Protestant woman would even have sought such recognition. Only on certain limited occasions might the artisanal status of a female be recognized by notary or political officer: when she was making a contract specifically related to her work (in other contracts she would be "Pernette Morilier, wife of Jean Yvard the goldsmith"); when she was responsible as a widow for taxes or a militiaman from her household; and when the consulate wanted to summon her and others in her trade, perhaps to tell them the fixed price of meat or bread.

The sense of craft for an independent artisanal woman probably arose, then, from the esteem in which she was held by those in her immediate environs: her husband and kin, her neighbors—and especially her female neighbors—and her clients. It was marked in small ways: the feminization of her last name (the silk-mistress Estiennette Léonard became Estiennette Léonarde; the tavernkeeper Estiennette Cappin became Estiennette Cappine); the attribution of nicknames (La chevauchée de Rohanne, the Cavalcade of Rohanne, for Jeanne Seiglevielle, hostess of the Ecu de France de Rohanne); and especially by addressing her as Dame, a worthy title not often accorded women of artisanal status. Her position was indicated by her frequent role as godmother, bringing with it influence over the gossip networks in the quarter; by the petty loans she made to kin and neighbors, listed and sometimes forgiven in her will; and by gifts of her clothing and money, bestowed on less fortunate women for whom she felt responsible. Some men played a similar role, but the master's prestige drew more heavily upon his excellence in his métier, and his connections and reputation stretched out through his craft beyond his street and beyond his parish. The Dames among the *menu peuple* were noted for a cluster of womanly achievements, of which work skill was only one, and they were primarily rooted in their neighborhood.

The one exception was in the printing trade, where the names of eight females in Lyon were carried far and wide on the title pages or in the colophons of books. Or rather, in most cases their names were listed as widows of printers or booksellers whose trade they were continuing—"La vefve de Balthazar Arnoullet," "La vevfe de Gabriel Cotier." Some of the women may have been content to entrust the "governance" of the atelier wholly to a senior journeyman or a male relative; but not a woman like Antoinette Peronet who outlived two husbands, the first a printer, the second a bookseller, to marry a publisher younger than herself in 1555. Gabriel Cotier's publishing business was financed by her dowry of 2,080 *livres* in books, tools, money, and rents, from which she carefully reserved dowries for her daughters and income "for her small pleasures and wishes." After Cotier's death in 1565, she maintained the publishing house at the Sign of Milan for eleven years, using his mark, reissuing some of his editions, and accepting the services of a scholarly translator who had worked with the firm earlier. But she also addressed herself to a new printer and brought out some fresh works, obtaining a royal privilege to protect them against being pirated. In one of these, a French translation of a work by Marcus Aurelius Antoninus, she wrote a dedicatory letter to the governor of the Lyonnais, taking credit for initiating the edition, so important for teaching how to conduct oneself happily and to govern. Although she spoke conventionally of her "smallness," praising the governor as "the true asylum for poor widows charged with orphans," she signed herself firmly with her own name, "Antoynette Peronnet."

And what of Jeanne Giunta whose praise of women in the crafts we heard in the opening of this essay? She published under her own name, as did Sibille de La Porte, because they were carrying on their father's house. Indeed, both women were somewhat at odds with their spouses: Giunta sued for separation of her goods and return of her dowry in 1572 because of her husband's poor management of the business (he died the next year). La Porte, as a new widow, left Calvinist Geneva where her publisher husband had taken refuge, to return to Lyon and ultimately to Catholicism. Neither woman was an artisan, of course; by birth and marriage they were part of the rich Consular elite of Lyon, and their publishing houses were great commercial enterprises. Neither woman was educated or experienced enough to be involved in the daily administration of firms publishing religious, legal, and scholarly texts in Latin; this they left to their sons, to editors, and male employees. Yet Giunta frequently intervened to keep the business going in the wake of religious turmoil and family quarreling; she presented herself in a 1579 dedication (presumably dictated in French to a Latin translator) as devoted to the typographical art, lest the honor that her father and Florentine ancestors had won thereby be lost. And La Porte may have helped compose the letter from the Bibliopola to the Benevolent Reader which insists on the correctness of her 1591 edition of the Commentaries on Aristotle's *De Anima* by the Jesuit François Tolet. At any rate, these two women are the closest we come in sixteenth-century Lyon to the high-level female entrepreneur. It is perhaps no accident that it is a merchant-publisher who raises a lone female voice in that city to celebrate woman's work.

No one perceived these widows as dangerous competition to other printers and publishers; there were too few of them, and, in any case, they were maintaining family firms, not creating new ones. In some trades, however, the independent female artisan was eyed with suspicion as a slippery opening (cold and wet?) for interlopers. (Already, royal edicts were trying to curb the use of property by widows who remarried and to constrain married women to make contracts only with their husbands' consent.)

The unbridled female could be a matter of concern even in a free trade, where supposedly anyone could set up shop without hindrance. A 1554 ruling for silk manufacture had made no effort to limit access to the craft. But in 1561, the market began to look uncertain, and about 158 merchants and masters engaged in various kinds of silkmaking met before a notary to set up "good order" among them, prevent "ruin," and "obviate disturbance, debates and disputes." The number of male apprentices in silkweaving was limited to two per master, with a duration of four to five years. *Apprentisses* ("female apprentices") were to be eliminated from the trade entirely, except for the daughters and sisters of masters. All masters were to send away their *apprentisses* within the month under penalty of twenty-five *livres* to the Aumône Générale, and this because of the "great prejudice and danger" they offered to the craft, especially because some of them were married to men in other arts. *Compagnonnes* ("journeywomen") who had already done an apprenticeship could be hired for wages, but were not to be supplied with work they could do "apart" in their rooms, unless they were married to men in the trade. Wives and widows of master silkmakers could work on the looms, but could take no apprentices, male or female, except their own children. In short, mastership was to go from male to male and not pass through the female line.

In fact, these provisions were not fully realized. A 1583 ruling for the master silkmakers was still trying to limit male apprentices to two per master, but in regard to females it now prescribed that there could be no *apprentisses ex-cept* girls taken from Saint Catherine's orphan hospital or "poor orphan girls" begging in the master's quarter. Nevertheless, in both cases we see fearful action against the independent female artisan, generated by hard times in an industry under the control of commercial capitalism.

Among the barber-surgeons, the quarrel broke out in prosperous times and was connected with the attempt of the sworn guildmasters to control the quality of practice in their art. Already in the fall of 1540, the Parlement of Paris was judging a case between thirteen sworn masters of Lyon on the one hand, and five *varlets* ("journeymen"), barber-surgeons, and three widows on the other hand. The journeymen were ordered to close their *boutiques,* and the widows were told they could keep shops open only for shaving beards and simple wounds (penalty for violation—1,000 livres parisis). In 1548–52, there were more cases before the Sénéchausée of Lyon. Now the masters would no longer tolerate journeymen who gave shaves and minor care from time to time in their own rooms. Now the widows would have to be constrained "because of the masterships and shops that they are renting out day after day to journeymen barbers, incapable and ignorant, leading to accidents and misfortunes." The letters of *maîtrise* must be turned in, and the women would be compensated with the small sum of nine *livres* per year.

As with the widows of master printers and booksellers, some of these widows may have participated little in the shops they rented out. But Dame Marguerite Roybet was actually called a *barbière* in the 1550s after the death of her husband, a master barber-surgeon. And we can find a few other women so described, perhaps widows, perhaps females carrying on their art in defiance of the sworn masters. At any rate, the renting out of shops by widows continued unabated. From 1552 to 1565, Master Simon Guy was trying to put a stop to such activity; in 1571 his widow, Claudine Cazot, was renting out his kerchiefs and other barber's equipment. Perhaps these women obeyed their husbands while they were still alive, but when they were dead it was another matter.

One last group of women should be mentioned among practitioners of the medical art: the midwives. In sixteenth-century Lyon, they were not yet experiencing the competition with male midwives that the royal midwife Louise Bourgeois was to complain of in Paris in 1609. And the physicians of Lyon, eager though they were to have some kind of control over the surgeons and apothecaries, were not yet interested in the *sages-femmes,* as the midwives were called. The latter went about their business freely on their street or at the Rhône Bridge Hospital: Etiennette Jay, widow of a printer and of a collar-maker; Françoise Ru, a currier's wife; Anne Beauroy, godmother to an illegitimate child she had delivered in the parish of Saint Nizier; and others. These were Dames par excellence, pride in their manual skills merging with the sense of their importance at critical moments in a woman's life. Perhaps, too, they enjoyed the devotion from their female neighbors that Louise Bourgeois described in Paris in the old days: "When their midwives died, the women went into deep mourning and prayed God not to send them children any longer."

CONCLUSIONS

Women's work was important in this sixteenth-century city for the products created and sold and the services performed, and also for the flexibility it introduced into the craft economy and the economy of the family. That flexibility was prepared for by the girls' relatively informal training and was maintained by some of the other features of female life we have considered: weak connection with organizational structures in shop and craft, relatively weak work identity, and high identity as a member of a family and neighborhood. In good times and in bad times, the female adapted her skills and work energies to the stages of her life cycle and to the states of her body; to the needs of the families of which she was part successively as a daughter, wife, mother, and if she lived long enough, as widow and second wife. A craft as a whole could expand on semiskilled female labor, could respond to busy periods by adding low-paid or unpaid female labor, could allow some vertical mobility through shops run by females, and could contract by shedding or curbing female work.

Male artisans could also display such flexibility on occasion. The painter Mathieu Charrier married and decided to go into innkeeping with his wife's brother; musician Hélie Gachoix took up glovemaking during a slack season. At the construction site, most of the mason's helpers were male, not female; in a large shop, young semiskilled males as well as females could be found in peripheral jobs. Through thick and thin, however, the male artisan held on to his work identity: Gachoix was called *musicien* even when he was buying his calf leather and paying his hired glover; Jacques Lescuyer, alias *Le Boiteux* ("The Limper"), changed his abode "to earn his living" as a printer rather than remain in Lyon and do something different. The female, in contrast, stayed put and improvised, patched together what work she could to fit her family requirements. In her availability for multiple uses, she prefigures the casual worker in industrial society.

Finally, we return to those features of Lyon life which may account for the scope of female work and for efforts to limit female autonomy in the crafts. Neither the guild nor capitalism were to blame by themselves. On the one hand, the complex economy of a large city offered a wide range of jobs for both sexes and included many textile shops and taverns in which female work was welcome. On the other hand, the craft economy was unsteady, social inequality in the city had much increased since the days of the medieval commune, and the interest of the citydwellers in private property—in maintaining, increasing, and passing on the family's private property—was intensifying. These factors usually acted to enhance the patriarchal character of institutions and values inherited from the past and to give a patriarchal twist to new ones; the wives went along with conventions which represented the husband as The Artisan in a métier to which the whole household had in fact contributed. Therefore, the guild, which in principle could be (and in some cities sometimes was) an apparatus available for mistresses in a trade, served in Lyon as a means for sworn master surgeons to limit female activity, along with that of journeymen competitors. So entrepreneurs and masters in the "free" trade of silkmaking tried to achieve the same goals by informal combination.

The regime of "free work" was a mixed blessing for women as it was for poor journeymen. It encouraged the establishment of new industries in Lyon and of work unwinding cocoons, embroidery with gold thread, and so forth. It made it easier for women to use their ingenuity to get around economic restrictions aimed at them, their husbands, and other male accomplices. But it also facilitated the capitalist organization of wholesale manufacture, and important female entrepreneurs were almost as rare as mistress masons and much rarer than mistress butchers. Lyon tradeswomen had enough credit and cash to take out and make small loans, but patriarchal society did not entrust the weaker and slippery sex with the control of large amounts of capital or with the direction of a major industrial enterprise. Compare the genteel, all-female shops of silkmakers in medieval Paris or London, limited in output, with the female and mixed shops of Lyon's busy export industry, their few mistresses and many masters dominated by entrepreneurs. By the eighteenth century, the women would be clustered at the bottom of the trade.

Still other factors shaped the character of day-to-day work in the shop. The politics of the property-oriented family, supported by the politics of the slowly building state, was gradually concentrating decisions for everyone's good in the husband's hands. This could compromise the authority of the female, both in dealing with male workers and in working in the trade at large. Then, too, the strongly held attitudes which sorted out the technical work appropriate to each sex seemed to be favoring the male. Either sex could now make silk, with only the watery process of unwinding cocoons left to females; but manual operations at the printing press, the forge, and the foundry were to be confined to males. Men could also dominate the mixed atelier by their articulated and public associational life: the magical culture of female work had less bite to it, especially when one had to be wary of witchcraft accusations.

For a time, the Protestant movement may have assigned more sanctity to women's work as it did to all lay vocations ("You can even say sacramental words in the kitchen, washing the dishes," said a male proselytizer), and the Dames among the *menu peuple* were often converts to the new religion. Merchant-shoemaker Jean Pierre, who acknowledged the contribution of his linen-making wife to the family's profits, was an elder of the Reformed Consistory. In the longer run, the Reformation strengthened the hand of the father and energetically proscribed fairies and devotions to the Virgin from the workshop. Artisanal women in seventeenth century Geneva were to have no more scope than those in Catholic Lyon.

Within all these constraints, women worked however and wherever they could, helping husbands and making anything from pins to gloves. "The highest of praise," they may have received for the exercise of their craft, as Jeanne Giunta said, but it usually remained within the world of their street, their gossip network, their tavern, their kin—unpublished and unsung.

LITERARY CREDITS

BEN-AMOS-Ilana Krausman Ben-Amos, *Adolescence and Youth in Early Modern England*, 1994 (pp. 100–108, 170–175.) Reprinted by permission of Yale University Press.

BENNETT-"Public Power and Authority in the Medieval English Countryside" by Judith M. Bennett in *Women and Power in the Middle Ages* by Erler and Kowaleski (pp. 18–29). Reprinted by permission of The University of Georgia Press.

BLUNDELL-Reprinted by permission of the publisher from *Women in Ancient Greece* by Sue Blundell, Cambridge, Mass.: Harvard University Press, Copyright © 1995 by Sue Blundell.

BOUCHARD-*Strong of Body, Brave & Noble* by Constance Bouchard, pp. 67–74, 86–91, 87–101. Copyright Cornell University Press. Used by permission of Cornell University Press.

BRADLEY-Keith Bradley, *Slavery and Society at Rome* pp. 24–30, 65–66, 67–71, 71–76, 76–77. Copyright Cambridge University Press. Reprinted with the permission of Cambridge University Press.

CHAZAN-Robert Chazan, *Medieval Jewry in Northern France: A Political and Social History*, pp. 2–29. Reprinted by permission of Johns Hopkins University Press.

DAVIS-Excerpt from *Women in the Crafts* reprinted by permission of Natalie Davis.

GEREMEK-Bronisław Geremek; Jean Birrell (trans.). *The Margins of Society in Late Medieval Paris*, pp. 96–105, 106–117, 118–121. Copyright Cambridge University Press. Reprinted by permission of Cambridge University Press.

HANAWALT-From *Growing Up in Medieval London: The Experience of Childhood in History* by Barbara A. Hanawalt. Copyright © 1995 by Oxford University Press, Inc. Used by permission of Oxford University Press, Inc.

HANAWALT-From *The Ties that Bound: Peasant Families in Medieval England* by Barbara A. Hanawalt. Copyright © 1986 by Oxford University Press, Inc. Used by permission of Oxford University Press, Inc.

HERLIHY-Reprinted by permission of the publisher from *Medieval Households* by David Herlihy, Cambridge, Mass.: Harvard University Press, Copyright © 1985 by the President and Fellows of Harvard College.

KEEGAN-From *The Face of Battle* by John Keegan. Copyright © 1976 by John Keegan. Used by permission of Viking Penguin, a division of Penguin Putnam Inc.

LAWRENCE-C. H. Lawrence, *Medieval Monasticism: Forms of Religious Life in Western Europe in the Middle Ages*, pp. 111–127. Copyright Addison Wesley Longman Ltd. Reprinted with permission of Addison Wesley Longman Ltd.

LAZENBY-"The Killing Zone" by John Lazenby from *Hoplites* by Victor Davis Hanson, ed., pp. 87, 88–108. Reprinted by permission of Routledge.

OZMENT-Steven Ozment, "The Private Life of an Early Modern Teenager," *Journal of Family History*, 21(1), pp. 22–32, 36–37, 37–38, copyright by Sage Publications, Inc. Reprinted by permission of the publisher.

PAINTER-Sidney Painter, *William Marshall: Knight-Errant*, pp. 13–29. Reprinted by permission of Johns Hopkins University Press.

RUGGIERO-From *Binding Passions: Tales of Magic, Marriage, and Power at the End of the Renaissance* by Guido Ruggiero. Copyright © 1993 by Oxford University Press, Inc. Used by permission of Oxford University Press, Inc.

SHAHAR-Shulamith Shahar, *Childhood in the Middle Ages*. pp. 32–39, 43–44, 77, 92–93, 97–108. Reprinted by permission of Routledge and the author.

STAMBAUGH-John E. Stambaugh, *The Ancient Roman City*, pp. 225–237. Reprinted by permission of Johns Hopkins University Press.

SUMPTION-*Pilgrimage and Medieval Travel* by Jonathan Sumption. Reprinted by permission of Littlefield, Adams Co.

THORNTON-Dora Thornton, *The Scholar in His Study* (1997) pp. 27–29, 29–30, 31–33, 35–36, 36, 176–178. New Haven, CT: Yale University Press. Reprinted by permission of Yale University Press.

WALLACE-HADRILL-Excerpts from *The Frankish Church* by J.M. Wallace-Hadrill (1983) reprinted by permission of Oxford University Press.

WATT-From Tessa Watt, *Cheap Print and Popular Piety, 1550–1640*, pp. 193–205, 208–216. Reprinted by permission of Cambridge University Press.

YEGÜL-Fikret Yegül, *Baths and Bathing in Classical Antiquity*, pp. 30–35, 37–43. Reprinted by permission of The MIT Press.